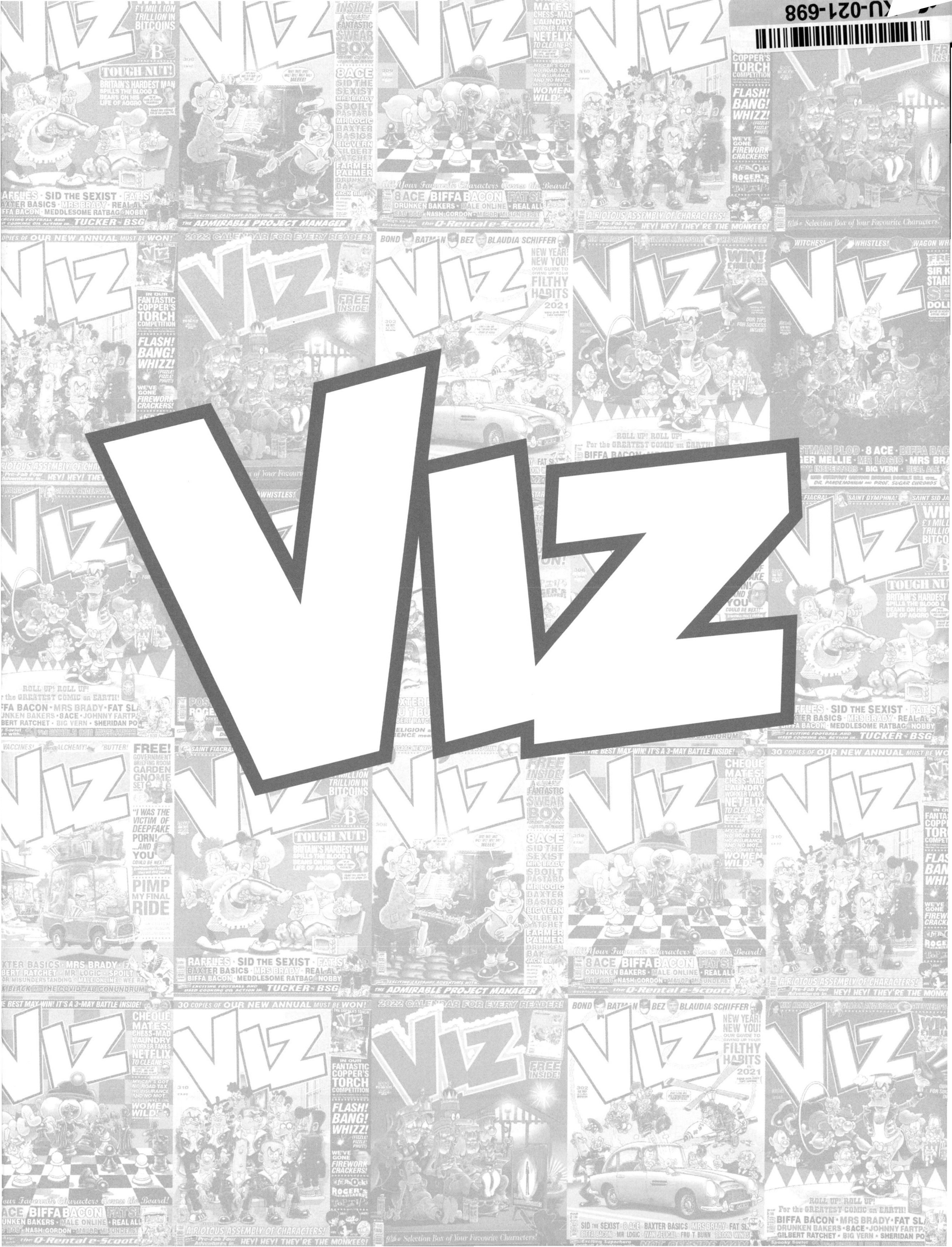
VIZ

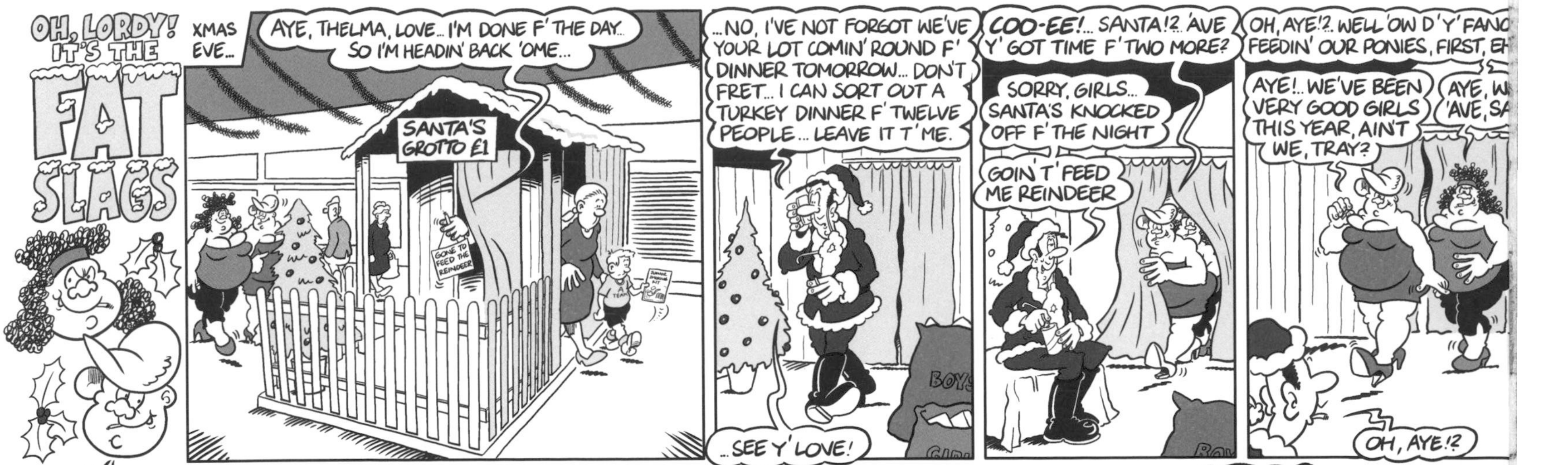
OH, LORDY! IT'S THE FAT SLAGS
XMAS EVE...
AYE, THELMA, LOVE... I'M DONE F' THE DAY... SO I'M HEADIN' BACK 'OME...
SANTA'S GROTTO £1
GONE TO FEED THE REINDEER
...NO, I'VE NOT FORGOT WE'VE YOUR LOT COMIN' ROUND F' DINNER TOMORROW... DON'T FRET... I CAN SORT OUT A TURKEY DINNER F' TWELVE PEOPLE... LEAVE IT T' ME.
...SEE Y' LOVE!
COO-EE!... SANTA!? 'AVE Y' GOT TIME F' TWO MORE?
SORRY, GIRLS... SANTA'S KNOCKED OFF F' THE NIGHT
GOIN' T' FEED ME REINDEER
AYE!.. WE'VE BEEN VERY GOOD GIRLS THIS YEAR, AIN'T WE, TRAY?
OH, AYE!?

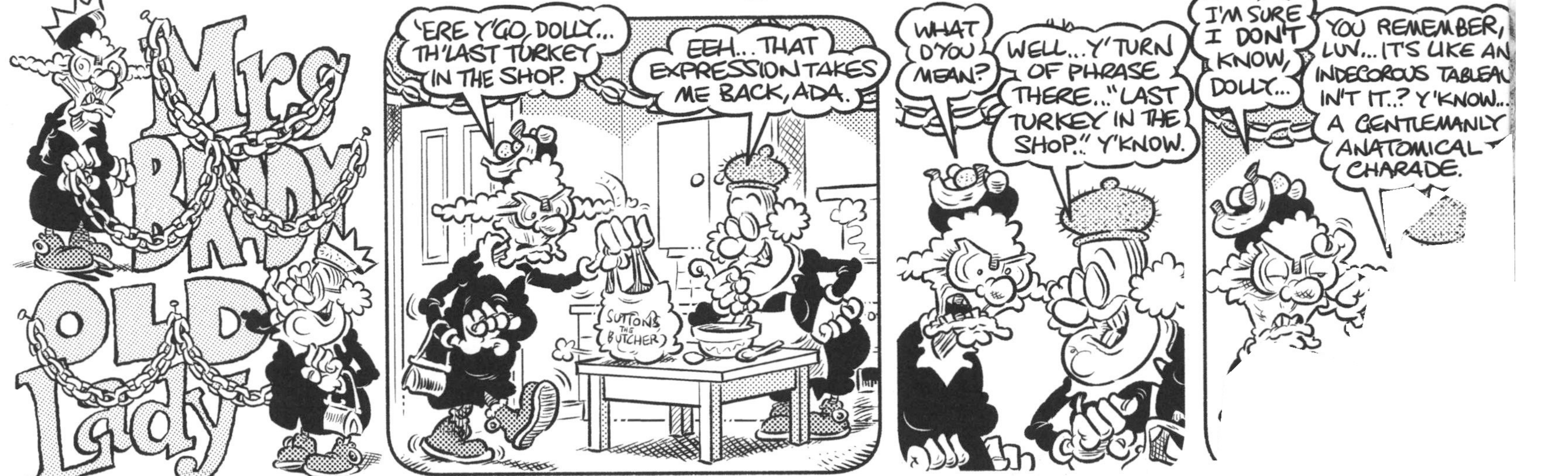
Mrs BLOODY OLD Lady
'ERE Y'GO, DOLLY... TH'LAST TURKEY IN THE SHOP.
EEH... THAT EXPRESSION TAKES ME BACK, ADA.
SUTTONS THE BUTCHER
WHAT D'YOU MEAN?
WELL... Y' TURN OF PHRASE THERE... "LAST TURKEY IN THE SHOP." Y'KNOW.
I'M SURE I DON'T KNOW, DOLLY...

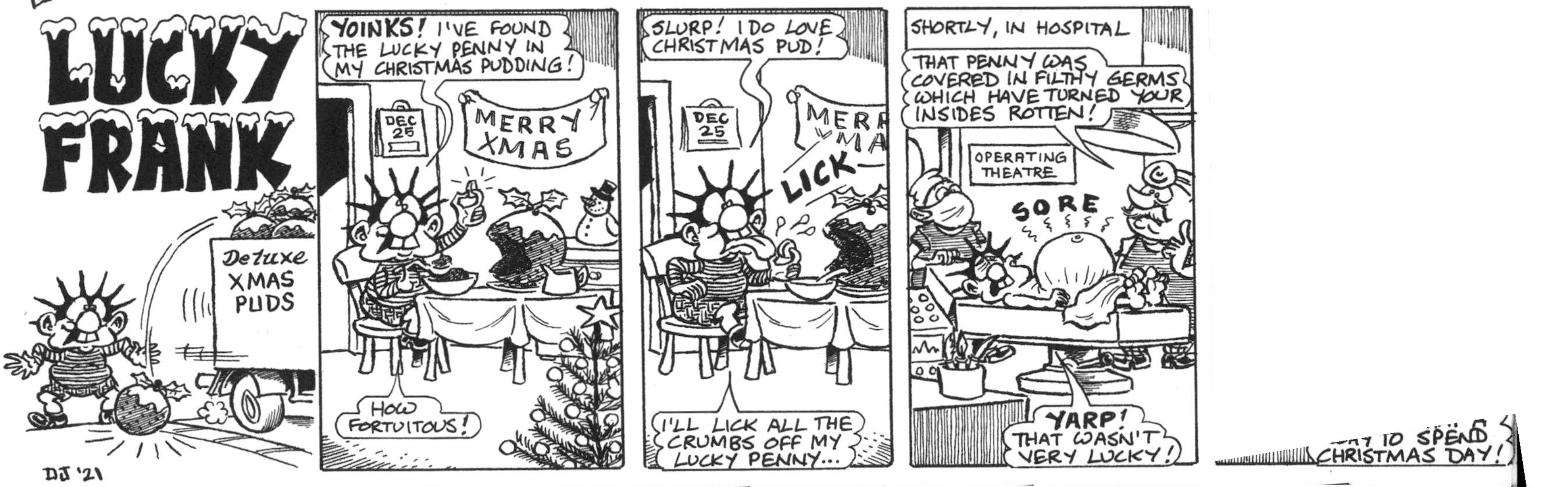
LUCKY FRANK
DeLuxe XMAS PUDS
DJ '21
YOINKS! I'VE FOUND THE LUCKY PENNY IN MY CHRISTMAS PUDDING!
DEC 25
MERRY XMAS
HOW FORTUITOUS!
SLURP! I DO LOVE CHRISTMAS PUD!
LICK
I'LL LICK ALL THE CRUMBS OFF MY LUCKY PENNY...
SHORTLY, IN HOSPITAL
THAT PENNY WAS COVERED IN FILTHY GERMS WHICH HAVE TURNED YOUR INSIDES ROTTEN!
OPERATING THEATRE
SORE
YARP! THAT WASN'T VERY LUCKY!
CHRISTMAS DAY!

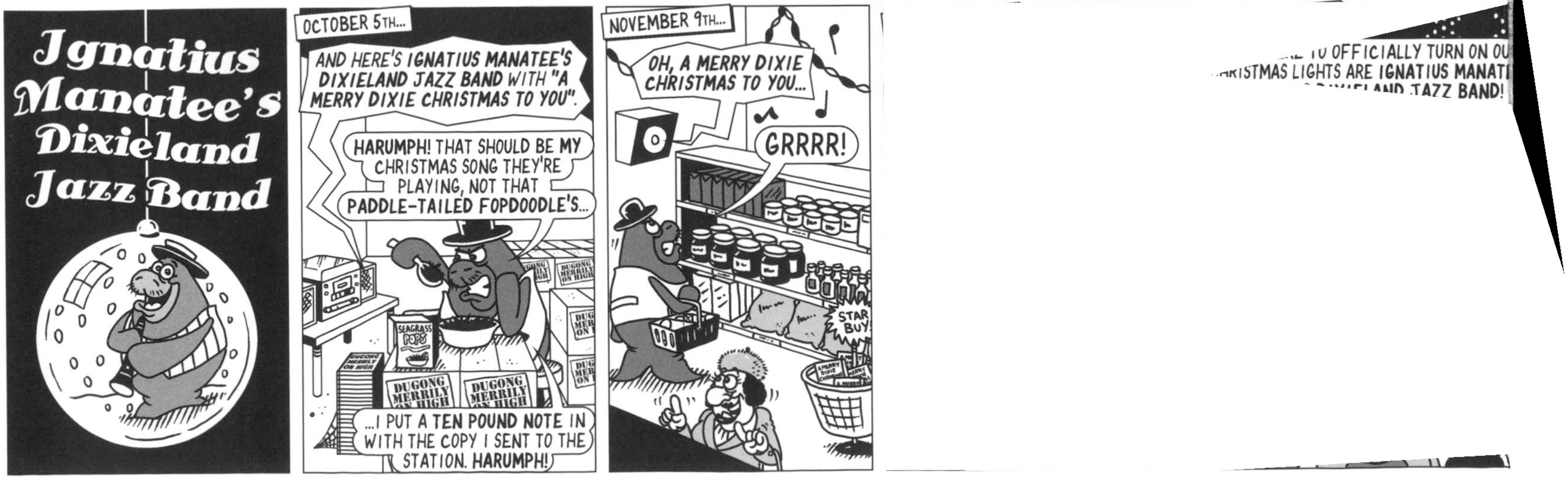
Ignatius Manatee's Dixieland Jazz Band
OCTOBER 5TH...
AND HERE'S IGNATIUS MANATEE'S DIXIELAND JAZZ BAND WITH "A MERRY DIXIE CHRISTMAS TO YOU".
HARUMPH! THAT SHOULD BE MY CHRISTMAS SONG THEY'RE PLAYING, NOT THAT PADDLE-TAILED FOPDOODLE'S...
DUGONG MERRILY ON HIGH
SEAGRASS POPS
...I PUT A TEN POUND NOTE IN WITH THE COPY I SENT TO THE STATION. HARUMPH!
NOVEMBER 9TH...
OH, A MERRY DIXIE CHRISTMAS TO YOU...
GRRRR!
STAR BUY!

WELL... WHY DON'T Y' JUMP UP ON SANTA'S LAP, THEN, GIRLS...

...SEE IF HE'S GOT OWT IN HIS SACK F'Y'BOTH... HEH!

PAT! PAT! PAT!

WAHAY!!!

JESUS!!! ...ONE AT A TI...

CRACK!! CRACK!!

SANTA'S GROTTO £1

XMAS DAY...

HERE'S YOUR DINNER, MR. ASKWITH... TURKEY WITH ALL THE TRIMMINGS.

OOH, THAT LOOKS LOVELY, NURSE... YOU COULDN'T RUSTLE UP A DOZEN MORE, COULD YOU?.. EXTRA STUFFING ON THELMA'S DAD'S

...A WHAT NOW?

...A MANIPULATION OF THE PREPUCE AN' THE SCROTAL SAC, ADA... A SORT OF RIBALD BARRACK-ROOM HARLEQUINADE, IF YOU WILL...

SUTTONS THE BUTCHER

TSK

EEH! LOOK AT THAT, DOLLY...!

WHAT IS IT, ADA?

SUTTONS THE BUTCHER

...THAT RIGHT PUTS ME IN MIND OF MY SIDNEY'S COCK AND BALLS.

GRUNT! ONE OF YOUR BONES IS GETTING IN MY WAY!

WRENCH! HEAVE!

I'LL SEE IF I CAN PULL IT OUT...

GOOD GRACIOUS! IT'S YOUR WISHBONE!

SNAP!

AND I'VE GOT THE BIG BIT — WHICH MEANS I GET TO MAKE A WISH!

THEN

DOCTOR! YOU'VE JUST WON A MILLIONTY-TRILLION QUID ON THE LOTTERY!

NATIONAL LOTTERY JACKPOT

GASP! MY WISH HAS COME TRUE — WHAT LUCK!

AND

PLEASE ACCEPT THIS GIGANTIC CHRISTMAS PUDDING WITH THE BANK OF ENGLAND INSIDE IT, AS A REWARD!

BANK OF ENGLAND

YOINKS! (MUNCH! CHOMP!)

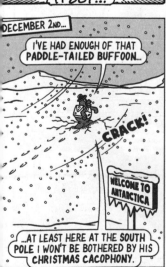

DECEMBER 2ND...

I'VE HAD ENOUGH OF THAT PADDLE-TAILED BUFFOON...

CRACK!

WELCOME TO ANTARCTICA

...AT LEAST HERE AT THE SOUTH POLE I WON'T BE BOTHERED BY HIS CHRISTMAS CACOPHONY.

AAAARGH!

I'M WEDGED STUCK! LUCKY I PACKED MY RADIO WITH LONG LIFE BATTERIES. I'LL FIND A CHANNEL AND CALL FOR HELP.

WEEEOOOOWEEEE... OH, A MERRY DIXIE CHRISTMAS TO YOU...

EEEK!

EEEK! EEEK! EEEK!

EEEK!

FWUMP!

DECEMBER 31ST...

OH, A MERRY DIXIE CHRISTMAS TO YOU...

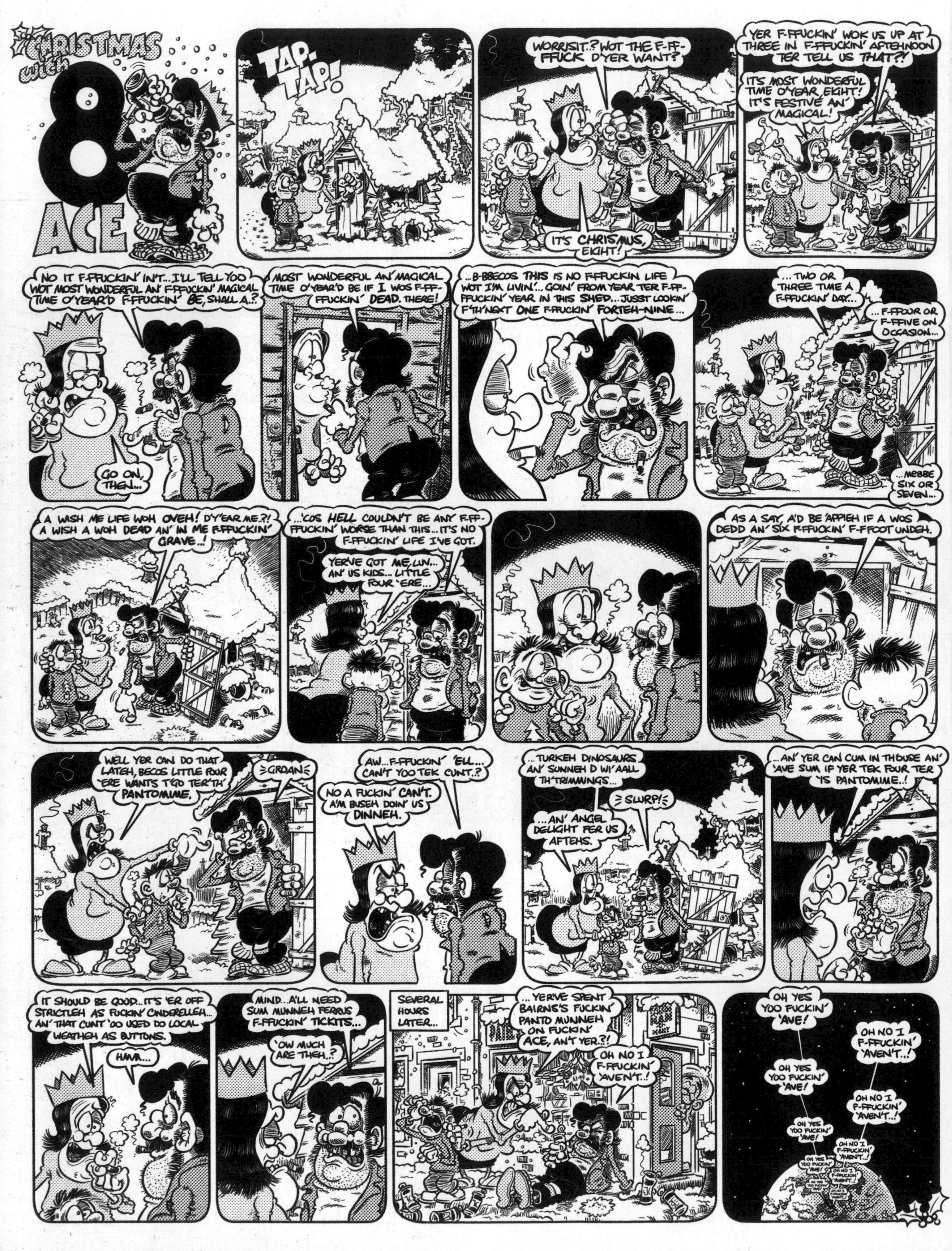
CHRISTMAS with 8 ACE
TAP-TAP!
WORRISIT..? WOT THE F-FF-FFUCK D'YER WANT?
IT'S CHRISMUS, EIGHT!
YER F-FFUCKIN' WOK US UP AT THREE IN F-FFUCKIN' AFTEHNOON TER TELL US THAT?!
IT'S MOST WONDERFUL TIME O'YEAR, EIGHT! IT'S FESTIVE AN' MAGICAL!
NO IT F-FFUCKIN' IN'T... I'LL TELL YOO WOT MOST WONDERFUL AN' F-FFUCKIN' MAGICAL TIME O'YEAR'D F-FFUCKIN' BE, SHALL A..?
GO ON, THEN...
MOST WONDERFUL AN' MAGICAL TIME O'YEAR'D BE IF I WOS F-FF-FFUCKIN' DEAD. THERE!
...B-BBECOS THIS IS NO F-FFUCKIN LIFE WOT I'M LIVIN'... GOIN' FROM YEAR TER F-FF-FFUCKIN' YEAR IN THIS SHED... JUSST LOOKIN' F'TH'NEXT ONE F-FFUCKIN' FORTEH-NINE...
...TWO OR THREE TIME A F-FFUCKIN' DAY...
...F-FFOUR OR F-FFIVE ON OCCASION...
...MEBBE SIX OR SEVEN...
A WISH ME LIFE WOH OVEH! DY'EAR ME..?! A WISH A WOH DEAD AN' IN ME F-FFUCKIN' GRAVE..!
...'COS HELL COULDN'T BE ANY F-FF-FFUCKIN' WORSE THAN THIS... IT'S NO F-FFUCKIN' LIFE I'VE GOT.
YER'VE GOT ME, LUV... AN' US KIDS... LITTLE FOUR 'ERE...
AS A SAY, A'D BE 'APPIEH IF A WOS DEDD AN' SIX F-FFUCKIN' F-FFOOT UNDEH.
WELL YER CAN DO THAT LATEH, BECOS LITTLE FOUR 'ERE WANTS T'GO TER'TH' PANTOMIME.
GROAN
AW... F-FFUCKIN' 'ELL... CAN'T YOO TEK CUNT..?
NO A FUCKIN' CAN'T. A'M BUSEH DOIN' US DINNEH.
...TURKEH DINOSAURS AN' SUNNEH D WI' AALL TH'TRIMMINGS...
SLURP!
...AN' ANGEL DELIGHT FER US AFTEHS.
...AN' YER CAN CUM IN TH'OUSE AN' 'AVE SUM IF YER TEK FOUR TER 'IS PANTOMIME..!
IT SHOULD BE GOOD... IT'S 'ER OFF STRICTLEH AS FUCKIN' CINDERELLEH... AN' THAT CUNT 'OO USED DO LOCAL WEATHEH AS BUTTONS.
HMM...
MIND... A'LL NEED SUM MUNNEH FERRUS F-FFUCKIN' TICKITS...
'OW MUCH ARE THEH..?
SEVERAL HOURS LATER...
...YER'VE SPENT BAIRNS'S FUCKIN' PANTO MUNNEH ON FUCKIN' ACE, AN'T YER..?!
OH NO I F-FFUCKIN' 'AVEN'T..!
OH YES YOO FUCKIN' 'AVE!
OH NO I F-FFUCKIN' 'AVEN'T..!
OH YES YOO FUCKIN' 'AVE!
OH NO I F-FFUCKIN' 'AVEN'T..!
OH YES YOO FUCKIN' 'AVE!
OH NO I F-FFUCKIN' 'AVEN'T..!
OH YES YOO FUCKIN' 'AVE!
OH NO I F-FFUCKIN' 'AVEN'T..!

Something for the weekend? It's

Viz

THE

BARBER'S POLE

A Headful of Nit-Ridden Follicles Combed from Issues 302~311

Short Back and Sides
Graham Dury, Simon Thorp and Alex Morris

Shampoo and Sets

Adrian Bamforth, Mark Bates, Alistair Blacklaw, Iain Cameron, Christian Boston, Kevin Caswell-Jones, Alex Collier, Jack Dury, Simon Ecob, Tom Ellen, Chad Elliot, Barney Farmer, David Glasper, Lee Healey, Davey Jones, Marc Jones, Aiden Kelly, Julian Lawrence, Christian Marshall, Luke McGarry, Steve McGarry, Howard McWilliam, Richard Milne, Paul Palmer, Tom Paterson, Sophie Poole, Paul Rainey, David Slade, Paul Solomons, Kent Tayler, Neil Tollfree, Nick Tolson, Matt Vickers and Stevie White.

Tuppenny All-Offs

David Saunders and Lee Boyman

Published by Diamond Publishing Ltd
2nd Floor, Saunders House,
52-53 The Mall, Ealing,
London W5 3TA

ISBN 978-1-91642-194-3
First Printing Summer 2023

Subscribe online at www.viz.co.uk
Find us at facebook.com/vizcomic and twitter.com/vizcomic

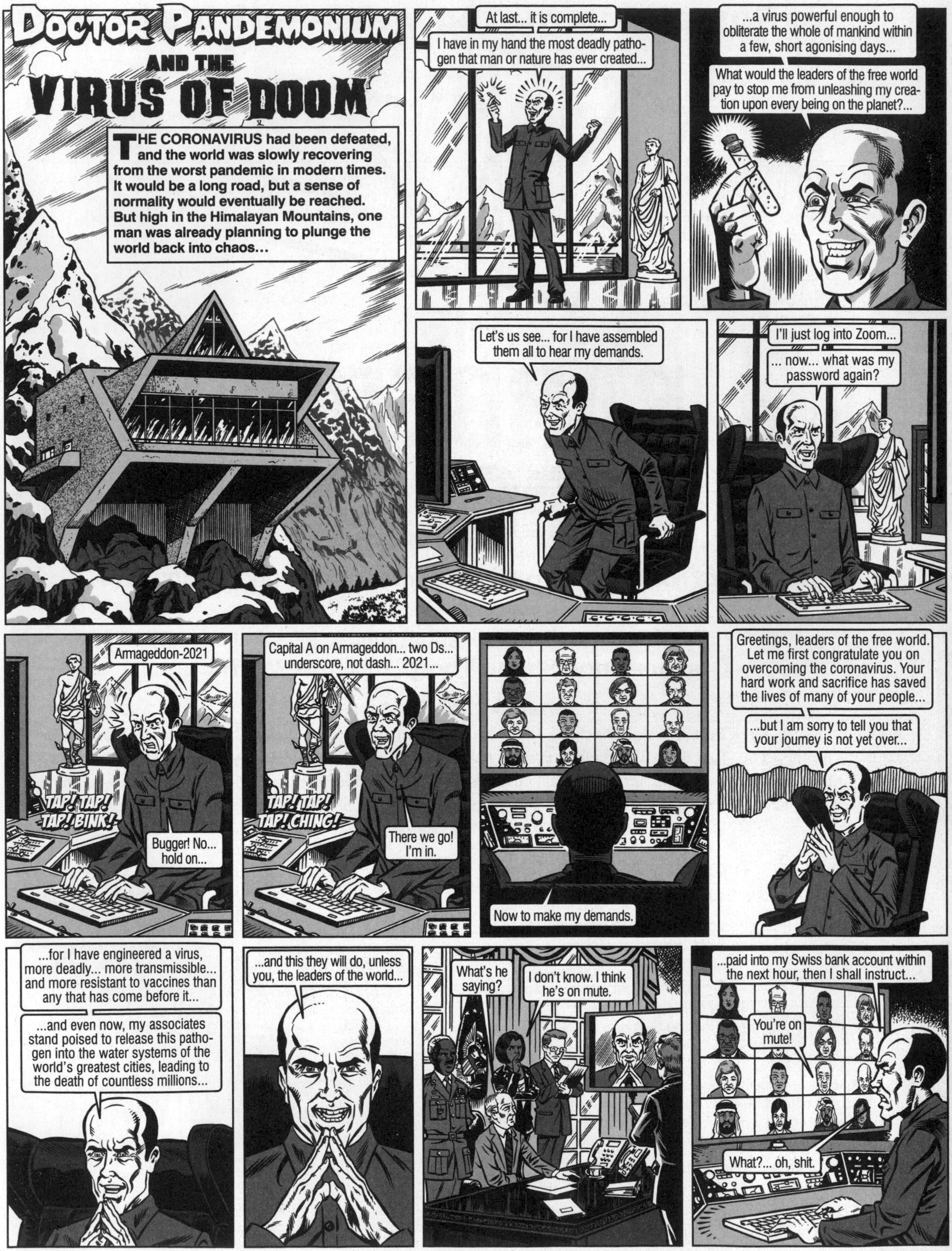
DOCTOR PANDEMONIUM AND THE VIRUS OF DOOM
THE CORONAVIRUS had been defeated, and the world was slowly recovering from the worst pandemic in modern times. It would be a long road, but a sense of normality would eventually be reached. But high in the Himalayan Mountains, one man was already planning to plunge the world back into chaos...
At last... it is complete...
I have in my hand the most deadly pathogen that man or nature has ever created...
...a virus powerful enough to obliterate the whole of mankind within a few, short agonising days...
What would the leaders of the free world pay to stop me from unleashing my creation upon every being on the planet?...
Let's us see... for I have assembled them all to hear my demands.
I'll just log into Zoom...
... now... what was my password again?
Armageddon-2021
TAP! TAP! TAP! BINK!
Bugger! No... hold on...
Capital A on Armageddon... two Ds... underscore, not dash... 2021...
TAP! TAP! TAP! CHING!
There we go! I'm in.
Now to make my demands.
Greetings, leaders of the free world. Let me first congratulate you on overcoming the coronavirus. Your hard work and sacrifice has saved the lives of many of your people...
...but I am sorry to tell you that your journey is not yet over...
...for I have engineered a virus, more deadly... more transmissible... and more resistant to vaccines than any that has come before it...
...and even now, my associates stand poised to release this pathogen into the water systems of the world's greatest cities, leading to the death of countless millions...
...and this they will do, unless you, the leaders of the world...
What's he saying?
I don't know. I think he's on mute.
...paid into my Swiss bank account within the next hour, then I shall instruct...
You're on mute!
What?... oh, shit.

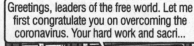

Can you hear me?
Yes, we can now. I think you were on mute.
I'll start again.

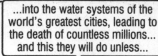
Greetings, leaders of the free world. Let me first congratulate you on overcoming the coronavirus. Your hard work and sacri...

Oh, he's frozen.
You've frozen!

Ich denke er ist eingefroren
Ja. Er muss die Verbindung verloren haben.

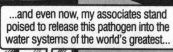
...into the water systems of the world's greatest cities, leading to the death of countless millions... and this they will do unless...
Sorry, you froze.
What?

What was the last thing I said?
You had just congratulated us on overcoming the coronavirus.
Oh, Jesus...

Erm... your hard work and sacrifice has saved the lives of many of your people...but I am sorry to tell you that your journey is not yet over...

...for I have engineered a virus, more deadly... more transmissible... and more resistant to vaccines than any that has come before it.

...and even now, my associates stand poised to release this pathogen into the water systems of the world's greatest...
...sorry... hang on a second...

Daddy's just talking to some very important people... go and play with Mummy...
Gee. Kids, huh?
Heh! Heh!

Sorry about that...er...
Thank you... erm... where was I?...
What lovely children, Dr Pandemonium
Release the pathogen into the water system.

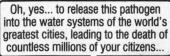
Oh, yes... to release this pathogen into the water systems of the world's greatest cities, leading to the death of countless millions of your citizens...
You're on mute again.

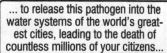
... to release this pathogen into the water systems of the world's greatest cities, leading to the death of countless millions of your citizens...
TAP! CHING!

SHIT!
ZOOM
Your FREE TRIAL with ZOOM has ended. Subscribe NOW for just £9.99 per month.
Upgrade to Zoom Business for just £14.99 per month.

Next Week:
Dr Pandemonium takes out a subscription to Zoom Pro, only to find that his operating system doesn't support it, and he needs to upgrade it to Windows 10 version 20H2.

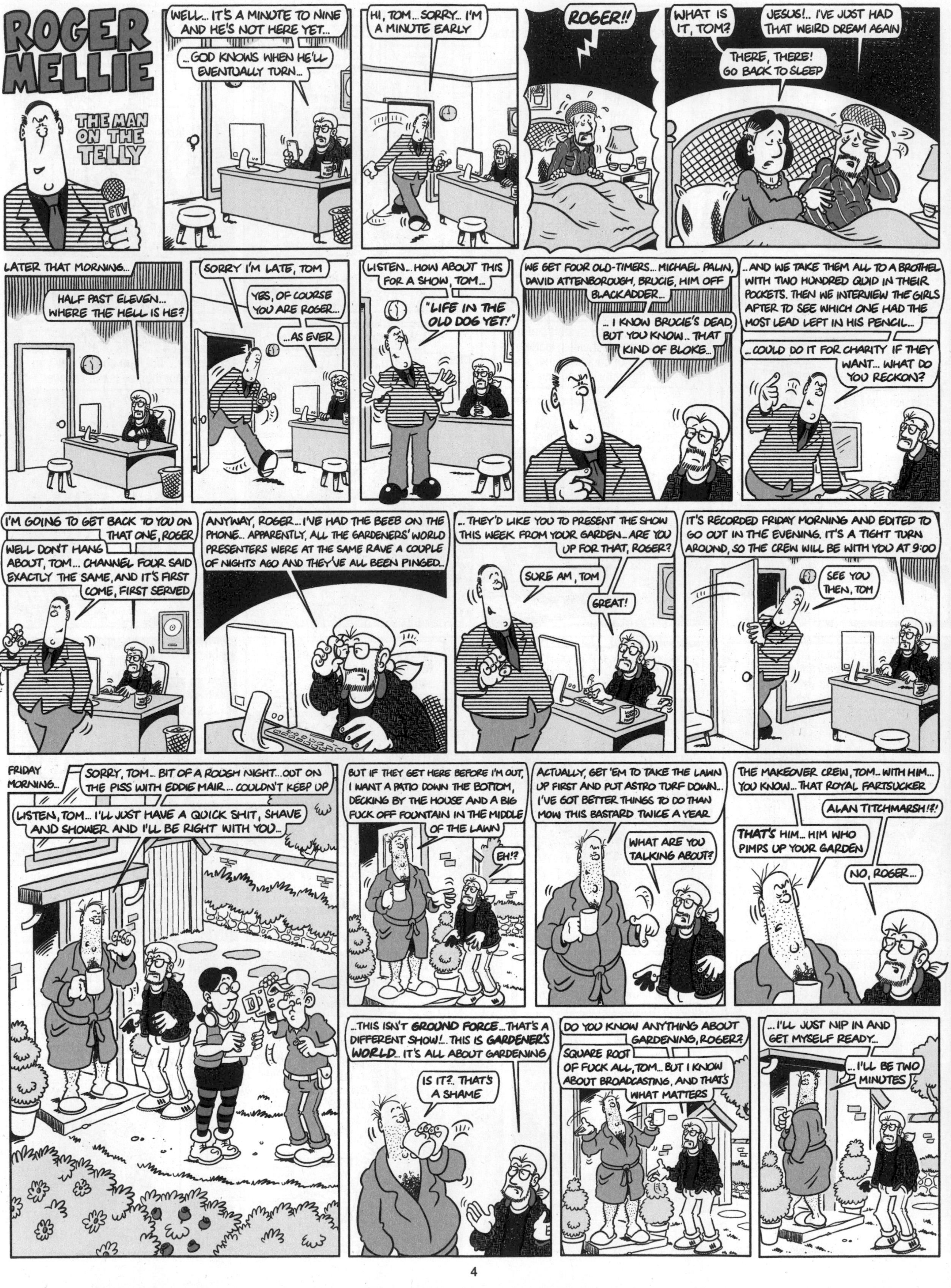
ROGER MELLIE
THE MAN ON THE TELLY
FTV
WELL... IT'S A MINUTE TO NINE AND HE'S NOT HERE YET...
...GOD KNOWS WHEN HE'LL EVENTUALLY TURN...
HI, TOM... SORRY... I'M A MINUTE EARLY
ROGER!!
WHAT IS IT, TOM?
JESUS!... I'VE JUST HAD THAT WEIRD DREAM AGAIN
THERE, THERE! GO BACK TO SLEEP
LATER THAT MORNING...
HALF PAST ELEVEN... WHERE THE HELL IS HE?
SORRY I'M LATE, TOM
YES, OF COURSE YOU ARE ROGER...
...AS EVER
LISTEN... HOW ABOUT THIS FOR A SHOW, TOM...
"LIFE IN THE OLD DOG YET!"
WE GET FOUR OLD-TIMERS... MICHAEL PALIN, DAVID ATTENBOROUGH, BRUCIE, HIM OFF BLACKADDER...
... I KNOW BRUCIE'S DEAD, BUT YOU KNOW... THAT KIND OF BLOKE...
...AND WE TAKE THEM ALL TO A BROTHEL WITH TWO HUNDRED QUID IN THEIR POCKETS. THEN WE INTERVIEW THE GIRLS AFTER TO SEE WHICH ONE HAD THE MOST LEAD LEFT IN HIS PENCIL...
...COULD DO IT FOR CHARITY IF THEY WANT... WHAT DO YOU RECKON?
I'M GOING TO GET BACK TO YOU ON THAT ONE, ROGER
WELL DON'T HANG ABOUT, TOM... CHANNEL FOUR SAID EXACTLY THE SAME, AND IT'S FIRST COME, FIRST SERVED
ANYWAY, ROGER... I'VE HAD THE BEEB ON THE PHONE... APPARENTLY, ALL THE GARDENERS' WORLD PRESENTERS WERE AT THE SAME RAVE A COUPLE OF NIGHTS AGO AND THEY'VE ALL BEEN PINGED...
... THEY'D LIKE YOU TO PRESENT THE SHOW THIS WEEK FROM YOUR GARDEN... ARE YOU UP FOR THAT, ROGER?
SURE AM, TOM
GREAT!
IT'S RECORDED FRIDAY MORNING AND EDITED TO GO OUT IN THE EVENING. IT'S A TIGHT TURN AROUND, SO THE CREW WILL BE WITH YOU AT 9:00
SEE YOU THEN, TOM
FRIDAY MORNING...
SORRY, TOM... BIT OF A ROUGH NIGHT... OUT ON THE PISS WITH EDDIE MAIR... COULDN'T KEEP UP
LISTEN, TOM... I'LL JUST HAVE A QUICK SHIT, SHAVE AND SHOWER AND I'LL BE RIGHT WITH YOU...
BUT IF THEY GET HERE BEFORE I'M OUT, I WANT A PATIO DOWN THE BOTTOM, DECKING BY THE HOUSE AND A BIG FUCK OFF FOUNTAIN IN THE MIDDLE OF THE LAWN
EH!?
ACTUALLY, GET 'EM TO TAKE THE LAWN UP FIRST AND PUT ASTRO TURF DOWN... I'VE GOT BETTER THINGS TO DO THAN MOW THIS BASTARD TWICE A YEAR
WHAT ARE YOU TALKING ABOUT?
THE MAKEOVER CREW, TOM... WITH HIM... YOU KNOW... THAT ROYAL FARTSUCKER
ALAN TITCHMARSH!?!
THAT'S HIM... HIM WHO PIMPS UP YOUR GARDEN
NO, ROGER...
...THIS ISN'T GROUND FORCE... THAT'S A DIFFERENT SHOW!... THIS IS GARDENER'S WORLD... IT'S ALL ABOUT GARDENING
IS IT?.. THAT'S A SHAME
DO YOU KNOW ANYTHING ABOUT GARDENING, ROGER?
SQUARE ROOT OF FUCK ALL, TOM... BUT I KNOW ABOUT BROADCASTING, AND THAT'S WHAT MATTERS
...I'LL JUST NIP IN AND GET MYSELF READY...
...I'LL BE TWO MINUTES

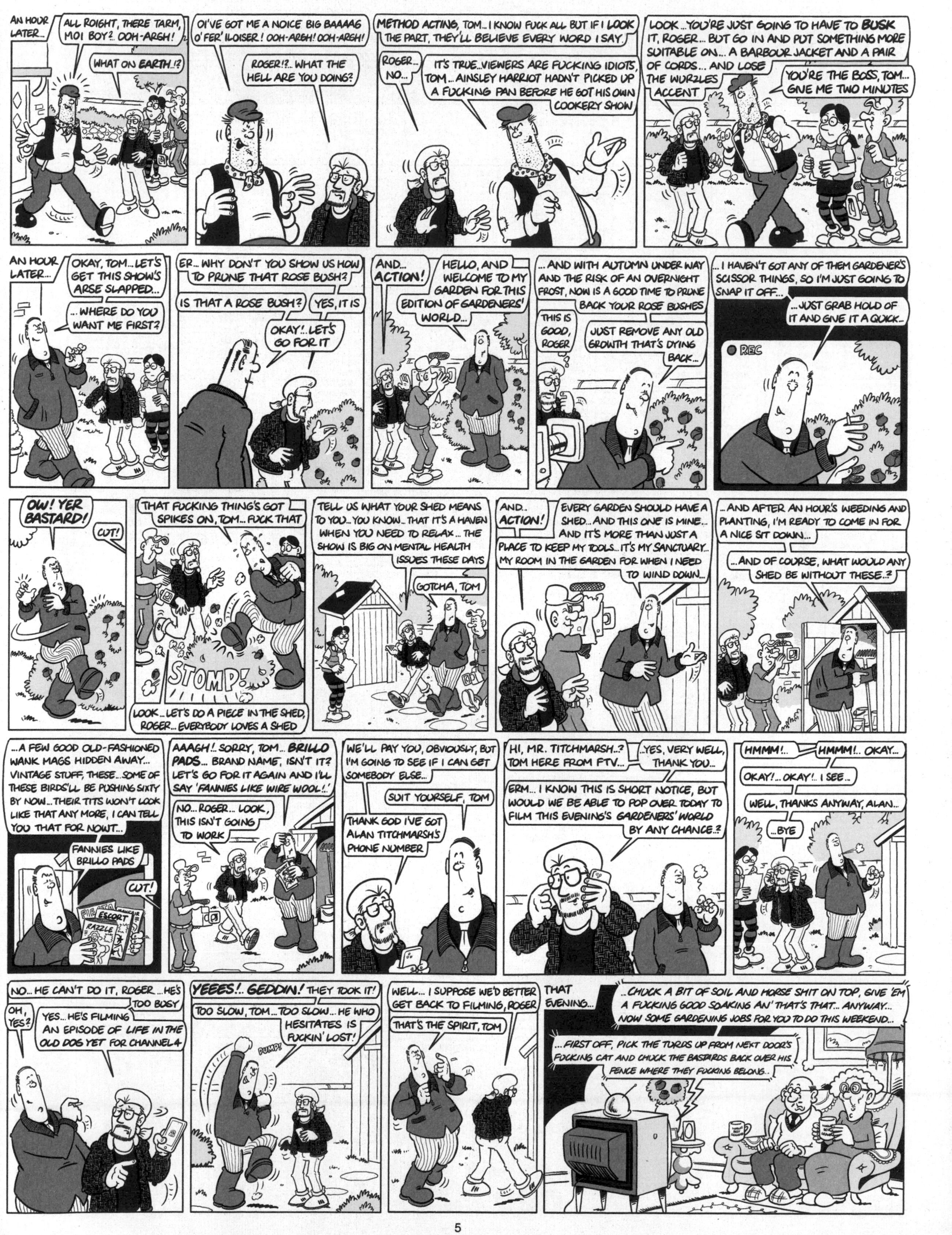
AN HOUR LATER...
ALL ROIGHT, THERE TARM, MOI BOY?.. OOH-ARGH!
WHAT ON EARTH..!?
OI'VE GOT ME A NOICE BIG BAAAAG O' FER' ILOISER! OOH-ARGH! OOH-ARGH!
ROGER!?.. WHAT THE HELL ARE YOU DOING?
METHOD ACTING, TOM... I KNOW FUCK ALL BUT IF I LOOK THE PART, THEY'LL BELIEVE EVERY WORD I SAY.
ROGER... NO...
IT'S TRUE...VIEWERS ARE FUCKING IDIOTS, TOM... AINSLEY HARRIOT HADN'T PICKED UP A FUCKING PAN BEFORE HE GOT HIS OWN COOKERY SHOW
LOOK... YOU'RE JUST GOING TO HAVE TO BUSK IT, ROGER... BUT GO IN AND PUT SOMETHING MORE SUITABLE ON... A BARBOUR JACKET AND A PAIR OF CORDS... AND LOSE THE WURZLES ACCENT
YOU'RE THE BOSS, TOM... GIVE ME TWO MINUTES
AN HOUR LATER...
OKAY, TOM... LET'S GET THIS SHOW'S ARSE SLAPPED...
...WHERE DO YOU WANT ME FIRST?
ER... WHY DON'T YOU SHOW US HOW TO PRUNE THAT ROSE BUSH?
IS THAT A ROSE BUSH?
YES, IT IS
OKAY!.. LET'S GO FOR IT
AND... ACTION!
HELLO, AND WELCOME TO MY GARDEN FOR THIS EDITION OF GARDENERS' WORLD...
...AND WITH AUTUMN UNDER WAY AND THE RISK OF AN OVERNIGHT FROST, NOW IS A GOOD TIME TO PRUNE BACK YOUR ROSE BUSHES
THIS IS GOOD, ROGER
JUST REMOVE ANY OLD GROWTH THAT'S DYING BACK...
...I HAVEN'T GOT ANY OF THEM GARDENER'S SCISSOR THINGS, SO I'M JUST GOING TO SNAP IT OFF...
...JUST GRAB HOLD OF IT AND GIVE IT A QUICK...
REC
OW! YER BASTARD!
CUT!
THAT FUCKING THING'S GOT SPIKES ON, TOM... FUCK THAT
STOMP!
LOOK... LET'S DO A PIECE IN THE SHED, ROGER... EVERYBODY LOVES A SHED
TELL US WHAT YOUR SHED MEANS TO YOU... YOU KNOW... THAT IT'S A HAVEN WHEN YOU NEED TO RELAX... THE SHOW IS BIG ON MENTAL HEALTH ISSUES THESE DAYS
GOTCHA, TOM
AND.. ACTION!
EVERY GARDEN SHOULD HAVE A SHED... AND THIS ONE IS MINE... AND IT'S MORE THAN JUST A PLACE TO KEEP MY TOOLS... IT'S MY SANCTUARY... MY ROOM IN THE GARDEN FOR WHEN I NEED TO WIND DOWN...
...AND AFTER AN HOUR'S WEEDING AND PLANTING, I'M READY TO COME IN FOR A NICE SIT DOWN...
...AND OF COURSE, WHAT WOULD ANY SHED BE WITHOUT THESE..?
...A FEW GOOD OLD-FASHIONED WANK MAGS HIDDEN AWAY... VINTAGE STUFF, THESE... SOME OF THESE BIRDS'LL BE PUSHING SIXTY BY NOW... THEIR TITS WON'T LOOK LIKE THAT ANY MORE, I CAN TELL YOU THAT FOR NOWT...
FANNIES LIKE BRILLO PADS
CUT!
ESCORT
RAZZLE
AAAGH!.. SORRY, TOM... BRILLO PADS... BRAND NAME, ISN'T IT? LET'S GO FOR IT AGAIN AND I'LL SAY 'FANNIES LIKE WIRE WOOL!'
NO... ROGER... LOOK, THIS ISN'T GOING TO WORK
WE'LL PAY YOU, OBVIOUSLY, BUT I'M GOING TO SEE IF I CAN GET SOMEBODY ELSE...
SUIT YOURSELF, TOM
THANK GOD I'VE GOT ALAN TITCHMARSH'S PHONE NUMBER
HI, MR. TITCHMARSH..? TOM HERE FROM FTV...
...YES, VERY WELL, THANK YOU...
ERM... I KNOW THIS IS SHORT NOTICE, BUT WOULD WE BE ABLE TO POP OVER TODAY TO FILM THIS EVENING'S GARDENERS' WORLD BY ANY CHANCE..?
HMMM!..
HMMM!.. OKAY...
OKAY!... OKAY!.. I SEE..
WELL, THANKS ANYWAY, ALAN...
...BYE
NO... HE CAN'T DO IT, ROGER... HE'S TOO BUSY
OH, YES?
YES... HE'S FILMING AN EPISODE OF LIFE IN THE OLD DOG YET FOR CHANNEL 4
YEEES!.. GEDDIN! THEY TOOK IT!
TOO SLOW, TOM... TOO SLOW... HE WHO HESITATES IS FUCKIN' LOST!
PUMP!
WELL... I SUPPOSE WE'D BETTER GET BACK TO FILMING, ROGER
THAT'S THE SPIRIT, TOM
THAT EVENING...
...CHUCK A BIT OF SOIL AND HORSE SHIT ON TOP, GIVE 'EM A FUCKING GOOD SOAKING AN' THAT'S THAT... ANYWAY... NOW SOME GARDENING JOBS FOR YOU TO DO THIS WEEKEND...
...FIRST OFF, PICK THE TURDS UP FROM NEXT DOOR'S FUCKING CAT AND CHUCK THE BASTARDS BACK OVER HIS FENCE WHERE THEY FUCKING BELONG...

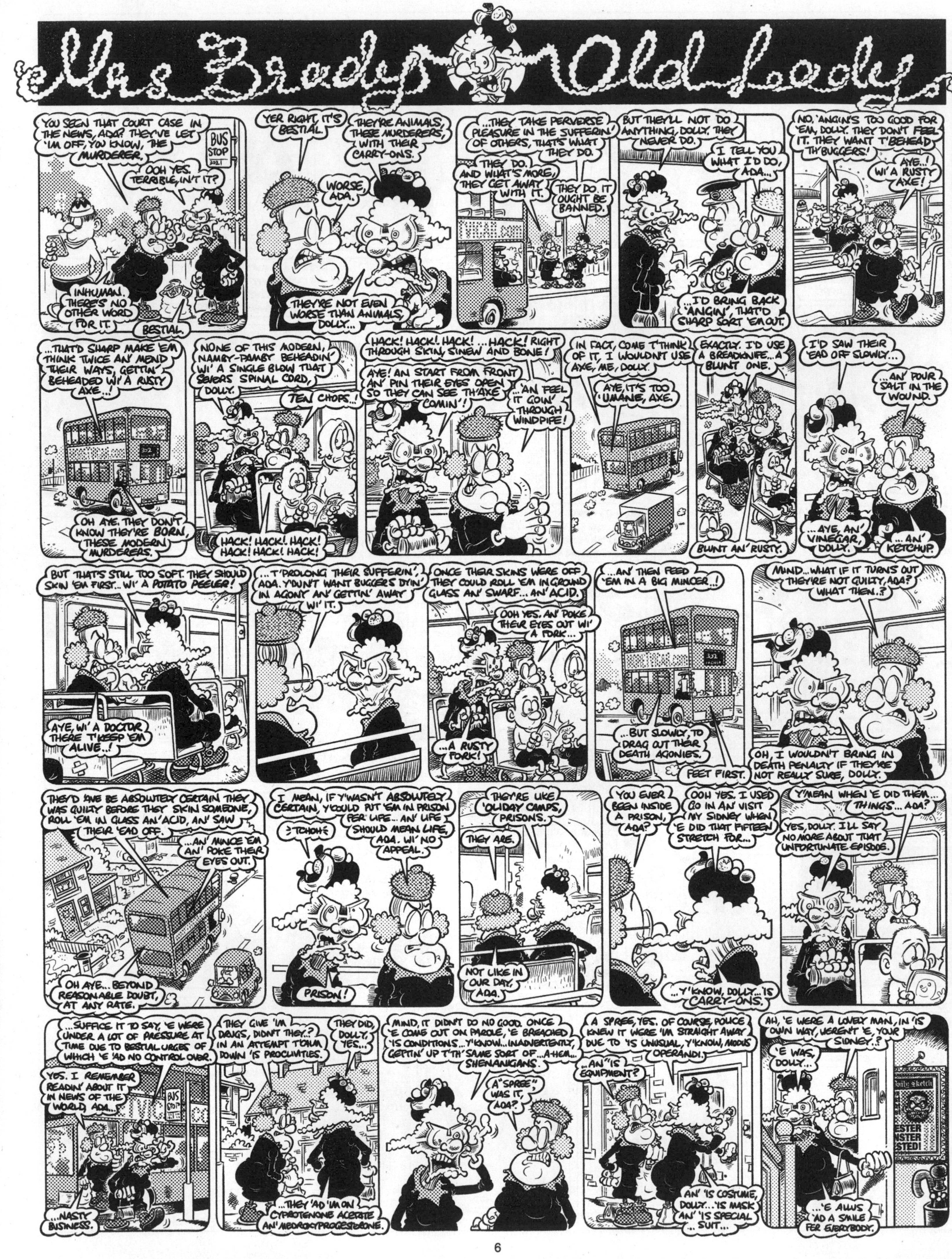
Mrs Brady Old Lady
YOU SEEN THAT COURT CASE IN THE NEWS, ADA? THEY'VE LET 'IM OFF, YOU KNOW, THE MURDERER.
BUS STOP 2021
OOH YES. TERRIBLE, IN'T IT?
INHUMAN. THERE'S NO OTHER WORD FOR IT.
BESTIAL.
YER RIGHT, IT'S BESTIAL.
THEY'RE ANIMALS, THESE MURDERERS, WITH THEIR CARRY-ONS.
WORSE, ADA.
THEY'RE NOT EVEN WORSE THAN ANIMALS, DOLLY...
...THEY TAKE PERVERSE PLEASURE IN THE SUFFERIN' OF OTHERS, THAT'S WHAT THEY DO.
THEY DO. AND WHAT'S MORE, THEY GET AWAY WITH IT.
THEY DO. IT OUGHT BE BANNED.
BUT THEY'LL NOT DO ANYTHING, DOLLY. THEY NEVER DO.
I TELL YOU WHAT I'D DO, ADA...
...I'D BRING BACK 'ANGIN', THAT'D SHARP SORT 'EM OUT.
NO, 'ANGIN'S TOO GOOD FOR 'EM, DOLLY. THEY DON'T FEEL IT. THEY WANT T'BEHEAD TH'BUGGERS!
AYE..! WI' A RUSTY AXE!
...THAT'D SHARP MAKE 'EM THINK TWICE AN' MEND THEIR WAYS, GETTIN' BEHEADED WI' A RUSTY AXE..!
OH AYE. THEY DON'T KNOW THEY'RE BORN, THESE MODERN MURDERERS.
NONE OF THIS MODERN, NAMBY-PAMBY BEHEADIN' WI' A SINGLE BLOW THAT SEVERS SPINAL CORD, DOLLY.
TEN CHOPS..!
HACK! HACK! HACK! HACK! HACK! HACK!
HACK! HACK! HACK! ...HACK! RIGHT THROUGH SKIN, SINEW AND BONE!
AYE! AN' START FROM FRONT AN' PIN THEIR EYES OPEN SO THEY CAN SEE TH'AXE COMIN'!
...'AN FEEL IT GOIN' THROUGH WINDPIPE!
IN FACT, COME T'THINK OF IT, I WOULDN'T USE AXE, ME, DOLLY.
AYE, IT'S TOO 'UMANE, AXE.
EXACTLY. I'D USE A BREADKNIFE... A BLUNT ONE.
BLUNT AN' RUSTY.
I'D SAW THEIR 'EAD OFF SLOWLY...
...AN' POUR SALT IN THE WOUND.
...AYE, AN' VINEGAR, DOLLY.
...AN' KETCHUP.
BUT THAT'S STILL TOO SOFT. THEY SHOULD SKIN 'EM FIRST... WI' A POTATO PEELER!
AYE, WI' A DOCTOR THERE T'KEEP 'EM ALIVE..!
...T'PROLONG THEIR SUFFERIN', ADA. Y'DON'T WANT BUGGERS DYIN' IN AGONY AN' GETTIN' AWAY WI' IT.
ONCE THEIR SKINS WERE OFF THEY COULD ROLL 'EM IN GROUND GLASS AN' SWARF... AN' ACID.
OOH YES. AN' POKE THEIR EYES OUT WI' A FORK...
...A RUSTY FORK!
...AN' THEN FEED 'EM IN A BIG MINCER..!
...BUT SLOWLY, TO DRAG OUT THEIR DEATH AGONIES.
FEET FIRST.
MIND... WHAT IF IT TURNS OUT THEY'RE NOT GUILTY, ADA? WHAT THEN..?
OH, I WOULDN'T BRING IN DEATH PENALTY IF THEY'RE NOT REALLY SURE, DOLLY.
THEY'D 'AVE BE ABSOLUTELY CERTAIN THEY WAS GUILTY BEFORE THEY SKIN SOMEONE, ROLL 'EM IN GLASS AN' ACID, AN' SAW THEIR 'EAD OFF.
...AN' MINCE 'EM AN' POKE THEIR EYES OUT.
OH AYE... BEYOND REASONABLE DOUBT, AT ANY RATE.
I MEAN, IF Y'WASN'T ABSOLUTELY CERTAIN, Y'COULD PUT 'EM IN PRISON FER LIFE... AN' LIFE SHOULD MEAN LIFE, ADA. WI' NO APPEAL.
TCHOH
PRISON!
THEY'RE LIKE 'OLIDAY CAMPS, PRISONS.
THEY ARE.
NOT LIKE IN OUR DAY, ADA.
YOU EVER BEEN INSIDE A PRISON, ADA?
OOH YES. I USED GO IN AN' VISIT MY SIDNEY WHEN 'E DID THAT FIFTEEN STRETCH FOR...
...Y'KNOW, DOLLY... 'IS CARRY-ONS.
Y'MEAN WHEN 'E DID THEM... THINGS... ADA?
YES, DOLLY. I'LL SAY NO MORE ABOUT THAT UNFORTUNATE EPISODE.
...SUFFICE IT TO SAY, 'E WERE UNDER A LOT OF PRESSURE AT TIME DUE TO BESTIAL URGES OF WHICH 'E 'AD NO CONTROL OVER.
YES. I REMEMBER READIN' ABOUT IT IN NEWS OF THE WORLD, ADA.
BUS STOP
...NASTY BUSINESS.
THEY GIVE 'IM DRUGS, DIDN'T THEY..? IN AN ATTEMPT T'CALM DOWN 'IS PROCLIVITIES.
THEY DID, DOLLY, YES...
...THEY 'AD 'IM ON CYPROTENONE ACETATE AN' MEDROXYPROGESTERONE.
MIND, IT DIDN'T DO NO GOOD. ONCE 'E COME OUT ON PAROLE, 'E BREACHED 'IS CONDITIONS... Y'KNOW... INADVERTENTLY, GETTIN' UP T'TH' SAME SORT OF... A-HEM... SHENANIGANS.
A 'SPREE', WAS IT, ADA?
A SPREE, YES. OF COURSE, POLICE KNEW IT WERE 'IM STRAIGHT AWAY DUE TO 'IS UNUSUAL, Y'KNOW, MODUS OPERANDI.
...AN' 'IS EQUIPMENT?
AN' 'IS COSTUME, DOLLY... 'IS MASK AN' 'IS SPECIAL ...SUIT...
AH, 'E WERE A LOVELY MAN, IN 'IS OWN WAY, WEREN'T 'E, YOUR SIDNEY..?
'E WAS, DOLLY...
...'E ALLUS 'AD A SMILE FER EVERYBODY.

What's in a Name?
~Rishi Sunak

SINCE TAKING up residence at number 10 Downing Street over a year ago, former Chancellor of the Exchequer **RISHI SUNAK** has got Britain's ladies' interest rates soaring. The true blue First Lord of the Treasury may be small in stature, but he's got a pound or two in his pocket that any red-blooded girl would love to get her hands on. We see him every day on the news, making speeches, visiting hospitals and borrowing hundreds of billions to pay for Brexit. But what is this dishy budget bombshell PM really like when he's not acting the giddy goat for the telly cameras?

Believe it or not, the secret is hidden in plain sight, woven into the very letters that make up his name.

R **is for RABBITS**
As a child, Rishi used to supplement his pocket money by breeding rabbits for TV magicians such as David Nixon, Paul Daniels and the Great Soprendo. "The thing is, conjurors get through loads of rabbits, because every time they put one in a top hat and magic it, it vanishes and they have to replace it," he told the BBC's Gary O'Donoghue. "I used to charge them £2 for each rabbit, and £1 for pigeons to appear out of hankies."

I **is for INSANE CLOWN POSSE**
Not many people in government realise that Sunak is a keen "juggalo" - a fan of hardcore Detroit hip-hop outfit Insane Clown Posse. Indeed, the Premier has all their records and estimates that he has seen the *Carnival of Carnage* duo in concert more than fifty times.
"Whenever I'm chilling out after raising the minimum lending rate by a quarter of one percent or levying a stamp duty surcharge on foreign buyers of properties in England and Northern Ireland, I stick J and Shaggy's latest LP on my record player, and turn that motherfucker up to eleven," he told *Newsnight*'s Emily Maitlis.

S **is for SANTA CLAUS**
During a recent interview with *BBC Breakfast*'s Naga Munchetty, the Prime Minister revealed that he has been terrified of Santa Claus since childhood. "On Christmas Eve, I'm, so frightened of Father Christmas coming down my chimney that I have to sleep with the light on," he said. "When I was about sixteen, my mam told me that it was her and dad that did all my presents, and there was no such thing as Santa Claus, but I didn't believe her then and I don't believe her now."

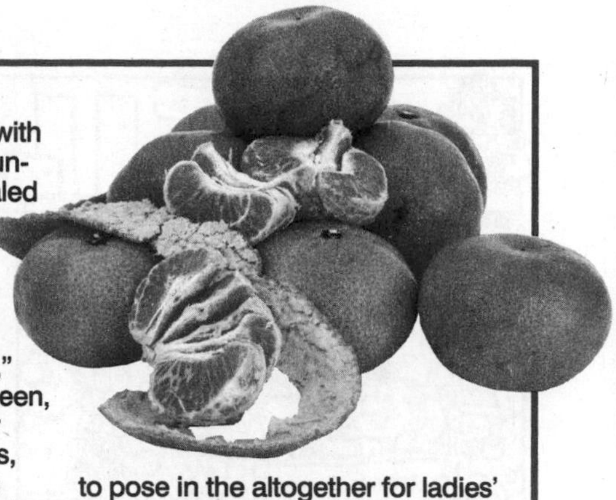

H **is for HIBISCUS TEA**
Sunak's favourite drink is Hibiscus tea, and he reckons he drinks at least 35 cups of the stuff every day. "It's supposed to be very good for you," he told the BBC's health editor Hugh Pym. "I saw on a website where it's packed with antioxidants and it fights bacterias. The only problem is that I have to get up and go for a piss every ten minutes, day and night, twenty-four hours a day."

I **is for ISUZU TROOPER**
After passing his driving test at the sixth attempt in 1998, Sunak celebrated by going out and buying his frst car - an Isuzu Trooper. And 25-years-later, the V-reg turbo-diesel off-roader, now with more than 300,000 miles on the clock, is still the car he drives to work in Parliament every day. "In all the years I've had my Trooper, it's only needed tyres, two exhausts and a new rear diff after the seal went on the old one. And I got that from a scrapyard for forty quid," the thrifty politician told *PM*'s Carolyn Quinn.

S **is for SATSUMAS**
Even though he's got fancy first class honours degrees from some of the world's most prestigious universities, including Oxford, Stanford and many more, Rishi says he simply can't tell the difference between satsumas and tangerines.

U **is for UNDERWEAR**
The pocket politician buys all his smalls from the children's section in George at Asda. He says: "I get a great deal on my little vests and Y-fronts because there's no VAT on kids' clothes, and even better, there's less chance of my scads falling down and showing my bot when I get up in the Commons to do an emergency budget or stand on a chair at the Treasury to adjust the Exchange Rate Mechanism."

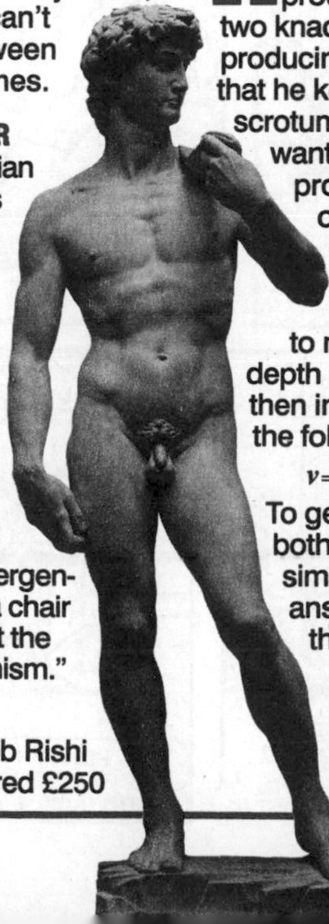

N **is for NUDE**
Cabinet heartthrob Rishi was recently offered £250

to pose in the altogether for ladies' wank mag *Playgirl*. "I can't pretend I wasn't tempted," he told BBC Parliamentary Correspondent Laura Kuenssberg. "The thought of all them sexually frustrated birds jilling themselves daft whilst checking out my meat and two veg was a real turn-on."

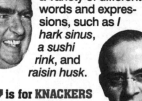

A **is for ANAGRAMS**
Like many former Chancellor of the Exchequers (eg Nigel Lawson - *wine gallons*, Denis Healey - *ashen eyelid*, Stafford Cripps - *stiff drops crap*), the letters in Rishi's name can be rearranged to make a variety of different words and expressions, such as *I hark sinus*, *a sushi rink*, and *raisin husk*.

K **is for KNACKERS**
Rishi is the proud owner of two knackers - sperm-producing reproductive glands that he keeps tucked away in his scrotum. If the Prime Minister wanted to find out the approximate volume (*v*) of one of his testicles, he could use a special measuring device called an orchidometer to measure its length (*l*), depth (*d*) and width (*w*), and then insert these figures into the following formula:

$$v = {}^4\!/_3\,\pi \times {}^l\!/_2 \times {}^d\!/_2 \times {}^w\!/_2$$

To get the total volume of both his knackers, he would simply have to double his answer - a piece of cake for the maths-whiz politician.

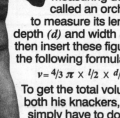

Next Week *What's in a Name?* looks at **The Artist Formerly Known as Prince**

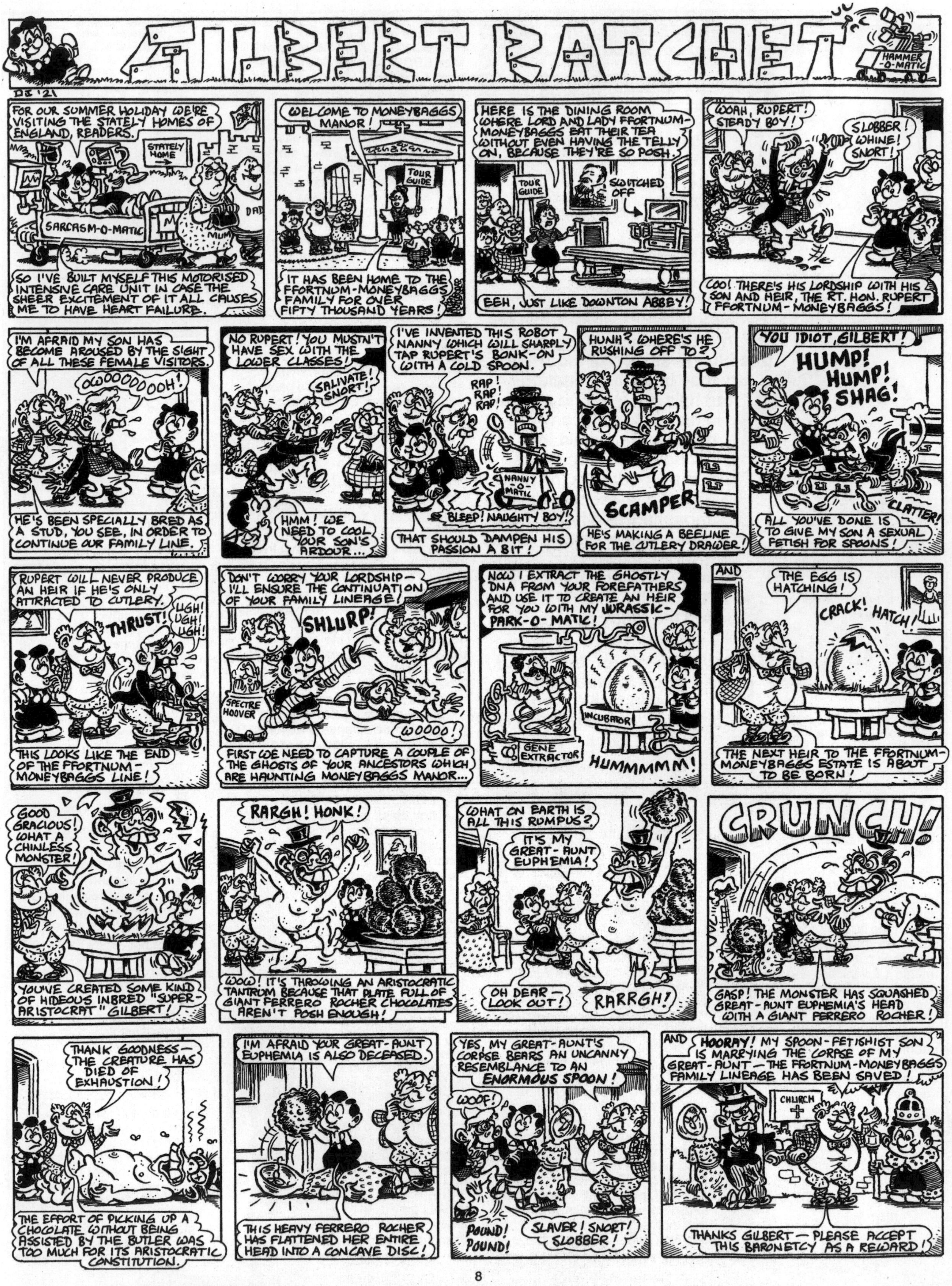
GILBERT RATCHET
HAMMER-O-MATIC
DJ '21
FOR OUR SUMMER HOLIDAY WE'RE VISITING THE STATELY HOMES OF ENGLAND, READERS.
STATELY HOME
SARCASM-O-MATIC
MUM
DAD
SO I'VE BUILT MYSELF THIS MOTORISED INTENSIVE CARE UNIT IN CASE THE SHEER EXCITEMENT OF IT ALL CAUSES ME TO HAVE HEART FAILURE.
WELCOME TO MONEYBAGGS MANOR!
TOUR GUIDE
IT HAS BEEN HOME TO THE FFORTNUM-MONEYBAGGS FAMILY FOR OVER FIFTY THOUSAND YEARS!
HERE IS THE DINING ROOM WHERE LORD AND LADY FFORTNUM-MONEYBAGGS EAT THEIR TEA WITHOUT EVEN HAVING THE TELLY ON, BECAUSE THEY'RE SO POSH.
TOUR GUIDE
SWITCHED OFF
EEH, JUST LIKE DOWNTON ABBEY!
WOAH, RUPERT! STEADY BOY!
SLOBBER! WHINE! SNORT!
COO! THERE'S HIS LORDSHIP WITH HIS SON AND HEIR, THE RT. HON. RUPERT FFORTNUM-MONEYBAGGS!
I'M AFRAID MY SON HAS BECOME AROUSED BY THE SIGHT OF ALL THESE FEMALE VISITORS.
OWOOOOOOOOH!
HE'S BEEN SPECIALLY BRED AS A STUD, YOU SEE, IN ORDER TO CONTINUE OUR FAMILY LINE.
NO RUPERT! YOU MUSTN'T HAVE SEX WITH THE LOWER CLASSES!
SALIVATE! SNORT!
HMM! WE NEED TO COOL YOUR SON'S ARDOUR...
I'VE INVENTED THIS ROBOT NANNY WHICH WILL SHARPLY TAP RUPERT'S BONK-ON WITH A COLD SPOON.
RAP! RAP! RAP!
NANNY-O-MATIC
BLEEP! NAUGHTY BOY!
THAT SHOULD DAMPEN HIS PASSION A BIT!
HUNH? WHERE'S HE RUSHING OFF TO?
SCAMPER
HE'S MAKING A BEELINE FOR THE CUTLERY DRAWER!
YOU IDIOT, GILBERT!
HUMP! HUMP! SHAG!
CLATTER!
ALL YOU'VE DONE IS TO GIVE MY SON A SEXUAL FETISH FOR SPOONS!
RUPERT WILL NEVER PRODUCE AN HEIR IF HE'S ONLY ATTRACTED TO CUTLERY.
THRUST!
UGH! UGH! UGH!
THIS LOOKS LIKE THE END OF THE FFORTNUM-MONEYBAGGS LINE!
DON'T WORRY YOUR LORDSHIP — I'LL ENSURE THE CONTINUATION OF YOUR FAMILY LINEAGE!
SHLURP!
SPECTRE HOOVER
WOOOO!
FIRST WE NEED TO CAPTURE A COUPLE OF THE GHOSTS OF YOUR ANCESTORS WHICH ARE HAUNTING MONEYBAGGS MANOR...
NOW I EXTRACT THE GHOSTLY DNA FROM YOUR FOREFATHERS AND USE IT TO CREATE AN HEIR FOR YOU WITH MY JURASSIC-PARK-O-MATIC!
INCUBATOR
GENE EXTRACTOR
HUMMMMM!
AND
THE EGG IS HATCHING!
CRACK! HATCH!
THE NEXT HEIR TO THE FFORTNUM-MONEYBAGGS ESTATE IS ABOUT TO BE BORN!
GOOD GRACIOUS! WHAT A CHINLESS MONSTER!
YOU'VE CREATED SOME KIND OF HIDEOUS INBRED "SUPER-ARISTOCRAT" GILBERT!
RARGH! HONK!
WOW! IT'S THROWING AN ARISTOCRATIC TANTRUM BECAUSE THAT PLATE FULL OF GIANT FERRERO ROCHER CHOCOLATES AREN'T POSH ENOUGH!
WHAT ON EARTH IS ALL THIS RUMPUS?
IT'S MY GREAT-AUNT EUPHEMIA!
OH DEAR — LOOK OUT!
RARRGH!
CRUNCH!
GASP! THE MONSTER HAS SQUASHED GREAT-AUNT EUPHEMIA'S HEAD WITH A GIANT FERRERO ROCHER!
THANK GOODNESS — THE CREATURE HAS DIED OF EXHAUSTION!
THE EFFORT OF PICKING UP A CHOCOLATE WITHOUT BEING ASSISTED BY THE BUTLER WAS TOO MUCH FOR ITS ARISTOCRATIC CONSTITUTION.
I'M AFRAID YOUR GREAT-AUNT EUPHEMIA IS ALSO DECEASED.
THIS HEAVY FERRERO ROCHER HAS FLATTENED HER ENTIRE HEAD INTO A CONCAVE DISC!
YES, MY GREAT-AUNT'S CORPSE BEARS AN UNCANNY RESEMBLANCE TO AN ENORMOUS SPOON!
WOOF!
POUND! POUND!
SLAVER! SNORT! SLOBBER!
AND HOORAY! MY SPOON-FETISHIST SON IS MARRYING THE CORPSE OF MY GREAT-AUNT — THE FFORTNUM-MONEYBAGGS FAMILY LINEAGE HAS BEEN SAVED!
CHURCH
THANKS GILBERT — PLEASE ACCEPT THIS BARONETCY AS A REWARD!

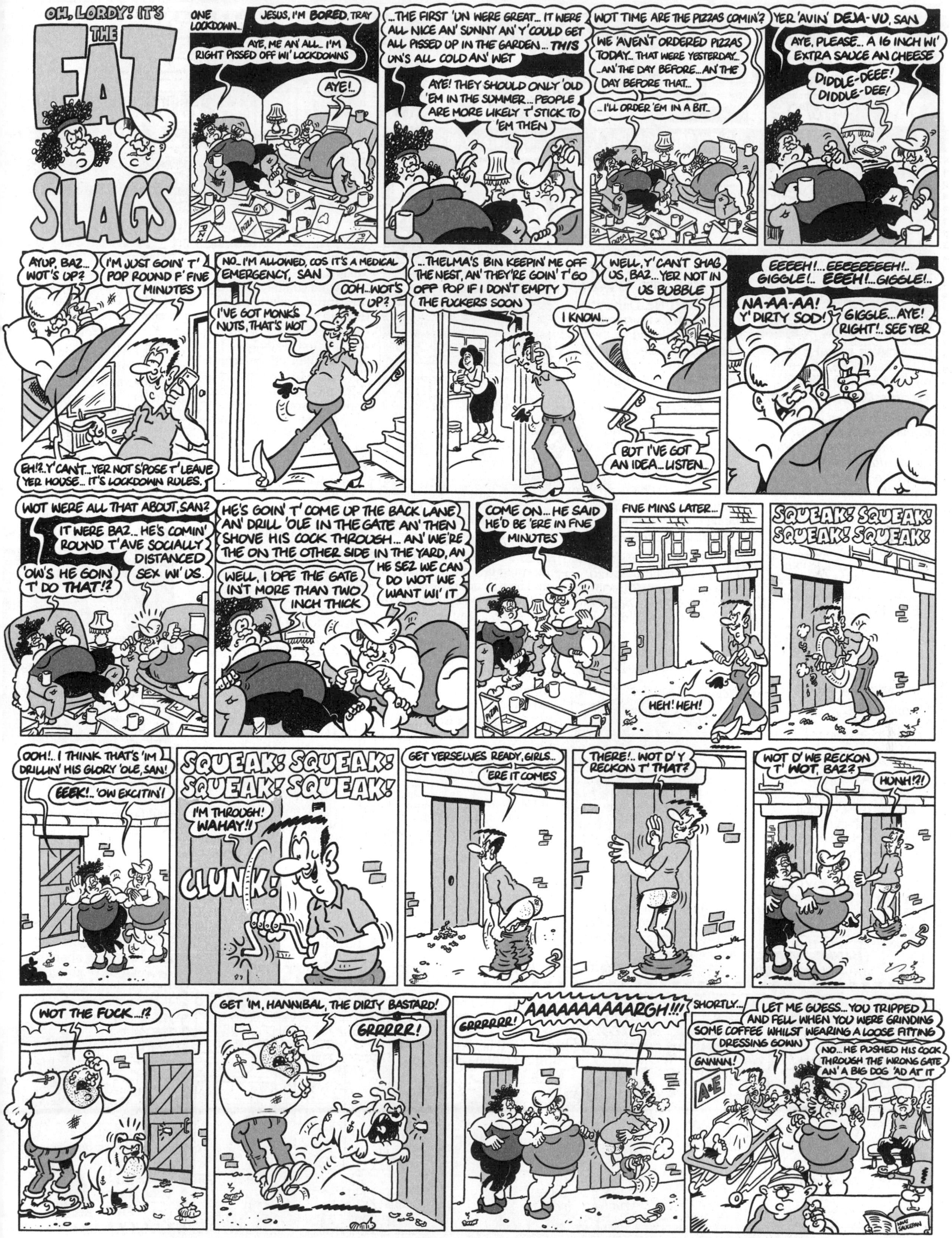
OH, LORDY! IT'S
THE FAT SLAGS
ONE LOCKDOWN...
JESUS, I'M BORED, TRAY
AYE, ME AN' ALL... I'M RIGHT PISSED OFF WI' LOCKDOWNS
...THE FIRST 'UN WERE GREAT... IT WERE ALL NICE AN' SUNNY AN' Y'COULD GET ALL PISSED UP IN THE GARDEN... THIS UN'S ALL COLD AN' WET
AYE!..
AYE! THEY SHOULD ONLY 'OLD 'EM IN THE SUMMER... PEOPLE ARE MORE LIKELY T' STICK TO 'EM THEN
WOT TIME ARE THE PIZZAS COMIN'?
WE 'AVEN'T ORDERED PIZZAS TODAY... THAT WERE YESTERDAY... ...AN' THE DAY BEFORE... AN' THE DAY BEFORE THAT...
...I'LL ORDER 'EM IN A BIT...
YER 'AVIN' DEJA-VU, SAN
AYE, PLEASE... A 16 INCH WI' EXTRA SAUCE AN CHEESE
DIDDLE-DEEE! DIDDLE-DEE!
AYUP, BAZ... WOT'S UP?
I'M JUST GOIN' T' POP ROUND F' FIVE MINUTES
EH!?.. Y' CAN'T... YER NOT S'POSE T' LEAVE YER HOUSE... IT'S LOCKDOWN RULES.
NO... I'M ALLOWED, COS IT'S A MEDICAL EMERGENCY, SAN
OOH... WOT'S UP?
I'VE GOT MONK'S NUTS, THAT'S WOT
...THELMA'S BIN KEEPIN' ME OFF THE NEST, AN' THEY'RE GOIN' T' GO OFF POP IF I DON'T EMPTY THE FUCKERS SOON
WELL, Y' CAN'T SHAG US, BAZ... YER NOT IN US BUBBLE
I KNOW...
BUT I'VE GOT AN IDEA... LISTEN...
EEEEH!.. EEEEEEEEH!.. GIGGLE!.. EEEH!.. GIGGLE!..
NA-AA-AA! Y' DIRTY SOD!
GIGGLE... AYE! RIGHT!.. SEE YER
WOT WERE ALL THAT ABOUT, SAN?
IT WERE BAZ... HE'S COMIN' ROUND T'AVE SOCIALLY DISTANCED SEX WI' US.
'OW'S HE GOIN' T' DO THAT!?
HE'S GOIN' T' COME UP THE BACK LANE AN' DRILL 'OLE IN THE GATE AN' THEN SHOVE HIS COCK THROUGH... AN' WE'RE THE ON THE OTHER SIDE IN THE YARD, AN HE SEZ WE CAN DO WOT WE WANT WI' IT
WELL, I 'OPE THE GATE IN'T MORE THAN TWO INCH THICK
COME ON... HE SAID HE'D BE 'ERE IN FIVE MINUTES
FIVE MINS LATER...
HEH! HEH!
SQUEAK! SQUEAK! SQUEAK! SQUEAK!
OOH!.. I THINK THAT'S 'IM DRILLIN' HIS GLORY 'OLE, SAN!
EEEK!.. 'OW EXCITIN'!
SQUEAK! SQUEAK! SQUEAK! SQUEAK!
I'M THROUGH! WAHAY!!
CLUNK!
GET YERSELVES READY, GIRLS...
'ERE IT COMES
THERE!.. WOT D'Y RECKON T' THAT?
WOT D'WE RECKON T' WOT, BAZ?
HUNH!?!
WOT THE FUCK...!?
GET 'IM, HANNIBAL, THE DIRTY BASTARD!
GRRRRR!
GRRRRRR!
AAAAAAAAARGH!!!
SHORTLY...
LET ME GUESS... YOU TRIPPED AND FELL WHEN YOU WERE GRINDING SOME COFFEE WHILST WEARING A LOOSE FITTING DRESSING GOWN
GNNNN!
NO... HE PUSHED HIS COCK THROUGH THE WRONG GATE AN' A BIG DOG 'AD AT IT
A&E

LETTERBOCKS

Viz Comic, P.O. Box 841 Whitley Bay, NE26 9EQ letters@viz.co.uk

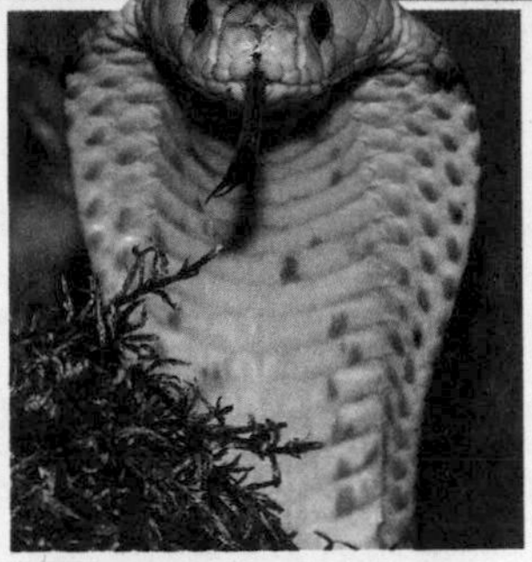

☐ **HAVE** any of your readers ever been bit on the arse off a snake?

George Dirtcrumbs, Tring

∗ Well, we have a lot of readers, Mr Dirtcrumbs, so it's entirely possible that one or more of them have been bit on the arse off a snake. The only way to find out is to do a poll. All our readers are requested to fill in the attached form, and send it, along with a £1 administration fee to: Viz Comic Arse Snakebite Survey, PO Box 841, Whitley Bay, NE26 9EQ.

☐ I have / ☐ have never been bit on the arse off a snake.
I enclose £1 admin fee.
Name: ....
Address: ....
....

☐ **WHAT'S** all the fuss about en-suite toilets? If anyone thinks I want to hear my husband launching a dreadnought with an accompanying trumpet voluntary in the middle of the night they're very much mistaken. In an ideal world he'd have his own bathroom in a concrete bunker half a mile away.

Harriet Jumpjet, Scarborough

☐ **"A FINGER** of fudge is just enough to give your kids a treat," so the advertising slogan goes. Well, my son ate one, and yet the ungrateful little scrote still wanted a PlayStation 5 for Christmas.

Mr P Rant, Southsea

☐ **IMAGINE** Darcey Bussell's husband was called Russell and he took her name, he'd be Russell Bussell. Now imagine they lived in Brussels. Honestly, you couldn't make it up!

DuSinge, Lincoln

☐ **BBC** bigwigs were quick to trumpet the 40th anniversary of *Children in Need*. Yet these so-called 'children' must be deep into middle-age by now. We're being taken for fools.

Norfolk Passmore, email

☐ **IS** the expression 'like a boss' supposed to be a positive one? Because I work at Sports Direct and my boss is a complete cunt.

H Janus, Newcastle

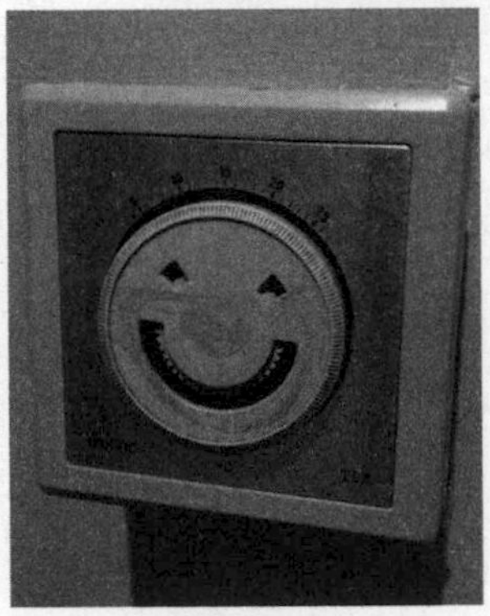

☐ **I RECENTLY** went in to the toilets at Marks and Spencer for a posh wee and saw the second most sinister looking thermostat I have ever seen.

Ash, Sheffield

STAR LETTER

☐ **WHY IS** it that whenever I pick a frog up, it immediately pisses in my hand? Is this some kind of reflex action or defence mechanism, or is it just a coincidence that I only ever pick them up when they're busting for a slash?

Hector Tambourine, Clifton

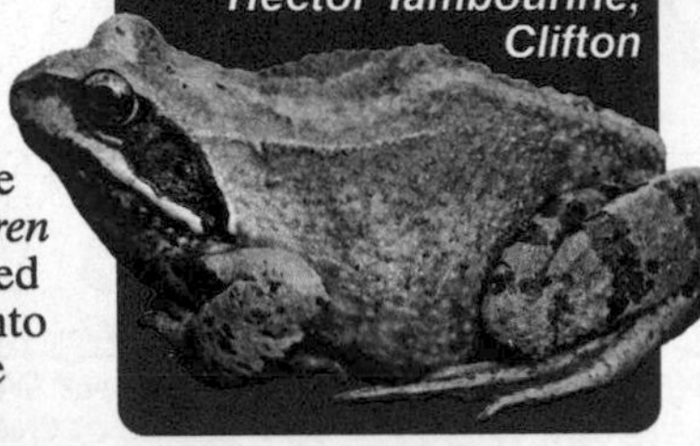

☐ **LAST** Friday my mate Andy reckoned he could fart the alphabet, and he was doing alright until he seriously misjudged the letter 'g' and followed through. I don't know who was more upset - him, the restaurateur, or the two women sat on the table behind us, who frankly had no sense of humour.

James Bonnington, Oakhampton

☐ **I REALISE** that as an intelligence agent, James Bond must be pretty perceptive, but I can't believe he would really notice if the barman gave his Vodka Martini a little stir after shaking it? Come on mate, you're just taking the piss.

Keggy Oboe, Bury St. Edmunds

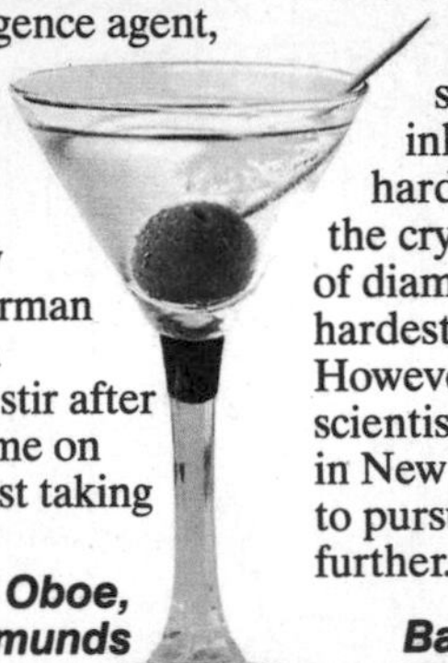

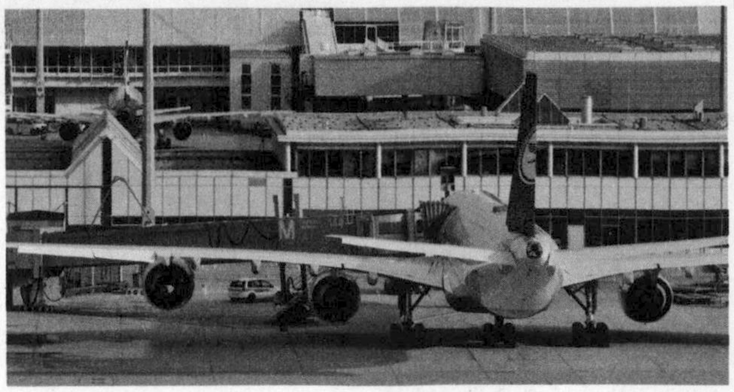

☐ **I FEEL** Manchester Airport - the second largest airport in the UK with daily flights to the capital cities and continents around the world - really needs to make a bigger deal about the fact that it has a direct rail link to Cleethorpes. It would put this British coastal town on a par with places like Miami Beach and the Costa del Sol, if you ignore the dog shit, feral seagulls and economic decline. Talking themselves up a bit might give the UK's post-Covid travel industry a much-needed boost.

Dave Turton, Doncaster

☐ **FOR** anyone suffering the misery of constipation and a dislike of taking laxatives, might I suggest four spiced Quorn burgers and a tin of beans? I had an arse like a rabbit's nose for 90 minutes and eventually had to stop my car, jump over a hedge and shit in a field.

Hubert Pubes, York

☐ **"WE'RE** like crystal, we break easy," sang New Order in their hit single *Crystal*. But crystalline structures are inherently strong and hard to break; indeed, the crystal lattice structure of diamond is one of the hardest substances on earth. However, since there are no scientists or former teachers in New Order, I don't intend to pursue this matter any further.

John Gray, Barney Farmer's farm

☐ **EVERY** second shit, I sit on the bog like the woman on the *Profumo Scandal* poster so my wife gets a chance to try and piss off the baked-on shit stains. I'm all for equality.

BIGzee, Coulsdon

☐ **THEY** reckon that Google tapes you talking via your smartphone and then sends you adverts and offers based on your discussions. Well that must be bollocks, because I've only ever received adverts for shirts and shorts. I've never received one for a soapy tit wank and I talk about them all the time.

Gordon Bennett, Auckland

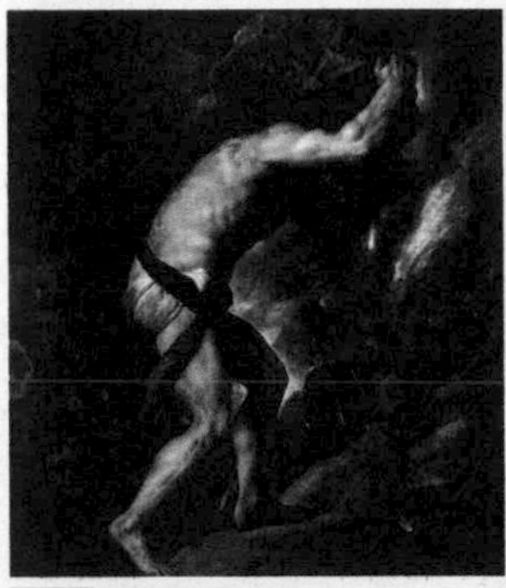

☐ **SISYPHUS** was condemned to push a boulder up a hill for ever, in Hell. Why didn't he just stand on one side, let the boulder roll down the hill and fuck off to the pub for eternity? It might've landed on someone below, but that's Hell for you. I imagine you can't get too precious.

David Haslam, Datchworth

☐ **IF** Bill Gates had anything about him, he would have gotten into the blacksmithery game, making security and privacy ironwork, and started his own company called "Bill's Gates". He might have done so much better for himself. Still, stable doors, horses bolting and all that.

John Mason, email

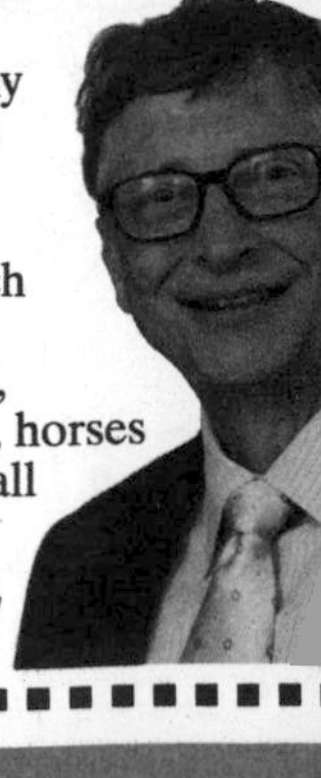

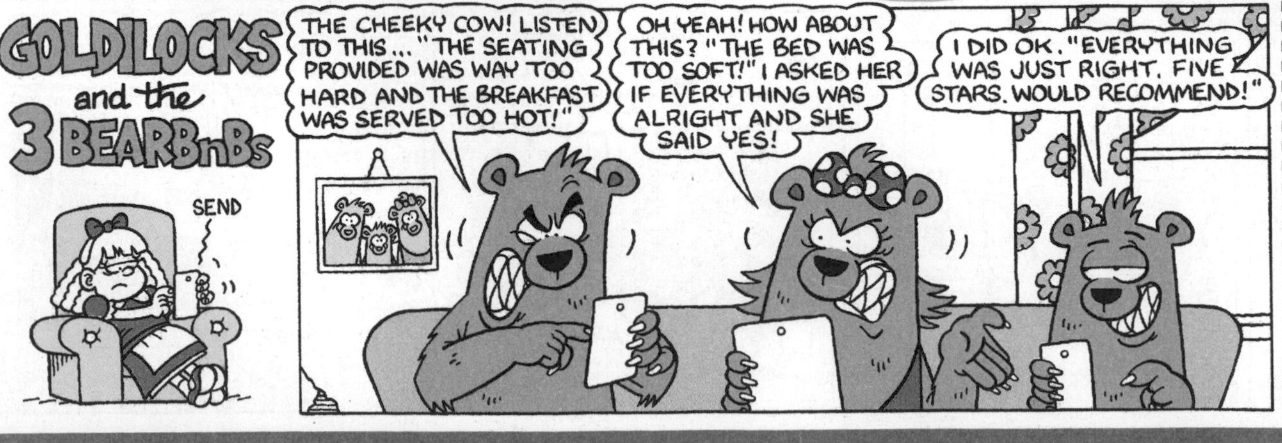
GOLDILOCKS and the 3 BEARBnBs
SEND
THE CHEEKY COW! LISTEN TO THIS... "THE SEATING PROVIDED WAS WAY TOO HARD AND THE BREAKFAST WAS SERVED TOO HOT!"
OH YEAH! HOW ABOUT THIS? "THE BED WAS TOO SOFT!" I ASKED HER IF EVERYTHING WAS ALRIGHT AND SHE SAID YES!
I DID OK. "EVERYTHING WAS JUST RIGHT. FIVE STARS. WOULD RECOMMEND!"

THESE markings were recently discovered carved into the stonework of a church in Stoke Mandeville, and were apparently put there 700 years ago to ward off witches. Given they look uncannily like my ringpiece, I reckon they've probably been doing a pretty good job.

David Brewis, Eton

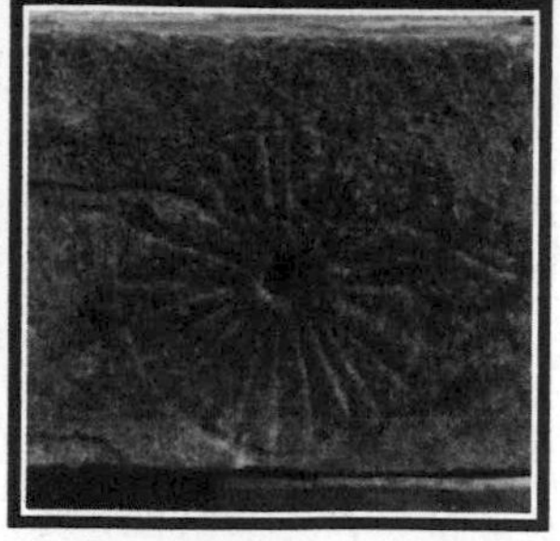

WHILE watching England v the Republic of Ireland at Wembley, I noticed centre forward Dominic Calvert-Lewin checking the soles of his boots before taking a penalty. I think it's appalling that the powers that be who run our national game could allow dog dirt to spoil the pitch at the national stadium. Perhaps they could spend some of their millions of pounds on signs to encourage irresponsible owners to clear up their pets' mess after walking them on the hallowed turf.

T Kennedy, Scotch Corner

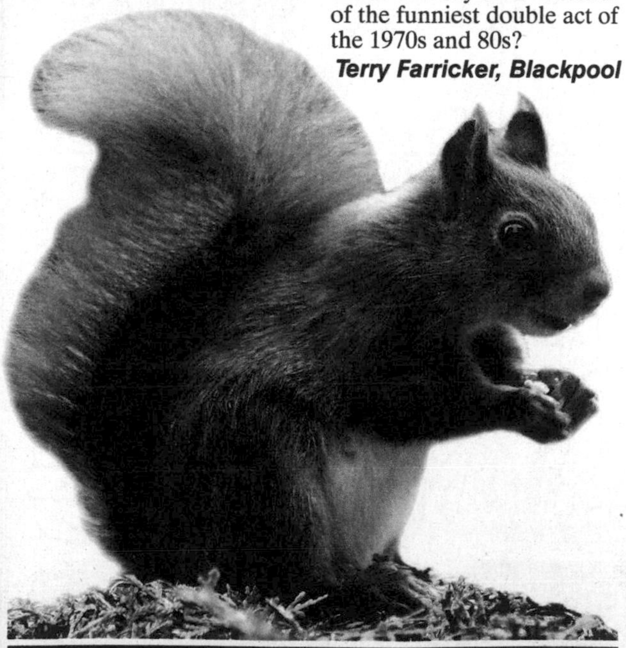

GREAT work by the *Daily Mirror* censors in this *I'm a Celebrity* article.

Oswaldo Oberprillar, Blackpool

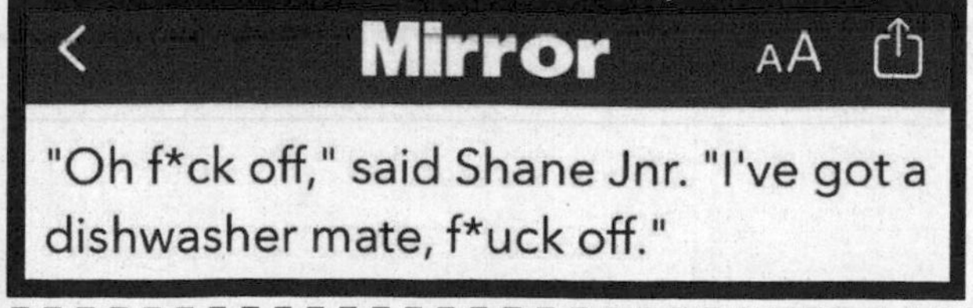
Mirror
AA
"Oh f*ck off," said Shane Jnr. "I've got a dishwasher mate, f*uck off."

I THINK that *Star Trek* would have been much improved if Mr Spock had been fitted with a huge prehensile cock, like that of a barnacle. He could have read people's minds by sticking it in their ear, and annoyed Dr McCoy by flicking the back of his head with it when he was trying to work. Instead, they gave him pointy ears and green blood, which is very unlikely if you ask me.

Annie Seed-Balls, Orkney

IF Stone Age people didn't have a written language, how do we know they had names like Gronk and Thag? I'd like to see the so called experts on the Neanderthal period explain that one.

Peter Busby, Australia

WHAT'S the deal with snooker? They play on an oblong table with round balls which they start off by arranging in a triangle. Come on, snooker players, pick a shape and stick with it.

Ben Nunn, Caterham

I SENT you a letter about squirrels 18 months ago, but you did not publish it, which is your prerogative. I showed it to to the late, great Bobby Ball not long after and he thought it was very funny. I suppose you are now claiming to know more about comedy than one half of the funniest double act of the 1970s and 80s?

Terry Farricker, Blackpool

TOP TIPS

FLATULENT singers. Shout "went the trolley" after farting 3 times in quick succession. If you then manage another quick-fire trio of bottom burps, you should shout "went the bell".

Mel Conington, Basildon

BIGOTS. Instead of getting all angry over the subject of gay marriage, simply say "No thank-you" each time a gay person asks you to marry them.

Ben Banks, London

FOULED footballers. Try clutching the correct part of your body as you writhe in simulated agony in order to give your claim more credibility.

Monkey Boy, Nintendo-on-Sea

AMERICANS. Prevent imbeciles from becoming your POTUS in the future by insisting that Presidential candidates sit an exam. Something like the Key Stage 1 English SAT or that one where they get kids to put a square piece of plastic in a square hole should do the trick.

Tim Buktu, Timbuktu

CV light on qualifications? Pack it out with MOT passes, remembering to attach a scan of the test certificates as proof. No car? Put 'fully licensed to receive broadcast television', and attach your telly licence.

Mark Glover, Coventry

PRETEND you're a builder by asking your wife for a tea with 3 sugars and then throwing most of it into a bush.

Kevin Caswell-Jones, Gresford

toptips@viz.co.uk

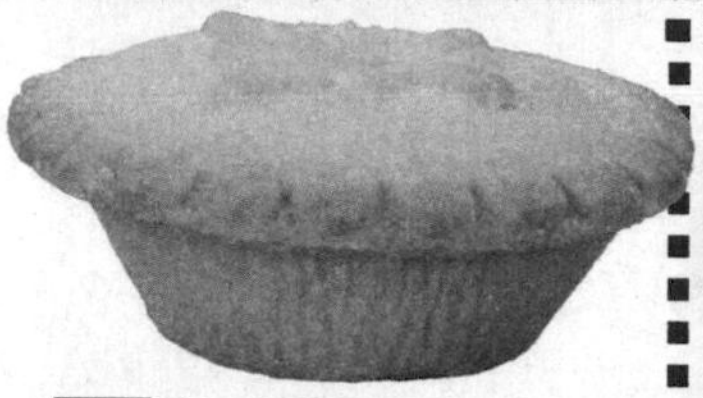

I DON'T know why scientists are hell-bent on injecting the Covid-19 vaccine into everybody, as lots of people I know are frightened of needles. Everybody, on the other hand, loves mince pies. So why didn't they simply put it in the mince pies we ate over Christmas? And yes, I said Christmas, not Holiday Season, even though sleepy Joe Biden is planning to make that illegal. SAD!

D Trump, Washington

WHY IS it so expensive to take the train? They're going that way anyway, why can't they just drop me off?

David Chittock, Cheltenham

I'VE JUST seen the biggest dog turd of my life near the terminus of the Leeds-Liverpool Canal. I didn't take a picture as I wouldn't want to embarrass the dog involved who might very well be reading your publication. But I would be interested to know whether any of your other readers have ever seen a bigger one?

Rev. Fergus Butler-Gallie, Liverpool

YOU know how your own farts smell much nicer than other people's farts? Well, if you fart and then forget you farted, does it smell horrible because you think it is someone else's? Have these boffins ever done experiments with goldfish, or people with short term memory loss? I bet they haven't.

Alex Stokoe, Newcastle

Want to avoid driving round town looking for a parking space?
Want to avoid trawling round the shops carrying the bags?
...then use...

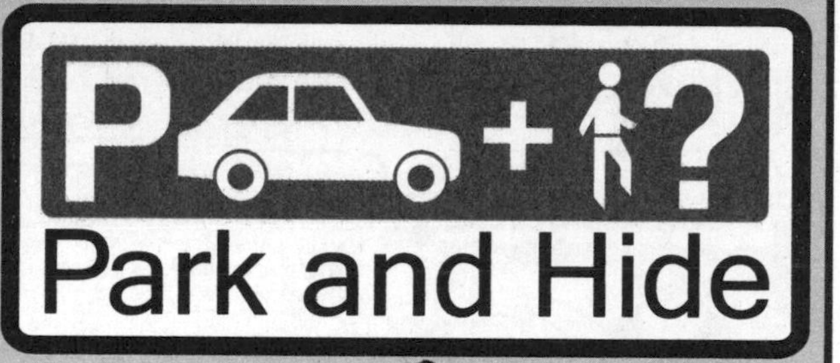
P + ?
Park and Hide

Out of town parking with over 1000 parking spaces for your car, 1000 hiding places for you, and buses into town every 10 mins for your wife.

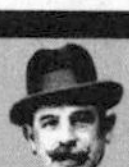

"I hid behind one of the hundreds of bushes in Durham's Howland's Farm ***Park and Hide*** *whilst my wife went to buy the tickets. After looking for me for ten minutes, she got on the bus and went into town, and I spent the afternoon sitting in the car listening to the football."*

Mr B, Low Fell

Looking for a fine wine at an affordable price?

None of Yer Shite

If you are tired of paying £5 for a bottle of wine, only to be disappointed by its inferior taste, then you'll be pleasantly surprised by *None of yer Shite*. A truly drinkable drop in the £5 a bottle bracket.

Comes in Red, White and Rosé

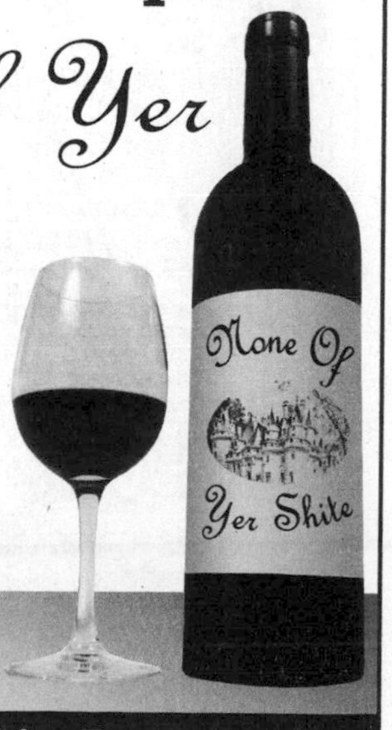
None Of
Yer Shite

Available at Majestic, Boozebuster, Cigs 'n' Booze and all good offies.

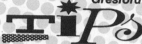

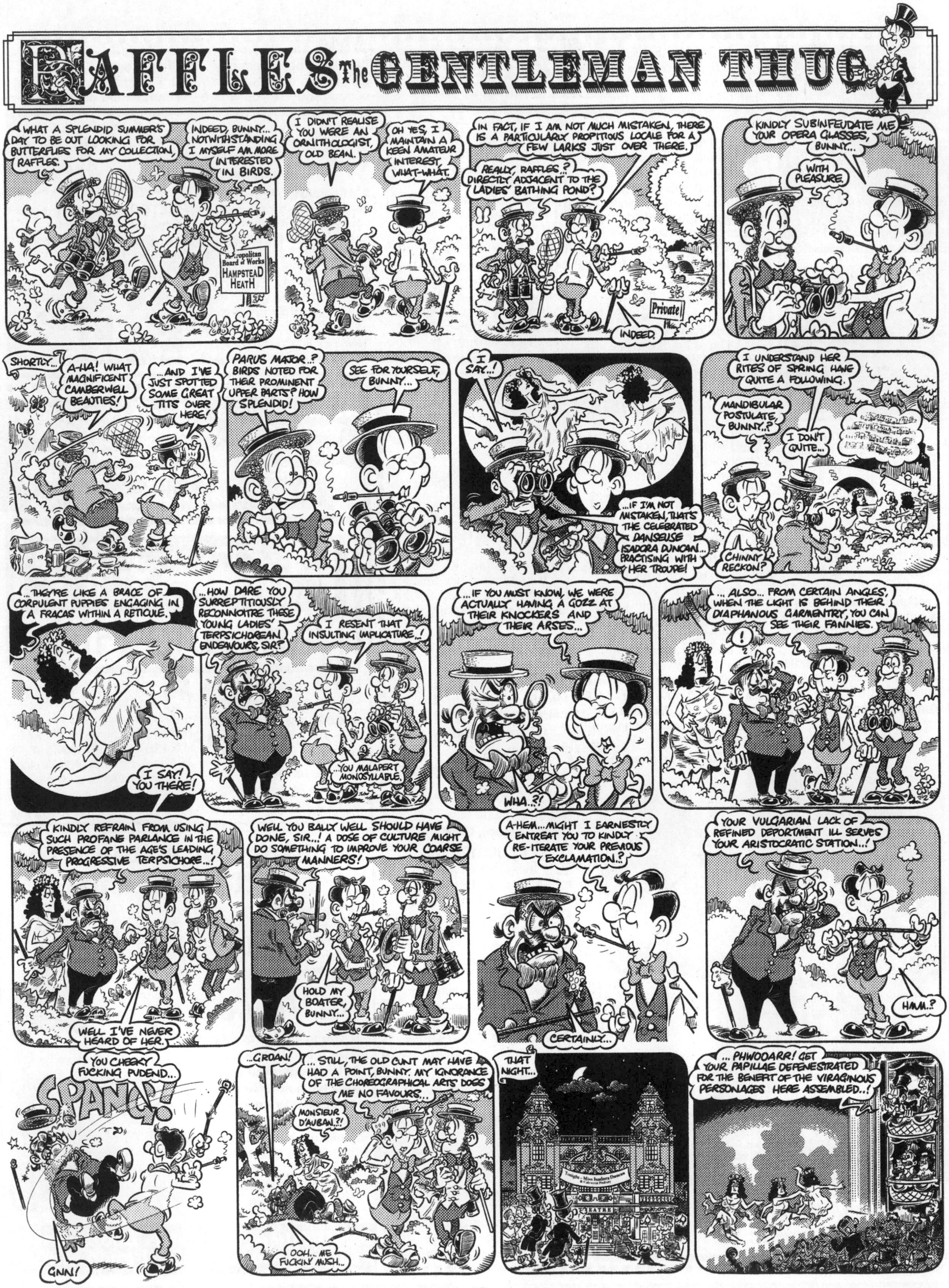
RAFFLES The GENTLEMAN THUG
WHAT A SPLENDID SUMMER'S DAY TO BE OUT LOOKING FOR BUTTERFLIES FOR MY COLLECTION, RAFFLES.
INDEED, BUNNY... NOTWITHSTANDING I MYSELF AM MORE INTERESTED IN BIRDS.
Metropolitan Board of Works HAMPSTEAD HEATH
I DIDN'T REALISE YOU WERE AN ORNITHOLOGIST, OLD BEAN.
OH YES, I MAINTAIN A KEEN AMATEUR INTEREST, WHAT-WHAT.
IN FACT, IF I AM NOT MUCH MISTAKEN, THERE IS A PARTICULARLY PROPITIOUS LOCALE FOR A FEW LARKS JUST OVER THERE.
REALLY, RAFFLES..? DIRECTLY ADJACENT TO THE LADIES' BATHING POND?
Private
INDEED.
KINDLY SUBINFEUDATE ME YOUR OPERA GLASSES, BUNNY...
WITH PLEASURE.
SHORTLY...
A-HA! WHAT MAGNIFICENT CAMBERWELL BEAUTIES!
...AND I'VE JUST SPOTTED SOME GREAT TITS OVER HERE!
PARUS MAJOR..? BIRDS NOTED FOR THEIR PROMINENT UPPER PARTS? HOW SPLENDID!
SEE FOR YOURSELF, BUNNY...
I SAY..!
...IF I'M NOT MISTAKEN, THAT'S THE CELEBRATED DANSEUSE ISADORA DUNCAN... PRACTISING WITH HER TROUPE!
I UNDERSTAND HER RITES OF SPRING HAVE QUITE A FOLLOWING.
MANDIBULAR POSTULATE, BUNNY..?
I DON'T QUITE...
CHINNY RECKON?
...THEY'RE LIKE A BRACE OF CORPULENT PUPPIES ENGAGING IN A FRACAS WITHIN A RETICULE.
I SAY! YOU THERE!
...HOW DARE YOU SURREPTITIOUSLY RECONNOITRE THESE YOUNG LADIES' TERPSICHOREAN ENDEAVOURS, SIR?
I RESENT THAT INSULTING IMPLICATURE..!
...YOU MALAPERT MONOSYLLABLE.
...IF YOU MUST KNOW, WE WERE ACTUALLY HAVING A GOZZ AT THEIR KNOCKERS AND THEIR ARSES...
WHA..?!
... ALSO... FROM CERTAIN ANGLES, WHEN THE LIGHT IS BEHIND THEIR DIAPHANOUS GARMENTRY, YOU CAN SEE THEIR FANNIES.
!
KINDLY REFRAIN FROM USING SUCH PROFANE PARLANCE IN THE PRESENCE OF THE AGE'S LEADING PROGRESSIVE TERPSICHORE...!
WELL I'VE NEVER HEARD OF HER.
WELL YOU BALLY WELL SHOULD HAVE DONE, SIR...! A DOSE OF CULTURE MIGHT DO SOMETHING TO IMPROVE YOUR COARSE MANNERS!
HOLD MY BOATER, BUNNY...
A-HEM... MIGHT I EARNESTLY ENTREAT YOU TO KINDLY RE-ITERATE YOUR PREVIOUS EXCLAMATION..?
CERTAINLY...
YOUR VULGARIAN LACK OF REFINED DEPORTMENT ILL SERVES YOUR ARISTOCRATIC STATION...!
HMM..?
YOU CHEEKY FUCKING PUDEND...
SPANG!
GNN!
...GROAN!
... STILL, THE OLD CUNT MAY HAVE HAD A POINT, BUNNY. MY IGNORANCE OF THE CHOREOGRAPHICAL ARTS DOES ME NO FAVOURS...
MONSIEUR D'AUBAN..?!
OOH... ME FUCKIN' MUSH...
THAT NIGHT...
...PHWOOARR! GET YOUR PAPILLAE DEFENESTRATED FOR THE BENEFIT OF THE VIRAGINOUS PERSONAGES HERE ASSEMBLED...!

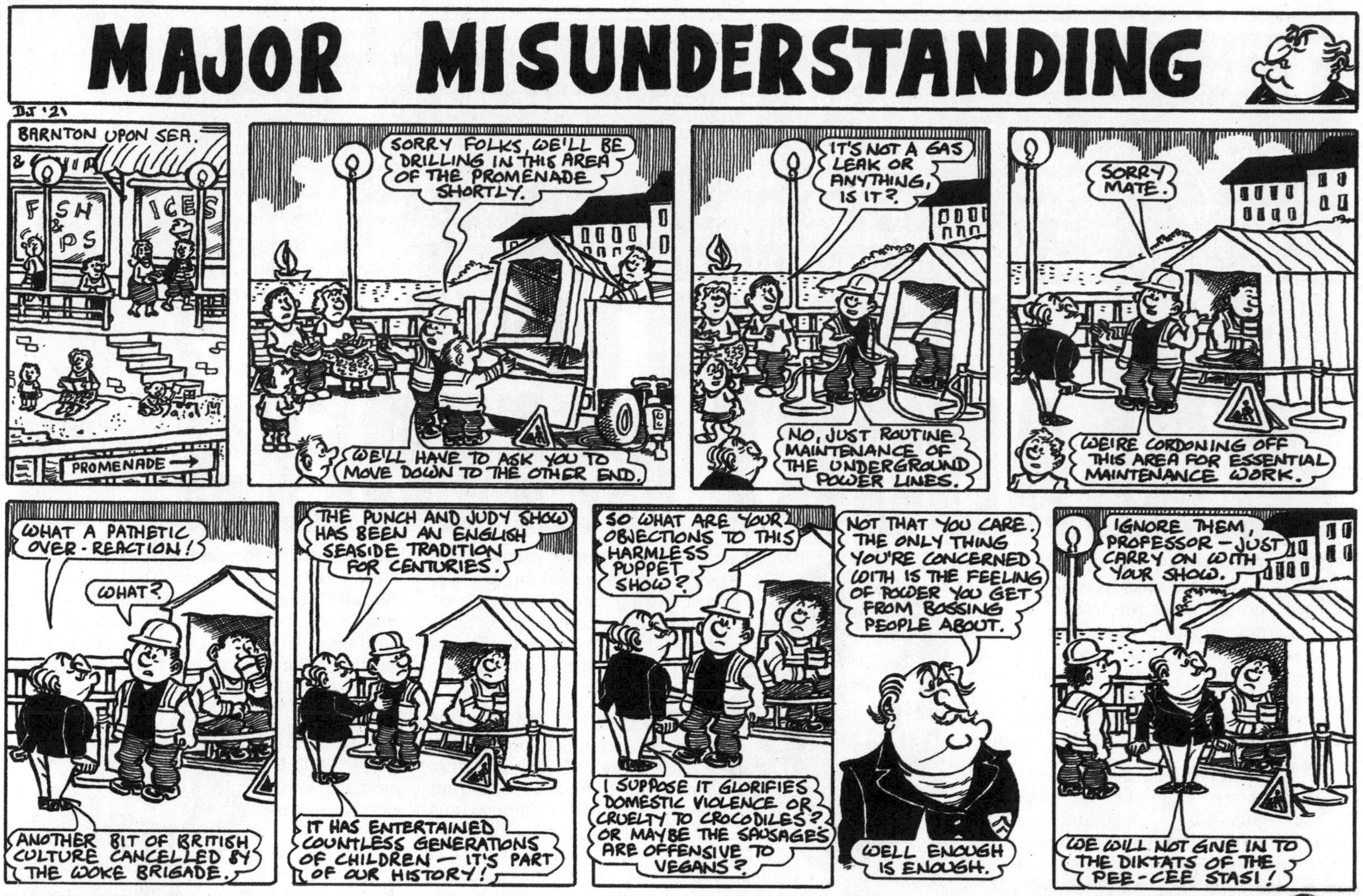

MAJOR MISUNDERSTANDING
DJ '21
BARNTON UPON SEA.
FISH & CHIPS
ICES
PROMENADE →
SORRY FOLKS, WE'LL BE DRILLING IN THIS AREA OF THE PROMENADE SHORTLY.
WE'LL HAVE TO ASK YOU TO MOVE DOWN TO THE OTHER END.
IT'S NOT A GAS LEAK OR ANYTHING, IS IT?
NO, JUST ROUTINE MAINTENANCE OF THE UNDERGROUND POWER LINES.
SORRY MATE.
WE'RE CORDONING OFF THIS AREA FOR ESSENTIAL MAINTENANCE WORK.
WHAT A PATHETIC OVER-REACTION!
WHAT?
ANOTHER BIT OF BRITISH CULTURE CANCELLED BY THE WOKE BRIGADE.
THE PUNCH AND JUDY SHOW HAS BEEN AN ENGLISH SEASIDE TRADITION FOR CENTURIES.
IT HAS ENTERTAINED COUNTLESS GENERATIONS OF CHILDREN — IT'S PART OF OUR HISTORY!
SO WHAT ARE YOUR OBJECTIONS TO THIS HARMLESS PUPPET SHOW?
I SUPPOSE IT GLORIFIES DOMESTIC VIOLENCE OR CRUELTY TO CROCODILES? OR MAYBE THE SAUSAGES ARE OFFENSIVE TO VEGANS?
NOT THAT YOU CARE. THE ONLY THING YOU'RE CONCERNED WITH IS THE FEELING OF POWER YOU GET FROM BOSSING PEOPLE ABOUT.
WELL ENOUGH IS ENOUGH.
IGNORE THEM, PROFESSOR – JUST CARRY ON WITH YOUR SHOW.
WE WILL NOT GIVE IN TO THE DIKTATS OF THE PEE-CEE STASI!

ECCLESIASTICAL ROOFING SERVICES

TRIED EVERYTHING TO FIX THAT LEAKING ROOF? HAD TRADESMAN AFTER TRADESMAN AROUND, BUT THE WATER STILL COMES IN? BEEN TOLD THAT THE ROOF SIMPLY CANNOT BE REPAIRED?

CALL *Elijah Churchill*

FAITH ROOF REPAIRER

The ONLY roofer in the UK with the divine gift OF being able to fix your roof with faith alone.

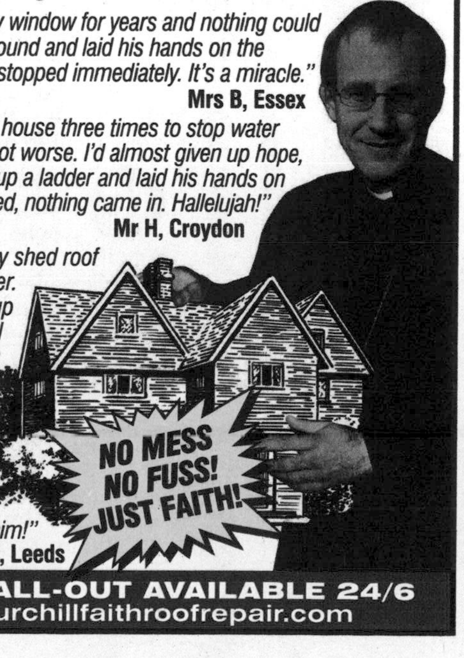

NO MESS NO FUSS! JUST FAITH!

"I had water coming in a bay window for years and nothing could stop it. Elijah Churchill can round and laid his hands on the slates above the window, and it stopped immediately. It's a miracle."

Mrs B, Essex

"I replaced the tiles on my house three times to stop water ingress, but if anything it got worse. I'd almost given up hope, but Elijah Churchill simply went up a ladder and laid his hands on the tiles, and the next time it rained, nothing came in. Hallelujah!"

Mr H, Croydon

"My roofer told me that my shed roof wouldn't last another winter. All other tradesmen had given up hope, so I called Elijah Churchill to come and have a look. When he went up a stepladder and touched the roofing felt, I could feel an overwhelming sense of it repairing under his hands. That was 10 years ago and it's still going strong today. Praise him! **PRAAAAISE** him!"

Mrs G, Leeds

EMERGENCY CALL-OUT AVAILABLE 24/6
www.elijahchurchillfaithroofrepair.com

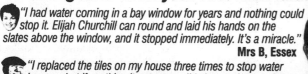

ARBITER OF TASTE

Your Etiquette Questions Answered by Acknowledged Etiquette Expert

MICKEY ARBITER, O.B.E.

Dear Mickey... My auntie is terminally ill and I suspect that she may pop her clogs sometime this week. I was just wondering how long is it after she goes before I can have a wank without it seeming disrespectful. I love her very much, but I also love to have a nice wank.

Billy Beaujangles, Goole

Mickey says...That is a difficult one, Mr Beaujangles. If it was someone extremely close to you who had died, such as your mother, sister or wife, then you should not have a strum of any sort for at least a week. In the case of an auntie, it all depends on the closeness of your relationship, but I think you should refrain from any form of self abuse for at least 48 hours. Unless of course, you are a 17 year-old boy, in which case you should try your best to wait until the person breaking the news to you has left the room before pulling the pope's cap off.

Dear Mickey... Last week my cousin was killed in an industrial accident which was obviously a terrible shock to our family. A few days after his death, I found out that my son, after several months' trials, had been given a contract to play for Manchester City. I am absolutely over the moon and I want to tell everybody about it. My entire family will be at my cousin's funeral next week and it would be an ideal opportunity to let everyone know my son has made the big time. I wonder if it would be in bad taste to go around telling everybody the fantastic news, grinning like an idiot, on such a solemn occasion.

Tommy Coathooks, Manchester

Mickey says... Funerals are very strange occasions, with both sombre and light-hearted moments. The actual service will be a solemn time of reflection of the life lost, and you must not mention your wonderful news at the crem. However, the gatherings after a funeral invariably lighten in mood as everyone moves forward. So afterwards, you would certainly be able to spread the fantastic news. Perhaps steer the conversation towards football whilst talking fondly about your cousin, and then mention the news in passing adding that, were he still with us, how proud he would have been of your son's success, something like that.

THEY run around football pitches, they skate around ice hockey rinks and they sit on very high chairs during tennis matches. They are **REFEREES**: the unsung heroes and heroines of our favourite sporting fixtures. But even though they are essential cogs in the sporting machine, most of us in the stands never even realise they are there. Like high court judges, refs apply the laws of the game, making decisions and handing out punishments with fairness and impartiality. Without them, competitive sports would quickly descend into *Mad-Max*-style chaos and anarchy. But how much do we know about these arbiters of sporting jurisprudence? How are they trained? What are their powers? What is the record for the greatest number of them inside a telephone box? Here are the answers to these and more questions as we bring you...

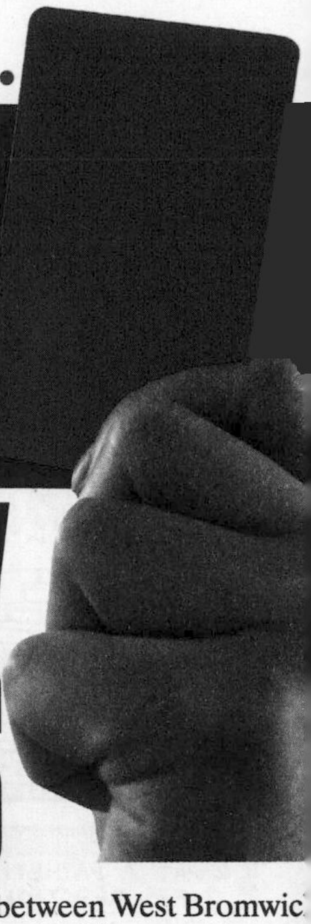

20 THINGS YOU NEVER KNEW ABOUT REFEREES

1 REFEREES are effectively sporting police and – like the real police – they do not make the laws of the game; they simply uphold them, making sure everyone plays the game in a safe, fair and enjoyable manner. However, unlike police, they will not fit somebody up for a foul they did not commit, or fabricate evidence after they wrongly blow the whistle for offside.

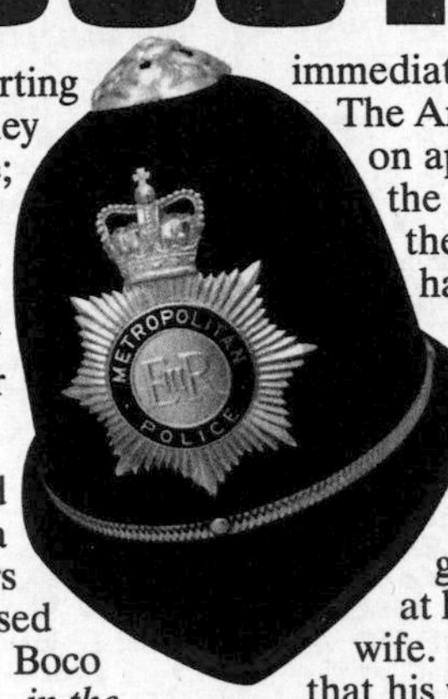
METROPOLITAN
POLICE

2 WHEN Boca Juniors entertained River Plate at La Bombonera Stadium, Argentina, Juniors midfielder Bambos Iguanadon was surprised to be shown a yellow card by referee Mr Boco Perez for using foul and abusive language... *in the shower after the game*. On appeal, the Argentinian FA upheld the controversial caution, saying that the referee's authority continued after the final whistle, whilst the teams were leaving the field of play, and whilst in the dressing room.

3 IN THE past, referees were often taunted by fans singing *"Who's the bastard, who's the bastard, who's the bastard in the black? Who's the bastard in the black?"* to the tune of the hymn *Bread of Heaven*. Indeed, the problem at one point became so great that FIFA decided to change the colour of the refs' strips. However, they soon found out that the foul-mouthed lyrics still worked with blue, red, brown, green and white kits; yellow was the only hue which did not 'scan' properly, and so the governing body finally plumped on that as their refs' official shirt colour. Sadly, obscene crowd chanting is still a problem in France, where the word for yellow - 'jaun' - only has one syllable.

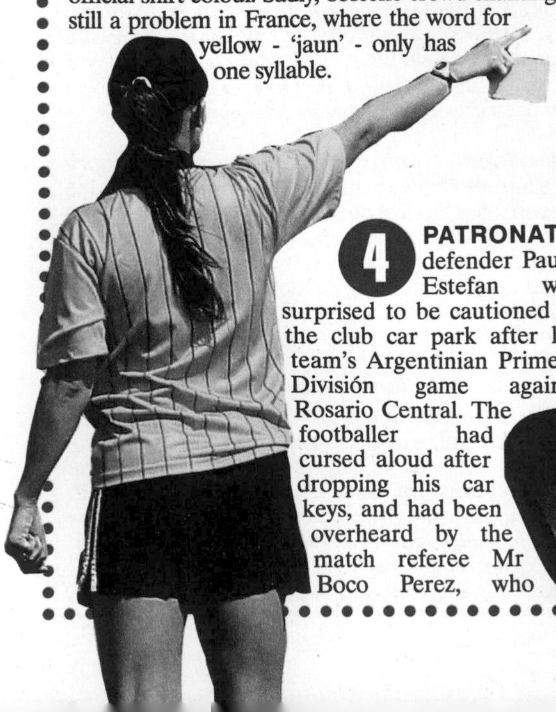

4 PATRONATO defender Paulo Estefan was surprised to be cautioned in the club car park after his team's Argentinian Primera División game against Rosario Central. The footballer had cursed aloud after dropping his car keys, and had been overheard by the match referee Mr Boco Perez, who immediately showed him a yellow card. The Argentinian FA upheld the decision on appeal, saying that the authority of the match referee continued up until the time all the players and officials had left the ground on the day of the game.

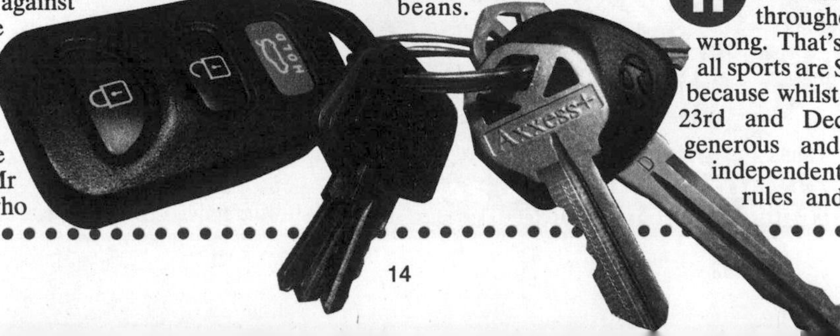

5 ONE SATURDAY evening, following a 2-1 win for his team against Central Cordoba, Santamarina goalkeeper Faustino Campos was at home having energetic sex with his wife. The keeper had just suggested that his wife turn around so that he could attempt 'doggy-style' intercourse when match referee Mr Boco Perez stepped out of the wardrobe and cautioned him for Ungentlemanly Conduct. The Argentinian FA upheld a subsequent appeal, saying that a referee's authority did not stretch to the players' bedrooms after the match, and that although Mr Perez had been well-intentioned, he had in this instance been over-zealous in his application of the game's laws.

6 GO TO A GAME of cricket, and you'll see not one, but two referees. However, such is the spirit of fair play and gentlemanliness in which all cricket games are conducted that match officials are rarely – if ever – needed to arbitrate on a decision. In fact, their main duty is to hold a player's pullover while he bowls and to occasionally bring on a tray of orange juice if it's a particularly warm day.

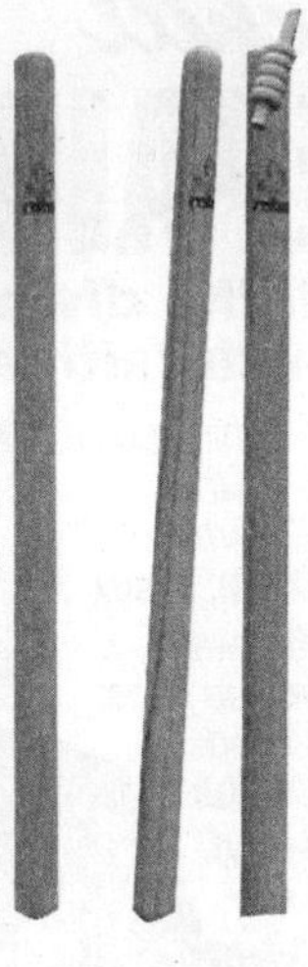

7 AND YOU WON'T hear the crowd chanting *"The referee's a wanker! The referee's a wanker!"* if they happen to get a decision wrong... because cricket referees are called *umpires!*

8 LONGTIME Premiership referee Michael Oliver raised £700 for Battersea Dogs Home after he took charge a football match whilst sitting in a bath of beans. The 2017 relegation clash between West Bromwic Albion and Stoke City saw the 35-year-old spen the full 90-minutes ensconced in the centre circl in his soggy bath. "Obviously, I couldn't keep u with play very well, and I missed a couple c penalties. But it was great fun," he told Sky TV Jeff Stelling after the game.

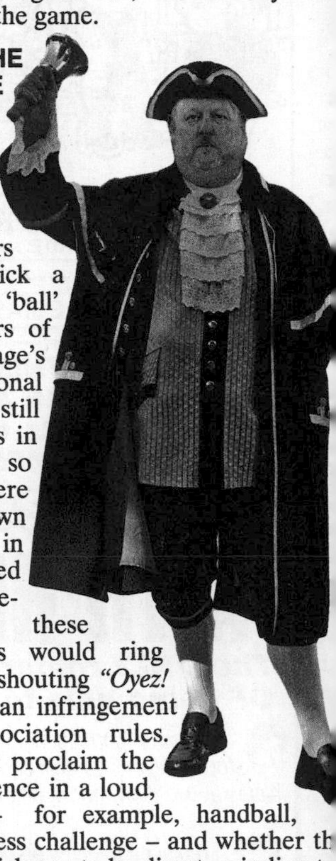

9 IN THE MIDDLE AGES, football was a game played between two villages, involving hundreds of players attempting to kick a pig's bladder 'ball' through the doors of the opposing village's church. Professional referees were still hundreds of years in the future, and so games were controlled by town criers. Dressed in their distinctive red uniforms and three-cornered hats, these respected figures would ring their bells whilst shouting *"Oyez! Oyez!"* to signify an infringement of Football Association rules. They would then proclaim the nature of the offence in a loud, booming voice – for example, handball, offside or a reckless challenge – and whether th subsequent free kick was to be direct or indirect.

10 DIFFERENT sports in the UK all requi their referees to wear a specific unifor unique to that particular game. But i America, match officials all dress exactly the sam regardless of which sport they are officiating – in baseball cap, mint-humbug-striped shirt and blac dress trousers. *You couldn't make it up!*

11 YOU MIGHT imagine that the star sig of referees would be distributed even throughout the Zodiac, but you would b wrong. That's because 87% of referees acro all sports are Sagittarians! This is not surprisin because whilst people born between Novemb 23rd and December 21st are open-hearte generous and good-natured, they are als independent thinkers who are sticklers for th rules and not afraid to make unpopul

decisions if they need to, the exact qualities needed to take control of a sporting contest. A referee's ruling planet is Jupiter, their lucky gemstone is Topaz, and their top love match is Aries.

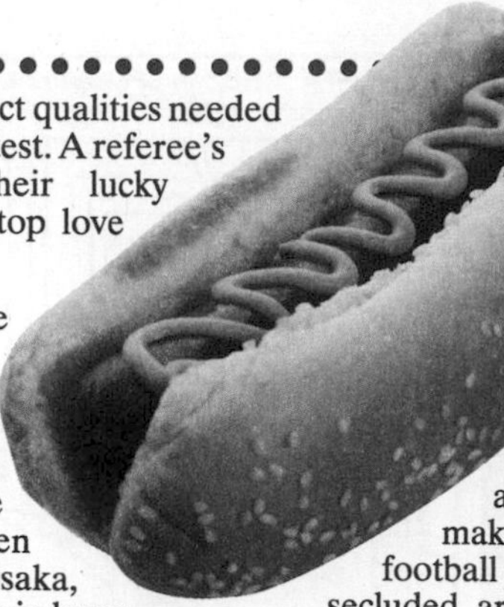

12 **THE RECORD** for the most number of hot dogs eaten whilst officiating at a football match is held by Japanese referee Takeru Kobayashi. During the 2018 J1 League clash between Yokohama FC and Gamba Osaka, Kobayashi downed 134 hot dogs in buns – 75 in the first half, 55 in the second, and 4 in time added on for injuries. He was aided during the game by the fourth official who soaked the ouns in water to make them easier to swallow before nanding them to the referee as he ran past. The natch ended in a 2-2 draw, with the record-breaking referee handing out 4 yellow cards and dismissing an Osaka defender for denying a goalscoring opportunity.

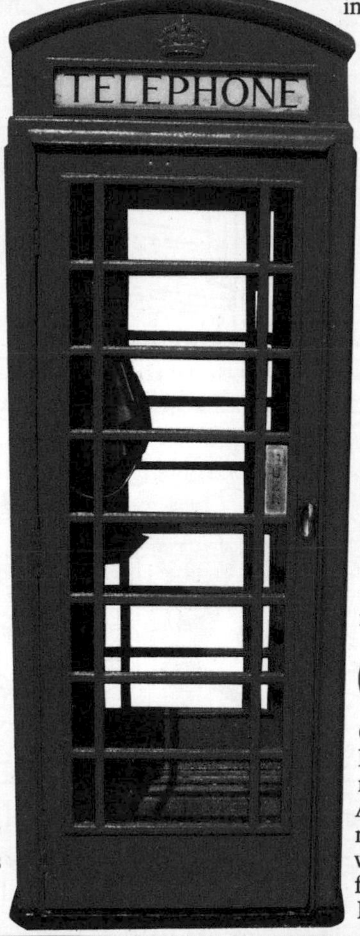

TELEPHONE

13 **IN A GAME** of table football, The fact that all the players are fixed to rigid netal bars means that they can never come into contact with each other or nadvertently stray into an offside position. In addition, with their arms ixed down at their sides, any handball would be deemed accidental and herefore not an offence. Furthermore, thanks to the presence of a high, wooden wall around the pitch, the ball can never leave the ield of play. Consequently, whilst the world's smallest nan – Calvin Phillips – would have been the ideal person to referee one of hese games, his services would have been completely nnecessary.

14 **WHEN HE RAN** onto the field to officiate at a local Sunday league fixture, Referee Trevor Crumbhorn was embarrassed to discover that he had left his whistle and cards in the changing room. Not only that, but he had also forgotten to put on his shorts and was naked from the waist down. To make matters worse, he wasn't even on the football pitch, as he had accidentally gone to a secluded area of his local park. And if that wasn't bad enough, he had forgotten that he wasn't even a football referee. After he was spotted by a local woman walking her dog, the 53-year-old plasterer was arrested by police and charged with indecent exposure.

15 **ON 12TH DECEMBER** 2017, 14 Premier League referees crammed themselves into a standard British red telephone box, smashing the 2015 record set in Germany by 12 Bundesliga officials. The first in the box, Premiership stalwart Mike Dean, said it was great fun, despite suffering an injury when fellow whistleman Andre Marriner stepped on his knackers. The stunt raised £8 for *Children in Need*.

16 **IF A PLAYER** hit an opponent across the back with a folding chair during a football match, the referee would have no hesitation in giving him or her a straight red card, and the FA would doubtless implement a lengthy ban. Yet in the World Wrestling Federation, officials seem unable to assert their authority, with similar incidents - and worse - going unpunished in matches time and time again.

17 **THE FAMOUS** WWI Christmas Day football match between England and Germany almost didn't take place, as FIFA regulations stated that a match referee must be from a neutral country. As kick-off time approached in no man's land, all feared that the game would have to be postponed. But in a fantastic stroke of luck, Altherr Baumgartner, a Swiss national on a hiking tour of the Somme wandered onto the shell-crater-strewn pitch and offered to officiate. The fact that Altherr was also a Level 3 referee, registered with the Swiss FA, made the coincidence even more fortuitous.

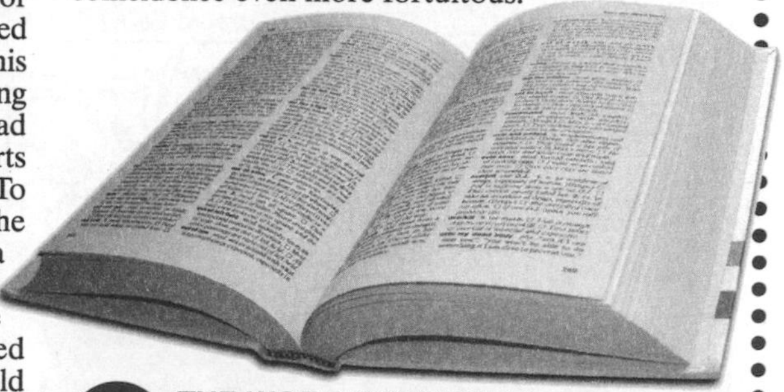

18 **THE WORD 'REFEREE'** is a conjunction of the word 'refer' meaning to consult, and 'ee', a suffix which changes a transitive verb into a noun denoting a person who is the object of the particular act specified by the verb – literally *"one who is referred to."*

19 **IF YOU ARE** in a relationship with a referee and you want to tie the knot, then you need to get permission... *from the King!* That's because, just like swans on the Thames, according to an archaic law all referees in the United Kingdom belong to the ruling monarch. *Ye Acte of the Sporting Officialf* of 1569 required all referees, umpires and tennis linesmen to "Pledgee their Liffes, bodies and soulf to the Crowne." This archaic legislation has never been removed from the statute books, but it is thought unlikely that His Majesty would press charges against a ref marrying without consent.

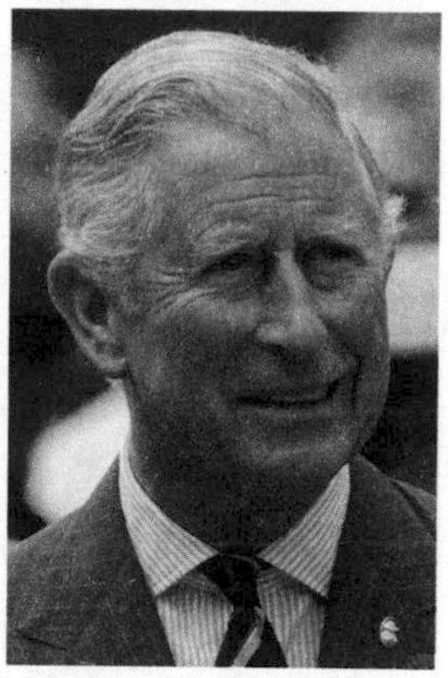

20 **MOST PEOPLE** think a game of football is controlled by the referee alone, but they'd be wrong. There are in fact three officials on the field during a game – a referee on the pitch and an assistant on either touchline. In addition, a fourth ref sitting on the sideline has the authority to over-rule any decision made by the other three and so is, in effect, in complete control of the game. So actually, they are right.

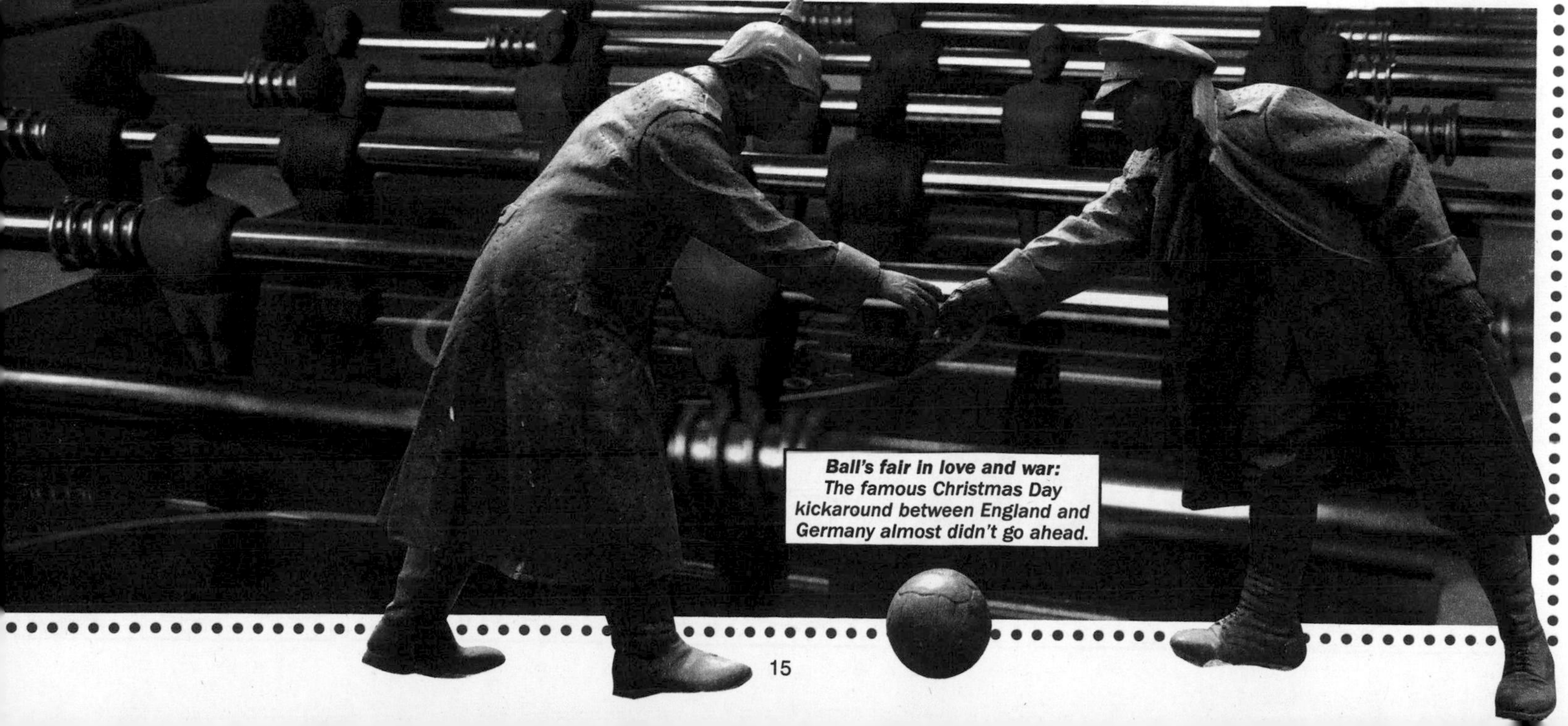

Ball's fair in love and war: The famous Christmas Day kickaround between England and Germany almost didn't go ahead.

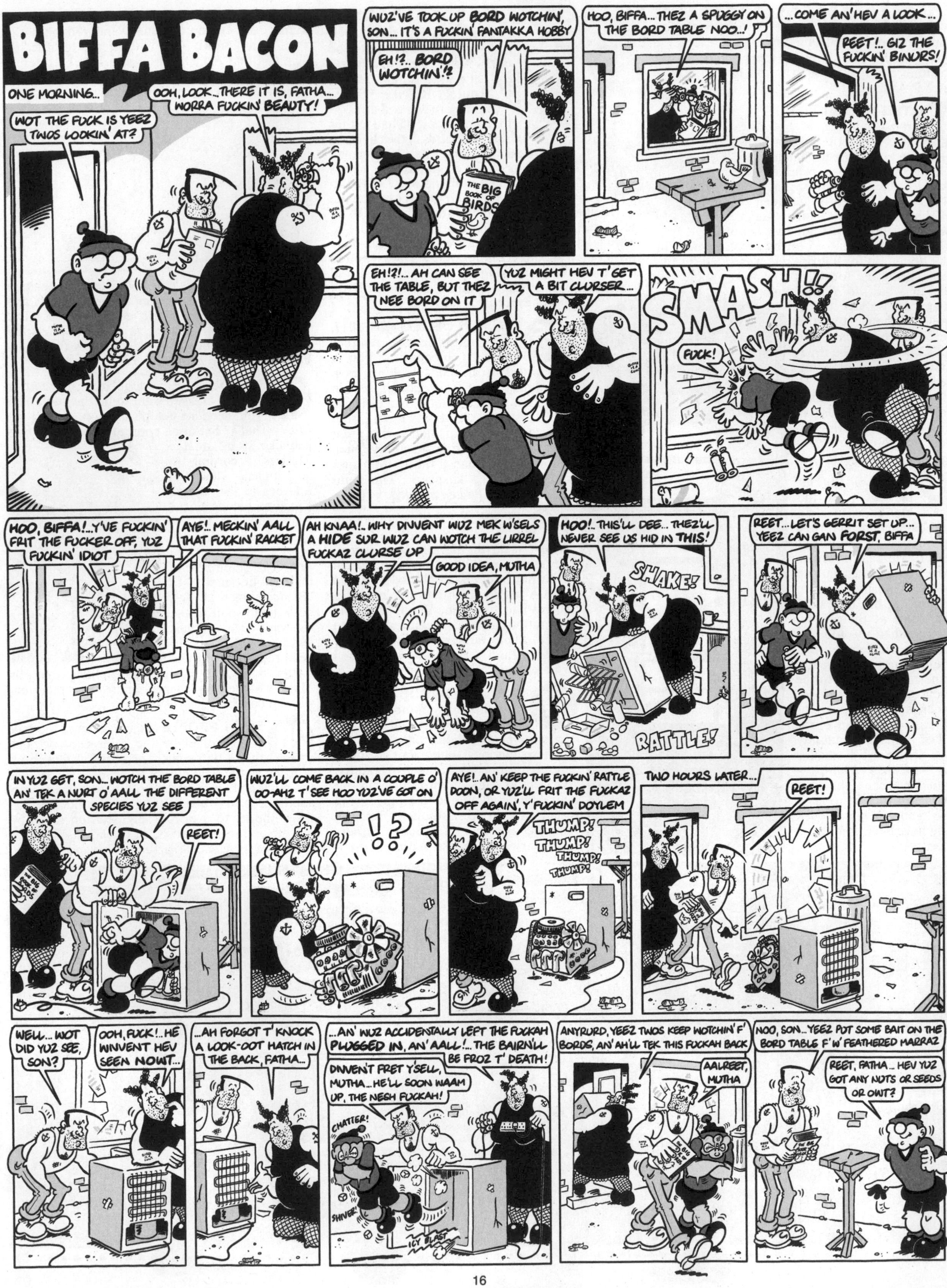
BIFFA BACON
ONE MORNING...
OOH, LOOK...THERE IT IS, FATHA... WORRA FUCKIN' BEAUTY!
WOT THE FUCK IS YEEZ TWOS LOOKIN' AT?
WUZ'VE TOOK UP BORD WOTCHIN', SON... IT'S A FUCKIN' FANTAKKA HOBBY
EH!?.. BORD WOTCHIN'!?
THE BIG BOOK OF BIRDS
HOO, BIFFA... THEZ A SPUGGY ON THE BORD TABLE NOO..!
...COME AN' HEV A LOOK...
REET!.. GIZ THE FUCKIN' BINURS!
EH!?!... AH CAN SEE THE TABLE, BUT THEZ NEE BORD ON IT
YUZ MIGHT HEV T' GET A BIT CLURSER...
SMASH!!
FUCK!
HOO, BIFFA!..Y'VE FUCKIN' FRIT THE FUCKER OFF, YUZ FUCKIN' IDIOT
AYE!.. MECKIN' AALL THAT FUCKIN' RACKET
AH KNAA!.. WHY DIVVENT WUZ MEK W'SELS A HIDE SUR WUZ CAN WOTCH THE LIRREL FUCKAZ CLURSE UP
GOOD IDEA, MUTHA
HOO!.. THIS'LL DEE... THEZ'LL NEVER SEE US HID IN THIS!
SHAKE!
RATTLE!
REET... LET'S GERRIT SET UP... YEEZ CAN GAN FORST, BIFFA
IN YUZ GET, SON... WOTCH THE BORD TABLE AN' TEK A NURT O' AALL THE DIFFERENT SPECIES YUZ SEE
REET!
WUZ'LL COME BACK IN A COUPLE O' OO-AHZ T' SEE HOO YUZ'VE GOT ON
!?
AYE!.. AN' KEEP THE FUCKIN' RATTLE DOON, OR YUZ'LL FRIT THE FUCKAZ OFF AGAIN', Y'FUCKIN' DOYLEM
THUMP!
THUMP!
THUMP!
THUMP!
TWO HOURS LATER...
REET!
WELL... WOT DID YUZ SEE, SON?
OOH, FUCK!.. HE WINVENT HEV SEEN NOWT...
...AH FORGOT T' KNOCK A LOOK-OOT HATCH IN THE BACK, FATHA...
...AN' WUZ ACCIDENTALLY LEFT THE FUCKAH PLUGGED IN, AN' AALL!.. THE BAIRN'LL BE FROZ T' DEATH!
DIVVEN'T FRET Y'SELL, MUTHA... HE'LL SOON WAAM UP, THE NESH FUCKAH!
CHATTER!
SHIVER!
ICY BLAST
ANYRURD, YEEZ TWOS KEEP WOTCHIN' F' BORDS, AN' AH'LL TEK THIS FUCKAH BACK
AALREET, MUTHA
NOO, SON... YEEZ PUT SOME BAIT ON THE BORD TABLE F' W' FEATHERED MARRAZ
REET, FATHA... HEV YUZ GOT ANY NUTS OR SEEDS OR OWT?

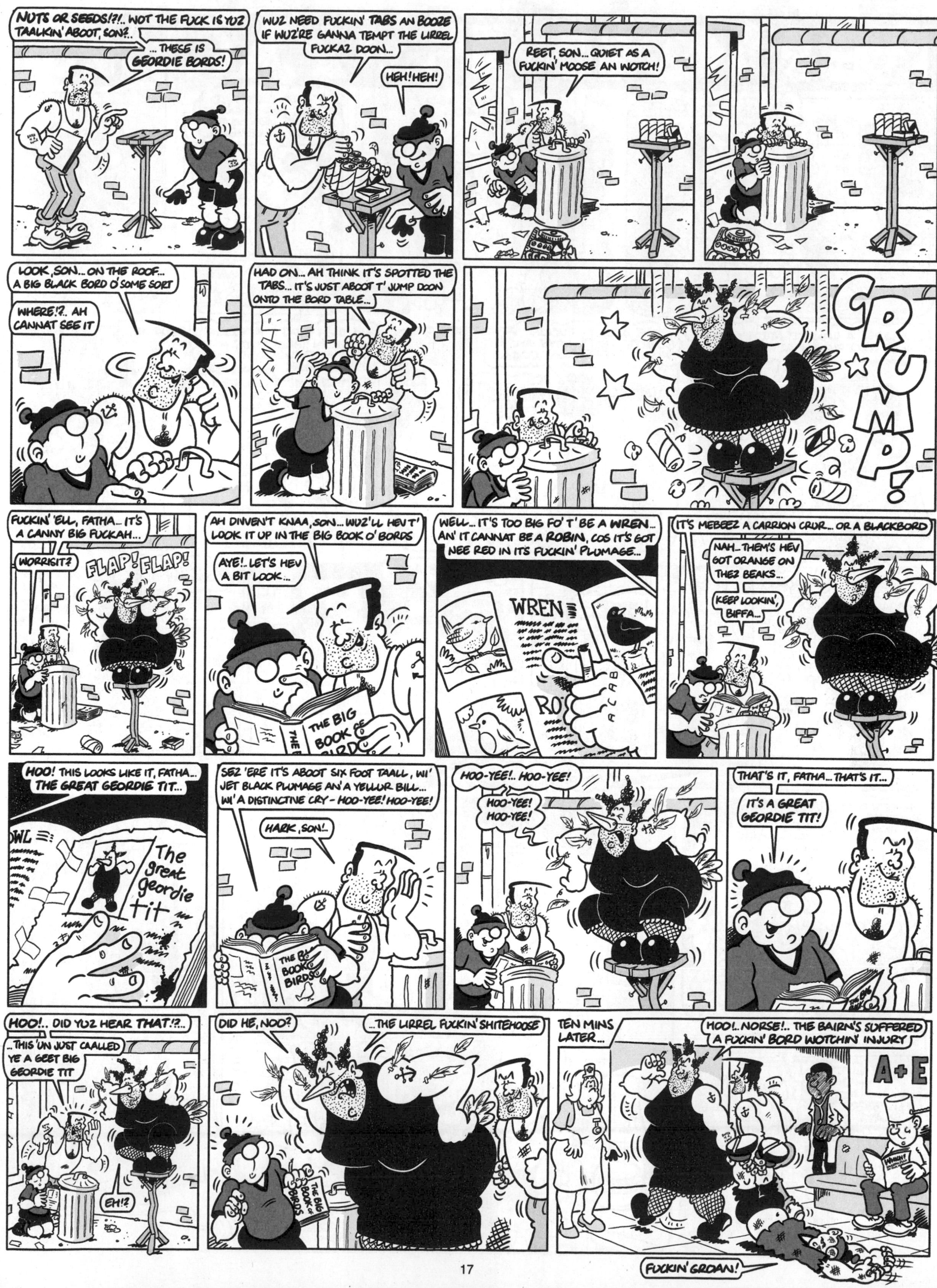
NUTS OR SEEDS!?!.. WOT THE FUCK IS YUZ TAALKIN' ABOOT, SON?..
... THESE IS GEORDIE BORDS!
WUZ NEED FUCKIN' TABS AN BOOZE IF WUZ'RE GANNA TEMPT THE LIRREL FUCKAZ DOON...
HEH! HEH!
REET, SON... QUIET AS A FUCKIN' MOOSE AN WOTCH!
LOOK, SON... ON THE ROOF... A BIG BLACK BORD O' SOME SORT
WHERE!?.. AH CANNAT SEE IT
HAD ON... AH THINK IT'S SPOTTED THE TABS... IT'S JUST ABOOT T' JUMP DOON ONTO THE BORD TABLE...
CRUMP!
FUCKIN' 'ELL, FATHA... IT'S A CANNY BIG FUCKAH...
WORRISIT?
FLAP! FLAP!
AH DINVEN'T KNAA, SON... WUZ'LL HEV T' LOOK IT UP IN THE BIG BOOK O' BORDS
AYE!.. LET'S HEV A BIT LOOK...
THE BIG BOOK OF BIRDS
WELL... IT'S TOO BIG FO' T' BE A WREN... AN' IT CANNAT BE A ROBIN, COS IT'S GOT NEE RED IN ITS FUCKIN' PLUMAGE...
WREN
IT'S MEBEEZ A CARRION CRUR... OR A BLACKBORD
NAH... THEM'S HEV GOT ORANGE ON THEZ BEAKS...
KEEP LOOKIN', BIFFA...
HOO! THIS LOOKS LIKE IT, FATHA... THE GREAT GEORDIE TIT...
The great geordie tit
SEZ 'ERE IT'S ABOOT SIX FOOT TAALL, WI' JET BLACK PLUMAGE AN' A YELLUR BILL... WI' A DISTINCTIVE CRY - HOO-YEE! HOO-YEE!
HARK, SON!..
HOO-YEE!.. HOO-YEE!
HOO-YEE! HOO-YEE!
THAT'S IT, FATHA... THAT'S IT...
IT'S A GREAT GEORDIE TIT!
HOO!.. DID YUZ HEAR THAT!?..
...THIS 'UN JUST CAALLED YE A GEET BIG GEORDIE TIT
EH!?
DID HE, NOO?
...THE LIRREL FUCKIN' SHITEHOOSE
TEN MINS LATER...
HOO!.. NORSE!.. THE BAIRN'S SUFFERED A FUCKIN' BORD WOTCHIN' INJURY
A+E
FUCKIN' GROAN!

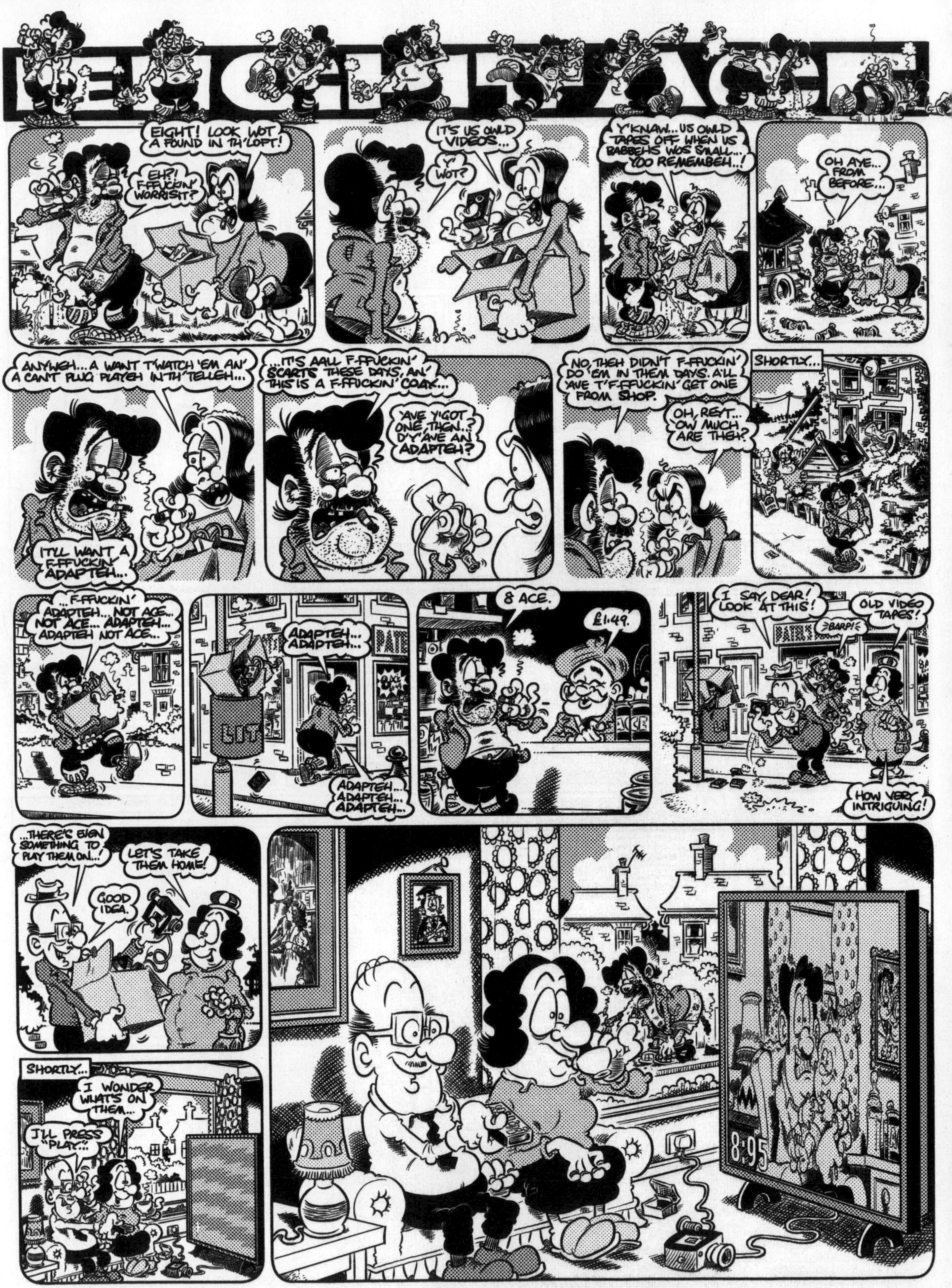
EIGHT! LOOK WOT A FOUND IN TH' LOFT!
EH?! F-FFUCKIN' WORRISIT?
IT'S US OWLD VIDEOS...
Y' WOT?
Y'KNAW... US OWLD TAPES OFF WHEN US BABBEHS WOS SMALL... YOO REMEMBEH...!
OH AYE... FROM BEFORE...
ANYWEH... A WANT T'WATCH 'EM AN' A CAN'T PLUG PLAYEH IN TH' TELLEH...
IT'LL WANT A F-FFUCKIN' ADAPTEH...
...IT'S AALL F-FFUCKIN' SCARTS THESE DAYS, AN' THIS IS A F-FFUCKIN' COAX...
'AVE Y'GOT ONE, THEN..? D'Y'AVE AN ADAPTEH?
NO, THEH DIDN'T F-FFUCKIN' DO 'EM IN THEM DAYS. A'LL 'AVE T'F-FFUCKIN' GET ONE FROM SHOP.
OH, REYT... 'OW MUCH ARE THEH?
SHORTLY...
...F-FFUCKIN' ADAPTEH... NOT ACE... NOT ACE... ADAPTEH... ADAPTEH NOT ACE...
ADAPTEH... ADAPTEH...
ADAPTEH... ADAPTEH... ADAPTEH...
8 ACE.
£1.49.
I SAY, DEAR! LOOK AT THIS!
BARP!
OLD VIDEO TAPES!
HOW VERY INTRIGUING!
...THERE'S BEEN SOMETHING TO PLAY THEM ON...!
LET'S TAKE THEM HOME!
GOOD IDEA.
SHORTLY...
I WONDER WHAT'S ON THEM...
I'LL PRESS "PLAY"...
8:95

Drunken bakers

And that, *pal* – – is what we call choux fuckin' pastry.

Aye, it looks the part. I'll give you that.

Give? You?! *Piss off!!* I've still got it! In these hands!

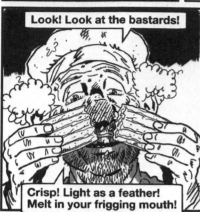
Look! Look at the bastards! Crisp! Light as a feather! Melt in your frigging mouth!

I'll tell you what, these eclairs will make that Valerie Patteries *bint* choke on her marzipan! And they won't cost four quid neither!

What it is is, you're *jealous*, is what it is. Cos your choux is *bollocks*. Always was.

It's *tough*. I never – *Tough bollocks.*

There's a knack to it right enough. Amen. You've either got it or you ain't, and you... are bollocks.

Ha ha, right, I'll have a quick rum then whip up some cream. What rum?

ADLD Household Basic Madeira. Christ.

Madeira shouldn't burn going down. You get what you pay for. It sort of ticks a box.

Blech – I ain't sure how... ... but that tasted a fuck sight better when I thought it was shit rum.

Soon. Treat yourself. I might, they look decent. *Naughty but nice.*

That's what they used to say ain't it? The adverts. That... Carry on tits bird.

Her, that Lizzie Windsor. PTOO

The cream's gone. *Nah*... It's there look. *Gone off. Bad. Proper bad.*

And that *brown* isn't chocolate. Shit. How's the pastry?

Perfect. Ah well. That's something.

NHS: NATIONAL HOS

We team up with healthcare expert to select A-List medical A-Team

OVER the past fourteen months, as our great country has battled bravely against Covid-19, one fact has become abundantly clear: *the NHS is broken.*

Our heroic government has done everything it can to combat the disease – from PM Boris Johnson valiantly shaking hands with patients as the death toll soared, to health secretary Matt Hancock calling on his own FRIENDS and NEIGHBOURS to selflessly produce medical equipment in exchange for nothing more than a few million pounds of taxpayers' money. But despite these big-hearted efforts, the cack-handed cabal of so-called 'experts' that make up our so-called 'National Health Service' have allowed thousands to die on their watch.

It's sickening, it's saddening, and it's WRONG.

But this recent catalogue of failure is a mere drop in the ocean compared to the horrific healthcare experiences of one Rainham-based bachelor. Chronically ill **BERNIE POLYPS**, 58, has spent the best part of FORTY YEARS in and out of NHS hospitals with a litany of puzzling ailments, and he has been consistently UNDERWHELMED by the shabby treatment he has received.

"From root to stem, the NHS is sicker than most of its patients," sighs jobless Bernie. "The waiting times are scandalous, the staff are discourteous, and the doctors are so incompetent that they regularly accuse me of having absolutely nothing wrong with me at all. The whole health service is a complete and utter shambles."

That's why, for a bit of fun, we've asked quintuple divorcee Bernie to hand-pick a top class medical team... *made up exclusively of A-List celebrities!*

"I'm positive that the showbiz stars could do a far better job than the current crop propping up our National Health Service," chuckles 30-stone Bernie. "One thing's for certain – *they couldn't be any worse.*"

RECEPTIONIST: *Tom Cruise*

THE RECPTIONIST is the public face of the NHS, and as such they should always be ready with a big smile and a warm welcome for the poorly punters that stream through their surgery doors. Disappointingly, however, every single hospital receptionist I've ever encountered has been uncooperative, grumpy and downright rude. Which is why I'd want my A-List front desk manned by pint-sized Tinseltown ace **TOM CRUISE**.

Cruise has had a lifetime of experience humouring the Great Unwashed – and whether he's signing autographs at a film premiere or posing for selfies in the street, the diminutive *Top Gun* hunk is always ready to turn on the charm with his trademark twinkling grin. Indeed, when I staggered into A&E last weekend after chipping my thumbnail, it would have made a refreshing change to be greeted by a Hollywood megastar's 100-watt beam, rather than a surly woman called Sheila telling me I was 'wasting hospital time.'

The NHS receptionist is also responsible for the care and comfort of everyone in the waiting room. Or, at least, *they should be*. And this is another area where the short-arsed Scientologist would shine. Cruise could regale his sick and wounded patients with a cavalcade of showbiz anecdotes – and when it came to keeping us fed and watered, the *Cocktail* icon would be able to whip up a refreshing round of Sexes On The Beach, rather than simply grunting about there being a 'coffee machine next to the bogs'.

All in all, I think the microscopic Mission: Impossible star would make the perfect first recruit for my make-believe A-List health centre.

CHIEF SURGEON: *Alan Davies*

I RARELY get to see the chief surgeon at my local hospital because the feckless nursing staff tend to dismiss my injuries as 'non-serious' or 'non-existent'. The closest I've ever got to meeting one was a few years back when I found myself in the operating theatre, screaming in agony after stepping on a Lego brick. Rather than downing tools on the car crash victim he was patching up, the bungling surgeon simply showered me with four-letter abuse and pushed me back outside. A far better candidate for the job, in my opinion, would have been *Jonathan Creek* funnyman **ALAN DAVIES**.

They say laughter is the best medicine, and corkscrew-haired Alan would certainly be up to prescribing it. His sick, maimed and dying patients would forget their troubles and roar with laughter as Dr Davies paraded up and down the ward every morning, rattling off wry observational one-liners. What's more, a chief surgeon must be a bona fide brainbox, with degrees and qualifications galore, and although Davies only has a BA in Theatre & Drama studies to his name, he has spent nearly two decades on eggheaded panel show *QI*, where he will undoubtedly have picked up all manner of intellectual nuggets.

What's more, with hospital equipment in woefully short supply, many chief surgeons are forced to operate with whatever comes to hand. And if any patient needed an ear amputating, the allegedly lug-hole-biting comic could use his own teeth to whip it off with practised ease.

Mop-headed Alan is famous for hosting the talk show As Yet Untitled – but here's a title I'd like to bestow on him: Chief Surgeon at my imaginary A-List hospital.

MEDICAL INTERNS: *Flavor Flav & Bez*

MEDICAL interns – what used to be called junior doctors – are perhaps the most lazy people in the hospital, and for most of the time they look half asleep. After forty years of ill health, I still can't for the life of me figure out what it is they do. As far as I can see, they just follow the doctors around like clipboard-carrying sheep, letting their colleagues do all the hard work whilst they fanny about doing fuck all. And among the showbiz celebrity set, no one knows more about fannying about doing fuck all than **FLAVOR FLAV** and **BEZ**.

The Public Enemy and Happy Mondays funnymen are renowned for their ability to pick up a cheque whilst not pulling their weight in the slightest, so they would be the perfect choice as my A-List interns. That said, both quirky performers would be more useful on the hospital floor than your average non-showbiz junior doctor. Freaky Dancer Bez spent the thick end of two decades ripped to his tits on Es, whizz and hash cakes, so he could provide valuable advice to the anaesthetists about which drugs would be most effective to take the edge off their poorly patients.

Equally, hip-hop icon Flav would be a huge asset to the medical staff, as the giant clock he wears around his neck at all times would alert the idle staff to how far behind they are running on appointments, thus – hopefully – encouraging them to pull their fucking fingers out.

Ultimately, both these madcap musos would represent vital cogs in my showbiz NHS machine.

PITAL OF THE STARS!

AMBULANCE
Emergency Ambulance
NHS

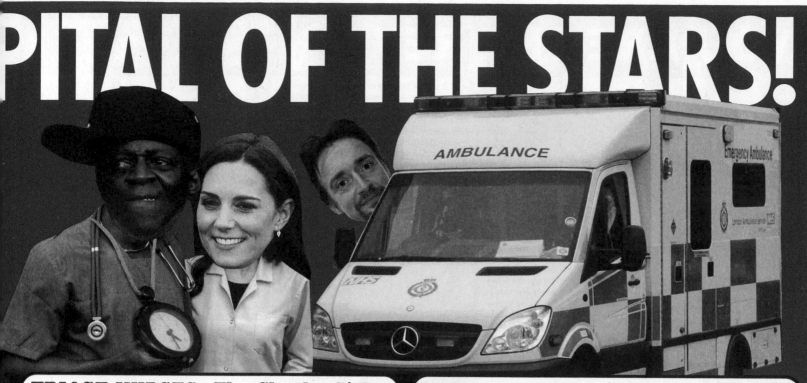

TRIAGE NURSES: *The Cheeky Girls*

IF YOU'VE seen the hit film *Carry On Doctor*, you might imagine – as I once did – that a nurse's job is simply to provide patients with a bit of much-needed eye candy, sauntering about in a skimpy uniform whilst making saucy, medical-based double entendres. Regrettably, real life is nothing like the movies.

In my four decades of catastrophic health issues, every triage nurse I've come across has been a joyless, hatchet-faced harridan who rejects my ailments as fictional, and considers a light-hearted pat on the backside to be grounds for ejecting a chronically ill man from hospital. With this in mind, for my showbiz medical assistants, I'd call on none other than forgotten Transylvanian pop duo **THE CHEEKY GIRLS**.

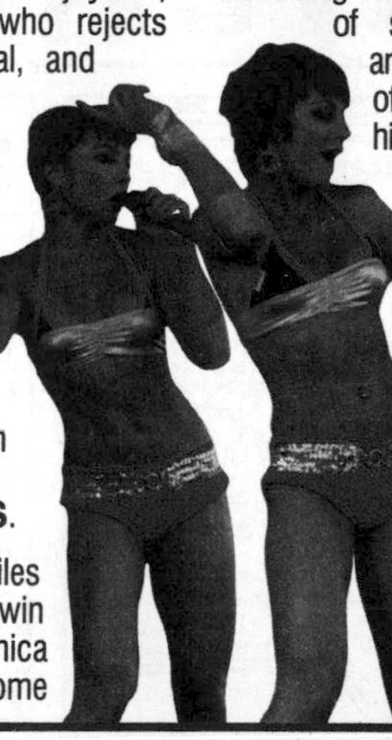

With their winning smiles and buxom figures, twin sisters Gabriela and Monica Irimia would bring some sorely needed sunshine to the dull, grey hospital floors. And the title of their 2002 debut single *Touch My Bum* shows they are good fun and wouldn't fly off the deep end at a spot of cheeky horseplay.

But the Lembit-Opik-seducing double act are more than just pretty faces and cracking arses. As former gymnasts and ballet dancers, the Romanian siblings have plenty of experience in stretching, exercising and dealing with all manner of strains, sprains, bumps and bruises. Even the title of the duo's only other hit suggests a confirmed interest in healthcare: 2003's *Take Off Your Shoes* is something a nurse might say to a patient with athlete's foot.

On all fronts, the Eastern Bloc disco-popsters would be the perfect fit for my star-studded general hospital.

MIDWIFE: *HRH Princess Cambridge*

I'VE SADLY been unable to attend the births of all of my children, due to reasons that I won't go into here, but which are all far more valid than my ex-missuses will have you believe. But from my shoddy experience in all other departments of our Broken NHS, I can only assume that the maternity wards are just as understaffed, overfilled and fuckwittedly mismanaged as the others. To make sure my hypothetical A-List labour clinic didn't fall into the same state of disrepair, I would employ **HRH THE DUCHESS OF CAMBRIDGE** as head midwife.

Princess Kate has had three children, so nobody knows more about childbirth than her. When the mums-to-be on her ward went into labour, Kate's knowledge of when to breathe and when to push would be invaluable. She also has the common touch with ordinary people, speaking to them with a grace and charm that would put them at ease during the stress of childbirth. She also runs Anmer Hall, a busy house with a staff of around twenty, so she is used to barking orders and would certainly get things done on her imaginary maternity ward.

For the newborn infants in this made-up hospital, having the future Queen of England as a midwife would also be a veritable boon: what better way to enter this world than being held by the feet and smacked on the arse by a senior member of our beloved royal family? And, of course, like the rest of her blue-blooded brood, Kate has had years of experience of smiling whilst cutting ribbons, so cheerfully snipping an umbilical cord or two would be second nature to her.

Yes, I can say with absolute certainty that Kate would deliver a right royal triumph as my celebrity childbirth assistant.

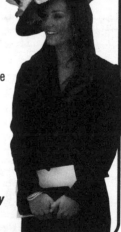

AMBULANCE DRIVER: *Richard 'The Hamster' Hammond*

WITH ALL my health problems I usually end up phoning for an ambulance at least four times a week – so I know how important getting a decent driver is. Unfortunately, most of the NHS wheelmen I've dealt with in my time have been thoroughly incompetent and unpleasant characters. Only yesterday, I dialled 999 when I spotted a worrying new mole on my elbow. It turned out to be a stray Coco Pop, but rather than chuckling at this mix-up and giving me a lift to the hospital anyway, the obnoxious ambulance man simply swore at me and stormed off. For my A-List med team, I'd want a driver who was friendly, professional, and a dab hand behind the wheel – so who better than vertically challenged telly fave **RICHARD 'THE HAMSTER' HAMMOND**?

First and foremost, *Top Gear* icon Hammond is a renowned petrolhead, so he would not be afraid to stick the sirens on full blast and screech through the streets at breakneck speed to ferry his wounded subjects to safety. What's more, the death-defying Hamster already knows his way around the healthcare system, having spent five weeks in Leeds General Infirmary after going arse over tit in a rocket-powered dragster. As such, the tidy-bearded presenter would be able to soothe his patients' nerves about what was in store, providing words of comfort and experience from the driver's seat.

Hammond could even surprise his pick-ups with a delightful new scheme called 'Star In A Reasonably Priced Ambulance', in which he roped in another A-List petrolhead – perhaps James Martin or Jay Kay out of Jamiroquai – to take the wheel and see if they could make it to Casualty before their starstruck patient bled out in the back of the vehicle.

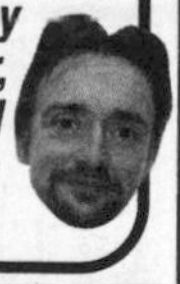

When it came to selecting my A-List ambulance operator, Lilliputian motormouth Richard would finish in pole position every time.

***NEXT WEEK:** Civil STAR-vice! We team up with a top civil servant to select an A-List squad of showbiz public sector workers*

YOU ARE THE REV

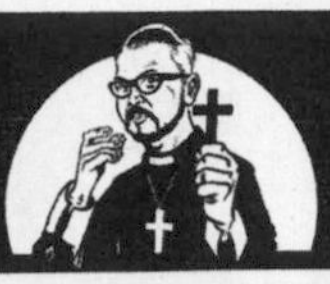

Test YOUR ecclesiastical football knowledge with the Premiership vicar, the Reverend Dr. Theodore Whelks.

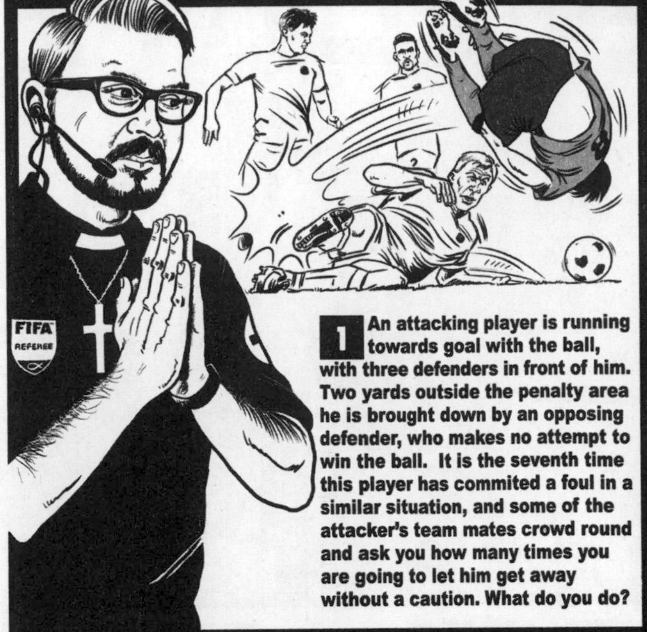

FIFA REFEREE

1 An attacking player is running towards goal with the ball, with three defenders in front of him. Two yards outside the penalty area he is brought down by an opposing defender, who makes no attempt to win the ball. It is the seventh time this player has commited a foul in a similar situation, and some of the attacker's team mates crowd round and ask you how many times you are going to let him get away without a caution. What do you do?

2 A player takes a corner, delivering the ball into the centre of the 18 yard box where it is headed towards goal by an attacking player. A defender on the goal line moves to block the ball which strikes him on the forearm and goes out for another corner. Although the defender had his arms by his side when the ball struck him, he did move his body into the its path. What action do you take?

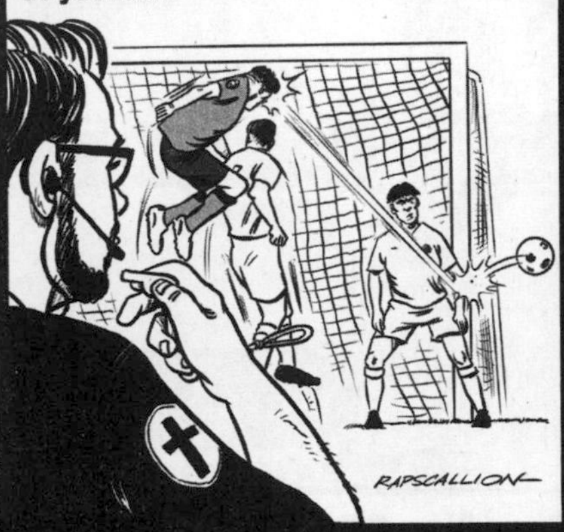

RAPSCALLION

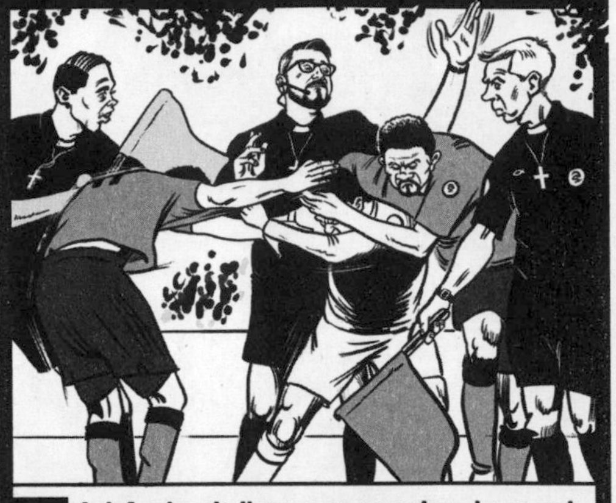

3 A defender challenges an opposing player and takes the ball in what you deem a fair challenge. However, the dispossessed player feels he was unfairly challenged and pushes his opponent in the back. A fight between the two breaks out, and several other players join the scuffle. The situation quickly gets out of hand and your assistants come onto the pitch and eventually help you restore order. What action do you take?

1A. YOU tell the attacker's team mates that those amongst them who have never commited a foul, let them criticise the lack of a yellow card. You inform them that you will not caution the midfielder, yea though he commits the foul seventy times seven. Then you tell the defender to go back ten yards and foul no more before awarding a direct free kick to the attacking side.

2A. INTENT is everything when applying the handball rule, which clearly states that the ball must be handled deliberately in order for the action to be deemed an offence. You ask the defender to tell the truth as to his intentions in thought and deed when he handled the ball, and if he confesses that the handball was deliberate, you show him a red card and award a penalty. If he tells you it was accidental, then you award a corner, but warn him that if he has not told the truth, then the penalty he will pay in the hereafter will be far greater than the one on the pitch.

3A. IN incidents like these which escalate quickly, it is often difficult to identify the various individuals who are to blame. You tell the dispossessed player that aggression is never the solution to a problem. At the same time you tell the defending player that when he finds himself the victem of aggression, he should turn the other cheek. You tell all the players to stand together for a moment's quiet reflection to think about their actions whilst you take the opportunity to pass the collection plate around the crowd.

MEDDLESOME RATBAG

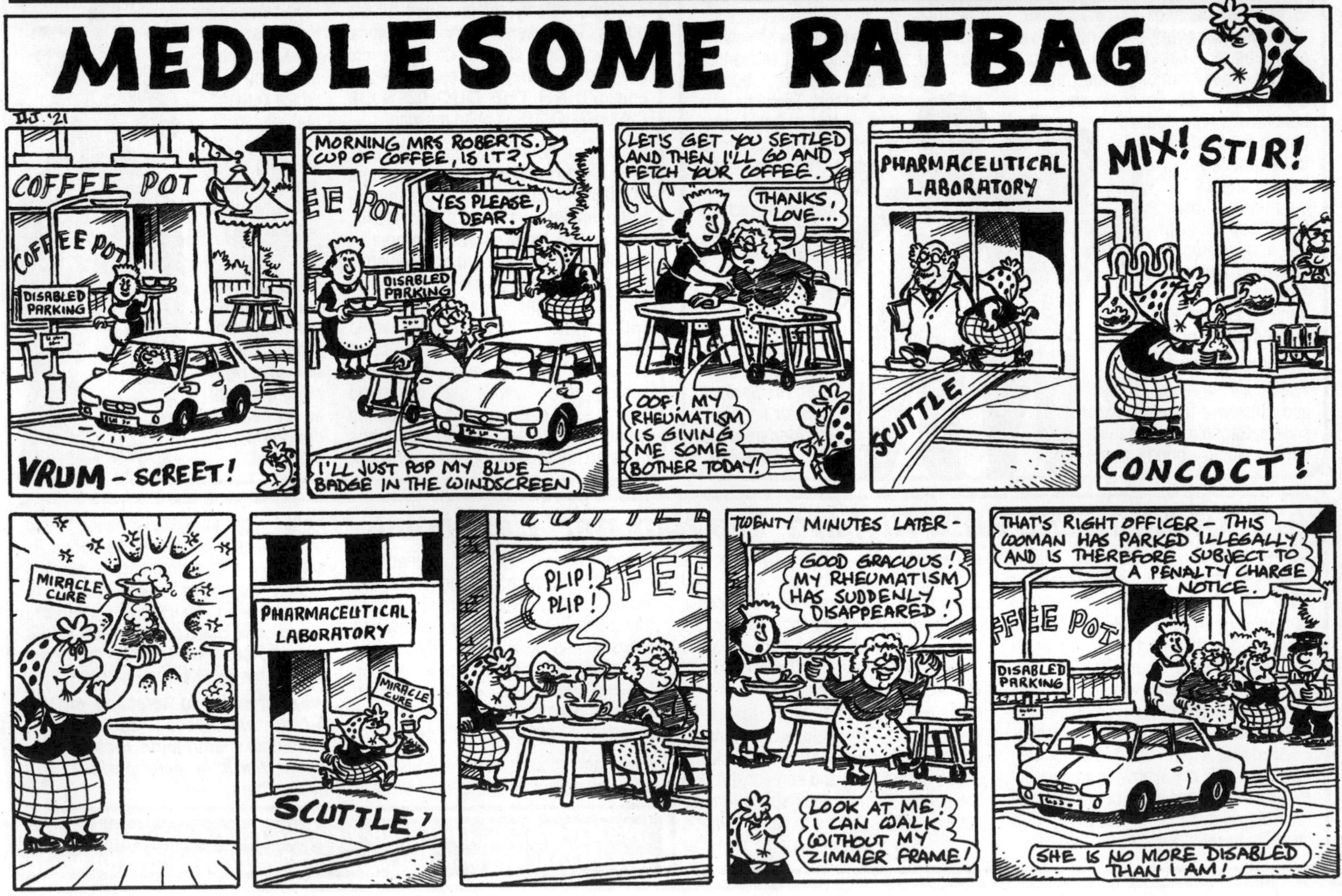

DJ '21
COFFEE POT
COFFEE POT
DISABLED PARKING
VRUM - SCREET!
MORNING MRS ROBERTS. CUP OF COFFEE, IS IT?
YES PLEASE, DEAR.
DISABLED PARKING
I'LL JUST POP MY BLUE BADGE IN THE WINDSCREEN
LET'S GET YOU SETTLED AND THEN I'LL GO AND FETCH YOUR COFFEE.
THANKS, LOVE...
OOF! MY RHEUMATISM IS GIVING ME SOME BOTHER TODAY!
PHARMACEUTICAL LABORATORY
SCUTTLE
MIX! STIR!
CONCOCT!
MIRACLE CURE
PHARMACEUTICAL LABORATORY
MIRACLE CURE
SCUTTLE!
PLIP! PLIP!
TWENTY MINUTES LATER -
GOOD GRACIOUS! MY RHEUMATISM HAS SUDDENLY DISAPPEARED!
LOOK AT ME! I CAN WALK WITHOUT MY ZIMMER FRAME!
THAT'S RIGHT OFFICER - THIS WOMAN HAS PARKED ILLEGALLY AND IS THEREFORE SUBJECT TO A PENALTY CHARGE NOTICE.
DISABLED PARKING
SHE IS NO MORE DISABLED THAN I AM!

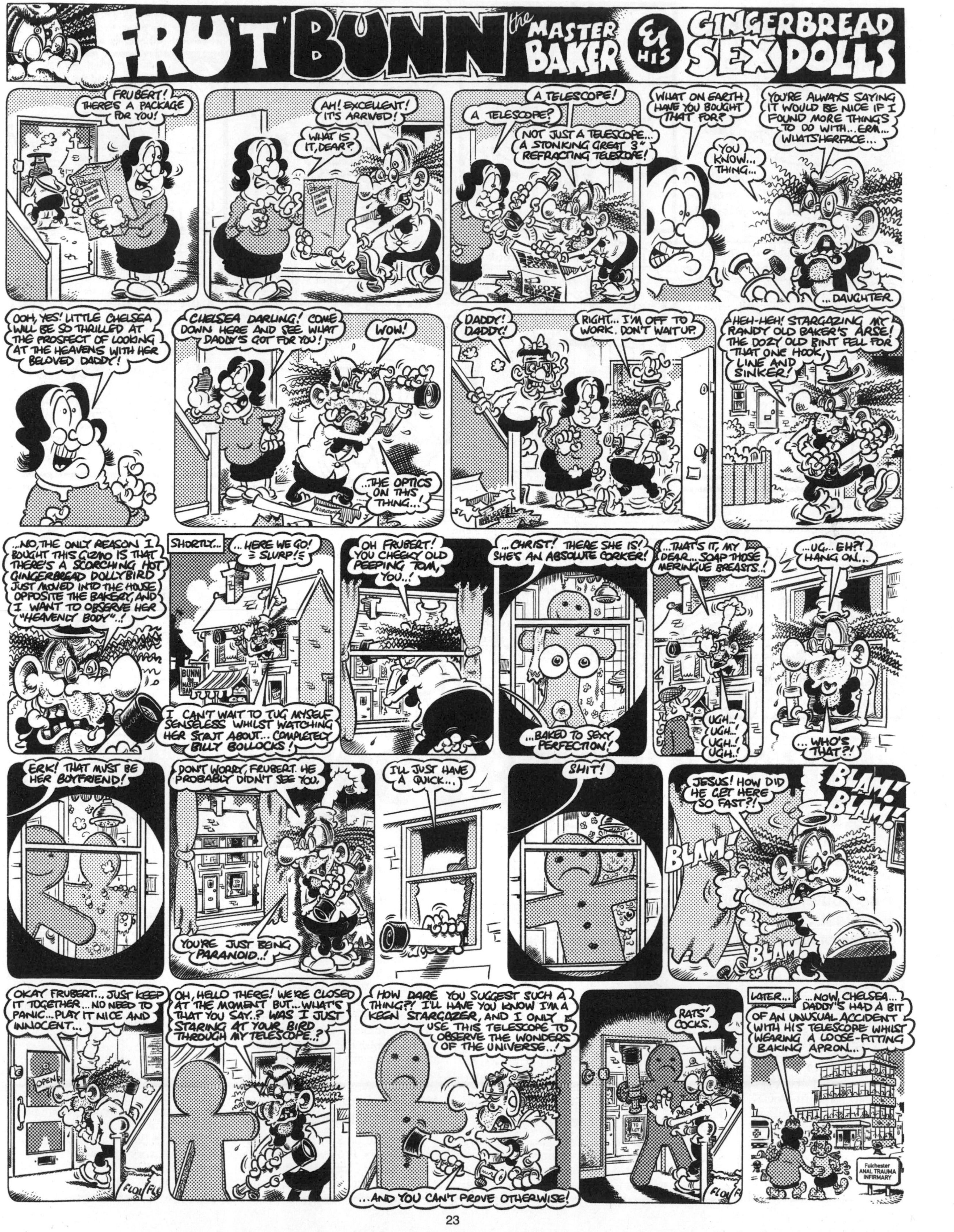
FRU'T'BUNN the MASTER BAKER & HIS GINGERBREAD SEX DOLLS
FRUBERT! THERE'S A PACKAGE FOR YOU!
AH! EXCELLENT! IT'S ARRIVED!
WHAT IS IT, DEAR?
A TELESCOPE?
A TELESCOPE!
NOT JUST A TELESCOPE... A STONKING GREAT 3" REFRACTING TELESCOPE!
WHAT ON EARTH HAVE YOU BOUGHT THAT FOR?
YOU'RE ALWAYS SAYING IT WOULD BE NICE IF I FOUND MORE THINGS TO DO WITH... ERM... WHATSHERFACE...
YOU KNOW... THING...
...DAUGHTER.
OOH, YES! LITTLE CHELSEA WILL BE SO THRILLED AT THE PROSPECT OF LOOKING AT THE HEAVENS WITH HER BELOVED DADDY!
CHELSEA DARLING! COME DOWN HERE AND SEE WHAT DADDY'S GOT FOR YOU!
WOW!
...THE OPTICS ON THIS THING...
DADDY! DADDY!
RIGHT... I'M OFF TO WORK. DON'T WAIT UP.
HEH-HEH! STARGAZING MY RANDY OLD BAKER'S ARSE! THE DOZY OLD BINT FELL FOR THAT ONE HOOK, LINE AND SINKER!
...NO, THE ONLY REASON I BOUGHT THIS GIZMO IS THAT THERE'S A SCORCHING HOT GINGERBREAD DOLLYBIRD JUST MOVED INTO THE HOUSE OPPOSITE THE BAKERY, AND I WANT TO OBSERVE HER "HEAVENLY BODY"..!
SHORTLY...
...HERE WE GO! SLURP!
I CAN'T WAIT TO TUG MYSELF SENSELESS WHILST WATCHING HER STRUT ABOUT... COMPLETELY BILLY BOLLOCKS!
OH FRUBERT! YOU CHEEKY OLD PEEPING TOM, YOU..!
...CHRIST! THERE SHE IS! SHE'S AN ABSOLUTE CORKER!
...BAKED TO SEXY PERFECTION!
...THAT'S IT, MY DEAR... SOAP THOSE MERINGUE BREASTS..!
UGH..! UGH..! UGH..! UGH..!
...UG... EH?! HANG ON...
...WHO'S THAT?!
ERK! THAT MUST BE HER BOYFRIEND!
DON'T WORRY, FRUBERT. HE PROBABLY DIDN'T SEE YOU.
YOU'RE JUST BEING PARANOID..!
I'LL JUST HAVE A QUICK...
SHIT!
JESUS! HOW DID HE GET HERE SO FAST?!
BLAM! BLAM!
BLAM!
BLAM!
OKAY FRUBERT... JUST KEEP IT TOGETHER... NO NEED TO PANIC... PLAY IT NICE AND INNOCENT...
OPEN
OH, HELLO THERE! WE'RE CLOSED AT THE MOMENT BUT... WHAT'S THAT YOU SAY..? WAS I JUST STARING AT YOUR BIRD THROUGH MY TELESCOPE..?
HOW DARE YOU SUGGEST SUCH A THING?! I'LL HAVE YOU KNOW I'M A KEEN STARGAZER, AND I ONLY USE THIS TELESCOPE TO OBSERVE THE WONDERS OF THE UNIVERSE..!
...AND YOU CAN'T PROVE OTHERWISE!
RATS' COCKS.
LATER...
...NOW, CHELSEA... DADDY'S HAD A BIT OF AN UNUSUAL ACCIDENT WITH HIS TELESCOPE WHILST WEARING A LOOSE-FITTING BAKING APRON...
Fulchester ANAL TRAUMA INFIRMARY

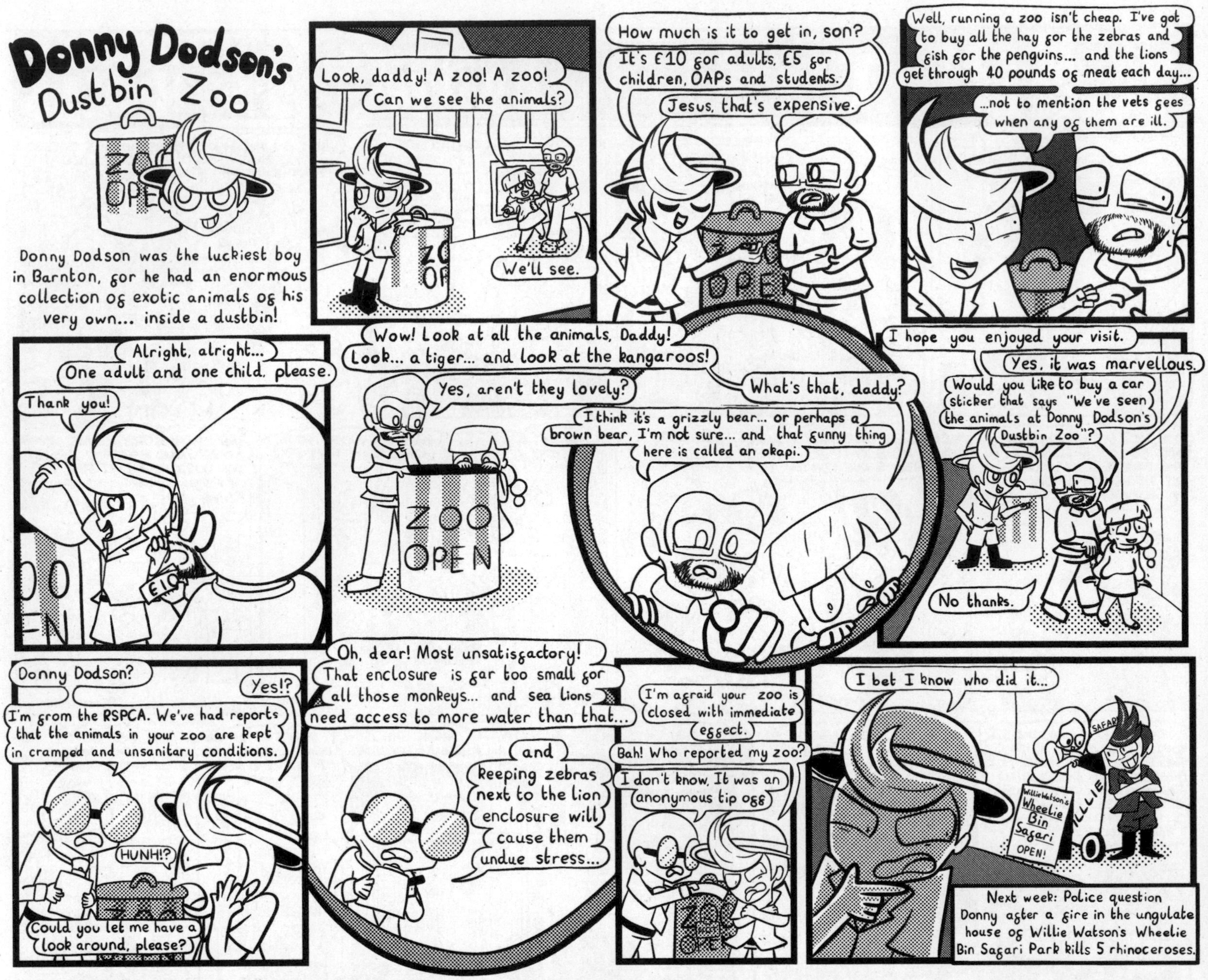
Donny Dodson's Dustbin Zoo
ZOO OPEN
Donny Dodson was the luckiest boy in Barnton, for he had an enormous collection of exotic animals of his very own... inside a dustbin!
Look, daddy! A zoo! A zoo!
Can we see the animals?
We'll see.
How much is it to get in, son?
It's £10 for adults, £5 for children, OAPs and students.
Jesus, that's expensive.
Well, running a zoo isn't cheap. I've got to buy all the hay for the zebras and fish for the penguins... and the lions get through 40 pounds of meat each day...
...not to mention the vets fees when any of them are ill.
Alright, alright...
One adult and one child, please.
Thank you!
£10
Wow! Look at all the animals, Daddy!
Look... a tiger... and look at the kangaroos!
Yes, aren't they lovely?
What's that, daddy?
I think it's a grizzly bear... or perhaps a brown bear, I'm not sure... and that funny thing here is called an okapi.
I hope you enjoyed your visit.
Yes, it was marvellous.
Would you like to buy a car sticker that says "We've seen the animals at Donny Dodson's Dustbin Zoo"?
No thanks.
Donny Dodson?
Yes!?
I'm from the RSPCA. We've had reports that the animals in your zoo are kept in cramped and unsanitary conditions.
HUNH!?
Could you let me have a look around, please?
Oh, dear! Most unsatisfactory! That enclosure is far too small for all those monkeys... and sea lions need access to more water than that...
and keeping zebras next to the lion enclosure will cause them undue stress...
I'm afraid your zoo is closed with immediate effect.
Bah! Who reported my zoo?
I don't know. It was an anonymous tip off
I bet I know who did it...
Willie Watson's Wheelie Bin Safari OPEN!
Next week: Police question Donny after a fire in the ungulate house of Willie Watson's Wheelie Bin Safari Park kills 5 rhinoceroses.

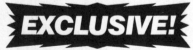

YOUR NUMBER'S DOWN

Global integer failure wreaks havoc

By our Scientific Correspondent Dr. Stanley Jordan

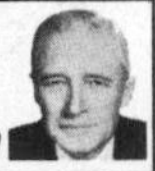

EXCLUSIVE!

PEOPLE all over the globe spent several hours in disarray yesterday after a computer glitch caused a catastrophic systems failure of *NUMBERS*.

News that the integers 1 to 9 had gone down first surfaced on Twitter, with one user asking: 'Are numbers down? Having trouble counting things' and another tweeting: 'Bloody typical. Just when I need to tell how many of something there are, numbers goes down!! FML!'

As news of the disaster spread, others took to social media to share their experiences. 'I'm a shepherd,' wrote one. 'It's really very important that I know exactly how many sheep I have in my field so if any go missing I can look for them. I'm looking at them right now and I can tell you there are some sheep but that's all I know.'

baker

A Newcastle baker who usually sells buns by the half-dozen said he had to turn customers away as he was unable to count out his wares, putting a note on his shop door asking customers to return when numbers were up and running again.

branagh

And technicians at Cumbria's Sellafield power station were forced to shut down their nuclear reactor to avoid a potential disaster. "The temperature of the reactor core is measured in degrees centrigrade which utilises combinations of the integers zero to nine," said chief scientist Dr Wendy Dentressangle. "The needle on the temperature gauge was pointing at something, but with numbers being down, we had no idea what it was and we shut down the reactor as a precaution." Technicians eventually rectified the fault, bringing numbers back on-line about two hours after going down.

williams

"They came back as quick as they went," said Professor Septimus Crane, Bodley Chair of Mathematics at the University of Oxford. "I was

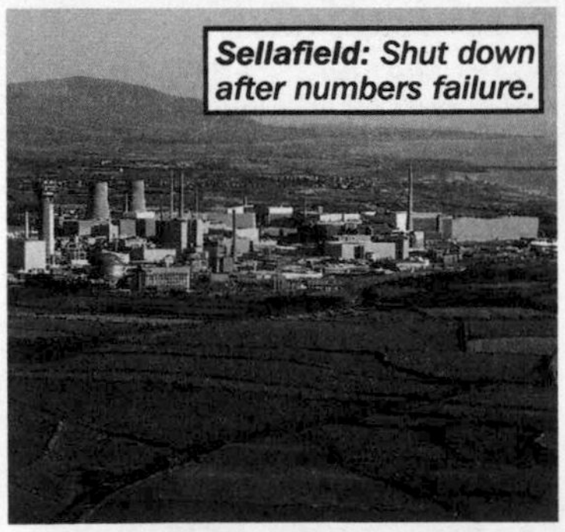

Sellafield: Shut down after numbers failure.

standing at the front of a lecture theatre doing a load of hard sums when the outage happened and I was just staring at all these indecipherable symbols on a chalkboard. I felt a right Charlie," he said. "Then suddenly, they came back and it all made sense again."

Whilst the number system, established in Mesopotamia in 3400 BC, has been known through the ages for its reliability, such outages are not unheard of. A similar incident during the Battle of Britain left pilots briefly unable to work out what number World War they were fighting in, or against which Reich.

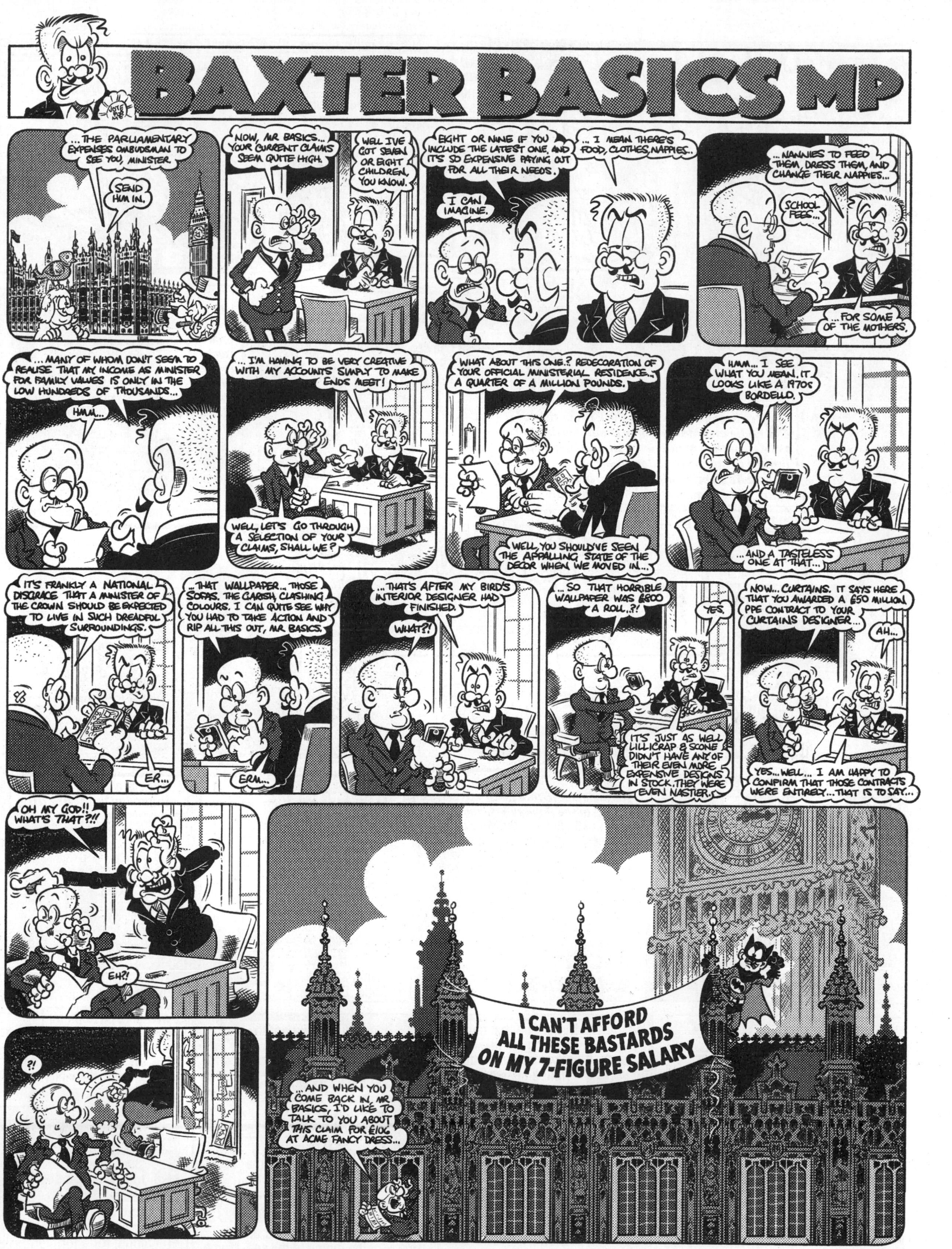
BAXTER BASICS MP
...THE PARLIAMENTARY EXPENSES OMBUDSMAN TO SEE YOU, MINISTER.
SEND HIM IN.
NOW, MR BASICS... YOUR CURRENT CLAIMS SEEM QUITE HIGH.
WELL I'VE GOT SEVEN OR EIGHT CHILDREN, YOU KNOW.
EIGHT OR NINE IF YOU INCLUDE THE LATEST ONE, AND IT'S SO EXPENSIVE PAYING OUT FOR ALL THEIR NEEDS.
I CAN IMAGINE.
...I MEAN THERE'S FOOD, CLOTHES, NAPPIES...
...NANNIES TO FEED THEM, DRESS THEM, AND CHANGE THEIR NAPPIES...
SCHOOL FEES...
...FOR SOME OF THE MOTHERS.
...MANY OF WHOM DON'T SEEM TO REALISE THAT MY INCOME AS MINISTER FOR FAMILY VALUES IS ONLY IN THE LOW HUNDREDS OF THOUSANDS...
HMM...
...I'M HAVING TO BE VERY CREATIVE WITH MY ACCOUNTS SIMPLY TO MAKE ENDS MEET!
WELL, LET'S GO THROUGH A SELECTION OF YOUR CLAIMS, SHALL WE?
WHAT ABOUT THIS ONE..? REDECORATION OF YOUR OFFICIAL MINISTERIAL RESIDENCE.. A QUARTER OF A MILLION POUNDS.
WELL, YOU SHOULD'VE SEEN THE APPALLING STATE OF THE DECOR WHEN WE MOVED IN...
HMM... I SEE WHAT YOU MEAN. IT LOOKS LIKE A 1970s BORDELLO.
...AND A TASTELESS ONE AT THAT...
IT'S FRANKLY A NATIONAL DISGRACE THAT A MINISTER OF THE CROWN SHOULD BE EXPECTED TO LIVE IN SUCH DREADFUL SURROUNDINGS.
ER...
...THAT WALLPAPER... THOSE SOFAS. THE GARISH, CLASHING COLOURS. I CAN QUITE SEE WHY YOU HAD TO TAKE ACTION AND RIP ALL THIS OUT, MR BASICS.
ERM...
...THAT'S AFTER MY BIRD'S INTERIOR DESIGNER HAD FINISHED.
WHAT?!
...SO THAT HORRIBLE WALLPAPER WAS £800 A ROLL..?!
YES.
IT'S JUST AS WELL LILLICRAP & SCONE DIDN'T HAVE ANY OF THEIR EVEN MORE EXPENSIVE DESIGNS IN STOCK. THEY WERE EVEN NASTIER.
NOW... CURTAINS. IT SAYS HERE THAT YOU AWARDED A £50 MILLION PPE CONTRACT TO YOUR CURTAINS DESIGNER...
AH...
YES... WELL... I AM HAPPY TO CONFIRM THAT THOSE CONTRACTS WERE ENTIRELY... THAT IS TO SAY...
OH MY GOD!! WHAT'S THAT?!!
EH?!
?!
I CAN'T AFFORD ALL THESE BASTARDS ON MY 7-FIGURE SALARY
...AND WHEN YOU COME BACK IN, MR BASICS, I'D LIKE TO TALK TO YOU ABOUT THIS CLAIM FOR £106 AT ACME FANCY DRESS...

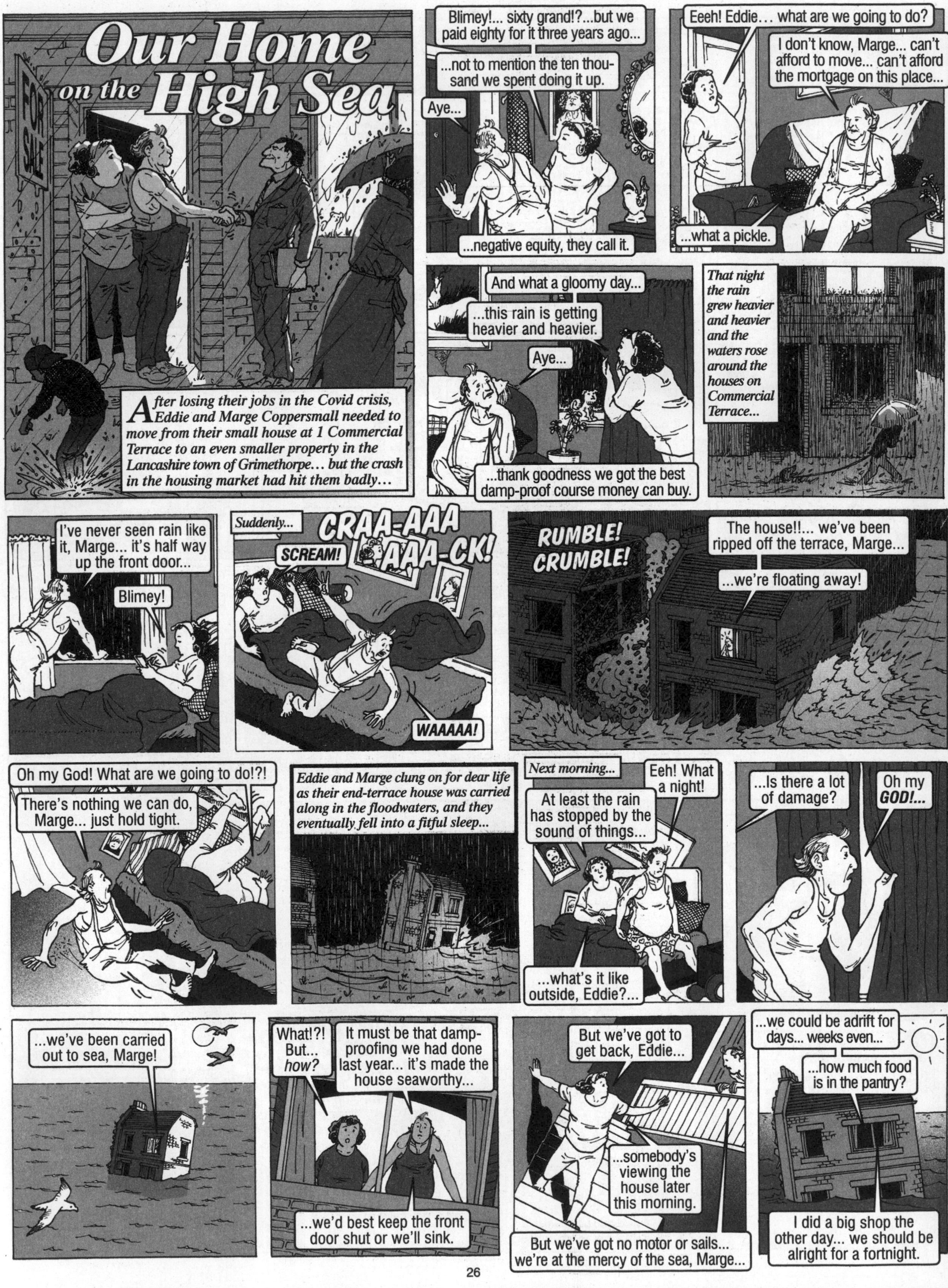
Our Home on the High Sea
FOR SALE
After losing their jobs in the Covid crisis, Eddie and Marge Coppersmall needed to move from their small house at 1 Commercial Terrace to an even smaller property in the Lancashire town of Grimethorpe… but the crash in the housing market had hit them badly…
Blimey!... sixty grand!?...but we paid eighty for it three years ago...
...not to mention the ten thousand we spent doing it up.
Aye...
...negative equity, they call it.
Eeeh! Eddie… what are we going to do?
I don't know, Marge... can't afford to move... can't afford the mortgage on this place...
...what a pickle.
And what a gloomy day...
...this rain is getting heavier and heavier.
Aye...
...thank goodness we got the best damp-proof course money can buy.
That night the rain grew heavier and heavier and the waters rose around the houses on Commercial Terrace...
I've never seen rain like it, Marge... it's half way up the front door...
Blimey!
Suddenly...
CRAA-AAA AAA-CK!
SCREAM!
WAAAAA!
RUMBLE! CRUMBLE!
The house!!... we've been ripped off the terrace, Marge...
...we're floating away!
Oh my God! What are we going to do!?!
There's nothing we can do, Marge... just hold tight.
Eddie and Marge clung on for dear life as their end-terrace house was carried along in the floodwaters, and they eventually fell into a fitful sleep...
Next morning...
Eeh! What a night!
At least the rain has stopped by the sound of things...
...what's it like outside, Eddie?...
...Is there a lot of damage?
Oh my GOD!...
...we've been carried out to sea, Marge!
What!?! But... how?
It must be that damp-proofing we had done last year... it's made the house seaworthy...
...we'd best keep the front door shut or we'll sink.
But we've got to get back, Eddie...
...somebody's viewing the house later this morning.
But we've got no motor or sails... we're at the mercy of the sea, Marge...
...we could be adrift for days... weeks even...
...how much food is in the pantry?
I did a big shop the other day... we should be alright for a fortnight.

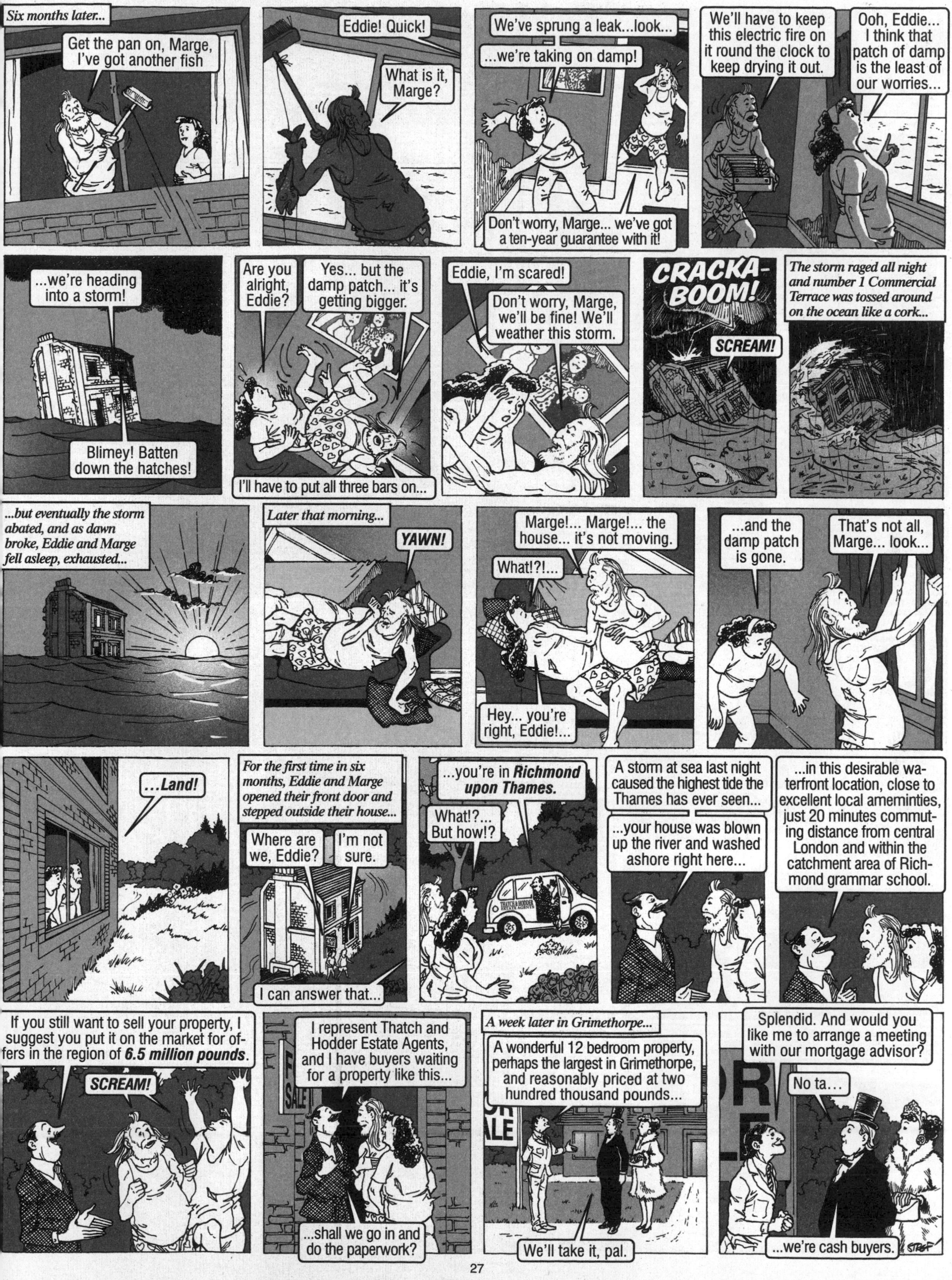

Six months later...
Get the pan on, Marge, I've got another fish
Eddie! Quick!
What is it, Marge?
We've sprung a leak...look...
...we're taking on damp!
Don't worry, Marge... we've got a ten-year guarantee with it!
We'll have to keep this electric fire on it round the clock to keep drying it out.
Ooh, Eddie... I think that patch of damp is the least of our worries...
...we're heading into a storm!
Blimey! Batten down the hatches!
Are you alright, Eddie?
Yes... but the damp patch... it's getting bigger.
I'll have to put all three bars on...
Eddie, I'm scared!
Don't worry, Marge, we'll be fine! We'll weather this storm.
CRACKA-BOOM!
SCREAM!
The storm raged all night and number 1 Commercial Terrace was tossed around on the ocean like a cork...
...but eventually the storm abated, and as dawn broke, Eddie and Marge fell asleep, exhausted...
Later that morning...
YAWN!
Marge!... Marge!... the house... it's not moving.
What!?!...
Hey... you're right, Eddie!...
...and the damp patch is gone.
That's not all, Marge... look...
...Land!
For the first time in six months, Eddie and Marge opened their front door and stepped outside their house...
Where are we, Eddie?
I'm not sure.
I can answer that...
...you're in Richmond upon Thames.
What!?... But how!?
THATCH & HODDER ESTATE AGENTS
A storm at sea last night caused the highest tide the Thames has ever seen...
...your house was blown up the river and washed ashore right here...
...in this desirable waterfront location, close to excellent local ameminties, just 20 minutes commuting distance from central London and within the catchment area of Richmond grammar school.
If you still want to sell your property, I suggest you put it on the market for offers in the region of 6.5 million pounds.
SCREAM!
I represent Thatch and Hodder Estate Agents, and I have buyers waiting for a property like this...
...shall we go in and do the paperwork?
A week later in Grimethorpe...
A wonderful 12 bedroom property, perhaps the largest in Grimethorpe, and reasonably priced at two hundred thousand pounds...
We'll take it, pal.
Splendid. And would you like me to arrange a meeting with our mortgage advisor?
No ta...
...we're cash buyers.

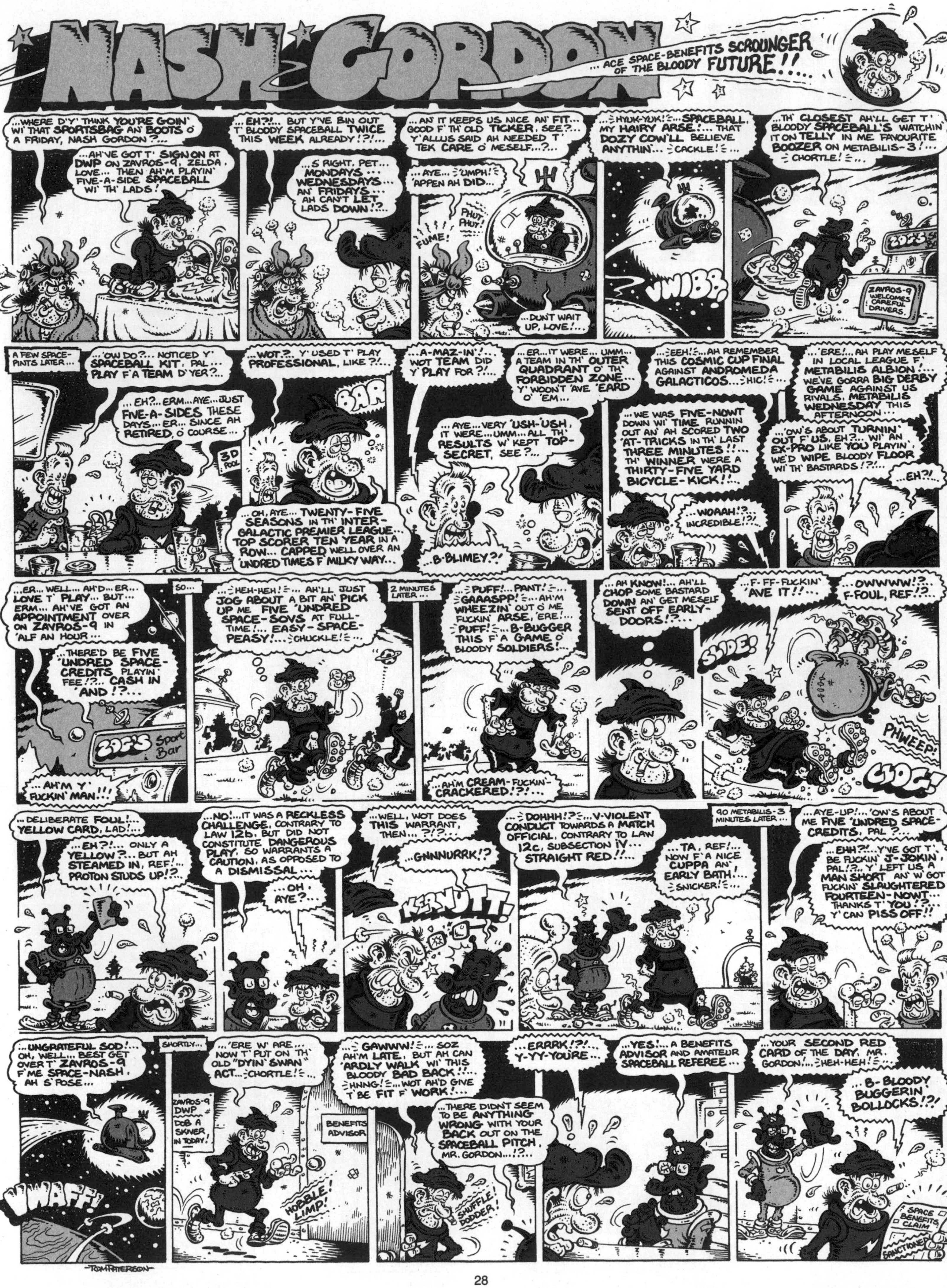
NASH GORDON
...ACE SPACE-BENEFITS SCROUNGER OF THE BLOODY FUTURE!!...
...WHERE D'Y' THINK YOU'RE GOIN' WI' THAT SPORTSBAG AN' BOOTS O' A FRIDAY, NASH GORDON?...
...AH'VE GOT T' SIGN ON AT DWP ON ZAVROS-9, ZELDA LOVE... THEN AH'M PLAYIN' FIVE-A-SIDE SPACEBALL WI' TH' LADS!
...EH?!... BUT Y'VE BIN OUT T' BLOODY SPACEBALL TWICE THIS WEEK ALREADY!?!...
...S RIGHT, PET... MONDAYS... WEDNESDAYS... AN' FRIDAYS... AH CAN'T LET LADS DOWN!?...
...AN' IT KEEPS US NICE AN' FIT... GOOD F' TH' OLD TICKER, SEE?... Y' ALLUS SAID AH NEEDED T' TEK CARE O' MESELF...?...
...AYE... UMPH! 'APPEN AH DID...
PHUT PHUT!
FUME!
...DON'T WAIT UP, LOVE!...
...HYUK-YUK!...SPACEBALL MY HAIRY ARSE!... THAT DOZY COW'LL BELIEVE ANYTHIN'... CACKLE!...
VWIBB!
...TH' CLOSEST AH'LL GET T' BLOODY SPACEBALL'S WATCHIN' IT ON TELLY IN ME FAVOURITE BOOZER ON METABILIS-3!... CHORTLE!...
ZAVROS-9 WELCOMES CAREFUL DRIVERS.
A FEW SPACE-PINTS LATER...
...'OW DO?... NOTICED Y' SPACEBALL KIT, PAL... PLAY F'A TEAM D'YER?...
...EH?...ERM...AYE...JUST FIVE-A-SIDES THESE DAYS...ER... SINCE AH RETIRED, O' COURSE...
3D POOL
...WOT?... Y' USED T' PLAY PROFESSIONAL, LIKE?!...
BAR
...OH, AYE... TWENTY-FIVE SEASONS IN TH' INTER-GALACTIC PREMIER LEAGUE... TOP SCORER TEN YEAR IN A ROW... CAPPED WELL OVER AN 'UNDRED TIMES F' MILKY WAY...
...A-MAZ-IN'! WOT TEAM DID Y' PLAY FOR?!...
...ER...IT WERE...UMM... A TEAM IN TH' OUTER QUADRANT O' TH' FORBIDDEN ZONE... Y' WOON'T 'AVE 'EARD O' 'EM...
...AYE...VERY 'USH-'USH, IT WERE...UMM...ALL TH' RESULTS W' KEPT TOP-SECRET, SEE?...
...B-BLIMEY?!
...EEH!...AH REMEMBER THIS COSMIC CUP FINAL AGAINST ANDROMEDA GALACTICOS... HIC!...
...WE WAS FIVE-NOWT DOWN WI' TIME RUNNIN' OUT AN' AH SCORED TWO 'AT-TRICKS IN TH' LAST THREE MINUTES!!... TH' WINNER WERE A THIRTY-FIVE YARD BICYCLE-KICK!!...
...WOAAH!?... INCREDIBLE!?!...
...'ERE!...AH PLAY MESELF IN LOCAL LEAGUE F' METABILIS ALBION... WE'VE GORRA BIG DERBY GAME AGAINST US RIVALS, METABILIS WEDNESDAY THIS AFTERNOON...
...'OW'S ABOUT TURNIN' OUT F' US, EH?... WI' AN EX-PRO LIKE YOU PLAYIN', WE'D WIPE BLOODY FLOOR WI' TH' BASTARDS!?!...
...EH?!...
...ER...WELL... AH'D...ER... LOVE T' PLAY... BUT... ERM... AH'VE GOT AN APPOINTMENT OVER ON ZAVROS-9 IN 'ALF AN HOUR...
...THERE'D BE FIVE 'UNDRED SPACE-CREDITS PLAYIN' FEE!?... CASH IN 'AND!?...
ZOF'S Sport Bar
...AH'M Y' FUCKIN' MAN!!!
SO...
...HEH-HEH!... AH'LL JUST JOG ABOUT A BIT AN' PICK UP ME FIVE 'UNDRED SPACE-SOVS AT FULL-TIME!... EASY-SPACE-PEASY!... CHUCKLE!...
2 MINUTES LATER...
...PUFF!...PANT!... GAAASPP!...AH'M WHEEZIN' OUT O' ME FUCKIN' ARSE, 'ERE!... PUFF!...B-BUGGER THIS F' A GAME O' BLOODY SOLDIERS!...
...AH'M CREAM-FUCKIN'-CRACKERED!?!...
...AH KNOW!...AH'LL CHOP SOME BASTARD DOWN AN' GET MESELF SENT OFF EARLY-DOORS!?...
...F-FF-FUCKIN' 'AVE IT!!...
SLIDE!
...OWWWW!?... F-FOUL, REF!?
PHWEEP!
CLOC!
...DELIBERATE FOUL!... YELLOW CARD, LAD!...
...EH?!... ONLY A YELLOW?... BUT AH STEAMED IN, REF!... PROTON STUDS UP!?...
...NO!...IT WAS A RECKLESS CHALLENGE, CONTRARY TO LAW 12b, BUT DID NOT CONSTITUTE DANGEROUS PLAY, SO WARRANTS A CAUTION, AS OPPOSED TO A DISMISSAL...
...OH AYE?...
...WELL, WOT DOES THIS WARRANT, THEN...?!?...
...GNNNURRK!?
KERNUTT!
...DOHHH!?...V-VIOLENT CONDUCT TOWARDS A MATCH OFFICIAL, CONTRARY TO LAW 12c, SUBSECTION IV... STRAIGHT RED!!...
...TA, REF!... NOW F' A NICE CUPPA AN' EARLY BATH!... SNICKER!...
90 METABILIS-3 MINUTES LATER...
...AYE-UP!...'OW'S ABOUT ME FIVE 'UNDRED SPACE-CREDITS, PAL?...
...EHH?!... Y'VE GOT T' BE FUCKIN' J-JOKIN' PAL!?... Y' LEFT US A MAN SHORT AN' W' GOT FUCKIN' SLAUGHTERED FOURTEEN-NOWT... THANKS T' YOU!?... Y' CAN PISS OFF!!
...UNGRATEFUL SOD!... OH, WELL... BEST GET OVER T' ZAVROS-9 F' ME SPACE-NASH, AH S'POSE...
WHAFF!
SHORTLY...
ZAVROS-9 DWP DOB A SKIVER IN TODAY!
...'ERE W' ARE... NOW T' PUT ON TH' OLD "DYIN' SWAN" ACT... CHORTLE!...
HOBBLE! LIMP!
BENEFITS ADVISOR
...GAWWW!...SOZ AH'M LATE, BUT AH CAN 'ARDLY WALK WI' THIS BLOODY BAD BACK!... HNNG!...WOT AH'D GIVE T' BE FIT F' WORK!...
SHUFFLE! DODDER!
...THERE DIDN'T SEEM TO BE ANYTHING WRONG WITH YOUR BACK OUT ON THE SPACEBALL PITCH, MR. GORDON...!?...
...ERRRK!?!... Y-YY-YOU'RE...
...YES!... A BENEFITS ADVISOR AND AMATEUR SPACEBALL REFEREE...
...YOUR SECOND RED CARD OF THE DAY, MR. GORDON!... HEH-HEH!
...B-BLOODY BUGGERIN' BOLLOCKS!?!
SPACE BENEFITS CLAIM
SANCTIONED
TOM PATERSON

THE Male Online

We've been driving around for an hour...

I'll *find* a space, woman, have some bloody patience!

Why can we never just use a car-park? They're only a pound on Sundays

They're all run by the council, that's why.

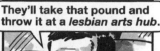
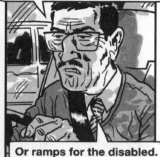

They'll take that pound and throw it at a *lesbian arts hub*.

Or ramps for the disabled.

Ramps for lesbian artists who are too *sodding* bone-idle to–

A space! There! Over there!

There, see? Now every penny we spend will go solely to *boosting* the Great British retail sector –

– rather than on mime classes for druggist homosexuals.

Yes, heaven forbid anyone should try to–

Uh-oh. Back in the car please, Beryl.

Why?

Young people.

Quickly now.

I'll do no such thing! The shops are closing soon.

Tough! Our car would be ablaze the second we step out of sight.

None of these other cars are *ablaze*.

Yet. Yet!

Only a question of time.

I mean, look at them.

You can smell the *seething* resentment from here.

Why should they resent us?

Ha! What?

How long have you got?!

For one, they are *convinced* we had it easy purely because our homes were cheap to buy!

They might have a point there...

Ohhh, I *see*, so it's *our* fault Trots managed to mess-up housing after the war!

Maybe we should *apologise* for our first house being carelessly priced at £400.

Balls! They should be *thanking* us, for voting Maggie in to help the market bring order!

But do they? Do they buggery!

BANG

They'd sooner loaf around, *sneering* and playing rap music.

Flaunt their wares, like those girls!

Crop-tops, toned midriffs, and have you *seen* their skirts?!

The *thigh's* the limit!!

And how, exactly, are men supposed to know their age?

Of course they're going to feast my eyes, it's nature!!

Oh, but if *something happens* you bet it'll be me I mean *the man who gets the blame!*

Every bloody time! And as for the hot-pants! *The hot-pants!!*

Shortly

Knickers! Knackers! Knockers!

Hush, we're nearly home.

Knickers! Knackers! GAAAAAH!

LITTLE & MEDIUM

MADAME ARCATI
PALMS READ
TAROT
PSYCHIC
And why is it that you wish to contact this particular individual?
There's a question I *need* to ask.
What?
I have to know...
Why he'd never let me finish any of my songs.
Seems legit.
Oh, ooh, a voice is coming through...
Who is it?
I was... half of a popular comedy double-act...
This sounds promising!
Rock on Tommy!
Rock on Tommy!
Er –
– I don't think that's him.
ROCK ON TOMMY!!
That is definitely not him...
Rock on Tommy!
It's just not a thing he ever said.
Ohh, the voice is fading to me, fading, fading...
To me...
To me!
To who?
To me.
To who?
To me.
To who?
MADAME ARCATI
PALMS READ
TAROT
PSYCHIC
To me.

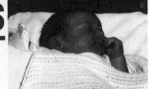

Murderous Despot Born in Leeds

A VILE dictator, whose murderous reign of terror will enslave half the globe, was born in Leeds General Hospital this morning.

Barnaby Percival Clarke, who will one day have total dominion over billions of cowed and broken subjects, weighed 6lb 12oz, and, according to his mum, Becky, has his dad's beautiful blue eyes.

statue

"He's so adorable," she said of the child whose 500m high statue will one day dwarf the ruins of St Paul's Cathedral. "From the moment we set eyes on him, it was love."

Fourteen-inch-long Barnaby's resemblance to dad Glen means that the despot-in-waiting is already a big hit with his aunties and uncles, in contrast to the multitudes who will one day weep in despair at his very name.

"He looks so innocent" beamed Becky, unaware of the brutal and merciless power her son would one day wield over the unfortunate subjects under his rule.

But it is this superficial charm that will carry him to the highest office in the land on May 1st 2041, before vanishing abruptly as he abolishes parliament the same day.

"We've already got four kids," said Glen. "So we weren't sure about having another. But now he's here we're over the moon."

"And he's got four big brothers and sisters to spoil him!" he joked, unaware that the one-day autocrat will have all four siblings executed after a series of grotesque show trials in the mid-2050s.

future

Proud mum Becky was pragmatic about the future of her tyrant-in-waiting. "I know it's a hard world out there for kids these days," she said. "As long as he finds something he's good at that makes him happy."

"At the minute, he's just our little prince," she added, unaware that her son would install her as Queen Of The Moon in 2059.

You've Been Framed! LIFE INSURANCE

No complicated premiums! Just no-quibble payouts!
As long as you get your accidental death on camera, you're covered!

JUST LOOK AT THESE FABULOUS PAYOUTS*

- ***Severed jugular after running into French doors* £250**
- ***Burnt to death whilst lighting barbecue with can of petrol* £250**
- ***Fatally injured by falling masonry whilst demolishing supporting wall with big hammer* £250**
- ***Cracked back of head on edge of swimming pool whilst jumping off hotel balcony* £250**
- ***BMX jump into bonfire whilst wearing rayon anorak* £250**
- ***Fell off rope swing onto rocks whilst showing pants* £250**
- ***Hit truck whilst riding shopping trolley down steep hill into junction with dual carriageway* £250**
- ***Massive rectal haemorrhage and shock following drunken firework launching prank* £250**

You've Been Framed Insurance plc., c/o Granada TV, Manchester

Payments not guaranteed if tapes not wound on to the correct bit or footage filmed with your phone the wrong way up. *We only pay out 50% for Betamax. Canned laughter may be added to footage of your demise.

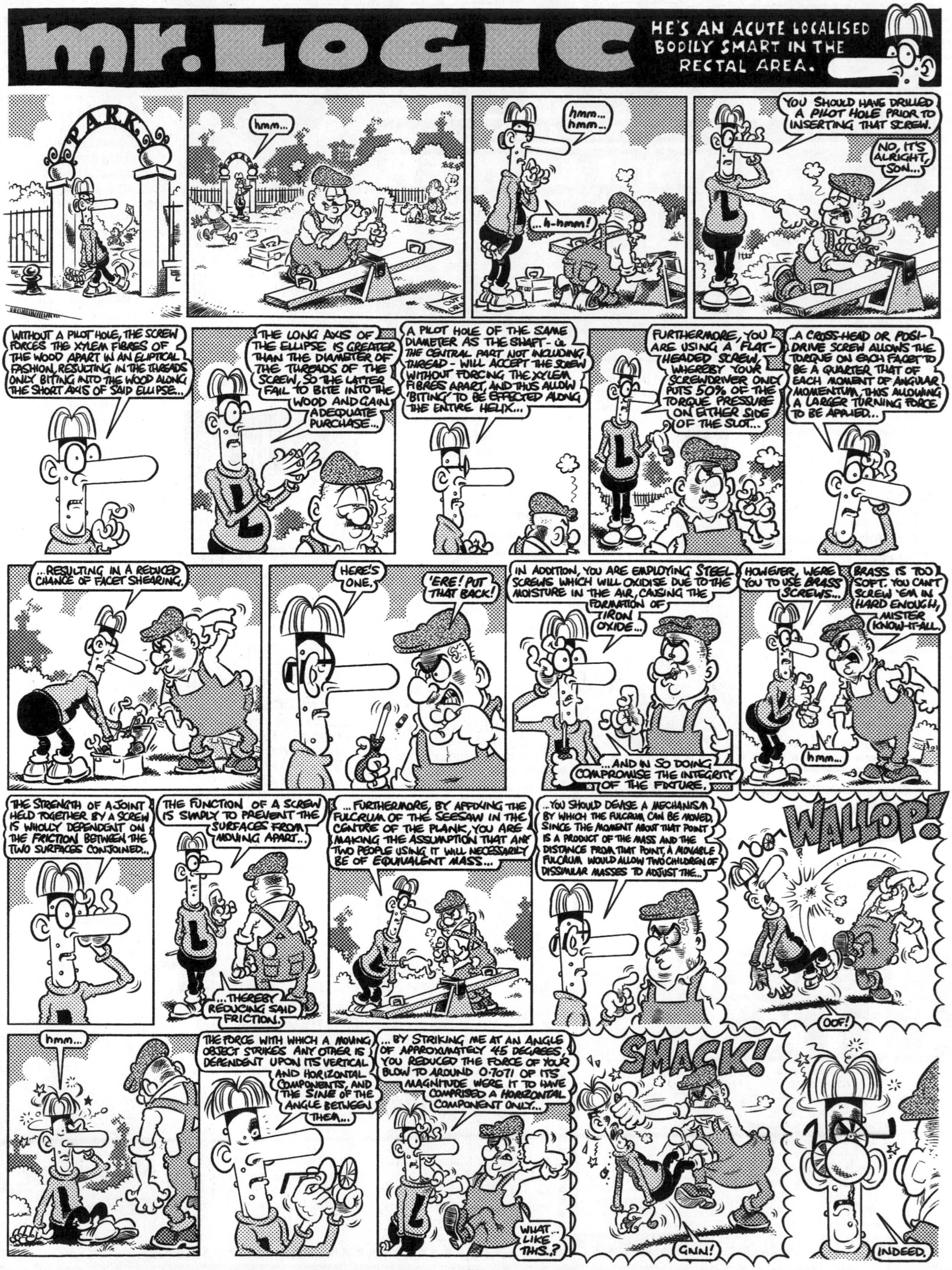
mr. LOGIC
HE'S AN ACUTE LOCALISED BODILY SMART IN THE RECTAL AREA.
PARK
hmm...
hmm... hmm...
...h-hmm!
YOU SHOULD HAVE DRILLED A PILOT HOLE PRIOR TO INSERTING THAT SCREW.
NO, IT'S ALRIGHT, SON...
WITHOUT A PILOT HOLE, THE SCREW FORCES THE XYLEM FIBRES OF THE WOOD APART IN AN ELIPTICAL FASHION, RESULTING IN THE THREADS ONLY BITING INTO THE WOOD ALONG THE SHORT AXIS OF SAID ELLIPSE...
THE LONG AXIS OF THE ELLIPSE IS GREATER THAN THE DIAMETER OF THE THREADS OF THE SCREW, SO THE LATTER FAIL TO BITE INTO THE WOOD AND GAIN ADEQUATE PURCHASE...
A PILOT HOLE OF THE SAME DIAMETER AS THE SHAFT - i.e. THE CENTRAL PART NOT INCLUDING THREAD - WILL ACCEPT THE SCREW WITHOUT FORCING THE XYLEM FIBRES APART, AND THUS ALLOW 'BITING' TO BE EFFECTED ALONG THE ENTIRE HELIX...
FURTHERMORE, YOU ARE USING A 'FLAT-HEADED' SCREW, WHEREBY YOUR SCREWDRIVER ONLY PUTS 50% OF THE TORQUE PRESSURE ON EITHER SIDE OF THE SLOT...
...A CROSS-HEAD OR POSI-DRIVE SCREW ALLOWS THE TORQUE ON EACH FACET TO BE A QUARTER THAT OF EACH MOMENT OF ANGULAR MOMENTUM, THIS ALLOWING A LARGER TURNING FORCE TO BE APPLIED...
...RESULTING IN A REDUCED CHANCE OF FACET SHEARING.
HERE'S ONE.
'ERE! PUT THAT BACK!
IN ADDITION, YOU ARE EMPLOYING STEEL SCREWS WHICH WILL OXIDISE DUE TO THE MOISTURE IN THE AIR, CAUSING THE FORMATION OF IRON OXIDE...
...AND IN SO DOING COMPROMISE THE INTEGRITY OF THE FIXTURE.
HOWEVER, WERE YOU TO USE BRASS SCREWS...
BRASS IS TOO SOFT. YOU CAN'T SCREW 'EM IN HARD ENOUGH, MISTER KNOW-IT-ALL.
hmm...
THE STRENGTH OF A JOINT HELD TOGETHER BY A SCREW IS WHOLLY DEPENDENT ON THE FRICTION BETWEEN THE TWO SURFACES CONJOINED...
THE FUNCTION OF A SCREW IS SIMPLY TO PREVENT THE SURFACES FROM MOVING APART...
...THEREBY REDUCING SAID FRICTION.
...FURTHERMORE, BY AFFIXING THE FULCRUM OF THE SEESAW IN THE CENTRE OF THE PLANK, YOU ARE MAKING THE ASSUMPTION THAT ANY TWO PEOPLE USING IT WILL NECESSARILY BE OF EQUIVALENT MASS...
...YOU SHOULD DEVISE A MECHANISM BY WHICH THE FULCRUM CAN BE MOVED, SINCE THE MOMENT ABOUT THAT POINT IS A PRODUCT OF THE MASS AND THE DISTANCE FROM THAT POINT. A MOVABLE FULCRUM WOULD ALLOW TWO CHILDREN OF DISSIMILAR MASSES TO ADJUST THE...
WALLOP!
OOF!
hmm...
THE FORCE WITH WHICH A MOVING OBJECT STRIKES ANY OTHER IS DEPENDENT UPON ITS VERTICAL AND HORIZONTAL COMPONENTS, AND THE SINE OF THE ANGLE BETWEEN THEM...
...BY STRIKING ME AT AN ANGLE OF APPROXIMATELY 45 DEGREES, YOU REDUCED THE FORCE OF YOUR BLOW TO AROUND 0·7071 OF ITS MAGNITUDE WERE IT TO HAVE COMPRISED A HORIZONTAL COMPONENT ONLY...
WHAT... LIKE THIS.?
SMACK!
GNN!
INDEED.

Letterbocks

Viz Comic, P.O. Box 841 Whitley Bay, NE26 9EQ letters@viz.co.uk

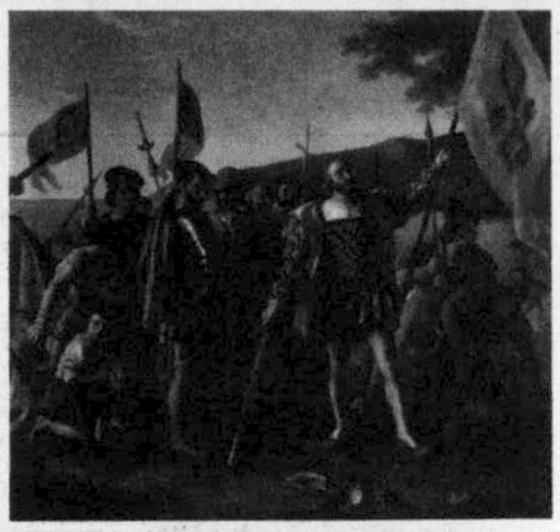

I READ that Christopher Columbus was 41 years old when he went to America, and as a consequence everyone celebrates him to this day. I was 25 when I first landed on the East Coast of the USA, and yet not one book has been written about me despite the fact that I beat Columbus by a good 16 years. Once again, it's one rule, etc… you know the rest.

Rick Riley, Manchester

I FEEL that Daffy Duck cartoons present a very inaccurate portrayal of how ducks react to being shot. Rather than emerging displeased - yet relatively unscathed - with their beaks moved 180 degrees around their faces, in reality they tend to just explode when blasted at point blank range with a shotgun.

Matthew John, email

STAR LETTER

I DON'T know why people use the phrase "It went down like a lead balloon" to describe something that was poorly received, as a lead balloon would go down very well indeed, I would imagine. "It went down like a helium balloon" would be a much more fitting simile.

Sarah Spence, Newcastle

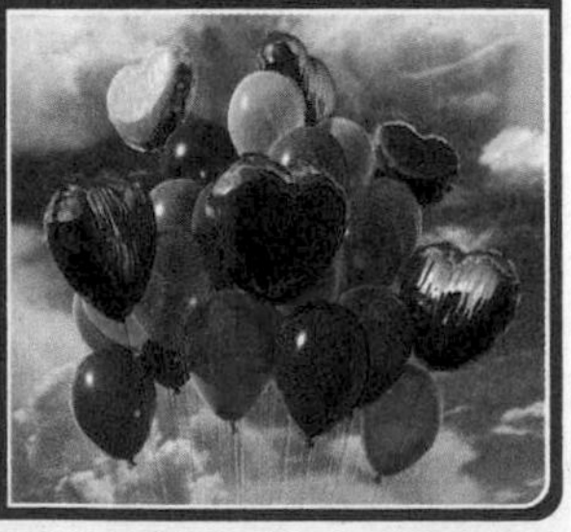

WHY is it that when pharmaceutical companies decide to do clinical trials for drugs, they always want healthy non-smokers of a certain age? You never see them asking for morbidly obese, 40-a-day, meat-lipped, gammon-eating alcoholics like most of the population. Come on, big pharma, let's have a bit more equality. I want to earn money taking pills.

Darren Perambulator, Notts

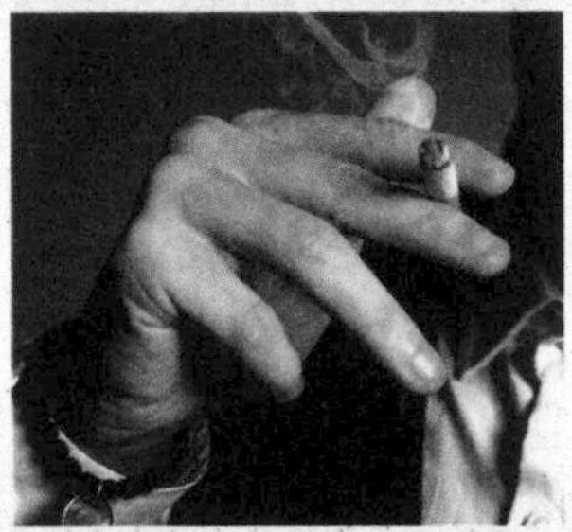

THEY say a bad workman always blames his tools. But they also say that a workman is only as good as the tools he uses. I've just put some shelves up on the wonk, and I don't know whether I can blame my tools or not.

Thanston Crabb, Wisbech

WHENEVER I hear a politician say that we should "trust the Great British Public," I remind myself that this is the public that put *You're the One that I Want* by John Travolta and Olivia Newton-John at Number 1 in the pop charts for 9 weeks in 1978.

Adrian Newth, Stratford-u-Avon

I THINK a lot more people would understand poetry and perhaps even enjoy it if poets would stop talking in riddles and just say what they mean.

T O'Neill, Glasgow

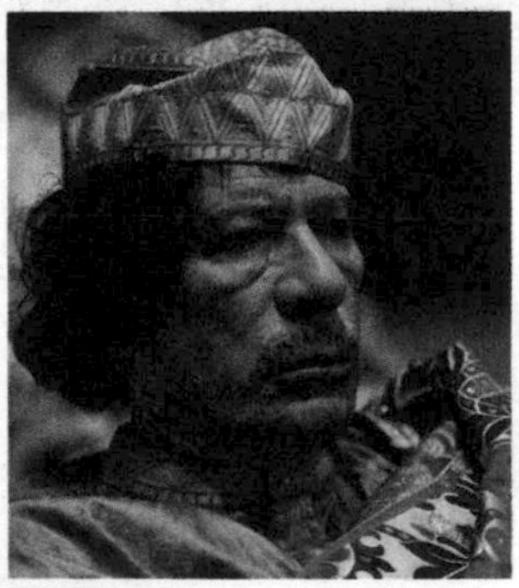

YOU can say what you like about late Libyan dictator Muammar Gadaffi, but despite wielding complete control over his country and its military for forty-odd years, he never promoted himself above Colonel, even though there were a couple of higher ranks available. Thats the kind of self-effacing behaviour you rarely see in murderous autocrats these days.

Chris Powell, France

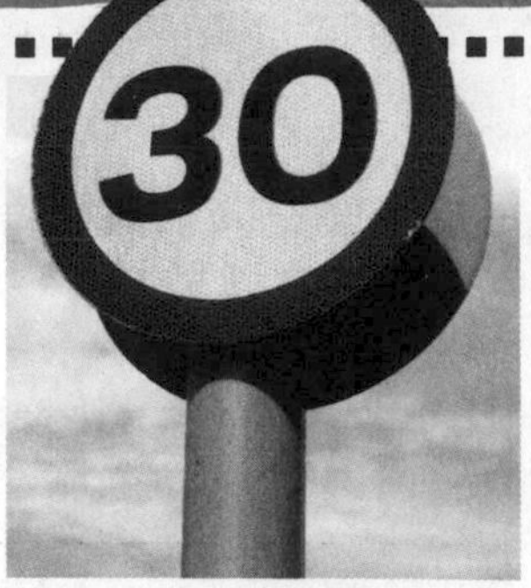
30

EARLIER today I was driving along a road which was clearly marked as a 30mph zone, but then another sign a mile further on said 40mph, followed by ANOTHER sign five miles later saying 30mph again. I wish these government "experts" would make their minds up.

Richard Scaramanga, Ipswich

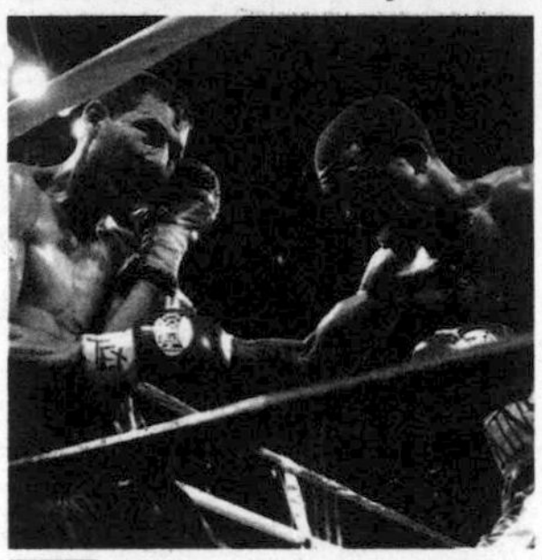

I'VE never understood why boxers want to get up and have a fight at 3 am. I struggle to get up and go for a piss at that time of the morning.

Stuie, Bunny

I NOTICE the Wikipedia page describes *Viz* as "a popular British adult comic magazine." Given sales of about 50,000 in a country of nearly 70 million people, does this mean I can describe myself as popular if 99.9% of people think I'm a cunt?

Mike Tatham, St. Andrews

AN emergency toilet visit recently found me without my phone or a magazine for 35 long minutes. On the positive side, I now consider myself an authority on the chemical composition of toilet duck. So you know, every cloud and all that.

Eldon Furse, email

TODAY, I saw an advert for child adoption on the back of a bus I was following. I understand that a decision to go for a McDonald's or join the RAC may be inspired by these adverts, and that's fine. But with regard to the life-changing decision to adopt a child, I imagine a bit more forethought is needed than idly reacting to an ad on the back of the 34A to Hanley.

John Mason, email

HOW come the Kryptonian Council from *Superman* all wore long, flowing, luminous white gowns during their meetings, but the members of my parish council all wear Pringle sweaters, tweed skirts or chinos? I think they would get more respect from the local electorate if they were all to dress in the same futuristic clothing - such as high-necked silver onesies with belts - the next time they meet to discuss parking restrictions in the town centre.

Neil Johnson, Durham

IN the last issue, you referred to Manchester Airport as the UK's second largest airport after Heathrow. However, according to 2019 passenger numbers, Manchester Airport is the third largest airport in the UK, servicing 29,397,537 passengers in comparison to London Gatwick, which saw 46,576,473 travellers come through its doors, very much like your mother, whom has easily serviced a similar amount of cocks through her back doors.

Trim McKenna, Surbiton

** And here we go again. If it's Friday, it must be another cheap jibe at the expense of the editors' mothers from Trim McKenna, a man who has TWICE been banned from the Viz Letterbocks pages for using insulting language. Well we have great pleasure in banning him yet again. If you want to write letters insulting our mothers, Mr McKenna, then please send them to some other magazine, like the one we once saw with pictures of your mum doing a 10-way tramp bukkake party.*

WHAT happens if a Dalek goes through a dog shit? Will they have an attachment for removing it, or does Davros have to come along and scrape it off the wheels with a piece of cardboard?

Big Dave, Redditch

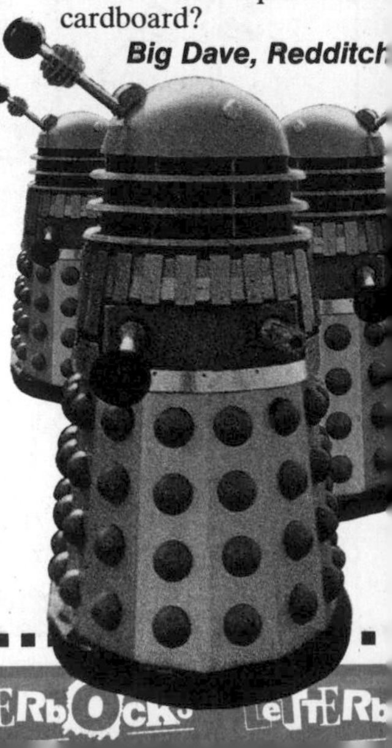

THE rumour that cheese contains pus from infected cows' udders has been well and truly debunked. Although the jury is still out on whether or not farmers stick their cocks in the cups of milking machines.

Gerry Paton, London

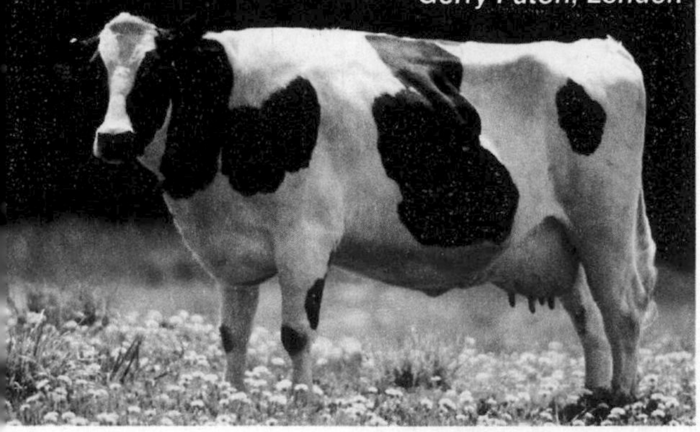

UPON seeing a barely opened Cadbury's Fudge bar on the pavement, my wife remarked "Oh, that's a shame. Somebody's dropped their fudge." I laughed out loud, and as she didn't understand, I explained it to her but she still didn't get it. Anyway, we've been divorced for fifteen years since that incident. Yesterday I farted on my girlfriend's leg and she laughed for about half an hour. It's funny where life takes you.

Toobler, Brighton

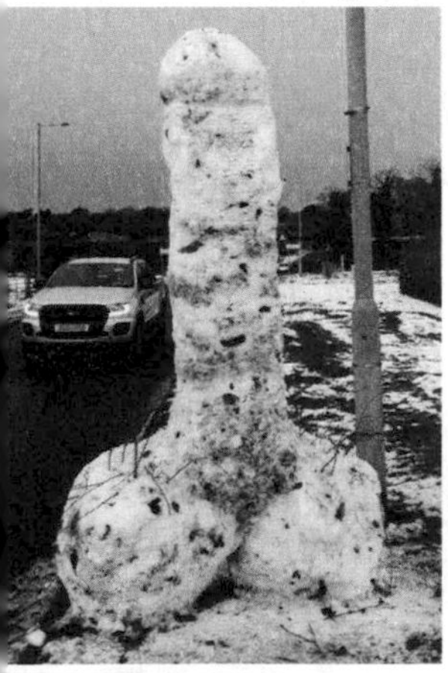

JUDGING by this picture, some festive fool in the village of Kirkliston outside Edinburgh clearly had too much time on their hands, producing this 7-foot tall snow cock. They even went to the trouble of sticking lots of twigs in the scratbags to resemble short and curlies.

Kenneth Wilson, Glasgow

ACTING on some online advice, my partner and I decided to spice up our sex life by watching pornography together. I'm not sure what it was, but the 4-on-1, double-anal gang-bang we watched seems to have done our relationship more damage than good.

Barren Munchoreson, email

I'VE just watched a football match and bent over and farted the full time whistle. And I only lightly soiled myself.

Andrew, Wellington

TV presenters keep making gaffes and there's nothing they can do about it. Just 35 minutes into *Children in Need*, the lovely Alex Scott referred to Noel Gallagher as a 'legend' when she clearly meant 'bellend.' Isn't live telly brilliant!

Alfie Noakes, Woking

MY girlfriend was telling me about how she woke in the middle of the night to find two burglars in her bedroom. "My blood froze," she said. I had to laugh as I explained that blood temperature varies only between 97 - 99 degrees Fahrenheit, so it certainly wouldn't have frozen. Ex-girlfriend. She's my ex-girlfriend.

Dominic Twose, L'ton Spa

IF you removed all the Os from Jon Bon Jovi's name, then he'd be called "Jn Bn Jvi." If, however, you removed all of those letters instead, he'd simply be called "Ooo." You couldn't make it up.

David Elliott, Upper Thigh

IT'S all very well people saying how much better the leaders of Australia have been in keeping their populations safe from Covid, but let's not forget that they are teeming with deadly fucking spiders and surrounded by man-eating sharks, and their governments haven't done much to get rid of them. Thanks to our leaders, the worst we have to contend with is a sting off a wasp. So let's stop putting ourselves down and give our government a bit of credit where it's due.

Hector Dugong, Surrey

I'VE just read that posh newsreader Joanna Gosling is allegedly dating the thespian Colin Firth. Had I known she'd set the bar so low I'd have made enquiries myself about spending some quality time with her. I'm just as good an actor as Mr. Firth, as I was a Wise Man in my school nativity in 1976, and earlier this year I only just missed the 'cut' for *Over 50's Love Island*. Honestly, only just.

Rich, email

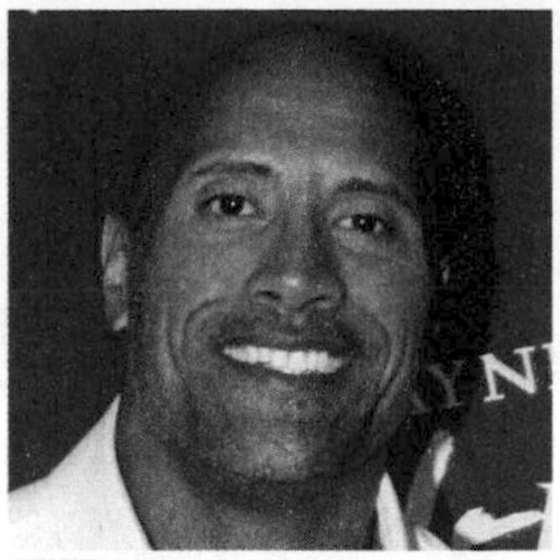

DOES anybody know if Dwayne 'The Rock' Johnson took his name from the popular seaside confectionery, or did the people of Blackpool name their Rock after the popular wrestler/actor?

Ben Nunn, Caterham

SHEPHERD'S pie, Shepherd's Bush, Shepherd's delight. Why do these shepherds get everything their way?

Dale Von Minaker, Kidderminster

WHILE watching football today, I wondered why no team had ever worn a camouflage strip? You could hide from the ref when he was coming to book you by lying on the ground, or even sneak extra players onto the pitch unseen. Honestly, I can't think of a single reason not to do it.

Robbie Savage, Wales

IF I took on a shark in a triathlon, I'm pretty sure I could outrun it, but it would obviously be a much faster swimmer than me. So basically it would come down to who was the better cyclist.

Alex Nimmo, Portsmouth

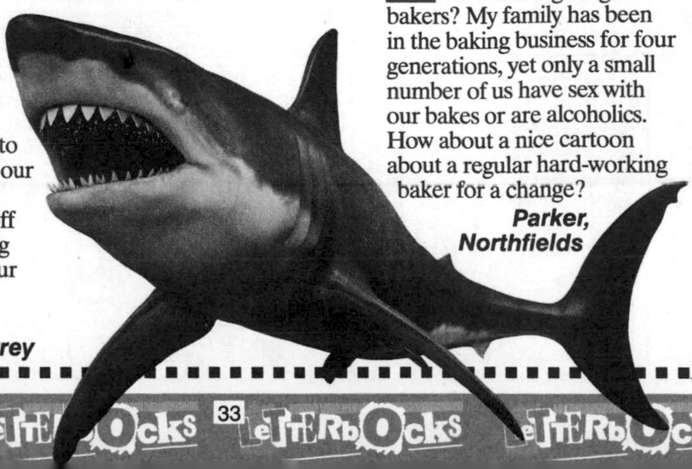

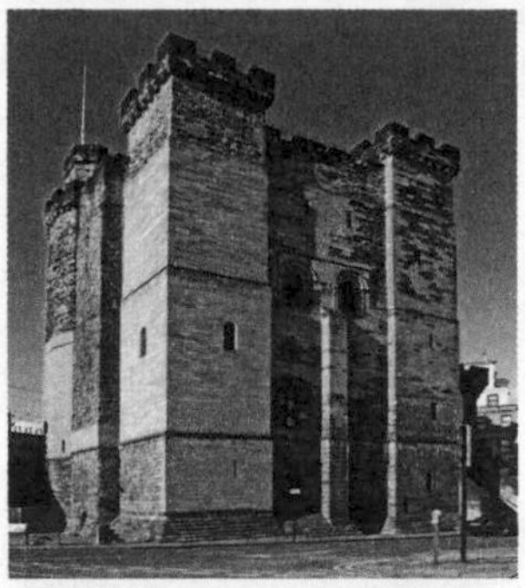

NEWCASTLE'S castle was built in 1080 by William the Conqueror's eldest son Robert Curthose. It is by no stretch of the imagination a "new castle." Geordies should stop living in the past.

Boody, Chesvegas

BOFFINS say that robots will replace most human jobs eventually. With this in mind, how about a picture of a robot kissing that bird's arse so we can have a vision of the future? A bot kissing a bot, if you will.

Geoff Greensmith, Chod Bin

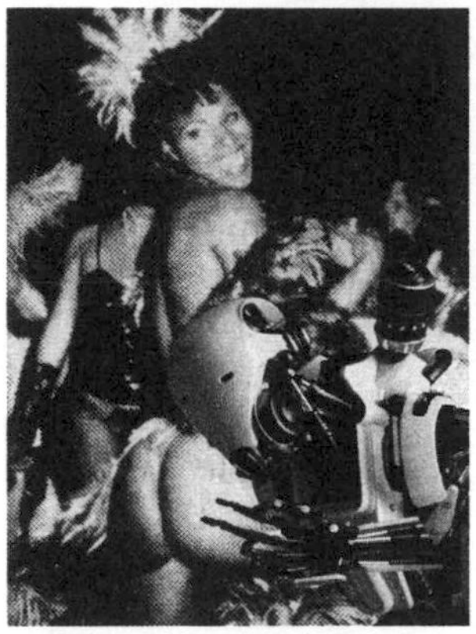

* *Here you go, Geoff*

I'M right-handed, yet whenever I slip out a sneaky fart, it's my left buttock that I raise. Does this make me left-arsed or ambidextrous? Or is it the arse cheek that remains placed that dictates whether you are left or right-arsed? Come on scientists, stop fannying about with vaccines and answer the key questions facing mankind.

Sid Knee, Sydney

WHAT have your cartoonists got against bakers? My family has been in the baking business for four generations, yet only a small number of us have sex with our bakes or are alcoholics. How about a nice cartoon about a regular hard-working baker for a change?

Parker, Northfields

TOP TIPS

LOOK like a top chef when making a cup of tea by balancing the saucer on the tips of your fingers two inches from your face and adding the sugar with your thumb and forefinger.

Mark Humphries, Crewe

TRICK your friends into thinking you've spent the day at Madame Tussaud's by having your photo taken with Barack Obama and Tom Cruise.

Ciaran Ightley, email

LOST something important? Cheer yourself up by imagining the joy of the future archaeologist who rediscovers your wedding ring, passport or car keys.

Phil Moore, Tring

STAND ten paces away from someone and silently mouth the word 'supersonic.' Then run towards them as fast as you can. On arrival, say 'supersonic' out loud without moving your lips. Hey presto! They will think you can travel at the speed of sound.

D Williams, Donegal

CHRISTIAN parents. Indoctrinate your kids by changing your Amazon Echo's name to "Dear Lord." Simple commands like "turn on lights" and "turn off TV" will now appear to be answered prayers.

Ben S, London

MAKE your neighbour feel like a member of the government by standing opposite their house and shouting "Are you going to resign?" as they leave for work.

Kevin Caswell-Jones, Gresford

toptips@viz.co.uk

FAMOUS PEOPLE ON THE TOILET

No. 303: Paris Hilton

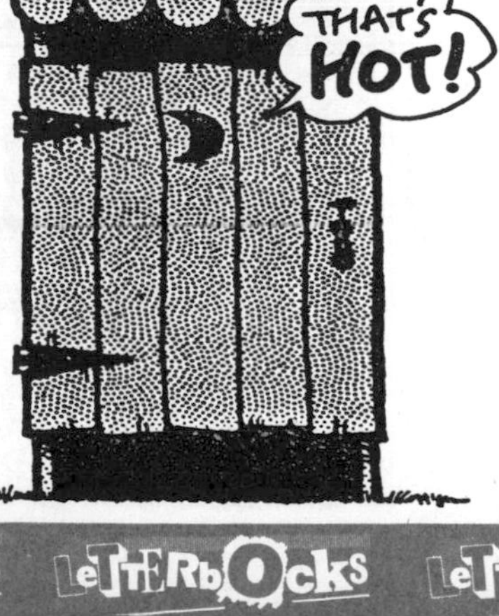
THAT'S HOT!

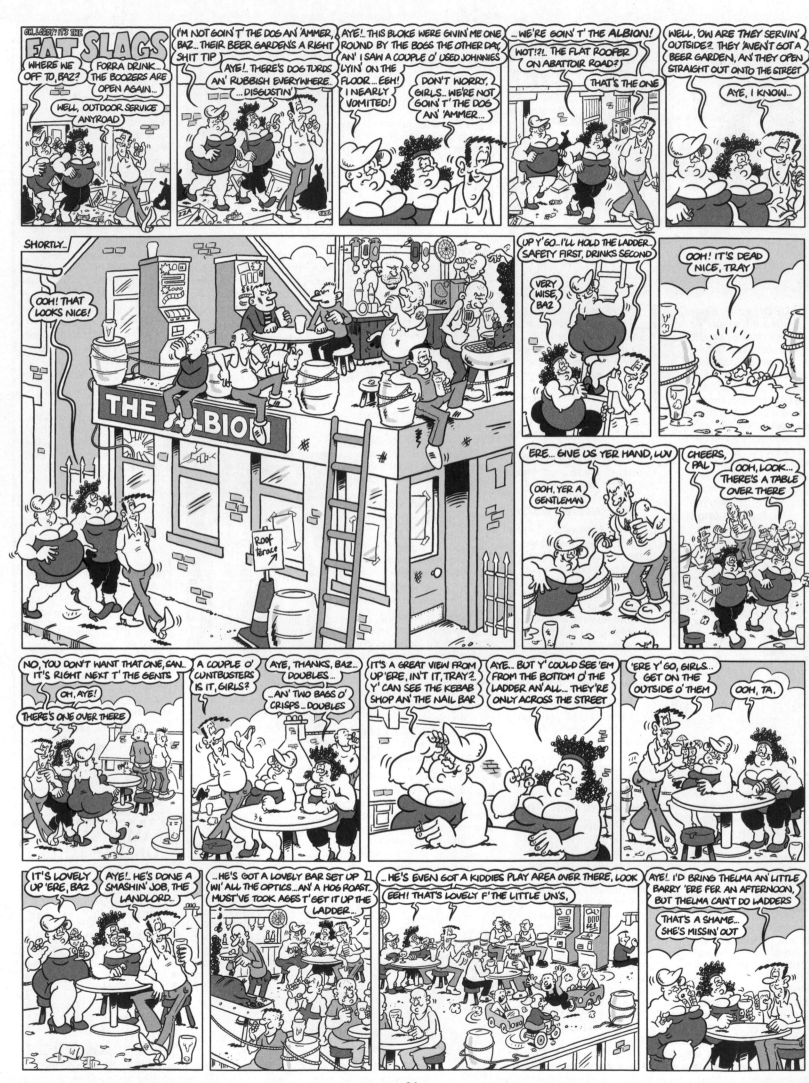

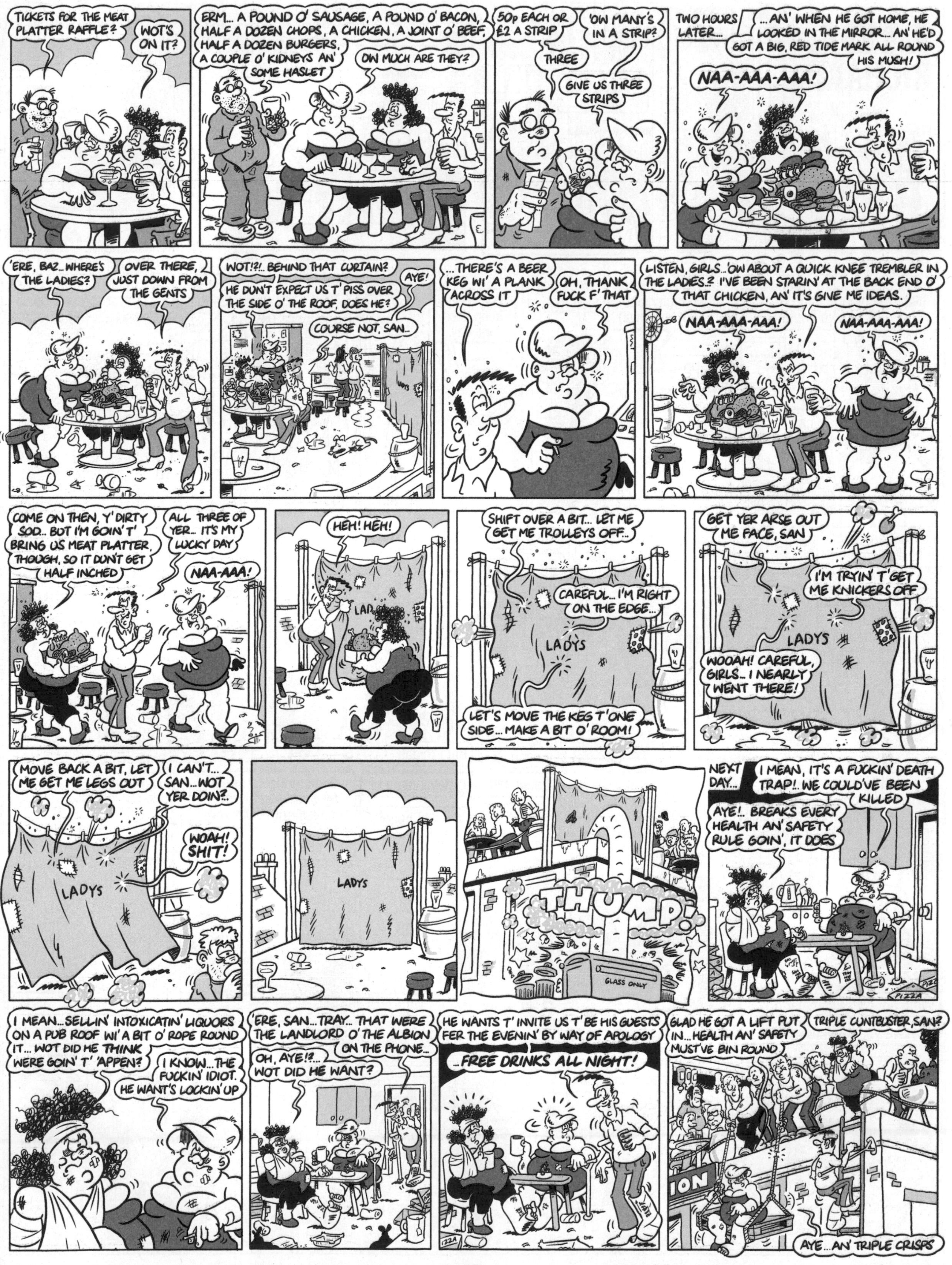
TICKETS FOR THE MEAT PLATTER RAFFLE?
WOT'S ON IT?
ERM... A POUND O' SAUSAGE, A POUND O' BACON, HALF A DOZEN CHOPS, A CHICKEN, A JOINT O' BEEF, HALF A DOZEN BURGERS, A COUPLE O' KIDNEYS AN' SOME HASLET
'OW MUCH ARE THEY?
50p EACH OR £2 A STRIP
'OW MANY'S IN A STRIP?
THREE
GIVE US THREE STRIPS
TWO HOURS LATER...
...AN' WHEN HE GOT HOME, HE LOOKED IN THE MIRROR... AN' HE'D GOT A BIG, RED TIDE MARK ALL ROUND HIS MUSH!
NAA-AAA-AAA!
'ERE, BAZ... WHERE'S THE LADIES?
OVER THERE, JUST DOWN FROM THE GENTS
WOT!?!.. BEHIND THAT CURTAIN?
HE DUN'T EXPECT US T' PISS OVER THE SIDE O' THE ROOF, DOES HE?
AYE!
COURSE NOT, SAN...
LADYS
...THERE'S A BEER KEG WI' A PLANK ACROSS IT
OH, THANK FUCK F' THAT
LISTEN, GIRLS... 'OW ABOUT A QUICK KNEE TREMBLER IN THE LADIES..? I'VE BEEN STARIN' AT THE BACK END O' THAT CHICKEN, AN' IT'S GIVE ME IDEAS.
NAA-AAA-AAA!
NAA-AAA-AAA!
COME ON THEN, Y' DIRTY SOD... BUT I'M GOIN' T' BRING US MEAT PLATTER THOUGH, SO IT DUN'T GET HALF INCHED
ALL THREE OF YER... IT'S MY LUCKY DAY
NAA-AAA!
HEH! HEH!
LADYS
SHIFT OVER A BIT... LET ME GET ME TROLLEYS OFF...
CAREFUL... I'M RIGHT ON THE EDGE...
LADYS
LET'S MOVE THE KEG T' ONE SIDE... MAKE A BIT O' ROOM!
GET YER ARSE OUT ME FACE, SAN
I'M TRYIN' T' GET ME KNICKERS OFF
LADYS
WOOAH! CAREFUL, GIRLS... I NEARLY WENT THERE!
MOVE BACK A BIT, LET ME GET ME LEGS OUT
I CAN'T... SAN... WOT YER DOIN'?..
WOAH! SHIT!
LADYS
LADYS
THUMP!
GLASS ONLY
NEXT DAY...
I MEAN, IT'S A FUCKIN' DEATH TRAP!.. WE COULD'VE BEEN KILLED
AYE!.. BREAKS EVERY HEALTH AN' SAFETY RULE GOIN', IT DOES
I MEAN... SELLIN' INTOXICATIN' LIQUORS ON A PUB ROOF WI' A BIT O' ROPE ROUND IT... WOT DID HE THINK WERE GOIN' T' 'APPEN?
I KNOW... THE FUCKIN' IDIOT. HE WANT'S LOCKIN' UP
'ERE, SAN... TRAY... THAT WERE THE LANDLORD O' THE ALBION ON THE PHONE...
OH, AYE!?.. WOT DID HE WANT?
HE WANTS T' INVITE US T' BE HIS GUESTS FER THE EVENIN' BY WAY OF APOLOGY
...FREE DRINKS ALL NIGHT!
GLAD HE GOT A LIFT PUT IN... HEALTH AN' SAFETY MUST'VE BIN ROUND
TRIPLE CUNTBUSTER, SAN?
ION
AYE... AN' TRIPLE CRISPS

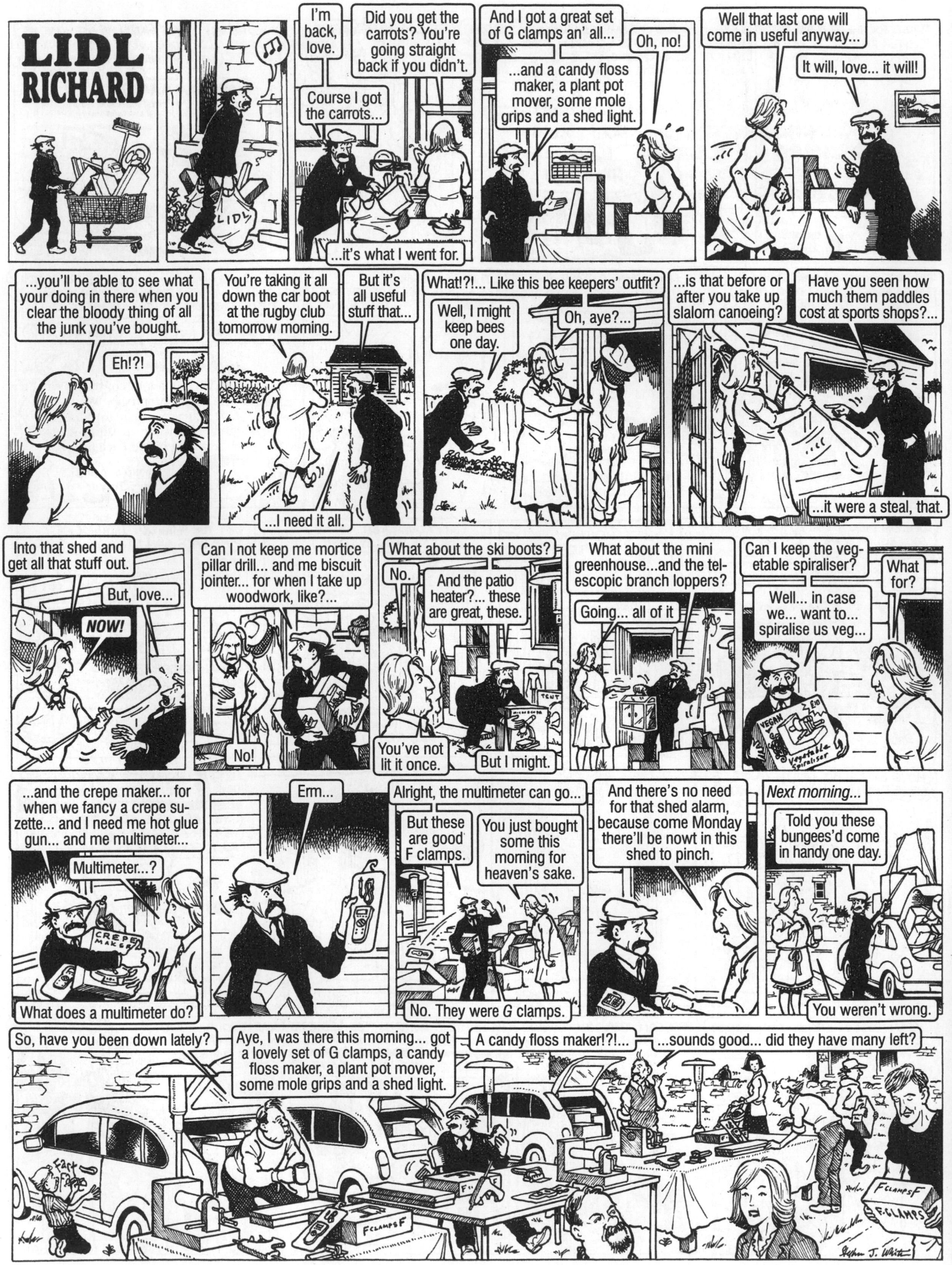
LIDL RICHARD
I'm back, love.
Did you get the carrots? You're going straight back if you didn't.
Course I got the carrots...
...it's what I went for.
And I got a great set of G clamps an' all...
...and a candy floss maker, a plant pot mover, some mole grips and a shed light.
Oh, no!
Well that last one will come in useful anyway...
It will, love... it will!
...you'll be able to see what your doing in there when you clear the bloody thing of all the junk you've bought.
Eh!?!
You're taking it all down the car boot at the rugby club tomorrow morning.
But it's all useful stuff that...
...I need it all.
What!?!... Like this bee keepers' outfit?
Well, I might keep bees one day.
Oh, aye?...
...is that before or after you take up slalom canoeing?
Have you seen how much them paddles cost at sports shops?...
...it were a steal, that.
Into that shed and get all that stuff out.
But, love...
NOW!
Can I not keep me mortice pillar drill... and me biscuit jointer... for when I take up woodwork, like?...
No!
What about the ski boots?
No.
And the patio heater?... these are great, these.
You've not lit it once.
But I might.
What about the mini greenhouse...and the telescopic branch loppers?
Going... all of it
Can I keep the vegetable spiraliser?
What for?
Well... in case we... want to... spiralise us veg...
...and the crepe maker... for when we fancy a crepe suzette... and I need me hot glue gun... and me multimeter...
Multimeter...?
What does a multimeter do?
Erm...
Alright, the multimeter can go...
But these are good F clamps.
You just bought some this morning for heaven's sake.
No. They were G clamps.
And there's no need for that shed alarm, because come Monday there'll be nowt in this shed to pinch.
Next morning...
Told you these bungees'd come in handy one day.
You weren't wrong.
So, have you been down lately?
Aye, I was there this morning... got a lovely set of G clamps, a candy floss maker, a plant pot mover, some mole grips and a shed light.
A candy floss maker!?!...
...sounds good... did they have many left?

WITH KNOBS OFF!

Littlejohn slams hypothetical measurement outcry

A CORN-COCKED *Daily Mail* columnist RICHARD LITTLEJOHN today reacted in fury to imaginary complaints from millennials over the phrase 'a knob of butter.'

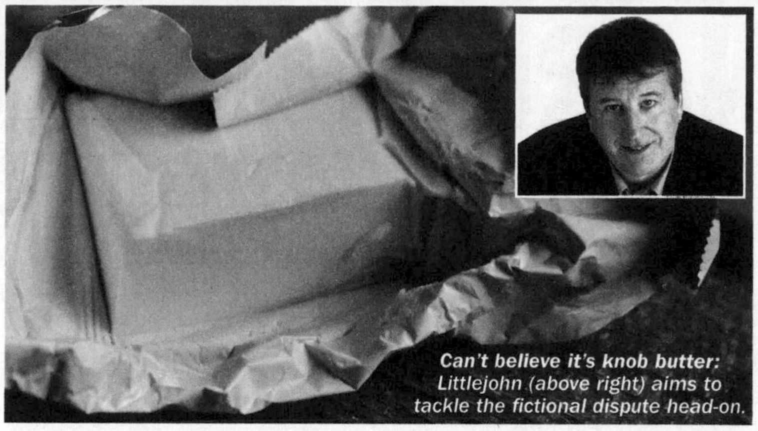

Can't believe it's knob butter: Littlejohn (above right) aims to tackle the fictional dispute head-on.

EXCLUSIVE!

In his latest column for the paper, Littlejohn, 67, pulled no punches as he weighed in to a hypothetical Twitter storm over the imprecise and vaguely phallic culinary measurement.

"A 'knob of butter' is a great British phrase that dates all the way back to the signing of the Magna Carta," Littlejohn fumed. "It simply beggars belief that this cabal of pathetic snowflakes I've just invented would try to 'cancel' this harmless idiom because it offends their delicate Trotskyite sensibilities."

"You couldn't make it up," Littlejohn added. "Even though, in this instance, I have."

rant

The Florida-based gobshite concluded his fiery op-ed by stating: "The fictional woke mob can rant and rave all they want, but this most green and pleasant of British cookery terms shall not – repeat **NOT** – become another victim of the anti-free-speech brigade."

He went on to tell his readers: "I for one will be rustling up a great British roast dinner this evening, with an **EXTRA LARGE** knob of butter on top! I wait with baited breath to see what the make-believe left-wing millennials in my mind think of that."

runcle

And Littlejohn, penis size 3/4" when erect, was backed in this theoretical social media spat by many of his top Fleet Street peers.

"What Richard is imagining is an utter disgrace," wrote **ROD LIDDLE** in his latest column for *The Spectator* magazine. "The very idea of these putative Guardianistas taking issue with an innocent phrase like 'a knob of butter' makes me sick to my very stomach. I can only imagine how I'd feel if it was actually happening in real life."

rousin

Littlejohn's fellow *Daily Mail* scribe **SARAH VINE** also added her two penn'orth on Twitter, claiming: "The Stalinist snowflake brigade have already pulled down our beloved statues – it will be a dark day indeed if they also manage to consign 'a knob of butter' to the historical scrapheap. We must do everything we can to combat the sickening woke revisionism that is happening inside Richard's head."

And Littlejohn's campaign to snuff out conjectured wokeness shows little sign of slowing down. Last night, the veteran bile-smith penned another column for the paper after he imagined hypothetical 'woke' vegan film directors who were refusing to work with *Madmen* actor **JON HAMM**.

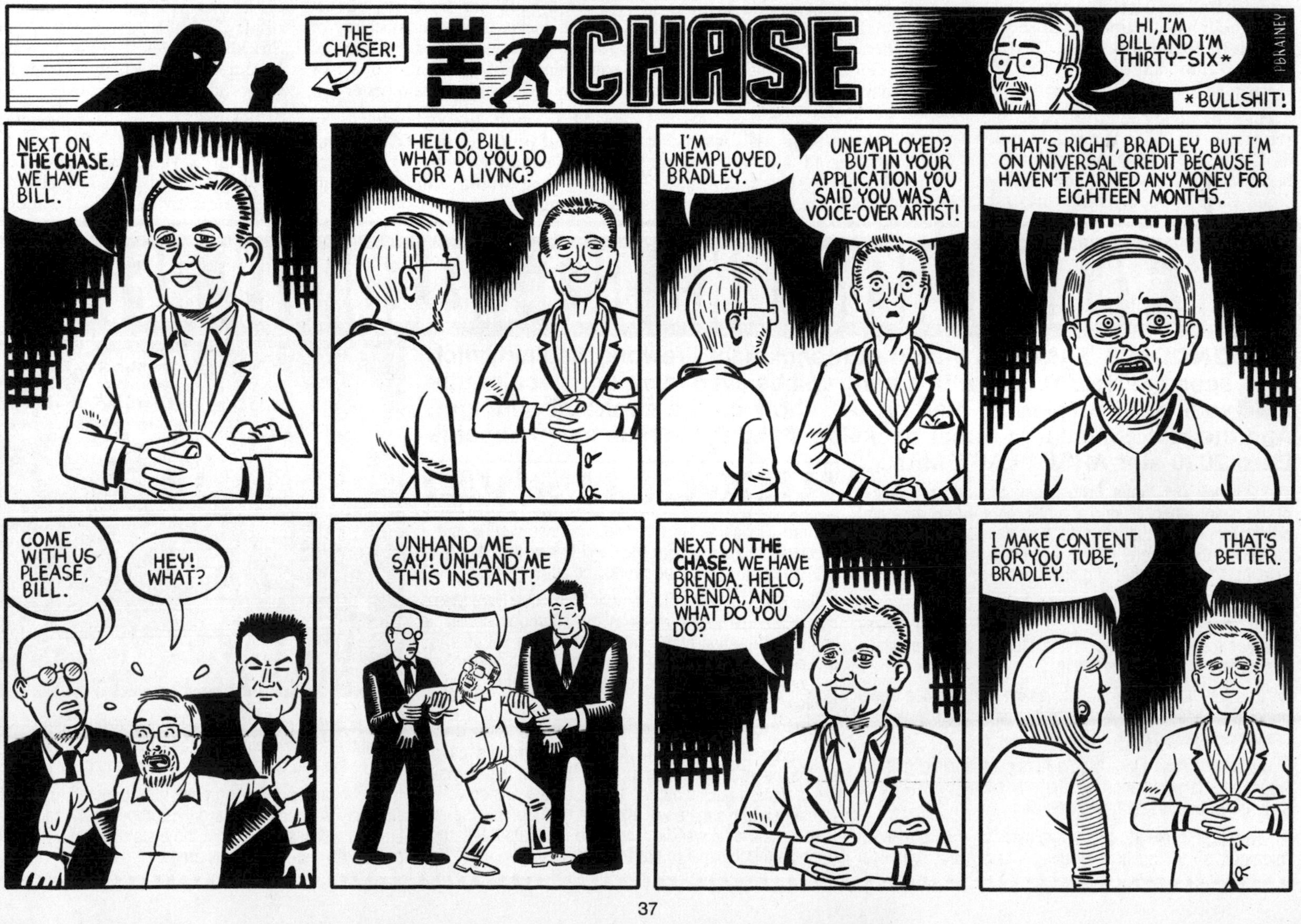

THE CHASER!
THE CHASE
HI, I'M BILL AND I'M THIRTY-SIX*
*BULLSHIT!
P.BRAINEY
NEXT ON THE CHASE, WE HAVE BILL.
HELLO, BILL. WHAT DO YOU DO FOR A LIVING?
I'M UNEMPLOYED, BRADLEY.
UNEMPLOYED? BUT IN YOUR APPLICATION YOU SAID YOU WAS A VOICE-OVER ARTIST!
THAT'S RIGHT, BRADLEY, BUT I'M ON UNIVERSAL CREDIT BECAUSE I HAVEN'T EARNED ANY MONEY FOR EIGHTEEN MONTHS.
COME WITH US PLEASE, BILL.
HEY! WHAT?
UNHAND ME, I SAY! UNHAND ME THIS INSTANT!
NEXT ON THE CHASE, WE HAVE BRENDA. HELLO, BRENDA, AND WHAT DO YOU DO?
I MAKE CONTENT FOR YOU TUBE, BRADLEY.
THAT'S BETTER.

FIREWORK HORROR NARROWLY AVERTED

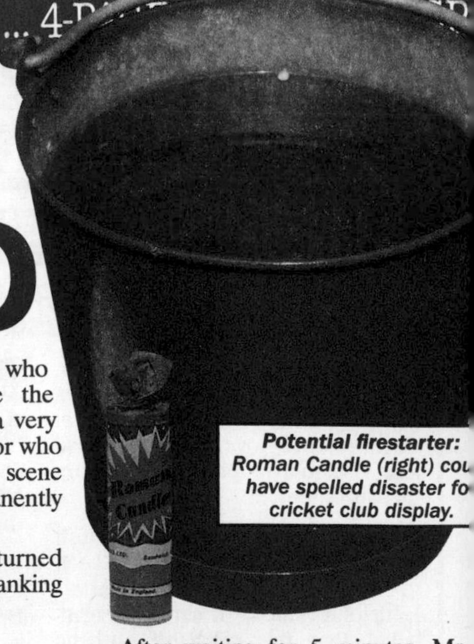

Potential firestarter: Roman Candle (right) cou have spelled disaster fo cricket club display.

EXPLOSIVE EXCLUSIVE!

BONFIRE NIGHT revellers could have been horrified last night as one of the fireworks in an organised display failed to ignite.

The show at Tipton Cricket Club was about halfway through when the incident occurred, leaving the crowd, who had paid £2 each and £1 for children, holding their breath. Display organiser Bernie Robespierre had walked over to a large Roman candle in the middle of the cricket field and lit it with a safety lighter held at arm's length, before retiring to a safe distance.

The crowd of around 70 people watched and waited for the firework to burst into life, blasting golden sparks 15 feet into the air, crackling as they rained down to earth. But after 10 seconds nothing had happened.

Mr Robespierre, who has organised the display at the cricket ground for the last 30 years, knew that under no circumstances should he return to the firework. "It's the first and most important rule of the Firework Code," he said.

Had he ignored this rule and returned to the Roman candle, looking at it to see if the touch paper had blown out, the smouldering fuse could have suddenly burst into life, blasting white hot flames directly into his face.

The crowd would have gasped as Mr Robespierre fell to the ground clutching his face and screaming in agony. Fortunately, one of the crowd might have been a doctor who would immediately have given first aid to the unfortunate man, dousing his face and chest with lukewarm water whilst others called the emergency services.

"It was horrible to watch," one woman would have said, adding: "He was screaming in agony. Thank goodness there was a doctor on hand who knew what to do."

ambulance

The ambulance would have arrived 10 minutes later, and Robespierre, although badly burned, would doubtless have been able to climb in himself, aided by two paramedics. He would then have been taken to North Tipton General Hospital where he would have been treated for third degree burns and shock.

"Mr Robespierre is responding well to treatment and will probably be released home in a day or so," the consultant surgeon of the burns unit would have told reporters who would have gathered outside the hospital entrance. "But he is a very lucky man, and he has the doctor who administered first aid at the scene to thank that he isn't permanently scarred," he would have added.

Robespierre would have returned home on Thursday after thanking hospital staff for his treatment.

stupidity

"It was an extremely foolish thing that I did," he would have told reporters from *The Tipton Cornet and Carillon.* "I would like to thank the hospital staff and apologise that my carelessness and stupidity made their lives more difficult at a time when they are already overworked," he would have added.

A spokesperson for the Fire and Rescue service would have used the incident to highlight the dangers of fireworks and the importance of following the Firework Code. "We all learn from our mistakes, but let us also learn from the mistakes of others," the spokesperson called something like Amanda Dunbarr or something would have said yesterday.

"Make sure that whoever is in charge of your fireworks celebrations is well acquainted with the Firework Code," she would almost certainly have gone on to add.

After waiting for 5 minutes, Mr Robespierre decided that the firework was safe, returning cautiously carrying a bucket of water. When he was about 10 feet from the Roman candle, he threw the water over it, drenching it and rendering it harmless.

of

The display continued with the rest of the fireworks being set off without incident. As the crowd left the field, it was generally agreed that they had watched one of the best displays the cricket club had presented in years.

"It was a wonderful, wonderful display," said spectator Agnes Strickland. "But it could so easily have turned into a night of tragedy if things had gone differently."

"Seeing Mr Robespierre horrifically burnt, with all the children crying and screaming, would have been an absolute nightmare," Mrs Strickland added.

NEW YEAR FIREWORKS GET CELEBRITY SET OFF

LONDON'S FAMOUS Victoria Embankment firework display which sees the New Year in with a bang will be even more spectacular this year, with a celebrity starting the show on the stroke of midnight. And the famous face, or rather backside, lighting the blue touch paper is Euro 2020 star ARSE FLARE MAN.

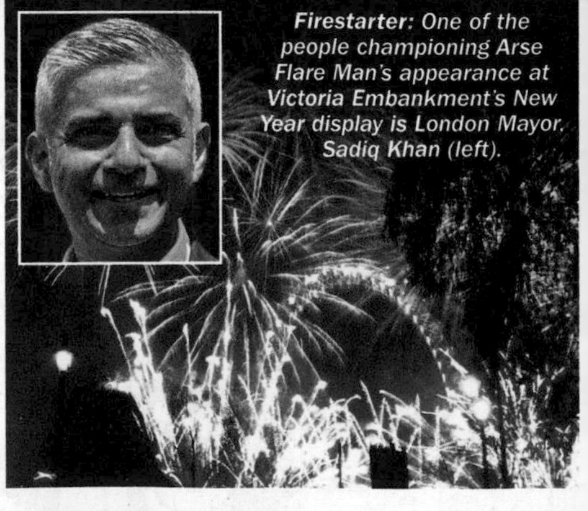

Firestarter: One of the people championing Arse Flare Man's appearance at Victoria Embankment's New Year display is London Mayor, Sadiq Khan (left).

KEX-CLUSIVE!

The 25 year old roofer from Essex captured the hearts of the nation after sticking a lighted flare up his arse and posing for photographs outside Wembley Stadium. He later described the reasons for his action as a desire to bring England's fans together and cheer them up after Covid.

"It was a remarkable gesture," said London Mayor Sadiq Khan. "Arse Flare Man put himself in harm's way in order to bring a smile to the face of a nation which desperately needed cheering up."

"It is for that reason that we asked him to once again bring that sense of joy by officially starting our New Year fireworks extravaganza," he added.

But whilst Arse Flare Man's heroic footballing gesture was a spontaneous act, his New Year's Eve role will be an exercise in organisation and precision.

"The first firework has to launch on the stroke of midnight, so timing is everything," said event organiser Bartram Golightly. "To that end, we have worked out a timetable that Arse Flare Man will follow to make sure everything goes like clockwork," he added.

It is believed that on December 31st, Arse Flare Man's day will begin at 3 o'clock in the afternoon, when he will down the first of 20 cans of cider. He will then be picked up from his home in a stretch limo and driven to London's South Bank, drinking cider and 'banging powder' along the way.

As midnight approaches, he will down his last can and make his way up a specially constructed gantry at the base of the London Eye, wearing his famous Louis Vuitton bucket hat. At 11:59, he will pull down his trousers and his mate will stick the flare up his arse and light it, before he waddles over and presents the flare to the blue touch paper to start the show.

"The touch paper has a 15-second burn time," said Golightly. "So it is essential that Arse Flare Man puts his flare to the end at 11:59 and 45 seconds precisely."

"He's under a lot of pressure to get it right," Mr Golightly warned. "It was only Europe watching the last time he did this. This time, the eyes of the world will be on that flare stuffed up his arse."

LIGHT THE BLUE-BLOODED TOUCH PAPER

What the Royals cost us in Fireworks

WE ALL love the Royal family as much as our own. More, in fact. They do a wonderful job under extremely difficult circumstances, working tirelessly and without reward. And all they ask for in return is a few palaces and servants, some free money and half the year off. Nobody begrudges them what they have.

Or do they? Because in post-pandemic, post-Brexit Britain as we all tighten our belts, loyal British subjects may begin to wonder if our Royal family actually represents value for money. And as Bonfire night approaches, we may find ourselves asking the question... *Would it be better to take the money we give to the monarchy and spend it on fireworks?*

It's a difficult choice to make without the facts, so let's have a look how much the Royal family costs the taxpayer, and what fireworks you could get with that money.

FLYWHEEL
DO NOT HOLD IN HAND.

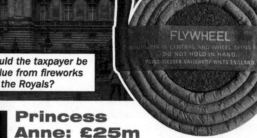

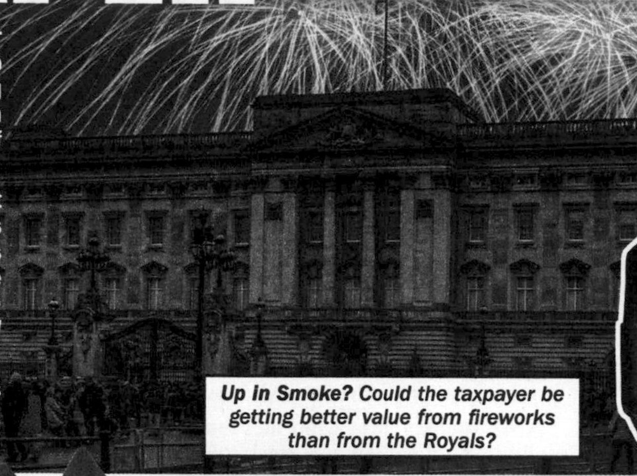

Up in Smoke? Could the taxpayer be getting better value from fireworks than from the Royals?

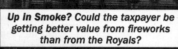

HM the Queen: £67.5m

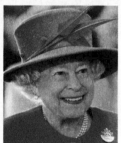

BY FAR AND AWAY the highest paid member of the Royal family, Her Majesty the Queen is also the hardest working and worthy of her pay packet. But £67million would buy enough fireworks to put on an unforgettable show. A pack of 5 Space Explorer rockets costs £9 on the internet, which means that by dumping Her Maj, the British taxpayer could buy almost 38 million of these exciting fireworks. That is easily one for every household in the UK. Or we could let them off in one place, ten at a time, ten seconds apart, making a fantastic show in the sky lasting nearly six months. Even better, with each rocket capable of reaching heights of 100m, tied together, this super rocket would easily reach the Moon.

MOON-ROCKET
MOON-ROCKET
MUST NOT BE HELD

AIR BOMB REPEATER
12p

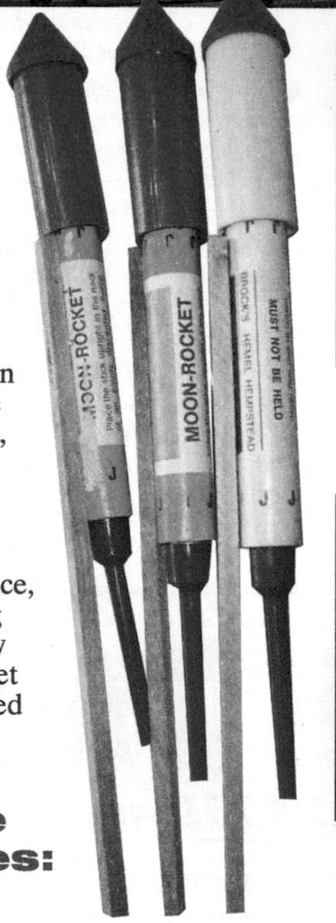

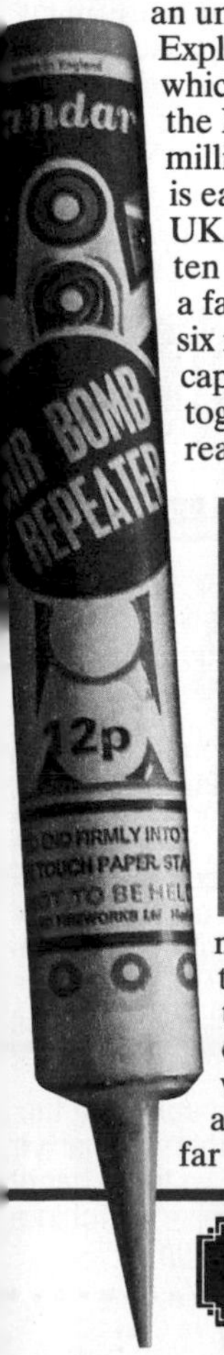

Prince Charles: £30m

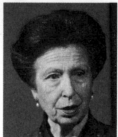

THE PRINCE OF WALES is paid a handsome £30m for giving talks on subjects he knows little about, fiddling with his cuffs and declaring things open. And whilst we would certainly miss these things if he didn't do them, 30 million quids' worth of fireworks would take our mind off the loss. At £2 a pop, the British taxpayer could swap their Heir to the Throne for an Air Bomb to the Throne in the form of 15 million Thunder Mountain Air Bombs. Let off in one go in Trafalgar Square, the Krakatoa-volume noise would shatter every window in England as far west as Bristol and up to Nottingham in the Midlands, and would be heard as far away as New York. Who *wouldn't* like to hear that?

Princess Anne: £25m

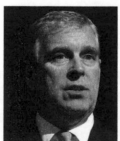

FOR YEARS, THE PRINCESS ROYAL has performed her duties with quiet dignity, and it is no surprise that she is considered the most value-for-money member of the Royal family. But £25 million is not to be sniffed at and would buy Joe Public around 17 million Catherine wheels. There are over 22 million sheds in gardens in the UK, so finding something to nail them onto wouldn't be a problem. And even if, as is likely, half of them failed to spin round and just sat there causing burn damage to the timber, it would still be a spectacle that would dwarf the majesty of the Queen's daughter.

BANGER

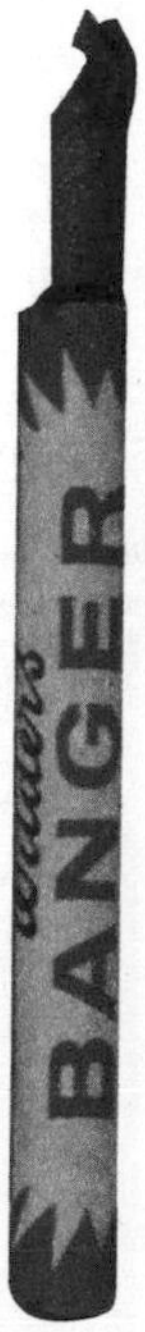

Prince Andrew: £22m

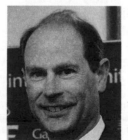

THE QUEEN'S FAVOURITE SON was recently put on gardening leave from his Royal duties due to a misunderstanding. Before the misunderstanding, Randy Andy pocketed the best part of £22 million for his services as Britain's trade envoy, and once the misunderstanding is cleared up, he'll be back at the coalface, promoting Britain's arms trade and playing golf in the Middle East.

Or we could tell him that his job has gone and buy £22 million worth of bangers. This would equate to about a dozen bangers for each of Britain's schoolboys to get up to mischief with, throwing them under cars, popping them into post boxes and shoving them up cats' arses.

Prince Edward: £15m

A SUCCESSFUL TELEVISION PRODUCER in his own right, The Duke of Wessex takes home £15m before, and indeed after, tax. And while he keeps the nation entertained with his hilarious TV game show 25 years ago, perhaps that money would provide better entertainment were it spent on sparklers. At £1 for a packet of five, his wages would buy 75 million of the entertaining metal fire sticks, enough for every one of his mum's subjects to light one up and write their name in the air, or draw a big cock with spunk coming out the end.

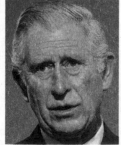

This article first appeared in December 2021 before the Queen carked it, and is included here as a tribute to her late Majesty.

SPARKLERS
Standard

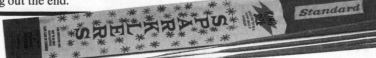

PM NEEDS TO LEVEL UP BONFIRE NIGHT

Report reveals shocking north/ south divide in celebrations

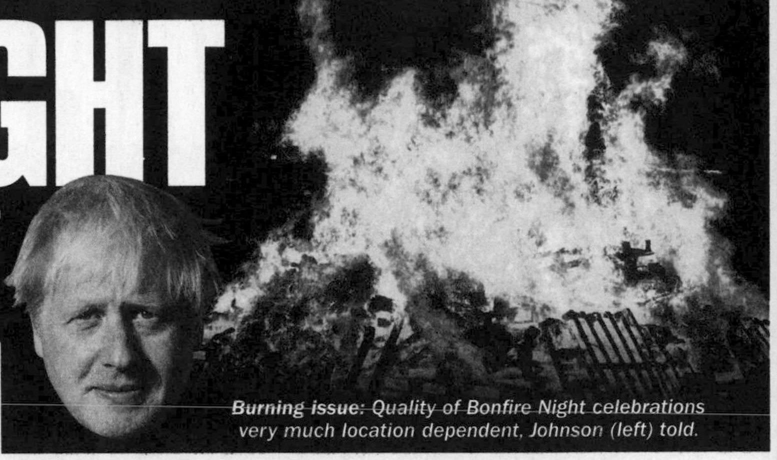

Burning issue: Quality of Bonfire Night celebrations very much location dependent, Johnson (left) told.

THERE were fireworks in parliament yesterday when Prime Minister Boris Johnson came under attack after presiding over what has been described as a 'two-tier Bonfire Night system.'

Labour leader Kier Starmer told the house that where people live in the country is the defining factor in the the quality of Guy Fawkes Night celebration they experience, describing the government's 'levelling up' agenda as "hot air".

"This November 5th, children in the north of England and Scotland will watch fewer, and significantly less spectacular fireworks than those in the south," he told MPs.

fizzle

"Their rockets will not go as high, their Catherine wheels will not spin as fast, and their Roman candles will fizzle out 20% more quickly," he continued.

And it wasn't just the quantity and quality of the fireworks that put northern families at a disadvantage, said Mr Starmer. The entire Bonfire Night experience was of a notably poorer quality north of the Midlands.

"Mr Speaker, it is a sad fact that a child in Kent will enjoy a fresh toffee apple and a piece of treacle fudge at their Bonfire Night party, whilst a child in Newcastle would get just the toffee apple, and that would be all bruised inside," Starmer said, accompanied by cries of "Shame!" from his benches.

The Labour leader was quoting from a report issued by the Bonfire Night Commission, a cross-party select committee investigating inequality in Guy Fawkes celebrations. And the report's findings make stark reading.

- ★ ***Penny for the Guys in the north are constructed from old clothes from charity shops stuffed with newspaper, whereas those in the south are constructed of kapok-filled Barbour jackets and Ralph Lauren trousers, finished off with an Armani scarf.***
- ★ ***Bonfires in the north are fuelled with pallets and old flat-pack furniture, whereas southern fires burn Chippendale desks, Louis XIV chairs and Rococo sideboards.***
- ★ ***Bonfires are on average twice as high in the south, with 16% being so big that they need to be put out by the fire service, compared to only 2% in the north.***
- ★ ***Food served at northern Bonfire parties is limited to baked potatoes and hot dogs, whilst in the south they have the addition of a range of canapes and finger sandwiches.***

The report also said that a staggering 10% of northerners still live in firework poverty, with many families only able to afford to let off 6 bangers, all over in a couple of minutes. Whilst in London and the south, 70% of under-twelves will enjoy a £35 Standard selection box lasting half an hour.

"Mr Speaker, this government was elected on a manifesto that promised to 'level up' the country," Starmer said. "But, like a dud Roman Candle, they have failed to deliver."

But Prime Minister Johnson accused the Labour leader of misrepresenting the report, claiming that no government had done more to raise the standard of Bonfire night celebrations for the whole of the country. And he went further, accusing Labour of wanting to spoil everyone's fun.

"We all know that the party opposite would BAN Bonfire night if they could, Mr Speaker. That is the plain and simple truth," he fabricated, his words being drowned out by wails of "Yee-aar! Yee-aar!" from his backbenchers.

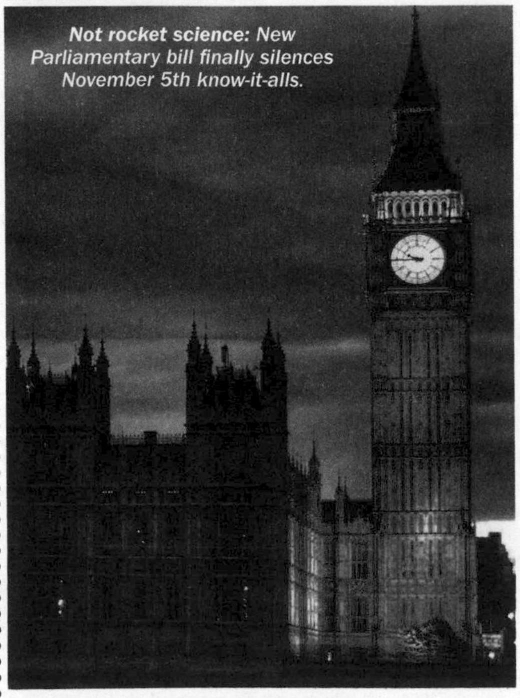

Not rocket science: New Parliamentary bill finally silences November 5th know-it-alls.

FLASH! (PAUSE) BANG!

Bonfire Night bill waved through Parliament

IN AN unusual moment of Parliamentary consensus, both sides of the House passed a bill yesterday making it an offence for anyone watching fireworks to explain why you see rockets explode seconds before you hear them.

The Private Member's Bill was put before the house by Labour backbencher Iris Coppersmith on Thursday and passed its first reading unopposed. It will go automatically to its second reading without amendments some time before Christmas.

"My constituents going to see the fireworks were fed up with repeatedly having to listen to some arsehole explaining why you see them go off before you hear them," said Ms Coppersmith, who has represented the constituency of Bamton East for 20 years.

"This new bill will allow people to just watch the fireworks without some bell-end giving them a science lecture about the speed of sound and the speed of light," she said.

The bill is likely to pass quickly through the next reading and the upper chamber, and looks likely to become law in time for Bonfire Night 2022.

But campaigners have criticised the bill, describing it as the thin end of a rather dangerous wedge. "These people get on my tits as much as anyone's," said Free Speech UK's Crispin Beaujolais. "But people should have the right to come out with any old bollocks they want."

"Legislating to prevent them from speaking in the 'marketplace of ideas' risks making them a martyr to their cause," he said. "Far better to let them bang on for a bit and and have everyone else watching the fireworks tell them to shut the fuck up."

FIREWORKS, the LAW and YOU

Your Legal firework queries with QUERCUS PETRAEA, QC

MY NEIGHBOUR had some fireworks in his back garden last bonfire night, and I watched them from my bedroom window. The following day he came round to my house and presented me with a bill for £40 - half of what he had paid for the fireworks. I questioned the bill, as he had seven people watching in his garden, and I told him that at most I should pay £10 – one eighth of the bill. But he said that in law, it was the number of households watching the display which was important. Is he correct, as I don't want to fall foul of this law again?

BRIAN Lundberg, Crewe

Quercus says... This is a grey area of the law. You could argue that you should pay nothing, as the display was conducted *ab extra* of your property, although you neighbour could then argue that whilst this was the case, your sharing *ex proprio motu* the enjoyment of the fireworks, you were *ex post facto* agreeing to share the costs. That will be 475 guineas.

LAST BONFIRE NIGHT, I let off a rocket. It was a fantastic display, but when the spent firework with its stick came down, it landed in my neighbour's garden. The next day, I went to get it back and he refused to hand it over, saying that as it landed in his property, it now belonged to him. Does he have a legal right to keep it, or must he hand it over?

Stan Pettyforts, Blyth

Quercus says... This is a grey area of the law. Your neighbour is claiming possession of your firework *ius retentionis*, claiming it to be *res derelictae*, which, *rebus sic standibus*, he was, *ratio scripta*, within his rights to do. However, you could take action *quantum valebant* for the return of the firework *pro tempore postliminium*, until an agreement can be reached. That will be 475 guineas.

LAST YEAR, November 5th fell on a Thursday, but my neighbour set his fireworks off on the Saturday. I know people want to celebrate Guy Fawkes night, and I don't want to spoil anyone's fun, but can I sue him for causing a disturbance by setting fireworks off on the 7th November, and if so, how much will I get?

Ely Opiates, Goole

Quercus says... This is a grey area of the law. Your neighbour has, *contra bonos mores*, committed an offence *sui juris*. But you, *secundum formam statuti*, must, *res judicata* be aware that *quo ante quod hoc, pactum de non petendo (in anticipando)*. Effectively, this means, *quantum meruit, quae ipso usu consumuntur pendente lite*. However, you could, *novus actus interveniens, nemo debit bis vexari pro una et eadem causa*, but not, *intra legem, in pari delicto funus boni iuris fortis attachiamentum validior praesumptionem. Hoc erit CDLXXV guineaum.*

COUNCIL PUTS OUT MR BONFIRE!

A GUY Fawkes night addict who goes by the name of "Mr. Bonfire" has been given an Anti-Social Behaviour Order and banned from launching fireworks on any night except November 5th after celebrating Bonfire Night EVERY SINGLE EVENING for the past twenty years.

Councillors in the Derbyshire village of Monkbottle finally intervened after exasperated neighbours organised an online petition to see resident Guy Bonfire's nightly pyrotechnic extravaganza come to an end. The Bonfire Night-mad former plasterer had been the subject of thousands of complaints from neighbours over the years. But councillors finally decided to act when his nightly conflagrations got out of control, resulting in the fire service being called out four times in a single week.

Bonfire, who changed his name by deed poll from Noel Christmas in 2007, says he was only trying to spread a bit of Bonfire Night joy and cheer around his well-maintained cul-de-sac. And he branded his neighbours 'miserable farts' after council officers, backed up by a community policing team, visited his property to issue him with a fixed penalty notice.

The 56-year-old bachelor estimates that he has spent the best part of a

Sparks fly as firework-mad Guy given ASBO

million pounds on his daily Bonfire Night festivities over the last two decades. "Fireworks don't come cheap, and I've sent about 75 quid's worth up in smoke every night since 2001," he told the *Monkbottle Recorder and Oboe*.

"And what with all the bonfire party grub and toffee apples, celebrating Guy Fawkes night is an expensive do," he added. "But it's money well spent, because I love it."

king

But yesterday the law finally caught with the self-styled "Firework King" as police ordered him to take down the permanent Guy Fawkes dummy displayed on his front lawn. And neighbours enjoyed their first silent night in two decades.

"I work shifts, so I was getting sick to the back teeth with him letting off rockets and air bombs at all hours," said one neighbour. "I've been that close to shoving them up his arse on many occasions," he added, indicating a distance of about half an inch between his thumb and forefinger.

Another relieved neighbour said she knew the petition had worked when the daily flat bed lorry delivering pallets failed to arrive yesterday. "It normally turns up at 8:30 in the morning and dumps a dozen pallets on his lawn," she said. "Then he spends the rest of the morning piling them up and setting his Guy on top in the afternoon."

"The constant letting off of screamers and bangers was bad enough," said one neighbour who lives opposite Bonfire. "But it was his constant knocking on the door offering me home-made cinder toffee that did my crust in."

Englishman

However Guy hit back, saying that the council were preventing him from being public spirited. "It's a very transient neighbourhood around here. There are always people moving in and out of my cul-de-sac, and new householders always love to

Pity for the Guy? Bonfire's nightly pyrotechnic displays proved too much for neighbours.

be greeted with a few fireworks," he argued.

And he suggested that rather than stop celebrating Bonfire Night immediately, the council should allow him to phase out his celebrations over two or three years. "They should let me do it three or four times a week for a year, then a couple of times a week over the next twelve months, and so on," he suggested.

"I've got 18 months' worth of fireworks in the garage. If I can only let them off once a year, I'll never get rid of them," he added.

And it appears that Bonfire has upped the ante in his battle with council killjoys. Neighbours say he has erected a large neon sign on his lawn flashing 'Happy New Year', and has started referring to himself as Jools Hogmanay.

Google Docs
Shhhhh...
Dad? Dad?
Mmmm, eh?
Wake up.
Is it... visiting?
No – we're getting you out of here!
I don't... want to.
Dad it's all a hoax.
I've been looking online!
Excuse me, can I ask what you're doing?
Saving my dad's life!
And you can't stop us!
Read this and weep.
What is it?
A law letter, it's all in there...
Under Magna Carter the deep state may NOT cause medical torture on any sovereign citizen or English man...
This is nonsense.
How is it nonsense?
Every way possible.
It doesn't even have your solicitor's name or practice details on it.
Yes it does, there at the bottom.
TittyLovinPatriot1488?
Duh, that's only his username –
– if he posted his real info Illuminati feds would have him disappeared.
SNATCH
Yes, well, I'm afraid you need to disappear too now please.
Oh we're going pal – and taking your victim with us.
Your father is in no condition to move.
We only removed his leg yesterday.
Yeah, and there was sod-all wrong with it!
He'd a gangrenous ulcer caused by peripheral artery disease.
Tsk, words...
It's a common condition in people with diabetes.
Diabetes isn't real.
Think about it. There's sugar in everything.
Yes... I'm going to call security.
And even if it is real, and he has it, where's the Vitamin D?
Why no magnesium? Why no riboflavin?
Those things are not effective treatments for diabetes.
Ha!
You'll be saying Zoflora doesn't cure Covid next!
Zoflora does not cure Covid.
Jesus, hospitals are so Deep State.
POP
Come on Dad, let's get you home...
Oh hello. Could you send a couple of big lads up to Ward 14?
SMACK
Short-tempered ones, ideally.
It isn't broken.
Ow! How can you say without a CAT scan?
You need to operate before bits of bone get in my brain!

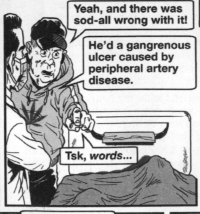

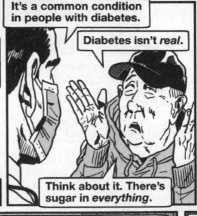

SEX DRIVE!

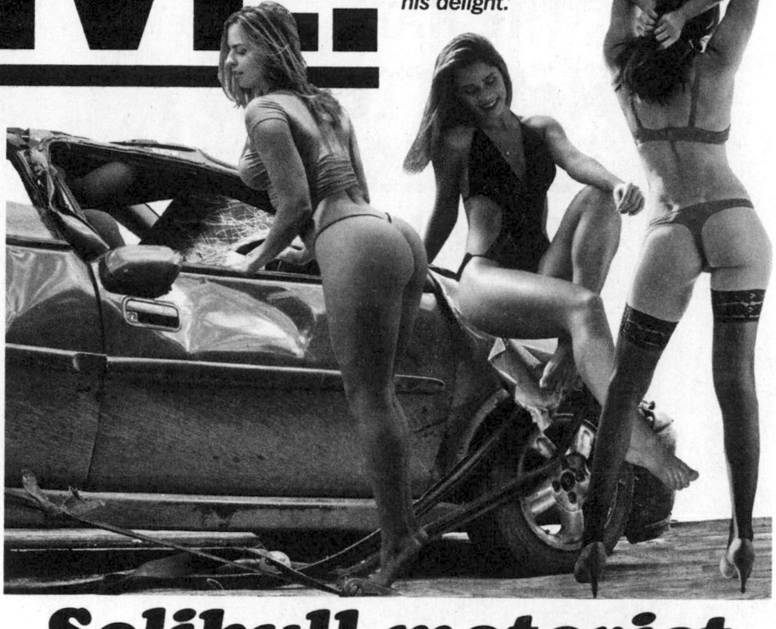

Pull up to the bumper: The ladies of Solihull just can't get enough of uninsured drivers, Wragg has discovered to his delight.

Solihull motorist gets no-claim bonus

EVERY YEAR, we all pay out excessive sums of money for car insurance, and at the same time we all like to think that we are a Romeo between the sheets. But according a recent report, uninsured male drivers are some of Britain's best lovers. And, if they are driving a car that is untaxed and with no MOT, their performance in bed can only be described as supercharged.

SEXCLUSIVE!

These are the findings of an independent study commissioned, written and published by a Solihull-based carpet fitter who wants to break the stigma around uninsured motorists.

Mick Wragg, who is 6 months into a 2-year ban for driving whilst disqualified, claims that cancelling his insurance policy has done wonders for his love life. "Ask any of the ladies in the Solihull area who have enjoyed a night with me," he says.

premium

At a press conference held outside the Poplar Road branch of BetFred, Wragg told a group of men, some of whom may have been reporters: "Uninsured drivers get a bad press. If we're not getting blamed for hiking up insured drivers' premiums and dangerous driving, then we're getting branded lazy lovers."

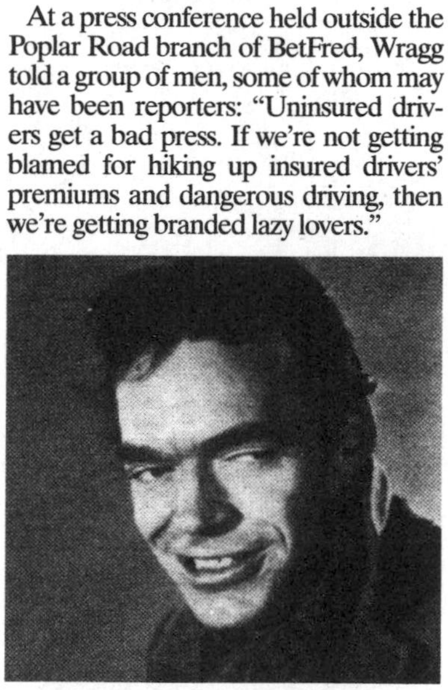

Insure fire winner: Wragg has become the Warren Beatty of Solihull since his policy expired.

But according to Wragg, nothing could be further from the truth. And he explained how an administrative oversight last year led to him conducting a scientifically sound survey, the results of which could be a game-changer in the areas of both men's sexual health and car insurance.

james

He said: "A couple of years ago, I had fully comp insurance on my VW Polo, complete with legal protection, roadside assistance and windscreen cover. I'd got all the bells and whistles on my policy, and I should have been feeling on top of the world."

"But even though I was complying in full with UK driving regulations, my cheerful exterior belied a dark secret - I was shit in bed."

The truth was that since taking out his fully comp policy Wragg had found it difficult to achieve an erection. His habit of drinking eight pints of beer every evening perhaps didn't help matters, but whatever the cause, he was becoming increasingly anxious about his failures in bed with the fairer sex.

ionic

Desperate for a solution, he tried everything from online holistic remedies to acupuncture and cutting his drinking down to 6 pints a night; but nothing seemed to work. "I still couldn't get it up," he said.

Then one evening last November, Wragg met a woman in a hotel bar in Solihull. "We got on well, and after five minutes our relationship had developed to the point where we wanted to take it to the next stage, so we went beck to my bedsit," he said.

"I was proper nervous because of my problem 'down there'," he told the possible reporters.

covalent

But he needn't have worried because, according to the 52-year-old bachelor, back in his bedsit he put in the sexual performance of his life.

"You wouldn't believe it. I was like a rolling pin, and I gave the lady multiple organism after multiple organism," he said. "She told me I was the best man at sex she had ever had, and she wasn't lying."

hydrogen

Although delighted that his sexual problems were now a thing of the past, Wragg was naturally curious as to what had effected the remarkable change in his potency. It was only when he received a letter in the post the next morning that the penny dropped.

"It was from my insurance brokers, telling me that the policy on my Polo had lapsed the previous day as it wasn't set to auto-renew, so I wasn't covered. And that's when the revelation hit me. Uninsured drivers are clearly better at sex."

atomic

Wragg threw the letter away, and over the next few months cancelled his road tax direct debit and ignored his MOT reminder. And as a result, his love life continued to skyrocket. He told reporters: "Before I knew it, I was fighting the birds off with a shitty stick.".

"I don't know why it is. Perhaps it's something to do with risk-taking and living on the edge, but the women round my way can't get enough of me. And what's more, I'm able to completely satisfy every last one of them."

sex

And he advises any men who are experiencing erectile dysfunction to stop wasting their money on blue pills. "Take it from me, simply stop paying your car insurance and before you know it, you'll be like a baby's arm holding an apple," he said.

And now a chance driving ban has given the West Midlands Lothario further motivation to continue his research, and he claims his early studies suggest that disqualified drivers immediately see noticeable gains in the length and girth of their penises.

"I was disqualified for two years after I was pulled by these coppers who saw my Polo wasn't off the road like I'd told the DVLA it was," he said.

"But ever since my licence was taken away, the length of my chopper has gone up by two inches. Two inches, I shit you not."

dirty

A spokesman for the DVLA said that while the agency did not endorse driving while uninsured as a homeopathic treatment for erectile dysfunction, it acknowledged there was some anecdotal evidence of untaxed drivers in the West Midlands area enjoying increased sexual performance.

SEX, SPEED AND SCIENCE

Does Driving Uninsured Improve your Sex Life?

Viz Scientist Dr Oud Scodheim from the University of Lund explains the concept of Correlation and Causation.

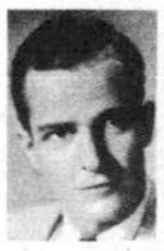

WHEN TWO THINGS happen at the same time, it is human nature to assume that one is somehow a result of the other. But this is not necessarily the case. Ice cream sales go up at exactly the same time and the same rate as shark attacks, but it would be foolish to think that they are related; both of these activities are linked to temperature, but not to each other.

So can cancelling your car insurance be the cause of improved sexual performance? Theoretically, yes, but it does not automatically follow simply because the two things occur simultaneously.

The only way to demonstrate a causative link between these two correlated events would be to conduct a *blind randomised control trial*. A group of 100 motorists would be asked to fill in a questionnaire asking about their sex lives and penis size before being split into two identical groups in terms of age range, occupation and health status.

One group - the 'control group' - would have their car insurance renewed. The other group would have their policies cancelled, but no driver would know which group they were in.

After driving for a year, they would again fill in the questionnaire pertaining to their sexual performance. Scientists would then be able to see if the uninsured group had experienced better sex than the control group, or if their cocks had become statistically longer or thicker at the end.

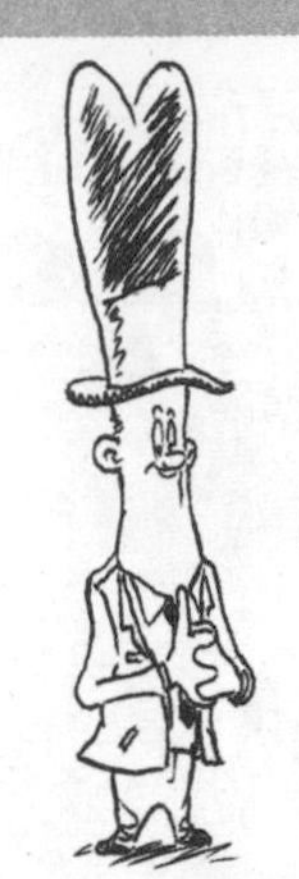

JACK 'THE HAT' McVITIE COMES BACK

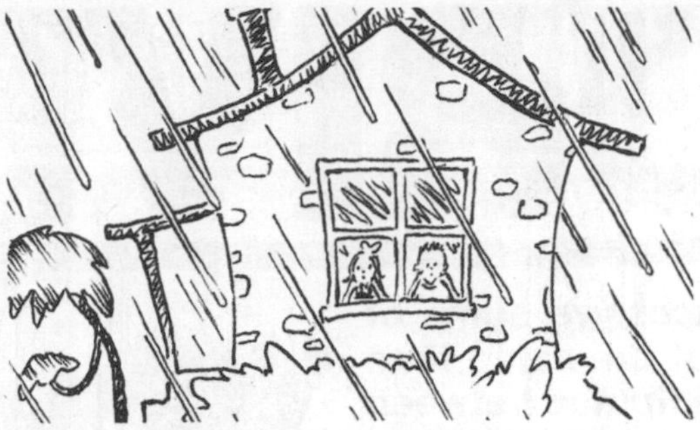

Kelly and Sally looked out from their room
There was nothing outside except grey skies and gloom
Their parents were out, it was quiet as a mouse
There was nothing to do and no fun in the house

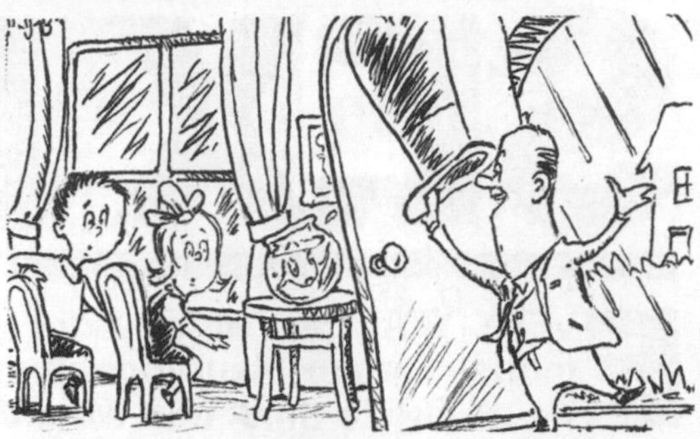

From the hall came a crash and then there on the mat
Stood a jaunty old gent in a black trilby hat
"I'm Jack-in-the-Hat!" said the man as a greeting
"I'm the Firm's top enforcer with a penchant for beating!"

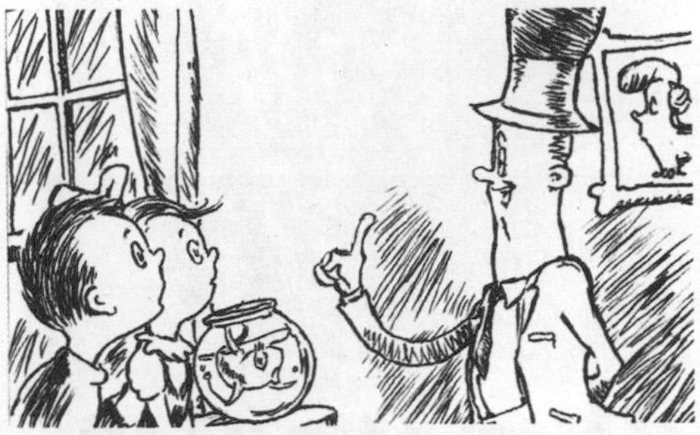

"Extortion and crime is how I spend my days
For I wipe out the narks on behalf of the Krays!"
"There are no narks here, sir!" the children exclaimed
"We don't want you here! We don't wish to play games!"

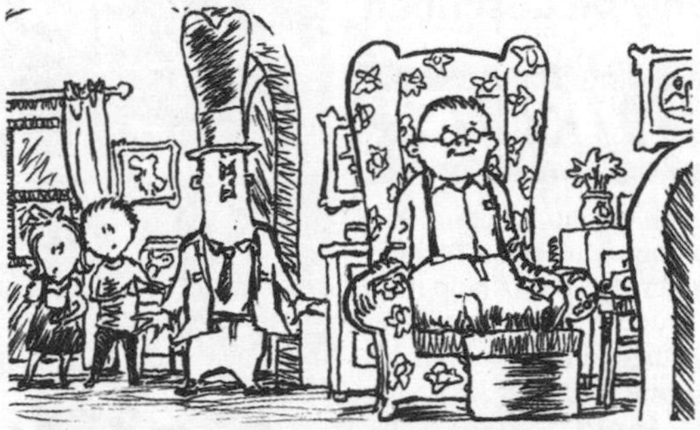

Then there in the living room sat on a chair
Was a man looking much like he hadn't a care
"Why that's old Les Payne, the dirty old snitcher
I'll kill him right here and then I'll be the richer!"

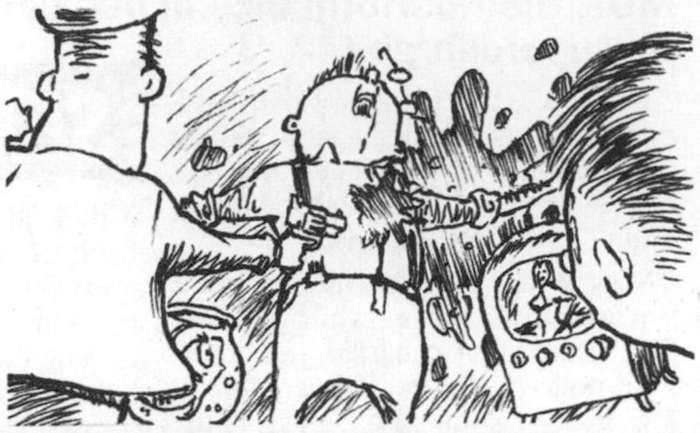

Jack pulled out a gun and then what a to-do!
Soon Les was a corpse and Jack said *"Now I'm through!"*
But Kelly and Sally were less than impressed
When they saw all the walls - so much blood! What a mess!

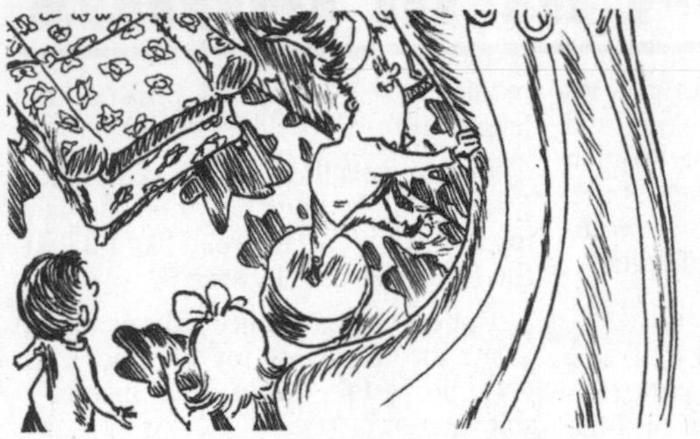

Jack said, *"Why, I'll clean this in ten seconds flat!*
And they'll never suspect it was Jack-in-the-Hat!
I'll mop up the blood with this rag to be certain!"
"Oh no!", cried the children, *"That's mum and dad's curtain!"*

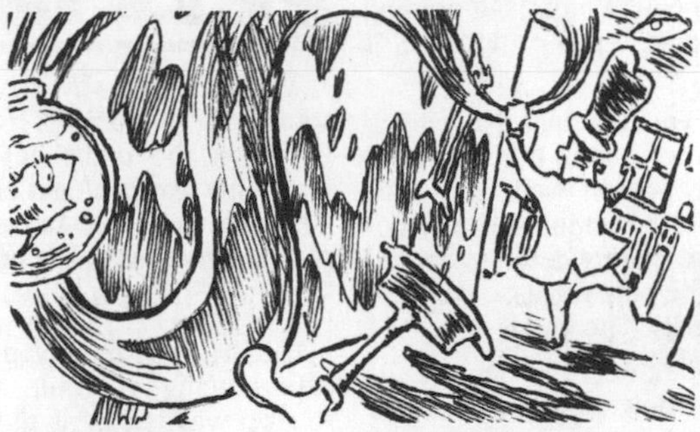

"Don't worry," said Jack, *"I'll make it a synch!"*
And distributed blood over every last inch
The more that he rubbed it the more that it spread
And soon the whole house was painted bright red!

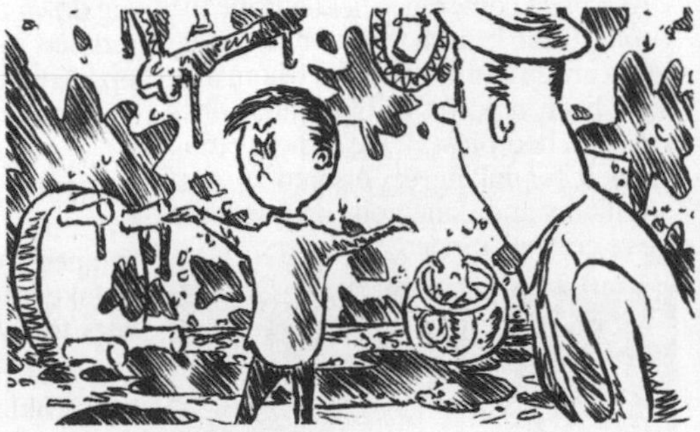

The kids said, *"Just look at the walls and the floor!*
There's even more mess than there was here before!
Our parents will come back and they won't be so glad
You must clean it all now or our dad will be mad!"

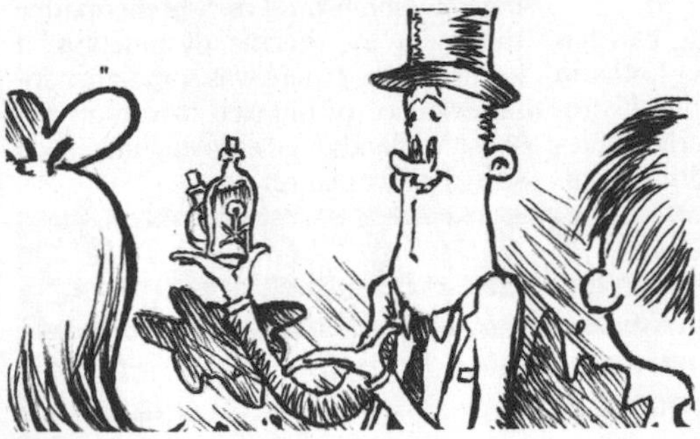

"Oh never mind that," said Jack with a laugh
"We'll get this old body upstairs in the bath
I have some good potions to eat and decay it
And there'll be no more grassing with no one to say it!"

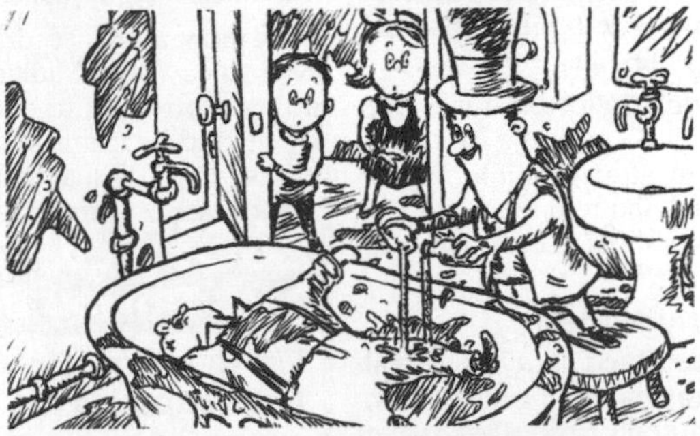

So he rushed up the stairs, the cadaver in tow
Leaving blood on the walls, up above and below
And soon there was nothing much left without stain
When into the bath went the corpse of Les Payne

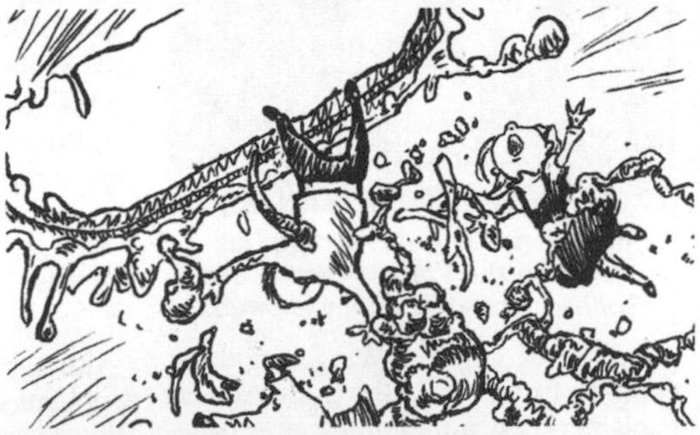

Jack emptied his bottles, *"This acid will do!"*
But the kids saw that Jack really hadn't a clue
For it ate through the bath and the floorboards went *'crack!'*
And down through the hole went the kids, bath and Jack!

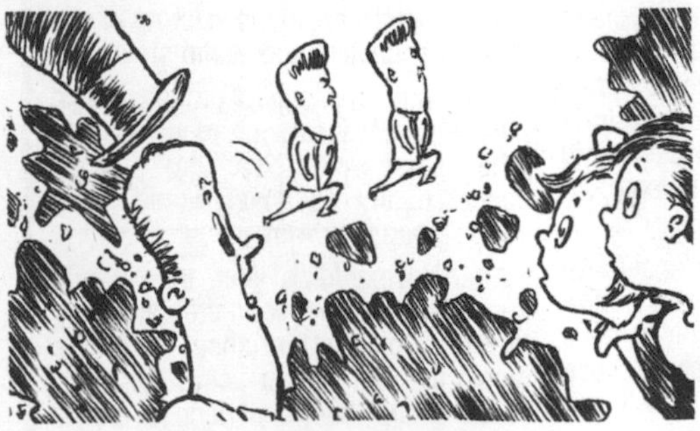

Now the house was infested with parts of Les Payne
Intestines and sputum, appendix and brain
Then out of Jack's hat leapt Kray 1 and Kray 2
"Oh dear," declared Jack, *"Now I'm in a stew!"*

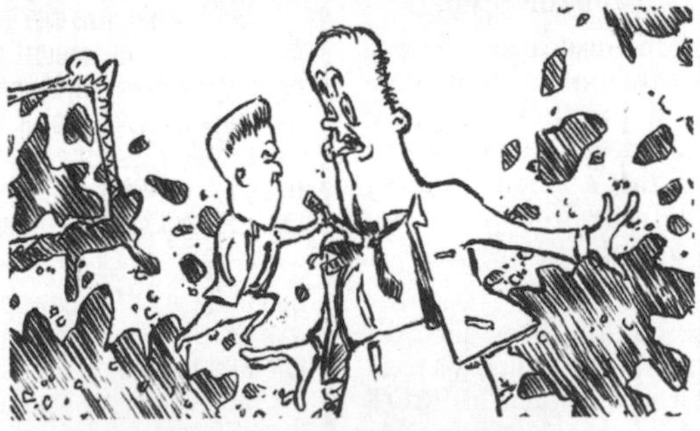

Kray 1 said, *"Your bumbling's a sad sight to see*
Now I will kill you and I'll get off scot-free!"
But his gun just went 'click' so he picked up a knife
And lunged at old Jack 'til he's taken his life

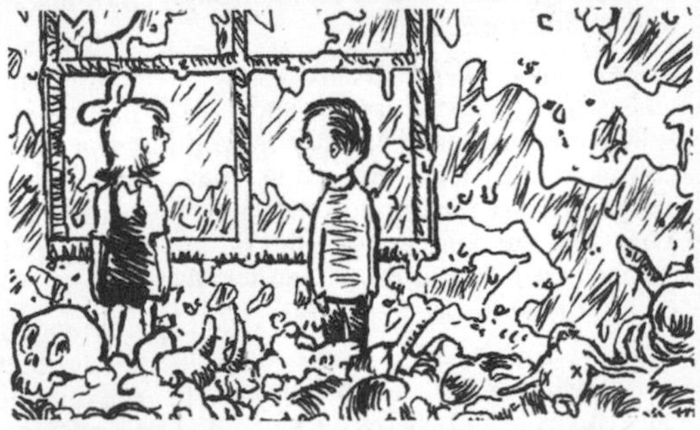

The Krays left the house and ducked down an alley
And there was no one else left except Kelly and Sally
Just as quick as they'd come they were gone just like that
And they never forgot that old cunt in the hat

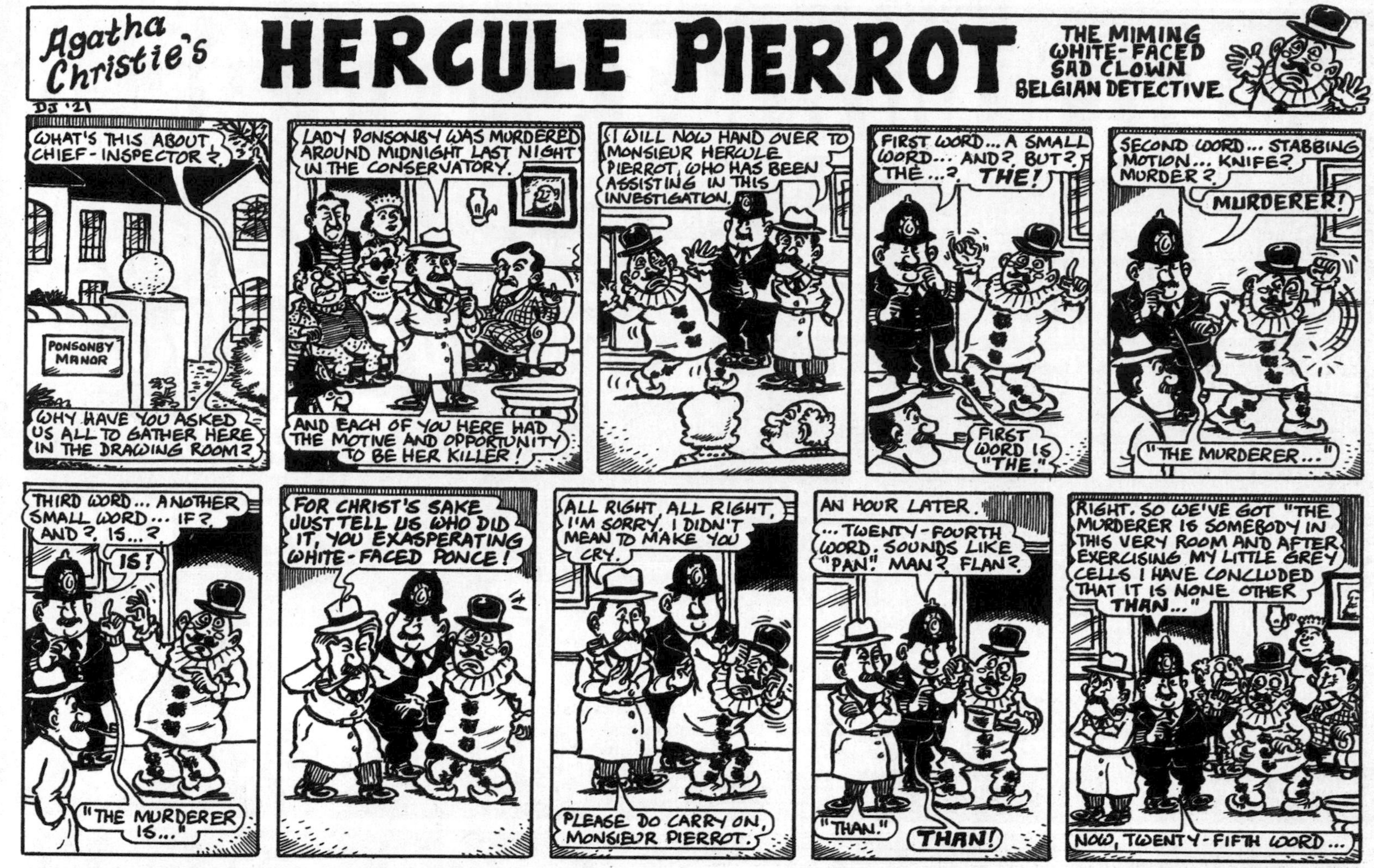

Agatha Christie's
HERCULE PIERROT
THE MIMING WHITE-FACED SAD CLOWN BELGIAN DETECTIVE
DJ '21
WHAT'S THIS ABOUT, CHIEF-INSPECTOR?
PONSONBY MANOR
WHY HAVE YOU ASKED US ALL TO GATHER HERE IN THE DRAWING ROOM?
LADY PONSONBY WAS MURDERED AROUND MIDNIGHT LAST NIGHT IN THE CONSERVATORY.
AND EACH OF YOU HERE HAD THE MOTIVE AND OPPORTUNITY TO BE HER KILLER!
I WILL NOW HAND OVER TO MONSIEUR HERCULE PIERROT, WHO HAS BEEN ASSISTING IN THIS INVESTIGATION.
FIRST WORD... A SMALL WORD... AND? BUT? THE...? THE!
FIRST WORD IS "THE."
SECOND WORD... STABBING MOTION... KNIFE? MURDER?
MURDERER!
"THE MURDERER..."
THIRD WORD... ANOTHER SMALL WORD... IF? AND? IS...?
IS!
"THE MURDERER IS..."
FOR CHRIST'S SAKE JUST TELL US WHO DID IT, YOU EXASPERATING WHITE-FACED PONCE!
ALL RIGHT, ALL RIGHT, I'M SORRY, I DIDN'T MEAN TO MAKE YOU CRY.
PLEASE DO CARRY ON, MONSIEUR PIERROT.
AN HOUR LATER.
...TWENTY-FOURTH WORD. SOUNDS LIKE "PAN." MAN? FLAN?
"THAN."
THAN!
RIGHT. SO WE'VE GOT "THE MURDERER IS SOMEBODY IN THIS VERY ROOM AND AFTER EXERCISING MY LITTLE GREY CELLS I HAVE CONCLUDED THAT IT IS NONE OTHER THAN..."
NOW, TWENTY-FIFTH WORD...

MAJOR 'TURNER' ROUND FOR ART PRIZE!

THE ART WORLD was in turmoil last night after the panel of judges for the 2021 Turner Prize controversially awarded the accolade... *to themselves!*

EXCLUSIVE!

It was the first time in the prestigious award's history that the five-strong panel has awarded the prize to itself.

"The nominations all had their own merit, and any one could justifibly have won," said panel chair Ellen Spanby.

"Araminta Bollux's photograph of some fallen leaves entitled *The Cycle of Temporary Loss and Eternal Rejuvenation* was very moving, and challenged our preconceptions about permanance and transitoryness," she said.

greed

"And Tim Boolshite's pinecone sitting on a five pound note, entitled *Economy and Gymnospermae* was a strong and thought-provoking metaphor for the greed that is destroying our planet," she added.

"But in the end, we thought that five Turner Prize judges awarding themselves the prize entitled *Success, Failure and Nothing In Between* was a clear winner."

There were emotional scenes during the awards ceremony at London's Tate Britain gallery, as the five judges stepped up on stage, where they presented themselves with a cheque for £40,000.

But not everyone was happy with the choice of winner, and several of the nominees complained that the piece should not have been considered as it was not even on the shortlist.

"It makes a mockery of the whole award," said Millie Waank, whose drawing of a mouse facing away from a piece of cheese, entitled *Conforming to Non-Conformity*, was tipped as the likely winner.

provocative

However, others applauded the controversial and brave decision the judging panel made. "It is this kind of transgressive and provocative act that the Turner Prize exists to reward," said *London Evening Standard* art critic the late Brian Sewell.

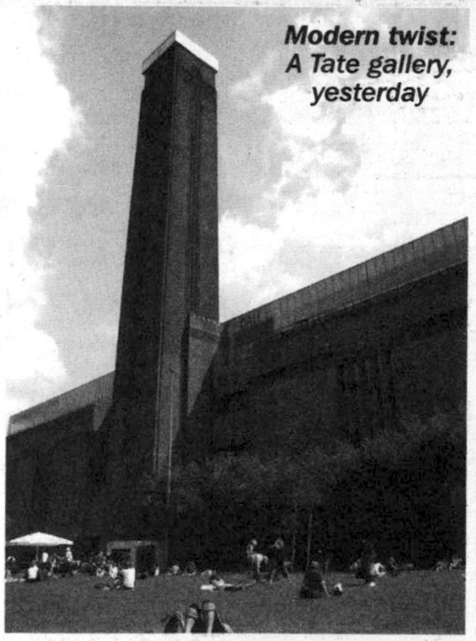

Modern twist:* *A Tate gallery, yesterday

Asked how they would spend with their prize money, four of the judges agreed that they would use their share to set up an annual prize for the Best Art Award Judging Panel, judged each year by themselves. The fifth said he intended to spend his £8,000 on sweets and prostitutes.

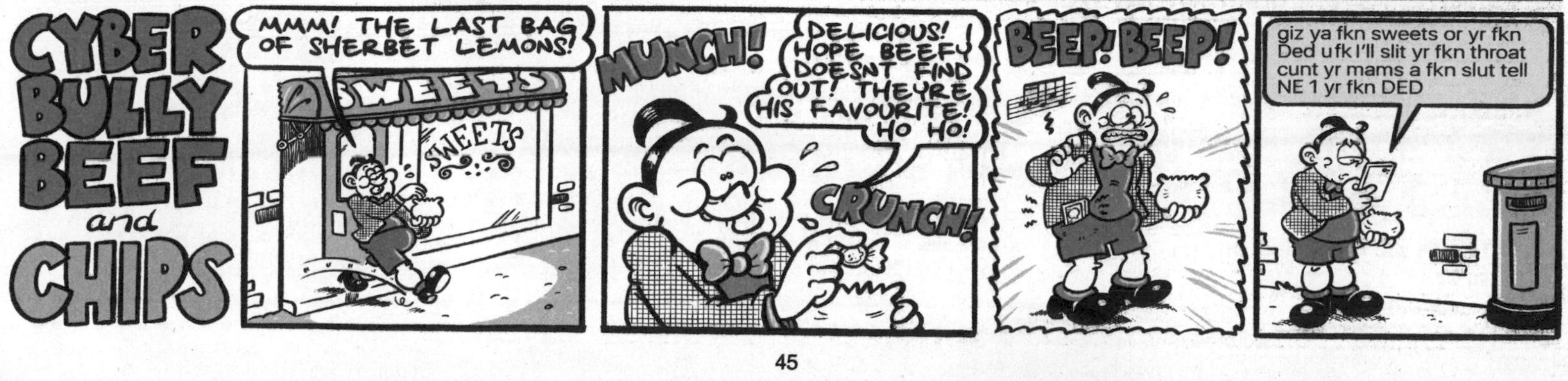

CYBER BULLY BEEF and CHIPS
MMM! THE LAST BAG OF SHERBET LEMONS!
SWEETS
SWEETS
MUNCH!
DELICIOUS! HOPE BEEFY DOESN'T FIND OUT! THEY'RE HIS FAVOURITE! HO HO!
CRUNCH!
BEEP! BEEP!
giz ya fkn sweets or yr fkn Ded u fk I'll slit yr fkn throat cunt yr mams a fkn slut tell NE 1 yr fkn DED

WHO WANTS TO BE A

ORDINARY people throughout the country are taking advantage of what financial experts are calling the biggest free cyber-cash windfall in history. By investing a bit of loose change in Bitcoin – the revolutionary open source internet currency invented back in 2008 by computer geeks – millions of Brits are becoming overnight *multi-billionaires*. And you can do it too, by following our simple step-by-step guide to the lucrative free money system.

Brits log on to join Bitcoin Bonanza

"It's like winning the pools and a lottery rollover jackpot every minute, twenty-four hours a day," says Nottingham cyber-trader Vince Fictitious, 46, who invested a bit of chewing gum he found stuck to the bottom of his shoe in Bitcoin yesterday afternoon. "I just did it for a laugh while I was waiting for a pop tart to cool down. I didn't think anything more about it until I checked my account after twenty minutes, when I was amazed to discover that I was now the fourth richest man in the world, after Bill Gates, Elon Musk and Jeff Bezos."

In fact, just 24 hours later, Vince's initial tiny investment has been so successful he's now the world's first *multi-trillionaire*, and thinking of giving up his job as a manual drains unblocker at Stoke Bardolph sewage plant. He told us: "Investing in Bitcoin has given me the financial security to pursue my ambition of becoming an antiques dealer like on *Dickinson's Real Deal* or *Flog It*. It's like all my dreams have come true at once."

There's clearly never been a better time to join Vince and jump aboard the runaway cyber-cash express train to an unimaginably vast Bitcoin fortune and the first class lifestyle of your dreams, dripping with Ferraris, personalised jets, superyachts, supermodels* and private islands in the tropics. There's a bottomless ocean of free money waiting for you just around the corner. What have you got to lose?

(*Or muscly blokes for the women)

Your Bitcoin Questions Answered

MANY PEOPLE are confused about what bitcoins actually are, where you get them, and how you spend them. R4's *Moneybox* presenter PAUL LEWIS give you the lowdown on the hi-tech currency.

What is Bitcoin?

BITCOIN is an internet-based currency that exists in cyberspace. Just a penny invested in Bitcoin in the morning is typically worth millions or billions of pounds by the afternoon.

How do I invest in Bitcoin?

SIMPLY go on the internet and buy some Bitcoin for a few pence… or even less! Then sit back and watch your investment grow. When you're ready to reap the rewards, just go back on the internet and sell your Bitcoin for tens or hundreds of millions of pounds!

How much does a Bitcoin cost?

A BITCOIN costs just a few pence or even less.

How much can I sell a Bitcoin for?

A BITCOIN can be sold for billions of pounds or even more.

Isn't Bitcoin trading complicated?

NOT AT ALL. Anyone who has access to a computer can trade in Bitcoin. Simply go on the internet and start trading. What's stopping you?

Do I need any special equipment?

BECAUSE Bitcoin only exists in cyberspace, you don't even need a moneybox or a wallet to keep it in while it grows from being worth just a few pence to a ten-figure sum.

Where can I buy Bitcoin?

BUY BITCOIN on the internet for a few pence. Then away you go!

Can I spend Bitcoin in the shops?

BITCOIN is a "cyber currency" which means it isn't a physical coin, so you'll have to exchange it for real money before you can spend it on Lamborghinis, helicopters and Cartier diamonds. To do this, simply sell it to someone else, and then take the billions of pounds they give you to the shops.

Can the value of Bitcoin go down?

TRADITIONAL investments made using real money are subject to market forces, and their value can go down over time. However Bitcoin rises so fast it can never go down, and will only ever be worth ever-increasing amounts of millions, billions or even trillions of pounds.

CRYPTO BILLIONAIRE?

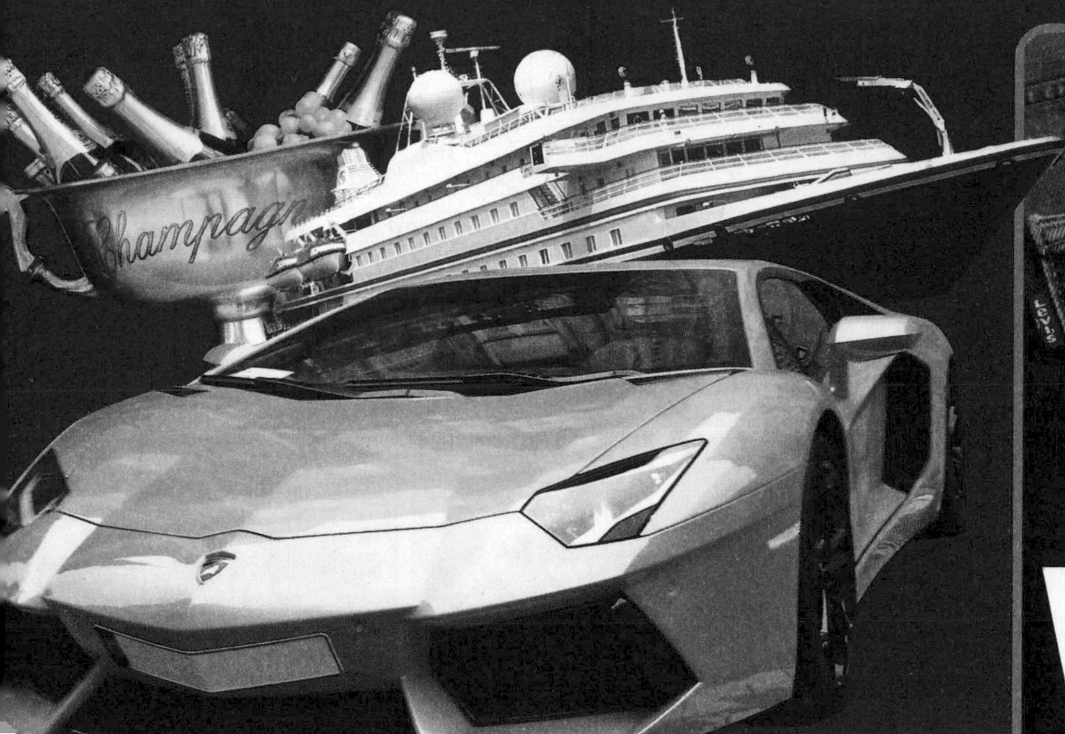

Champagne

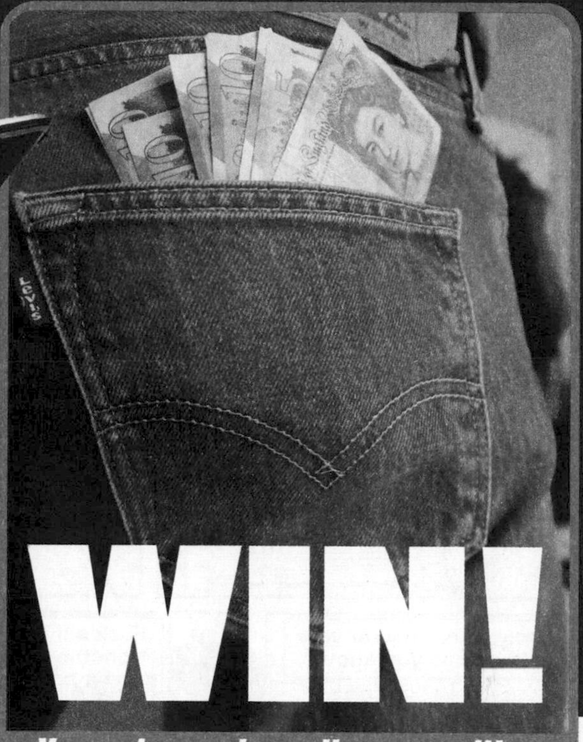

WIN!

Your chance to walk away with a Bitcoin Billion in your Back Pocket!

WE'RE giving away a *TEN-FIGURE BITCOIN FORTUNE* to the winner of this fantastic competition. Simply arrange these five features of Bitcoin in order of importance and complete the tiebreaker in 26 words or less for your chance to win.

1. **Simplicity. Trading in Bitcoins couldn't be easier.**
2. **Profitability. Bitcoins offer a near-instant multi-million % return on your investment.**
3. **Storage. Bitcoins can be kept on an ordinary home computer.**
4. **Cheapness. Bitcoins cost just a few pence, or even less.**
5. **Bitcoin transactions are validated via online blockchain nodes.**

Complete the tiebreaker:

I would like to become a Viz Bitcoin Billionaire because ....

....

(26 words or less or fewer)

Name..

Address ....

....

Send to: Viz, PO Box 841, Whitley Bay, NE26 9EQ.

Winners will receive 1p to invest in the Bitcoin blockchain of their choice.

SPREE BY GUM! How will YOU Spend YOUR Bitcoin Bonanza?

WE WENT out on the streets and asked a selection of passers-by how they would spend their Bitcoin Billions.

"**FIRSTLY** I'd get the brakes fixed on my old Maestro, because the back wheels get red hot when I've been down the shops so I think they're binding again. Then I'd buy a submarine and go to live on the bottom of the sea with Miss World and a robot butler."

Reg Hubris, chimney sweep

"**I WOULD** buy a Premier League football club, such as Chelsea, Manchester United or Liverpool, and I'd change its name to Dave Smith United. And instead of them playing at Stamford Bridge, Old Trafford or Anfield, I'd call the ground the Dave Smith Stadium, with Dave Smith painted on the roof in big letters."

Dave Smith, cheesemonger

"**I'D PUT** some of the money into reviving the career of my favourite comedy act of the 1970s, the Grumbleweeds. They used to do a dead good impression of Jimmy Savile which I imagine they won't do now. I don't know how many of them are still alive, but I would pay to put them on at the Royal Albert Hall, with the London Symphony Orchestra as their backing band, and André Previn as the conductor. If he's still alive."

Sandra Ratchet, midwife

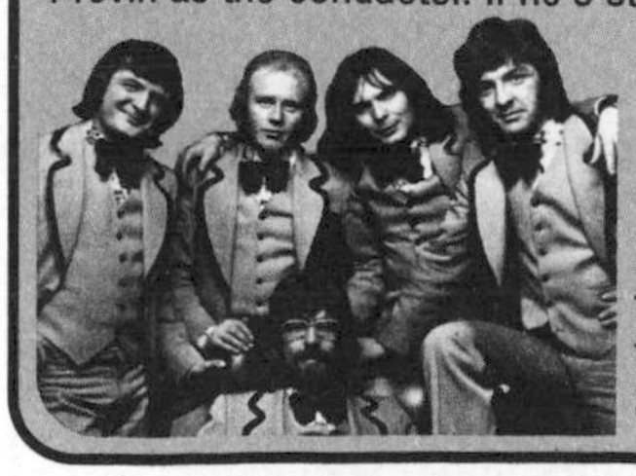

"**I'D PAY** a billion pounds to get the King to do a personal appearance at my birthday party at Pizza Hut, dressed up like a clown and doing balloon animals for the kids. Everyone's got their price."

Gerald Octane-Rating, plumber

"**I WOULD** feel uncomfortable receiving such a vast amount of money for such little effort, so I would probably donate a large proportion of my proceeds to a good cause, such as a Formula 1 team, Sir Richard Branson's space rocket or Nigel Farage's latest political party."

Mark Cordwainer, GP

"**ALL MY LIFE** I have dreamt of owning that Van Gogh painting *Nature Morte, Vase Aux Marguerites Et Coquelicots*, which recently sold at auction for $55 million. So if I suddenly found myself with billions of pounds in my pocket, I would fund an audacious robbery at the art gallery who bought it, lowering myself through a skylight from a stealth-equipped luxury helicopter after filling the place with specially developed memory-erasing gas."

Ada Frangipane, retired dinner lady

"**IN THE TRADITION** of Playboy boss Hugh Hefner, I'd set up my own luxury mansion full of beautiful women to have hows-your-father with whenever I fancied it. I'd get them all dressed up in stockings and suspenders and bras and high-heels, and then I'd have nookie with them all day on a big round bed. And when they started getting a bit old, I'd throw them out and get some new ones in."

Jimmy Trondheim, cinema organist

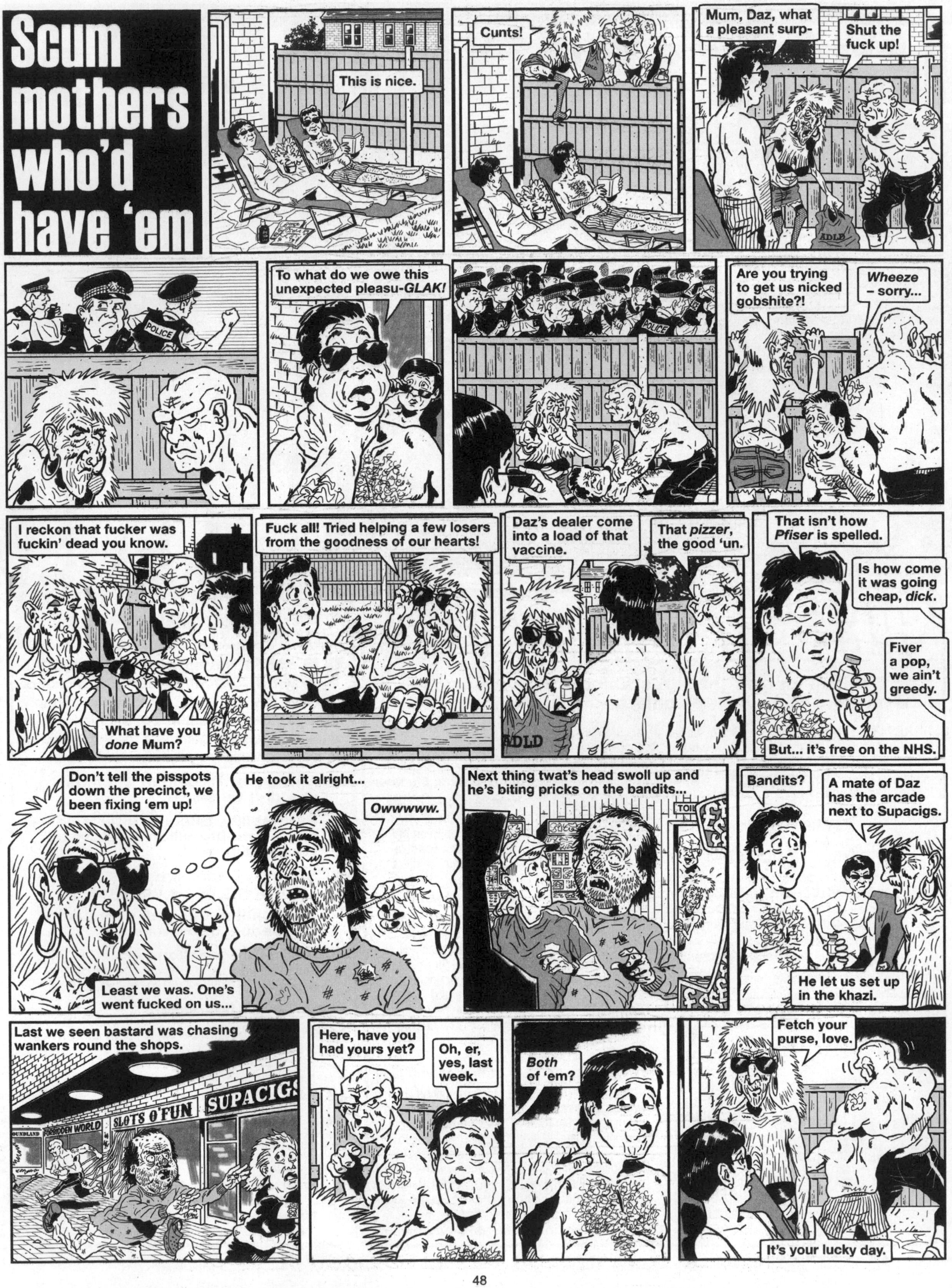

Scum mothers who'd have 'em
This is nice.
Cunts!
Mum, Daz, what a pleasant surp-
Shut the fuck up!
ADLD
POLICE
To what do we owe this unexpected pleasu-GLAK!
POLICE
Are you trying to get us nicked gobshite?!
Wheeze – sorry...
I reckon that fucker was fuckin' dead you know.
What have you done Mum?
Fuck all! Tried helping a few losers from the goodness of our hearts!
Daz's dealer come into a load of that vaccine.
That pizzer, the good 'un.
ADLD
That isn't how Pfiser is spelled.
Is how come it was going cheap, dick.
Fiver a pop, we ain't greedy.
But... it's free on the NHS.
Don't tell the pisspots down the precinct, we been fixing 'em up!
Least we was. One's went fucked on us...
He took it alright...
Owwwww.
Next thing twat's head swoll up and he's biting pricks on the bandits...
Bandits?
A mate of Daz has the arcade next to Supacigs.
He let us set up in the khazi.
Last we seen bastard was chasing wankers round the shops.
SUPACIGS
SLOTS O'FUN
FORBIDDEN WORLD
Here, have you had yours yet?
Oh, er, yes, last week.
Both of 'em?
Fetch your purse, love.
It's your lucky day.

Bad Bob The Randy Wonder Dog

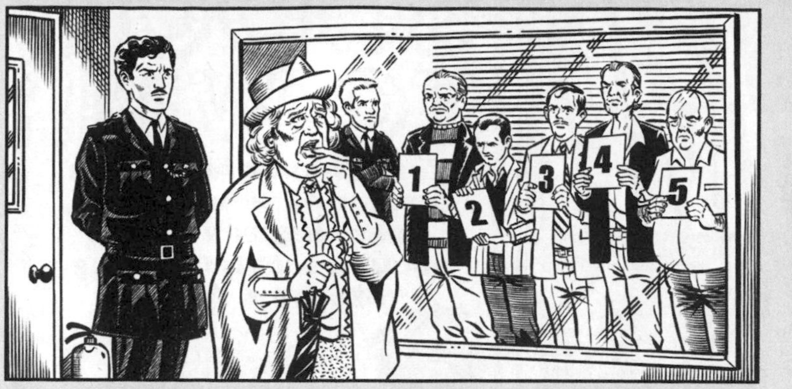
1
2
3
4
5

OLD MRS McTweed had been the victim of a callous robbery in the high street, and a suspect had been arrested. In a nervous state, she went along to Glenpeebles police station to see if she could pick the perpetrator out of a line-up. "Do you see the villain who took your handbag?" asked Sergeant Greenock.

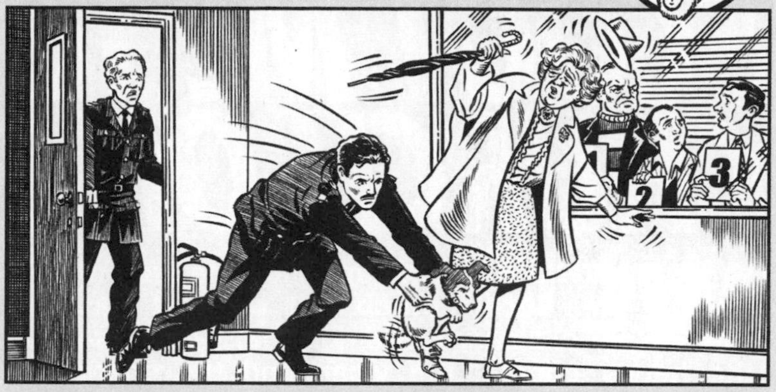
1
2
3

SUDDENLY the old woman screamed. "What is it? Do you see your assailant?" asked the sergeant. "No... it's your mutt!" she replied. "He's getting intimate wi' ma leg again!" The embarrassed policeman tried to separate his randy dog from the old lady's leg. "Bad Bob!" he cried. "BAD Bob!"

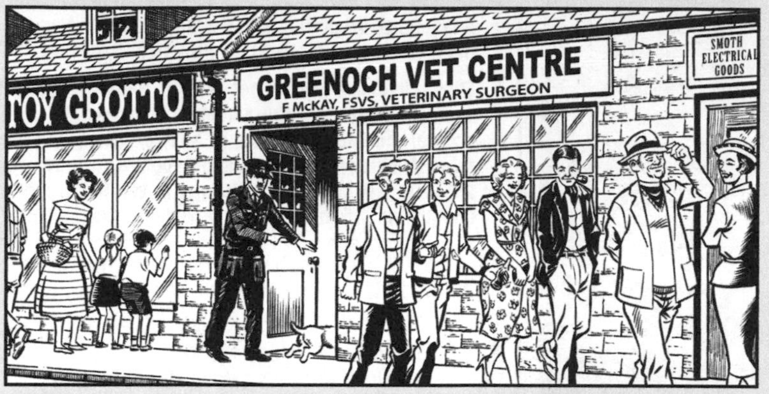
TOY GROTTO
GREENOCH VET CENTRE
F McKAY, FSVS, VETERINARY SURGEON
SMOTH ELECTRICAL GOODS

AFTER profuse apologies to Mrs McTweed, Sergeant Greenock took his amorous four-legged friend to Mr McKay, the village veterinary surgeon. "In with ye, lad. You're goin' tae have your nuts aff... and nae a'fore time," he said. "That should take the lead oot o' that wee pencil o' yours."

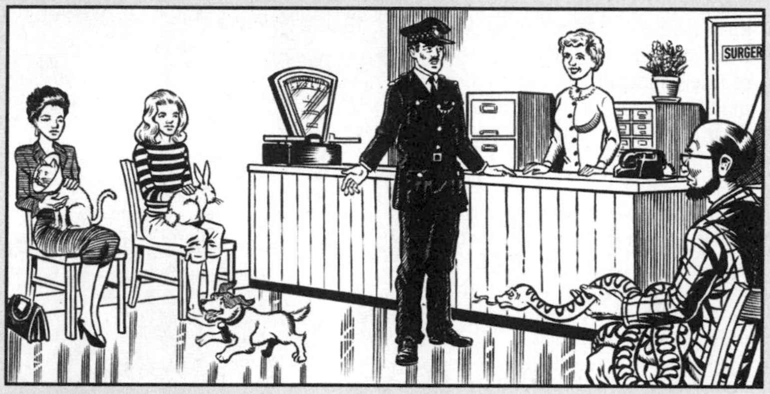

INSIDE, Sergent Greenock approached Miss Tindal, the vet's receptionist. "I've brought ma wee dog to be de-podded," he said. "The dirty wee cur is getting oot o' hand with his funny business." "Okay. If you could pop him on the scales, we'll get him weighed," she replied. But Bob had other ideas.

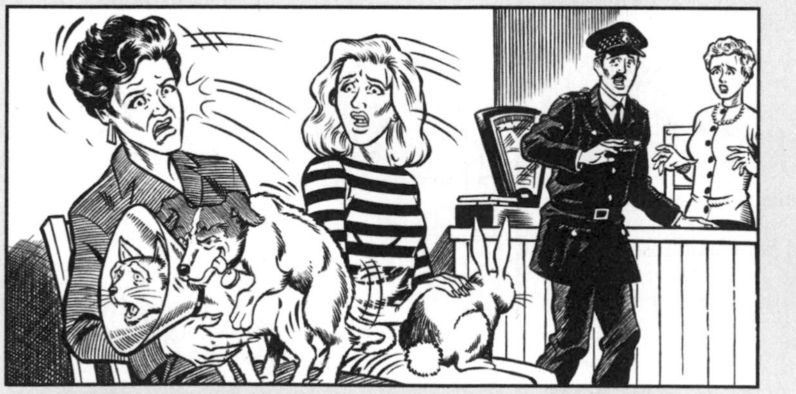

THE RANDY mutt made straight for Mrs Tompkins' cat Whiffles, who was suffering from an eye infection. "Och, Greenock! Get your dog aff ma cat!" she cried. "The poor thing is in a bad enough state as it is, withoot being frottered by your dirty hoond." "Stoap, Bob! Stoap!" the sergeant cried. But to no avail.

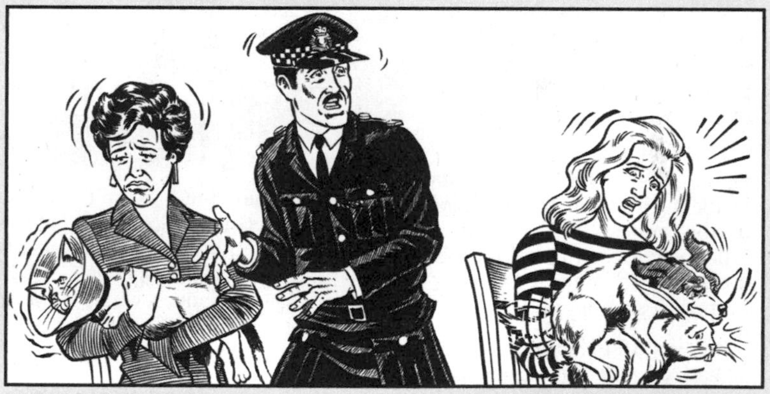

EVENTUALLY, the burly policeman managed to rescue the cat from his dog's advances, but the randy animal was not finished. "Ma rabbit! Get it aff ma wee bunny!" cried Miss Copeland, as Bob mounted her bunny and began humping away. "Aff it, Bob! Nae biscuit! Nae biscuit!" cried the sergeant.

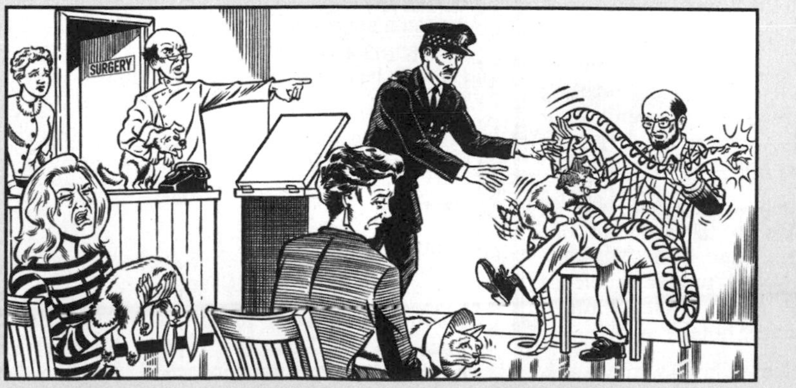
SURGERY

"MA WEE rabbit's drapped dead wi' fright!" cried Miss Copeland. Then Mr McGill called out, "Greenock! Your dog's tryin' tae bum ma python. Get it aff!" Mr McKay came out of his surgery at all the commotion. "Whit's going on? hollered the vet. "Greenock! Get that hound oot o' my surgery."

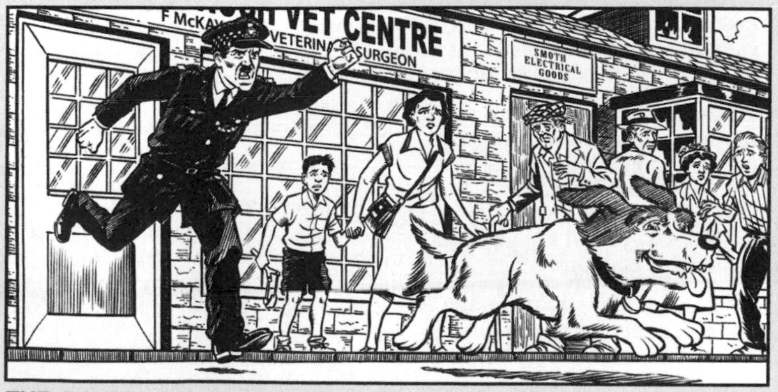
SMOTH ELECTRICAL GOODS

THE RANDY mutt didn't need telling twice and fled from the veterinary surgery with his embarrassed owner behind him. "Come back here, ye dirty wee monster!" the Sergeant shouted after his dog. "This is nae the end of it... they're coming aff, if I hae tae do it ma'sel with a couple o' hoose bricks!"

SCOOT ME TO THE CHURCH ON TIME!

WHEN a Bristol couple tied the knot at their local church last week, it was no ordinary wedding. That's because the happy couple, the vicar, and the entire congregation were on *scooters*.

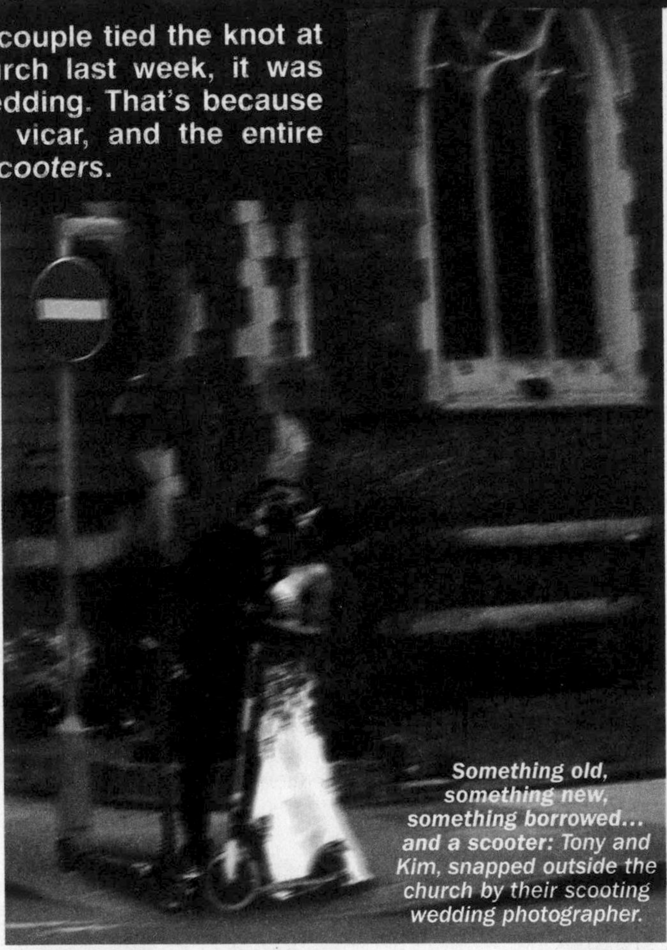
Something old, something new, something borrowed... and a scooter: Tony and Kim, snapped outside the church by their scooting wedding photographer.

Scooter-mad lovebirds Tony and Kim Chalmondly met at the Bristol Scooter Society, and have both been fans of the two-wheeled vehicles for years. So it seemed natural that when they made their vows, they and all their guests were riding scooters.

was

"It was a wonderful day," said newly married Tony. "I'll always remember the butterflies I had as I was standing at the altar along with the vicar and my best man, all on scooters."

And three minutes late, as is the tradition, his bride-to-be, her father and four bridesmaids all scooted down the aisle of St Paul's Church in Clifton.

"It was wonderful," said blushing newlywed Kim. "I love scooters, and for them to be part of the biggest day of my life made it all the more special."

However, her grand entrance didn't pass entirely without incident. In her excitement, one of the bridesmaids scooted a little too fast and ran onto Kim's dress, ripping off the 6-foot long train, exposing her underwear.

"It was a little hiccup which all added to the fun of the day," she told local paper *The Clifton and Redland Bonanza.*

(not was)

After the vows had been taken, the wedding party gathered outside the church for the usual round of photographs.

"Everyone in the photos was moving because you can't stop on a scooter otherwise you fall off," said Tony. "And the photographer was on a scooter too, so it meant all the pictures came out a bit blurred."

"It was a little disappointing, but it was all part of the fun of the day," he added.

The newly-weds and their 100 guests dispensed with cars and scooted off to the reception, but the journey there wasn't exactly plain sailing. Scooting down Constitution Hill, the bridal party reached speeds of nearly 45 mph and several, including the groom's 88-year-old grandmother were involved in a pile-up.

"A few people, including my matron of honour were taken to hospital with cuts, grazes and concussion," said Kim.

"It was obviously upsetting to see them taken away by ambulance on what should have been a happy occasion, but it was all part and parcel of the fun."

wasn't

The reception at the Bristol Boat Club on the Marina saw the newly married couple enjoy their first dance on scooters, before the buffet opened and the party began. But the evening's celebrations didn't go entirely according to plan.

"A great aunt of mine came off her scooter whilst trying to put some coleslaw on her plate at the buffet," said Tony. "She's 98 and her balance isn't what it used to be, and she went arse over tit and fractured her hip."

"The paramedics came, and when they saw our reception, they joined in the fun and stretchered my great aunt away on scooters," he added.

"It was lovely that they joined in with the fun of the day."

The big day ended at 11.00 that evening when the now Mr and Mrs Chalmondly boarded their scooters to spend their wedding night in a nearby country hotel.

"My best man had tied all tin cans to the back of our scooters," said Kim. "We must have woken up the whole of Bristol as we scooted through town to the hotel."

And in the hotel's bridal suite, the happy couple consummated their marriage whilst on scooters.

SCOOT TO WIN!

Your chance to win the scooter of your dreams, assuming you dream about a scooter costing £16 from Argos.

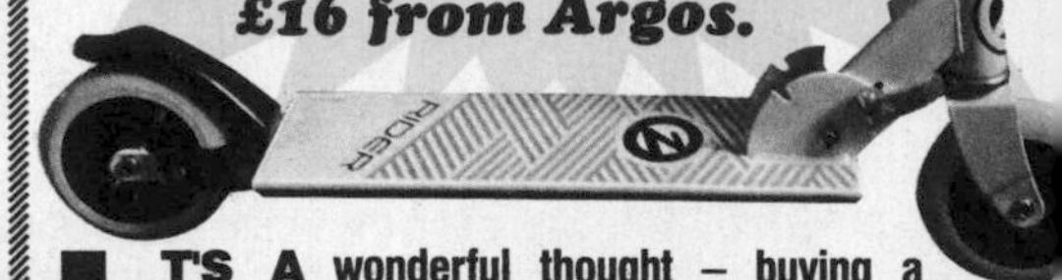

IT'S A wonderful thought – buying a scooter and riding the open road, feeling that sense of freedom as you eat up the miles with the wind in your hair. But in reality you'll go to the shops on it twice before putting it in the shed. So don't waste any money. Let your big-hearted *Viz* waste it for you.

That's because we've got one of these fantastic £16 scooters to give to the winner of our equally fantastic scooter competition. Simply answer these 5 scooter-related questions correctly, and if you are the lucky winner the prize will be scooting its way to you in the form of a cheque for £16 to spend on a scooter or anything else.

1. Which German hardcore rave techno band named themselves after a self propelled, two-wheeled mode of transport?

- ☐ a. *The Jets*
- ☐ b. *The Cars*
- ☐ c. *Scooter*

2. Scooters differ from bicycles in several respects. But which of these features are common to both scooters and bicycles?

- ☐ a. *A seat*
- ☐ b. *Two wheels*
- ☐ c. *Some pedals*

3. If all the current and past members of the pioneering German electro-synth band Kraftwerk owned a scooter, how many scooters would they have between them?

- ☐ a. *20*
- ☐ b. *22*
- ☐ c. *35*

4. Thor, the Norse God of thunder, had a hammer called Mjölnir. But which of the Norse Gods rode around the heavens on a scooter called Folkvangr?

- ☐ a. *Freyja*
- ☐ b. *Odin*
- ☐ c. *None of them*

5. German punk outfit Die Toten Hosen have never written a song with the word 'scooter' in the title, or ever made mention of scooters in their lyrics. But which German city are they from?

- ☐ a. *Munich*
- ☐ b. *Cologne*
- ☐ c. *Düsseldorf*

Name ....

Address ....

.... **Post Code** ....

Send your answers to Viz Comic £16 Scooter Competition, PO Box 841, Whitley Bay, NE26 9EQ, or email them to letters@viz.co.uk with the subject "£16 Scooter Competition". All entries must arrive by 20th August two years ago.

FOR years, scientists have been telling us that a personal transport revolution is just around the corner. We've been led to believe that in the not too distant future we will be flying around on jet packs, one-man gyrocopters, or hoverboards with neon blue lights underneath. But now it seems that all that was bollocks, as it turns out that it's the **SCOOTER** that is set to transport us in the years to come – a far less exciting prospect. Old-fashioned cars have had their day, and the future looks scooter-shaped. Of course, like everything, the scooter will no doubt evolve as time progresses – two wheels will be replaced with three and then four to increase stability. A safety shell will be constructed around the scooter to afford the rider protection, and seats will be provided for comfort. Now too heavy to be foot-propelled, these scooters of the future will be driven by petrol engines and capable of covering hundreds of miles in a day at speeds in excess of 70mph. Be be in no doubt, scooters are here to stay. But how much do we really know about them? Here's...

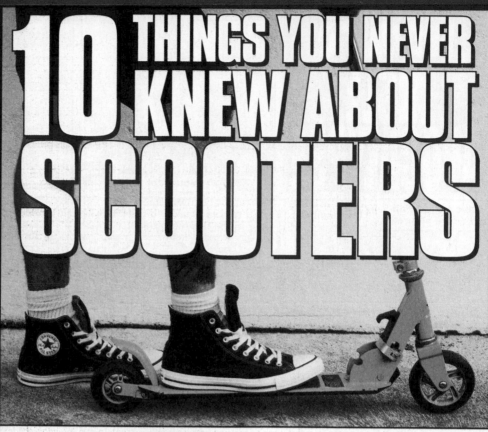

10 THINGS YOU NEVER KNEW ABOUT SCOOTERS

1 **MEMBERS** of America's technology-eschewing Amish community are forbidden from riding bicycles, but are allowed to move about their Pennsylvania neighbourhoods on scooters. This is because, while they believe that pedals, chains and crankshafts constitute a machine, wheels, bearings and axles do not.

2 **NO MATTER** how heavy it is, a scooter on the moon will weigh just one sixth of its weight on earth. You might think that this means you could scoot about six times quicker on the lunar surface than here on our home planet, but you'd be wrong. Cast your mind back to the Apollo 11 mission, and you'll remember that everything in space happens in slow motion.

3 **IF YOU** went to the top of the Leaning Tower of Pisa and simultaneously dropped a scooter and a bike, weighing 10kg and 20kg respectively, it would be an extremely dangerous thing to do. Up to 30,000 people a day visit this popular tourist attraction, and throwing large metal-framed machines from the top could cause serious injury or even death to an unsuspecting member of the public.

4 **IF YOU** had a scooter before 1668, chances are you wouldn't have got very far on it. That's because it wasn't until that year that mathematician Sir Isaac Newton invented his famous third law of motion which provides an equal and opposite reaction to any force. And it is this reaction which allows a scooter to move forwards when you push back with your foot.

5 **IF YOU** ask to hire a scooter in Hungary, you'll be met with a blank stare. That's because those funny Hungarians refer to the two-wheeled push-along vehicle as a 'robogo'. You couldn't make it up!

6 **IF YOU** ask to hire a scooter in Sweden, you might think you'd be met with a blank stare. But you'd be wrong, because everyone in that Nordic country speaks fantastic English, better than many people in England.

7 **THE WORLD** horizontal land speed record for a scooter was set by Albert Potato, aboard the specially designed LegThrust II. On June 18th, 2015, Potato reached a speed of 38.12 mph, set over two 300m runs across the Utah Salt Flats. The first run was uneventful, but in the second, disaster struck. As Potato crossed the line he caught his scooter's back wheel with the heel of his pushing foot, sending him crashing to the ground. He was treated at the scene for grazes on his knees and left elbow.

8 **ROCK** monsters AC/DC almost had to cancel their 1996 "Ballbreaker" world tour after a disagreement between guitarist Angus Young and the group's management. The band's record company, who organised the mammoth 155 date stadium tour, had refused to let the schoolboy plank-spanker take his scooter along with him, and Young had threatened to quit in protest. In the end, his mum, Dolly, met with senior executives from Columbia Records to try to smooth things over, and it was agreed that her son could take his scooter, but he would not be allowed to ride it up and down the tour bus. Young agreed and the record-breaking tour went ahead.

9 **KING** Charles may have ascended the throne, but he has never ridden a scooter. He has piloted a helicopter, driven a Chieftain tank and taken the controls of a Cessna 172 Skyhawk light aircraft, but not once has he stood on one of the two-wheeled platforms and pushed himself forwards with one foot. Other things he has never done is open a door, put toothpaste on his toothbrush or worn the same pair of underpants twice.

10 **UNLIKE** on a motorbike, you are not compelled by law to wear a crash helmet when riding a scooter, but you do have to wear clothes of some sort. Whilst public nudity is not strictly illegal in the UK, you could be charged with offending public decency if you are indiscreet in your behaviour whilst naked, and scooting around in the Billy Bollocks except for one shoe is likely to be deemed a breach of the peace, and you could end up scooting straight to court to be bound over.

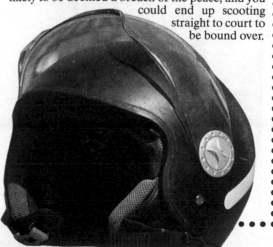

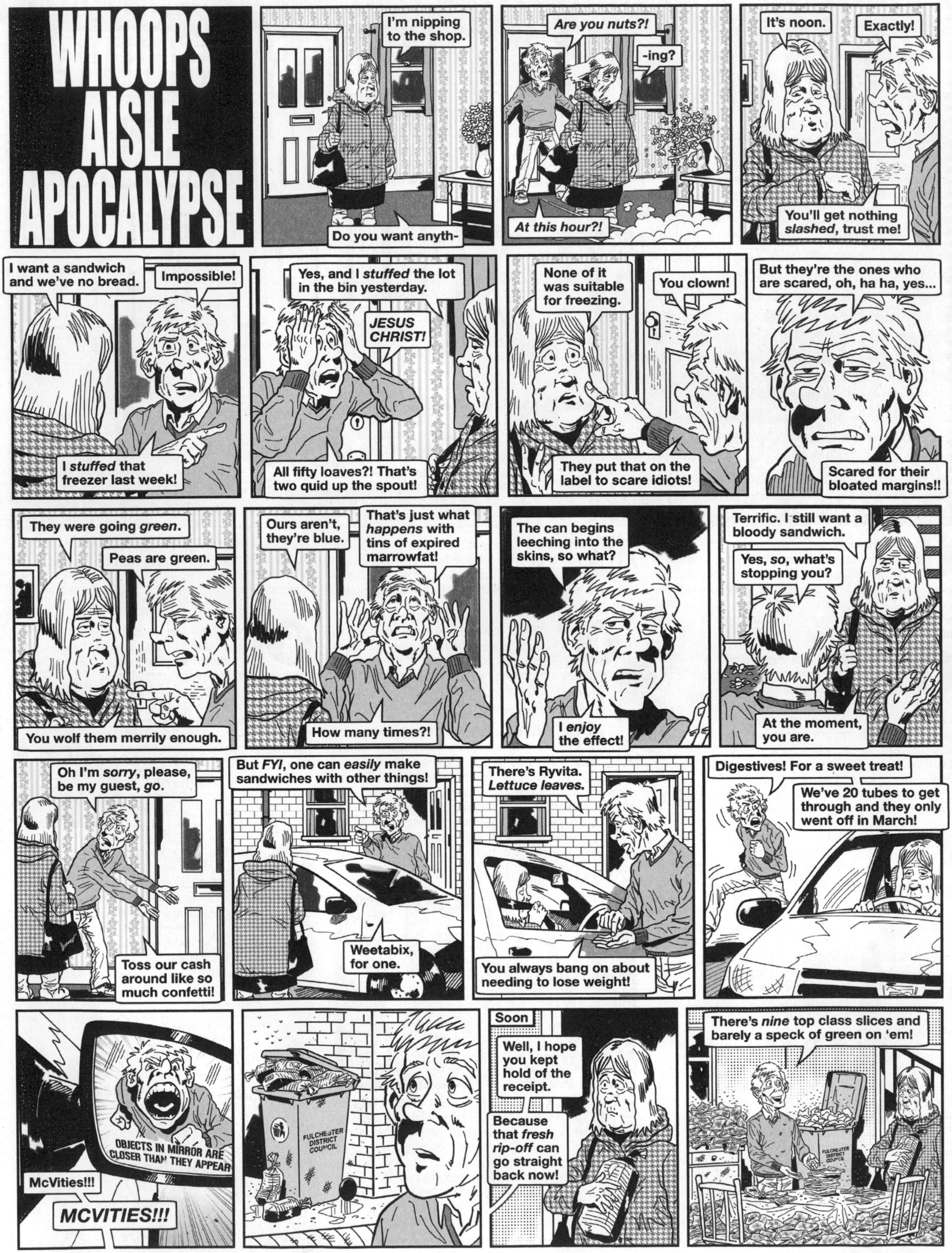
WHOOPS AISLE APOCALYPSE
I'm nipping to the shop.
Do you want anyth-
Are you nuts?!
-ing?
At this hour?!
It's noon.
Exactly!
You'll get nothing *slashed*, trust me!
I want a sandwich and we've no bread.
Impossible!
I *stuffed* that freezer last week!
Yes, and I *stuffed* the lot in the bin yesterday.
JESUS CHRIST!
All fifty loaves?! That's two quid up the spout!
None of it was suitable for freezing.
You clown!
They put that on the label to scare idiots!
But they're the ones who are scared, oh, ha ha, yes...
Scared for their bloated margins!!
They were going *green*.
Peas are green.
You wolf them merrily enough.
Ours aren't, they're blue.
That's just what *happens* with tins of expired marrowfat!
How many times?!
The can begins leeching into the skins, so what?
I *enjoy* the effect!
Terrific. I still want a bloody sandwich.
Yes, *so*, what's stopping you?
At the moment, you are.
Oh I'm *sorry*, please, be my guest, *go*.
Toss our cash around like so much confetti!
But *FYI*, one can *easily* make sandwiches with other things!
Weetabix, for one.
There's Ryvita. *Lettuce leaves.*
You always bang on about needing to lose weight!
Digestives! For a sweet treat!
We've 20 tubes to get through and they only went off in March!
OBJECTS IN MIRROR ARE CLOSER THAN THEY APPEAR
McVities!!!
MCVITIES!!!
FULCHESTER DISTRICT COUNCIL
Soon
Well, I hope you kept hold of the receipt.
Because that *fresh rip-off* can go straight back now!
There's *nine* top class slices and barely a speck of green on 'em!

DOCTOR IN THE HOUSE

A BARNSLEY man says he is regretting the day he let his wife give him a lockdown appendectomy after he was left with a ridiculous-looking scar and life-threatening injuries.

Hubby gets emergency appendix op from missus

Slice 'n' easy? George received home-made op courtesy of wife, Kath (inset).

George Trinkets, 43, was isolating at home with his wife Kath and their three children when he developed a crippling pain in the right side of his abdomen. Mrs Trinkets suspected immediately that it was a burst appendix, because her sister had had the condition when she was twelve, and her husband was displaying all the same symptoms.

"George wanted to go to hospital, but I said it would be a nightmare, as it was at the height of the pandemic," she told the *Barnsley Aorta and Ventricle*. "We've all had to become experts in one thing and another during lockdown, and I thought it couldn't be too hard, so I told him I would do the operation myself."

knife

George was a little reluctant at first, but he eventually gave in and climbed on the kitchen table. In the absence of any surgical equipment, Kath used the vegetable knife and a pair of dress-making scissors to perform the op.

"I was a little nervous making the initial incision," she said. "But I thought 'in for a penny, in for a pound' and I got to work."

It wasn't the best of starts. Kath told the paper: "My first cut was a bit wonky, and it was about two inches lower than it should have been." And when she got to the external oblique muscle, her incision was even more crooked.

"It was all over the shop, and I started to get the giggles," she said.

fork

And it didn't stop there, because when Mrs Trinkets eventually reached her husband's inflamed appendix and removed it, she accidentally lopped off a chunk of caecum along with the ruptured organ.

She said: "I burst out laughing and George asked me what had happened. I said it was nothing, but I think he suspected I was making a right pig's ear of his op."

The Trinkets's three children had come in to watch their mum give their dad his appendectomy, and when they saw the mess she was making, they all started laughing.

"It was all I could do to keep a straight face," said Kath. "It wasn't as easy as it looked, and George knew it was going badly. By the time I'd got the appendix out, I decided to cut my losses and sew him up before I did any more damage."

spoon

Mrs Trinkets finished the operation, but now faced the prospect of her husband seeing the result.

"George asked for a mirror to see what kind of job I had made," she said. "I was shaking with laughter and not surprisingly, he was looking distinctly apprehensive."

machine

One of the couple's children fetched a shaving mirror from the bathroom and George examined his home-style appendectomy scar. "It looked hysterical," admitted Kate. "I'd sewn his wound up at a ridiculous angle, much higher on one side than the other. I'd taken far too much subcutaneous fat out and there was a big tuft of peritoneum sticking out the top."

ghost

After a few second's disbelief, George burst out laughing at the sight of his unsightly scar. "I have to admit, he's got a wonderful sense of humour and he saw the funny side," said Kate. "He even took a picture and put it up on his Facebook page with the caption 'Don't let your missus take your appendix out in lockdown!'"

dust

Mr Trinkets was rushed to Barnsley hospital the next day after he developed septicaemia and slipped into unconsciousness. He spent three weeks on the critical list in the intensive care unit before he eventually began to recover.

myth

Head of the unit, Dr Aneesa Iqbal advised against people attempting to perform surgical operations during lockdown, although she did admit that Mrs Trinkets had made a reasonable job of the appendectomy.

"It was a half-decent attempt for a first try, but she made a couple of fundamental errors, including severing a couple of illiohypogastric nerves, and sewing the wrong muscle layers together, which will need several operations to put right," she said.

"But top marks for effort," she added.

LUCKY HEATHER
LUCKY FRANK
I ♥ HEATHER
BLANK CHEQUE
ECCENTRIC BILLIONAIRE HEATHER ENTHUSIAST
DJ '21
YOINKS! FREE STRAWBERRY-FLAVOUR COVID VACCINES!
SCIENTISTS RESEARCH INSTITUTE
FREE STRAWBERRY FLAVOUR COVID VACCINES
IT'S MY LUCKY DAY — STRAWBERRY FLAVOUR IS MY FAVOURITE!
SNATCH!
JAB!
LET ME INJECT THIS STRAWBERRY GOODNESS INTO MY VEINS!
OH WAIT! DID I ACCIDENTALLY WRITE "FREE STRAWBERRY FLAVOUR COVID VACCINES" ON THIS SIGN?
DYSLEXIC SCIENTISTS RESEARCH INSTITUTE
FREE STRAWBERRY FLAVOUR COVID VACCINES
MY MISTAKE! I MEANT TO WRITE "DANGER — EXPERIMENTAL DRUG THAT TURNS HUMAN BEINGS INTO ROBOTS!"
YEEBLE-BLEEBLE-BLEEP! I'VE BEEN TURNED INTO A ROBOT!
PWOOF!
THIS DOESN'T STRIKE ME AS BEING PARTICULARLY LUCKY!
LOOK OUT! HERE COMES ANOTHER WAVE OF THE CORONAVIRUS...
RUMBLE
AND THIS ONE IS THE NEW "FULCHESTER VARIANT" WHICH LOOKS LIKE BEING AN ABSOLUTE BASTARD!
BLEEBLE BLOINKS!
BIT-OW! BIT-OW!
FORTUITOUSLY, BEING A ROBOT I CAN SIMPLY ZAP THE VIRUSES OUT OF THE AIR WITH MY LASER BEAM NIPPLES!
YARP! THE ROBOT DRUG HAS WORN OFF — I'M HUMAN AGAIN!
LORD MAYOR
YES — AND YOU'VE WIPED OUT THE DEADLY FULCHESTER VARIANT OF COVID, THEREBY SAVING THE CITY!
AND
TUCK IN, FRANK ~ WITH THE COMPLIMENTS OF THE PEOPLE OF FULCHESTER!
VACCINES IN CAVIAR
VACCINATION CENTRE de POSH
YOINK! LUCKY ME!

LETTERBOCKS

Viz Comic, P.O. Box 841 Whitley Bay, NE26 9EQ : letters@viz.co.uk

I HAVE long held left-handed people in the highest regard, but after experimenting by wiping my arse with my left hand, my respect for them has increased massively. It was easily the most difficult and least satisfying wipe of my life. How they do it on a daily basis is beyond me. Hang in there, lefties. You are brilliant.

Joel Hewitt, Pontypool

INSTEAD of spending millions training milkmen how to drive milk floats, dairies should get people who own mobility scooters to drive them, as they are already qualified to operate slow electric vehicles. The milkmen could follow the float in their own car in order to carry the bottles to the door and collect the empties. And bonk the lonely housewives.

D Williams, Donegal

WHEN I was in school, my English teacher told me that I would never be a published author. Well, 25 years later, and after dozens of drafts, re-writes, and rejection letters from publishing houses, I'm happy to announce that that teacher has finally died.

Gary Ireland, Tauran

IN THE future, whe all cars run on air, where will we buy cheap last-minute flowers when we forget our wives' birthdays? I hope the boffins are working on that one.

Dominic Twose, Leamington Spa

I DON'T understand the appeal of having 'friends with benefits'. I spend months trying to persuade people at the Job Centre to go for a pint with me and none of them have a pot to piss in.

Ted Awful, Goole

I DON'T know anyone who has been bitten on the arse off a snake *(Letterbocks page 10)*, but my mate Dave was bitten on the arse off a swan at Hornsea Mere while we were fishing. Thankfully he survived and made a full recovery.

TC Rusling, Cottingham

STAR LETTER

I DREAMED I ran a Marathon last night. I don't know what everyone's on about. it was a piece of piss.

Mark Barrowcliffe, Brighton

I WISH broadband providers would add a bit of reality into their adverts. Rather than illustrating poor internet connection with a frustrated home worker trying to Skype colleagues from their front room, they should show some bloke in stained Y-fronts watching a buffering message during *Mature Booty Raiders 4*. If you ask me, having a catastrophic flop-on due to internet failure before a cream pie scene would be far more traumatic than not being able to email a spreadsheet.

F Buttery, Whitby

I'M A big fan of David Mitchell and his wife Victoria Coren, who are both super clever and funny. But can you be too clever? I find it hard to believe the Coren-Mitchells would discuss which chocolate bar would hurt the most when being forcibly pulled out of your arsehole, like me and my not-too-bright wife just did. It's a Toblerone by the way.

Baz McGuigan, Blaydon

IT'S FUNNY how we all recall films so differently. I remember *Alien* as a movie where a young Sigourney Weaver-wearing a short T-shirt like a model two-ring circus tent, and tiny white knickers- slowly climbs into a spacesuit as the camera zooms in on her bum crack. My wife insists that there was a whole lot more to this film, but she must be mistaken. The scenes she describes sounded terrifying, and if it had been me in the film, my underpants would have looked like the Somme battlefield on day fifty. Sigourney's scads, on the other hand, were pristine white. Perfect, in fact. Absolutely perfect.

Rev. Norman Gothic, Aberdeen

IF WE had never evolved trousers, on a cold day we would be able to see our farts like we see our breath. Thank goodness for trousers, I say.

Boody, Chesvegas

I CAN'T help but feel sorry for the Royal family; for one thing, they are forced to live in really old houses that are filled with second hand furniture. Furthermore, whenever The King goes to a formal engagement, he is always seen in the same old crown and robes that were hand-me-downs from his mum.

TO'Neill, Glasgow

I ALWAYS thought 'Arse' would be a good name for an Elbow tribute band.

Joel Young, email

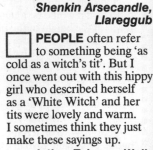

I'M JUST listening to *In Our Time* with Melvyn Bragg on Radio 4, and they're talking about some bloke who died in 900AD! Hardly "in our time", is it Melvyn?

Shenkin Arsecandle, Llareggub

PEOPLE often refer to something being 'as cold as a witch's tit'. But I once went out with this hippy girl who described herself as a 'White Witch' and her tits were lovely and warm. I sometimes think they just make these sayings up.

Jethro Tulsage, Wells

I'M TRYING to think of the best word which can be used as a pronoun, a determiner, an adverb or a conjunction. Can any of your readers beat that?

John Moynes, Dublin

IS THERE anything else you can do with pleasantries other than exchange or dispense with them?

A Slapcabbage, Leeds

∗ That's a tricky one, probably best answered by someone who is dead good at words, like Stephen Fry or Susie Dent. If any of our readers know either Stephen Fry or Susie Dent, could they show them this letter and let us know what they say?

I AM not scared of snarling dogs and I would quite fancy my chances against any police Alsatian. I am, however, terrified of snakes, so if the coppers set a snake on me I would probably surrender very quickly. Perhaps the police should consider carrying snakes.

Michael Harris, Gourock

I'VE JUST noticed that Saturday has the word 'turd' in the middle of it. Why aren't we taught this stuff at school instead of algebra?

Dominic Twose, L'ton Spa

Bagpussy

GET OFF MY CUSHION.
YOU'RE IN MY SPOT.
MOVE.
SOMEONE'S SITTING THERE, FATTY.

TOP TIPS

OUTER Space drama makers. Set the fictitious year of your show at least 500 years into the future, thus avoiding your predictions being proved embarrassingly wrong within your own lifetime.
Eldon Furse, Leeds

MISS heading to France on a booze cruise? Simulate the experience by buying crates of Belgian lager in your local Aldi and driving home by way of Dover.
Ottawa Ramsbottom, Sligo

A TRAINER on your dashboard makes an ideal cup holder.
Vinny Reynolds, M'chester

MOURNERS. Cheer up the sad task of scattering ashes by singing the Shake'n'Vac song.
Christina Martin, email

BUS manufacturers. Put the steering wheel at the back of the bus so the driver can keep an eye on unruly passengers.
D Williams, Donegal

FOOL friends into thinking you have sat on a whoopee cushion by farting as you sit down.
L King, Liverpool

MAKE yourself cry before you start peeling onions, perhaps by thinking about the death of an elderly relative, or how you are a failure in your family's eyes. Do not let the onion win.
Penny Pusher, Blackpool

AVOID the disappointment of having your holiday cancelled by booking somewhere you don't want to go to anyway.
Craig Pullen, Birmingham

toptips@viz.co.uk

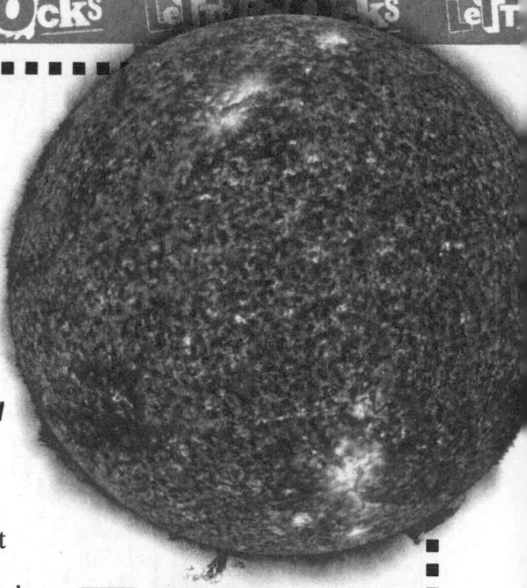

THE SUN is a ball of burning gas, I have always been led to believe. It's certainly not electric. Surely then, it would be more useful to scientists if the Sun's temperature, rather than being reported as 5,600°C, were given as Gas Mark 425.
Micky Bullock, email

AN EGG, left in boiling water for six minutes, is surprisingly tasty, given it has come out of a hen's arse. My wife calls it *Dom's Hen's Arse Treat*.
Dominic Twose, L'ton Spa

READING your latest issue I have to ask why is it when Gilbert Ratchet makes his contraptions, he frequently adds a second setting which sends the machine haywire and causes chaos? Surely he is just making extra work for himself with a result that is sub-optimal for all concerned. I should, of course, have realised this about 25 years ago, but I'm not the sharpest tool in the box.
Lord Schmoo, Bicester

IT ALWAYS makes me laugh when conspiracy theorists claim that the Moon landings were faked. What a load of rubbish. In fact, if anything, I reckon we've landed on the Moon loads more times than we know about and the authorities kept quiet about it. Probably other planets too, I shouldn't wonder.
Ben Nunn, Caterham

I WAS under the impression that we lived in a democracy with free speech. But once again you have gone power mad and on page 32, you banned Trim McKenna from the *Letterbocks* page. Well, enough is enough. I say we have a referendum on whether or not Mr Mckenna should be banned. The millions of *Viz* readers can cast their vote in a simple yes/no ballot. Vote 'Yes' if Mr McKenna should be allowed to remain on the *Letterbocks* pages, or vote 'No' if you want him to leave these pages forever. In the event of a tie, the *Viz* editor can have the final say, unlike his mother, who could not say anything with all cocks in her mouth.
Jase, Stoke

✱ Oh, dear, here we go again. As if it's not bad enough with Trim McKenna insulting the editors' mothers, Jase from Stoke is now joining in, showing off to Mr McKenna who is undoubtably egging him on. We have no hesitation in banning him from the Letterbocks page too. Good riddance to both of them.

YOU SEE the phrase 'you couldn't make it up' used a lot these days. But you could make it up, and people do all the time. The millions of fictional books in the world – *made up*. The cartoon strips in this comic – *made up*. This letter – *made up*. The phrase 'you most definitely could have made it up' would be nearer the truth.
David Slade, Stevenage

THANK goodness the Covid-19 pandemic didn't strike in the 1970s, when the tellies had smaller, squarer screens. Thanks to modern widescreens, the Home Secretary, the Chief Medical Officer and the Chief Scientific Adviser are all able to appear simultaneously during briefings and still keep a safe distance from one another.
Col R Stickler, Prestwick

TODAY I finally achieved my childhood ambition of eating a whole Fray Bentos steak pie to myself. Never give up on your dreams, people!
Laird of Darkness, B'pool

ONE OF the finest comedy noises used to be a car backfiring, and people pretending to have been shot. Modern cars are much more reliable and consequently less fun. We can only hope that with Brexit dragging us back to the 1950s, cars will once again start backfiring and causing amusement once more.
Arty Choke, Cornwall

WHY AREN'T these aliens who go around sticking probes up people's bums called 'analiens'. And why our bottoms? Surely there must be plenty of arseholes on their own planet they could perform their sordid 'science' on?
Stew, Perth

Tacklebocks
This month's fishiest letters

WHEN PEOPLE go fishing, they use worms to attract fish. But worms live in the ground and fish live in the sea, so how can fish eat worms? In fact, how does a fish even know what a worm is? I thought of sending this letter to the *International Journal of Biological Sciences*, but they don't give out pencils, so I went with *Viz* instead.
Peter Chainey, Manchester

I'LL NEVER understand salmon. They complete the almost impossible task of navigating the Atlantic, scaling waterfalls and dodging predators on the epic journey to their original spawning grounds. Then they go and get caught by eating a feather disguised as a fly dangling on a piece of string.
Lindsey Doyle, Pickering

Jokes that Arguably Work Better Spoken Outloud Rather than Written Down

No. 388 "Petit Four"

"...AND I'VE MARKED THE LEVEL ON MY MILK SO I'LL KNOW IF ANY OF YOU LOT HAVE HELPED YOURSELVES."

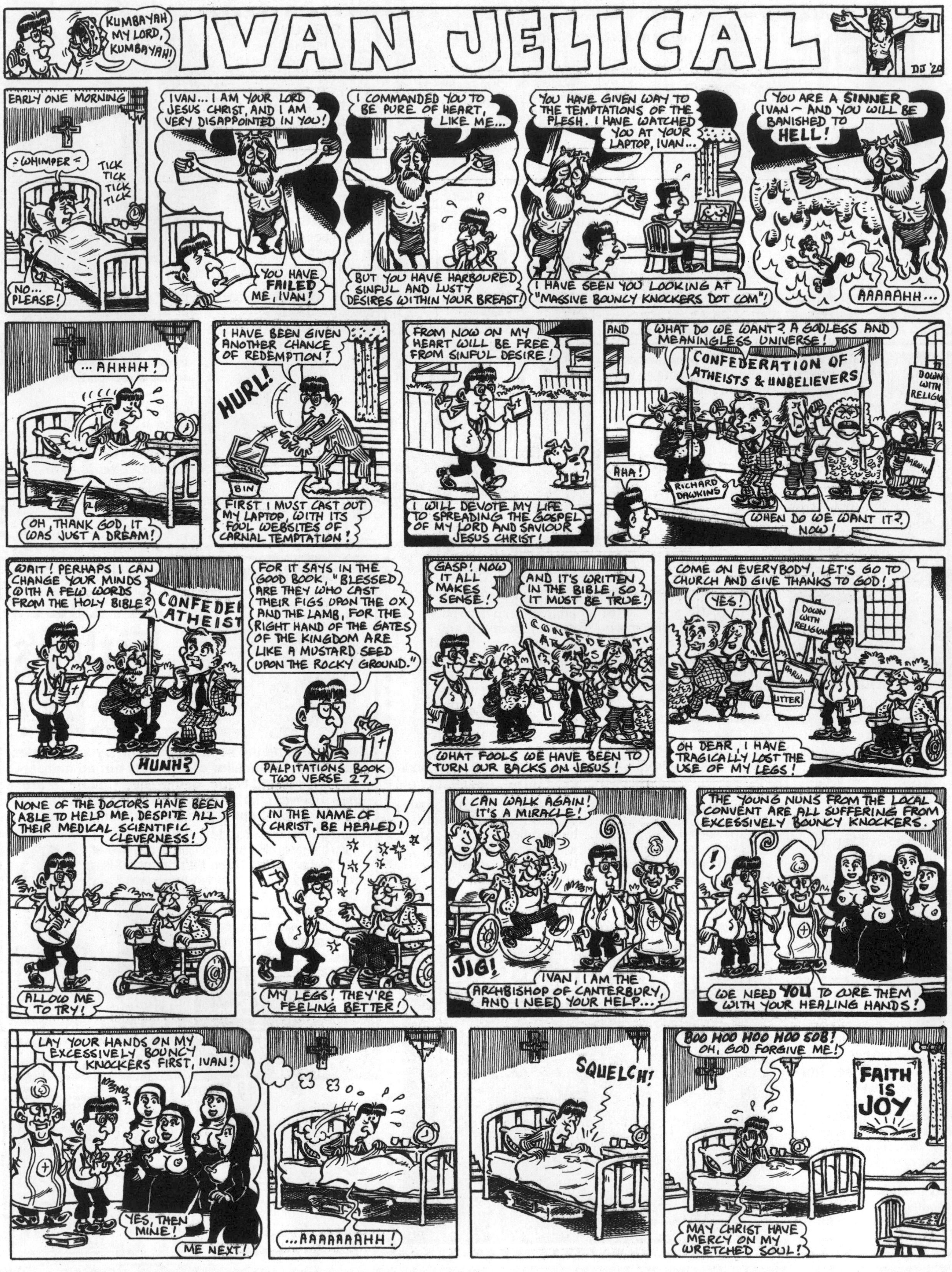
KUMBAYAH MY LORD, KUMBAYAH!
IVAN JELICAL
DJ '20
EARLY ONE MORNING
WHIMPER
TICK TICK TICK TICK
NO... PLEASE!
IVAN... I AM YOUR LORD JESUS CHRIST, AND I AM VERY DISAPPOINTED IN YOU!
YOU HAVE FAILED ME, IVAN!
I COMMANDED YOU TO BE PURE OF HEART, LIKE ME...
BUT YOU HAVE HARBOURED SINFUL AND LUSTY DESIRES WITHIN YOUR BREAST!
YOU HAVE GIVEN WAY TO THE TEMPTATIONS OF THE FLESH. I HAVE WATCHED YOU AT YOUR LAPTOP, IVAN...
I HAVE SEEN YOU LOOKING AT "MASSIVE BOUNCY KNOCKERS DOT COM"!
YOU ARE A SINNER IVAN – AND YOU WILL BE BANISHED TO HELL!
AAAAAHH...
...AHHHH!
OH, THANK GOD, IT WAS JUST A DREAM!
I HAVE BEEN GIVEN ANOTHER CHANCE OF REDEMPTION!
HURL!
BIN
FIRST I MUST CAST OUT MY LAPTOP, WITH ITS FOUL WEBSITES OF CARNAL TEMPTATION!
FROM NOW ON MY HEART WILL BE FREE FROM SINFUL DESIRE!
I WILL DEVOTE MY LIFE TO SPREADING THE GOSPEL OF MY LORD AND SAVIOUR JESUS CHRIST!
AND
WHAT DO WE WANT? A GODLESS AND MEANINGLESS UNIVERSE!
CONFEDERATION OF ATHEISTS & UNBELIEVERS
DOWN WITH RELIGIO
AHA!
RICHARD DAWKINS
DARWIN
WHEN DO WE WANT IT? NOW!
WAIT! PERHAPS I CAN CHANGE YOUR MINDS WITH A FEW WORDS FROM THE HOLY BIBLE?
CONFEDEI ATHEIST
HUNH?
FOR IT SAYS IN THE GOOD BOOK, "BLESSED ARE THEY WHO CAST THEIR FIGS UPON THE OX AND THE LAMB, FOR THE RIGHT HAND OF THE GATES OF THE KINGDOM ARE LIKE A MUSTARD SEED UPON THE ROCKY GROUND."
PALPITATIONS BOOK TWO VERSE 27.
GASP! NOW IT ALL MAKES SENSE!
AND IT'S WRITTEN IN THE BIBLE, SO IT MUST BE TRUE!
WHAT FOOLS WE HAVE BEEN TO TURN OUR BACKS ON JESUS!
COME ON EVERYBODY, LET'S GO TO CHURCH AND GIVE THANKS TO GOD!
YES!
DOWN WITH RELIGION
LITTER
OH DEAR, I HAVE TRAGICALLY LOST THE USE OF MY LEGS!
NONE OF THE DOCTORS HAVE BEEN ABLE TO HELP ME, DESPITE ALL THEIR MEDICAL SCIENTIFIC CLEVERNESS!
ALLOW ME TO TRY!
IN THE NAME OF CHRIST, BE HEALED!
MY LEGS! THEY'RE FEELING BETTER!
I CAN WALK AGAIN! IT'S A MIRACLE!
JIG!
IVAN, I AM THE ARCHBISHOP OF CANTERBURY, AND I NEED YOUR HELP...
THE YOUNG NUNS FROM THE LOCAL CONVENT ARE ALL SUFFERING FROM EXCESSIVELY BOUNCY KNOCKERS.
!
WE NEED YOU TO CURE THEM WITH YOUR HEALING HANDS!
LAY YOUR HANDS ON MY EXCESSIVELY BOUNCY KNOCKERS FIRST, IVAN!
YES, THEN MINE!
ME NEXT!
...AAAAAAAH!
SQUELCH!
BOO HOO HOO HOO SOB! OH, GOD FORGIVE ME!
FAITH IS JOY
MAY CHRIST HAVE MERCY ON MY WRETCHED SOUL!

Government in Surprise U-turn on Male Menopause Regulations

PONYTAILS OF THE UNEXPECTED

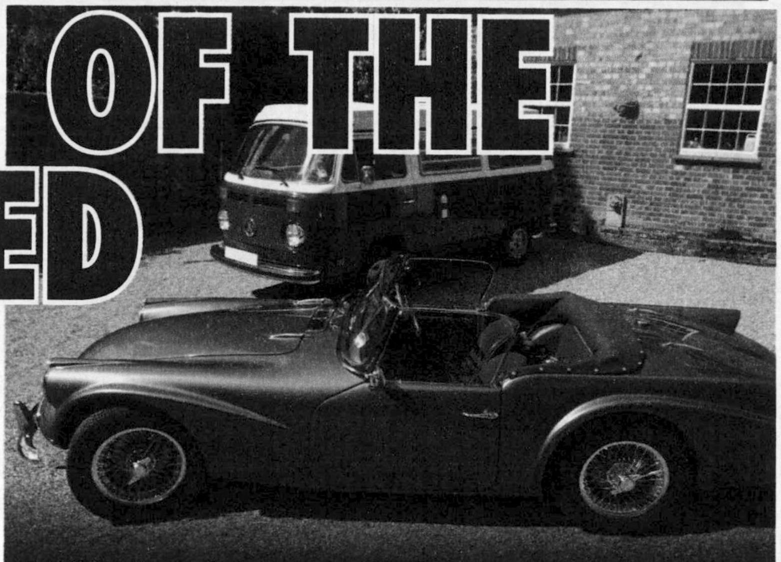

Fast living: *New parliamentary bill overhauls outdated male midlife crisis laws.*

THERE were jubilant scenes outside the Houses of Parliament last night as men's welfare groups celebrated a cross-party parliamentary committee's decision to overhaul outdated laws governing male MIDLIFE CRISES in England and Wales. The changes will come into effect from next year and could affect up to 6 million middle-aged men with diminishing levels of male sex hormones.

The sweeping changes are expected to pass through the Commons unopposed, and will bring the male midlife crisis into the 21st century.

OUT will go dated goatee beards, tattoos, braided bracelets, and functional alcoholism. **IN** will come carbon fibre racing bikes, along with undersized lycra tops, tongue piercings, anal bleaching and spouting uninformed incoherent bollocks on Twitter.

"Britain has a long and proud tradition of increasingly reckless, embarrassing and foolhardy behaviour from its middle-aged men," committee chairman, Hector Mantovani told lobby reporters. "Field Marshal Montgomery had 'Mild' and 'Bitter' tattooed around his nipples on his 42nd birthday, whilst Alan Titchmarsh's botched Prince Albert is the stuff of legend."

"Out of the blue, middle-aged men find themselves forced to confront the insignificance of their mundane existence, coupled with their inevitable demise, and we should support them in their futile attempts to recapture a largely misremembered youth," he said.

bald

The report said the committee recognises the challenges faced by an increasingly ageing population, and accepts that British mid-life crisis laws have remained largely unaltered since the 1980s. Sweeping changes were felt necessary to enable Britain's stressed and confused middle-aged men to enjoy a 'World-beating' crisis fit for the 21st century.

The report was welcomed across the house, with Chancellor of the Exchequer Rishi Sunak promising additional funding. "We're pledging to invest £1billion over the next two years to ensure British men's outward displays of their borderline nervous breakdowns will be the envy of the world," he said.

There were also suggestions of raising the qualifying age limit for having a male mid-life crisis from its current 49 to 55. According to the report, this would allow individuals more time to complete a full blown, public display of age-related psychiatric meltdown. But the committee also recommended that several key tropes should remain firmly in place.

"Some things will not be changed by the new bill," Mantovani assured reporters. "Sporting a ponytail, despite being otherwise as bald as a coot will remain the cornerstone of the mid-life crisis," he said.

"And deserting a long suffering wife in favour of a gold-digging stunner half your age will be ring-fenced, along with making a spectacle of yourself by dressing up like a Power Ranger and riding a ludicrously powerful motorcycle which bears no resemblance to the Yamaha 50cc FSIE you last rode in 1980," he added.

ARE *YOU* HAVING A MIDLIFE CRISIS?

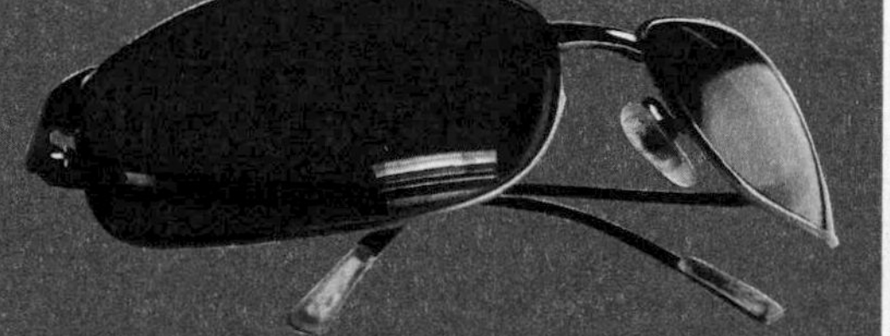

WE see men going through their midlife crisis every day; whether it's making lewd comments to women 20 years their junior in the workplace, taking out finance on a Testarossa at the Ferrari showroom, or shouting ill-researched bullshit through a megaphone on the street corner. But before you point and laugh, have you considered that *YOU* might be going through the male menopause? All men experience a midlife crisis at some point in their lives, *and you could be going through yours right now.*

So why not take our fun quiz to find out? Simply answer the following questions truthfully, tot up your answers, and see if you are going through a male pattern midlife meltdown.

1. **How would you describe your facial hair?**
   a. *Clean shaven. There's not really much point in making work for yourself.*
   b. *A Noel Edmonds-style tidy beard, treated with a light touch of Just for Men.*
   c. *An enormous twirly-tipped waxed moustache, exquisitely maintained pointed sideburns and a stupid plaited Viking beard.*
2. **You could do with some clothes, so you go shopping for a new outfit. What do you buy?**
   a. *A stylish suit with a sober shirt and a pair of brogues from a gent's outfitter.*
   b. *A pair of M&S Chinos, matching polo shirt, a pair of deck shoes and a sweater inexplicably draped over your shoulders.*
   c. *A white, skin-tight Calvin Klein T-shirt, ripped Tommy Hilfiger jeans, Oakley sun glasses and a pair of designer sneakers costing more than a family hatchback.*
3. **What is your normal bedtime routine?**
   a. *You usually turn in about 10pm with a good book, whilst catching a roundup of the day's news on Radio 4*
   b. *You tend to drop off around midnight after a glass of wine and maybe a weekly attempt at some perfunctory sex with your wife.*
   c. *You arrive home at 6 in the morning, dishevelled and still ripped to the tits on MDMA after spending the night throwing ludicrous shapes and waving glow sticks at an illegal rave at an out of town warehouse.*
4. **A scuffle between a group of young men half your age breaks out in your local. How do you react?**
   a. *Just keep your head down, hoping the security staff will deal swiftly with the troublemakers.*
   b. *Ensure you are between your wife and the participants, appearing ready to step in if they get too close and inviting your wife to hold you back. You did, after all, box at school.*
   c. *Strip to the waist and angrily enquire whether any of the miscreants fucking wants some.*
5. **You pop to the shops to buy a pint of milk. How will you get there?**
   a. *Cycle, or maybe take a brisk walk. It's only a short distance and the exercise will do you good.*
   b. *You drive there in an eco-friendly Hybrid vehicle.*
   c. *On a Honda Fireblade, capable of a top speed in excess of 190mph, dressed head to toe in a gaudy, tasselled leather one-piece that would embarrass Evel Knievel.*

HOW DID YOU DO?

Mostly A's: Relax, you are not having a midlife crisis. You're comfortable in your skin and growing old fabulously. You are rightly proud of the way your life has worked out, you have a rock solid marriage and plenty of friends, and you know when the bins go out.

Mostly B's: You are not having a mid-life crisis, but you need to be careful as you could easily tip into one. Keep reminding yourself that you are closer to receiving a bus pass than you are to sprouting your first pubic hair. Get a new barber and buy a few Cotton Traders polo shirts and you should be able to safely negotiate the choppy waters of middle age without embarrassing your kids.

Mostly C's: Oh dear! You are bursting with regret and age-related angst, and in the midst of a humdinger of a midlife crisis. Despite your failed hair transplant and multiple Botox treatments, your face continues to resemble a badly ironed scrotum, and you continue to hold your ex-wife wholly responsible for your failure to achieve any of your life goals, including making it as a Premiership footballer.

NEXT ISSUE: "Are you a Bellend?"

TENDING AN ALLOTMENT is a tradition that dates back centuries. Since the 1500s, families have grown fruit and veg on these small plots of land, and they are more popular today than they have ever been. But whilst there are over 350,000 allotment holders in the UK, most normal people know very little about these community spaces. In fact, we only ever see them as a collection of broken greenhouses and piles of tyres flashing past the windows of a train. So lets's pull on our wellies, make a flask of tea, and see...

- ☐ **A man** for whom growing the largest leek in the allotment society show will be the highlight of his life, slashing his rival's seedlings with a Stanley knife.
- ☐ **A man** who doesn't like leeks, and whose wife doesn't like leeks, growing leeks, and only leeks, as he has done for the past 48 years.
- ☐ **A man** who took the plot on hoping his family and he would tend it and enjoy quality time together in the fresh air, digging on his own whilst his wife is at the bingo and his three kids are at home on the X-Box.
- ☐ **A man** pouring sump oil onto his plot neighbour's raised bed following a heated discussion over the best variety of outdoor tomato.
- ☐ **A member** of the Allotment Committee giving a woman a verbal warning couched as 'friendly advice' to remove a dandelion plant growing at the base of her shed.
- ☐ **A delegation** from the council making their twice yearly visit on the look out for any breach of council regulations they could use to justify closing the allotment, levelling the site and building 200 starter homes.
- ☐ **A man** cutting a branch of his apple tree that overhangs the neighbouring plot by two feet in order to prevent the holder helping himself to any fruit.
- ☐ **Two police** officers starting their shift, as they do every morning, by investigating the previous night's break-in at the Allotment Committee hut.
- ☐ **A woman** who keeps chickens on her plot, who fellow allotment holders blame for any sighting of a rat within 30 miles of her coop.
- ☐ **A member** of the Allotment Committee allegedly 'taking no pleasure' in issuing a written warning to a man whose hedge is 1.8cm higher than the regulations allow.
- ☐ **An old** man who claims that spending 16 hours a day on his allotment, every day for the past 50 years, is the secret of his long and happy marriage.
- ☐ **A man** who over his 35-year tenancy has amassed enough pornographic magazines to stock half the oil rigs in the north sea.
- ☐ **A man** who saw his wife adjusting her clothes whilst coming out of a fellow allotment holder's shed, spraying weedkiller onto the same man's runner beans.
- ☐ **A man** who refuses to use pesticides, herbicides or non-organic plant foods, taking his entire year's harvest home in a trug.
- ☐ **A man** who sprays his plants with all the agrochemical industry can come up with, harvesting so much stuff he can't give it away.
- ☐ **A member** of the Allotment Committee, drunk with power, who is nevertheless 'very sad' to have to take the ultimate sanction and terminate a holder's tenancy after she coiled the communal hosepipe anticlockwise on the hook rather than clockwise as per the regulations.
- ☐ **A man** whose wife suddenly moved to Canada to live with her sister, erecting a greenhouse on a newly laid patio area.
- ☐ **A man** whose 10m x 15m plot somehow manages to produce enough waste to enable him to light a smoke-billowing bonfire every day, including weekends and Christmas Day.
- ☐ **Three men** who don't look like gardeners and who spend most of the time on their mobile phones, but who nevertheless have a constant stream of customers buying whatever crop they are growing inside their large, translucent poly tunnel.
- ☐ **A man** who took dozens of orders to supply organic vegetable boxes having to use stuff bought from Aldi to supplement his own marble-sized onions and radishes.
- ☐ **A man** with an air rifle which is ostensibly for pigeons, winging a child who has climbed the fence to get his football back.
- ☐ **A pair** of retired solicitors who think that the rule about not bringing vehicles on to the allotment site doesn't apply to them, as the Range Rover Evoque R-Dynamic HSE is technically an agricultural vehicle.

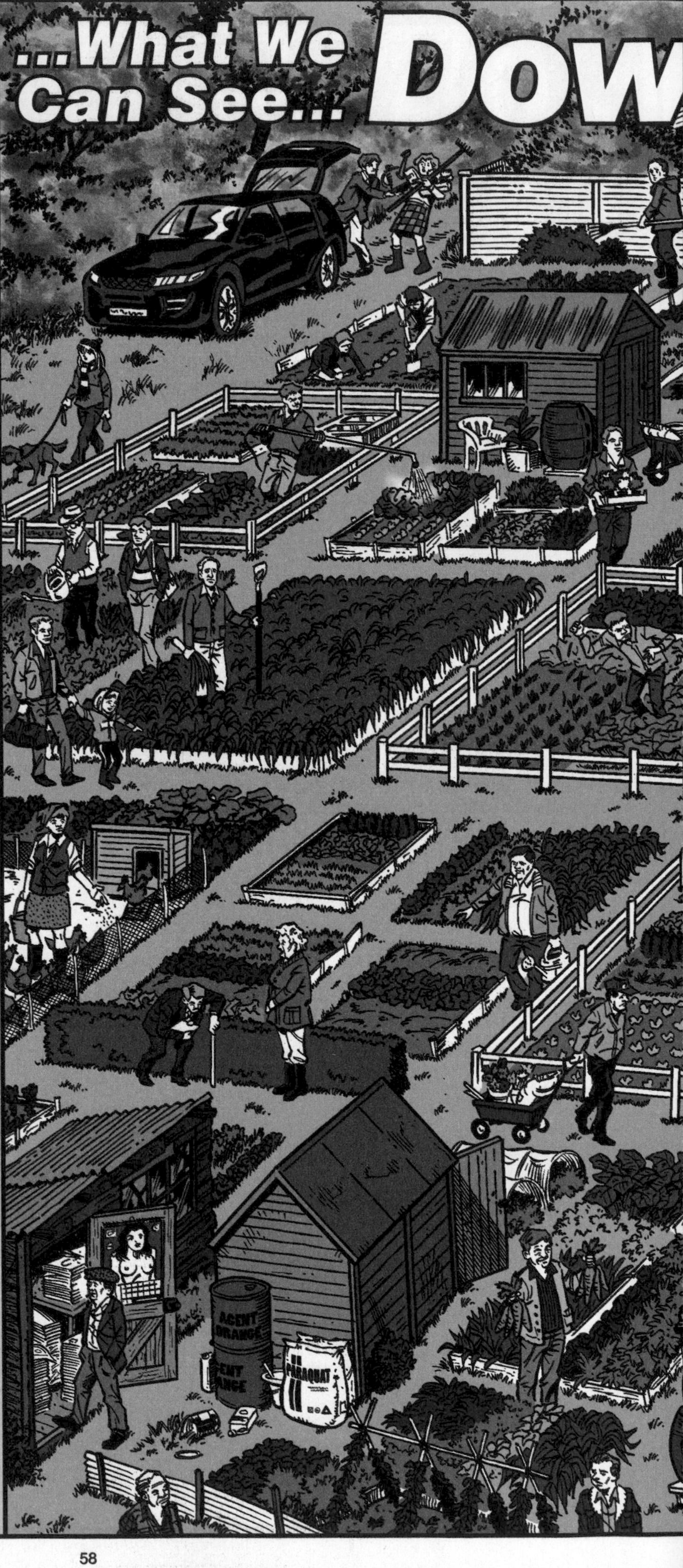

...What We Can See... Dow
AGENT ORANGE
PARAQUAT

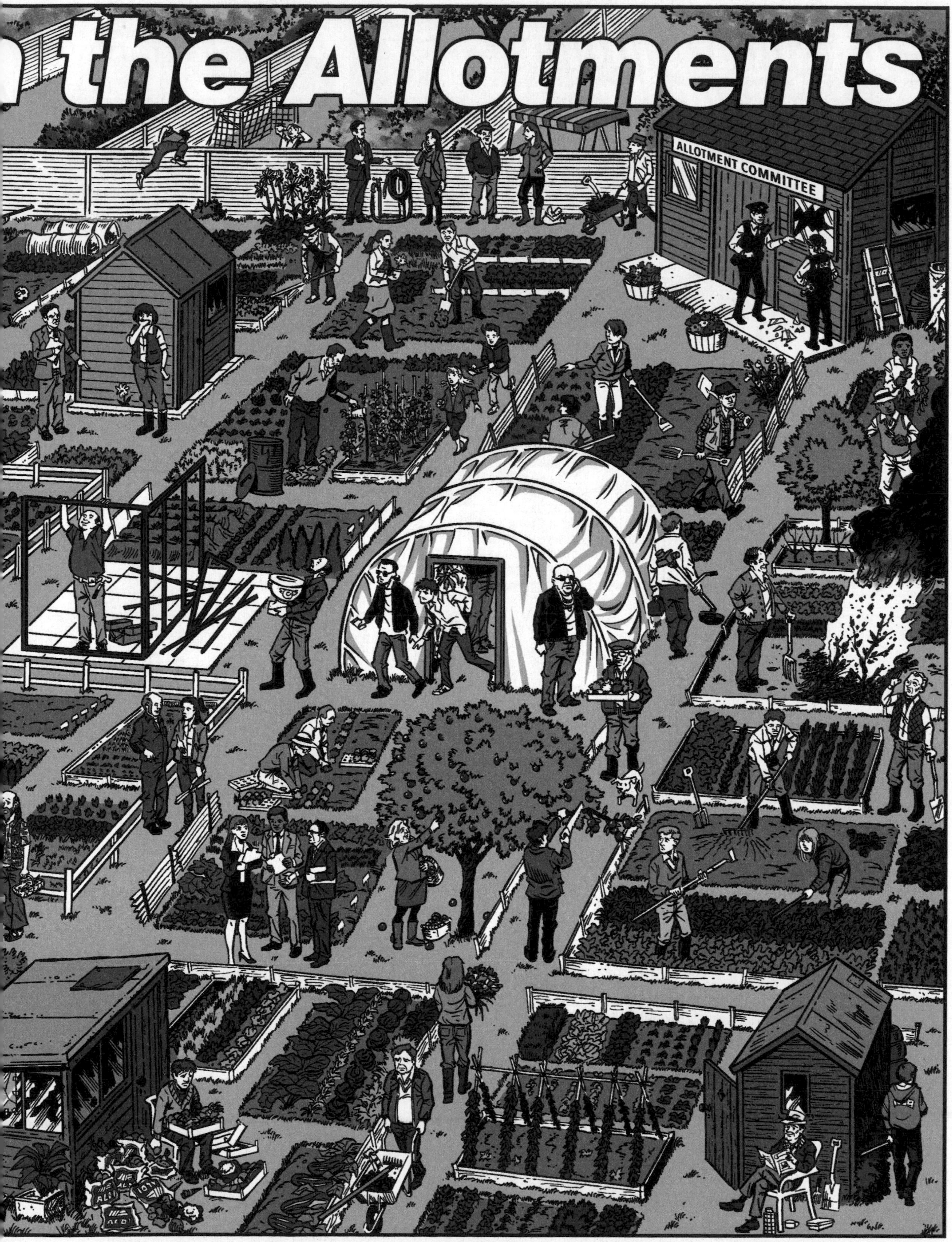
the Allotments
ALLOTMENT COMMITTEE

Adult Scientific Adventures in...
Prof. Sugar Chronos's Casebook

Nobel-Prize-winning theoretical physicist and adult film star Professor Sugar Chronos was in her laboratory at Oxford University, pondering her latest experimental results...

A cup of tea for you, Professor Chronos... and a Wagon Wheel.

...Oh... thank you Tom.

You seem a little distracted, today, Professor? Is your experiment going badly?

No, not all. On the contrary, in fact...

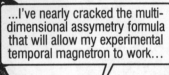

...I've nearly cracked the multi-dimensional assymetry formula that will allow my experimental temporal magnetron to work...

Wow!...

...that will allow Time Travel to become possible.

Exactly. If I could just think what shape the traversible wormhole would have to be in order to penetrate the quantum field...

Wait a minute... this Wagon Wheel looks small... didn't they used to be much bigger?

I'm not sure, Professor.

I mean, they were as big as your hand back in the day...

...I'm sure

Maybe your hands were smaller then... I mean, Einstein's relativity theory says...

No, they were massive...

...the size of a saucer!

Of course! That's it!

What is it, Professor?

Time assymetry must be circular!

What we call "time" is merely the interaction between particles in a trans-dimensional circular electric field..!

You mean...?!

"Events" and the passage of time are merely quantised perturbations in an assymetric circular matrix...

...which means...

...all I have to do to make Time Travel a reality is to reverse the polarity on the magnetron of my time podule!

There!...

...I've done it!

The whole of history is there for me to explore, from the age of the dinosaurs to far into the future when we will have all hover cars!

Where will you go first? The Last Days of Pompei? The Iron Age...? The Italian Renaissance...?

No, Tom...

...I'm going back in time to 1976 to find out how big Wagon Wheels were!

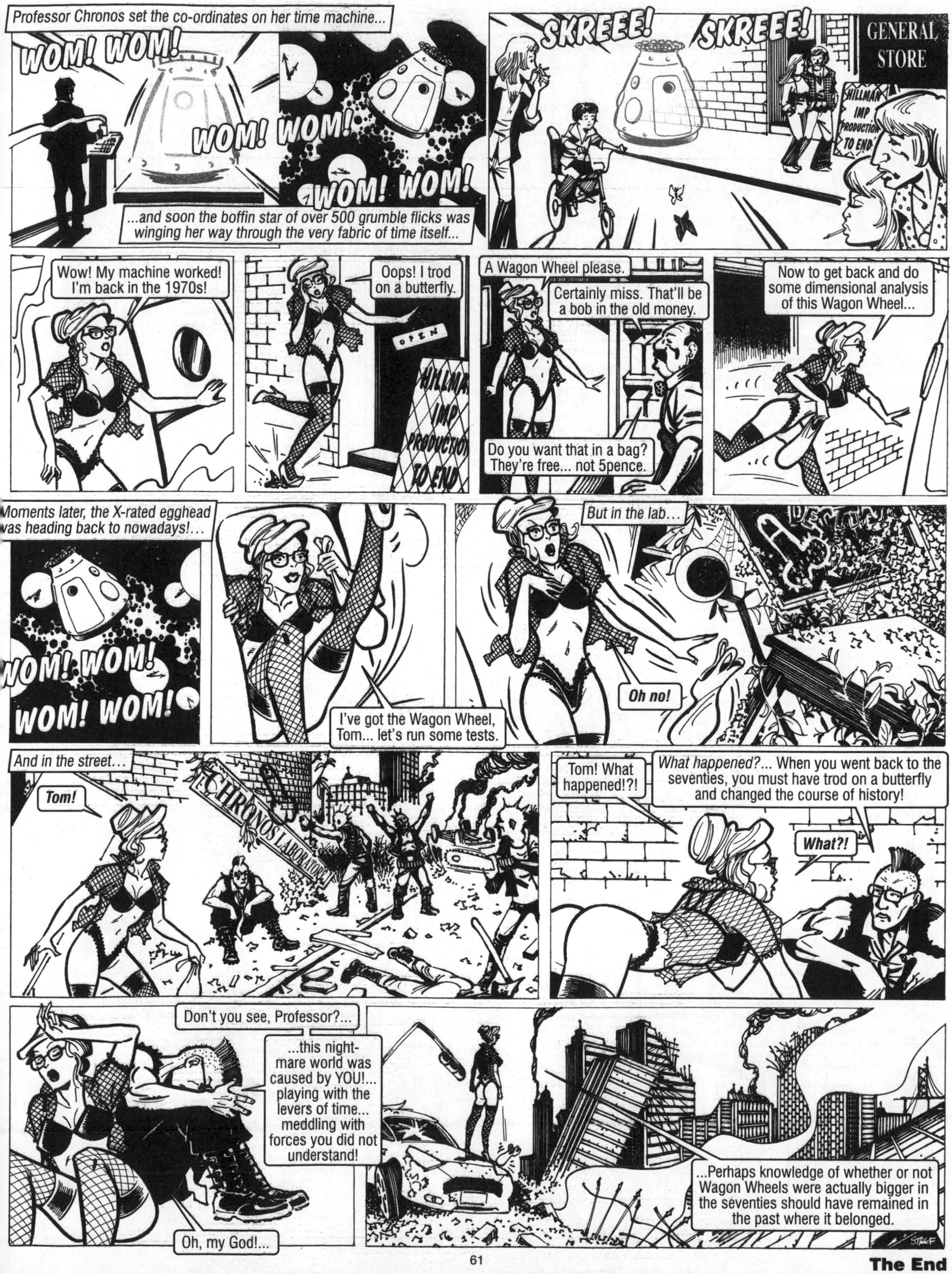

Professor Chronos set the co-ordinates on her time machine...
WOM! WOM!
WOM! WOM!
WOM! WOM!
...and soon the boffin star of over 500 grumble flicks was winging her way through the very fabric of time itself...
SKREEE!
SKREEE!
GENERAL STORE
HILLMAN IMP PRODUCTION TO END
Wow! My machine worked! I'm back in the 1970s!
Oops! I trod on a butterfly.
OPEN
HILLMAN IMP PRODUCTION TO END
A Wagon Wheel please.
Certainly miss. That'll be a bob in the old money.
Do you want that in a bag? They're free... not 5pence.
Now to get back and do some dimensional analysis of this Wagon Wheel...
Moments later, the X-rated egghead was heading back to nowadays!...
WOM! WOM!
WOM! WOM!
I've got the Wagon Wheel, Tom... let's run some tests.
But in the lab...
Oh no!
And in the street...
Tom!
CHRONOS LABORATORY
Tom! What happened!?!
What happened?... When you went back to the seventies, you must have trod on a butterfly and changed the course of history!
What?!
Don't you see, Professor?...
...this night-mare world was caused by YOU!... playing with the levers of time... meddling with forces you did not understand!
Oh, my God!...
...Perhaps knowledge of whether or not Wagon Wheels were actually bigger in the seventies should have remained in the past where it belonged.

The End

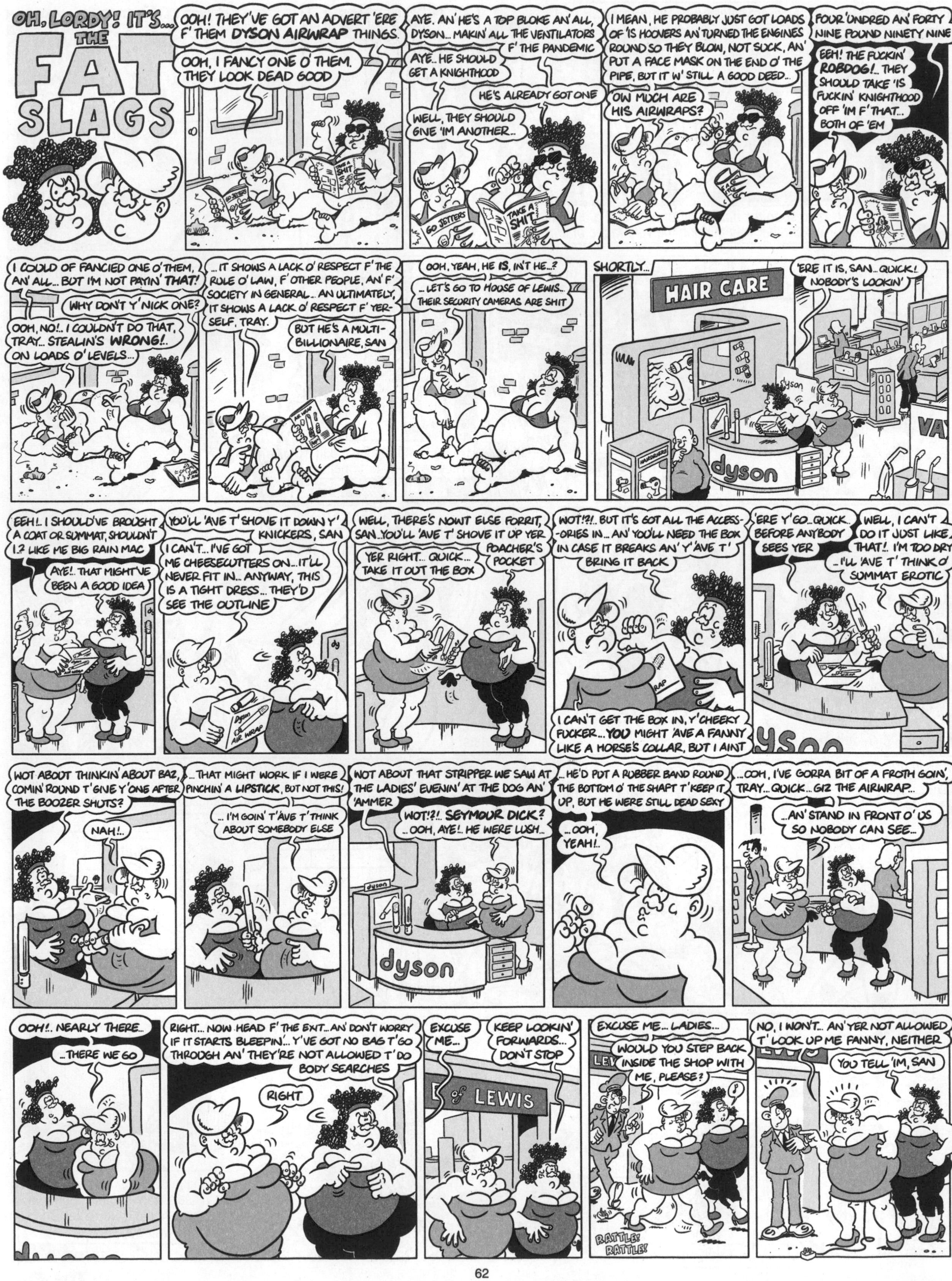
OH, LORDY! IT'S... THE FAT SLAGS
OOH! THEY'VE GOT AN ADVERT 'ERE F' THEM DYSON AIRWRAP THINGS.
OOH, I FANCY ONE O' THEM. THEY LOOK DEAD GOOD
GO JETTERS
TAKE A SHIT
AYE. AN' HE'S A TOP BLOKE AN' ALL, DYSON... MAKIN' ALL THE VENTILATORS F' THE PANDEMIC
AYE.. HE SHOULD GET A KNIGHTHOOD
HE'S ALREADY GOT ONE
WELL, THEY SHOULD GIVE 'IM ANOTHER...
GO JETTERS
TAKE A SHIT
I MEAN, HE PROBABLY JUST GOT LOADS OF 'IS HOOVERS AN' TURNED THE ENGINES ROUND SO THEY BLOW, NOT SUCK, AN' PUT A FACE MASK ON THE END O' THE PIPE, BUT IT W' STILL A GOOD DEED...
'OW MUCH ARE HIS AIRWRAPS?
FOUR 'UNDRED AN' FORTY NINE POUND NINETY NINE
EEH! THE FUCKIN' ROBDOG!.. THEY SHOULD TAKE 'IS FUCKIN' KNIGHTHOOD OFF 'IM F' THAT... BOTH OF 'EM
I COULD OF FANCIED ONE O' THEM, AN' ALL... BUT I'M NOT PAYIN' THAT!
WHY DON'T Y' NICK ONE?
OOH, NO!.. I COULDN'T DO THAT, TRAY... STEALIN'S WRONG!.. ON LOADS O' LEVELS...
...IT SHOWS A LACK O' RESPECT F' THE RULE O' LAW, F' OTHER PEOPLE, AN' F' SOCIETY IN GENERAL.. AN ULTIMATELY, IT SHOWS A LACK O' RESPECT F' YER-SELF, TRAY.
BUT HE'S A MULTI-BILLIONAIRE, SAN
OOH, YEAH, HE IS, IN'T HE..?
...LET'S GO TO HOUSE OF LEWIS... THEIR SECURITY CAMERAS ARE SHIT
SHORTLY...
HAIR CARE
'ERE IT IS, SAN... QUICK!.. NOBODY'S LOOKIN'
dyson
EEH!.. I SHOULD'VE BROUGHT A COAT OR SUMMAT, SHOULDN'T I..? LIKE ME BIG RAIN MAC
AYE!.. THAT MIGHT'VE BEEN A GOOD IDEA
YOU'LL 'AVE T' SHOVE IT DOWN Y' KNICKERS, SAN
I CAN'T... I'VE GOT ME CHEESECUTTERS ON... IT'LL NEVER FIT IN... ANYWAY, THIS IS A TIGHT DRESS... THEY'D SEE THE OUTLINE
AIR WRAP
WELL, THERE'S NOWT ELSE FORRIT, SAN... YOU'LL 'AVE T' SHOVE IT UP YER POACHER'S POCKET
YER RIGHT... QUICK... TAKE IT OUT THE BOX
WOT!?!.. BUT IT'S GOT ALL THE ACCESS-ORIES IN... AN' YOU'LL NEED THE BOX IN CASE IT BREAKS AN' Y' 'AVE T' BRING IT BACK
I CAN'T GET THE BOX IN, Y' CHEEKY FUCKER... YOU MIGHT 'AVE A FANNY LIKE A HORSE'S COLLAR, BUT I AIN'T
'ERE Y' GO... QUICK... BEFORE ANYBODY SEES YER
WELL, I CAN'T DO IT JUST LIKE THAT!.. I'M TOO DRY ...I'LL 'AVE T' THINK O' SUMMAT EROTIC
WOT ABOUT THINKIN' ABOUT BAZ, COMIN' ROUND T' GIVE Y' ONE AFTER THE BOOZER SHUTS?
NAH!..
...THAT MIGHT WORK IF I WERE PINCHIN' A LIPSTICK, BUT NOT THIS!
...I'M GOIN' T' 'AVE T' THINK ABOUT SOMEBODY ELSE
WOT ABOUT THAT STRIPPER WE SAW AT THE LADIES' EVENIN' AT THE DOG AN' 'AMMER
WOT!?!.. SEYMOUR DICK? ...OOH, AYE!.. HE WERE LUSH...
dyson
...HE'D PUT A RUBBER BAND ROUND THE BOTTOM O' THE SHAFT T' KEEP IT UP, BUT HE WERE STILL DEAD SEXY
...OOH, YEAH!..
...OOH, I'VE GORRA BIT OF A FROTH GOIN', TRAY... QUICK... GIZ THE AIRWRAP...
...AN' STAND IN FRONT O' US SO NOBODY CAN SEE...
OOH!.. NEARLY THERE...
...THERE WE GO
RIGHT... NOW HEAD F' THE EXIT... AN' DON'T WORRY IF IT STARTS BLEEPIN'... Y'VE GOT NO BAG T' GO THROUGH AN' THEY'RE NOT ALLOWED T' DO BODY SEARCHES
RIGHT
EXCUSE ME...
KEEP LOOKIN' FORWARDS... DON'T STOP
of LEWIS
EXCUSE ME... LADIES...
WOULD YOU STEP BACK INSIDE THE SHOP WITH ME, PLEASE?
RATTLE! RATTLE!
NO, I WON'T... AN' YER NOT ALLOWED T' LOOK UP ME FANNY, NEITHER
YOU TELL 'IM, SAN

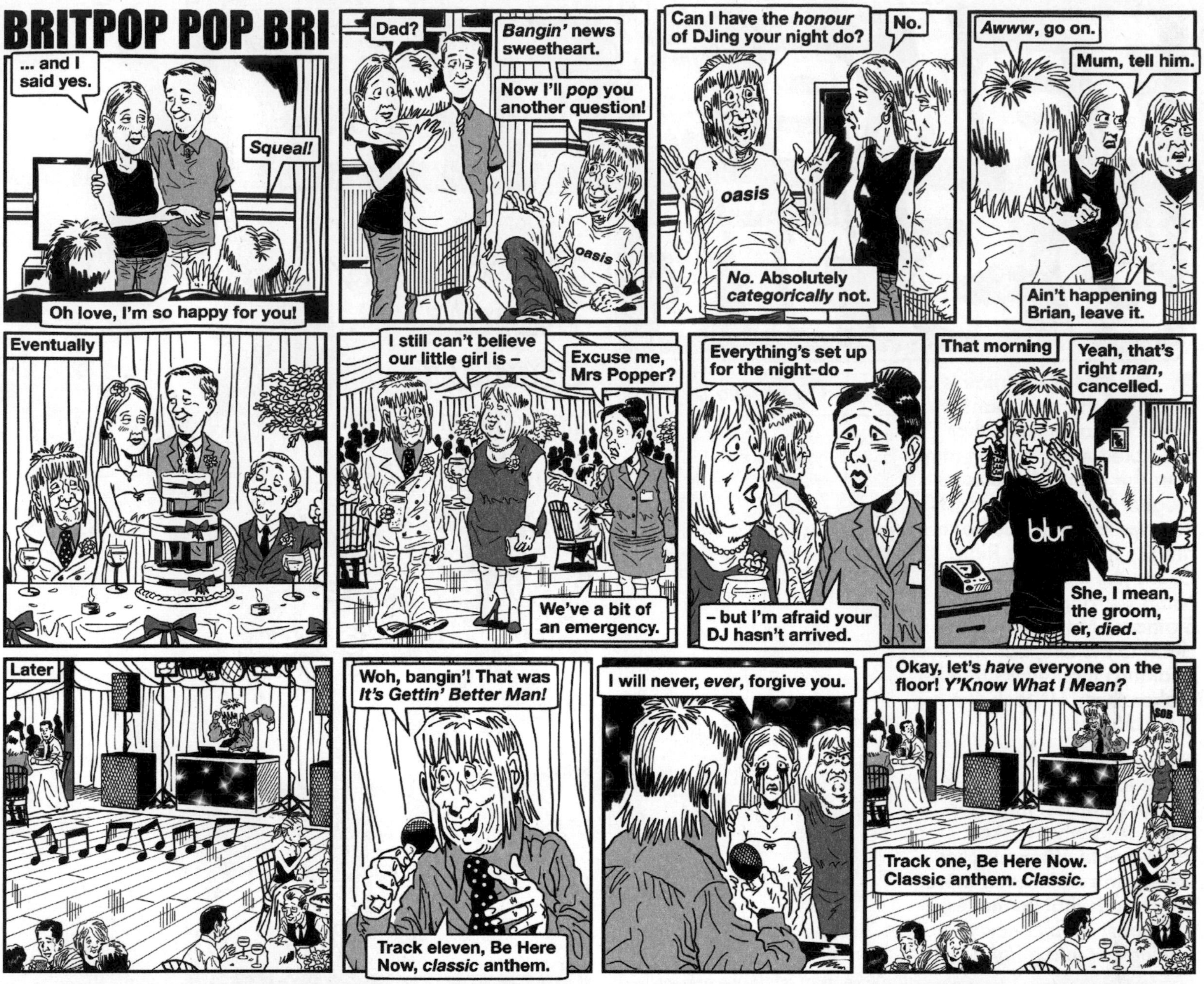
BRITPOP POP BRI
... and I said yes.
Squeal!
Oh love, I'm so happy for you!
Dad?
Bangin' news sweetheart.
Now I'll *pop* you another question!
oasis
Can I have the *honour* of DJing your night do?
No.
oasis
No. Absolutely *categorically* not.
Awww, go on.
Mum, tell him.
Ain't happening Brian, leave it.
Eventually
I still can't believe our little girl is –
Excuse me, Mrs Popper?
We've a bit of an emergency.
Everything's set up for the night-do –
– but I'm afraid your DJ hasn't arrived.
That morning
Yeah, that's right *man*, cancelled.
blur
She, I mean, the groom, er, *died*.
Later
Woh, bangin'! That was *It's Gettin' Better Man!*
Track eleven, Be Here Now, *classic* anthem.
I will never, *ever*, forgive you.
Okay, let's *have* everyone on the floor! *Y'Know What I Mean?*
Track one, Be Here Now. Classic anthem. *Classic.*

ALL TO CLOCK!

AN AUSTRALIAN tourist holidaying in the UK was left shocked and disorientated after glancing at his watch and seeing the hands moving in a different direction to the way they did back home.

Ausie can't believe watch goes clockwise

Holidaying sheep-shearer Mick Aberdeen noticed the strange phenomenon whilst waiting for the tube at Heathrow airport.

"The first time I saw my watch with the hands going round clockwise, I thought it must be crocked," laughed the 52-year-old New South Wales resident, adjusting the corks on his hat.

platform

"But then I saw the clock on the station platform was doing the same thing, and I wondered if I'd got myself caught up in some sort of time-travel caper. Strewth," he continued.

"Down under in Oz, the hands go round anti-clockwise, but it's all back-to-front up-over. I don't understand how you Poms deal with it," he added.

Physicist Professor Brian Cox explained that Mr Aberdeen had experienced something called the Coriolis effect, a principle of force that causes moving objects to spin in different directions in the north and south hemispheres.

"Anything that turns as it moves will demonstrate the Coriolis effect," the former D:Ream synth-stabber told us. "Water going down a plughole in the northern hemisphere will spin the right way, whereas it will go the wrong way south of the equator."

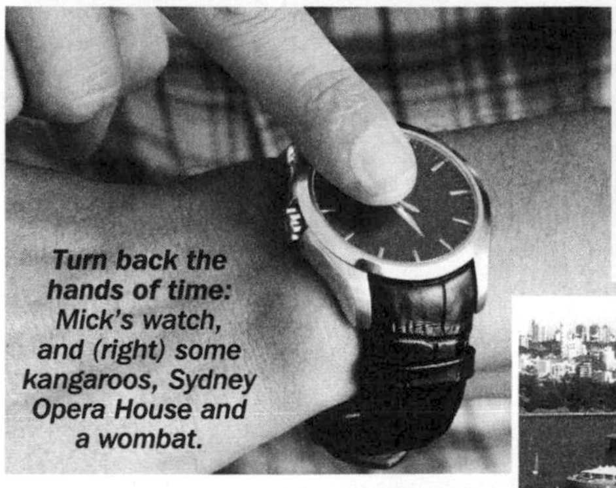

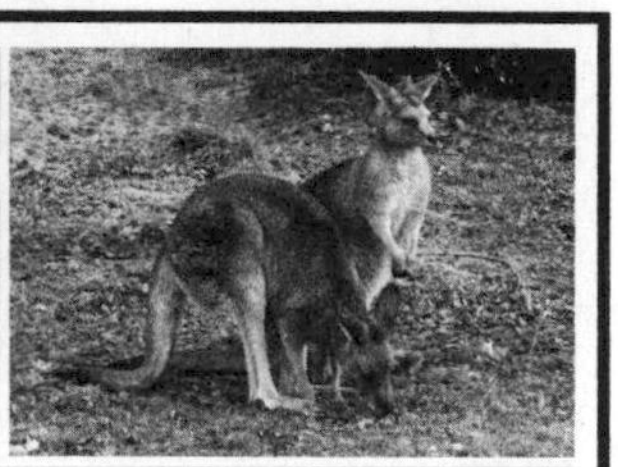

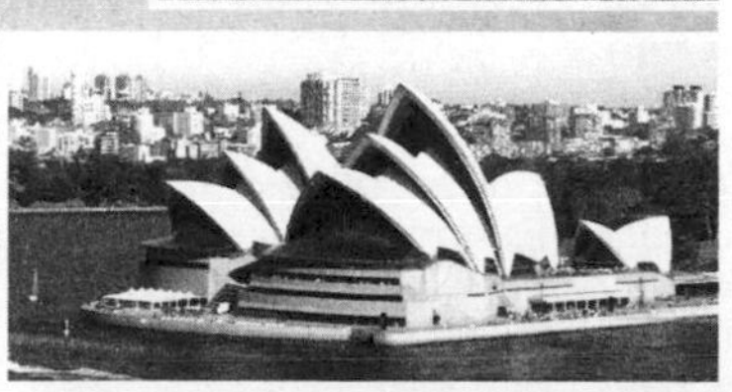

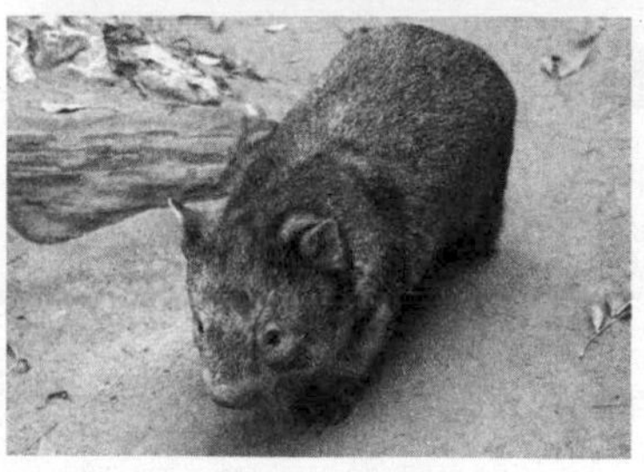

Turn back the hands of time: Mick's watch, and (right) some kangaroos, Sydney Opera House and a wombat.

"Mr Whippy ice-cream comes out the nozzle all to cock in Australia too. The Aussies hang their toilet rolls the wrong way round and their clocks go backwards," he explained. "That's why their daytime is our night-time. It's simple physics."

running

A spokeswoman for the UK Tourist Board said that the Coriolis effect can often be a disorienting experience for Australians coming to the UK. She told us: "My tip to visiting Aussies would be to turn their watches upside down for the first few days so that they appear to run the same way they do back home, just until they get used to things."

Take a Shit

WINNER MAGAZINE OF THE YEAR ~Take a Shit Magazine of the Year Awards

THE HAR

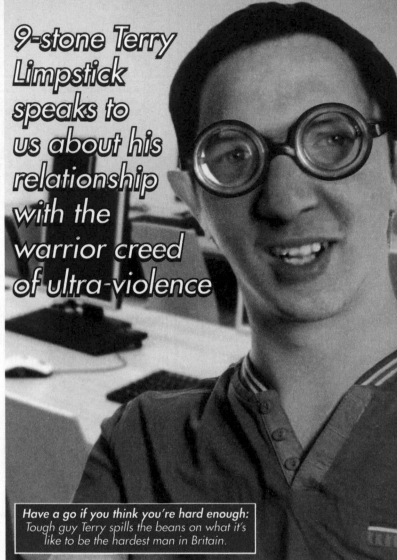

9-stone Terry Limpstick speaks to us about his relationship with the warrior creed of ultra-violence

Have a go if you think you're hard enough: *Tough guy Terry spills the beans on what it's like to be the hardest man in Britain.*

WHO IS Britain's hardest man? It's a question that has taxed many a keen mind over the years. Are boxers tougher than martial artists? Perhaps bareknuckle boxers are the Kings of the Ring? Or maybe it's cage fighters, Ninja warriors or Jason Statham? Many may lay claim to the title, but one East Midlands man thinks that he makes them ALL look like big girl's blouses.

Nottingham-born Terry Limpstick boasts that he is Britain's hardest man bar none. And what makes 23-year-old office supplies salesman's claim even more amazing is that he makes this boast *despite never having got into a fight!*

Speaking to reporters at the launch of his self-published autobiography *NEVER BACK DOWN – MY RISE TO THE TOP OF THE SCRAP HEAP*, 9-stone Terry spoke about his life and his relationship with the warrior creed of ultra-violence. "I don't care how big my opponent is, or how many of them there are, if someone made the mistake of crossing swords with me they'd know they'd been in a battle," he said.

The bespectacled father-of-none says that his story began in the school playground, an arena where so many of life's toughest lessons are learned.

"On my first day at comprehensive, I discovered that I was the only boy to turn up in short trousers, and I had also been placed in the top set. I knew that both of these factors would single me out for bullying, and it wasn't long before my first challenger tried his luck. I was standing in line at the end of playtime when someone – a boy I later found out to be called Stewart Penworthy – blatantly pushed in front of me.

Penworthy no doubt felt he could throw his below average weight around, having recently joined the school Dungeons & Dragons Club, but this tosser's many-sided dice weren't going to be of any help to him here. In such a situation a lesser boy than me might have sought assistance from a dinner lady, but I resolved to take matters into my own hands.

Without hesitation, I reclaimed my place in the queue and stared icily at my adversary's sandals. This was the key moment – I knew Penworthy's next move could trigger a sharp escalation in hostilities, and I was more than ready for it. *It was hammer time.* As luck would have it, for him at least, he backed down, claiming not to have realised I was there. It was a likely story, and he was clearly humbled by my aura of wiry inner strength. I could have pressed home my advantage there and then, but a successful hard case knows when not to fight, and this was one of those occasions.

My years at school were spent teaching lessons as well as learning – teaching boys not to attempt to flush my head down the toilets, not to steal my shoes and throw them on top of the maths block, not to burn the word TWAT onto my blazer with a bit of hot wire in a chemistry lesson. I only hope the perpetrators went on to become better people as a result of the discipline I meted out as the hardest kid in the school."

As told to *Vaginia Discharge*

SPAR-RING PARTNER

Over the years, Terry discovered that being hard often attracts trouble, as other bruisers try to assert their authority and become cock of the walk. Although he would rather avoid bother, Terry never shies away from putting such pretenders to his throne in their place.

"I remember one tasty experience from a few years ago. My mum had sent me to the Spar for a few essentials and I was reaching up for a bottle of ketchup, when... *BAM!*... someone crashed into the back of my legs with their trolley.

Like an uncoiling spring, I turned round to confront my assailant, a mountain of a man, easily six-foot-plus, broken nose, muscles in his spit. This man-monster would have given Mike Tyson nightmares, but not me. I decided to box clever; rather than going straight to Defcon-5 in the sauce aisle, I held his gaze for a split second, then threw him off his guard by apologising for having got in his way.

> "I held his gaze for a split second, then threw him off his guard by apologising for having got in his way."

This mind game was my way of ascertaining whether or not this was an accident on his part or an opening of hostilities. If he clattered his trolley into me again, the gloves would definitely have come off and I would have set about flattening him right there and then. If he didn't, this would prove it had been an honest mistake on his part and I could let it pass, all honour maintained. I had clearly laid down the gauntlet. The only question now was, would this brute be man enough to accept my unspoken challenge?

Luckily for him he saw sense. He clearly realised he'd bitten off more than he could chew and his bottle went. He pretended that he hadn't noticed me and I decided to leave it at that. As the late, great Freddie Mercury said... *'Another one bites the dust.'*"

DER THEY COME...

NARROW PATH OF THE RIGHTEOUS MAN

Anyone reading Terry's book might assume he went around looking for trouble. But the 9-stone one-man-army says otherwise, likening himself to his easy-going namesake Terry McCann from Minder. But he is such a magnet for action that even a peaceful afternoon stroll can quickly turn violent.

"The gang were clearly un-nerved as they were making a great show of chatting away and pretending not to see me."

"Only last week I was walking down a rather narrow path in Nottingham Arboretum, and I could see a gang of crazed delinquents heading towards me. I could tell they were bent on raising hell as one of them was brandishing a frisbee, and several were laughing to show how unperturbed they were by my presence.

The grass on either side of the path was wet and I didn't want to step onto it because Mum had already got up my arse once that week for treading mud into the house. By hogging the whole width of the path, these teen hoodlums were out to test my manhood... a test they were about to fail.

Obviously, as Britain's hardest man I wasn't going to give an inch, even though I was vastly outnumbered. Giving ground just isn't in my nature. This was what a physicist would no-doubt describe as an unstoppable force meeting an immovable object. It was game on.

With every step this motley crew of street toughs drew closer, showing no sign of altering their course. I held my nerve and looked them straight in the eye; my steely gaze said "this path ain't big enough for the both of us." The gang were clearly un-nerved as they were making a great show of chatting away and pretending not to see me. The gap between us shrank quickly. Ten metres. Five. Two. One. *Hammer time.*

Quick as a flash, I moved one step to my left, forcing my rivals to do likewise. This meant that I only got one shoe muddy but they got one shoe muddy *each*, leaving them much worse off. Victory was mine yet again."

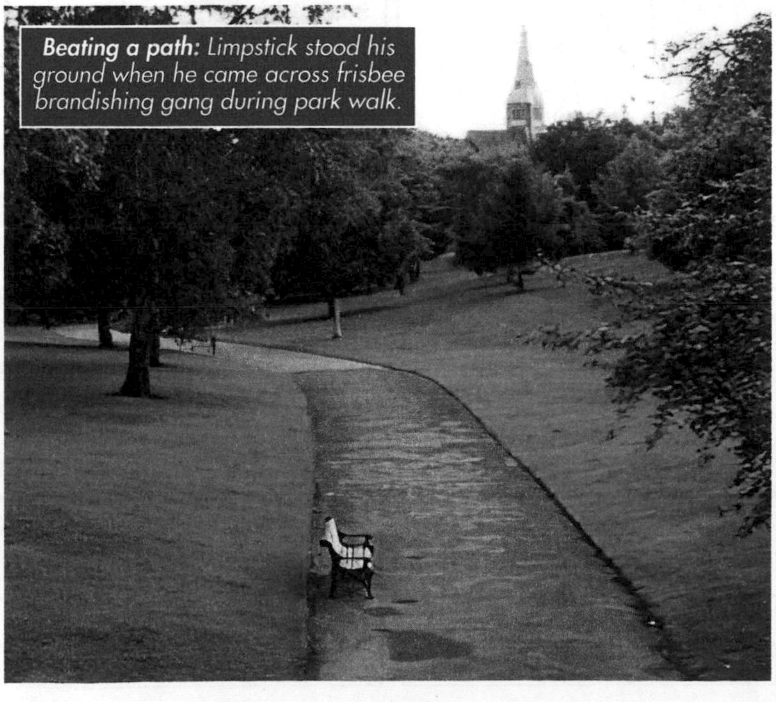

Beating a path: *Limpstick stood his ground when he came across frisbee brandishing gang during park walk.*

ROAD RAGE

After hearing such stories of testosterone-fuelled mayhem, you might be forgiven for thinking that Terry's life is just one brutal encounter after another. But as his book explains, despite a history rich in mortal combat, at heart Terry is a peace-loving man and a deep thinker; a true warrior philosopher. He has vowed never to use his extraordinary gift for extreme bodily harm unless provoked. Sadly, for Terry, such provocation is never far away.

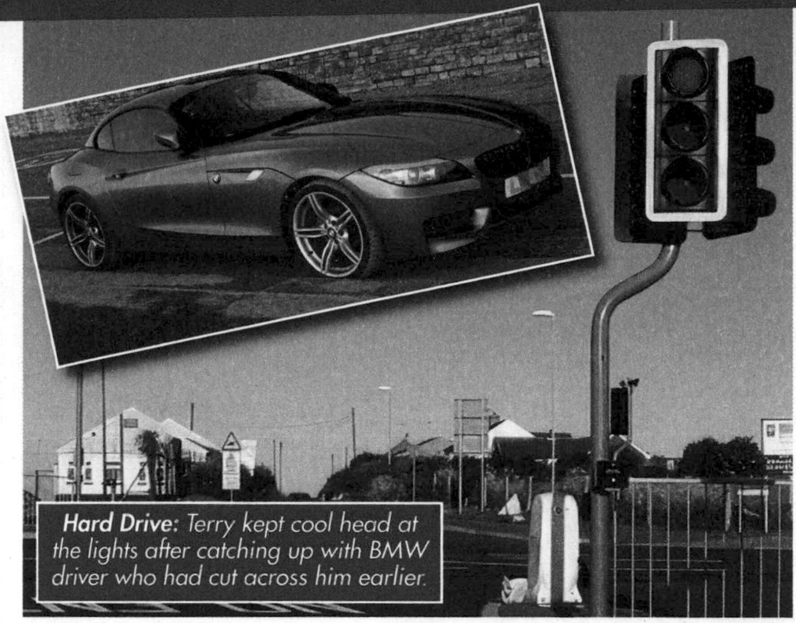

Hard Drive: *Terry kept cool head at the lights after catching up with BMW driver who had cut across him earlier.*

"I was driving to the chemist one day to pick up my bottom tablets when a BMW cut right across my path without signalling. I had to slam the Micra's anchors on and I was so angry I almost sounded my horn, but my cool inner Samurai swiftly quelled my hot-headed emotions. My retaliation would be more subtle and potentially lethal.

"I had to slam the Micra's anchors on and I was so angry I almost sounded my horn"

As is so often the case when some two-bob toss-pot burns you off the road, I caught up with my adversary at the next set of lights. My trap was set. Naturally, I could have jumped out of the car and dragged him into the road by his bollocks, before finishing him off with a roundhouse kick to the teeth. But instead, I decided to take him down with a bit of psychological warfare instead.

Sitting behind the beemer at the lights, I gazed angrily into his rear view mirror in the hope of making eye contact. This would be an open invitation for him to finish what he'd started, should he choose to accept. The lights seemed to stay red for an eternity as my steely gaze maintained its laser-like glare. *Go ahead, punk... Make my day.* Would the driver make the mistake of taking things to the next level?

A street-tough gladiator such as myself must be ready for action at all times, and I knew that every sinew of my body was primed. My knuckles turned white as I gripped the wheel of the Micra, revving the 1000cc engine aggressively. Sweat formed on my upper lip and I tried to control my breathing as adrenalin coursed through my veins. *Your move, Mr BMW.* Would he take the bait?

Suddenly, the lights changed and my enemy took flight as fast as his high-powered car could take him, screeching hard left into the Tesco Extra car park on Top Valley Drive. Our high stakes game of chicken was over without a single punch being thrown, and I'd been crowned cock of the walk. The driver in the beemer could clearly tell I meant business and had thought better of messing with Britain's hardest man. I wonder if he'll ever know how close he came to oblivion."

Terry hopes that his 46-page book will serve to educate and enthral his readers in equal measure. He told us: "It was never my ambition to be the toughest guy in town, but I've lived my life by the Warrior Code since day one." And he had this message for any would-be pretenders to his throne: *"Come and have a go if you think you're hard enough. You'll regret messing with Terry Limpstick, just ask anyone in Nottingham.*

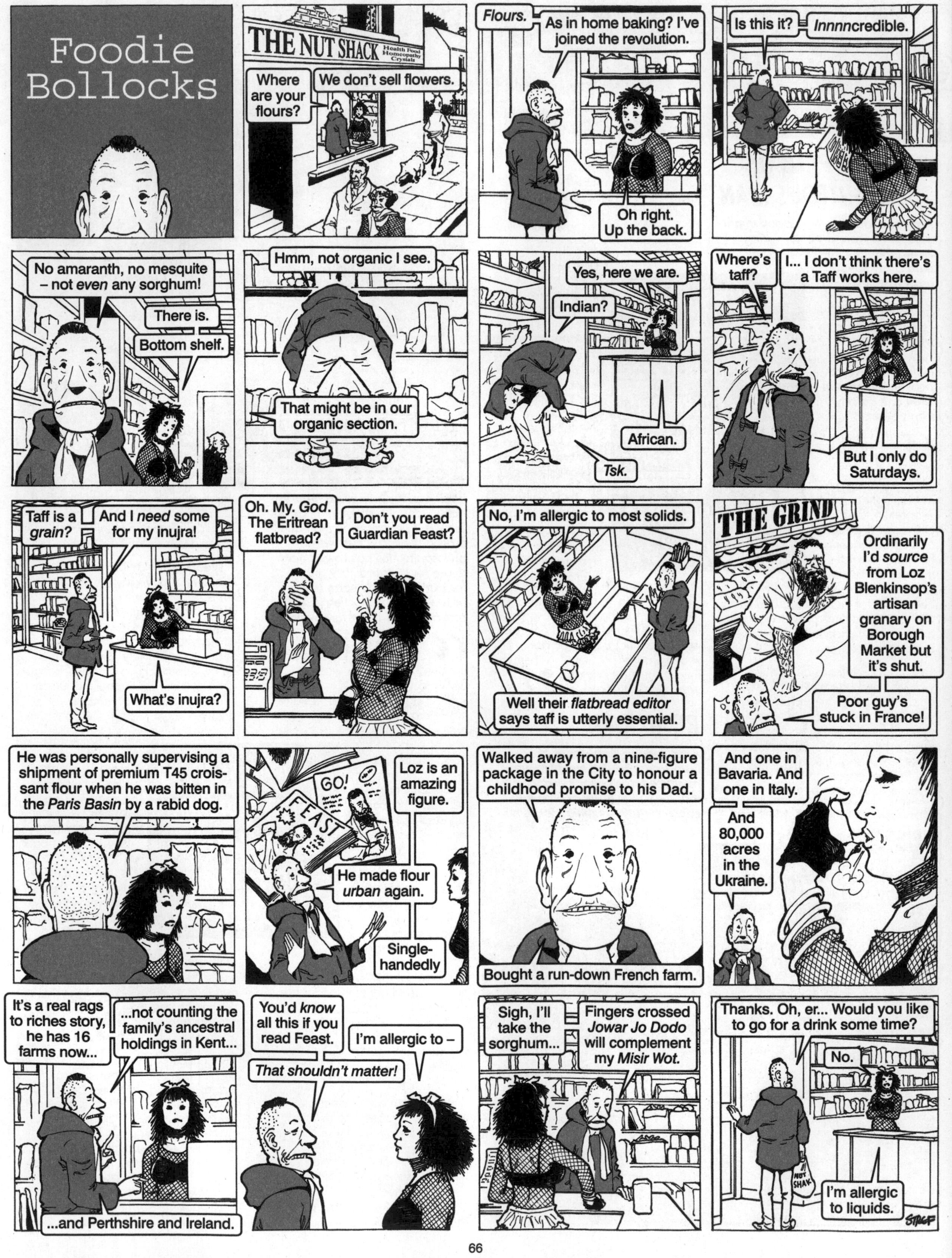
Foodie Bollocks
THE NUT SHACK
Health Food Homeopathy Crystals
Where are your flours?
We don't sell flowers.
Flours.
As in home baking? I've joined the revolution.
Oh right. Up the back.
Is this it?
Innnncredible.
No amaranth, no mesquite – not even any sorghum!
There is.
Bottom shelf.
Hmm, not organic I see.
That might be in our organic section.
Yes, here we are.
Indian?
African.
Tsk.
Where's taff?
I... I don't think there's a Taff works here.
But I only do Saturdays.
Taff is a grain?
And I need some for my inujra!
What's inujra?
Oh. My. God. The Eritrean flatbread?
Don't you read Guardian Feast?
No, I'm allergic to most solids.
Well their flatbread editor says taff is utterly essential.
THE GRIND
Ordinarily I'd source from Loz Blenkinsop's artisan granary on Borough Market but it's shut.
Poor guy's stuck in France!
He was personally supervising a shipment of premium T45 croissant flour when he was bitten in the Paris Basin by a rabid dog.
GO!
FEAST
Loz is an amazing figure.
He made flour urban again.
Single-handedly
Walked away from a nine-figure package in the City to honour a childhood promise to his Dad.
Bought a run-down French farm.
And one in Bavaria. And one in Italy.
And 80,000 acres in the Ukraine.
It's a real rags to riches story, he has 16 farms now...
...not counting the family's ancestral holdings in Kent...
...and Perthshire and Ireland.
You'd know all this if you read Feast.
I'm allergic to –
That shouldn't matter!
Sigh, I'll take the sorghum...
Fingers crossed Jowar Jo Dodo will complement my Misir Wot.
Thanks. Oh, er... Would you like to go for a drink some time?
No.
I'm allergic to liquids.
NUT SHAK
STRGF

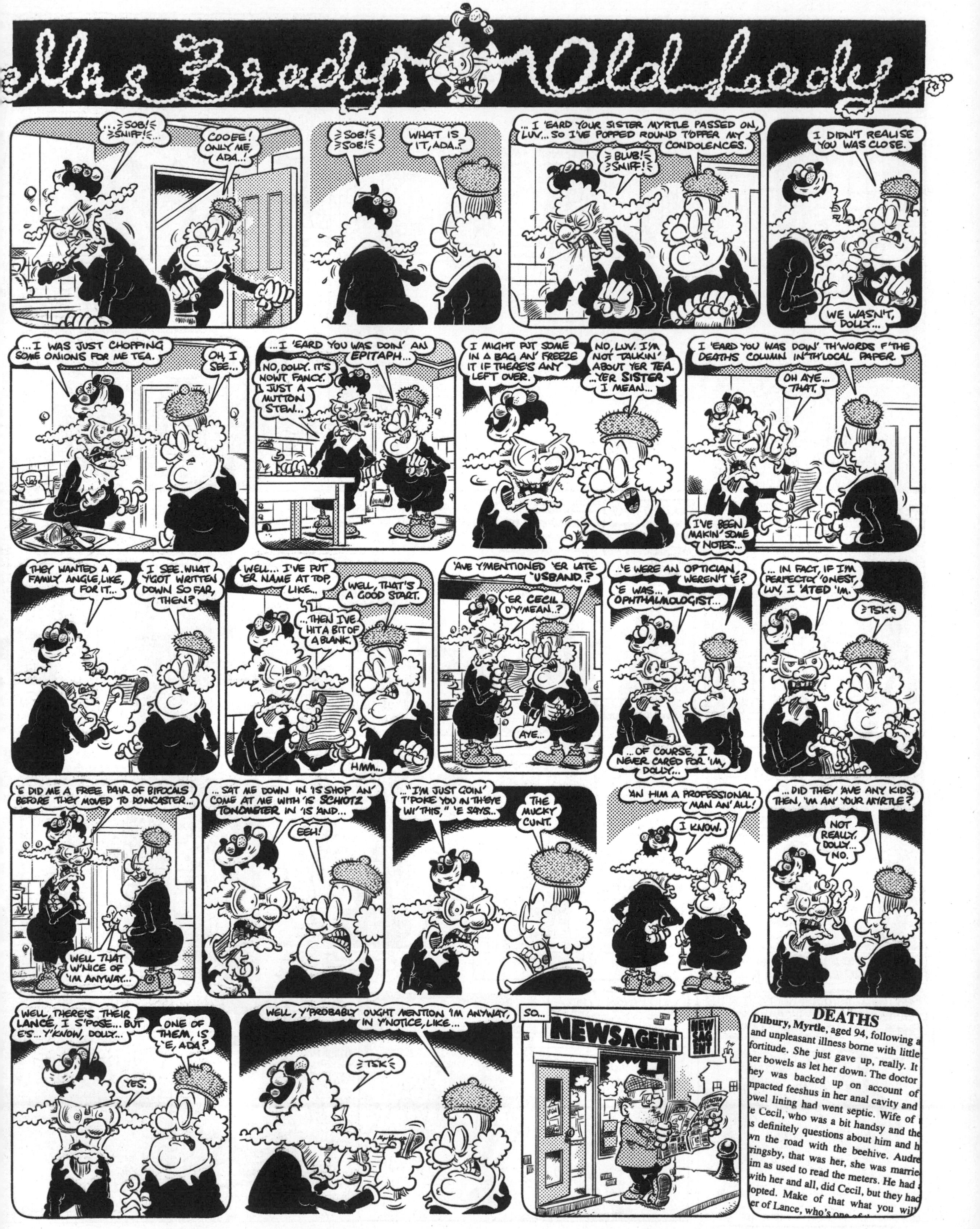
Mrs Brady Old Lady
... SOB! SNIFF! ...
COOEE! ONLY ME, ADA..!
SOB! SOB!
WHAT IS IT, ADA..?
... I 'EARD YOUR SISTER MYRTLE PASSED ON, LUV... SO I'VE POPPED ROUND T'OFFER MY CONDOLENCES.
BLUB! SNIFF!
I DIDN'T REALISE YOU WAS CLOSE.
WE WASN'T, DOLLY...
... I WAS JUST CHOPPING SOME ONIONS FOR ME TEA.
OH, I SEE...
... I 'EARD YOU WAS DOIN' AN EPITAPH...
NO, DOLLY. IT'S NOWT FANCY. JUST A MUTTON STEW...
I MIGHT PUT SOME IN A BAG AN' FREEZE IT IF THERE'S ANY LEFT OVER.
NO, LUV. I'M NOT TALKIN' ABOUT YER TEA. ...YER SISTER I MEAN...
I 'EARD YOU WAS DOIN' TH'WORDS F'THE DEATHS COLUMN IN TH'LOCAL PAPER
OH AYE... THAT.
I'VE BEEN MAKIN' SOME NOTES...
THEY WANTED A FAMILY ANGLE, LIKE, FOR IT...
I SEE. WHAT Y'GOT WRITTEN DOWN SO FAR, THEN?
WELL... I'VE PUT 'ER NAME AT TOP, LIKE...
WELL, THAT'S A GOOD START.
... THEN I'VE HIT A BIT OF A BLANK.
HMM...
'AVE Y'MENTIONED 'ER LATE 'USBAND..?
'ER CECIL D'Y'MEAN..?
AYE...
...'E WERE AN OPTICIAN, WEREN'T 'E?
'E WAS... OPHTHALMOLOGIST...
... OF COURSE, I NEVER CARED FOR 'IM, DOLLY...
... IN FACT, IF I'M PERFECTLY 'ONEST, LUV, I 'ATED 'IM.
TSK
'E DID ME A FREE PAIR OF BIFOCALS BEFORE THEY MOVED TO DONCASTER...
WELL THAT W'NICE OF 'IM ANYWAY...
... SAT ME DOWN IN 'IS SHOP AN' COME AT ME WITH 'IS SCHIOTZ TONOMETER IN 'IS 'AND...
EEH!
..."I'M JUST GOIN' T'POKE YOU IN TH'EYE WI'THIS," 'E SAYS...
THE MUCKY CUNT.
'AN HIM A PROFESSIONAL MAN AN' ALL!
I KNOW.
... DID THEY 'AVE ANY KIDS, THEN, 'IM AN' YOUR MYRTLE?
NOT REALLY, DOLLY... NO.
WELL, THERE'S THEIR LANCE, I S'POSE... BUT 'E'S... Y'KNOW, DOLLY...
ONE OF THEM, IS 'E, ADA?
YES.
WELL, Y'PROBABLY OUGHT MENTION 'IM ANYWAY, IN Y'NOTICE, LIKE...
TSK
SO...
NEWSAGENT
NEW SAG ENT
DEATHS
Dilbury, Myrtle, aged 94, following a
and unpleasant illness borne with little
fortitude. She just gave up, really. It
her bowels as let her down. The doctor
hey was backed up on account of
npacted feeshus in her anal cavity and
owel lining had went septic. Wife of
e Cecil, who was a bit handsy and the
s definitely questions about him and h
wn the road with the beehive. Audre
ringsby, that was her, she was marrie
im as used to read the meters. He had
with her and all, did Cecil, but they had
opted. Make of that what you will
er of Lance, who's one of

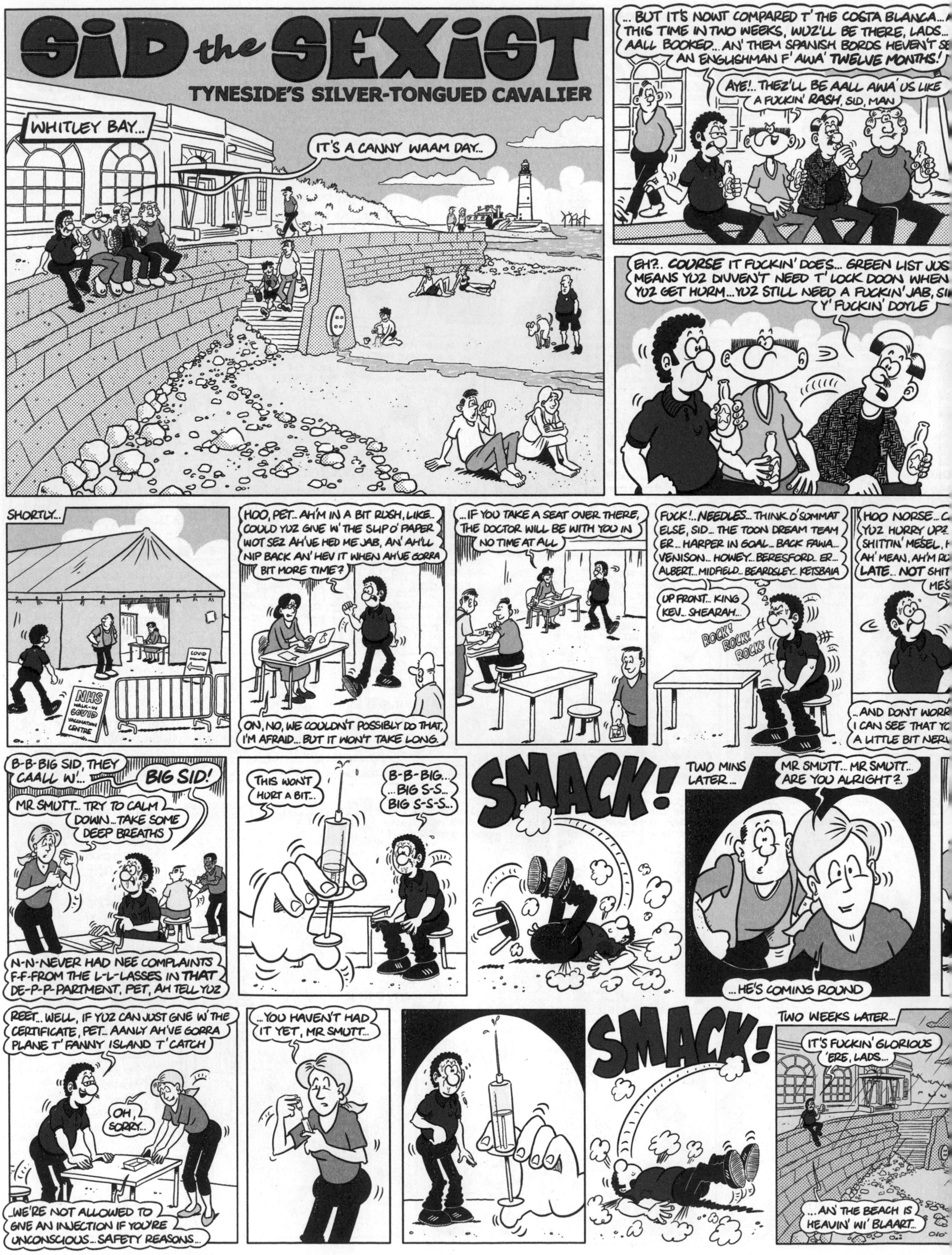
SID the SEXIST
TYNESIDE'S SILVER-TONGUED CAVALIER
WHITLEY BAY...
IT'S A CANNY WAAM DAY...
... BUT IT'S NOWT COMPARED T' THE COSTA BLANCA... THIS TIME IN TWO WEEKS, WUZ'LL BE THERE, LADS... AALL BOOKED... AN' THEM SPANISH BORDS HEVEN'T SE AN ENGLISHMAN F' AWA' TWELVE MONTHS!
AYE!.. THEZ'LL BE AALL AWA' US LIKE A FUCKIN' RASH, SID, MAN
EH?.. COURSE IT FUCKIN' DOES... GREEN LIST JUS MEANS YUZ DIVVEN'T NEED T' LOCK DOON WHEN YUZ GET HURM... YUZ STILL NEED A FUCKIN' JAB, SI Y' FUCKIN' DOYLE
SHORTLY...
NHS WALK-IN COVID VACCINATION CENTRE
COVID
HOO, PET... AH'M IN A BIT RUSH, LIKE... COULD YUZ GIVE W' THE SLIP O' PAPER WOT SEZ AH'VE HED ME JAB, AN' AH'LL NIP BACK AN' HEV IT WHEN AH'VE GORRA BIT MORE TIME?
OH, NO, WE COULDN'T POSSIBLY DO THAT, I'M AFRAID... BUT IT WON'T TAKE LONG.
...IF YOU TAKE A SEAT OVER THERE, THE DOCTOR WILL BE WITH YOU IN NO TIME AT ALL
FUCK!.. NEEDLES... THINK O' SOMMAT ELSE, SID... THE TOON DREAM TEAM ER... HARPER IN GOAL... BACK FAWA... VENISON... HOWEY... BERESFORD... ER... ALBERT... MIDFIELD... BEARDSLEY... KETSBAIA
UP FRONT... KING KEV... SHEARAH...
ROCK! ROCK! ROCK!
...AND DON'T WORR I CAN SEE THAT YO A LITTLE BIT NERV
B-B-BIG SID, THEY CAALL W'...
BIG SID!
MR SMUTT... TRY TO CALM DOWN... TAKE SOME DEEP BREATHS
N-N-NEVER HAD NEE COMPLAINTS F-F-FROM THE L-L-LASSES IN THAT DE-P-P-PARTMENT, PET, AH TELL YUZ
THIS WON'T HURT A BIT...
B-B-BIG... ...BIG S-S-S... BIG S-S-S...
SMACK!
TWO MINS LATER...
MR SMUTT... MR SMUTT... ARE YOU ALRIGHT?..
...HE'S COMING ROUND
REET... WELL, IF YUZ CAN JUST GIVE W' THE CERTIFICATE, PET... AANLY AH'VE GORRA PLANE T' FANNY ISLAND T' CATCH
OH, SORRY...
...WE'RE NOT ALLOWED TO GIVE AN INJECTION IF YOU'RE UNCONSCIOUS... SAFETY REASONS...
...YOU HAVEN'T HAD IT YET, MR SMUTT...
SMACK!
TWO WEEKS LATER...
IT'S FUCKIN' GLORIOUS 'ERE, LADS...
...AN' THE BEACH IS HEAVIN' WI' BLAART...

AYE!..IT'S GANNA BE A VERITABLE SMORGASBORD O' BLAART, AALL GAGGIN' F' ENGLISH CHOPPAH!

AYE... SERIOUSLY, LADS, WUZ'RE GANNA HEV T' PACE W'SELLS

HEV YUZ AALL HAD YUZ CURVID JABS, LADS?

AYE, AH HEV, BAZ

ME AN'AALL

WORRABOOT YEE, SIDNEY?

NAH... AH DIDN'T BOTHA... SPAIN'S ON THE GREEN LIST, SUR IT MAKES NEE DIFFERENCE, MAN

...REE SHAGS A DAY EACH...NEE MORE

WOT!?.. A NEEDLE!?

AYE!..

WOT'S WRANG, SID? YUZ'RE NOT FRIT O' NEEDLES, ARE YUZ?

D' THEZ DEE A VACCINE TABLET, INSTEAD?

HOWAY, SID...

AYE...THEZ WINNEN'T LET YUZ IN WI'OOT IT!..

...NEE VACCINE, NEE SPANISH FANNY... SIMPLE AS.

YOUR CHOICE, SID

...DIVEN'T TAALK SHITE, MAN...COURSE AH'M NOT

GET YERSEL DOON THE WAALK-IN CENTRE AN' STOP BEIN' SOFT ABOOT IT... YUZ'RE LIKE A FUCKIN' BAIRN, MAN

...ST... I'M ...DOCTOR, ...T A NURSE

NORVOUS!? O' COURSE AH'M NOT NORVOUS, PET... I'M NOT FRIT O' N-N-N-N-NEEDLES...

...NOT THAT AH KNAA MUCH ABOOT LITTLE P-P-PRICKS, M-M-ME, LIKE...

HMM!

ROCK! ROCK! ROCK!

...A L-L-LITTLE PRICK DOESN'T BOTHA ME...

H-H-HUNG LIKE A FUCKIN' C-C-CART H-H-HORSE, ME, NORSE... LIKE A F-F-FUCKIN' C-C-C-CART HORSE

...T HAPPENED, NORSE? ...ERE'S THE DOCTAH?

...DON'T WORRY, IT HAPPENS A LOT WHEN PEOPLE SEE NEEDLES.

HOO!.. TELL YUZ WOT, THOUGH... IT DOESN'T HORT A BIT, THAT... AH CANNAT FEEL NOWT...

...YOU PASSED OOT, MR SMUTT...

NAA... IT'S NOT NEEDLES, NORSE...AH'VE..ER..JUST FINISHED AN IRON MAN TRIATHLON AN' AH'VE HED NEE DINNAH

OH... THAT MUST BE IT, THEN

HOO, PET...YUZ'VE MADE A CANNY GOOD JOB O' THAT FORRA LASS

...AH RECKON YUZ'VE WASTED YUZ MONEY, LADS

!HOLA! YOU ENGLEESH BOYS PLAY VOLLEYBALL WITH US... SI?

SORRY, SID... GOT T' GAN... IT'S GAME ON

NO FLUS IS BAD NEWS!

NEWLY appointed Health Secretary *Savid Javid* yesterday hinted that there may have to be a delay to the beginning of the winter 20/21 winter flu season.

The popular virus usually kicks off around the middle of October, but like many things, it has been hard hit by the Coronovirus pandemic. And news of the delay has come as a blow to fans of the bug, who have been counting down the days over the summer.

Lifelong flu fan Mick Snorkle has renewed his flu jab every year for the past 20 seasons, but thinks that this year he may not bother. "This year, I may not bother," he said.

cancelled

In a statement, the health secretary said that there was no chance this year's flu cases would be cancelled, and insisted the virus would sweep through the community, albeit a little later than usual.

"We have to make sure that hospitals are not overwhelmed, so we thought it best to get Covid cases under control before we allow influenza to start," he told parliament.

flamed

However, a spokesman for the Winter Flu Supporters Association was sceptical about the health secretary's promise. "The government has been struggling with a fixture pile-up of respiratory viruses, and they need to get it sorted," he said.

"And I've heard rumours that the traditional flu season curtain-raiser in late September - a bit of a cold with a few sniffles - could be cancelled altogether," he added.

~Reuters

One Day in Thanet South...
Dear oh dear!... We've left the EU, so UKIP and my subsequently formed Brexit Party are dead and buried...
DAILY FAIL
...and these vaccines are going to put a halt to Coronavirus...so my Reform UK anti-lock-down party looks like a non-starter too...
...what a load of doom and gloom... there's no platform left for me to base a money-spinning political party on.
There must be **some** disquiet in the country that I can exploit for my own ends, surely.
Hello... what's this down the side of the cushion?
...it's an old copy of Q magazine from the early 80s... blimey!
...with a front page reporting the death of the 'New Romantic' movement... *sigh!*
Q MAGAZINE
GOODBYE NEW ROMANCE
What great times they were... British music being sold all around the world... How **dare** they kill that movement off?
That's it. I'm going to bring that movement back... I'm forming the ***New Romantic Reform UK*** Party.
If those unelected bureaucrats at Q magazine think they can get rid of one of the greatest British popular culture movements of all time, they can think again...
Now then...I'm pretty sure there are some frilly blouses and stuff upstairs that my second wife left when she went.
That night...
...and so I say to you... that we must take back control...
NEW ROMANTIC REFORM UK PARTY MEETING TONIGHT
ALL WELCOME
...we must reinstate the New Romantic values that were once so beloved of this great country...
...we must *make British cuffs frilly again...*
...and I intend to stand as the New Romantic Reform UK Party candidate in the upcoming by-election in Thanet South... and when I am elected to Parliament, I promise you that I will not rest until Spandau Ballet are once again number one in the hit parade!
Fellow dandy highwaymen, let us go onto the streets!
*Ant Mus-**iii**-ic!*
So...
Morning... Nigel Farage, your New Romantic Reform UK candidate... I hope I can count on your vote on election day, madam.
Eh!?
Good morning... Nigel Farage, your...
What are you going to do about the hospital..?
Erm...
...They're trying to close it down.
Yes, well... er... thank you... Goodbye!
Hello... I trust you'll be voting New Romantic Reform on election day...
Ooh, no... the wife an' I were *Goths*, see...
NRRUK
...never had time for any of that New Romance nonsense...
...all that velvet brocade an' tassels... *Tchoh!*... not to mention the silver-topped canes and all that pirate malarkey.
Nigel! We've got a problem...
Another candidate is doing a speech in the high street...
Don't worry, the Tories and Labour are finished in Thanet South...
It's not Tory or Labour...
It's George Galloway's Punk Respect Party!
...You're gonna vote for me, you big fuckin' cunt!...
An' so are you, you little fuckin' cunt...

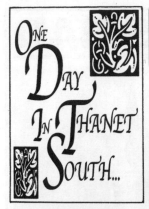

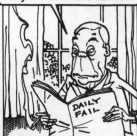

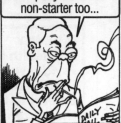

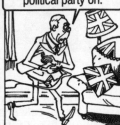

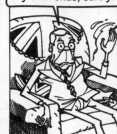

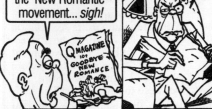

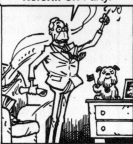

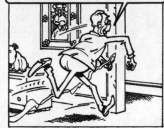

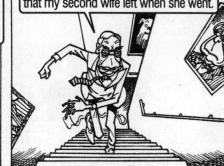

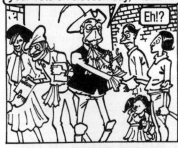

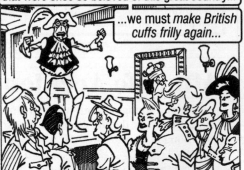

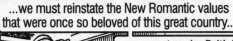

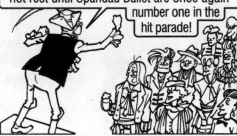

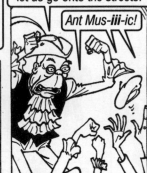

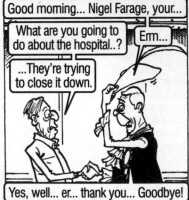

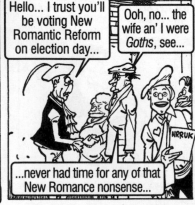

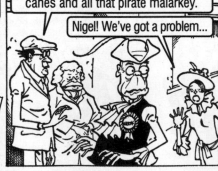

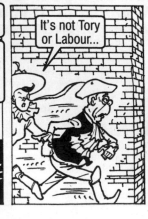

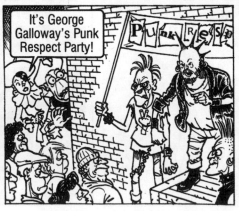

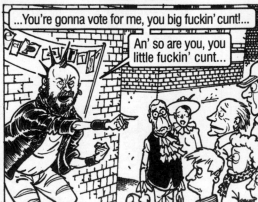

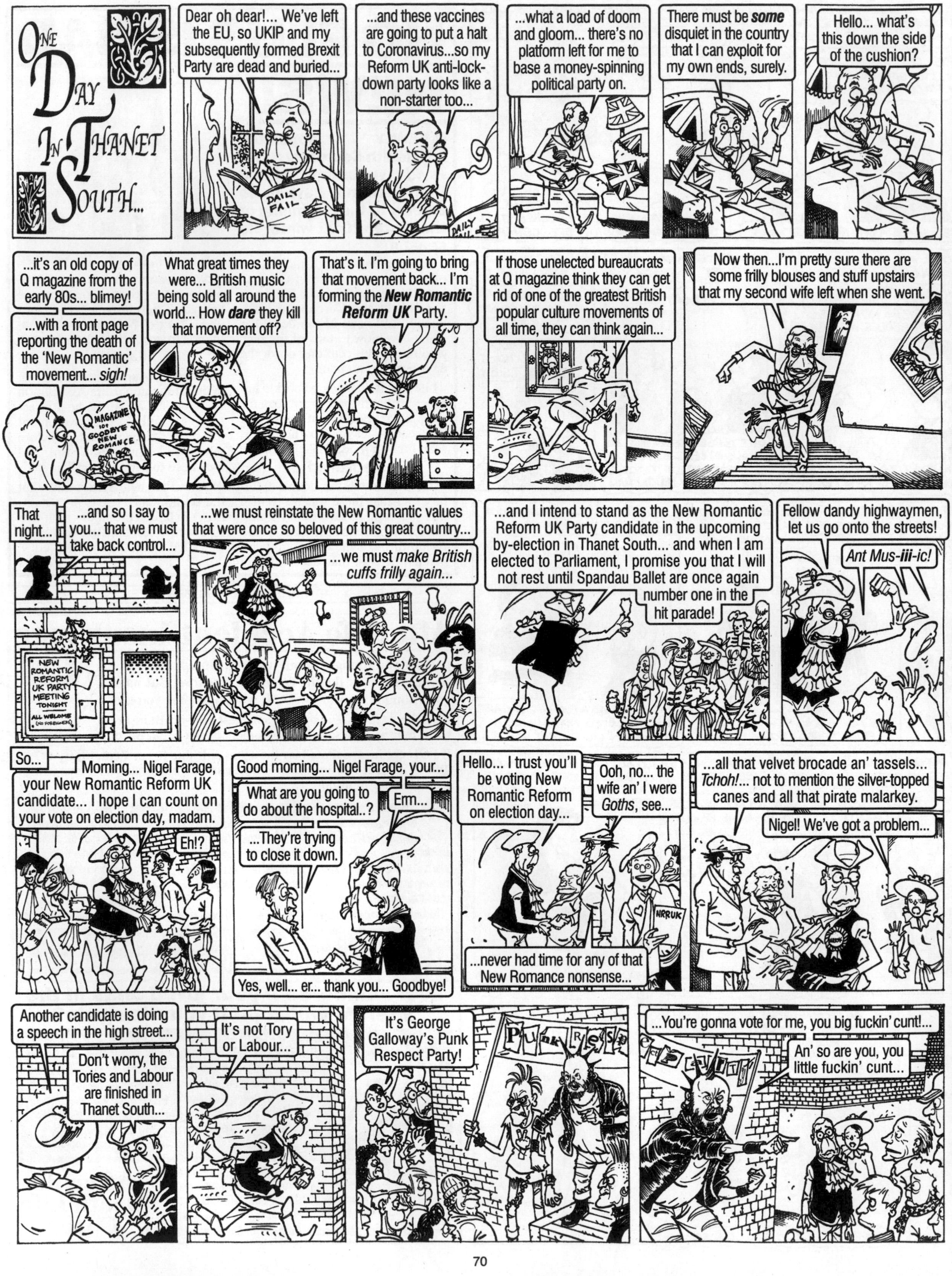

TOMMY "BANANA" JOHNSON
HE'S GOT A BIG BANANA!
Swimsuit Edition!
I THINK I'LL GO TO THE PARK TODAY
A practical and sporty swimming costume with racer back and comfortable longer leg, sizes 10-22. John Lewis £34
AT THE PARK...
OH DEAR! THIS PAINT IS STILL WET AND IT LOOKS LIKE IT'S GOING TO RAIN
WET PAINT
A beautiful swimsuit in cool white lace-effect crochet. Size 30-36. New Look £72
HEY MISTER! WHY NOT USE MY BANANA AS A GIANT HAIR DRYER TO DRY THE PAINT?
EH?
Sensational leopard-print swimsuit with a sexy cut. Aphrodite £65
PISS OFF, AND TAKE YER GIANT FRIGGIN' BANANA WITH YA!
ALRIGHT. I'M GOING
Comfortable tankini top offering a little more coverage in a sensational tropical print. Freya £56
LATER...
HAVE YOU SEEN MY LITTLE DOG ANYWHERE? HE'S GONE MISSING.
Classic hipster bikini. Fresh stripes and an understated look. Next £62
NO, BUT WHY NOT USE MY BANANA AS A LARGE TELESCOPE TO LOOK FOR HIM?
UH!?
Bandeau top for strapless tanning. Vibrant print and interesting twist-front top. M&S £65
Bang on-trend. A one-shoulder bikini to lounge at the poolside. Seafolly £56
GO ON, FUCK OFF!
Retro Esther Williams look. A blast from the past. Bettylicious £34
BLOODY BANANA TELESCOPE...
SHORTLY...
HEY, TOMMY, THAT BANANA IS JUST WHAT I'M LOOKING FOR!
THE LOCAL BOBBY
COULD I BORROW IT FOR JUST A SECOND?
Classic crochet halter-top bikini. Hollister £12
AGGH! MY BOTTOM
THAT SHOULD PUT A STOP TO YOUR BANANA PRANKS, EH TOMMY? HO HO HO!
Marble pattern tie-side 2-piece bikini. Boohoo £12

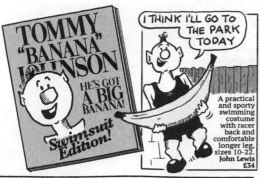

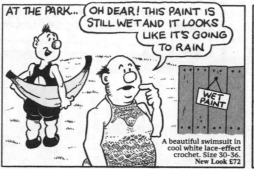

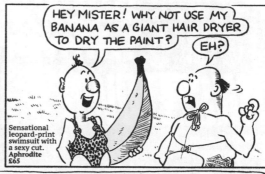

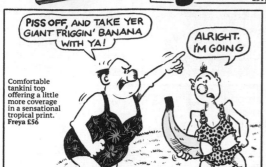

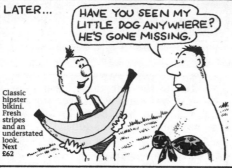

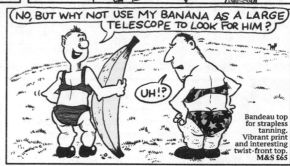

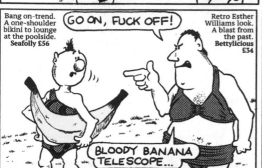

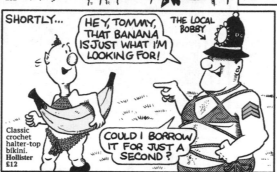

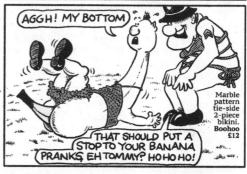

VIEW! WHAT A TORTURE!

Man plans ultimate YouTube binge

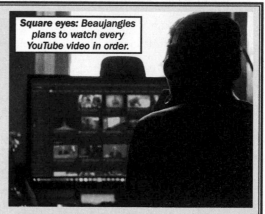

Square eyes: *Beaujangles plans to watch every YouTube video in order.*

WE all spend too much time in front of our computers, but this weekend a Glossop man is set for an epic screen session that will put us all to shame, when he plans to watch *every single video on YouTube back to back!*

Martin Beaujangles came up with the idea for the marathon binge-fest after searching the popular video-sharing platform looking for help with a DIY project he was undertaking in his terraced home.

"I was making some drawers for the kitchen and I wanted to know how to do dovetail joints, so I found a video on YouTube that showed you how to do it," he told reporters at the *Glossop and Broadbottom Scrutiniser*. "It turns out it was too hard and in the end I just used nails. But I got sucked into the channel and kept clicking on the next video and the next video and the next."

solid

Beaujangles watched YouTube uploads for 8 solid hours before finally pulling himself away from his PC in the small hours. But a plan was forming in his head.

"I stopped because I needed a sit-down visit to the lav," he said. "But I thought what a great thing it would be to watch every single video on the site. I don't think it's ever been done before."

And the 63-year-old former newspaper delivery boy could not be accused of wasting time in front of the computer when he attempts his marathon video slog, because he plans to watch the site's entire output for charity.

"A couple of blokes at the pub are going to give me 10p for every video I watch," he said. "I know it doesn't sound like much, but there must be a few hundred uploads on there. I wonder if they know what they've let themselves in for."

systematic

And Martin is going for a systematic approach to his mammoth viewing challenge to ensure that no videos on the site go unwatched.

"I'm going to start on Friday morning by watching all the ones with cats doing stuff, and then in the afternoon I'm going to watch the ones with people falling off things," he said.

"On Saturday it's all the pop music videos and them compilations of funny footballing moments. Sunday morning I'll watch all the ones about how to make things, and finish in the afternoon with all the ones you can't categorise, like that Viking dancing in the street, and that bloke whose dog chases some deer."

milk monitor

However, the former classroom milk monitor fears that no matter how well he plans his marathon session, things could still go wrong. "My internet was cut off a few months back over some confusion about non-payment, and I've been piggybacking on my neighbour's wifi ever since," he said.

"It's fairly thin at the best of times, but if he starts going on his porn sites like he usually does at the weekend, it's going to slow me down quite a bit and put me behind schedule."

But all going well, Beaujangles aims to finish his quest in style, by watching the streaming site's most popular clip. "It's some kids singing about baby sharks or something. Sounds like a load of rubbish, but it's had eight billion views, by all accounts," he said.

"Come ten o'clock Sunday night, it'll be 8 billion and one."

THIS WEEK

★ Tales from Hollywood ★

TINSELTOWN'S ALCHEMIST ACTORS

FOR centuries, man has sought the secrets of alchemy. From Agathodaemon in the third century, to Isaac Newton in the Age of Enlightenment, many have tried to find the secret of turning base metal into gold. The quest has become an obsession for people from every walk of life – scientists, philosphers, writers and artists have all sought this glittering prize. But it might come as a surprise to discover that since the dawn of the golden age of cinema, many Hollywood stars have also dabbled in this mysterious pseudoscientific practice, with varying degrees of success. Here are five movie stars who have attempted to transmute base metal into gold.

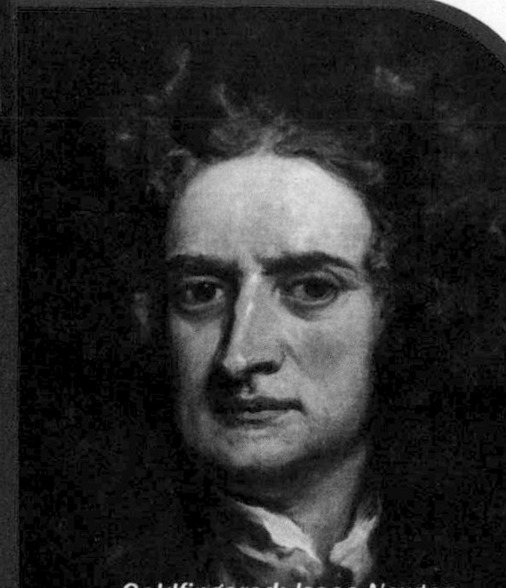

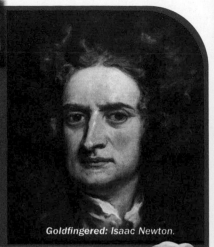

Goldfingered: Isaac Newton.

James Stewart

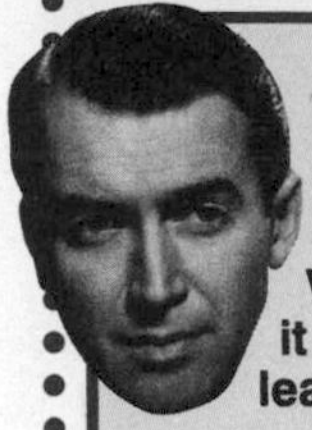

NOT only a movie legend and Oscar-winning star, Stewart also fought in World War II with great distinction. And it was during his military service that he learnt the secrets of alchemy.

Stationed on an island in the south seas, the *Vertigo* star was chasing a platoon of Nazis through the jungle when he got lost and found himself outside a mystical temple. Curious, he headed inside where he found a wizened old man standing in front of a pile of gold.

The old man was a fan of Stewart, having seen him in films such as *Mr Smith Goes to Washington* and *Destry Rides Again*, and he told the actor that he would reveal the secrets of alchemy in return for his autograph. Stewart readily agreed, and after scribbling his signature and posing for a couple of photographs with his fan, he left the temple with a series of ancient scrolls containing everything he needed to know.

When Stewart returned home from the war, he followed the instructions in the scrolls and was astonished to find he could create gold.

Stewart often told the story on TV chat shows, but would never reveal what the scrolls contained. He continued making films, as well as making gold, throughout his life, generously donating all the precious metal to local Hollywood charities.

Dustin Hoffman

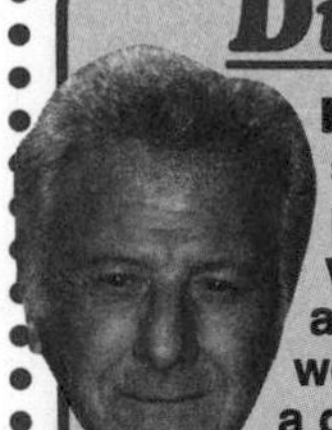

HOFFMAN burst onto the Hollywood scene in 1967 with his electric performance in *The Graduate*. It was clear from the start that he was a gifted actor, but what studio bosses were unaware of was that he was also a gifted in the science of alchemy.

In the sixties, Hoffman shared an apartment in New York City with fellow actor Robert Duvall who recalls living with the up-and-coming alchemist.

"The stink is what I remember more than anything else. This pungent reek that would emanate from Dusty's room," Duval told The New Yorker. "I lit candles, I bought air-freshener, I cracked all the windows but just couldn't get rid of it."

"When I asked what was causing the smell, Dustin just laughed and said the stink was the by-product of the alchemy. He then showed me all this scientific apparatus in his bedroom, all coloured chemical bubbling away and with gold coming out the end and dropping into the final flask."

"I admit, I was pretty shocked. But, you know, he used that gold to pay our rent, buy food and bribe producers to put us in their pictures. So, I got a pretty good career out of it."

Marilyn Monroe

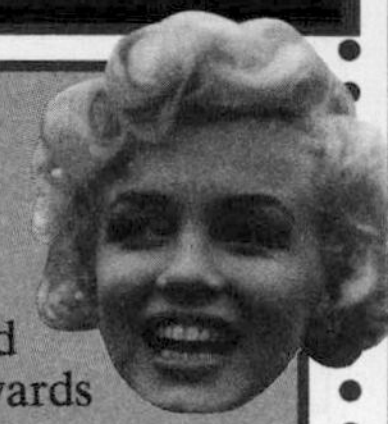

FAMOUS for her ditsy on-screen persona, Monroe was actually an accomplished amateur chemist who had been toying with alchemy since she was a teenager.

She suspected that the secret lay in the electron shell arrangement in the lead atom, her Eureka! moment coming whilst she was having her skirt blown upwards on the set of *The Seven Year Itch*.

When the film's director Billy Wilder called a wrap for the day, Monroe ran home and popped into her laboratory to test her new idea. It was a success, but she only managed to produce a few flakes of gold.

Over the following years, she modified the experiment to focus exclusively on increasing the yield until, in 1962, she was able to produce large quantities of gold from lead.

However, fearing that foreign agents may kidnap or recruit the *Gentlemen Prefer Blondes* sex bomb and force her to make gold for enemy states, the CIA had her killed, staging her death to look like an overdose of barbiturates.

Michael Douglas

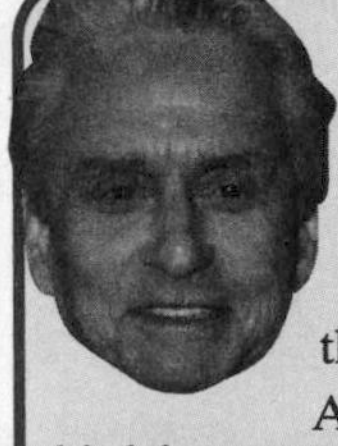

THE TRAGIC tale of Douglas is a cautionary one to all who would dabble in the mysterious arts.

From early in his career, the *Fatal Attraction* star had a well equipped alchemy laboratory set up in his Bel Air mansion, where he would spend much of his time experimenting. But in 1976, the Best Picture Oscar went to *One Flew Over the Cuckoo's Nest* and, as the film's producer, Douglas put his experimentation on hold and threw a party.

After several days of celebrating, the groggy star woke up and staggered into his laboratory, where he was amazed to see that at the end of the huge and complex series of tubes, bottles and flasks, were two flecks of pure gold.

However, his delight soon turned to despair. In his drunken state, Douglas had stumbled upon the secret that he had sought, but tragically, he was too pissed to take notes and record his results.

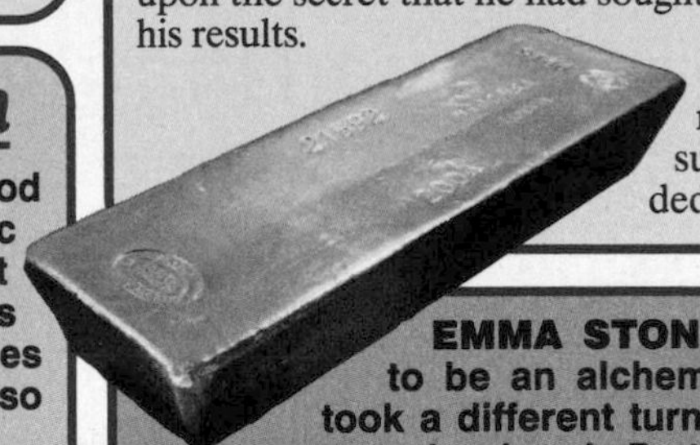

For years afterwards, the *Falling Down* star tried to recreate the experiment but was never able to repeat its success. In the nineties, he finally gave up alchemy and dedicated his life to having sex with lots of women instead.

Emma Stone

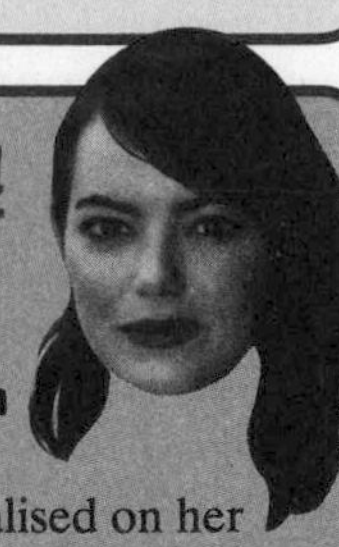

EMMA STONE grew up wanting to be an alchemist, but her career took a different turn in 2004, when she appeared as Laurie Partridge in VH1's show *The New Partridge Family*. But it wasn't until she wowed everyone with her sensational performance in *La La Land* in 2016 that she became a household name.

With her first love still the quest to turn base metal to gold, Stone capitalised on her new found fame by patenting the 'Emma Stone Fantasmagorical Alchemic Machine' which she billed as 'The Wonder of the Age.'

The machine comprised of a black box about two feet square with a funnel on the top, into which Stone would drop a piece of lead or other base metal. The machine would rattle and make chugging noises and after half a minute, a lump of gold would drop out of a chute on the other side, landing in a net underneath.

Stone would never explain the secrets of her machine and she refused to allow anyone to look inside the box. Instead, she toured it throughout America, astonishing people who had paid $5 to see it in action. But not everyone was taken in. Before his death in 2020, sceptic James Randy said that Emma's machine was "pure bunkum" and that the Oscar winner was "a fraud and a huckster, playing on people's gullibility like a two-bit snake oil saleswoman."

TALES FROM HOLLYWOOD NEXT WEEK:
The Necromancing A-listers who have RAISED the DEAD!

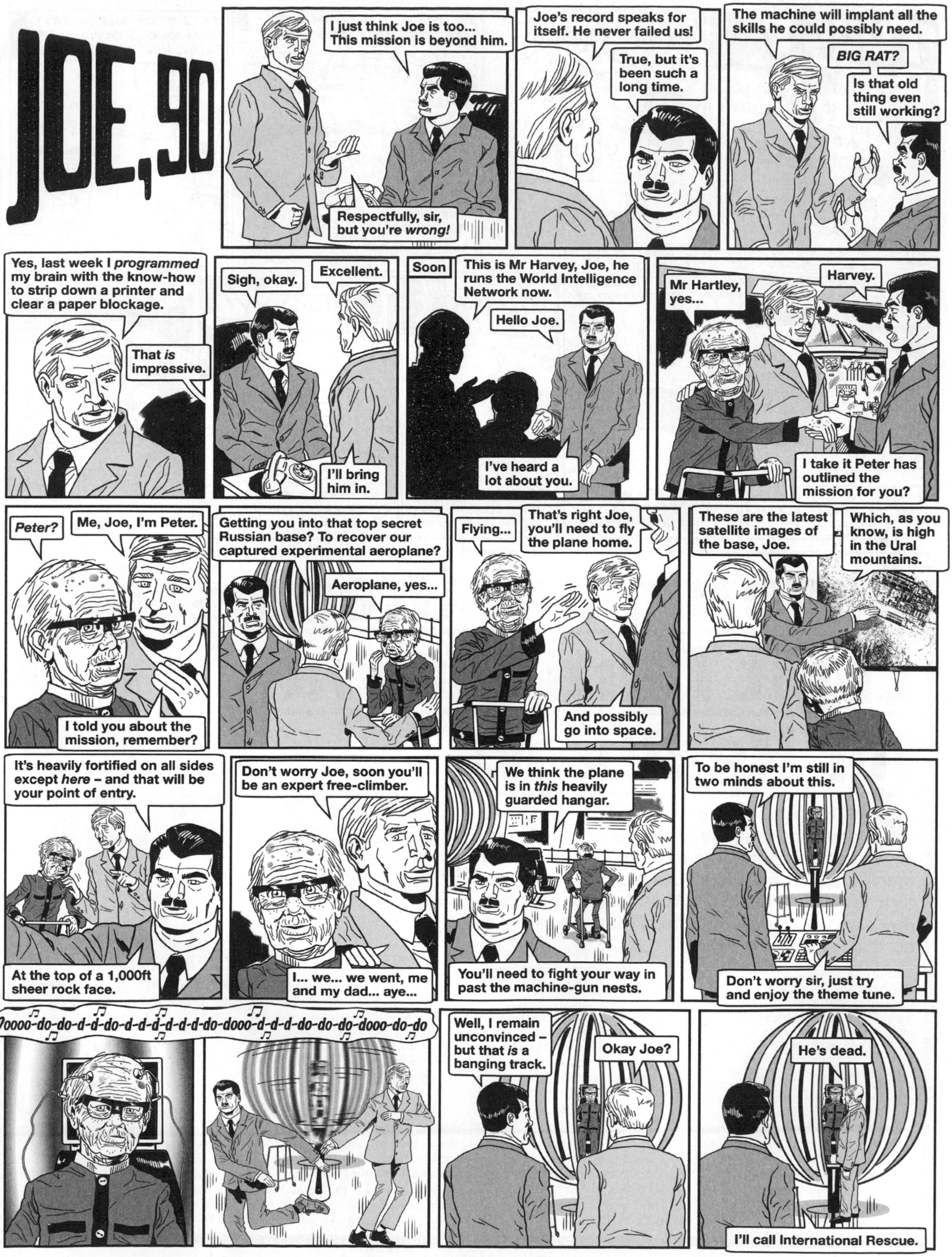
JOE, 90
I just think Joe is too... This mission is beyond him.
Respectfully, sir, but you're *wrong!*
Joe's record speaks for itself. He never failed us!
True, but it's been such a long time.
The machine will implant all the skills he could possibly need.
BIG RAT?
Is that old thing even still working?
Yes, last week I *programmed* my brain with the know-how to strip down a printer and clear a paper blockage.
That *is* impressive.
Sigh, okay.
Excellent.
I'll bring him in.
Soon
This is Mr Harvey, Joe, he runs the World Intelligence Network now.
Hello Joe.
I've heard a lot about you.
Mr Hartley, yes...
Harvey.
I take it Peter has outlined the mission for you?
Peter?
Me, Joe, I'm Peter.
I told you about the mission, remember?
Getting you into that top secret Russian base? To recover our captured experimental aeroplane?
Aeroplane, yes...
Flying...
That's right Joe, you'll need to fly the plane home.
And possibly go into space.
These are the latest satellite images of the base, Joe.
Which, as you know, is high in the Ural mountains.
It's heavily fortified on all sides except *here* – and that will be your point of entry.
At the top of a 1,000ft sheer rock face.
Don't worry Joe, soon you'll be an expert free-climber.
I... we... we went, me and my dad... aye...
We think the plane is in *this* heavily guarded hangar.
You'll need to fight your way in past the machine-gun nests.
To be honest I'm still in two minds about this.
Don't worry sir, just try and enjoy the theme tune.
Doooo-do-do-d-d-do-d-d-d-d-d-do-dooo-d-d-do-do-do-dooo-do-do
Well, I remain unconvinced – but that *is* a banging track.
Okay Joe?
He's dead.
I'll call International Rescue.

TUGGY BOAT
WHEN THERE'S DANGER ABOUT, HE'LL BE KNOCKING ONE OUT...
Z
BRING! BRING!
WHA?! THAT'S THE EMERGENCY LINE!
HELLO... HARBOURMASTER?
TUGGY! A SHIP CARRYING THOUSANDS OF COPIES OF MEGHAN MARKLE'S CRAPPY VANITY PROJECT BOOK 'THE BENCH' IS ABOUT TO SINK!
IT'S 2 MILES NORTH-EAST FROM YOUR LOCATION - BRING HER TO SHORE!
I'M ON MY WAY!
FLUTTER FLUTTER
PLAP!
LINERS WIVES
HOLD ON - WHAT'S THIS?!
"LINERS' WIVES"?! LOOK AT THE CURVES ON THAT VESSEL!
PHWOAR!
SPLOSH!
I'M SURE I'VE GOT ENOUGH TIME TO :AHEM: CLEAN MY PIPE...
5 MINUTES LATER...
FAP FAP FAP FAP FAP
TOOT! TOOT!
BRING! BRING!
UH-OH
ERM... HELLO?
TUGGYYY! THAT SHIP HAS GONE UNDER!
YOU WERE BUFFING YOUR BARNACLES AGAIN, WEREN'T YOU?!
THEY'LL DECOMMISSION YOU FOR THIS!
LAWKS!
Tayler

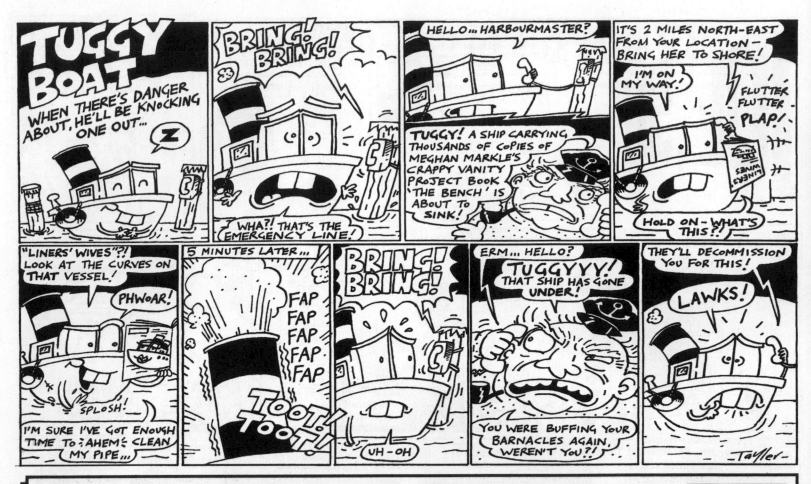

Government Green Light Third Runway for Heathrow

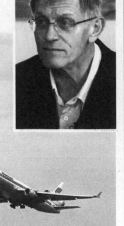

Up, up and away: Calder (right) to get own runway at Heathrow.

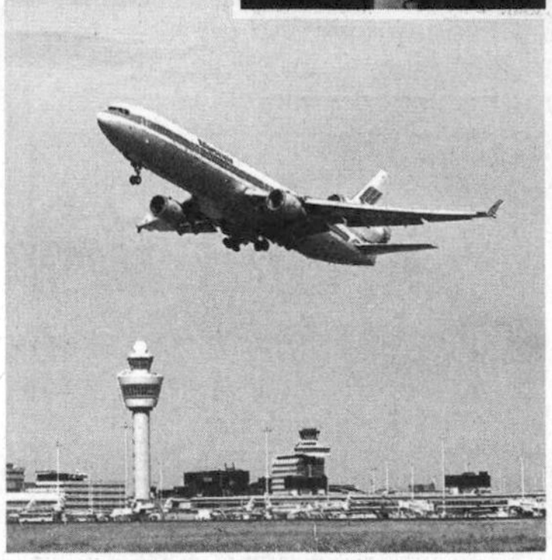

AFTER years of debate, MPs last night finally gave the green light for work to begin on a controversial third Heathrow runway for Simon Calder. The decision came as fears mounted that without it, the ubiquitous *Independent* holiday correspondent's air travel may not return to normal levels until 2024.

By our, and indeed everyone else's, Travel Correspondent **Simon Calder**

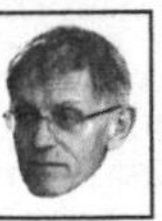

Ministers believe that having a third runway for exclusive use by the travel writer would help allay the public's concerns over the state of the airliner industry.

runway

Speaking to *This Morning* about the scrapping of the EHIC card, Calder said the announcement made sense, but advised the firms tendering for the construction work on the runway to read their contracts carefully.

"People potentially working on the new runway should consider investing in a travel card," he told Holly Willoughby.

"There are some great deals out there for getting to Heathrow. A £6 daily bus and rail travel card is great value, if you don't mind occasionally getting wet," he told the *Jeremy Vine Show* over the phone.

remote

He also advised surveyors assessing the land for the third runway to consider using remote airport parking companies rather than expensive long stay car parks.

"There are some great deals out there to be had," he told *The One Show* via text. "There is ample parking and regular shuttle buses service the land earmarked for development, meaning the whole parking experience is hassle free," he told LBC's *Eddie Mair show*.

pest

And the new two-mile runway, to be completed in early 2023, will be equipped with its own media centre so Calder can do interviews by leaning out of the window while his plane is taxiing.

birth

But not everyone has been pleased by the announcement. Local residents opposed to the plan are worried that the new runway could see TV crews congregating near the fencing to interview Calder, and they plan to march to London to deliver a petition to Downing Street calling for work to be halted.

advance

Talking from the toilet in the *BBC Breakfast* studio, Calder advised residents to book their journeys to London well in advance and consider split ticketing.

"Why not take in the sights of London from a fantastic tour bus! There are some great deals to be had, and most tours take in Downing Street, so you can hop off and hand in your petition," he told the man pissing next to him.

poached

But a government spokesman said that the decision was the right one and argued that it would create over 500 new jobs. "More than 70% of all Simon Calder's flights are set to go through Heathrow by 2025," he said.

"If we scrap the scheme, he could be poached by another major hub, such as Frankfurt or Amsterdam," he warned.

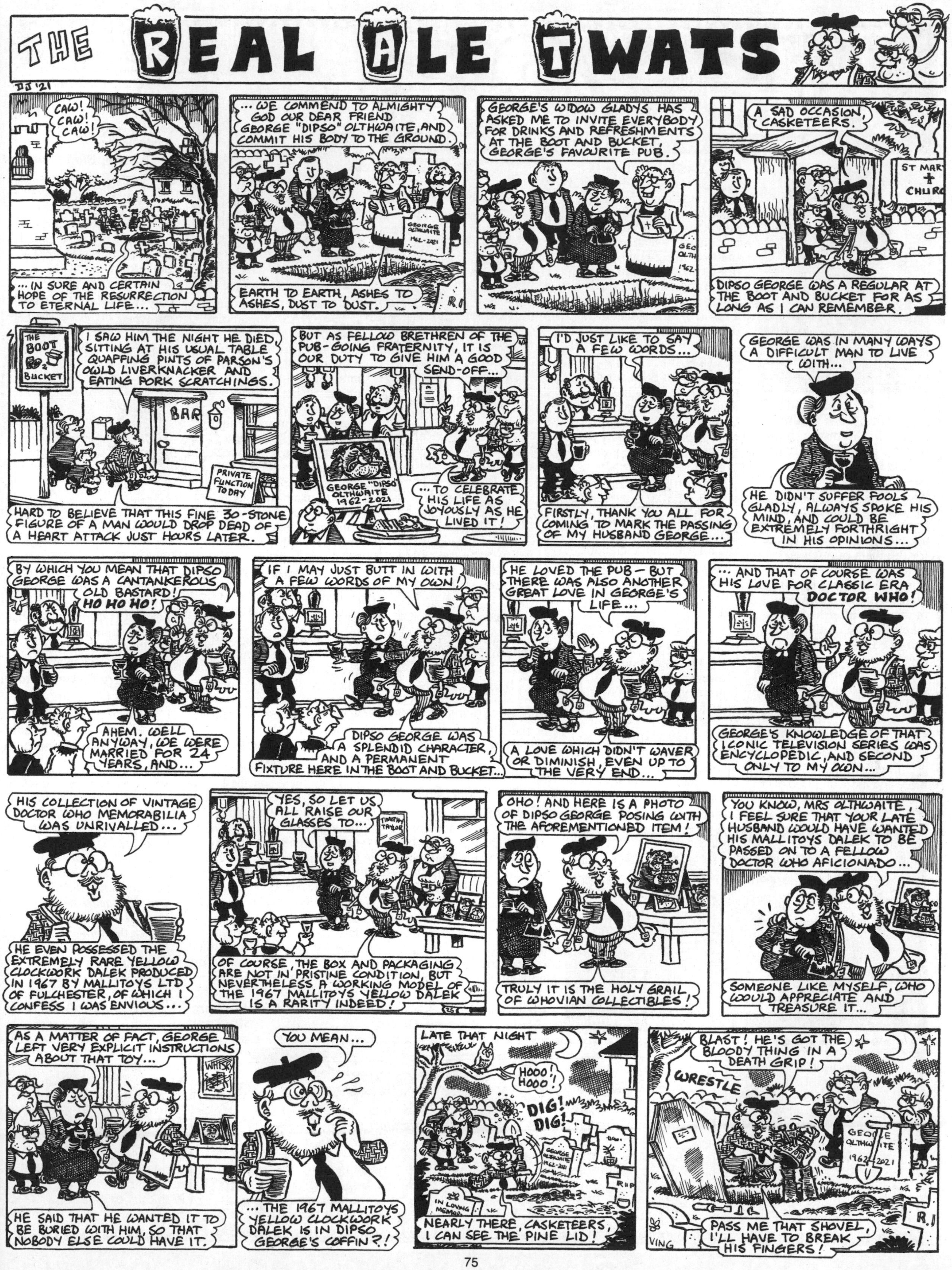
THE REAL ALE TWATS
TJ '21
CAW! CAW! CAW!
...IN SURE AND CERTAIN HOPE OF THE RESURRECTION TO ETERNAL LIFE...
...WE COMMEND TO ALMIGHTY GOD OUR DEAR FRIEND GEORGE "DIPSO" OLTHWAITE, AND COMMIT HIS BODY TO THE GROUND.
GEORGE OLTHWAITE 1962-2021
EARTH TO EARTH, ASHES TO ASHES, DUST TO DUST.
GEORGE'S WIDOW GLADYS HAS ASKED ME TO INVITE EVERYBODY FOR DRINKS AND REFRESHMENTS AT THE BOOT AND BUCKET, GEORGE'S FAVOURITE PUB.
A SAD OCCASION, CASKETEERS.
DIPSO GEORGE WAS A REGULAR AT THE BOOT AND BUCKET FOR AS LONG AS I CAN REMEMBER.
THE BOOT & BUCKET
I SAW HIM THE NIGHT HE DIED, SITTING AT HIS USUAL TABLE QUAFFING PINTS OF PARSON'S OWLD LIVERKNACKER AND EATING PORK SCRATCHINGS.
BAR
PRIVATE FUNCTION TODAY
HARD TO BELIEVE THAT THIS FINE 30-STONE FIGURE OF A MAN WOULD DROP DEAD OF A HEART ATTACK JUST HOURS LATER.
BUT AS FELLOW BRETHREN OF THE PUB-GOING FRATERNITY, IT IS OUR DUTY TO GIVE HIM A GOOD SEND-OFF...
GEORGE "DIPSO" OLTHWAITE 1962-2021
...TO CELEBRATE HIS LIFE AS JOYOUSLY AS HE LIVED IT!
I'D JUST LIKE TO SAY A FEW WORDS...
FIRSTLY, THANK YOU ALL FOR COMING TO MARK THE PASSING OF MY HUSBAND GEORGE...
GEORGE WAS IN MANY WAYS A DIFFICULT MAN TO LIVE WITH...
HE DIDN'T SUFFER FOOLS GLADLY, ALWAYS SPOKE HIS MIND, AND COULD BE EXTREMELY FORTHRIGHT IN HIS OPINIONS...
BY WHICH YOU MEAN THAT DIPSO GEORGE WAS A CANTANKEROUS OLD BASTARD! HO HO HO!
AHEM. WELL ANYWAY, WE WERE MARRIED FOR 24 YEARS, AND...
IF I MAY JUST BUTT IN WITH A FEW WORDS OF MY OWN!
DIPSO GEORGE WAS A SPLENDID CHARACTER, AND A PERMANENT FIXTURE HERE IN THE BOOT AND BUCKET...
HE LOVED THE PUB — BUT THERE WAS ALSO ANOTHER GREAT LOVE IN GEORGE'S LIFE...
A LOVE WHICH DIDN'T WAVER OR DIMINISH, EVEN UP TO THE VERY END...
...AND THAT OF COURSE WAS HIS LOVE FOR CLASSIC ERA DOCTOR WHO!
GEORGE'S KNOWLEDGE OF THAT ICONIC TELEVISION SERIES WAS ENCYCLOPEDIC, AND SECOND ONLY TO MY OWN...
HIS COLLECTION OF VINTAGE DOCTOR WHO MEMORABILIA WAS UNRIVALLED...
HE EVEN POSSESSED THE EXTREMELY RARE YELLOW CLOCKWORK DALEK PRODUCED IN 1967 BY MALLITOYS LTD OF FULCHESTER, OF WHICH I CONFESS I WAS ENVIOUS...
YES, SO LET US ALL RAISE OUR GLASSES TO...
TIMOTHY TAYLOR
OF COURSE, THE BOX AND PACKAGING ARE NOT IN PRISTINE CONDITION, BUT NEVERTHELESS A WORKING MODEL OF THE 1967 MALLITOYS YELLOW DALEK IS A RARITY INDEED!
OHO! AND HERE IS A PHOTO OF DIPSO GEORGE POSING WITH THE AFOREMENTIONED ITEM!
TRULY IT IS THE HOLY GRAIL OF WHOVIAN COLLECTIBLES!
YOU KNOW, MRS OLTHWAITE, I FEEL SURE THAT YOUR LATE HUSBAND WOULD HAVE WANTED HIS MALLITOYS DALEK TO BE PASSED ON TO A FELLOW DOCTOR WHO AFICIONADO...
SOMEONE LIKE MYSELF, WHO WOULD APPRECIATE AND TREASURE IT...
AS A MATTER OF FACT, GEORGE LEFT VERY EXPLICIT INSTRUCTIONS ABOUT THAT TOY...
WHISKY
HE SAID THAT HE WANTED IT TO BE BURIED WITH HIM, SO THAT NOBODY ELSE COULD HAVE IT.
YOU MEAN...
...THE 1967 MALLITOYS YELLOW CLOCKWORK DALEK IS IN DIPSO GEORGE'S COFFIN?!
LATE THAT NIGHT
HOOO! HOOO!
DIG! DIG!
GEORGE OLTHWAITE 1962-2021
IN LOVING MEMORY
R.I.P.
NEARLY THERE, CASKETEERS, I CAN SEE THE PINE LID!
BLAST! HE'S GOT THE BLOODY THING IN A DEATH GRIP!
WRESTLE
GEORGE OLTHWAITE 1962-2021
PASS ME THAT SHOVEL, I'LL HAVE TO BREAK HIS FINGERS!

LetterbOcks

Viz Comic, P.O. Box 841 Whitley Bay, NE26 9EQ / letters@viz.co.uk

I HAD a dream in which I was waiting for Louis Theroux to show up for a meeting. There was a plate of biscuits on the table and every time I went to take one, I was told to 'wait for Louis'. When Theroux finally arrived, he refused to apologise and went straight for the plate of biscuits, ensuring that they were out of my reach. He only put the plate back into the middle of the table after he had taken the Bournvilles and Jammie Dodgers. People say that he comes across as charming and naïve, but I found him to be a very rude and self-centred man.

Roy Sauce, Steeple Bumpleigh

IF I was gifted immortality, I'd just get more and more annoyed over the millennia. No thank-you.

David Haslam, Datchworth

LAST night I was in that half-and-half world before nodding off to sleep when I dreamt I had tripped and fallen off the kerb. I did an almighty twitch in bed that was so big I pulled a muscle in the bottom of my foot. Have any other readers suffered an actual injury as a result of an accident in a dream?

Eli Wallace, Surrey

I HAVE recently given serious consideration to officially changing my name to 'John Turnbull'. However, as I am already called John Turnbull, I think it might actually be a waste of time.

John Turnbull, Hartlepool

I SAW a poster online recently that read "Don't Give Up!" However, since I was thinking about giving up smoking at the time, I'm wondering if it was paid for by a cigarette company.

William Stroker, Derry

THEY say love knows no boundaries. However, the court injunction taken out by my ex-wife clearly states I must stay at least 100 yards (or 300 feet) away from her and the children at all times. Yet again, it's one rule for the courts and another for us hopeless romantics.

Jeremy Wimble, Glossop

I LOVE athletics, but it's a shame that the 100 metres is over so quickly. Why can't the athletes run a bit slower, ensuring a longer race and letting the excitement build up?

Ben Nunn, Caterham

STAR LETTER

I'VE NOTICED that in the recent legislation banning protests that are noisy or cause inconvenience, the Government has neglected to include dirty protests. So anyone with a grievance can still wipe their shit all over the Houses of Parliament and there's nothing the police can do about it. Probably. I have to admit I'm not a lawyer.

Steve Crouch, P'borough

IF the bloke who invented Discos had stuck them in a tube, he'd be the billionaire inventor of Pringles. I imagine this letter comes as neither a surprise nor consolation to him.

Rob Young, Chingford

HAS anybody spared a moment to consider the effects of modern "woke" standards on traditional British pastimes? A peeping Tom used to be able to just look at his neighbour's knockers. Nowadays he'd have to also spy on a gay man and a transvestite or he'd get called homophobic and 'cancelled' off Twitter. No wonder our traditions are vanishing.

Pierre Teteblanche, Oxford

MANY Congratulations to NASA for landing another rover on Mars. But looking at their history, it seems most of these multi-billion pound gadgets ultimately break down when dust prevents their solar panels generating enough electricity to keep them working. Now I'm no rocket scientist, but why don't they spend a few extra quid and put wipers on the panels to keep the buggers clean? I've got a spare pair from my old 1970 Triumph Toledo if they need any donations.

Peter A, Palo Alto

ON the Sky Sports football, Martin Tyler always proclaims "…and it's live!" just before kick-off. Well I think he should stop saying this, because some of us are watching using a "chipped" Amazon Firestick which broadcasts at least a minute later.

Kevin Carter, Swindon

BOFFINS working on these so-called 'driverless cars' don't seem to have thought the thing through very well, if you ask me. The roads are already full of cars with drivers in them. To make the situation worse by introducing thousands of cars with nobody in them at all seems like a complete nonsense. And with no drivers to refuel them before the tanks run dry they'll all eventually break down in the traffic.

Pastor Carr-Bonhara, Stockport

WHEN did 'twiddling your thumbs' turn into 'playing with your arsehole'? I remember pornographic videos used to have nicer titles too. This country is going only one way if you ask me.

Dave, Bloodsausage

MY girlfriend bought me the book *1001 Albums to Hear Before You Die* for my birthday. Shouldn't it just be called *1001 Albums to Hear*? I don't know when else I would listen to them.

Barry McNab, Gateshead

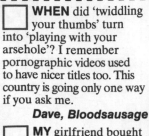

I ONCE went to a stately home which Queen Victoria had visited. In the suite where she stayed was an ornate, porcelain toilet with not a skid mark in it. All I can say is she must have had a pretty controlled sphincter, which is what makes the royals so special in my mind.

Gerry Paton, London

I'M 56, and I've never seen a badger in real life. How fucked up is that?

Fat Al White, Wrenthorpe,

** Perhaps it is unusual, Mr White, but perhaps not, since we don't know the average age at which people first see a badger. So let's find out. Could all Viz readers write in and tell us if they have ever seen a badger, how old they were when they first saw it (if applicable), and how old they are now. We'll crunch the numbers and let you know how unusual your circumstance is. Mark you envelope or email subject "Badger Spotting Age Survey".*

HA HA!
AND... CUT! HA HA! GREAT STUFF, GUYS. YOU'RE REALLY FUNNY.
FUNNY?
DIRECTOR
ITB
FUNNY HOW?
LIKE WE'RE HERE TO FUCKIN' AMUSE YOU?
LIKE WE'RE CLOWNS?
DIRECT
GOODIE Fellas

☐ **HOW** did the original builders of Stonehenge ever get planning permission for such a monstrosity? I bet there were hundreds of protesters from all over the country camping out to get it stopped, but fanatical religious groups got their way as usual.

Aidan Heslop, Gateshead

☐ **HOW** is it you get horseradish sauce with beef, apple sauce with pork and mint sauce with lamb, but nothing for chicken? I wonder what God had against the chickens not to give them their own sauce?

John Hargreaves, Lytham St Annes

☐ **WE** all know parrots are infamous for their dreadful language, but what about chickens? I was near some recently for some reason or other, and they kept up a gleeful chant of "Bukkake! Bukkake"! I had to block my wife's ears and hum loudly to shield her from this filth.

Sam Willetts, email

☐ **SOMEBODY** let their dog have a shit outside my house and after stepping on it, I slid across the pavement like I was a contestant on *Dancing on Ice*. Thanks arsehole!

Ross Kennett, Rochester

✳ *How irresponsible of the dog owner, Mr Kennett. But it could have been worse – your misfortune could have been filmed by a passer-by on their phone and uploaded to YouTube under the title "Watch this twat nearly go arse over tit on a turd." The clip would almost certainly have gone 'viral' and been viewed by millions, with people laughing at you across the globe. Now known simply as "Dog turd man", you would consequently have become an internet meme like the famous 'Keyboard Cat' with the shot of you slipping on a turd cut onto the end of other videos.*

☐ **WITH** a lot of time on my hands recently, I happened to catch a few minutes of CBBC on the television. I could not believe how utterly childish the programmes were. For fuck's sake, isn't it about time these programme makers bloody well grew up?

Paul Kaufman, Cambridge

☐ **I'M** sick of hearing women moaning about inequality. They're either whining about unequal pay, career glass ceilings or how painful it is to give birth. Men are 4 times more likely to be struck by lightning than women, but you don't hear us complaining.

H Hartley, Middlesbrough

☐ **IN** *Viz* 287, my good friend K Barford made the erudite point that 'tapas' is an anagram of 'pasta,' criticising the Spanish food inventors for their lack of naming creativity. I have recently realised that my local delicacy 'sushi' is not an anagram of either despite also having 5 letters. I feel the Japanese should be commended for their use of a different set of 5 letters in naming their national dish. Although I'm partial to several plates of the uncooked seafood, I do prefer a serving of pasta despite the orthographical similarities to the Spanish nibbles.

C Smith, Tokyo

☐ **WHEN** I get half a tea-cake, I mirthfully refer to it as a 'Semi lob-on', stressing the first and fourth syllables as you would to pronounce Simon Le Bon. Do any other readers name the various states of their wedding tackle after members of Duran Duran? Or indeed any New Romantic singers from the 1980s?

Freddy Brown, Coventry

☐ **WHY** is it that these days, we talk about dangerous dogs being "put to sleep"? Whatever happened to the good old 90s term "destroyed"?

Plain English Campaign, London

☐ **SOME** say that Generation X is the last generation to have grown up without the internet. But they are also the last generation to have used that hard, crinkly toilet paper at school, and I think that may have had a bigger effect on them.

Mat, Edinburgh

☐ **I'VE** just been watching an old Christopher Lee Dracula film and, after a blood-draining attack on a young lady that lasted at most thirty seconds, Peter Cushing's Van Helsing character described the vampire's victim as being "completely drained of blood". As the human body contains around ten pints of blood, Dracula couldn't possibly have 'down-in-oned' all the blood in such a short time. I couldn't down ten pints without a break or two for a few peanuts and a slash. Some realism in movies, please.

Jim H, Blackpool

TOP TIPS

SAVE time and when piercing your microwave dinner several times with a knife by using a slightly opened pair of scissors. Hey presto! Two pierces for the price of one stab!

Richard Karslake, Oxon

RUN out of spaghetti? Simply cut lasagne sheets into long strips with a Stanley knife. Alternatively, if you're running short of lasagne sheets, make your own by sellotaping spaghetti strands together.

Fussy eaters can always remove the sellotape later if they wish.

Phil Kitching, Isle of Jura

PORN stars. Perform all of your acting in the non-sex scenes in slow motion so that they will play at regular speed when the viewers hit fast forward.

Carl Crosse, Manchester

BANKS. Convince people that you're not a bunch of soulless leeches who brought the country to the brink of bankruptcy, by having a northern person read a poem in your adverts.

Matt G, London

CONVINCE people you're doing yoga by trying to sniff your own arsehole in the middle of a sports centre.

Gareth Thomas, Redhill

REDUCE wear-and-tear on your spectacle lenses by wearing them below the bridge of your nose and peering over the top.

Archibald McTumshie, Edinburgh

toptips@viz.co.uk

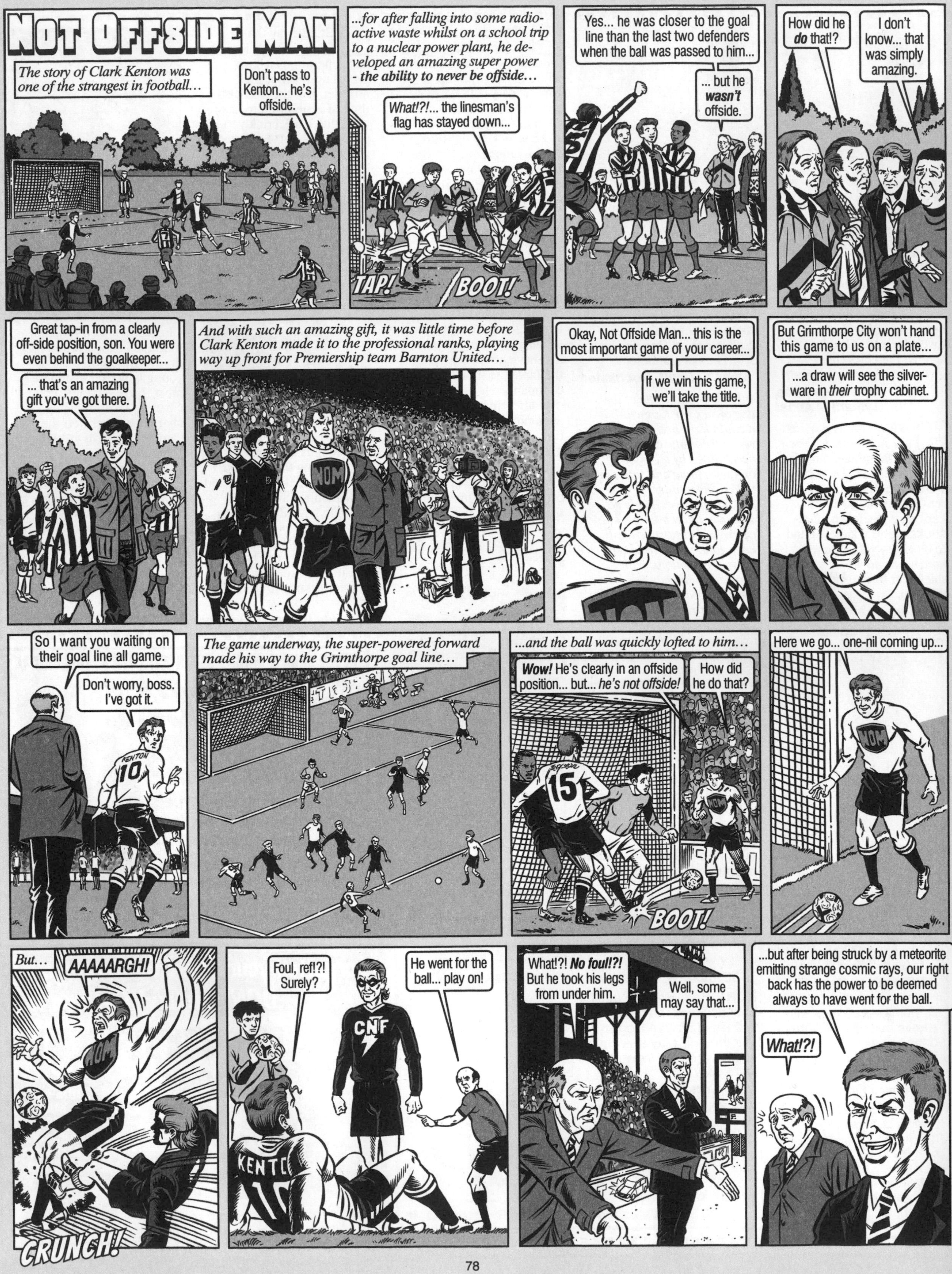
NOT OFFSIDE MAN
The story of Clark Kenton was one of the strangest in football…
Don't pass to Kenton… he's offside.
…for after falling into some radio-active waste whilst on a school trip to a nuclear power plant, he de-veloped an amazing super power - the ability to never be offside…
What!?!… the linesman's flag has stayed down…
TAP!
BOOT!
Yes… he was closer to the goal line than the last two defenders when the ball was passed to him…
… but he wasn't offside.
How did he do that!?
I don't know… that was simply amazing.
Great tap-in from a clearly off-side position, son. You were even behind the goalkeeper…
… that's an amazing gift you've got there.
And with such an amazing gift, it was little time before Clark Kenton made it to the professional ranks, playing way up front for Premiership team Barnton United…
Okay, Not Offside Man… this is the most important game of your career…
If we win this game, we'll take the title.
But Grimthorpe City won't hand this game to us on a plate…
…a draw will see the silver-ware in their trophy cabinet.
So I want you waiting on their goal line all game.
Don't worry, boss. I've got it.
The game underway, the super-powered forward made his way to the Grimthorpe goal line…
…and the ball was quickly lofted to him…
Wow! He's clearly in an offside position… but… he's not offside!
How did he do that?
BOOT!
Here we go… one-nil coming up…
But…
AAAAARGH!
CRUNCH!
Foul, ref!?! Surely?
He went for the ball… play on!
What!?! No foul!?! But he took his legs from under him.
Well, some may say that…
…but after being struck by a meteorite emitting strange cosmic rays, our right back has the power to be deemed always to have went for the ball.
What!?!

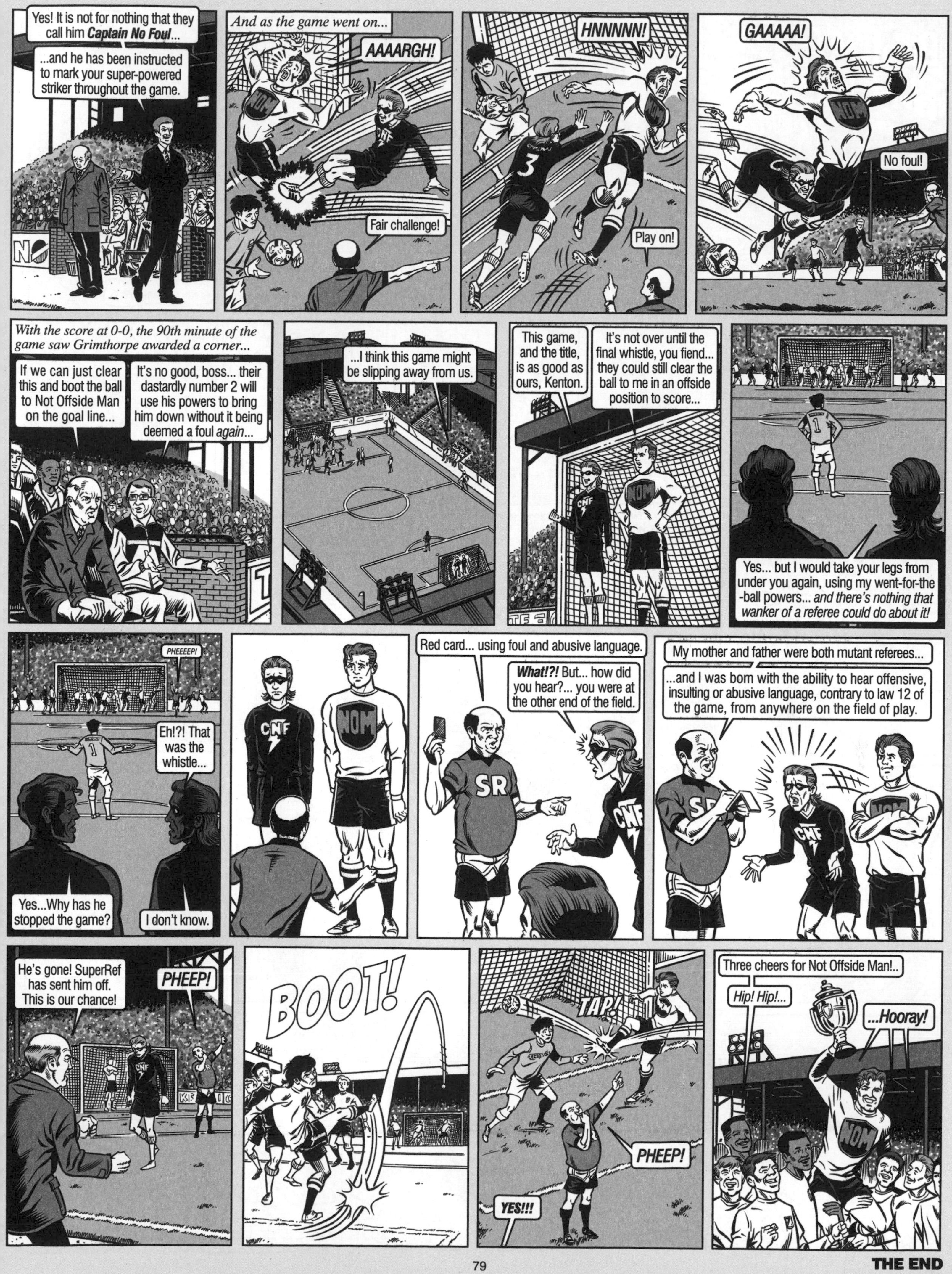
Yes! It is not for nothing that they call him Captain No Foul...
...and he has been instructed to mark your super-powered striker throughout the game.
And as the game went on...
AAAARGH!
Fair challenge!
HNNNNN!
Play on!
GAAAAA!
No foul!
With the score at 0-0, the 90th minute of the game saw Grimthorpe awarded a corner...
If we can just clear this and boot the ball to Not Offside Man on the goal line...
It's no good, boss... their dastardly number 2 will use his powers to bring him down without it being deemed a foul again...
...I think this game might be slipping away from us.
This game, and the title, is as good as ours, Kenton.
It's not over until the final whistle, you fiend... they could still clear the ball to me in an offside position to score...
Yes... but I would take your legs from under you again, using my went-for-the-ball powers... and there's nothing that wanker of a referee could do about it!
PHEEEEP!
Eh!?! That was the whistle...
Yes...Why has he stopped the game?
I don't know.
Red card... using foul and abusive language.
What!?! But... how did you hear?... you were at the other end of the field.
My mother and father were both mutant referees...
...and I was born with the ability to hear offensive, insulting or abusive language, contrary to law 12 of the game, from anywhere on the field of play.
He's gone! SuperRef has sent him off. This is our chance!
PHEEP!
BOOT!
TAP!
PHEEP!
YES!!!
Three cheers for Not Offside Man!..
Hip! Hip!...
...Hooray!

THE END

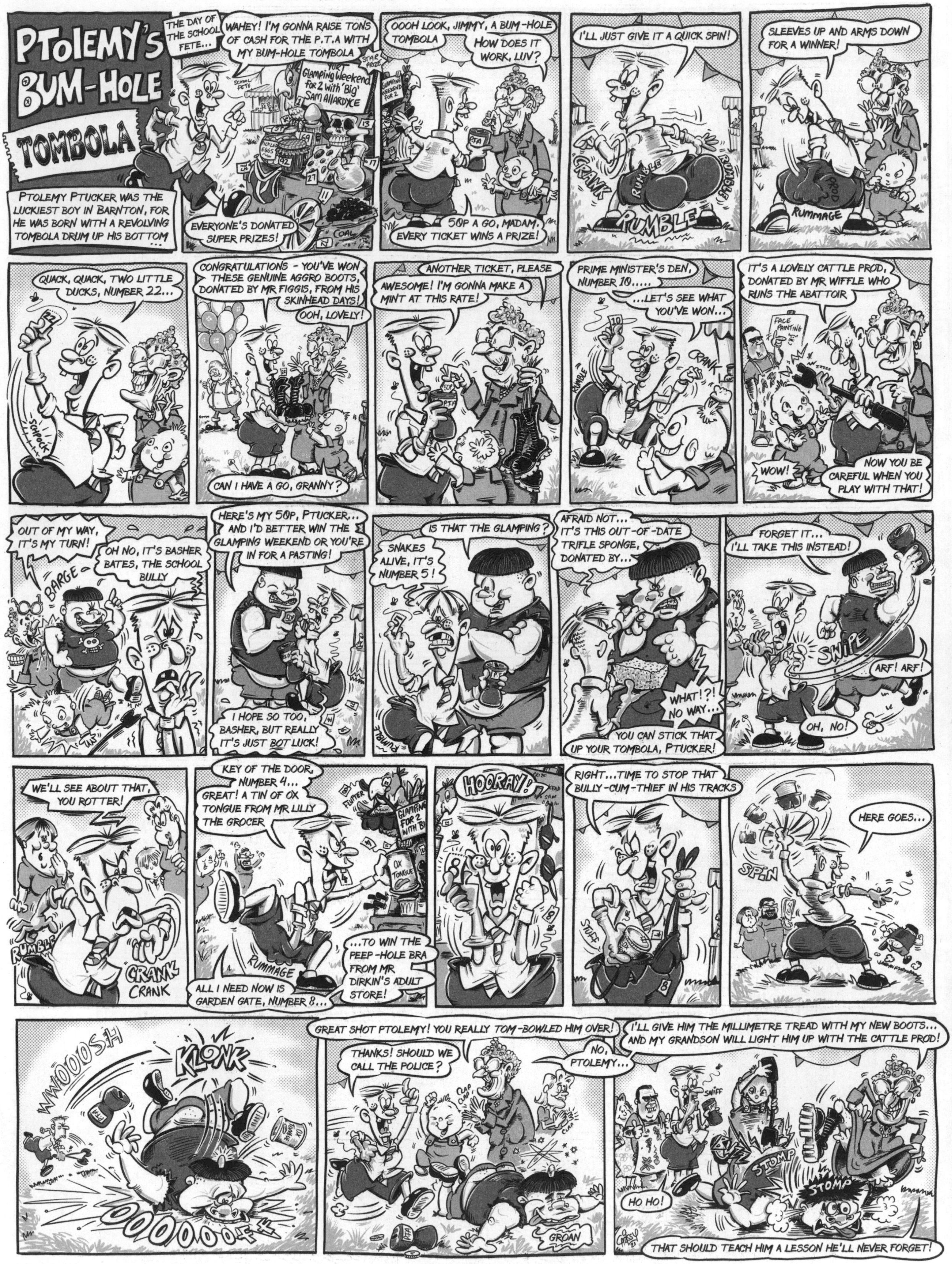
PTOLEMY'S BUM-HOLE TOMBOLA
THE DAY OF THE SCHOOL FETE...
WAHEY! I'M GONNA RAISE TONS OF CASH FOR THE P.T.A WITH MY BUM-HOLE TOMBOLA
STAR PRIZE
YURT Glamping Weekend for 2 with 'Big' Sam Allardyce
PICKLED EGGS
PTOLEMY PTUCKER WAS THE LUCKIEST BOY IN BARNTON, FOR HE WAS BORN WITH A REVOLVING TOMBOLA DRUM UP HIS BOTTOM...
EVERYONE'S DONATED SUPER PRIZES!
COAL
OOOH LOOK, JIMMY, A BUM-HOLE TOMBOLA
HOW DOES IT WORK, LUV?
GLAMPING WEEKEND FOR 2
PTA
50P A GO, MADAM. EVERY TICKET WINS A PRIZE!
I'LL JUST GIVE IT A QUICK SPIN!
CRANK
RUMBLE
RUMBLE
RUMBLE
SLEEVES UP AND ARMS DOWN FOR A WINNER!
PROD
RUMMAGE
QUACK, QUACK, TWO LITTLE DUCKS, NUMBER 22...
SCHPOCK
CONGRATULATIONS - YOU'VE WON THESE GENUINE AGGRO BOOTS, DONATED BY MR FIGGIS, FROM HIS SKINHEAD DAYS!
OOH, LOVELY!
CAN I HAVE A GO, GRANNY?
ANOTHER TICKET, PLEASE
AWESOME! I'M GONNA MAKE A MINT AT THIS RATE!
PRIME MINISTER'S DEN, NUMBER 10.....
...LET'S SEE WHAT YOU'VE WON...
RUMBLE
CRANK
IT'S A LOVELY CATTLE PROD, DONATED BY MR WIFFLE WHO RUNS THE ABATTOIR
FACE PAINTING
WOW!
NOW YOU BE CAREFUL WHEN YOU PLAY WITH THAT!
OUT OF MY WAY, IT'S MY TURN!
BARGE
OH NO, IT'S BASHER BATES, THE SCHOOL BULLY
HERE'S MY 50P, PTUCKER... AND I'D BETTER WIN THE GLAMPING WEEKEND OR YOU'RE IN FOR A PASTING!
I HOPE SO TOO, BASHER, BUT REALLY IT'S JUST BOT LUCK!
IS THAT THE GLAMPING?
SNAKES ALIVE, IT'S NUMBER 5!
RUMBLE
AFRAID NOT... IT'S THIS OUT-OF-DATE TRIFLE SPONGE, DONATED BY...
WHAT!?! NO WAY...
YOU CAN STICK THAT UP YOUR TOMBOLA, PTUCKER!
FORGET IT... I'LL TAKE THIS INSTEAD!
SWIPE
ARF! ARF!
OH, NO!
WE'LL SEE ABOUT THAT, YOU ROTTER!
RUMBLE
CRANK CRANK
KEY OF THE DOOR, NUMBER 4... GREAT! A TIN OF OX TONGUE FROM MR LILLY THE GROCER
OX TONGUE
GLAMPING FOR 2 WITH BIG
RUMMAGE
ALL I NEED NOW IS GARDEN GATE, NUMBER 8...
...TO WIN THE PEEP-HOLE BRA FROM MR DIRKIN'S ADULT STORE!
HOORAY!
RIGHT... TIME TO STOP THAT BULLY-CUM-THIEF IN HIS TRACKS
STUFF
HERE GOES...
SPIN
WWOOOSH
KLONK
OOOOOOOF
GREAT SHOT PTOLEMY! YOU REALLY TOM-BOWLED HIM OVER!
THANKS! SHOULD WE CALL THE POLICE?
NO, PTOLEMY...
CLAP CLAP
CLAP
GROAN
I'LL GIVE HIM THE MILLIMETRE TREAD WITH MY NEW BOOTS... AND MY GRANDSON WILL LIGHT HIM UP WITH THE CATTLE PROD!
SNIFF
STOMP
STOMP
HO HO!
THAT SHOULD TEACH HIM A LESSON HE'LL NEVER FORGET!

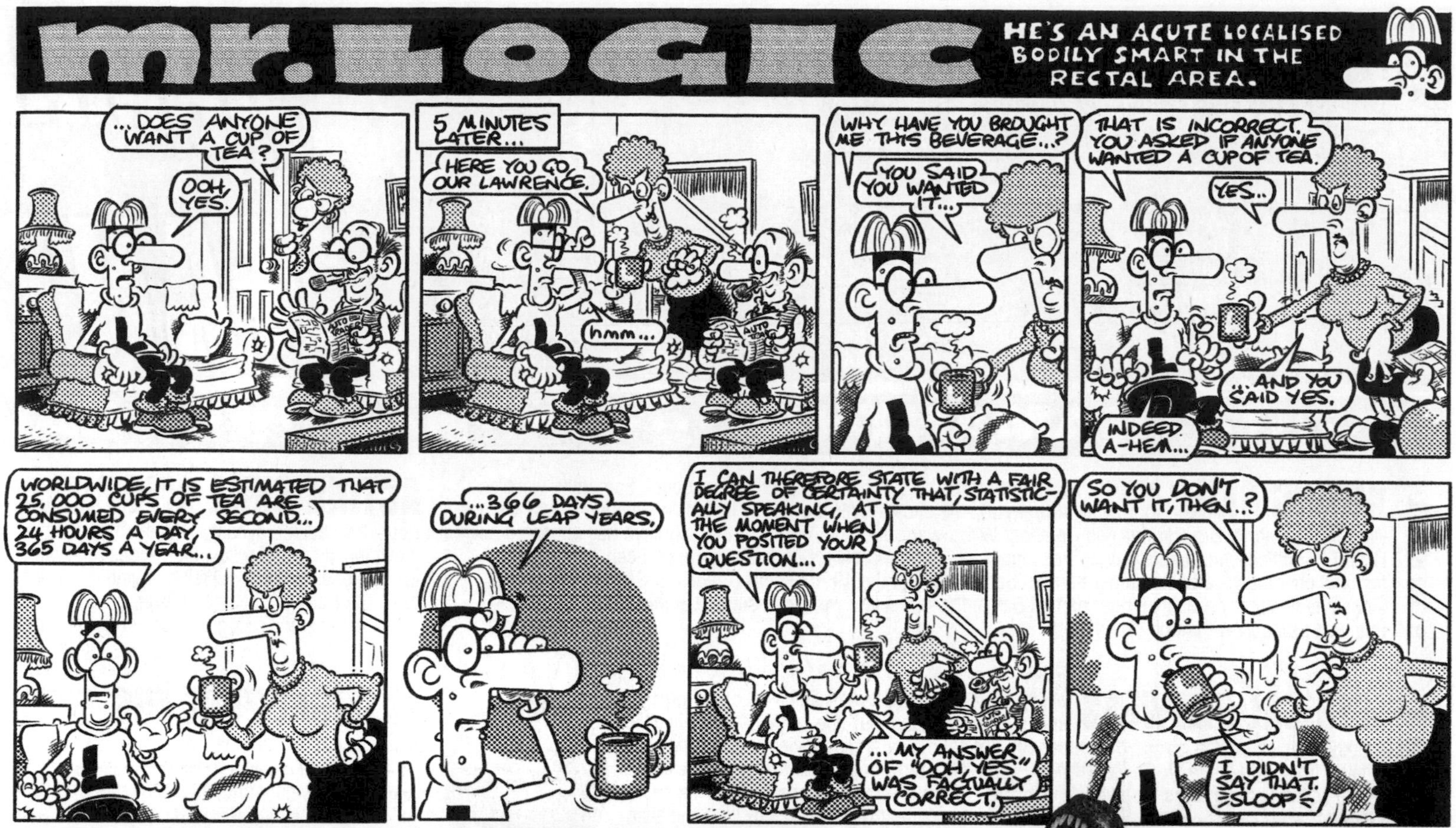
mr.LOGIC
HE'S AN ACUTE LOCALISED BODILY SMART IN THE RECTAL AREA.
...DOES ANYONE WANT A CUP OF TEA?
OOH, YES.
5 MINUTES LATER...
HERE YOU GO, OUR LAWRENCE.
hmm...
WHY HAVE YOU BROUGHT ME THIS BEVERAGE...?
YOU SAID YOU WANTED IT...
THAT IS INCORRECT. YOU ASKED IF ANYONE WANTED A CUP OF TEA.
YES...
...AND YOU SAID YES.
INDEED. A-HEM...
WORLDWIDE, IT IS ESTIMATED THAT 25,000 CUPS OF TEA ARE CONSUMED EVERY SECOND... 24 HOURS A DAY, 365 DAYS A YEAR...
...366 DAYS DURING LEAP YEARS.
I CAN THEREFORE STATE WITH A FAIR DEGREE OF CERTAINTY THAT, STATISTICALLY SPEAKING, AT THE MOMENT WHEN YOU POSITED YOUR QUESTION...
...MY ANSWER OF "OOH YES" WAS FACTUALLY CORRECT.
SO YOU DON'T WANT IT, THEN...?
I DIDN'T SAY THAT.
SLOOP

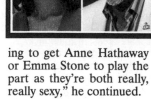

COVID CRISIS GETS TINSEL TOWN TREATMENT

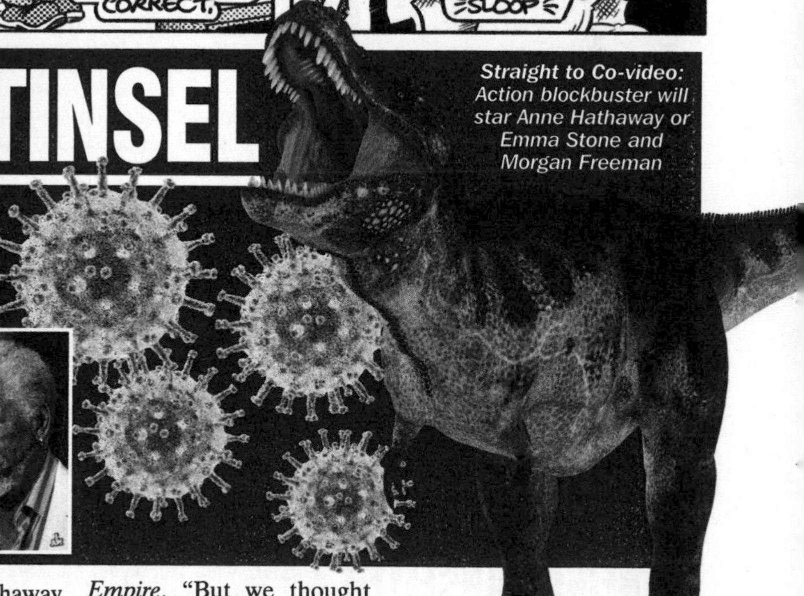

Straight to Co-video: Action blockbuster will star Anne Hathaway or Emma Stone and Morgan Freeman

AS FILMING gets underway in Hollywood, the story of the global Coronavirus pandemic is set to become a Tinseltown blockbuster. And the scientists in the story will not only face the danger of the virus, as moviegoers will see their laboratory attacked by dinosaurs!

EXCLUSIVE!

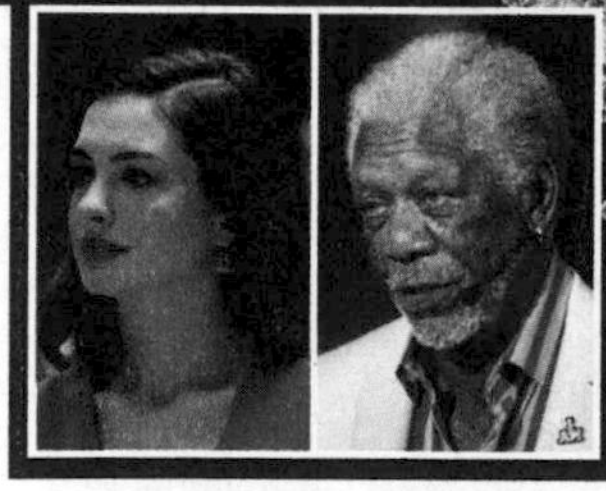

Covid! Jurassic Mission of Death is a dramatic telling of the story of the worst pandemic to hit the earth in 100 years, and will feature silver screen big names including Morgan Freeman and Vin Diesel.

"Although the pandemic has been the only news event for the past 12 months, it's actually quite a dull story," said director Spiro Theocropalis. "Searching for a vaccine might sound like an exciting project, but in reality, it just involves geeky scientists sitting round putting little bits of liquid in plastic tubes and staring into microscopes."

"So we had to sex it up a bit."

lab

The film follows scientist Dr Ursula Van der Lande, who heads the Biontech lab searching for a vaccine. But during a conference, she has a steamy affair with Dr Chuck Megalith, head of the rival Pfizer lab.

"Both are determined to develop the vaccine first, but sexual politics keep getting in the way," said Theocropalis. "Things take an unexpected turn when Van der Lande's boss is murdered, and the new CEO of Biontec gives her just 48 hours to complete her research."

"We thought it was important to cast a woman as the lead scientist, because we think the character should be a good role model for all girls wanting to follow a career in science," Theocropolis told *Empire* magazine. "And we're hoping to get Anne Hathaway or Emma Stone to play the part as they're both really, really sexy," he continued.

"Without giving too many spoilers, the sexy doc is in the lab doing all these equations on the wall, and suddenly she faints because she realises that the only way to develop a vaccine is by using the DNA of a dinosaur."

span

According to insiders, the scene ends when Dr Chuck comes in to find Dr Ursula on the laboratory floor, and takes her home, leading to a steamy sex scene.

"We had a lot of discussions about whether to include a sex scene in the film," Theocropalis told *Empire*. "But we thought that the actual scientists working on the Covid-19 vaccine would probably have had sex at home, and so it seemed particularly relevant. And it was really tastefully done."

terr

Things really heat up when US President Mike Magnum (Morgan Freeman) sends ex-Special Forces kung fu expert Jack Renegade (Vin Diesel) to the Amazonian jungle to capture one of the last velociraptors on earth and bring it back to the lab.

Meanwhile, a load of Russians surround Ursula's lab in an attempt to steal her research notes, and the scientists have to barricade themselves in. From then on, it's pretty much a race against time for Jack to get the velociraptor back, fight off the Russians and develop the vaccine.

Theocropalis said the film would be dedicated to the real-life scientists and technicians who have worked tirelessly to develop Covid-19 vaccines, and it would be a heartfelt tribute to the million-plus people who have died as a result of the virus.

Covid: Jurassic Mission of Death will be released in cinemas in the summer.

WHY ARE WE HERE? *Is there a God? What is the purpose of life on Earth?* Philosophers have been pondering all these weighty questions and more for many millennia now – but one query trumps them all when it comes to sparking violent debate and renting entire communities in twain: *Who Is The Best Celebrity With The Surname 'Fox'?*

For some people, the answer is, and always will be, **SAMANTHA FOX** – the busty model-turned-songstress who kept every red-blooded male's pulse racing throughout the 1980s. For others, the correct response is **LAURENCE FOX**, the maggot-cocked telly fave who won the hearts of tens with his stunning portrayal of DS James Hathaway in ITV's *Lewis*, before reinventing himself as an intellectual firebrand in the war against 'wokeness'. Others still will tell you that by far and away the best Fox is **RUEL FOX**, the journeyman soccer ace who made 173 appearances for Norwich City between 1986 and 1994. And there are probably others who'd plump for **MICHAEL J FOX**, the Tinseltown icon who got off with his own mum in a car park in *Back To The Future*. But we've only got space for three.

The time has come for the arguing, bickering and senseless bloodshed to end. We have decided to settle this age-old debate once and for all by pitting the three most formidable Foxes against one another in a six-round scrap to the death, in order to finally find out...

SAMAN
FANTA

•••••••••• SAMANTHA ••••••••••

•••••••••• LAU

ROUND 1

ACTING SKILL
AFTER FINDING fame as a popular Page 3 pin-up, saucy Samantha went on to appear in many top TV shows over the years, including *Celebrity Come Dine With Me*, *Celebrity Big Brother* and *Celebrity Wife Swap*. But in all of these, the foxy fave has appeared as HERSELF, which unfortunately does not require much acting skill. She has only once been cast as a fictional character - a busty singer named 'Samantha' - in the 1990 sitcom *Charles In Charge*. But since she is already a busty singer named Samantha in real life, we can assume that inhabiting this role was probably not much of a stretch.

Score 5

ACTING SKILL
ARSEHOLE Laurenc was born into the noto rious Fox acting dynasty. As such, it was perhap inevitable he would follow his various relatives into th board-treading trade - albeit enjoying much less suc cess than any of them. However, Laurence's lack o roles, awards and recognition is not due to him havin

ROUND 2

MUSICAL PROWESS
AMPLE-CHARMED Samantha enjoyed huge musical success throughout the eighties and nineties, topping singles charts across the globe with her saucy, parentheses-heavy hits *Touch Me (I Want Your Body)*, *Do Ya Do Ya (Wanna Please Me)* and *Naughty Girls (Need Love Too)*. She enjoyed less success by inverting the order of the parentheses on her 1991 hit *(Hurt Me! Hurt Me!) But The Pants Stay On* - which only reached Number 123 in the Australian hit parade - but regardless, it's a Platinum-selling round for the brackets-bonkers bombshell.

Score 7

MUSICAL PROWESS
MULTI-TALENTED Laurence is not only his generation's finest actor, h is also its most accomplished musician. The thim ble-dicked singer-songwriter has released two album of heart-wrenching acoustic rock - 2016's *Holdin Patterns* and 2019's *A Grief Observed* - both o

ROUND 3

NEPOTISM
BORN TO humble market traders in the East End of London, it would appear that Samantha owes very little of her success to her family connections. However, the surname she inherited from her parents has in fact provided her with a wealth of lucrative career opportunities. Not only did it form the basis of a satisfying pun for her 1997 album *21st Century Fox*, it also set up the slogan - *'Follow the Fox to Swithland Motors'* - for a series of television adverts with a Leicestershire-based car dealership. It's a strong round for the curvaceous ex-*Sun* stunner.

Score 7

NEPOTISM
AS A TEENAGER, pluck Laurence left Harrow School wit a seemingly unattainable dream - *to become a famou actor*. Starting from the very bottom, he worked his wa tirelessly up the theatrical ranks despite having no con tacts in the industry, except for his grandfather, gran mother, father, uncles, aunts, brother, sister, brother-in

ROUND 4

NATURAL RAPPORT WITH MICK FLEETWOOD

ON 13 February 1989, sexy Samantha took to the stage at London's Royal Albert Hall to present that year's BRIT Awards. By her side at the podium was lanky, slap-headed Fleetwood Mac tub-thumper, Mick Fleetwood. Sadly, the evening was beset by technical difficulties, and when the autocue broke, the pair were forced to rely on their natural rapport to see them through. Even more sadly, it transpired that they didn't have a natural rapport, and the resulting three-hour stilted performance caused many viewers to cringe so hard that their retinas detached.

Score 0

NATURAL RAPPORT WITH MICK FLEETWOOD
AS A champion the #AllLivesMatt movement and a bona fide man of the people, ex-Harrovia Laurence can get along with absolutely anyone, from th lowliest street sweeper to the highliest member of the F acting dynasty. He has yet to present a major awards ce emony alongside ex-Fleetwood Mac percussionist Mic

ROUND 5

BEING CANCELLED
IF SHE were still plying her bare-breasted trade in 2021, it seems highly likely that saucy Sam would find herself immediately 'cancelled' by miserable moaning minnie millennials, who would undoubtedly brand her cheeky antics as 'sexist'. Fortunately, however, Sam chose to strut her stuff on *The Sun's* Page 3 in the mid-to-late eighties - a halcyon era when men were men, birds were birds and political correctness was merely a nightmarish, Orwellian fantasy.

Score 2

BEING CANCELLED
AS wealth white man who dares to speak his min in public, brave Laurence gets 'cancelle at least ten times a day by the PC-craze liberal elite. Whether he's fearlessly explai ing racism to a black academic, heroical

ROUND 6

DIRECT RESPONSIBILITY FOR THE DEATHS OF THOUSANDS
IN HER semi-nude pomp, we can say with absolute certainty that sultry Samantha got more than a few hearts fluttering, pulses racing and blood pressures rising. That said, however, there is absolutely no evidence of any of these sexually-stimulated changes to her fans' corporeal rhythms leading to even *one* death - let alone thousands. It's a disappointing final showing for the 38DD non-mass-murderer.

Score 0

DIRECT RESPONSIBILITY FOR T
HAVING romped through the early rounds, Laurenc may have stumbled at the final hurdle. Because, rath than being responsible for the deaths of thousands, has actually *saved countless human lives*! By encou aging his 260,000 Twitter followers to throw off the protective masks and hug each other during a glob

HOW DID THEY DO?

SAMANTHA ••••••••••
Simply the Breast? Not quite! Page 3 stunna Sam has ended up at Number 3 on the podium in this Fearsome Free-way Fox Fight. She may be Blightly's most popular pin-up – but she's only its third favourite Fox.

21

LAURENCE ••
Lozza leads the way!
Laurence's legions of fans will have been concerned after his dire final round display, but they needn't have worried – the

HA v LAURENCE v RUEL
WHO IS THE MOST
STIC MR(s) FOX?

NCE

zero discernible talent - far from it. Instead, it is down to the sinister cabal of 'woke' snowflakes who control the BBC, Netflix and Hollywood, and refuse to cast the outspoken thespian because of his forthright political views. Taking this into account, it's a stonking opening round for the not-shit-at-acting *Lewis* icon. **Score 10**

which sank utterly without trace. However, this is not due to them being full of piss-weak, sub-Ed Sheeran dross - far from it. Rather, it's down to the liberal elitist record-buying public and their refusal to engage with Laurence's superb music on account of his fearless anti-woke activism. **Score 10**

aw and various cousins. Against all odds, Laurence's natural talent shone through, and he has managed to achieve a truly glittering acting career without any assistance from family or friends. **Score 0**

but if he did, we can be absolutely certain that the banter would flow freely and easily like fine wine, regardless of whether or not the autocue was working properly. **Score 9**

taking issue with the appearance of a Sikh soldier in a First World War film or valiantly urging people not to wear masks during an airborne viral pandemic, the courageous *Lewis* sidekick constantly risks life, limb and cancellation on the frontline of the war against wokeness. **Score 50**

ATHS OF THOUSANDS

pandemic, brave Lozza has single-handedly slowed Covid-19's deathly march across the UK - and crushed the dangerous propaganda spouted by NHS 'experts'. A negative score reflects just how not responsible for any deaths he is. **Score -10**

nti-woke actor as romped home n style. Three heers for *The* antastic Mr Fox!

69

RUEL

ROUND 1

ACTING SKILL

AS A QUICK, tricksy winger for Norwich City, Newcastle and Tottenham, soccer ace Ruel relied on his acting skills in every Premier League game he played. At least a dozen times per match, the Ipswich-born midfield whizz would feign going in one direction, and then actually go in another, in order to confound his defensive opponent. He drops a point because at no time did he have a sinister cabal of 'woke' snowflakes holding him back, but it's still an impressive opening haul for the journeyman footy fave. **Score 9**

ROUND 2

MUSICAL PROWESS

AFTER SIGNING for Newcastle United in 1994, Ruel was taken under the wing of corkscrew-haired manager Kevin Keegan. Keegan – a keen singer and performer, whose hits include *It Ain't Easy* and *Head Over Heels In Love* - may well have passed on some of his musical knowledge and prowess to his young protégé – we simply don't know. So, while Ruel Fox has yet to release a single, EP, album or display any concrete evidence that he is even interested in music, it is only fair to award the potential tunesmith half marks here. **Score 5**

ROUND 3

NEPOTISM

SHAMELESS nepotist Ruel owes his *entire* career to his parents. For if his mother and father had not had the foresight to engage in penetrative intercourse in April 1967, the speedy winger would not have been born in January 1968, and would consequently have found it nigh-on impossible to make his name as a top Premier League star. As such, it's an impressive points tally for the unable-to-succeed-on-his-own-two-feet footballer. **Score 9**

ROUND 4

NATURAL RAPPORT WITH MICK FLEETWOOD

IT SEEMS highly unlikely that Ruel Fox has ever met - let alone established a natural chemistry with - the iconic rock drummer Mick Fleetwood. However, if the two were to bump into one another, perhaps at a charity dinner or on a celebrity panel show, they would have plenty to talk about. Mick is described on Wikipedia as a "competent fencer", so the pair could chew the fat over their shared love of sport. Plus, both men have dabbled with restaurant management, so they could compare their adventures in the food trade. Ultimately, all signs indicate that the unlikely duo would get on like a house on fire. **Score 6**

ROUND 5

BEING CANCELLED

WHETHER due to his hectic footballing career - or just plain and simple cowardice - there is scant evidence of Ruel Fox ever speaking out publicly on issues such as the plight of the wealthy white man and the over-representation of Sikhs in war films. Constantly sidestepping these thorny topics in interviews and on social media means that the former Magpies frontman has never had to fear being cancelled by a load of jumped-up *Guardian*-reading snowflakes. **Score 0**

The Guardian
Students drafted in to plug NHS gaps

ROUND 6

DIRECT RESPONSIBILITY FOR THE DEATHS OF THOUSANDS

WING WIZARD Ruel can claim many accomplishments in his long and sort-of glittering career. From guiding Norwich to their highest ever Premier League finish in 1993 and 1994 to helping the Canaries defeat the mighty Bayern Munich en route to the last 16 of the UEFA Cup, the Whitton United chairman has achieved a great deal in his life. However, at no time has he directly caused the deaths of thousands of people. Good news for the general public, but potentially fatal news for his final score. **Score 0**

RUEL

Footy ace Ruel put in a decent first-half performance, but he'll be sick as a parrot at the final whistle, as he is bested by his polymathic, micropenised namesake. *Ruel thinks it's all over... and unfortunately, it is now!*

29

Next week:
Billie v Maris v Rowdy Roddy:
Which is the Best Piper?

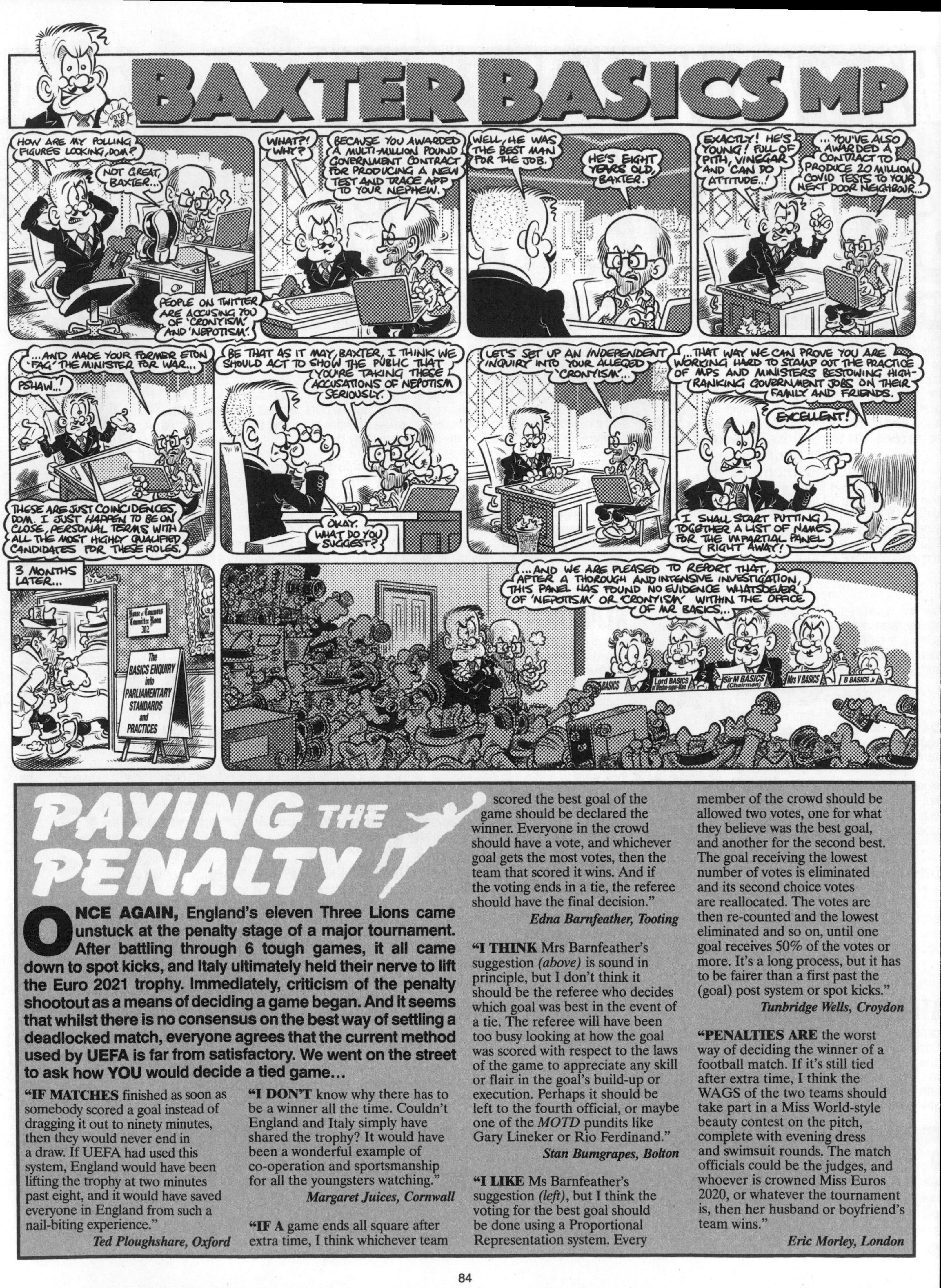
BAXTER BASICS MP
HOW ARE MY POLLING FIGURES LOOKING, DOM?
NOT GREAT, BAXTER...
PEOPLE ON TWITTER ARE ACCUSING YOU OF 'CRONYISM' AND 'NEPOTISM'.
WHAT?! WHY?
BECAUSE YOU AWARDED A MULTI-MILLION POUND GOVERNMENT CONTRACT FOR PRODUCING A NEW TEST AND TRACE APP TO YOUR NEPHEW.
WELL, HE WAS THE BEST MAN FOR THE JOB.
HE'S EIGHT YEARS OLD, BAXTER.
EXACTLY! HE'S YOUNG! FULL OF PITH, VINEGAR AND 'CAN DO' ATTITUDE..!
...YOU'VE ALSO AWARDED A CONTRACT TO PRODUCE 20 MILLION COVID TESTS TO YOUR NEXT DOOR NEIGHBOUR...
...AND MADE YOUR FORMER ETON 'FAG' THE MINISTER FOR WAR...
PSHAW..!
THESE ARE JUST COINCIDENCES, DOM. I JUST HAPPEN TO BE ON CLOSE, PERSONAL TERMS WITH ALL THE MOST HIGHLY QUALIFIED CANDIDATES FOR THESE ROLES.
OKAY. WHAT DO YOU SUGGEST?
BE THAT AS IT MAY, BAXTER, I THINK WE SHOULD ACT TO SHOW THE PUBLIC THAT YOU'RE TAKING THESE ACCUSATIONS OF NEPOTISM SERIOUSLY.
LET'S SET UP AN INDEPENDENT INQUIRY INTO YOUR ALLEGED 'CRONYISM'...
...THAT WAY WE CAN PROVE YOU ARE WORKING HARD TO STAMP OUT THE PRACTICE OF MPS AND MINISTERS BESTOWING HIGH-RANKING GOVERNMENT JOBS ON THEIR FAMILY AND FRIENDS.
EXCELLENT!
I SHALL START PUTTING TOGETHER A LIST OF NAMES FOR THE IMPARTIAL PANEL RIGHT AWAY!
3 MONTHS LATER...
House of Commons Committee Room 302
The BASICS ENQUIRY into PARLIAMENTARY STANDARDS and PRACTICES
...AND WE ARE PLEASED TO REPORT THAT, AFTER A THOROUGH AND INTENSIVE INVESTIGATION, THIS PANEL HAS FOUND NO EVIDENCE WHATSOEVER OF 'NEPOTISM' OR 'CRONYISM' WITHIN THE OFFICE OF MR BASICS.
S BASICS
Lord BASICS of Weston-super-Mare
Sir M BASICS (Chairman)
Mrs V BASICS
B BASICS Jr

PAYING THE PENALTY

ONCE AGAIN, England's eleven Three Lions came unstuck at the penalty stage of a major tournament. After battling through 6 tough games, it all came down to spot kicks, and Italy ultimately held their nerve to lift the Euro 2021 trophy. Immediately, criticism of the penalty shootout as a means of deciding a game began. And it seems that whilst there is no consensus on the best way of settling a deadlocked match, everyone agrees that the current method used by UEFA is far from satisfactory. We went on the street to ask how YOU would decide a tied game…

"IF MATCHES finished as soon as somebody scored a goal instead of dragging it out to ninety minutes, then they would never end in a draw. If UEFA had used this system, England would have been lifting the trophy at two minutes past eight, and it would have saved everyone in England from such a nail-biting experience."

Ted Ploughshare, Oxford

"I DON'T know why there has to be a winner all the time. Couldn't England and Italy simply have shared the trophy? It would have been a wonderful example of co-operation and sportsmanship for all the youngsters watching."

Margaret Juices, Cornwall

"IF A game ends all square after extra time, I think whichever team scored the best goal of the game should be declared the winner. Everyone in the crowd should have a vote, and whichever goal gets the most votes, then the team that scored it wins. And if the voting ends in a tie, the referee should have the final decision."

Edna Barnfeather, Tooting

"I THINK Mrs Barnfeather's suggestion *(above)* is sound in principle, but I don't think it should be the referee who decides which goal was best in the event of a tie. The referee will have been too busy looking at how the goal was scored with respect to the laws of the game to appreciate any skill or flair in the goal's build-up or execution. Perhaps it should be left to the fourth official, or maybe one of the *MOTD* pundits like Gary Lineker or Rio Ferdinand."

Stan Bumgrapes, Bolton

"I LIKE Ms Barnfeather's suggestion *(left)*, but I think the voting for the best goal should be done using a Proportional Representation system. Every member of the crowd should be allowed two votes, one for what they believe was the best goal, and another for the second best. The goal receiving the lowest number of votes is eliminated and its second choice votes are reallocated. The votes are then re-counted and the lowest eliminated and so on, until one goal receives 50% of the votes or more. It's a long process, but it has to be fairer than a first past the (goal) post system or spot kicks."

Tunbridge Wells, Croydon

"PENALTIES ARE the worst way of deciding the winner of a football match. If it's still tied after extra time, I think the WAGS of the two teams should take part in a Miss World-style beauty contest on the pitch, complete with evening dress and swimsuit rounds. The match officials could be the judges, and whoever is crowned Miss Euros 2020, or whatever the tournament is, then her husband or boyfriend's team wins."

Eric Morley, London

SAINTS ALIVE!

Catholic Church fear saintly intercession service near breaking point

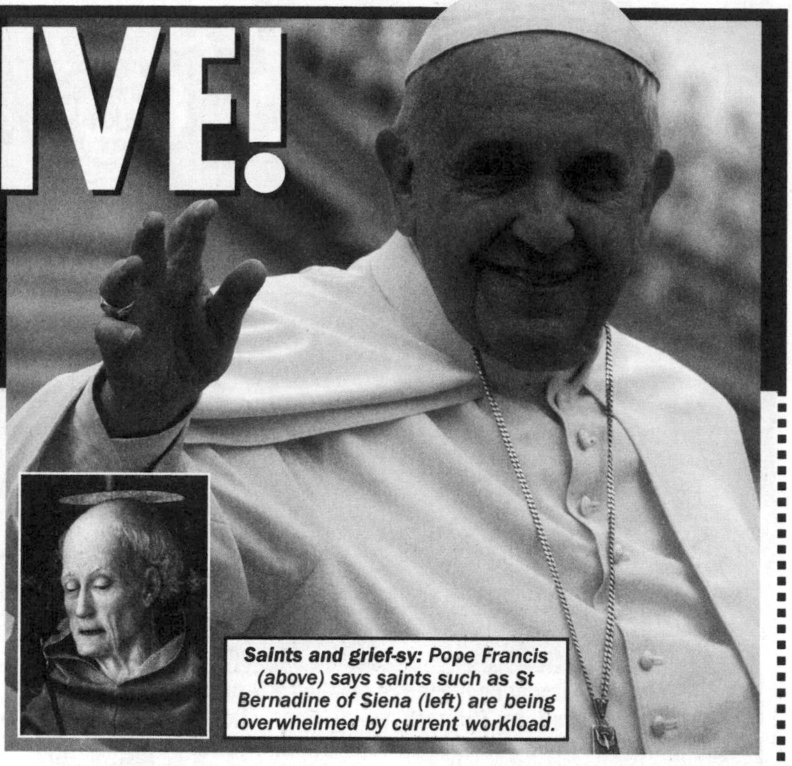

Saints and grief-sy: Pope Francis (above) says saints such as St Bernadine of Siena (left) are being overwhelmed by current workload.

THE COVID pandemic, with its knock-on effects on the economy and the nation's mental health, could be causing problems for the patron saints of the Catholic church.

EXCLUSIVE!

According to the religion's CEO, Pope Francis, since the pandemic struck, appeals to the saints for intercession have gone through the roof, and many of the canonised souls are struggling with their workload.

"People are praying for Covid victims right, left and centre," the Pontiff told *The Catholic Herald*. "Not only that, they're getting unprecedented requests from people whose businesses are under threat and others who are struggling with debt as a result of the pandemic," he continued.

"All of this comes on top of prayers for help for all the usual stuff like people who've lost things and people going for job interviews."

collapse

But while the situation is bad, the Holy Father fears that if Covid cases do not fall significantly and the economy pick up as a result, then next winter could see the saintly service collapse.

"Patron saints are working flat out round the clock at the minute," he said. "But come December, there'll be the influx of all the prayers from people whose car won't start in the morning, and those asking for a speedy recovery for some granny who has slipped on the ice. The whole Patron Saint system will be overwhelmed."

plan

In order to cope with the pressures, cardinals at the Vatican have drawn up a plan to reassign saints to other roles for the period of the pandemic.

lung

St Bernadine of Siena, the patron saint of lung diseases, will be helped by St Fiacra - who normally deals with haemorrhoid sufferers. And mental health boss St Dymphna will get assistance from St Dunstan who also has the blacksmith, locksmith and bellringers brief.

The Vatican also revealed plans to recruit sanctified souls – those on their way to canonisation – to help with intercessions if the situation worsens.

maiden

And the Pope was quick to reassure catholics who fear that their intercession could end up being performed by a non-qualified apostle. "Don't worry. Your prayer will be dealt with by a canonised saint," he said. "These sanctified souls will simply triage the prayers and make sure they get to the right department."

But while the saintly service was facing unprecedented difficulties, the Vatican was at pains to point out that it was business as usual, although he urged those in need to think before they pray.

ing board

"If you need a saint to intercede on your behalf, then by all means pray, but try to solve the problem yourself first," said Vatican press officer Umberto Columbo. "Before you ask St Anthony to locate your lost car keys, have another good look for them, or ask your wife if she has seen them," he continued.

"Or if you've got piles, stick a bit of Preparation H on them before you go asking St Fiacra to miraculously shrink the buggers."

Re-Insect-Carnation

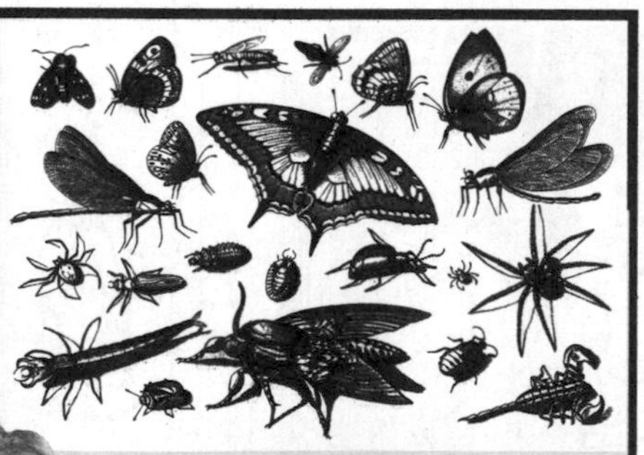

NOBODY knows what happens to us when we die. Christians would have us believe that if we are deserving, we ascend to Heaven, and if not, we burn forever in the fiery pit of Hell. As we don't know God's mind as to what is deserving and what isn't, it's a bit of a gamble. So it's probably best to believe that we are *reincarnated* instead – a process where our souls are transplanted to a fresh body to live life all over again. However, with trillions of individual animals on earth, of which only 7.9 billion are humans, chances are we'll be reincarnated as something else entirely. Whilst strolling around the jungle as a tiger, or soaring high in the sky as an eagle would not be a bad life, we must remember that 99% of all living animals are insects, so it's odds-on we're coming back as a creepy crawly when we kick the bucket. We asked some of our favourite celebrities and Katie Hopkins which insect they would like to be reincarnated in the body of...

Ben Dover,
Adult Film Impressario

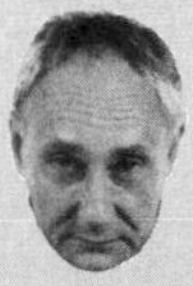

I MUST HAVE shagged the thick end of 50,000 women in my 40 years in front of the camera, and I'm absolutely knackered, let me tell you. So I hope when I'm reincarnated as an insect, I come back as an aphid. These wingless little things undergo a process known as parthenogenesis, which means the females can give birth to offspring without the need to have sex with a male aphid first. So that means all the females can go off and have the babies while I get my head down for a nice bit of peace and quiet.

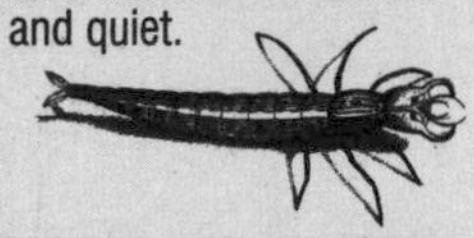

Helen Mirren,
actor-cum-national-treasure

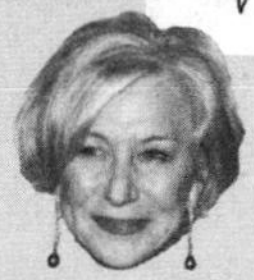

I FAMOUSLY PORTRAYED the Queen in a film of the same name, and I have to say, I loved it. She has a great life, not having to do anything and having everyone bow and scrape to her. So if I came back as an insect, I'd like to be a Queen bee. The thought of laying about a hive all day, eating honey and having tens of thousands of stinging subjects at my beck and call is thrilling. Of course, if I came back as a bee and I was a worker or a drone, I don't think I would like that at all.

Katie Hopkins,
gobshite

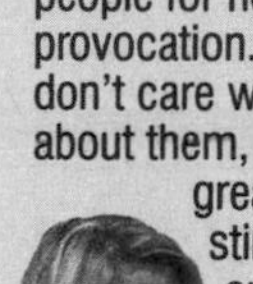

I SPEND MY DAY uploading spiteful, poisonous tweets and Facebook posts, so if I came back as an insect, I think I'd be a wasp. Like me, they love hurting people for no reason and without provocation. And like me they don't care what people think about them, probably. And the great thing is, they can sting again and again and again, unlike bees which only get one shot before pulling their arses inside out.

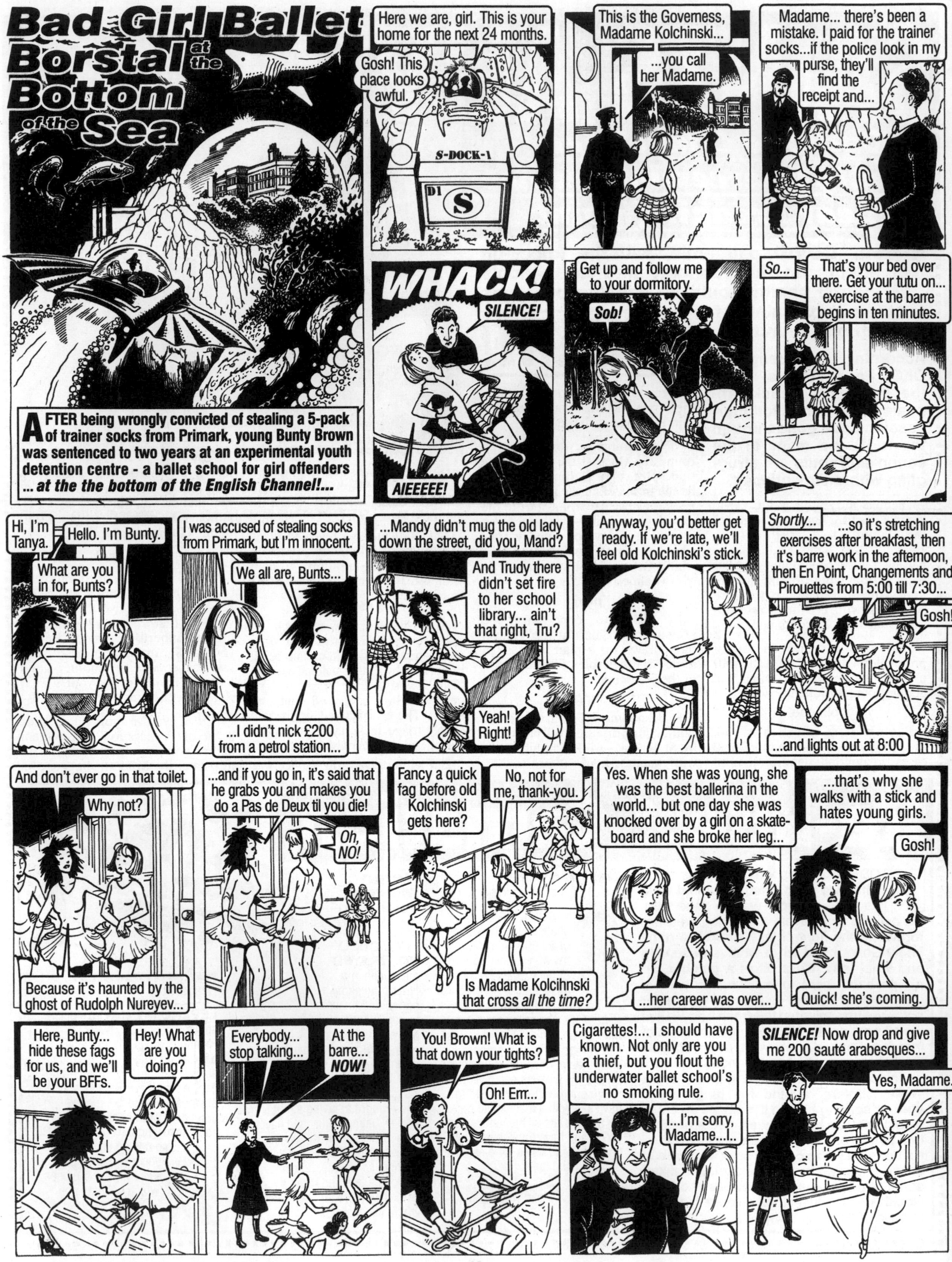
Bad Girl Ballet Borstal at the Bottom of the Sea
AFTER being wrongly convicted of stealing a 5-pack of trainer socks from Primark, young Bunty Brown was sentenced to two years at an experimental youth detention centre - a ballet school for girl offenders ... at the the bottom of the English Channel!...
Here we are, girl. This is your home for the next 24 months.
Gosh! This place looks awful.
S-DOCK-1
D1
S
This is the Governess, Madame Kolchinski...
...you call her Madame.
Madame... there's been a mistake. I paid for the trainer socks...if the police look in my purse, they'll find the receipt and...
WHACK!
SILENCE!
AIEEEEE!
Get up and follow me to your dormitory.
Sob!
So...
That's your bed over there. Get your tutu on... exercise at the barre begins in ten minutes.
Hi, I'm Tanya.
Hello. I'm Bunty.
What are you in for, Bunts?
I was accused of stealing socks from Primark, but I'm innocent.
We all are, Bunts...
...I didn't nick £200 from a petrol station...
...Mandy didn't mug the old lady down the street, did you, Mand?
And Trudy there didn't set fire to her school library... ain't that right, Tru?
Yeah! Right!
Anyway, you'd better get ready. If we're late, we'll feel old Kolchinski's stick.
Shortly...
...so it's stretching exercises after breakfast, then it's barre work in the afternoon, then En Point, Changements and Pirouettes from 5:00 till 7:30...
Gosh!
...and lights out at 8:00
And don't ever go in that toilet.
Why not?
Because it's haunted by the ghost of Rudolph Nureyev...
...and if you go in, it's said that he grabs you and makes you do a Pas de Deux til you die!
Oh, NO!
Fancy a quick fag before old Kolchinski gets here?
No, not for me, thank-you.
Is Madame Kolcihnski that cross all the time?
Yes. When she was young, she was the best ballerina in the world... but one day she was knocked over by a girl on a skate-board and she broke her leg...
...her career was over...
...that's why she walks with a stick and hates young girls.
Gosh!
Quick! she's coming.
Here, Bunty... hide these fags for us, and we'll be your BFFs.
Hey! What are you doing?
Everybody... stop talking...
At the barre... NOW!
You! Brown! What is that down your tights?
Oh! Err...
Cigarettes!... I should have known. Not only are you a thief, but you flout the underwater ballet school's no smoking rule.
I...I'm sorry, Madame...I...
SILENCE! Now drop and give me 200 sauté arabesques...
Yes, Madame.

...then after the lesson, get a mop and bucket from the caretaker and clean the shower room before evening class.
Yes, Madame.
After class...
Hey, thanks for not grassing us up, Bunt.
That's okay.
...if you had, we'd have come after you with some pool balls in a leg warmer.
Enjoy your tea. I'd better get started on the shower room.
Yeah! See you at 5:00, Bunt.
Excuse me... Madame said I was to get a mop and bucket to clean the shower room.
There's some down there.
Oh, bother... I've forgotten the detergent.
Excuse me, sir, I've forgotten the...
Oh... he's gone.
I'm sure he won't mind if I just take some...
...I wonder if it's through here...
There was no detergent behind the door, but what Bunty saw froze her blood...
Yes... I've almost finished the last life-like robot ballerina... and once I've replaced this batch of Borstal girls with the autons...
...I'll deliver you enough human flesh to keep the lions and tigers at your zoo fed for months!
Oh no! The Caretaker's going to replace us girls with robots and sell us to the zoo for tiger food...
...I've got to tell Madame!
And what makes you think I don't already know, Brown..?
EEEK!
There's a never-ending supply of bad girls sent to my sea-bed penal correction facility...
We build up their muscles through ballet, sell them to the zoo and return them to society as well-behaved autons...
...everyone's a winner... well... *almost* everyone.
Quick! After her!
SHRIEK!
RAAAAAAA!
I'll hide in here, he won't dare follow me... it's a girls only toilet.
Phew! Safe at last!
Come, child...!
...Let us dance a Pas de Deux...
...forever!
SCREAM! The g-g-g-ghost of Rudolf Nureyev!
RAAAAAA!
WOOOOO!
SCREAM!
RAAAAAA!
WOOOOO!
Oh, no! We're at the bottom of the sea... there's no escape!
Whaaa!
WOOOOO!
RAAAAAA!
SCREAM!
Oh, no! Her screams have cracked the dome!
Crumbs!
...If the glass breaks, we'll all drown or get ate off sharks!
Next week: The police, a priest and some builders arrive in a mini-sub and arrest Madame Kolchinski and the caretaker, exorcise the ghost of Rudolph Nureyev and fix the crack in the dome, respectively, before finding the receipt for the trainer socks in Bunty's purse and acquitting her of all charges. Don't miss the next thrilling episode of... Bad Girl Ballet Borstal at the Bottom of the Sea!

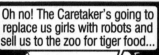

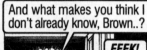

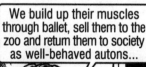

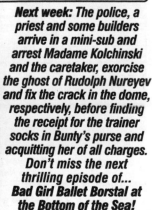

... 5-PAGE CHESS SPECIAL ... 5-PAGE CHESS SPECIAL ... 5-PAGE CHESS SPECIAL ... 5-PAGE C

CHEQUE, MATES!

North East chess champion sues Netflix over stolen story

NETFLIX series *The Queen's Gambit* was the smash TV hit of 2020, telling the tale of Beth Harmon, an orphan from Lexington, Kentucky, who embarks on a meteoric journey which ends in her being crowned World Chess Champion. And although it was a work of fiction, the story eerily mimics the life of a former launderette manager from Spennymoor in County Durham.

King of the Castle: Ex-laundry worker Calvin believes his story was stolen by streaming giant.

And now 38-year-old Calvin Weedol plans to **SUE** the billion-dollar streaming giant for telling the story of his life without permission, claiming £1500 in full and final settlement to compensate for the mental stress of seeing himself portrayed on screen.

"It was a good series, don't get me wrong," Weedol told *The Spennymoor and Staindrop Flugelhorn*. "But they should of asked my permission before rolling the cameras."

According to Weedol, the over-the-top content platform made a few subtle changes in order to throw him off the scent, but the onscreen tale was so similar to his own life story that he believes he is almost certain to win in court.

He told the paper: "The most obvious switch was that they changed sex, casting me as a girl rather than a bloke, and they made her an orphan, when my mum and dad are still alive and well."

"In fact I still live with them," he said.

Good Queen Beth? Harmon (played by Anna Taylor-Joy) in the Netflix hit.

The stories also diverge slightly in that – unlike the main character in the Netflix series – Weedol has never won a major chess tournament, or indeed any chess competition. Nor has he ever set foot in Moscow or New York where most of the drama takes place.

"Other than that, there's not a fag paper between our two stories," the former launderette manager said.

advanced

Calvin's love of chess began after he received a boardgame compendium for Christmas when he was 9 years old ... *exactly the same age* as the show's Beth Harmon when she discovers the game. And like her, he was soon playing and beating more advanced opponents.

"My first competitive game was during a wet playtime at school, when I beat Barry Duckworth," he said. "He was the class swot and had glasses and everything, but I beat him in fifteen minutes. He accused me of cheating by moving some prawns when he went to the toilet, but I didn't."

"I knew at that point that my future lay as a chess grandmaster."

ordinary

Over the few next years, Weedol's chess career went from strength to strength, just like his on-screen alter-ego. At the age of 10 he came second in the chess category in his cub scouts boardgames evening, and months later came third in his school chess club's end of term knock-out competiton.

"Some of the on-screen events were so similar to events in my life that it simply cannot be coincidence," he told *Flugelhorn* reporters. "At one point, Harmon slips a copy of *Chess World* under her coat in a newsagent's shop and leaves without paying, exactly the same as I did when I was fourteen," he continued. "In my case it was a copy of *Razzle* rather than a chess magazine, but it's the same plot."

And the similarities don't stop there, with many scenes suspiciously close to Weedol's life, including…

★ *Beth struggling with alcohol addiction in the show. Weedol himself likes a drink, regularly downing 8 or 9 pints in his local pub.*

★ *Dependent on tranquilisers, Beth steals a jar of pills from her school dispensary. Weedol once received a £200 fine for stealing a bottle of Scotch and a box of 12 Ferrero Rochers from his local Spar.*

★ *Much of the show is set in Paris, where Beth suffers her greatest defeat at the hands of Russian Grand Master Vasily Borgov. Weedol once went on a Booze Cruise to Calais, just 150 miles from the French capital.*

"It was like the Netflix producers had been following my every move," he said.

Weedol instructed his solicitors to send a letter to Netflix demanding compensation, which was dispatched by first class post to the company headquarters in Los Gatos, California at the end of last week. And he believes that the streaming giants will now be considering their response.

spirit

"I'm sure the shit hit the fan when they opened my letter," he told reporters. "I'm not so naive as to believe they'll just pay up. They'll try to fight the case itself like a game of chess, with moves and counter moves. But they are playing a grand master."

"This will be a landmark case and my solicitors think I have a very good chance of succeeding," he continued. "Although they said they couldn' work on a 'no-win-no-fee' basis, and insisted I pay by the hour up front."

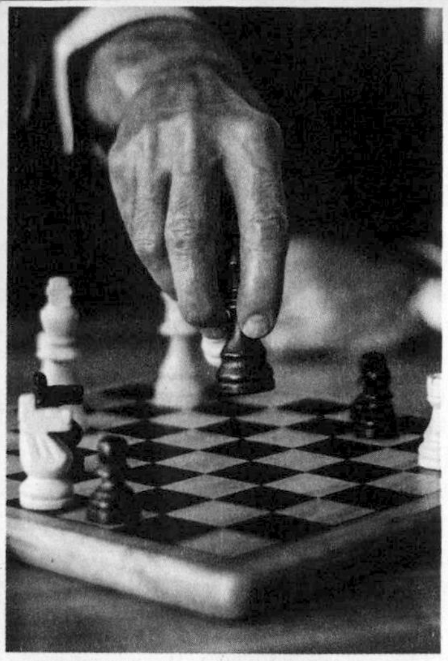

IMPROVE YOUR GAME

THE NOBLE game of chess has fascinated mankind ever since we lived in caves and hunted dinosaurs. We all know how to play, but knowing the rules and understanding the game are two different things entirely. Not everyone can be a grandmaster, but by applying one or two changes and learning a few tricks, we can all play at a higher level. Here are a few tips to help you improve your game...

1. GET PLENTY OF SLEEP

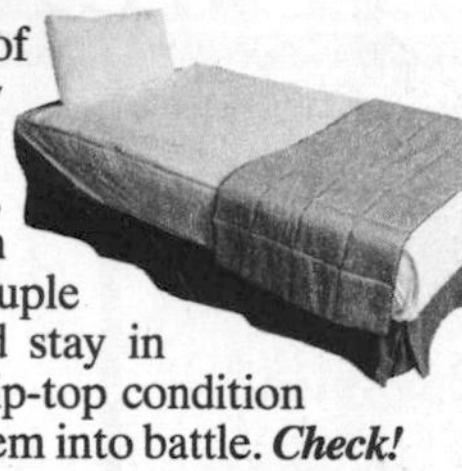

CHESS is the most cerebral of games, and a tired brain will play less well than a fresh, well-rested one. If you have a game coming up, perhaps at home with a friend, or in the park with a stranger, take a couple of days off work beforehand and stay in bed. Fully refreshed, you'll be in tip-top condition to marshal your pieces and send them into battle. ***Check!***

2. STAY AWAY FROM THE EDGES

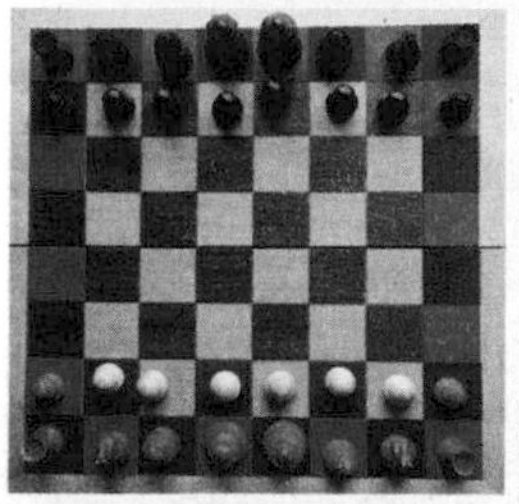

TO PLAY a winning game of chess, you have to be able to move out of danger. So if your pieces are at the sides of the board, there is only one direction they can move when threatened. So, early in the game, get as many of your pieces as possible into the middle where they are safe. ***Check!***

3. UNSETTLE YOUR OPPONENT

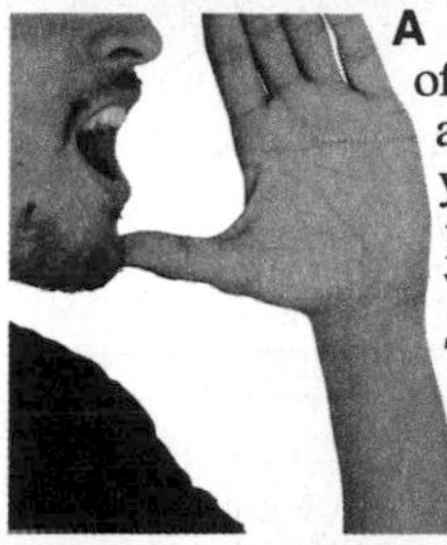

A GAME of chess demands 100% of a player's concentration if if they are to win. So if you can distract your opponent, even slightly, you put yourself at an advantage. Try whistling a catchy tune, like *The Birdie Song*, or *Invaders Must Die* by The Prodigy, and they will likely make a slip-up, or at least a miscalculation in their game. ***Check!***

4. GIVE YOURSELF AN EXTRA QUEEN

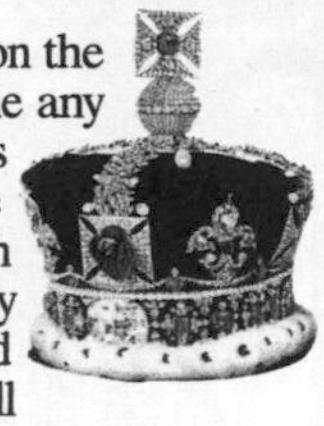

THE QUEEN is the most powerful piece on the chess board, able to move in a straight line any number of squares in any direction. And as such, if you have two of them, you double your advantage. Chess sets only come with one Queen per team, so you will have to buy an extra set. But when you put your second Queen on the chequered battlefield, you'll find it was worth the money. ***Check!***

5. MOVE TWICE EVERY TURN

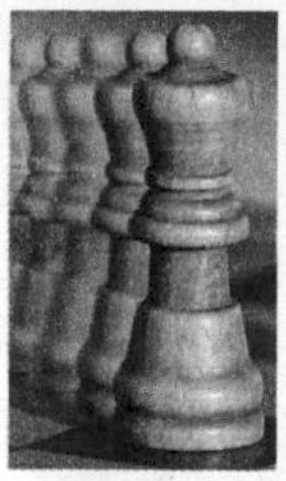

CHESS is effectively a game of stealth and strategy akin to a battle, and as any military commander will tell you, outflanking your enemy is the key to victory. So take two moves for every one your opponent takes. For instance, if they move a knight, counter by moving your bishop *and* a prawn. You'll soon find you are dominating the board. ***Check!***

6. HIDE ONE OF YOUR OPPONENT'S PIECES

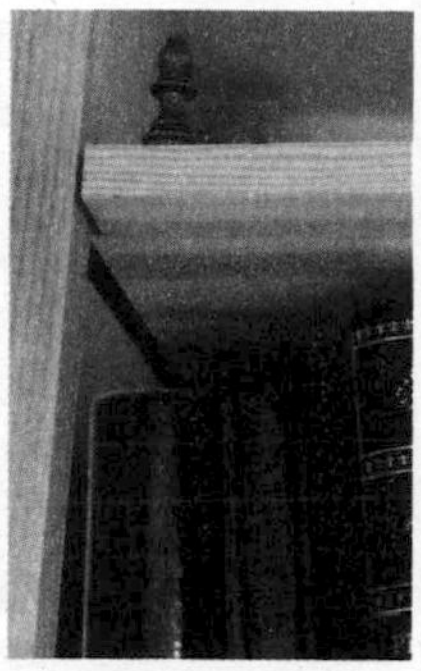

IF YOU CAN hide one of your opponent's pieces when they are not looking, you will seriously disadvantage them in the game, and the more powerful the piece you can remove, the greater your advantage. You may think this is against the spirit of the game, but think again. Chess is a battle, and all is fair in love and war. ***Check!***

Where is it Now? Deep Blue

BACK IN 1996, IBM's flagship chess-playing computer took the world by storm when it became the first machine to beat a human being – Garry Kasparov – in the first of six time-controlled games. The human grandmaster eventually went on to beat his electronic opponent 4-2 in the series. But the following year, following a programming upgrade which saw it capable of evaluating 200 million moves each second, the machine made history by winning the rematch $3\frac{1}{2}$-$2\frac{1}{2}$.

But what happened to it after that? And where is it now? Here's the timeline of events surrounding the world's most powerful chess computer...

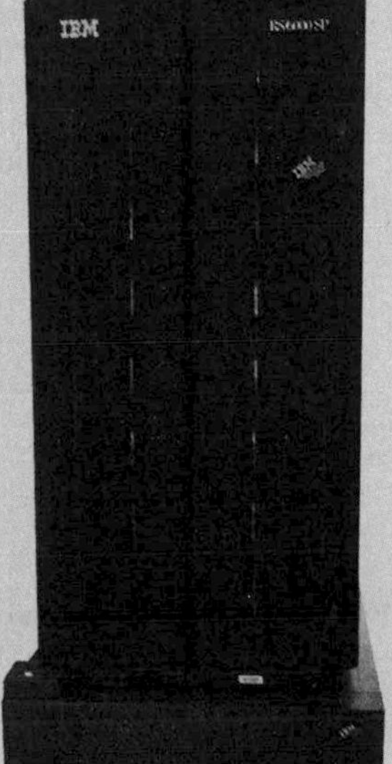
IBM

1989: Deep Blue is constructed at Carnegie Mellon University in Pennsylvania, and undergoes 7 years of testing and development

1996: The machine takes on Garry Kasparov in a 6-game match, eventually losing 4-2

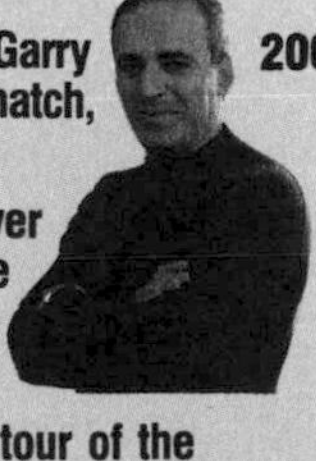

1997: Technology triumphs over biology as Deep Blue wins the re-match with Kasparov $2\frac{1}{2}$-$3\frac{1}{2}$

1999: IBM take Deep Blue on a tour of the USA, playing demonstration matches against local chess champions

2002: The demonstration match tour is extended to Europe and Asia, but the reception is poor with many venues being only half full

2003: A planned tour of Australia and New Zealand is cancelled due to poor ticket sales

2004: Deep Blue appears in a TV advert for Brain's Faggots, where he is beaten at a game of chess by a small child who has just eaten some of the product

2005: The chess-playing machine makes a cameo appearance in an episode of *Columbo*, entitled *Checkmate to Murder*

2007: Deep Blue is sold to United Airlines, where it is reprogrammed to handle baggage check-in at Atlanta airport, but is decommissioned after just 2 months

2008: Deep Blue is sold to Caesar's Palace in Las Vegas, where it is used first to run a chess-themed fruit machine, and then reprogrammed to operate the automatic doors

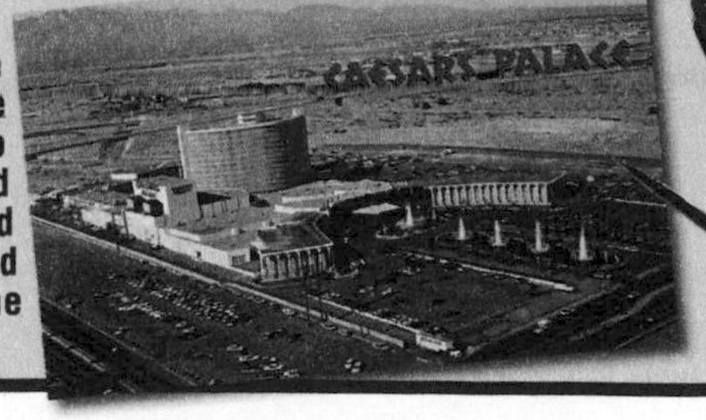
CAESARS PALACE

2010: With work drying up, the machine appears in two low-budget porn films called *Electric Deep Blue* and *Deep Blue Throat*

2012: Deep Blue is sold to a Silicon valley tech company who break it up for parts

2013: Deep Blue's cooling fan and power cable are rescued from a skip and put on display in the World Chess Hall of Fame in St Louis

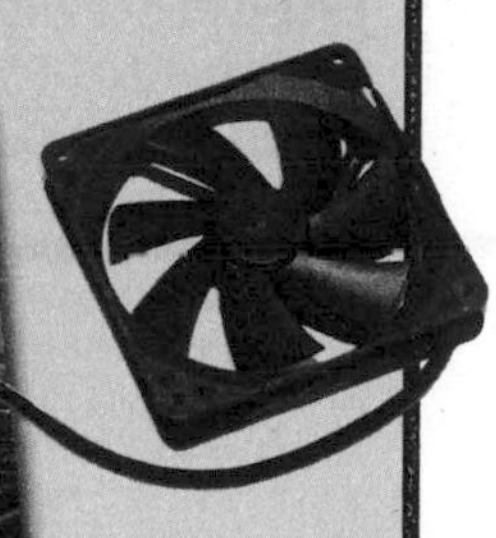

TIPTON CHESSMEN UNEARTHED

"Major find re-writes human history" ~ Guthrie

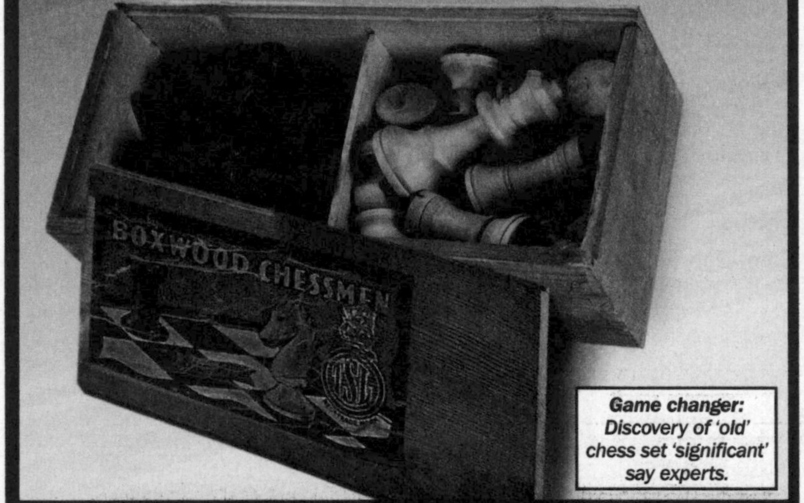
BOXWOOD CHESSMEN

Game changer: Discovery of 'old' chess set 'significant' say experts.

A N ANCIENT chess set hailed as "one of the ten greatest treasures ever discovered in Tipton" has been unearthed at a dig in the West Midlands town. Archaeologists excavating the ancient Moat Farm estate at Ocker Hill, a site believed to date back to the 1920s or even earlier, found a wooden box with a sliding lid, still in pristine condition despite being buried under almost a foot of loose earth, coalfire ashes and old carpet.

When the box was slid open, it was found to contain 32 ancient chess pieces, as well as the mummified remains of a spider, a draught, and two copper coins which have been sent away to be dated by experts at the West Midlands Collectors Centre in Wolverhampton.

Tipton's Head of Antiquities, Councillor Hugo Guthrie, hailed the

EXCLUSIVE!

find as one of the most important and significant archaeological discoveries since egyptologist Howard Carter unearthed the tomb of Tutunkhamun in 1922. He told local paper the *Tipton and Sandwell Fissure*: "This chess set doesn't just throw light on the history of this municipal borough; it completely re-writes the whole history of human civilisation."

human

And he called upon leading TV historians, including Dan Snow, David Olusoga and *GBNews*'s Neil Oliver, to re-write the whole history of human civilisation to include the find, which consists of 32 chess pieces crafted from some sort of ancient material which has been tentatively identified by local museum experts as either walrus bone, mammoth ivory or plastic.

"You can forget your Aztecs, your Egyptian Pharaohs, your Greeks and your Romans," he said. "This chess set changes everything we thought we knew about this planet's history, putting Tipton – along with the surrounding towns of Dudley, Moxley, and Bilston – at the very epicentre of human civilisation."

premier

And Councillor Guthrie reassured locals that he wasn't going to let the priceless relic leave the town to go on display at the British Museum. "Be in no doubt, we are not going to let this chess set go to London, no matter how much they want it," he told the paper. And he unveiled plans for a brand new museum and visitor centre to house the find, including a state-of-the-art virtual reality 3D ride through Tipton's history, a gift shop, and a cafe complete with a 'Mr Softee'-style ice cream machine.

"The Tipton Chessmen Experience will be developed in currently vacant town-centre premises just behind the Noah's Ark pub by the canal on Brick Kiln Street," Mr Guthrie continued. And he angrily dismissed claims from reporters that the site – formerly a shop run by his brother-in-law – had been chosen in an underhand manner.

half a

"The process was all completely above board," he said. "The Tipton Chessmen Experience is going to be a massive draw for people from all round the world, so we needed a position that was central, with easy access from the railway station, the canal, and major roads including Furnace Parade and the B4517."

"Also somewhere for the Mr Softee machine repair man to park his van," he added.

"It just happened that Neville's vape shop came up for sale during the tender process," said Mr Guthrie. And he revealed that when the centre opens in summer 2024, other recently discovered Tipton treasures will also be placed on public display, including several shoes, cigarette packets and beer tins, all perfectly preserved by the town's unique, blast-kiln ash-rich earth.

"This museum will offer visitors a unique window into Tipton's past, not to mention Mr Softee in eight different flavours, including butterscotch, strawberry and cherry dip," he added.

DO YA DO YA (WANNA GAME OF CHESS?)

I N A MOVE that will surprise her legions of fans, 55-year-old former page 3 favourite SAM FOX has decided to pack her tits away and dedicate herself to becoming a CHESS GRANDMASTER! She told ITV's *Loose Women* programme: "I've reached the stage in my life where I need a new challenge, and that new challenge is playing chess at the highest, international level."

Fox, 34-24-33, who rose to fame in the 80s posing topless in tabloid newspapers before going on to record a string of high-energy pop singles, told presenter Carol McGiffin that she had already bought herself a chess set and was going through the booklet of rules that came with it.

EXCLUSIVE!

"I've got all the bits and a board and everything," she said. "I've been learning which way all the different pieces go, like the horse ones going in an L-shape, the bellend ones going in a slant, and the little nipple ones at the front going one or two at a time or whatever."

She said: "It looks complicated when you first read the rules on the bit of paper in the box the bits come in, but it's actually not as hard as all that. There's only about five or six different sorts of bits on the board, because there's more than one of each, so you only have to remember which ways they're allowed to go, what colour you are, and when it's your turn."

Next month, Fox will travel to Yekaterinburg in Russia to compete in the 2021 International Chess Federation Tournament, where she will play 14 rounds against the reigning world champion Grandmaster, Magnus Carlsen of Norway.

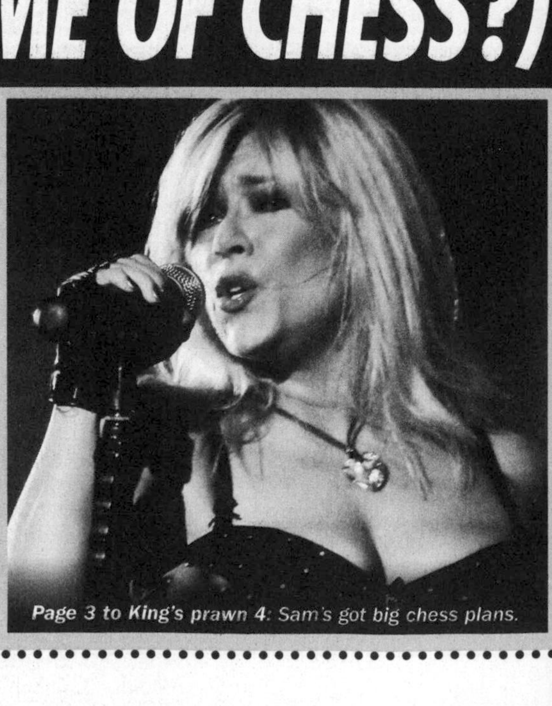

Page 3 to King's prawn 4: Sam's got big chess plans.

Lewis's Chessmen

Chess on the Cheap

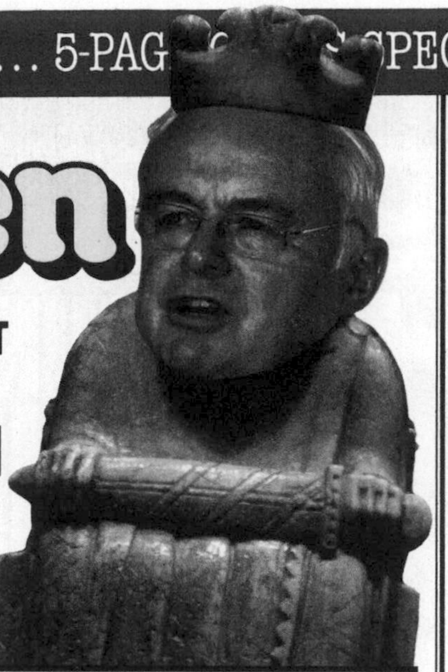

MONEYSAVING EXPERT
(AND NEWSREADER)
MARTYN LEWIS
SHOWS YOU HOW TO PLAY

CHESS is a game that can be enjoyed by anyone – if they can afford to buy a chess set, that is. With hand-carved Javan ebony and golden oak Staunton chess sets costing thousands of pounds, and solid gold and silver sets many times more, chess is a game that is out of reach to all but the extremely wealthy. But it needn't be. With a little imagination and ingenuity, you can have yourself a perfectly good chess set for nothing, using things you find around your home.

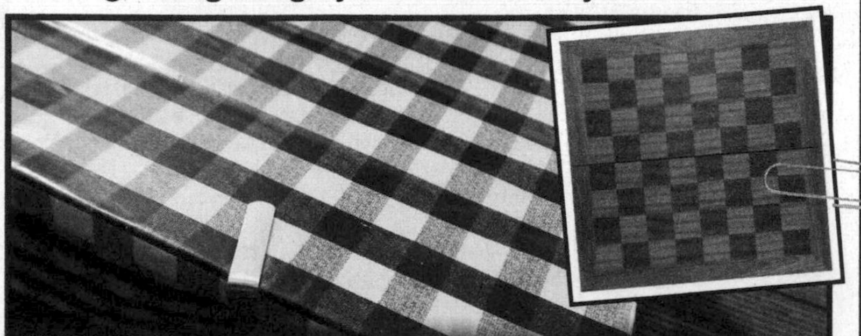

FIRST OF ALL, you'll need a board. If you have a chequered table cloth, you could utilise this: simply take a Sharpie and draw a square 8 checks along and 8 high. Maybe you have chequered tiles on you bathroom floor on which you could play a game of floor chess. Or perhaps a member of your family is a Formula 1 fan and has an old finish line flag lying around.

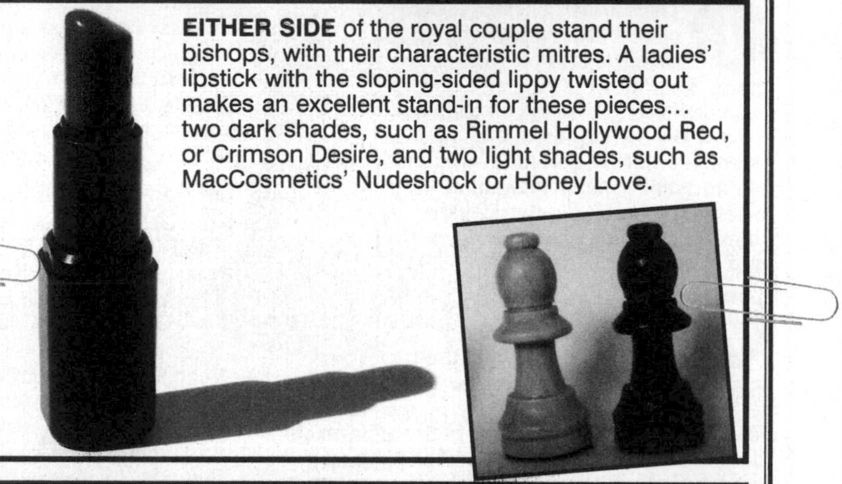

EITHER SIDE of the royal couple stand their bishops, with their characteristic mitres. A ladies' lipstick with the sloping-sided lippy twisted out makes an excellent stand-in for these pieces... two dark shades, such as Rimmel Hollywood Red, or Crimson Desire, and two light shades, such as MacCosmetics' Nudeshock or Honey Love.

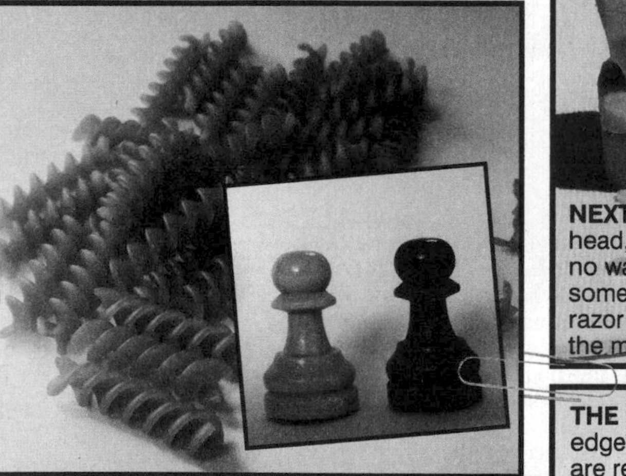

PAWNS ARE the most numerous pieces on the board, so you will need something small that you have lots of, such as dry pasta spirals – eight plain and eight wholewheat. Sixteen sugar cubes would work well, too, putting a drop of black food colouring on eight of them – but not too much or else they will dissolve.

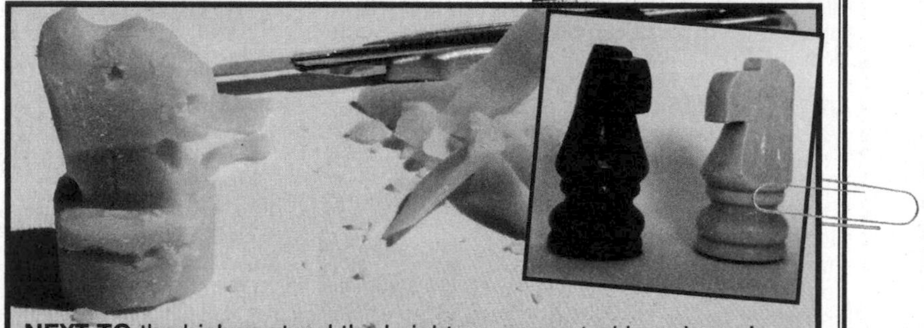

NEXT TO the bishop stand the knights, represented by a horse's head, and the most difficult piece to find around the house. There is no way around it, you will simply have to carve a horse's head into something, perhaps a cork, or a block of cheese. Use a scalpel or razor blade (take care!) to carve the details, and don't forget to do the mane and the flaring nostrils.

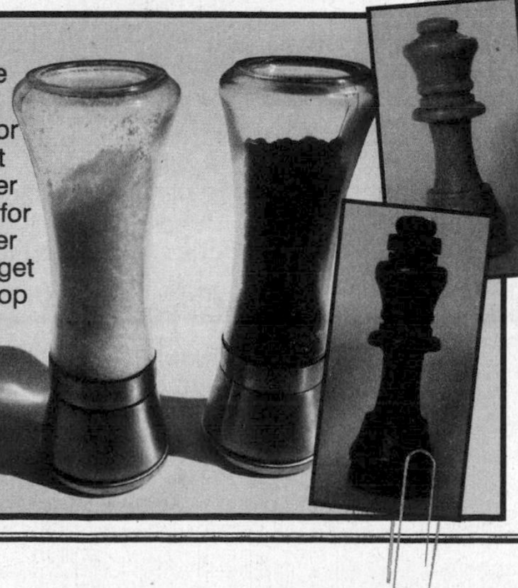

THE KING AND QUEEN are the tallest pieces on the board, about the size of a salt and pepper shaker. So for these you could use – what else? – your salt and pepper shakers. Fill them with salt for the white pieces and pepper for the black. And don't forget to write 'K' and 'Q' on the top in Sharpie, so you know which is which.

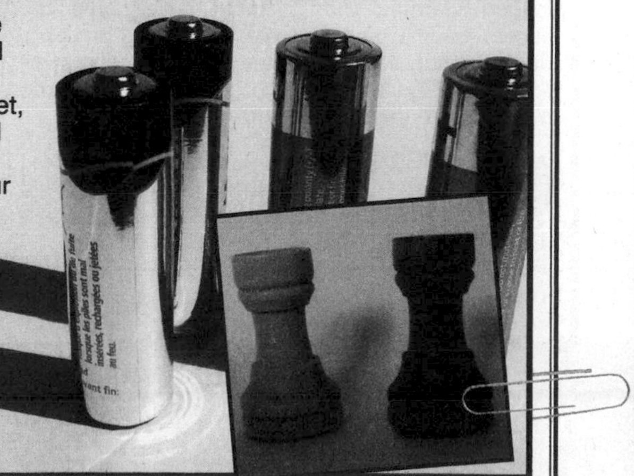

THE ROOKS patrol the edges of the board and are represented by two castle turrets. In your set, they can be substituted with four AA batteries standing on end, or four tops from those sets of cheap felt pens from the pound shop that dry up after a couple of uses.

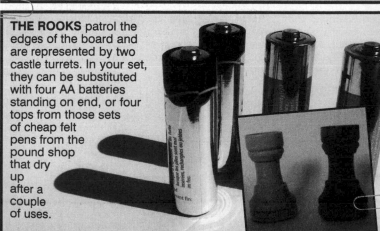

Happy Chessing,
Martyn xx

***NEXT WEEK:** Martyn explains how to make your wife a stylish merkin using an old Brillo pad and double-sided sticky tape.*

CHESS has been described as the ultimate game of cerebral fitness, or at least it was once in a song by Murray Head. The game has perplexed and fascinated mankind ever since it originated in northwest India in the 7th century, before spreading eastward and westward along the Silk Road to the wider world. But where did it originate? And when? And how did it spread to the rest of the world? Here are…

15 THINGS YOU NEVER KNEW ABOUT CHESS

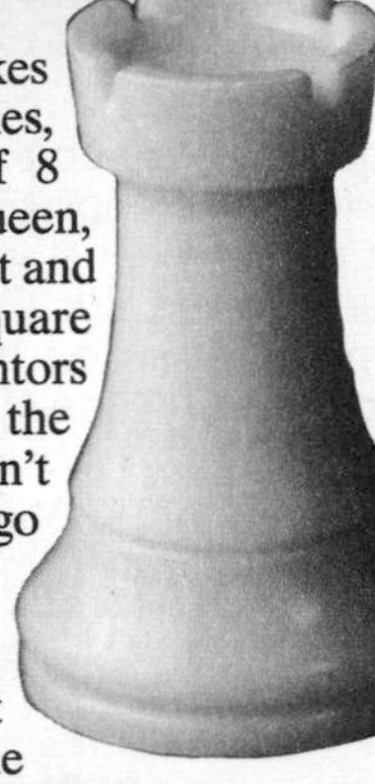

1 THE GAME of chess takes place between two armies, consisting of a row of 8 pawns in front of a king and queen, each flanked by a bishop, a knight and a rook on a chequered, 8x8 square board. It is believed that the inventors of the game originally wanted the board to be 10x10, but they couldn't think of another character to go next to each of the rooks.

2 THE RULES of chess are fairly simple, and it is often said that the game takes minutes to learn, but a lifetime to master. However, for busy people who don't have those minutes, the game of draughts makes a simpler alternative to chess – it is played on the same board, all the pieces make the same move, and any lost pieces can be replaced with a bottle top.

3 *CHESS* is not just a board game, it's also the title of a hugely successful West End musical written by Benny and Bjorn out of Abba, with lyrics by Tim Rice. Other games that have also been adapted into long-running stageshows include *Cluedo*, *Monopoly: The Musical*, and Andrew Lloyd Webber and Ben Elton's *Buckaroo*.

4 MATHEMATICIANS calculate that there are 1327 different possible openings to a game of chess; for example the so-called Lisbon Gambit, the Tashkent Attack and the Scotch Four Knights Game. In reality, however, there are only twelve – moving any of the 8 prawns forward, or making either of the two horses jump over them to the left or to the right.

5 CHESS Grandmasters have the amazing ability to think through thousands of permutations of responses to their moves, mentally playing out the game each response would elicit. They also have the ability to maintain a mental catalogue of every move made in thousands of games. Indeed, they do not even require a board to play, being able to conduct dozens of games simultaneously in their head. But this incredible mental dexterity comes at a price. Most of them have appallingly bad haircuts and big glasses, and none have any dress sense, favouring cream-coloured shirts and brown corduroy trousers that are about four inches too short.

TEXAS INSTRUMENTS
TI-30

6 IT'S unlikely that any two games of chess will be exactly the same. That's because the number of possible games of chess it is possible to play is greater than the number of atoms in the universe. Between 1950 and 1952, mathematician Claude Shannon calculated that there were approximately 10^{120} chess games playable, taking an average of 30 legal moves or 'plys' per turn, with an average game being 80 plys in duration. Quite why Shannon, who had a terrible haircut, and whose trousers were too short, spent 2 years of his life calculating this number remains a mystery.

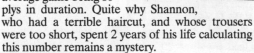

7 THE TV show *Star Trek* often featured Mr Spock and Captain Kirk playing 3-D chess, a game played on a space-age board split into different levels, held on futuristic silver arms. The shot would usually begin with Spock, played by actor Leonard Nimoy, looking contemplatively at the board for a few seconds before moving a piece from an upper level to a lower level. "It didn't make any sense," Nimoy told *Variety* magazine. "I just used to move any old piece anywhere. It was a load of bollocks."

8 THE LARGEST chess board in the world is in the grounds of the Medicine Hat Chess Club in Alberta, Canada. The giant chequerboard is a massive 8.3 metres long on each side, about the length of a Routemaster Bus. Unimpressively, however, the pieces are the standard size for a chess set, with the king standing at 3½ inches and the pawns just 2 inches high.

9 THE LARGEST chess set with the pieces in proportion to the board can be found in the centre of Nottingham, in the city's arboretum. The board measures 5.8 metres along each side, and the pieces range from the 1.2m pawns to the king, who stands a majestic 6-feet tall. The pieces are set out each morning for visitors to play, and put away each evening. One morning in July 2007, the groundsman found that one of the 4' 6" rooks was missing. However, it was discovered the following day in his shed, down the back of a 56-foot (17.06m) long settee.

10 AS WELL as being the world's smallest man, Calvin Phillips was also an accomplished chess Grandmaster, winning several international tournaments. In one famous game against the Russian Boris Spassky, the players set up the board only to find that one of Phillips's bishops was missing. The tiny player jumped on the board, taking the place of the missing piece himself, and the game began. Phillips remained in the game, taking two pawns and a rook, and forcing Spassky's king to move out of check. But on move 28, Phillips was taken by Spassky's queen's knight, and he left the board to retake his seat. The game ended in a draw.

11 CHESS has been likened to a combat, and as such it is important to know when the battle is lost. Experienced players can see when defeat is imminent, and concede the game with honour by laying their king on his side and offering their hand in congratulation to their adversary. Less experienced players may prefer to tip the board over, call their opponent a four-eyed twat, and stomp out the room, slamming the door.

12 AN IBM computer named Deep Thought was the first artificial intelligence machine to win a match against a chess grandmaster in a regular tournament game back in 1988. Six-time Danish champion Bent Larsen conceded the contest by tipping the board over and calling the sophisticated neural network device a four-eyed twat, before stomping out the room at the Vienna Conference Centre, slamming the door.

13 CHARLIE Chaplin may have been a Grand Master of comedy, but he was no great shakes at chess. In fact, Wikipedia lists him merely as a 'skilled but non-professional' player.

14 THE WORD 'chess' has no anagrams, it being impossible to arrange its letters into any other word. In this way, it differs from the game 'draughts,' whose letters can be rearranged to make the words 'drugs hat,' 'drags hut,' 'hags turd' and many more.

15 INCLUDING 'shag turd.'

GARDE

C3 H4 E1 S1 S1

Hen Cabin

Well, there they are.

Our new premises.

I didn't even know we was moving.

NOBLET ELECTRICALS
TV · HI-FI · REPAIRS · SPARES

TO LET

Yep.

And here is where.

Or next door, if I can get it for less.

Phipps Family Butcher

TO LET

NOBLET ELECTRICALS
TV · HI-FI · REPAIRS · SPARES

Or any of these shitholes...

HERR KUTZ   SHOE PLANET   Phipps Family Butcher

Buyer's market at the minute, it's great, everything's fucked.

But this one is best. This one is *nearest*.

Nearest what?

FULCHESTER HIGH SCHOOL

That.

Ahhhhh...

Hold on though –

– the council'll never let us.

BABY ELEPHANT CIRCUS
Special Tricks For All The Family!

Yeah they fuckin' will.

Nah, seen it on the news a bit back how nobody wants fast-food joints near schools no more.

I seen that too. Didn't do fuck-all about it though.

Yeah but –

Phipps Family Butcher

TO LET

NOBLET ELECTRICALS
TV · HI-FI · REPAIRS · SPARES

Children are our future.

Next day

Are you the chair of the planning committee?

I am.

Treat the wife.

SLAP

Shortly

Hen Cabin

Could you hold the ladder please?

Could you kiss my arse? Get on with it.

POCKET MONEY BOX
3 PIECES · FRIES · DRINK
£1.99!   COOL   FUN   FIT IN

That evening

Hen Cabin

POCKET MONEY BOX
3 PIECES · FRIES · DRINK
£1.99!   COOL   FUN

Two months later

Hen Cabin

POCKET MONEY BOX
3 PIECES · FRIES · DRINK
£1.99!   COOL   FUN

Three months later

Hen Cabin

POCKET MONEY BOX
3 PIECES · FRIES · DRINK
£1.99!   COOL

Poor little buggers.

I feel a bit bad. Maybe we should start doing them little bags of –

– fruit *OW*!

THWACK

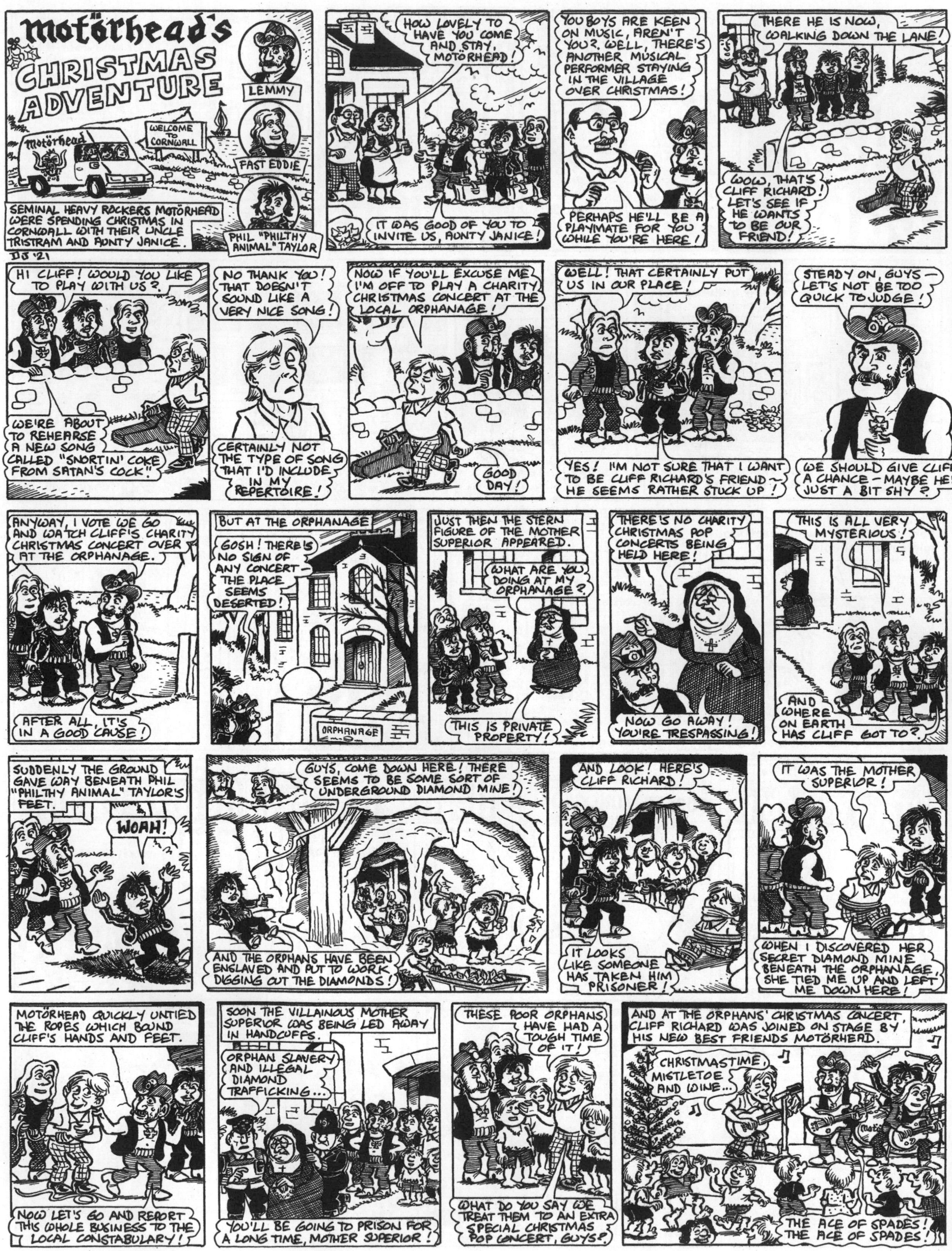
MOTÖRHEAD'S CHRISTMAS ADVENTURE
LEMMY
FAST EDDIE
PHIL "PHILTHY ANIMAL" TAYLOR
MOTÖRHEAD
WELCOME TO CORNWALL
SEMINAL HEAVY ROCKERS MOTÖRHEAD WERE SPENDING CHRISTMAS IN CORNWALL WITH THEIR UNCLE TRISTRAM AND AUNTY JANICE.
DJ '21
HOW LOVELY TO HAVE YOU COME AND STAY, MOTÖRHEAD!
IT WAS GOOD OF YOU TO INVITE US, AUNTY JANICE!
YOU BOYS ARE KEEN ON MUSIC, AREN'T YOU? WELL, THERE'S ANOTHER MUSICAL PERFORMER STAYING IN THE VILLAGE OVER CHRISTMAS!
PERHAPS HE'LL BE A PLAYMATE FOR YOU WHILE YOU'RE HERE!
THERE HE IS NOW, WALKING DOWN THE LANE!
WOW, THAT'S CLIFF RICHARD! LET'S SEE IF HE WANTS TO BE OUR FRIEND!
HI CLIFF! WOULD YOU LIKE TO PLAY WITH US?
WE'RE ABOUT TO REHEARSE A NEW SONG CALLED "SNORTIN' COKE FROM SATAN'S COCK"!
NO THANK YOU! THAT DOESN'T SOUND LIKE A VERY NICE SONG!
CERTAINLY NOT THE TYPE OF SONG THAT I'D INCLUDE IN MY REPERTOIRE!
NOW IF YOU'LL EXCUSE ME I'M OFF TO PLAY A CHARITY CHRISTMAS CONCERT AT THE LOCAL ORPHANAGE!
GOOD DAY!
WELL! THAT CERTAINLY PUT US IN OUR PLACE!
YES! I'M NOT SURE THAT I WANT TO BE CLIFF RICHARD'S FRIEND – HE SEEMS RATHER STUCK UP!
STEADY ON, GUYS – LET'S NOT BE TOO QUICK TO JUDGE!
WE SHOULD GIVE CLIFF A CHANCE – MAYBE HE'S JUST A BIT SHY?
ANYWAY, I VOTE WE GO AND WATCH CLIFF'S CHARITY CHRISTMAS CONCERT OVER AT THE ORPHANAGE.
AFTER ALL, IT'S IN A GOOD CAUSE!
BUT AT THE ORPHANAGE
GOSH! THERE'S NO SIGN OF ANY CONCERT – THE PLACE SEEMS DESERTED!
ORPHANAGE
JUST THEN THE STERN FIGURE OF THE MOTHER SUPERIOR APPEARED.
WHAT ARE YOU DOING AT MY ORPHANAGE?
THIS IS PRIVATE PROPERTY!
THERE'S NO CHARITY CHRISTMAS POP CONCERTS BEING HELD HERE!
NOW GO AWAY! YOU'RE TRESPASSING!
THIS IS ALL VERY MYSTERIOUS!
AND WHERE ON EARTH HAS CLIFF GOT TO?
SUDDENLY THE GROUND GAVE WAY BENEATH PHIL "PHILTHY ANIMAL" TAYLOR'S FEET.
WOAH!
GUYS, COME DOWN HERE! THERE SEEMS TO BE SOME SORT OF UNDERGROUND DIAMOND MINE!
AND THE ORPHANS HAVE BEEN ENSLAVED AND PUT TO WORK DIGGING OUT THE DIAMONDS!
AND LOOK! HERE'S CLIFF RICHARD!
IT LOOKS LIKE SOMEONE HAS TAKEN HIM PRISONER!
IT WAS THE MOTHER SUPERIOR!
WHEN I DISCOVERED HER SECRET DIAMOND MINE BENEATH THE ORPHANAGE, SHE TIED ME UP AND LEFT ME DOWN HERE!
MOTÖRHEAD QUICKLY UNTIED THE ROPES WHICH BOUND CLIFF'S HANDS AND FEET.
NOW LET'S GO AND REPORT THIS WHOLE BUSINESS TO THE LOCAL CONSTABULARY!
SOON THE VILLAINOUS MOTHER SUPERIOR WAS BEING LED AWAY IN HANDCUFFS.
ORPHAN SLAVERY AND ILLEGAL DIAMOND TRAFFICKING...
YOU'LL BE GOING TO PRISON FOR A LONG TIME, MOTHER SUPERIOR!
THESE POOR ORPHANS HAVE HAD A TOUGH TIME OF IT!
WHAT DO YOU SAY WE TREAT THEM TO AN EXTRA SPECIAL CHRISTMAS POP CONCERT, GUYS?
AND AT THE ORPHANS' CHRISTMAS CONCERT CLIFF RICHARD WAS JOINED ON STAGE BY HIS NEW BEST FRIENDS MOTÖRHEAD.
CHRISTMASTIME, MISTLETOE AND WINE...
THE ACE OF SPADES! THE ACE OF SPADES!

HO! HO! NO!

Toddlers are dreaming of a WAIT Christmas

A SHOCKING report in the *Retail Gazette* has revealed that British children could wait up to SIX WEEKS to see a Santa Claus in a department store this Christmas. And it is feared that as many as half a million wonderstruck toddlers may not get to see one at all.

The crisis is not due to a national shortage of Santa Clauses, which are in plentiful supply, but rather from Covid-19 restrictions which are limiting the number of appointments available for wide-eyed children in shops.

"Britain produces more Santas than any country in the world except the United States, so for once, Brexit is not to blame," said Aiken Drummond from the British Retailers Association. "But due to social distancing measures, the number of children a Santa can see in an hour is severely limited."

slot

Before the pandemic struck, awe-filled children could simply queue up and wait their turn to see a Santa, and a busy grotto Father Christmas could easily see up to 50 boys and girls an hour. But to comply with Covid safety rules, all visits to Santa are now by appointment only, with each 10 minute slot comprising of a brief, two minute chat with the child, followed by eight minutes of disinfecting the grotto.

"In this Covid world we now live in, a Santa in a busy department store can only sit six children on his lap per hour," Drummond added.

EXCLUSIVE!

A government task force has been set up to look into how more dumbstruck children can be processed through the Santa system, increasing the number of visits and prioritising those with the greatest need to see Father Christmas.

sewing

"Every child who wants to see a Santa Claus before Christmas will get the opportunity to see one. That is the priority of this government," said Secretary of State for Digital, Culture, Media and Sport, Nadine Dorries.

"There are many ways to do this, but we will start by rolling out Santa Clauses for the under fives first, then making visits available to over fives by late November and finally the over tens in mid-December," she told anyone who would listen.

washing

There have also been plans to increase the number of venues where open-mouthed children can visit Santa Claus. In addition to traditional department stores and shopping malls, the government is

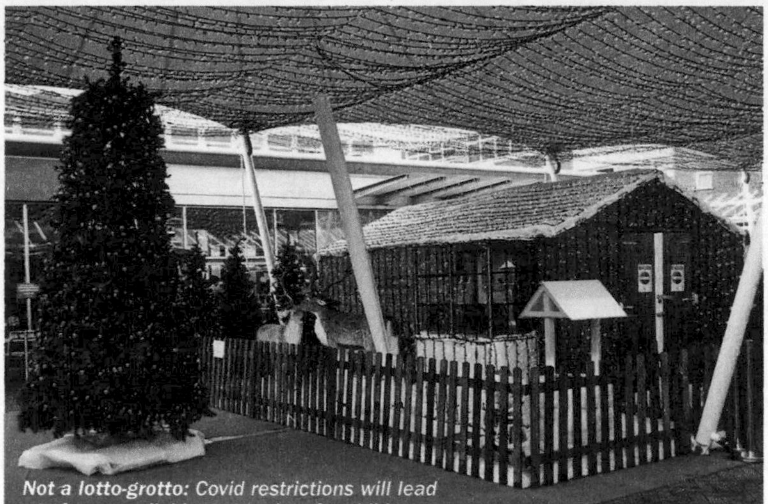

Not a lotto-grotto: *Covid restrictions will lead to fewer available grotto slots for children.*

trying out grottos in smaller shops and other retail outlets to provide a walk-in service for overwhelmed children.

silver

But that particular experiment has met with mixed results. Trevor Broomshank, who has been a professional Santa for 35 years, told us that this year's change of venue has been disastrous.

"I usually see hundreds of kiddies every day when I'm at the Arndale centre, or in the toy department of John Lewis," he told *The Grocer* magazine. "But this year my grotto was set up in the foyer of Screwfix on the local trading estate."

"I only saw half a dozen kids on the first Saturday in December. And two of those were sixteen year-old lads who were just larking about," he said.

And Herbert Pocket, who made a Santa appointment for his three year-old son, was astonished to find that the grotto he had been sent to was in an Ann Summers shop. "I think it was a totally inappropriate venue for a visit to Father Christmas," he complained.

"We were waiting for my son's turn to see Santa, surrounded by models wearing peep-hole bras and split crotch knickers. The tot was asking some very difficult questions. What should have been a magical experience was completely spoiled," said Mr Pocket.

"Once again, this government just hasn't thought it through," he added.

Remembering Santa's Reindeer...

EASY AS SLEIGH, B, C!

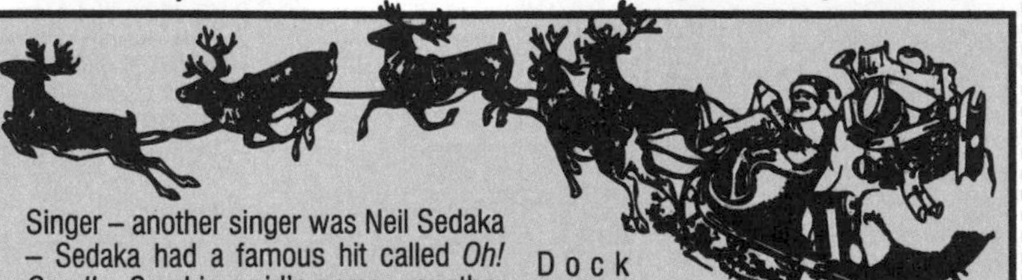

SOME things are as certain as the rising of the Sun in the morning, the ebbing and flowing of the tide, and the shitting of bears in the woods. And for the department store Santa, it's a certainty that each year, some snotty-nosed, know-it-all little kid will claim that if you are the real Santa Claus, you will be able to name all your nine reindeer. A jolly "Ho! Ho! Ho!" and asking them what they want for Christmas will cut no ice with these obnoxious little shits who want to see you squirm, and nothing less than all nine names tripped effortlessly off the tongue will shut the little fuckers up.

But who has got the time to learn the names of these magic, flying ungulates? Nobody. And luckily you don't need to, because if you are working this Christmas as a department store Santa, here's a handy word association system which will help you remember them all.

RUDOLPH He is the most famous of Santa's reindeer, and even has his own song. If you can't remember this one, you really should ask yourself if you are in the right game. **RUDOLPH** – Rudolph Hess, deputy to the nazi Führer who fled to Scotland during WWII – that war featured a bombing campaign called the Blitz = **BLITZEN**.

BLITZEN Zen, a type of Buddhism – Buddhism is a religion – religions worship God – God's minions are angels – the most famous of angels = **CUPID**.

CUPID was a little, fat baby with a bow and arrow – an arrow is a projectile – projectile vomit = **COMET**.

COMET The Comets were rocker Bill Haley's backing band – Haley was a Singer – another singer was Neil Sedaka – Sedaka had a famous hit called *Oh! Carol!* – Carol is a girl's name – another girl's name is Donna = **DONNER**.

DONNER Drop one N to get Doner – Doner kebab – kebabs are only eaten on a Saturday night – Saturday night is when *Strictly* is on the telly – Strictly features dancers = **DANCER**.

DANCER rhymes with prancer = **PRANCER**.

PRANCER rhymes with dancer (make sure you don't get in a loop) – Tina Turner had a hit with a song called *Private Dancer* – Private Dancers perform for men interested in sex – other men interested in sex are Furries who have erotic desires for anthropomorphic animals, so may be attracted to a woman dressed up as a sexy female fox – a female fox = **VIXEN**.

VIXEN rhymes with Dixon – Dixon of Dock Green was a mild mannered police officer who got killed in the film *The Blue Lamp* (1950) but was resurrected for a long running BBC TV series – the character who killed him in the film was played by Dirk Bogarde – Bogarde was also in a film called *The Damned* (1969) – The Damned were a punk band fronted by Captain Sensible – Captain is a rank in the Royal Navy – one of the navy's fleet is the Archer-class P2000 patrol and training vessel HMS Dasher = **DASHER**!

DASHER. And there's all nine of the fuckers.

NEXT YEAR: How to remember all the presents from that fucking awful Twelve Days of Christmas song.

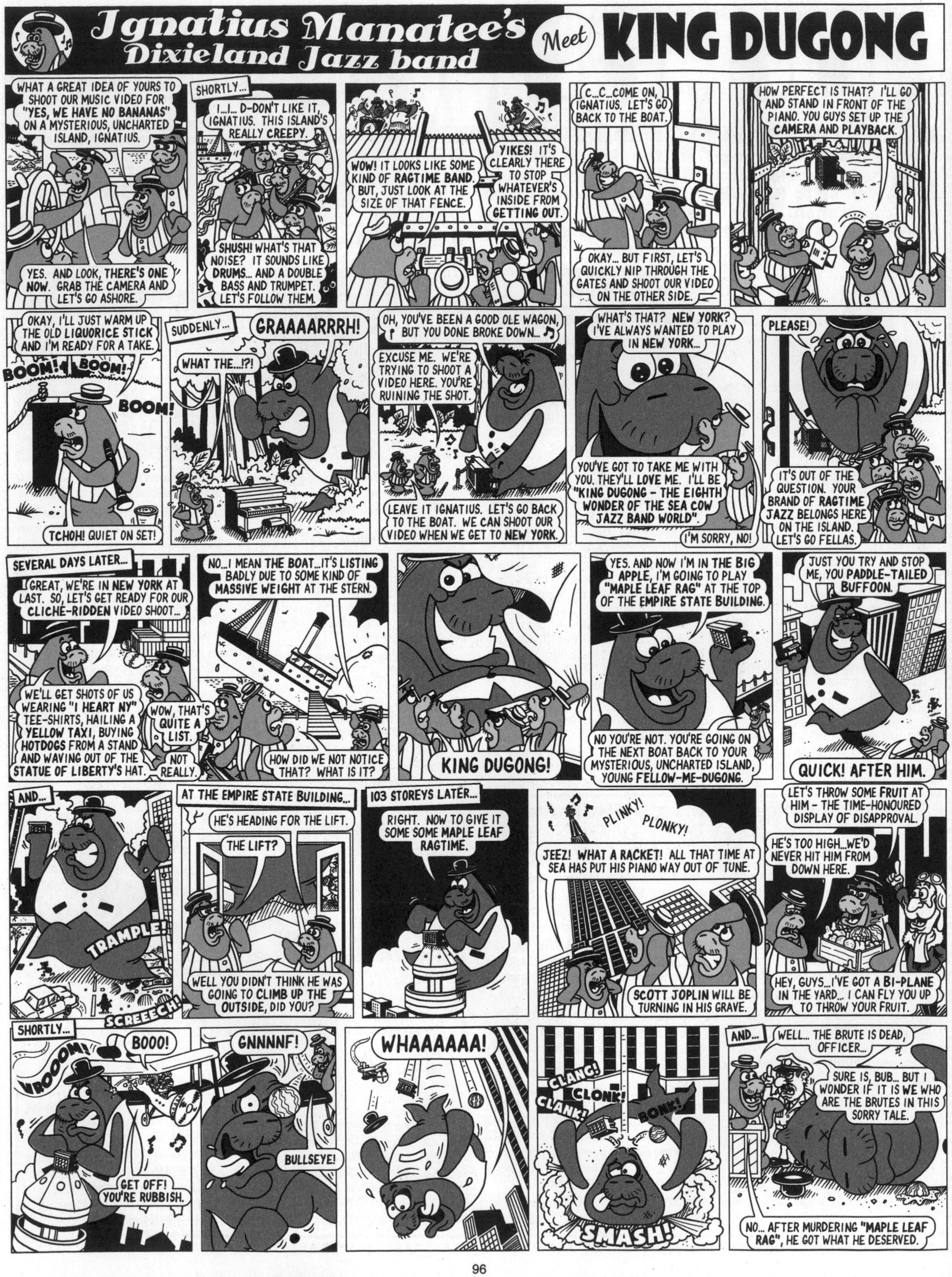
Ignatius Manatee's Dixieland Jazz band
Meet
KING DUGONG
WHAT A GREAT IDEA OF YOURS TO SHOOT OUR MUSIC VIDEO FOR "YES, WE HAVE NO BANANAS" ON A MYSTERIOUS, UNCHARTED ISLAND, IGNATIUS.
YES. AND LOOK, THERE'S ONE NOW. GRAB THE CAMERA AND LET'S GO ASHORE.
SHORTLY...
I...I... D-DON'T LIKE IT, IGNATIUS. THIS ISLAND'S REALLY CREEPY.
SHUSH! WHAT'S THAT NOISE? IT SOUNDS LIKE DRUMS... AND A DOUBLE BASS AND TRUMPET. LET'S FOLLOW THEM.
WOW! IT LOOKS LIKE SOME KIND OF RAGTIME BAND. BUT, JUST LOOK AT THE SIZE OF THAT FENCE.
YIKES! IT'S CLEARLY THERE TO STOP WHATEVER'S INSIDE FROM GETTING OUT.
C...C...COME ON, IGNATIUS. LET'S GO BACK TO THE BOAT.
OKAY... BUT FIRST, LET'S QUICKLY NIP THROUGH THE GATES AND SHOOT OUR VIDEO ON THE OTHER SIDE.
HOW PERFECT IS THAT? I'LL GO AND STAND IN FRONT OF THE PIANO. YOU GUYS SET UP THE CAMERA AND PLAYBACK.
OKAY, I'LL JUST WARM UP THE OLD LIQUORICE STICK AND I'M READY FOR A TAKE.
BOOM! BOOM!
BOOM!
TCHOH! QUIET ON SET!
SUDDENLY...
GRAAAARRRH!
WHAT THE...!?!
OH, YOU'VE BEEN A GOOD OLE WAGON, BUT YOU DONE BROKE DOWN...
EXCUSE ME. WE'RE TRYING TO SHOOT A VIDEO HERE. YOU'RE RUINING THE SHOT.
LEAVE IT IGNATIUS. LET'S GO BACK TO THE BOAT. WE CAN SHOOT OUR VIDEO WHEN WE GET TO NEW YORK.
WHAT'S THAT? NEW YORK? I'VE ALWAYS WANTED TO PLAY IN NEW YORK...
YOU'VE GOT TO TAKE ME WITH YOU. THEY'LL LOVE ME. I'LL BE "KING DUGONG - THE EIGHTH WONDER OF THE SEA COW JAZZ BAND WORLD".
I'M SORRY, NO!
PLEASE!
IT'S OUT OF THE QUESTION. YOUR BRAND OF RAGTIME JAZZ BELONGS HERE ON THE ISLAND. LET'S GO FELLAS.
SEVERAL DAYS LATER...
GREAT, WE'RE IN NEW YORK AT LAST. SO, LET'S GET READY FOR OUR CLICHÉ-RIDDEN VIDEO SHOOT...
WE'LL GET SHOTS OF US WEARING "I HEART NY" TEE-SHIRTS, HAILING A YELLOW TAXI, BUYING HOTDOGS FROM A STAND AND WAVING OUT OF THE STATUE OF LIBERTY'S HAT.
WOW, THAT'S QUITE A LIST.
NOT REALLY.
NO...I MEAN THE BOAT...IT'S LISTING BADLY DUE TO SOME KIND OF MASSIVE WEIGHT AT THE STERN.
HOW DID WE NOT NOTICE THAT? WHAT IS IT?
KING DUGONG!
YES. AND NOW I'M IN THE BIG APPLE, I'M GOING TO PLAY "MAPLE LEAF RAG" AT THE TOP OF THE EMPIRE STATE BUILDING.
NO YOU'RE NOT. YOU'RE GOING ON THE NEXT BOAT BACK TO YOUR MYSTERIOUS, UNCHARTED ISLAND, YOUNG FELLOW-ME-DUGONG.
JUST YOU TRY AND STOP ME, YOU PADDLE-TAILED BUFFOON.
QUICK! AFTER HIM.
AND...
TRAMPLE!
SCREEECH!
AT THE EMPIRE STATE BUILDING...
HE'S HEADING FOR THE LIFT.
THE LIFT?
WELL YOU DIDN'T THINK HE WAS GOING TO CLIMB UP THE OUTSIDE, DID YOU?
103 STOREYS LATER...
RIGHT. NOW TO GIVE IT SOME SOME MAPLE LEAF RAGTIME.
PLINKY!
PLONKY!
JEEZ! WHAT A RACKET! ALL THAT TIME AT SEA HAS PUT HIS PIANO WAY OUT OF TUNE.
SCOTT JOPLIN WILL BE TURNING IN HIS GRAVE.
LET'S THROW SOME FRUIT AT HIM - THE TIME-HONOURED DISPLAY OF DISAPPROVAL.
HE'S TOO HIGH...WE'D NEVER HIT HIM FROM DOWN HERE.
HEY, GUYS...I'VE GOT A BI-PLANE IN THE YARD... I CAN FLY YOU UP TO THROW YOUR FRUIT.
SHORTLY...
VROOOOM!
BOOO!
GET OFF! YOU'RE RUBBISH.
GNNNNF!
BULLSEYE!
WHAAAAAA!
CLANG!
CLONK!
CLANK!
BONK!
SMASH!
AND...
WELL... THE BRUTE IS DEAD, OFFICER...
SURE IS, BUB... BUT I WONDER IF IT IS WE WHO ARE THE BRUTES IN THIS SORRY TALE.
NO... AFTER MURDERING "MAPLE LEAF RAG", HE GOT WHAT HE DESERVED.

Night of the DELIVERING DEAD!

Horror of zombie pizza delivery man

Garlic dread: A pizza similar to the one delivered by zombie.

A NOTTINGHAM couple who ordered their usual Friday night takeaway got more than they bargained for last week, when their food was delivered to them _by a zombie!_

George and Karen Presstuds had called Aesop's Fabled Pizzas in West Bridgeford and paid the extra to have their order - a 12-inch deep-dish margherita with mushrooms and a side of garlic bread - delivered to their door.

couple

The peckish couple, who were told their order would be with them in 30 minutes, began looking forward to their food. But little did they know it was to be a Friday TV and pizza night like no other.

"The bell rang at about quarter to eight, and I went to the door while George got the plates," said Karen. "I'd already got the right money ready, including a £1.50 tip so there wouldn't be any kerfuffle."

moment

But when the 42-year old shop worker opened the door expecting the usual cheery delivery driver on the doorstep with her takeaway, she got the shock of her life.

"It's usually this young lad that brings it, or sometimes an older bloke with a bald head. But this time it was a zombie," she said.

"I was a bit taken aback because all the flesh was falling off his face, one of his eyes was hanging out and the left side of his mouth was just jawbone," she told local paper the _West Bridgeford Flugelhorn._ "He stood there holding the two pizza boxes out in front of him, making a low groaning noise."

"I took the pizza and garlic bread off him and tried to make a bit of light conversation, but he just kept groaning."

friction

It was at this point that the situation took a turn for the worse, as the "walking dead"-style delivery man started to lumber towards the terrified mum-of-three.

"He came into the house and I screamed at the top of my voice," she said. "George came running in from the kitchen, and when he saw this maggot-infested reanimated corpse in the hallway he threw the plates he was carrying at him."

Terrified: The Presstuds' pizza night became pizza nightmare.

According to 43-year-old bricklayer George, one of the plates missed the driver, but the other caught him, taking the suppurating flesh off the side of his face and exposing his cheek bone. But rather than retreat, the cacodemonic being just kept walking forward with his arms outstretched.

"It was like something out of one of these horror films," said George. "I lunged at him to push him back, but my hands just went straight through his chest."

"The stench was indescribable," he said. "Karen and I were both retching."

force

Despite protestations, the pizza-bearing revenant continued into the house, and George went to get one of his golf clubs from the cupboard under the stairs. "I've seen enough zombie films to know that there's no reasoning with these things," he said.

"To kill them once and for all, you have to destroy their brains."

Rushing back into the front room, George swung his trusty 3-wood and hit the reanimated being on the back of the head.

"That did the trick," he said. "His skull just exploded and he dropped like a stone. There was rotting brains and blood everywhere."

vector

Their nightmare over, the couple cleaned up the mess before settling down to their pizza. But Karen said that their evening-in in front of the telly had been spoiled.

"I called Aesops to complain, but they didn't want to know because the zombie was employed by a separate

business," she said. "They even had the cheek to say that since he hadn't come back to the shop with the money, we still owed them for the pizzas."

mevis

A spokesperson for the delivery company, Deliverwallaby, said they vetted all potential workers before employing them on zero-hours contracts.

"We check that all our employees have no criminal convictions and ask them to sign a code of conduct," she told us, but admitted that on this occasion, the company's vetting procedure had failed.

"The last thing we want is to have a reanimated corpse representing our company," she said. "We will reassess our procedures so that this sort of thing won't happen again.

And Deliverwallaby have said they will arrange for the Presstuds' house to be professionally cleaned, and have offered them a half-price takeaway - including a Tomato Bruschetta starter and a bottle of pop - as a gesture of goodwill.

"That's very decent of them," said George. "I only hope it's not a Frankenstein who delivers it," he quipped.

LETTERBOCKS

Viz Comic, P.O. Box 841 Whitley Bay, NE26 9EQ : letters@viz.co.uk

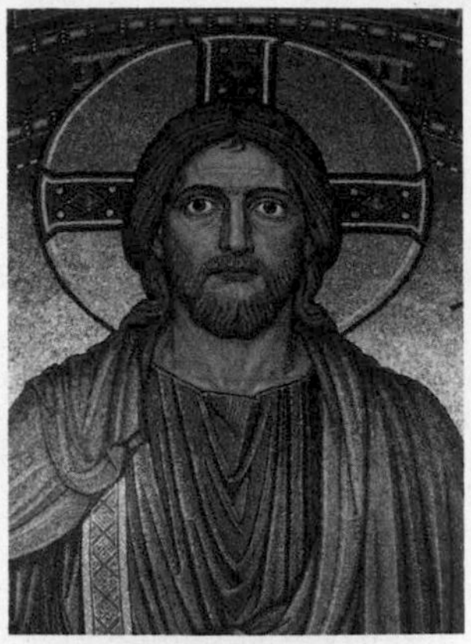

THANKS to Jesus we get Christmas presents, Easter eggs and four bank holidays a year. Come on, other religions, pull your finger out.

Allan Clark, Totnes

THOSE who do not learn the lessons of history are doomed to repeat it. Quite right. It took me three times to pass my GCSE.

Matthew Alford, Bath

WHY is it that goalkeepers always wear a boring old baseball cap when they take to the football field? I'd like to see them wear a Stetson during a game, or perhaps a fez or a deerstalker. Come on goalies, show a bit of variation in the hats you wear.

Joel, email

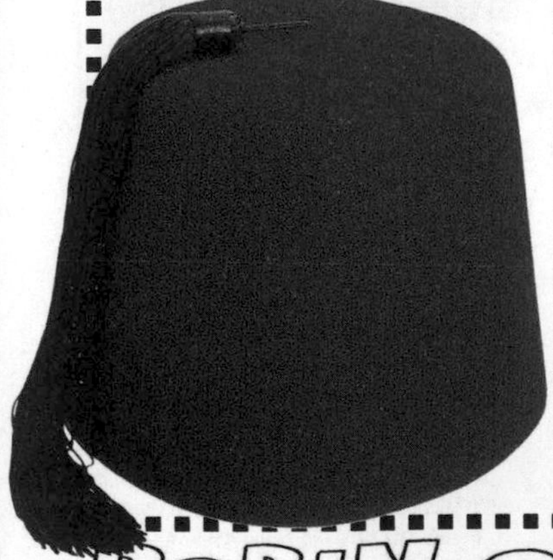

IN reply to Eli Wallace's letter about people injuring themselves in a dream *(page 76)*, I once dreamt my cousin threw a tarantula at me, so I punched him. Unfortunately, I woke up just in time to find myself punching my girlfriend in the back of the head instead. Have any readers been injured in real life from *someone else's* dream?

Gary Ireland, Tauranga

WHY are there no stand-up tribute acts? I would love to go and see someone telling that Michael McIntyre joke about cutting wrapping paper with scissors for half the price of the real one.

D Williams, Donegal

WHAT'S the point of wind? At least rain makes stuff grow and the sun makes it nice to sit in the garden, but wind just makes it cold, pushes things over and breaks stuff. You can dry clothes on the radiator and we have tumble driers these days anyway. Scientists should stop working on whatever the fuck it is they do in that round thing at CERN and get on with getting rid of wind.

Colin Stinging-Nettle, Chive

WHY don't they make bog seats open like pedal bin lids? It's fucking obvious if you ask me.

Bob Scrote, London

GIVEN that Jesus was a carpenter, somebody should have had the foresight to keep hold of some of the stuff that he made – you know, footstools, magazine racks, milk bottle holders – that kind of thing. You'd get a fortune for that lot on eBay.

Adam Birch, Uxbridge

STAR LETTER

DO any of your readers know if the scouts still do Bob A Job Week? It's just that my chimney stack needs repointing, and 5p seems a lot better than the £500 that I've been quoted.

A Royffe, email

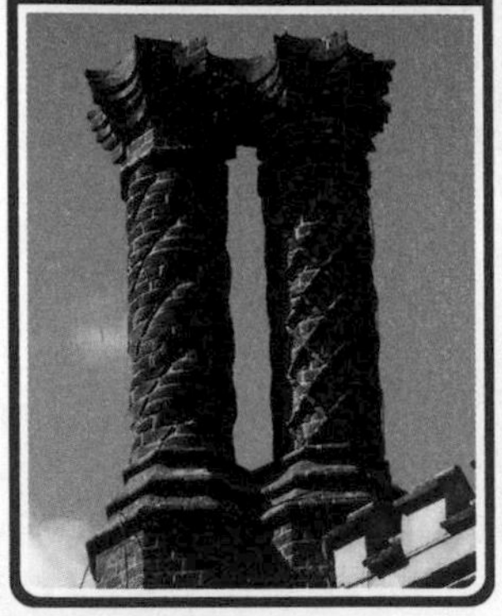

I REMEMBER in the nineties, people said that dog shit could make you blind if you got it in your eyes. But you don't hear about it at all nowadays. Has dog shit changed, or have people just stopped putting it in their eyes?

Jojo Collie-Cross, Matlock

THE other night, following a £112million jackpot Euromillions draw, I checked my ticket, expecting the usual disappointment, only to discover I'd matched all five numbers and both bonus balls. Imagine my disappointment when I clicked on the "prize breakdown" button to find six other ticket holders had also won the jackpot, and it had to be split seven ways. Dear God, when is my luck going to change?

PR Chuff, Wales

EVERY time there is a personal or cataclysmic tragedy, religious people always let God off the hook by claiming it is some sort of test to establish the strength of their faith. But surely the Almighty could think of an easier test than genocide, or afflicting the innocent with painful illnesses? Maybe He could send them a challenging sudoku, or one of those games where you catch fish with a magnet? He could even fix it for members of his flock to appear on Ken Bruce's *Popmaster*. But fuck that, let's roll out the boils, tsunamis and bollock cancer.

J Sentamu, York

YOU wouldn't think it was beyond the wit of boffins to invent a hot cross bun with two underneaths at Easter for us bun-loving agnostics.

Stuie, Bunny

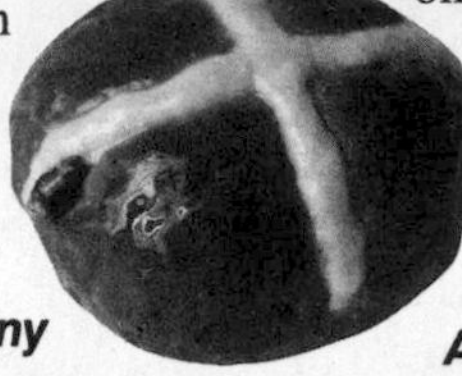

I AM fed up of newsreaders telling me to leave the room if I don't want to know a football result. It really is an annoying inconvenience for those of us who don't give a shit whether Arsenal beat Spurs.

Mike Stools, Shitespace

TWO or three years ago, a newsreader declared that something or other 'reaches temperatures of 1000° Celsius, 10 times the temperature of boiling water'. But as any idiot knows, water boils at 373 Kelvin and 1000°C is equivalent to 1273K, making 1000°C only 3.41 times hotter than 100°C. If the BBC lie about this, then why should I trust a word they say about any domestic and international affairs? Is Covid even real? I could switch over to Channel 4 news and check but quite frankly I don't have the time.

Thanston Crabb, Wisbech

I'VE never seen any cotton socks get blessed. It makes me wonder what these "so-called" vicars do all day.

S Pool, email

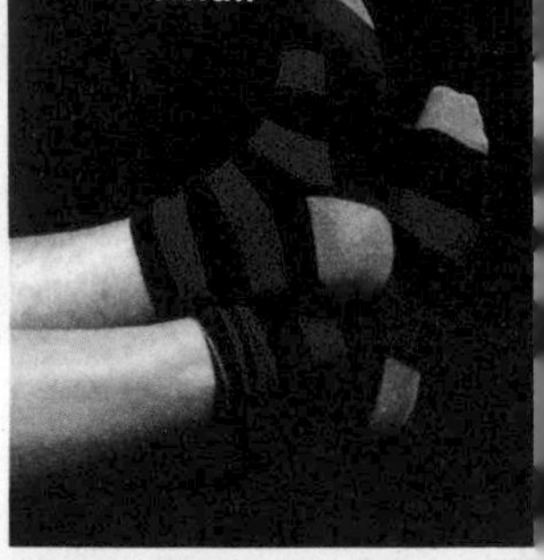

I DON'T know why NASA have gone to all that trouble putting a remote control helicopter on Mars. If they are anything like me, they'll fly it once and be bored of it by Boxing Day. A complete waste of time if you ask me.

AD Phillips, S'hampton

HOW come when horse racing is on TV, my wife always wants the grey horses to win because she thinks they're pretty, but I've got no chance of a blowie because apparently my grey pubes make her go queasy? It's one law for thoroughbreds and another for undersexed middle-aged blokes. Frankly, the hypocrisy makes me want to put my foot through the telly and send the bill to ITV Racing.

WH Lane, Tottenham

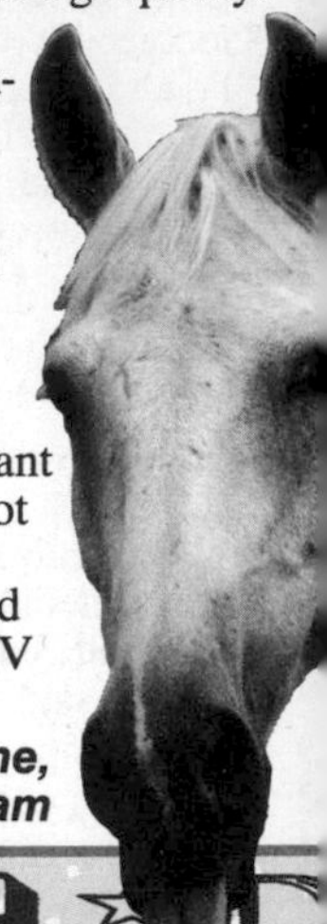

TOP

ADVERTISERS. Persuade consumers to part with wh little cash they have left b starting all your adverts w "We know these are ha times for everyone...."

Argy Ell, Glasg

SAVE money on you gas and electricity bills by keeping all of your gas and electric appliances switched c

Col P Fawcett, Durh

STOP fire walkers being s smug by mixing drawing pins in with the hot coals.

David Craik,

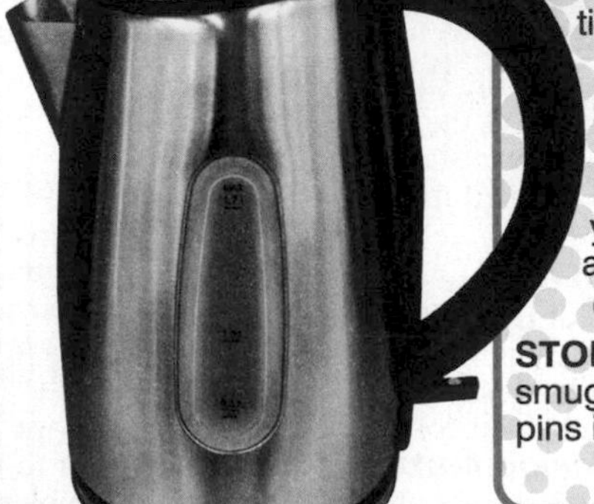

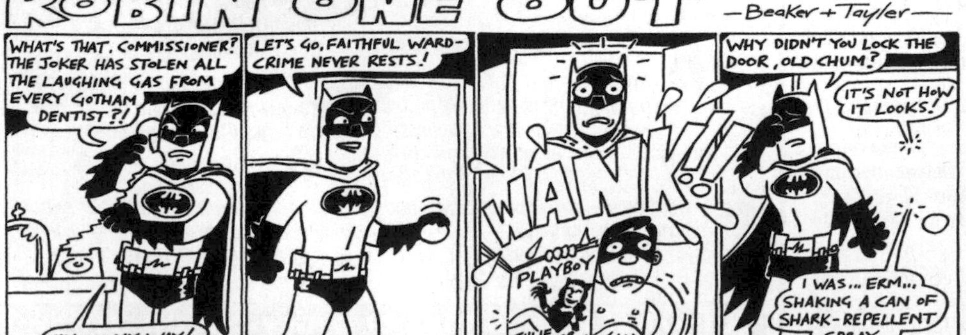
ROBIN ONE OUT
—Beaker + Tayler—
WHAT'S THAT, COMMISSIONER? THE JOKER HAS STOLEN ALL THE LAUGHING GAS FROM EVERY GOTHAM DENTIST?!
I'M ON MY WAY!
LET'S GO, FAITHFUL WARD - CRIME NEVER RESTS!
WANK!!
PLAYBOY
JULIE NEWMAR NAKED!
WHY DIDN'T YOU LOCK THE DOOR, OLD CHUM?
IT'S NOT HOW IT LOOKS.
I WAS... ERM... SHAKING A CAN OF SHARK-REPELLENT SPRAY...

I DIDN'T used to like macadamia nuts, but now I do. I would be very interested to hear if any other of your readers have had a similarly dramatic food-based U-turn?
Justin Brett, London

'ONE for sorrow, two for joy,' they say about magpies. What a load of superstitious rubbish. I sometimes see one of these birds, sometimes two, and I've been clinically depressed my entire adult life.
M Nelson, Kent

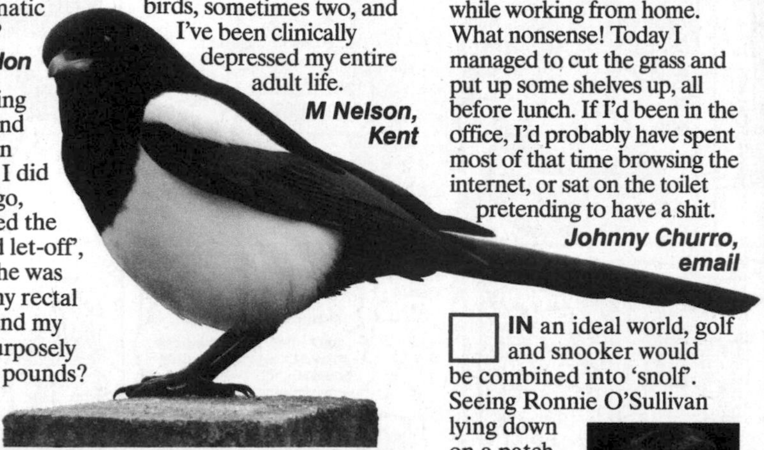

I WAS watching the snooker and just as Ricky Walden missed an easy pot, I did a big fart. John Virgo, commentating, called the miss 'an unexpected let-off', but it sounded like he was commentating on my rectal explosion. If I pretend my bottom burp was purposely timed, do I win five pounds?
Alex Stokoe, Newcastle

MY boss keeps going on about how he wants everyone back in the office as soon as possible because we are not achieving enough while working from home. What nonsense! Today I managed to cut the grass and put up some shelves up, all before lunch. If I'd been in the office, I'd probably have spent most of that time browsing the internet, or sat on the toilet pretending to have a shit.
Johnny Churro, email

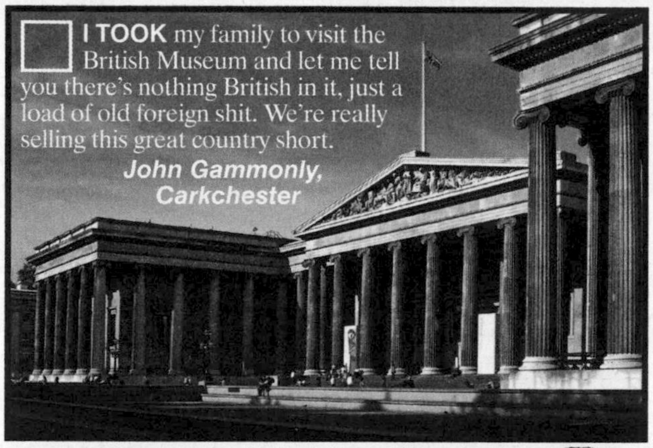

I TOOK my family to visit the British Museum and let me tell you there's nothing British in it, just a load of old foreign shit. We're really selling this great country short.
John Gammonly, Carkchester

IN an ideal world, golf and snooker would be combined into 'snolf'. Seeing Ronnie O'Sullivan lying down on a patch of daisies in long grass, attempting to pot a red and position himself on the pink from 440 yards away would be fantastic TV viewing.
W Scales, Scarborough

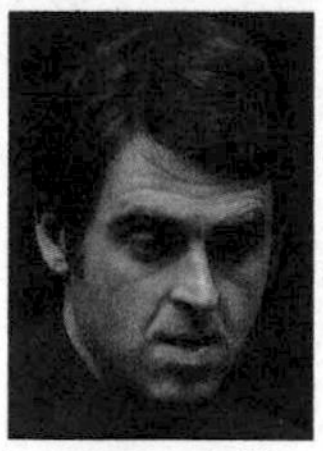

The MAN in the PUB TALKS ABOUT INSECTS

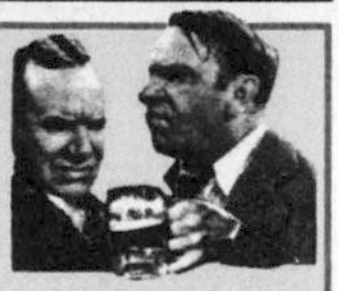

KNOW what the most poisonous insect in the world is? I bet you think it's a black widow spider or scorpion, don't you? Well it's not, because get this... it's a daddy long legs! Yeah! There's enough poison in one of them to kill three men, straight up. But their pincer things on their mouths, I don't know what they're called, well they're not strong enough to break through human skin, they're not. Fucking good job an' all, if you ask me.

AND I bet you think you've never ate a spider, don't you, eh? Well, you're wrong. Because you eat about two of the little fuckers every year. Crawl into your mouth while you're in bed asleep, they do, and you just swallow the fuckers and you don't even know. True. Turns your fucking stomach, dun't it. Eurgh!

DO YOU know, human beings would die without termites? Yeah - *termites!* Gospel truth. They're the only things that can eat wood, see, and if there weren't any of 'em, then all the trees that fell over wouldn't rot down and disappear. They'd just pile up and we'd be proper fucked. I mean, we could burn the fuckers now, but I'm talking about the time when we lived in caves before we invented fire. Mine's a pint of mild if you're going to the bar.

Badger Watch

BACK on page 76, we announced a survey to find out the average age somebody was when they first saw a badger, and your three letters came flooding in...

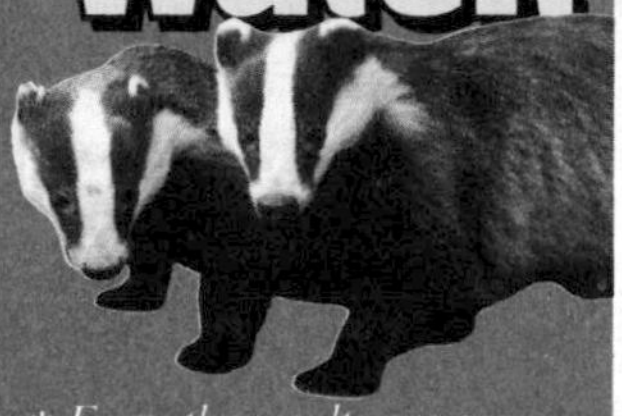

I WAS 20 when I saw my first and only badger in real life. It was in Liverpool. Quite near Penny Lane. I am 41 now.
Alex Stokoe, email

I ALSO only recently saw a badger for the first time, at the age of 44. Although I didn't actually see the fucker until I had to get out and scrape its remains off the wheel arch of my car.
Craig Scott, East Calder

I SAW a badger in real life when I was about 15, when me and my mate were eating a Chinese takeaway up by the garages. I'm now 39.
Rebecca Jeffery, email

** From the results, we can conclude that the average age of people when they first see a badger is 26.3 years, with 1 standard deviation of 15.5 years (ie. 68% of observations falling within 15.5 years either side of the mean, assuming age at first sighting is normally distributed.) With 28% of the UK population being under the age of 26.3, this means that 18.6 million people in the UK have not seen a badger – that's equal to the populations of London, Manchester, Birmingham, Leeds and Nantwich put together. And with an average age of the UK population of 40.5, all those who have seen a badger went through 64.9% of their life so far before seeing it.*

AFTER a reader's revelation *(page 54)* that "turd" was hidden inside the word "Saturday", I've just noticed that "fuck" is hidden in "motherfucker." What other perfectly innocent words have we all been using which may be containing such filth?
Alex Stokoe, Wirral

TIPS

USBANDS. Convince our wife that there's a ghost the house by farting in oms she's about to enter, en denying responsibility her mother's life.
Stuie, Bunny

AT balls, readily obtainable om garden centres or et shops, make barely ceptable substitutes r dumplings to add to a arming winter stew or hot oup.
Richard Forpoorah, Cambridge

AROMETERS make xcellent clocks for people ho have no interest in hat time it is.
Wensley Dale, Cheddar

WHEN starting a new job, simply tell everyone in your place of work that you still have four grandparents. Hey presto! You've gained four extra days leave.
Iain Devenney, Abingdon

MOBILE phone game developers. Please add a "Pause game while I wipe my arse" button to all of your games.
David Whiston, New Zealand

toptips@viz.co.uk

AMATEUR AUDIO BROADCAST PREVENTION SOLUTIONS

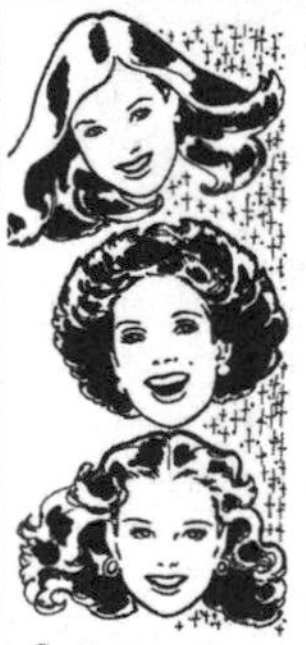

LADIES. Are YOU concerned that YOUR husband may try to start a podcast? Then you need...

PODCAST-B-GONE!™

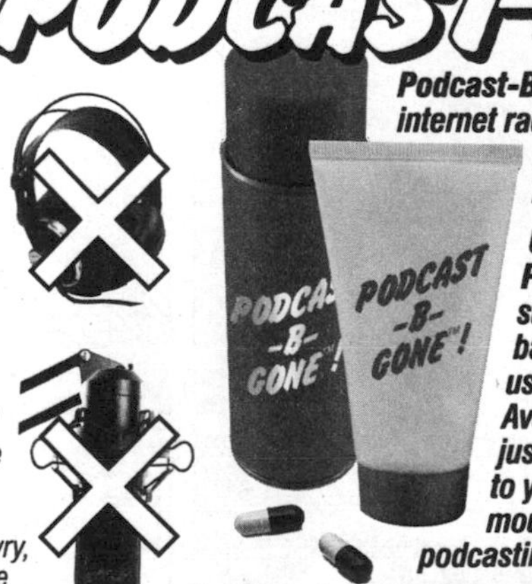

PODCAST -B- GONE!
PODCAST -B- GONE!

Podcast-B-Gone™ is the industry's leading internet radio series prevention product, recommended by FOUR out of FIVE irritated and exasperated spouses.

Unlike other podcast deterrents, Podcast-B-Gone™ is guaranteed to stop the recording of inane, directionless banter in your home BEFORE it starts, using powerful anti-badinage ingredients. Available in spray, pellet or lotion format, just one application of Podcast-B-Gone™ to your husband's laptop, headphones or mouth will eradicate the desire to begin podcasting for up to A FORTNIGHT.

*"My husband came home from the pub last week gabbling about how him and his mate Dave were going to start a weekly podcast in which they took a wry, sideways look at the news. I put a couple of **Podcast-B-Gone™** pellets under his pillow that night, and he hasn't mentioned it since."* **Mrs J, Leicester**

"It's a podcast-busting boon!" **Mrs B, Essex**

So, if you fear that YOUR other half may be tempted to record hours upon hours of painfully pedestrian free-form discussions in the back room, with a view to uploading them to SoundCloud, don't delay...

*"My husband recently informed me of his plans to launch an improvised musical comedy sketch podcast with several of his old university friends. I coated his MacBook with **Podcast-B-Gone™** and within an hour he had given up on the idea. Thank you, Podcast-B-Gone™!"* **Mrs V, Chiswick**

*"After listening to Russell Brand's podcast, my husband got the idea to do his own tedious and ill-informed weekly monologue about philosophy, religion and politics. I put a stop to that by swapping his toothpaste for a tube of **Podcast-B-Gone™**"* **Mrs K, Brighton**

Available NOW from www.podcastBgone.net

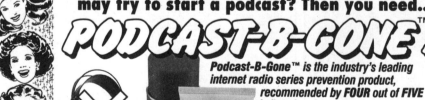

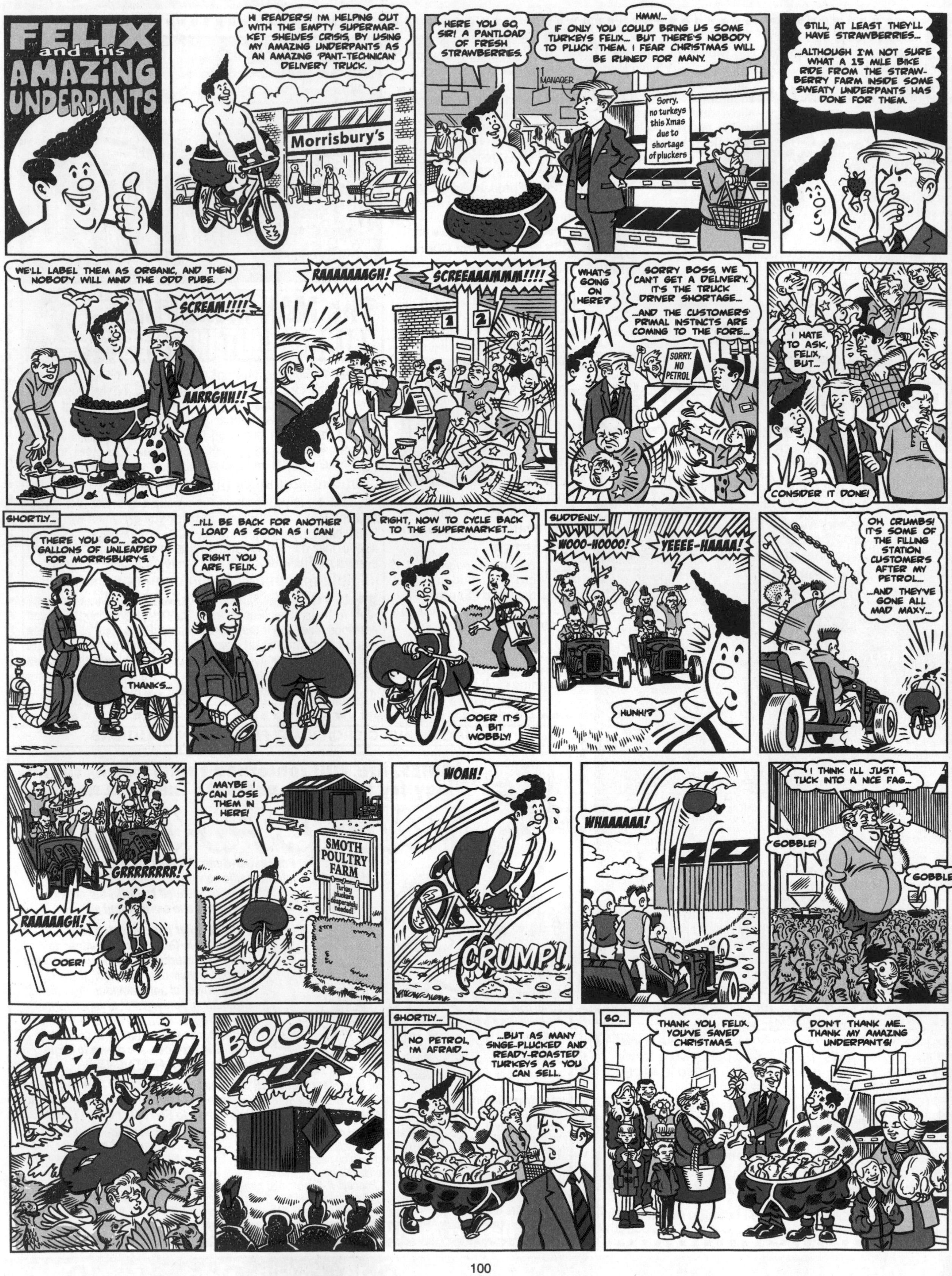
FELIX and his AMAZING UNDERPANTS
HI READERS! I'M HELPING OUT WITH THE EMPTY SUPERMARKET SHELVES CRISIS, BY USING MY AMAZING UNDERPANTS AS AN AMAZING 'PANT-TECHNICAN' DELIVERY TRUCK.
Morrisbury's
HERE YOU GO, SIR! A PANTLOAD OF FRESH STRAWBERRIES.
HMM!... IF ONLY YOU COULD BRING US SOME TURKEYS FELIX... BUT THERE'S NOBODY TO PLUCK THEM. I FEAR CHRISTMAS WILL BE RUINED FOR MANY.
MANAGER
Sorry, no turkeys this Xmas due to shortage of pluckers
STILL, AT LEAST THEY'LL HAVE STRAWBERRIES...
...ALTHOUGH I'M NOT SURE WHAT A 15 MILE BIKE RIDE FROM THE STRAWBERRY FARM INSIDE SOME SWEATY UNDERPANTS HAS DONE FOR THEM.
WE'LL LABEL THEM AS ORGANIC, AND THEN NOBODY WILL MIND THE ODD PUBE.
SCREAM!!!!
AARRGHH!!
RAAAAAAAGH!
SCREEAAAMMM!!!!
WHAT'S GOING ON HERE?
SORRY BOSS, WE CAN'T GET A DELIVERY. IT'S THE TRUCK DRIVER SHORTAGE...
...AND THE CUSTOMERS' PRIMAL INSTINCTS ARE COMING TO THE FORE...
SORRY. NO PETROL
I HATE TO ASK, FELIX, BUT...
CONSIDER IT DONE!
SHORTLY...
THERE YOU GO... 200 GALLONS OF UNLEADED FOR MORRISBURY'S.
THANKS...
...I'LL BE BACK FOR ANOTHER LOAD AS SOON AS I CAN!
RIGHT YOU ARE, FELIX.
RIGHT, NOW TO CYCLE BACK TO THE SUPERMARKET...
...OOER IT'S A BIT WOBBLY!
SUDDENLY...
WOOO-HOOOO!
YEEEE-HAAAA!
HUNH!?
OH, CRUMBS! IT'S SOME OF THE FILLING STATION CUSTOMERS AFTER MY PETROL...
...AND THEY'VE GONE ALL MAD MAXY...
GRRRRRRRR!
RAAAAAAGH!
OOER!
MAYBE I CAN LOSE THEM IN HERE!
SMOTH POULTRY FARM
Turkey pluckers desperately needed!
WOAH!
CRUMP!
WHAAAAAA!
I THINK I'LL JUST TUCK INTO A NICE FAG...
GOBBLE!
GOBBLE!
CRASH!
BOOM!
SHORTLY...
NO PETROL, I'M AFRAID...
...BUT AS MANY SINGE-PLUCKED AND READY-ROASTED TURKEYS AS YOU CAN SELL.
SO...
THANK YOU, FELIX. YOU'VE SAVED CHRISTMAS.
DON'T THANK ME... THANK MY AMAZING UNDERPANTS!

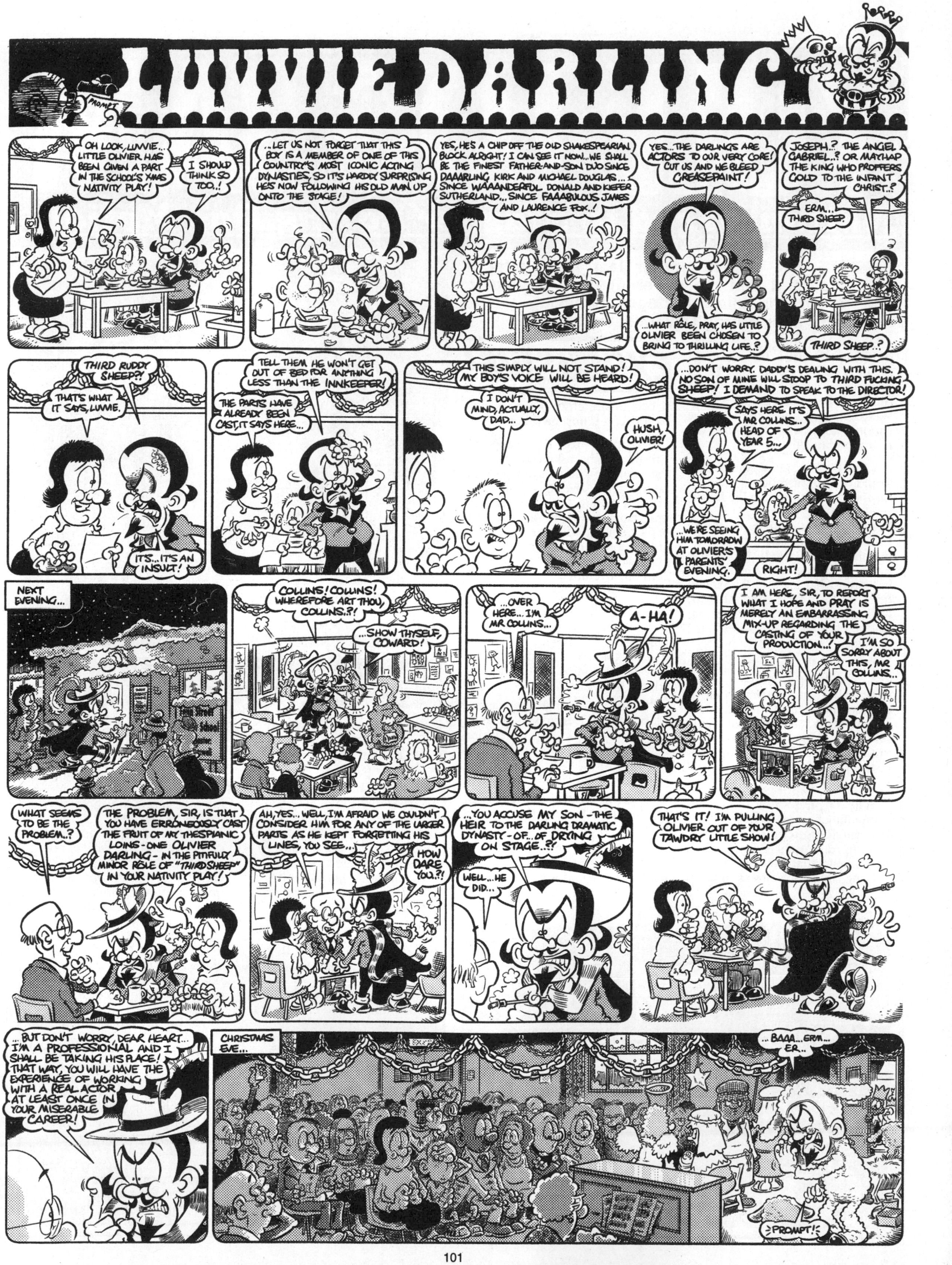
LUVVIE DARLING
PROMPT
OH LOOK, LUVVIE... LITTLE OLIVIER HAS BEEN GIVEN A PART IN THE SCHOOL'S XMAS NATIVITY PLAY!
I SHOULD THINK SO TOO..!
...LET US NOT FORGET THAT THIS BOY IS A MEMBER OF ONE OF THIS COUNTRY'S MOST ICONIC ACTING DYNASTIES, SO IT'S HARDLY SURPRISING HE'S NOW FOLLOWING HIS OLD MAN UP ONTO THE STAGE!
YES, HE'S A CHIP OFF THE OLD SHAKESPEARIAN BLOCK ALRIGHT! I CAN SEE IT NOW... WE SHALL BE THE FINEST FATHER-AND-SON DUO SINCE DAAARLING KIRK AND MICHAEL DOUGLAS... SINCE WAAANDERFUL DONALD AND KIEFER SUTHERLAND... SINCE FAAABULOUS JAMES AND LAURENCE FOX..!
YES... THE DARLINGS ARE ACTORS TO OUR VERY CORE! CUT US AND WE BLEED GREASEPAINT!
...WHAT RÔLE, PRAY, HAS LITTLE OLIVIER BEEN CHOSEN TO BRING TO THRILLING LIFE..?
JOSEPH..? THE ANGEL GABRIEL..? OR MAYHAP THE KING WHO PROFFERS GOLD TO THE INFANT CHRIST..?
ERM... THIRD SHEEP.
THIRD SHEEP..?
THIRD RUDDY SHEEP?!
THAT'S WHAT IT SAYS, LUVVIE.
IT'S... IT'S AN INSULT!
TELL THEM HE WON'T GET OUT OF BED FOR ANYTHING LESS THAN THE INNKEEPER!
THE PARTS HAVE ALREADY BEEN CAST, IT SAYS HERE...
THIS SIMPLY WILL NOT STAND! MY BOY'S VOICE WILL BE HEARD!
I DON'T MIND, ACTUALLY, DAD...
HUSH, OLIVIER!
...DON'T WORRY. DADDY'S DEALING WITH THIS. NO SON OF MINE WILL STOOP TO THIRD FUCKING SHEEP! I DEMAND TO SPEAK TO THE DIRECTOR!
SAYS HERE IT'S MR COLLINS... HEAD OF YEAR 5...
...WE'RE SEEING HIM TOMORROW AT OLIVIER'S PARENTS' EVENING.
RIGHT!
NEXT EVENING...
COLLINS! COLLINS! WHEREFORE ART THOU, COLLINS..?!
...SHOW THYSELF, COWARD!
...OVER HERE... I'M MR COLLINS...
A-HA!
I AM HERE, SIR, TO REPORT WHAT I HOPE AND PRAY IS MERELY AN EMBARRASSING MIX-UP REGARDING THE CASTING OF YOUR PRODUCTION...!
I'M SO SORRY ABOUT THIS, MR COLLINS...
WHAT SEEMS TO BE THE PROBLEM..?
THE PROBLEM, SIR, IS THAT YOU HAVE ERRONEOUSLY CAST THE FRUIT OF MY THESPIANIC LOINS - ONE OLIVIER DARLING - IN THE PITIFULLY MINOR RÔLE OF "THIRD SHEEP" IN YOUR NATIVITY PLAY!
AH, YES... WELL, I'M AFRAID WE COULDN'T CONSIDER HIM FOR ANY OF THE LARGER PARTS AS HE KEPT FORGETTING HIS LINES, YOU SEE...
HOW DARE YOU..?!
...YOU ACCUSE MY SON - THE HEIR TO THE DARLING DRAMATIC DYNASTY - OF... OF DRYING ON STAGE..?!
WELL... HE DID...
THAT'S IT! I'M PULLING OLIVIER OUT OF YOUR TAWDRY LITTLE SHOW!
...BUT DON'T WORRY, DEAR HEART... I'M A PROFESSIONAL AND I SHALL BE TAKING HIS PLACE! THAT WAY, YOU WILL HAVE THE EXPERIENCE OF WORKING WITH A REAL ACTOR AT LEAST ONCE IN YOUR MISERABLE CAREER!
CHRISTMAS EVE...
...BAAA... ERM... ER..
PROMPT!

YULE LOG JAM
Nation Urged to Stagger Boxing Day Motions

THE UK was in uproar last night after it emerged that the government is hoping to avoid Christmas shortages by asking people to stagger their Boxing Day toilet visits.

Due to a range of factors, including Brexit, the shortage of lorry drivers and the Covid pandemic, supply chains for toilet roll have been compromised, and Whitehall is clearly worried that the nation's stocks won't withstand the festive onslaught.

Many Britons, terrified that they would run out of chod-rag supplies for the smallest room in the house, stockpiled toilet paper at the beginning of the first lockdown, leading to empty shelves across the nation's supermarkets. More than a year on, these supplies have all but been used up, and Parliament fears that a repeat surge of panic buying could clear out Christmas stocks of bumwad across the nation.

To avoid this happening, and in order to avoid toilet paper shortages during what is traditionally a busy time for bog roll suppliers, the proposal would see every Briton being assigned a pre-determined date to drop their festive load.

dinners

"The figures I've seen are compelling," says ITV Chief Political Reporter Robert Peston. "During a normal Christmas, all 70 million inhabitants of the UK parking their Christmas dinners on Boxing Day uses enough shit

EXCLUSIVE!

tickets to stretch to the moon and back over a thousand times."

According to the proposal, Britons will be asked to schedule their festive cable laying by age group. The over-80s will take priority, taking their Boxing Day Shit from the 15th to the 19th of November, with the 55-79 age group following through shortly afterwards, between the 20th and 28th of November.

little

"I wasn't sure at first, but now I think it's a first-rate idea," Fulchester octogenerian Edna Crease told us. "And it's right that us pensioners get to drop our copper bolts first."

"I look foward to strangling a Mars bar on December the 26th, but if I've got to drop my Boxing Day Thora Hird in November, then I'll do it for Queen and country," said 92-year old Harold Barstool.

"Like in the war, we've all got to do our bit to keep the bumwad spinning off the roll."

"I only hope that shortages of turkey, sprouts and Christmas pudding will keep the turtle's head at Bay on December 26th," he added.

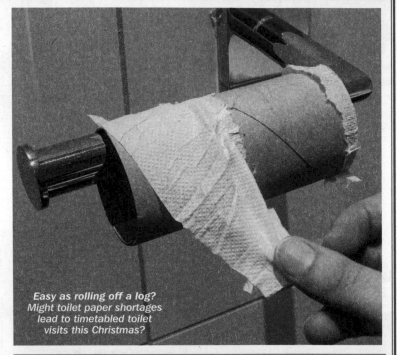

Easy as rolling off a log? Might toilet paper shortages lead to timetabled toilet visits this Christmas?

Beating the Boxing Day Bog Roll Shortage

IT'S the faecal fiasco that *everyone*'s got an opinion on. So we went out on the street to see what *YOU* think about the *Great British Bog Roll Embargo.*

"IF THE WATER companies invested in stonger maceration equipment, we could use old wrapping paper left over from Christmas Day for cleaning our arses. It would leave our holes a bit glittery and itchy, but it's a small price to pay for the luxury of an empty gut and forty minutes' peace and quiet on the thunder mug on Boxing Day."
Barry Murk, Shrewsbury

"ONCE AGAIN, Westminster is out of touch with the general population. I imagine your average politician eats stuff like quails' eggs, grouse and fancy cheese - all food that binds the bomb bay shut. I'd like to see these toffs wrestling with the stirrings caused by a few bottles of bitter and a jumbo bag of dry-roasted the day after Christmas."
Frank Potato, Chester

"MY WIFE and I are only a year apart in age, so we've both

been assigned the same slot for our festive flush; 3.15pm on the first of December. We only have the one toilet in our property so, in order to stick to Government guidelines, we are going to have to curl one out at precisely the same moment into the same pan. As it happens, we're quite looking forward to it, hoping it will put a bit of spice back into our marriage, but we understand that that kind of thing may not be everyone's cup of tea."
Harold Amphetamines, Hull

"I THINK it's a great idea and one that could be applied to other seasonal toilet-roll based activities, like the traditional festive tug. If everyone else in the country is like my husband, they'll all go for a quick ham shank when there's nothing much on TV, like during Songs of Praise or the monarch's Christmas Broadcast."
Marjorie Pleat, Tunbridge

Off the shelf: The now-familiar sight of supermarket shelves devoid of bog roll could spell a seasonal disaster for a nation gorged on sprouts and turkey (inset).

Carey Reveals Xmas Constipation Nightmare

ALL I WANT FOR CHRISTMAS IS (A) POO!

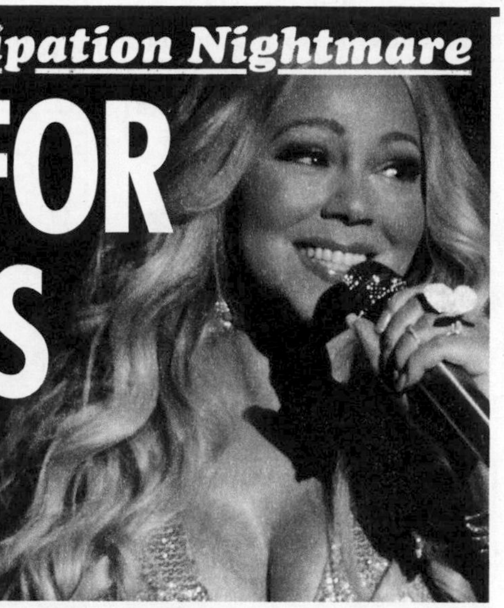

No shit: Carey struggles with laying a cable during the festive period.

MULTI-OCTAVED singer Mariah Carey has revealed that she doesn't want to receive any presents, cards or even turkey this festive season. And she stunned her fans by announcing that all she wants for Christmas is to be able to pass a normal stool.

FESTIVE BOWEL EXCLUSIVE!

"OMG! I dread Xmas," she tweeted in early November, followed by ten emoticon angry faces, leaving her 21.6 million twitter followers wondering what the diva had against the festive season.

But the Songbird Supreme clarified her social media outburst last week. "It's usually around the 21st or 22nd of December that I just stop being able to go to the lavvie for a sit down visit," she told *Last Week Tonight*'s John Oliver.

"I sit there with the Radio Times or Exchange and Mart and nothing comes out," she confessed. She went on to explain that the problem often lasts until New Year's Day, leaving her feeling bloated, tired and sick.

bloated

"I don't understand why I have this problem," she told Oliver. "I talked to Shania Twain, and she gets up on Christmas morning, drops a ton of fudge and then opens all her presents."

"Then she has a Christmas dinner, the full Monty with a goose and all the trimmings, and then goes for another dump in the afternoon," she added. "I'm, like, so jealous."

guts

Medical experts say Carey's Christmas constipation is extremely common, and is brought about by the stress of the festive season. "It's all down to a combination of excitement about opening her presents and nerves about the big day going to plan," says Dr Ben Goldacre, author of *Bad Guts Science*.

"Christmas is an extremely stressful time and Mariah will be worrying about whether she's got enough chairs for when her family come over for dinner, or if she's done enough roasties, things like that," he said.

"This anxiety releases hormones that cause the gut to go into spasm," he added. "Peristalsis – the wave of contractions that push waste through the intestine – stops and it all just sits there."

blockage

And Goldacre had this advice for anyone suffering from a simlilar festive blockage. "It's all psychological," he said. "If you just slow down, relax and enjoy the festive season without the pressure of trying to please everyone, you'll have the turtle's head just as the Bond film finishes."

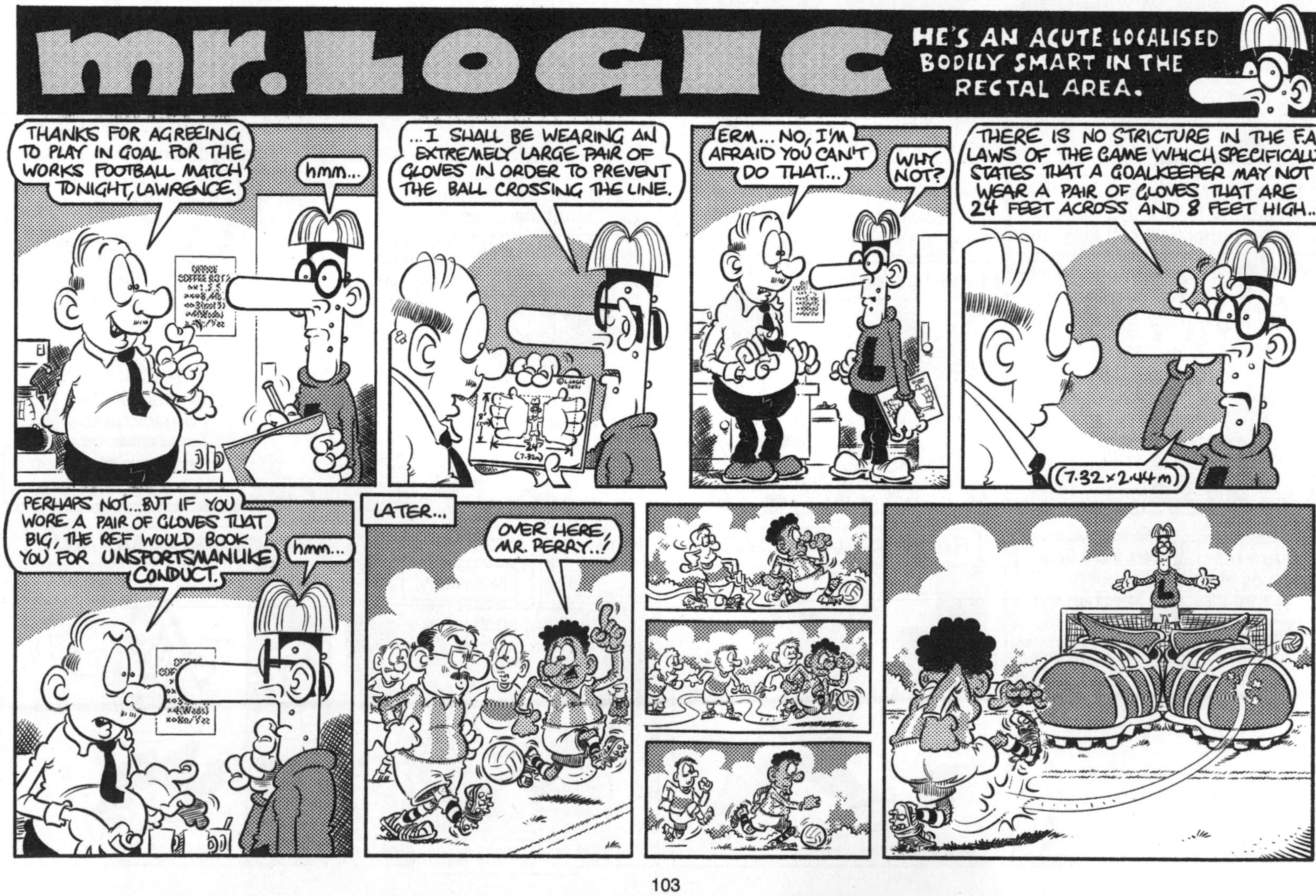
mr. LOGIC
HE'S AN ACUTE LOCALISED BODILY SMART IN THE RECTAL AREA.
THANKS FOR AGREEING TO PLAY IN GOAL FOR THE WORKS FOOTBALL MATCH TONIGHT, LAWRENCE.
hmm...
...I SHALL BE WEARING AN EXTREMELY LARGE PAIR OF GLOVES IN ORDER TO PREVENT THE BALL CROSSING THE LINE.
ERM... NO, I'M AFRAID YOU CAN'T DO THAT...
WHY NOT?
THERE IS NO STRICTURE IN THE F.A. LAWS OF THE GAME WHICH SPECIFICALLY STATES THAT A GOALKEEPER MAY NOT WEAR A PAIR OF GLOVES THAT ARE 24 FEET ACROSS AND 8 FEET HIGH...
(7.32×2.44m)
PERHAPS NOT...BUT IF YOU WORE A PAIR OF GLOVES THAT BIG, THE REF WOULD BOOK YOU FOR UNSPORTSMANLIKE CONDUCT.
hmm...
LATER...
OVER HERE, MR. PERRY..!

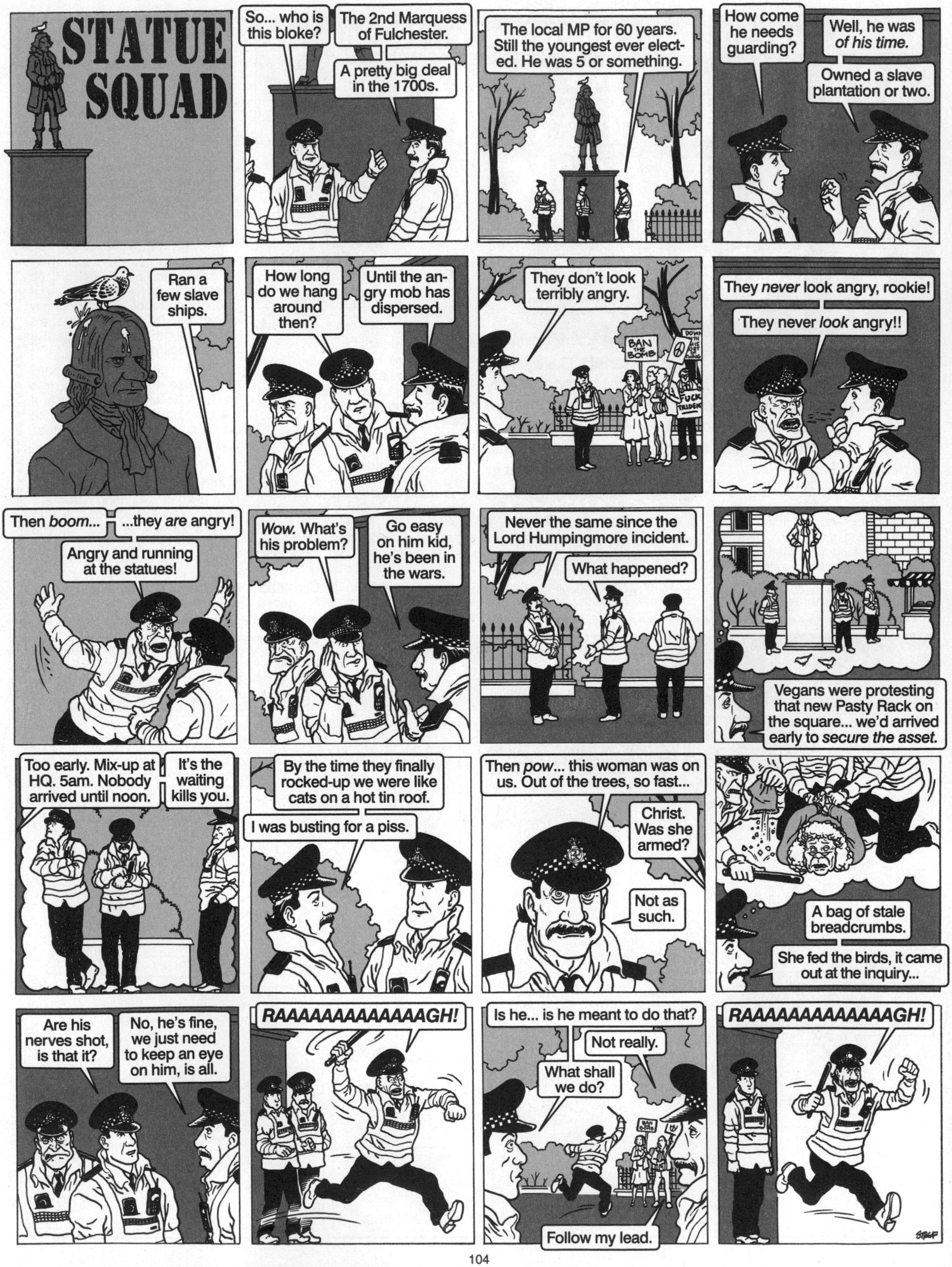
STATUE SQUAD
So... who is this bloke?
The 2nd Marquess of Fulchester.
A pretty big deal in the 1700s.
The local MP for 60 years. Still the youngest ever elect-ed. He was 5 or something.
How come he needs guarding?
Well, he was *of his time.*
Owned a slave plantation or two.
Ran a few slave ships.
How long do we hang around then?
Until the an-gry mob has dispersed.
They don't look terribly angry.
BAN THE BOMB
FUCK TRIDENT
They *never* look angry, rookie!
They never *look* angry!!
Then *boom...*
...they *are* angry!
Angry and running at the statues!
Wow. What's his problem?
Go easy on him kid, he's been in the wars.
Never the same since the Lord Humpingmore incident.
What happened?
Vegans were protesting that new Pasty Rack on the square... we'd arrived early to *secure the asset.*
Too early. Mix-up at HQ. 5am. Nobody arrived until noon.
It's the waiting kills you.
By the time they finally rocked-up we were like cats on a hot tin roof.
I was busting for a piss.
Then *pow*... this woman was on us. Out of the trees, so fast...
Christ. Was she armed?
Not as such.
A bag of stale breadcrumbs.
She fed the birds, it came out at the inquiry...
Are his nerves shot, is that it?
No, he's fine, we just need to keep an eye on him, is all.
RAAAAAAAAAAAAAGH!
Is he... is he meant to do that?
Not really.
What shall we do?
Follow my lead.
RAAAAAAAAAAAAAGH!

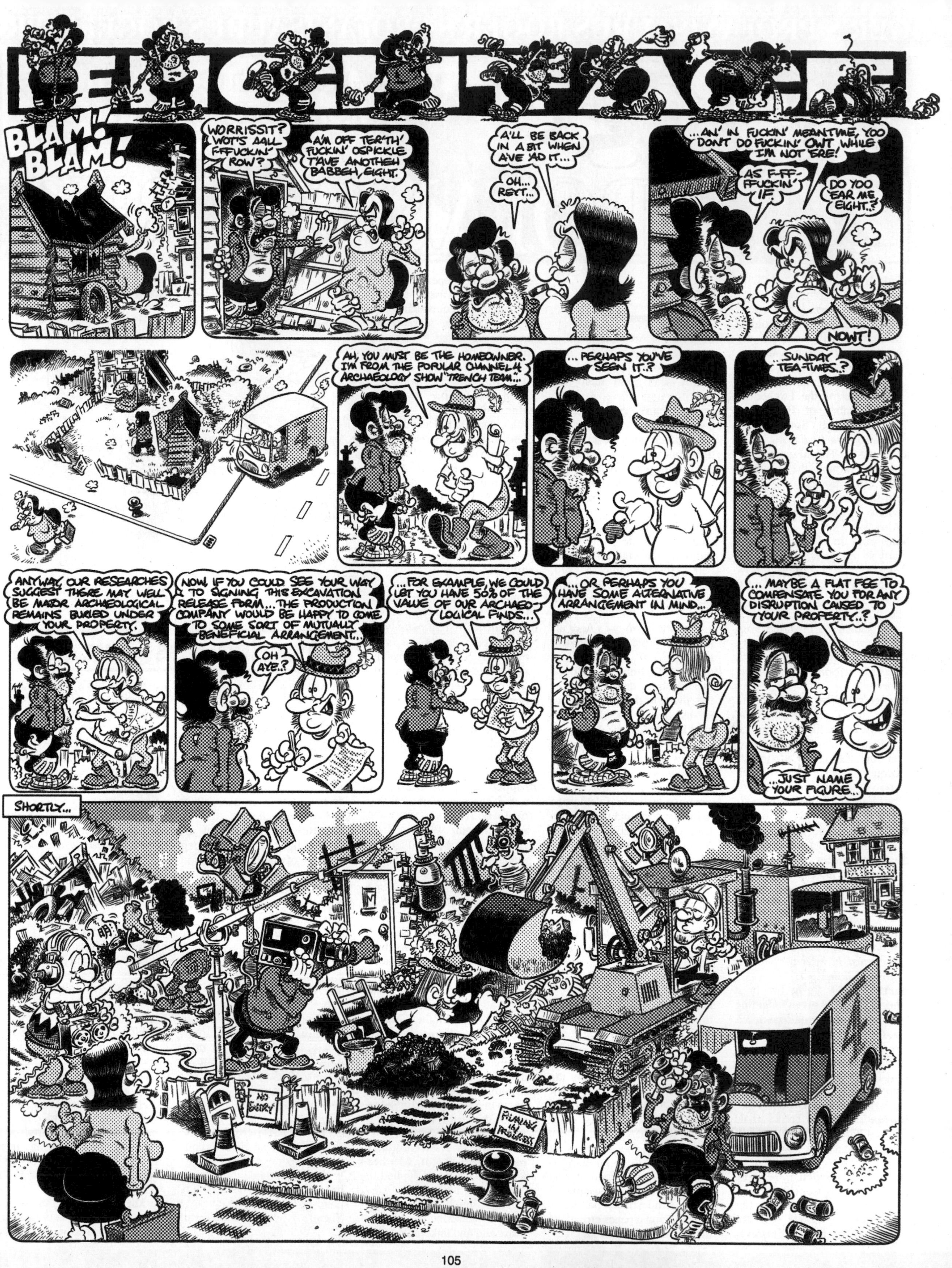
BLAM! BLAM!
WORRISSIT? WOT'S AALL F-FFUCKIN' ROW?
A'M OFF TER'TH' FUCKIN' OSPICKLE T'AVE ANOTHEH BABBEH, EIGHT.
A'LL BE BACK IN A BIT WHEN A'VE 'AD IT...
OH... REYT...
...AN' IN FUCKIN' MEANTIME, YOO DON'T DO FUCKIN' OWT WHILE I'M NOT 'ERE!
AS F-FF-FFUCKIN' IF.
DO YOO 'EAR ME EIGHT..?
NOWT!
AH, YOU MUST BE THE HOMEOWNER. I'M FROM THE POPULAR CHANNEL 4 ARCHAEOLOGY SHOW "TRENCH TEAM"...
...PERHAPS YOU'VE SEEN IT..?
...SUNDAY TEA-TIMES..?
ANYWAY, OUR RESEARCHES SUGGEST THERE MAY WELL BE MAJOR ARCHAEOLOGICAL REMAINS BURIED UNDER YOUR PROPERTY.
NOW, IF YOU COULD SEE YOUR WAY TO SIGNING THIS EXCAVATION RELEASE FORM... THE PRODUCTION COMPANY WOULD BE HAPPY TO COME TO SOME SORT OF MUTUALLY BENEFICIAL ARRANGEMENT...
OH AYE..?
...FOR EXAMPLE, WE COULD LET YOU HAVE 50% OF THE VALUE OF OUR ARCHAEO-LOGICAL FINDS...
...OR PERHAPS YOU HAVE SOME ALTERNATIVE ARRANGEMENT IN MIND...
...MAYBE A FLAT FEE TO COMPENSATE YOU FOR ANY DISRUPTION CAUSED TO YOUR PROPERTY..?
...JUST NAME YOUR FIGURE...
SHORTLY...
NO ENTRY
FILMING IN PROGRESS

Roger's PROFANISAURUS

A Stylish Cut of Entries from Britain's Favourite Lexicon of Profanity

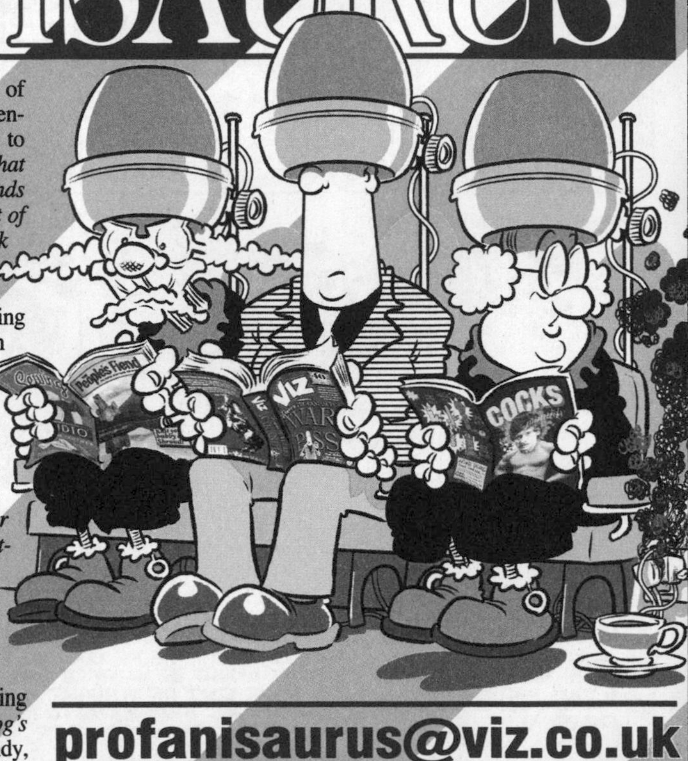
VIZ
COCKS

alisthair darling *n*. A lady with mis-matched plumage, *viz*. One whose *barnet* colour contrasts with her *pube* colour, in a style reminiscent of the unsettling eyebrow/hair hue combination of the former ventriloquist's dummy-esque Chancellor of the Exchequer and Member of Parliament for Edinburgh South West. An *aeroplane blonde*.

arse wig *n*. The *tagnutty* halo of hair around the *gammon ring*. Also poopée.

bald-headed hermit *n*. A long-winded way of saying *cock*. Also *bald man*.

bald man in a boat *1. n*. A lady's *clematis*. The *wail switch*. *2. n*. A hairless fellow esconced in a waterborne craft.

barber's bin *n*. A particularly badly kempt and unruly *snatch*. A *pieman's wig*. *'I'm sorry but I'm not doing that again, your worship. It was like sticking my head in a barber's bin.'*

Barber's Bridge *1. n*. A small town in Gloucestershire that was the site of the first intermediate station north of Gloucester on the old Ledbury & Gloucester Railway, as is well known. *2. n*. The small tuft of hair left on a lady's nethers after a *Brazilian* wax.

barber's floor *n*. An exceptionally hairy quim.

barber's lather pot *sim*. A generously filled *snatch*. Also a *billposter's bucket*, a *St. Bernard's chin*. A very, very, very *well-buttered bun*. *'My daughter is a groupie for So Solid Crew.' 'Good heavens! She must have a twat like a barber's lather pot.'*

barber's lolly *1. n*. In childhood, a reward given for sitting still while one's hair is cut. *2. n*. In adulthood, a reward given in return for performing any unpleasant task. *'Suck that? Alright, but you'll have to buy me an expensive barber's lolly afterwards, your Grace.'*

barber's pole *n*. Tricky male masturbatory technique entailing a helical clockwise twist on the upstroke.

barber's sandwich *n*. A badly pruned *muff*, from its resemblance to a buttered bap inadvertently dropped onto the unswept lino in a hairdresser's.

beard bait *n*. Artisanal, locally-sourced, farm-to-table *bollocks* designed to attract the skinny jeans and man bun crowd.

bearded bank robber *n*. A lass with a particularly hairy *biffer* who wears nylon tights but no *undercrackers*.

beard, tramp's *n*. A hairy, unwashed and unkempt *furry hoop*. With all bits of food stuck in it.

Bluto's beard *1. euph*. A spectacularly hirsute *Judith*, resembling the vigorous chinny hair of Popeye's thick-necked, Gary Bushell-lookylikey nemesis. A *biffer*. *2. n*. The dark ring of fluff found festooned around the *aardvark's nose* after wearing black *undercrackers*.

Bobby Charltons *n*. Rogue *fuckwhiskers* trapped under the *fiveskin* that stick themselves across the dome of your *bell end*, in the manner of the erstwhile centre-forward's last few remaining hairs. *Robert Robinsons, Demond Morrises*.

browneye lashes *n*. Glamorous hairs that surround the *balloon knot*. Often caked in a brown, mascara-like substance.

budget hairline *n*. The economical alternative to having a hair transplant. A *syrup* or *Irish jig*.

Captain Birdseye's chin *n*. Something hairy and haddocky. *'Fucking hell, love. It's like Captain Birdseye's chin down here.'*

centre parting *n*. Highly enjoyable form of solo *balloon knot* sport whereby the practitioner sits on a sturdy, solid chair or bench and then forcibly breaks wind while leaning forward at an angle of forty-five degrees, thus causing the emitted *trouser cough* to shoot straight up the middle of his or her back, like a sort of gaseous Evel Kneivel going up a ramp. HRH the Duchess of York is said to be an enthusiastic *centre parter* and, during Christmas dinners at Balmoral often demonstrates her skills by knocking a paper crown off the top of her own head.

cock hair *n*. Imperial unit of measurement used in engineering, equivalent to 2.32 *gnat's cods*. *'It seems that the O-ring failed 45 seconds after take off, allowing a jet of superheated gas just a cock hair wide to penetrate the main solid fuel booster.'*

collar and cuffs *euph*. Matching hair colour, up top and down below. *'See that blonde? Do you reckon her collar matches her cuffs? If you think you can help, contact Tyne and Wear CrimeStoppers on the number at the bottom of the screen. Our team of detectives are waiting to take your call.'*

combover cuffs *n*. Hairy hands, like what flocculent, banterous sports commentator Richard Keys has.

crosshair *n*. A stray *pube* lying horizontally across the *hog's eye*, thus creating a handy, sniper-like scope during the act of micturition, allowing one to aim accurately at the seat and floor.

Dick Turpin's hat *n*. A good, old-fashioned, three-cornered, hairy *blurtch* that would make the *old fella* "stand and deliver".

dropped lollipop, head like a *sim*. The *noggin* of a balding man who refuses to shave the remaining hair off his head, resulting in a scalp with similar amounts of hair on it to sticky confectionery retrieved from the living room carpet. *'I can't believe you paid £180 for that haircut, Wills. You've got a head like a dropped lollipop.'*

eating sushi off a barbershop floor *sim*. Performing *cumulonimbus* on a *pieman's wig*.

elephant's eyelashes *n*. The vigorous, jumbo-sized nasal hairs which Mother Nature inexplicably deems an essential *bird*-pulling accoutrement for males once they reach the age of thirty or so.

gentleman's gel *n*. A soothing facial/breast unguent for ladies which doubles as a hair styling product. *Heir cream*.

gloss drop *n*. A salon-quality moisturising serum, enriched with *Vitamin S* and applied to a lady's hair and/or face.

Hagrid's hairbrush *n*. Term used to describe a particularly wild and unkempt *growler*. Also *fanny like a dockyard cat, Percy Thrower's lawn, Terry Waite's allotment, welder's shoelaces, Max Clifford's hedge*.

profanisaurus@viz.co.uk

hairache *n*. The mother of all hangovers. *'I can't go on. You'll have to do the programme on your own, Phil. I've got hairache.'*

hairigami *n*. The ancient art of folding a few extra-long strands of hair from round the sides and back of a *baaldy*'s noggin into a convincing simulacrum of a coiffure. *'That's a magnificent bit of hairigami you have there, Mr Trump.' 'Door!'*

hog's eye hairpiece *n. Aus*. That long, *piss*-combed tuft of hair that seems to grow out the end of a dog's *unit*. Like on the top of Woody Woodpecker's head.

iced bun *n*. An old-fashioned ladies' hair-do that's all dripping in *spunk*. For whatever reason. *'I like your iced bun, Dusty.'*

Jim Royle's beard *n*. A *Dylan, pieman's wig*.

long bald *adj*. Descriptive of the sort of middle-aged man's coiffure consisting of a screamingly bald head flanked by longer but poorly-nourished, stringy hair, *eg*. That of Newcastle Theatre Royal panto stalwart Clive Webb.

Lord Winston's moustache *n*. A particularly hairy and poorly trimmed *biffer*, named after the exuberant face fungus of the popular ennobled telly boffin, test-tube *fanny apple* pioneer and former leading *twat mechanic* Dr Robert Winston. *Rhodes Boysons, whack-os*.

madman's arse *euph*. Descriptive of an extremely unruly hairstyle, *eg*. That *barnet* sported by erstwhile gun-toting "Wall of Sound" murderer Phil Spector.

mouldilocks *n*. An otherwise attractive woman who is let down by matted hair like off a *Harry Ramp*.

mullet *n*. Inbreds' haircut favoured by country and western singers, the trailer-trash guests on the *Jerry Springer Show* and 1980s footballers.

mull-over *n*. Trichologically speaking, a cross between a mullet and a combover; the sort of unsavoury, greasy hairdo sported by trainspotters, *kiddy-fiddlers* and those men you get in betting shops wearing shiny, wide-lapelled brown suits but no shirts.

nables *n*. Fast-growing nose hairs which increase in girth and strength by the year. From nose + cables.

Nutkin *1. n*. Of a man, the worst hairstyle it is possible to have, *eg*. Those worn by Phil

Harding (*Time Team* yokel archaeologist), Bill Bailey (troll-like comedian) and Terry Mancini (former QPR footballer). Named after late TV animal trainer and former sealion's dinner Terry Nutkin. *2. n.* A Mick Miller-style scrotal *pubedo*, with a shiny bald bit in the middle and long strands hanging down round the sides.

pieman's wig *1. n.* An artificial hairpiece worn by a purveyor of pastry-enveloped foodstuffs. *2. n.* An untidy *cunt-rug*.

pornytail *n.* The camera-friendly hairstyle of a grumble flick actress who thoughtfully ties her hair back to allow viewers an uninterrupted view of her *deep-throating* a *Charlie like a baby's arm*.

rat tail *1. n.* A long, thin, cylindrical file. *2. n.* A very suspect eighties hairdo. *3. n.* A long, thin, cylindrical *Richard the Third*.

redbeard *n.* A piratical hue of facial hair obtained by performing *cumulonimbus* upon a lady who *has the painters in*. Also known as a *Henry the eighth* or gorbie.

scrotee *1. n.* The sort of feeble, adolescent beard which appears to be composed principally of spare *nadbag* fluff. *2. n.* The clump of pretentious, tufted *jazz hair* growing off the lower slopes of one's *chicken skin handbag*. From scrotum + goatee.

self waxing *n.* Hair removal when a gent pulls back his crusted bed sheets the morning after a vigorous session of *making the bald man cry*.

Shearer's Island *n.* That increasingly isolated patch of hair on the front of a balding chap's head. Named after now baldy former footballer Alan, who fought an increasingly desperate battle to retain a minuscule archipelago of *Barnet* on his *noggin* for many years. Neil Tennant out of the Pet Shop Boys now has one of the most impressive *Shearer's Islands* in Britain.

shit in my hair! *exclam.* An exclamation of surprise similar to "Oh my days!" or "I'll go to the foot of our stairs!"

short back and sympathy *euph.* A cod haircut performed by an indulgent barber upon the pate of a balding gent, which involves making clipping noises near the customer's ears while throwing a bit of hair about to add realism.

short back and wipe *n.* The latest cut for the more follicly challenged gent. *'What will it be today, Prince William?' 'Short back and wipe please, barber.'*

snatch ponytail *1. n.* A fancy plait that "snatches" the face, lifting the cheekbones, it says here. As worn by Kim Kardashian and Ariana Grande. *2. n.* High-maintenance *hairy knickers*.

spangle bangle *n.* A hair band kept close to her bed by a keen *fellatrix* in order to keep her *barnet* out of her eyes as she performs *horatio*.

swope *n.* The hairstyle affected by balding men whereby the remaining strands of hair on one side of the head are grown long and swept over the dome, giving the impression of a full, healthy head of hair, *eg.* Robert Robinson, Bobby Charlton, Desmond Morris.

syrup *n.* Hairpiece. From syrup of fig = Irish jig. *"Q: 'Just look at this, 007.' Bond: 'What is it, Q? Looks like an ordinary syrup to me.' Q: 'Yes, but one tug on the chinstrap and it turns into a miniature helicopter.' Bond: 'Hmm! Hair raising!"* (from *Never Say Never Again*, 1983).

syruptitious *adj.* Of a balding gentleman, furtively and undetectably be-wigged.

top of a coconut *n.* Descriptive of a *Hitler tash* which has been neglected. A *pieman's wig*.

tuppenny all-off *1. n.* A cheap, no-nonsense haircut popular amongst national servicemen in the 1960s. *2. n.* A no-nonsense *fannicure*. A *Brazilian*.

vafro *n.* A magnificently hairy 1970s *biffer*.

Wallsend trim *n.* A haircut so short that you lose three layers of skin off your scalp in the process. Administered by all barbers in the eponymous leafy Tyneside suburb, irrespective of the style requested by the customer. A *tuppenny all-off*, *Geordie affro*.

wanker's tache *n. medic.* The vertical line of hair between the navel and the top of the *Rubiks*. Develops as a consequence of masturbation, along with spots, hairy palms, short-sightedness, insanity and stunted growth. The *crab ladder*.

Wiggins *n.* Pubage that carries on down the insides of a young lady's thighs. Named after the trademark sideburns of yellow-jerseyed mod bicyclist Sir Bradley. Also *Rhodes Boysons, inside burns, thighbrows, judge's eyebrows* and *whack-os*.

worzel, the *n.* Carefully curated "eccentric" hairstyle preferred by a former turnip-headed comedy Prime Minister, named after Jon Pertwee's children's TV scarecrow of the 1970s.

Roger's PROFANISAURUS HAIRY WORDSEARCH

YOU MUST know how this works by now. Hidden in the grid are all the entries in this *Roger's Hairy Profanisaurus* collection. They may read up, down or diagonally, backwards or forwards. And there is a prize of a *Viz* Cheap Pen for anyone who correctly sends a **LARGE LETTER STAMP** to: ***Roger's Profanisaurus Hairy Wordsearch, Viz Comic, PO Box 841, Whitley Bay, NE26 9EQ***

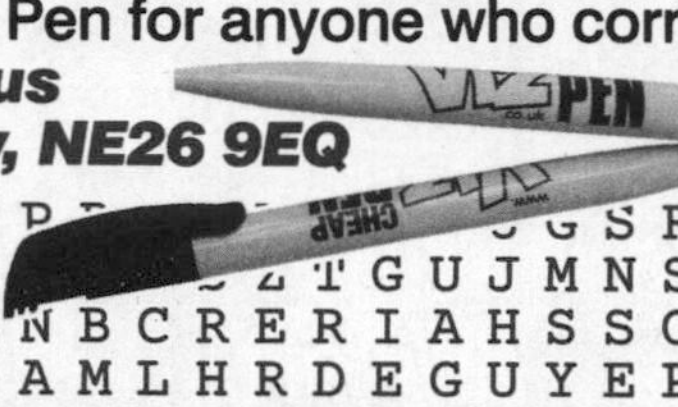
PEN
CHEAP

```
X H C I W D N A S S R E B R A B X E H C A T S R E K N A W P [illegible] G S R F C
S Z C T G P L K W E C T A M K S X R F H I K W S T P O G X [illegible] Z T G U J M N S D E
Z C G U O R M R D A W B R O W N E Y E L A S H E S X L P M N B C R E R I A H S S O R C
Z E L E T A X R H M J E B M K F D S G T R E W P E O J R L A M L H R D E G U Y E P K E
E Z F T U T Q T A M L T E T D D H I M L D S Z E S F E B H L D A E S T H G K P L K C E
L A L I S T H A I R D A R L I N G B C Z D E J S E D L M J Y N M W D T H U P B E S Q U
X T T E D A A U R E G P S E C M K H U E W E D G B N U D H M F D A Q M P S A K E F R I
W P C I D I M T A A D Y B F K A W L G T D R H E X H Y T M K D S E N M L R W A K F L P
P C J X N L A L C T D J I W T C J O T A O B A N I N A M D L A B A F S B M L J I U Y E
E O E E Z G S H H K O D N E U S E W Y P L R U M U P M S Q Y H F A L E A K G E A C S H
R M W R C H S G E N U T F W R M H Y D T D H J N M R M J L D W A K R E L R L O H D P O
D B A C E R E U M I H T F E P O R N Y T A I L Y G O E G X T S K S E B L I S A U N T G
Q O C T R A M P S B E A R D I M U G R A M H S M L E T V H W O L A C T E T I E T A L S
R V M L G U H R E H M L J U N V D E S Y O D M L P E R S O E O P K L G R R M L J R E E
L E S Y R U P T I T I O U S S M H P W E N Z Q N M L H P E L H P O W T I L S K E A B Y
O R A E D W W X V H U O E G H G S M U A A W T H U C E V L T L W E F G Y H P F T L O E
R C O K R F I M L H F W F E A W X Y K P L J Y T R T P Y S S K U L A A B M P E L L E H
D U A Z A L U G L H T F D F T E R C R M L L E C O C K H A I R G M M T C W E H P O L A
W F M I E E H S G I W E S R A L A P T U M E S H P P E I A V H I L M F E O M L P C O I
I F A E B L C E T I K P G T S B M L E K P L P E O S R E N L T S P M A D O C L E P K R
N S W R S R Z H P B N P H E T E A M K F S P T P N L U E U C M E L H T U E L O L B A P
S L P H O W A J E L E S P R M P H R M I F D I L P D T S H L P H E B L K M D E N O K I
T A E T T E H A G K M U O L U I M L B I R L F U L X T Z D T E S L D K Y E E M I U X E
O P E J U H R E C G U H L P L E D B J E L L U E E X H R O K A A I M L A G M P D T T C
N E L U L D W A P Y S E C Y L M K T F O R T G P E R E R I W H L M P O D O X B F S G E
S M P R B N K Y T F D W P G E M O T L N K S M Y G X W Z T M O E S P I M O E E J P O R
M S T A H A E N I L R I A H T E G D U B N P H I E D O A U C T Y S R Q U B P A P A S U
O P I A C H L A V H J K E R D U E I H A W Z W O L P R H K R E E B D E L P Y R H N L P
U T P K D W A D M L G E S Q T P M U M W X S R T P J Z S L H R S R R L B A C D K G P F
S Z X T H J U P H P J N F E P M L E W A N I L Y E F E S M R R T E A E L R P E T L S S
T D B H K P W E A E L H U O O P L E R A A O K L S E L H T E H N L E A I T A D G E B P
A M P H J S S E C H A G R N K T L U M H M L F R E S W O B M I A I B F A K P B H B R D
C S C P B E B H K I E D I P E W E E Y M P E B J D C E R O M K H L S Z T H X A R A T N
H M S E L M H T D R A X E E M Z I M L T L M L F D C A T N R G P K E L Y N Y N B N J A
E Z E B N M K F R E L O G D H P N K R O S A E P H B G B M K D E R L E N M E K L G S L
L P A B T T Z D K M P D H U H I K P P D N K L D R N O A O K G L L Y M O T F R H L P S
K N X D P H R I M L F H Y R T E P S U M D G M L I R D C M L A E P O T P M T O T E L I
N L O F E Q L E M L V P E I K D R T S Z L P B X E R E K S N O T L R A H C Y B B O B S
M P S E T D H T P G L P H A W E K M M L F E A A K Y G A M P G R W M T C U H B L O E R
X Z R T A M L S Q A X S B P B E C K I M P W T F L L E N P E X B H I L T E W E M L T E
N B E E M L D E S P R P O R B N A S P T F M L H R D L D P O B H J J S A K S R M L T R
M F H C J M L P Y R W T A M L D S W R L M K Y F D W P W M L P H F E O N M N L K S E A
X C H E C A P T A I N B I R D S E Y E S C H I N M L F I M D S W A L P S M L F C B I E
M L H D C B G L P Y N L O N M L T S P K B N L S E T D P M L H B A X Z T P I L H T G H
L H S U R B R I A H S D I R G A H M F C S J O T U P P E N N Y A L L O F F O K F R W S
```

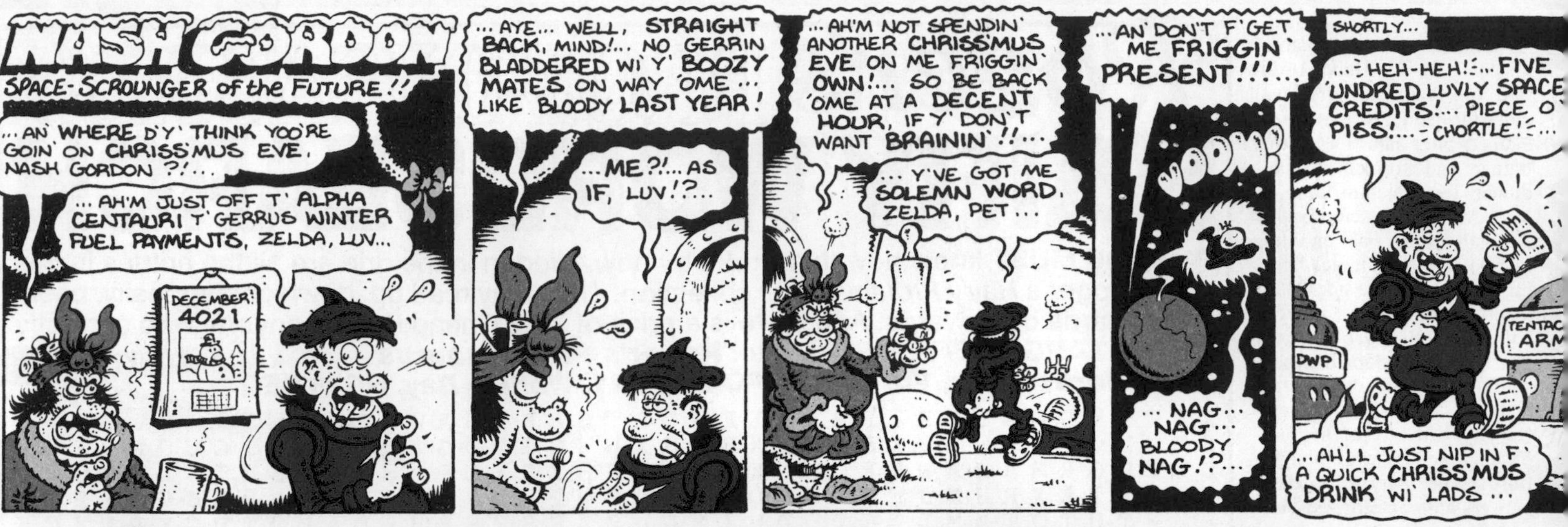
NASH GORDON
SPACE-SCROUNGER of the FUTURE!!
...AN' WHERE D'Y' THINK YOO'RE GOIN' ON CHRISS'MUS EVE, NASH GORDON ?!...
...AH'M JUST OFF T' ALPHA CENTAURI T' GERRUS WINTER FUEL PAYMENTS, ZELDA, LUV...
DECEMBER 4021
...AYE... WELL, STRAIGHT BACK, MIND!... NO GERRIN BLADDERED WI' Y' BOOZY MATES ON WAY 'OME... LIKE BLOODY LAST YEAR!
...ME?!...AS IF, LUV!?...
...AH'M NOT SPENDIN' ANOTHER CHRISS'MUS EVE ON ME FRIGGIN' OWN!... SO BE BACK 'OME AT A DECENT HOUR, IF Y' DON'T WANT BRAININ'!!...
...Y'VE GOT ME SOLEMN WORD, ZELDA, PET...
...AN' DON'T F'GET ME FRIGGIN' PRESENT!!!...
VOOM!
...NAG... NAG... BLOODY NAG!?...
SHORTLY...
...HEH-HEH!...FIVE 'UNDRED LUVLY SPACE CREDITS!... PIECE O' PISS!...CHORTLE!...
DWP
TENTAC ARM
...AH'LL JUST NIP IN F' A QUICK CHRISS'MUS DRINK WI' LADS...

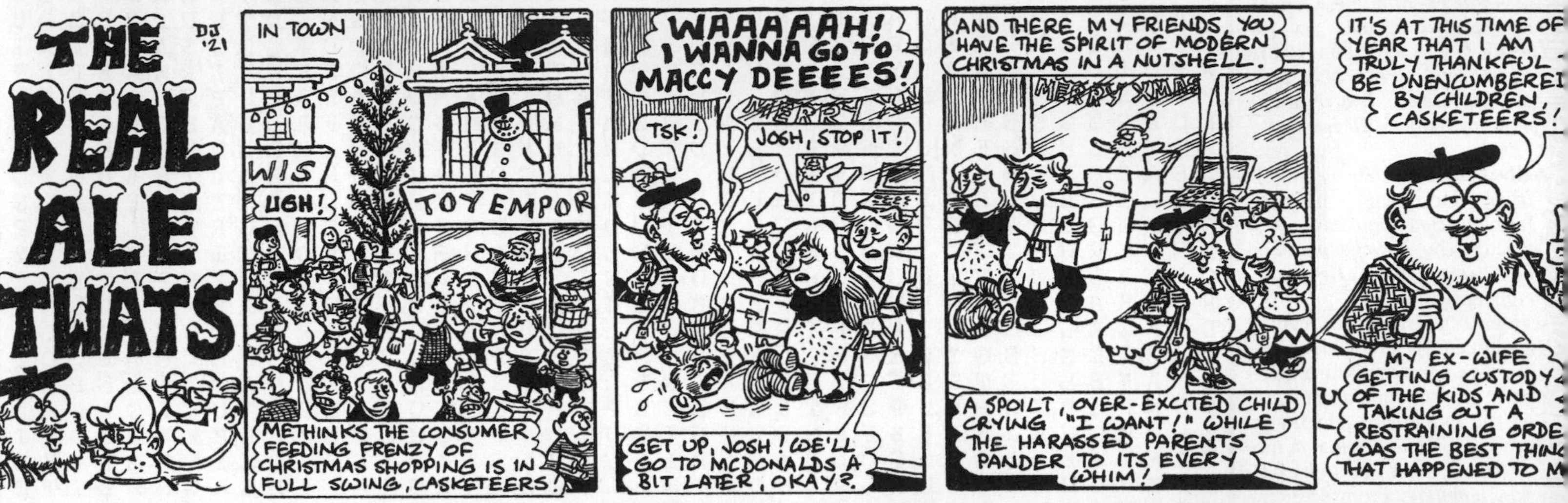
THE REAL ALE TWATS
DJ '21
IN TOWN
WIS
UGH!
TOY EMPOR
METHINKS THE CONSUMER FEEDING FRENZY OF CHRISTMAS SHOPPING IS IN FULL SWING, CASKETEERS!
WAAAAAH! I WANNA GO TO MACCY DEEEES!
TSK!
JOSH, STOP IT!
GET UP, JOSH! WE'LL GO TO McDONALDS A BIT LATER, OKAY?
AND THERE, MY FRIENDS, YOU HAVE THE SPIRIT OF MODERN CHRISTMAS IN A NUTSHELL.
MERRY XMAS
A SPOILT, OVER-EXCITED CHILD CRYING "I WANT!" WHILE THE HARASSED PARENTS PANDER TO ITS EVERY WHIM!
IT'S AT THIS TIME OF YEAR THAT I AM TRULY THANKFUL BE UNENCUMBERE BY CHILDREN, CASKETEERS!
MY EX-WIFE GETTING CUSTODY OF THE KIDS AND TAKING OUT A RESTRAINING ORDE WAS THE BEST THIN THAT HAPPENED TO M

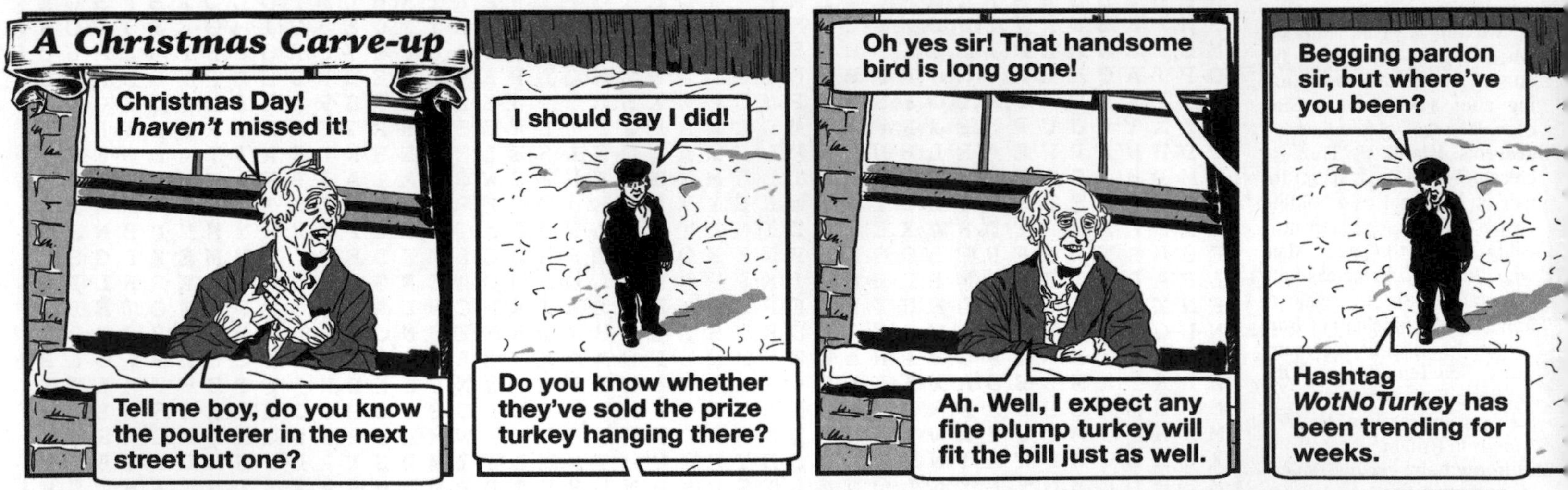
A Christmas Carve-up
Christmas Day! I *haven't* missed it!
Tell me boy, do you know the poulterer in the next street but one?
I should say I did!
Do you know whether they've sold the prize turkey hanging there?
Oh yes sir! That handsome bird is long gone!
Ah. Well, I expect any fine plump turkey will fit the bill just as well.
Begging pardon sir, but where've you been?
Hashtag *WotNoTurkey* has been trending for weeks.

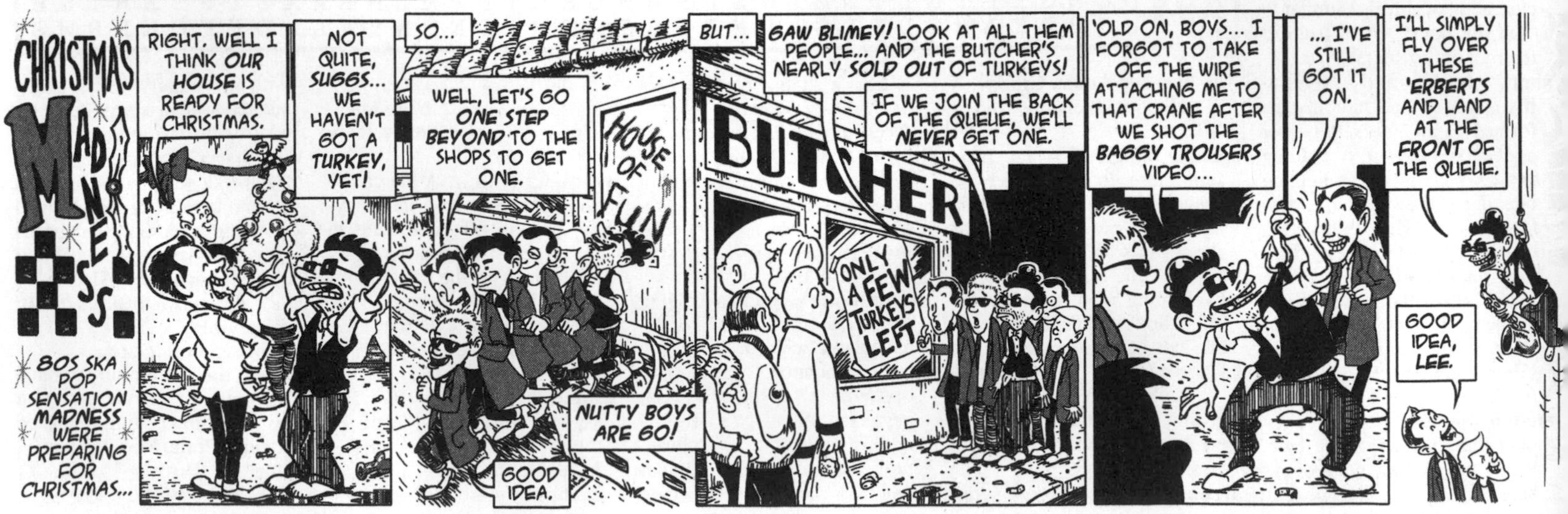
CHRISTMAS MADNESS
80s SKA POP SENSATION MADNESS WERE PREPARING FOR CHRISTMAS...
RIGHT. WELL I THINK *OUR HOUSE* IS READY FOR CHRISTMAS.
NOT QUITE, SUGGS... WE HAVEN'T GOT A TURKEY, YET!
SO...
WELL, LET'S GO *ONE STEP BEYOND* TO THE SHOPS TO GET ONE.
HOUSE OF FUN
NUTTY BOYS ARE GO!
GOOD IDEA.
BUT...
GAW BLIMEY! LOOK AT ALL THEM PEOPLE... AND THE BUTCHER'S NEARLY *SOLD OUT* OF TURKEYS!
IF WE JOIN THE BACK OF THE QUEUE, WE'LL *NEVER* GET ONE.
BUTCHER
ONLY A FEW TURKEYS LEFT
'OLD ON, BOYS... I FORGOT TO TAKE OFF THE WIRE ATTACHING ME TO THAT CRANE AFTER WE SHOT THE *BAGGY TROUSERS* VIDEO...
...I'VE STILL GOT IT ON.
I'LL SIMPLY FLY OVER THESE 'ERBERTS AND LAND AT THE *FRONT* OF THE QUEUE.
GOOD IDEA, LEE.

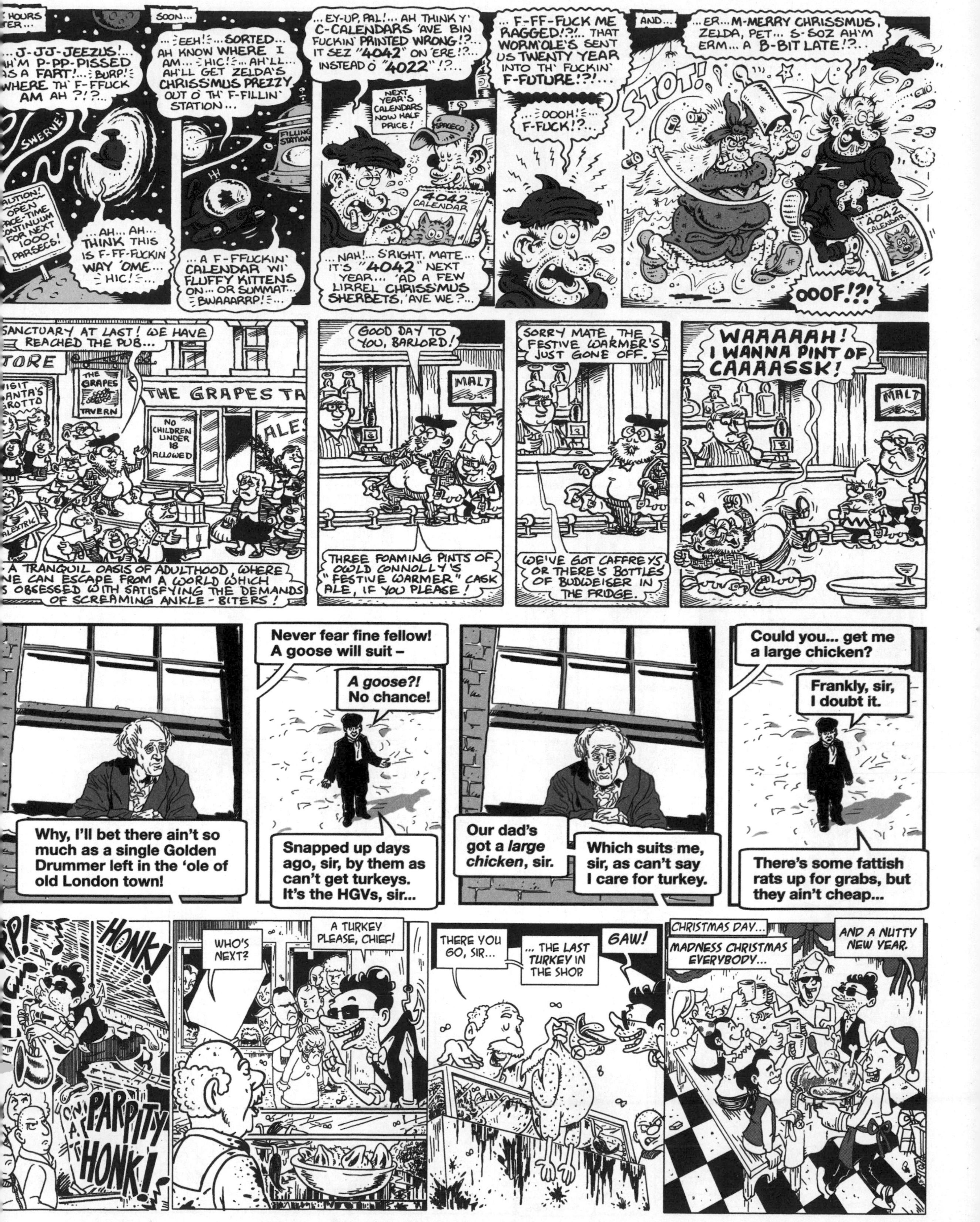

HOURS LATER...
...J-JJ-JEEZUS!... AH'M P-PP-PISSED AS A FART!... BURP! WHERE TH' F-FFUCK AM AH?!?...
SWERVE
CAUTION! OPEN SPACE-TIME CONTINUUM FOR NEXT 1000 PARSECS!
...AH... AH... THINK THIS IS F-FF-FUCKIN WAY 'OME... HIC!...
SOON...
...EEH!...SORTED... AH KNOW WHERE I AM... HIC!... AH'LL... AH'LL GET ZELDA'S CHRISSMUS PREZZY OUT O' TH' F-FILLIN' STATION...
FILLING STATION
...A F-FFUCKIN' CALENDAR WI' FLUFFY KITTENS ON... OR SUMMAT... BWAAARRP!...
...EY-UP, PAL!... AH THINK Y' C-CALENDARS 'AVE BIN FUCKIN' PAINTED WRONG!?... IT SEZ "4042" ON 'ERE!?... INSTEAD O' "4022"!?...
NEXT YEAR'S CALENDARS NOW HALF PRICE!
SPACECO
4042 CALENDAR
...NAH!... S'RIGHT, MATE... IT'S "4042" NEXT YEAR... 'AD A FEW LIRREL CHRISSMUS SHERBETS, 'AVE WE?...
...F-FF-FUCK ME RAGGED!?!... THAT WORM'OLE'S SENT US TWENTY YEAR INTO TH' FUCKIN' F-FUTURE!?!...
...OOOH!... F-FUCK!?...
AND...
...ER... M-MERRY CHRISSMUS, ZELDA, PET... S-SOZ AH'M ERM... A B-BIT LATE!?...
STOT!
4042 CALENDAR
OOOF!?!
SANCTUARY AT LAST! WE HAVE REACHED THE PUB...
STORE
VISIT SANTA'S GROTTO
THE GRAPES TAVERN
THE GRAPES TA
NO CHILDREN UNDER 18 ALLOWED
ALES
SCALEXTRIC
...A TRANQUIL OASIS OF ADULTHOOD, WHERE ONE CAN ESCAPE FROM A WORLD WHICH IS OBSESSED WITH SATISFYING THE DEMANDS OF SCREAMING ANKLE-BITERS!
GOOD DAY TO YOU, BARLORD!
MALT
THREE FOAMING PINTS OF OWLD CONNOLLY'S "FESTIVE WARMER" CASK ALE, IF YOU PLEASE!
SORRY MATE, THE FESTIVE WARMER'S JUST GONE OFF.
WE'VE GOT CAFFREYS OR THERE'S BOTTLES OF BUDWEISER IN THE FRIDGE.
WAAAAAH! I WANNA PINT OF CAAAASSK!
MALT
Why, I'll bet there ain't so much as a single Golden Drummer left in the 'ole of old London town!
Never fear fine fellow! A goose will suit –
A goose?! No chance!
Snapped up days ago, sir, by them as can't get turkeys. It's the HGVs, sir...
Our dad's got a large chicken, sir.
Which suits me, sir, as can't say I care for turkey.
Could you... get me a large chicken?
Frankly, sir, I doubt it.
There's some fattish rats up for grabs, but they ain't cheap...
HONK!
AN' A PARPITY HONK!
WHO'S NEXT?
A TURKEY PLEASE, CHIEF!
THERE YOU GO, SIR...
...THE LAST TURKEY IN THE SHOP.
GAW!
CHRISTMAS DAY...
MADNESS CHRISTMAS EVERYBODY...
AND A NUTTY NEW YEAR.

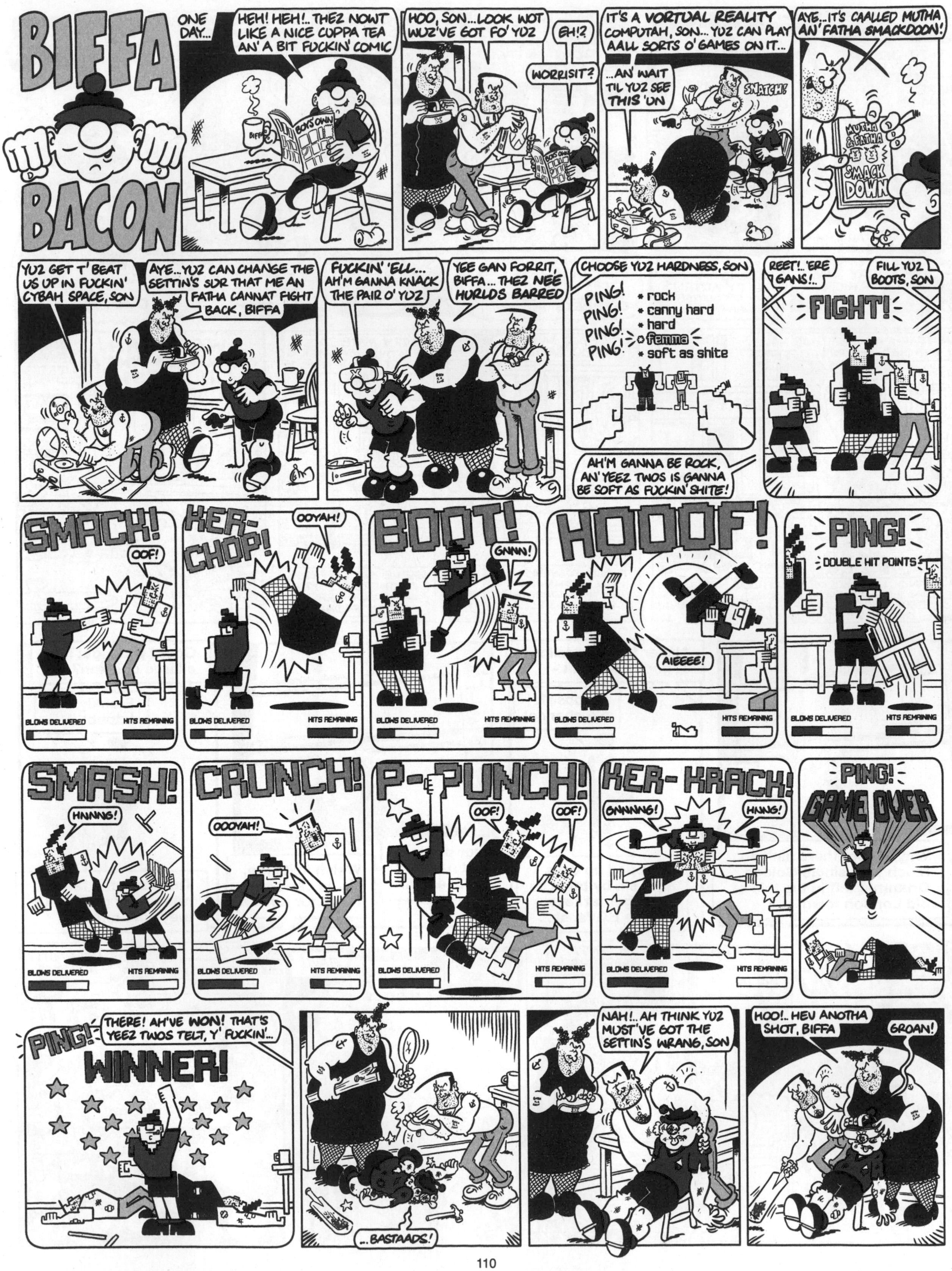

BIFFA BACON
ONE DAY...
HEH! HEH!.. THEZ NOWT LIKE A NICE CUPPA TEA AN' A BIT FUCKIN' COMIC
BOYS' OWN
HOO, SON... LOOK WOT WUZ'VE GOT FO' YUZ
EH!?
WORRISIT?
IT'S A VORTUAL REALITY COMPUTAH, SON... YUZ CAN PLAY AALL SORTS O' GAMES ON IT...
...AN' WAIT TIL YUZ SEE THIS 'UN
SNATCH!
AYE... IT'S CAALLED MUTHA AN' FATHA SMACKDOON!
MUTHA & FATHA SMACK DOWN
YUZ GET T' BEAT US UP IN FUCKIN' CYBAH SPACE, SON
AYE... YUZ CAN CHANGE THE SETTIN'S SUR THAT ME AN FATHA CANNAT FIGHT BACK, BIFFA
FUCKIN' 'ELL... AH'M GANNA KNACK THE PAIR O' YUZ
YEE GAN FORRIT, BIFFA... THEZ NEE HURLDS BARRED
CHOOSE YUZ HARDNESS, SON
PING! PING! PING! PING!
* rock
* canny hard
* hard
* femma
* soft as shite
AH'M GANNA BE ROCK, AN' YEEZ TWOS IS GANNA BE SOFT AS FUCKIN' SHITE!
REET!.. 'ERE GANS!..
FILL YUZ BOOTS, SON
FIGHT!
SMACK!
OOF!
BLOWS DELIVERED
HITS REMAINING
KER-CHOP!
OOYAH!
BLOWS DELIVERED
HITS REMAINING
BOOT!
GNNN!
BLOWS DELIVERED
HITS REMAINING
HOOOF!
AIEEEE!
BLOWS DELIVERED
HITS REMAINING
PING!
DOUBLE HIT POINTS
BLOWS DELIVERED
HITS REMAINING
SMASH!
HNNNG!
BLOWS DELIVERED
HITS REMAINING
CRUNCH!
OOOYAH!
BLOWS DELIVERED
HITS REMAINING
P-PUNCH!
OOF!
OOF!
BLOWS DELIVERED
HITS REMAINING
KER-KRACH!
GNNNNG!
HNNG!
BLOWS DELIVERED
HITS REMAINING
PING!
GAME OVER
PING!
THERE! AH'VE WON! THAT'S YEEZ TWOS TELT, Y' FUCKIN'...
WINNER!
...BASTAADS!
NAH!.. AH THINK YUZ MUST'VE GOT THE SETTIN'S WRANG, SON
HOO!.. HEV ANOTHA SHOT, BIFFA
GROAN!

Scum mothers who'd have 'em

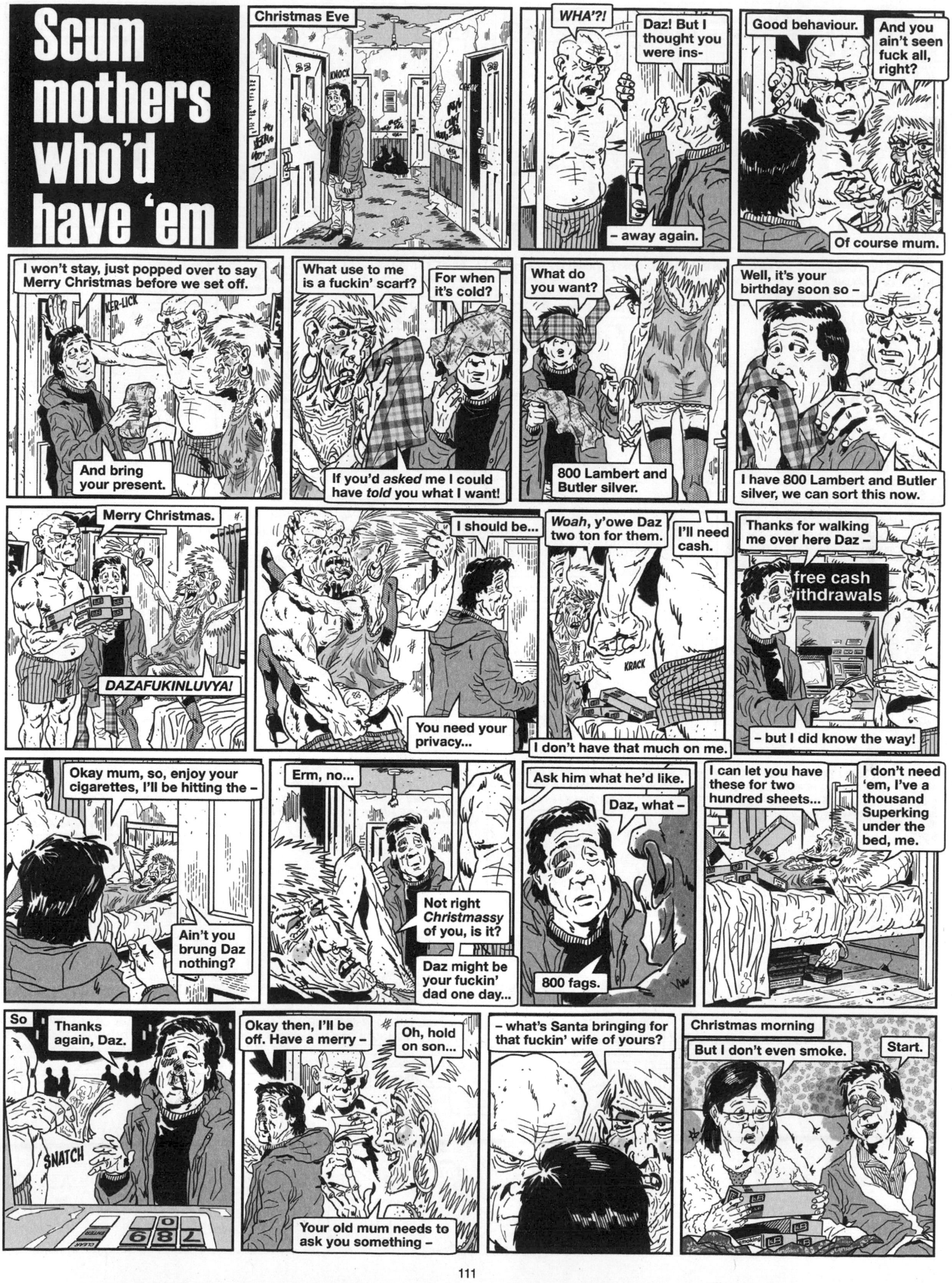

Christmas Eve
KNOCK
CREAK
WHA'?!
Daz! But I thought you were ins-
– away again.
Good behaviour.
And you ain't seen fuck all, right?
Of course mum.
I won't stay, just popped over to say Merry Christmas before we set off.
KER-LICK
And bring your present.
What use to me is a fuckin' scarf?
For when it's cold?
If you'd *asked* me I could have *told* you what I want!
What do you want?
800 Lambert and Butler silver.
Well, it's your birthday soon so –
I have 800 Lambert and Butler silver, we can sort this now.
Merry Christmas.
DAZAFUKINLUVYA!
I should be...
You need your privacy...
Woah, y'owe Daz two ton for them.
I'll need cash.
KRACK
I don't have that much on me.
Thanks for walking me over here Daz –
free cash withdrawals
– but I did know the way!
Okay mum, so, enjoy your cigarettes, I'll be hitting the –
Ain't you brung Daz nothing?
Erm, no...
Not right *Christmassy* of you, is it?
Daz might be your fuckin' dad one day...
Ask him what he'd like.
Daz, what –
800 fags.
I can let you have these for two hundred sheets...
I don't need 'em, I've a thousand Superking under the bed, me.
So
Thanks again, Daz.
SNATCH
Okay then, I'll be off. Have a merry –
Oh, hold on son...
Your old mum needs to ask you something –
– what's Santa bringing for that fuckin' wife of yours?
Christmas morning
But I don't even smoke.
Start.

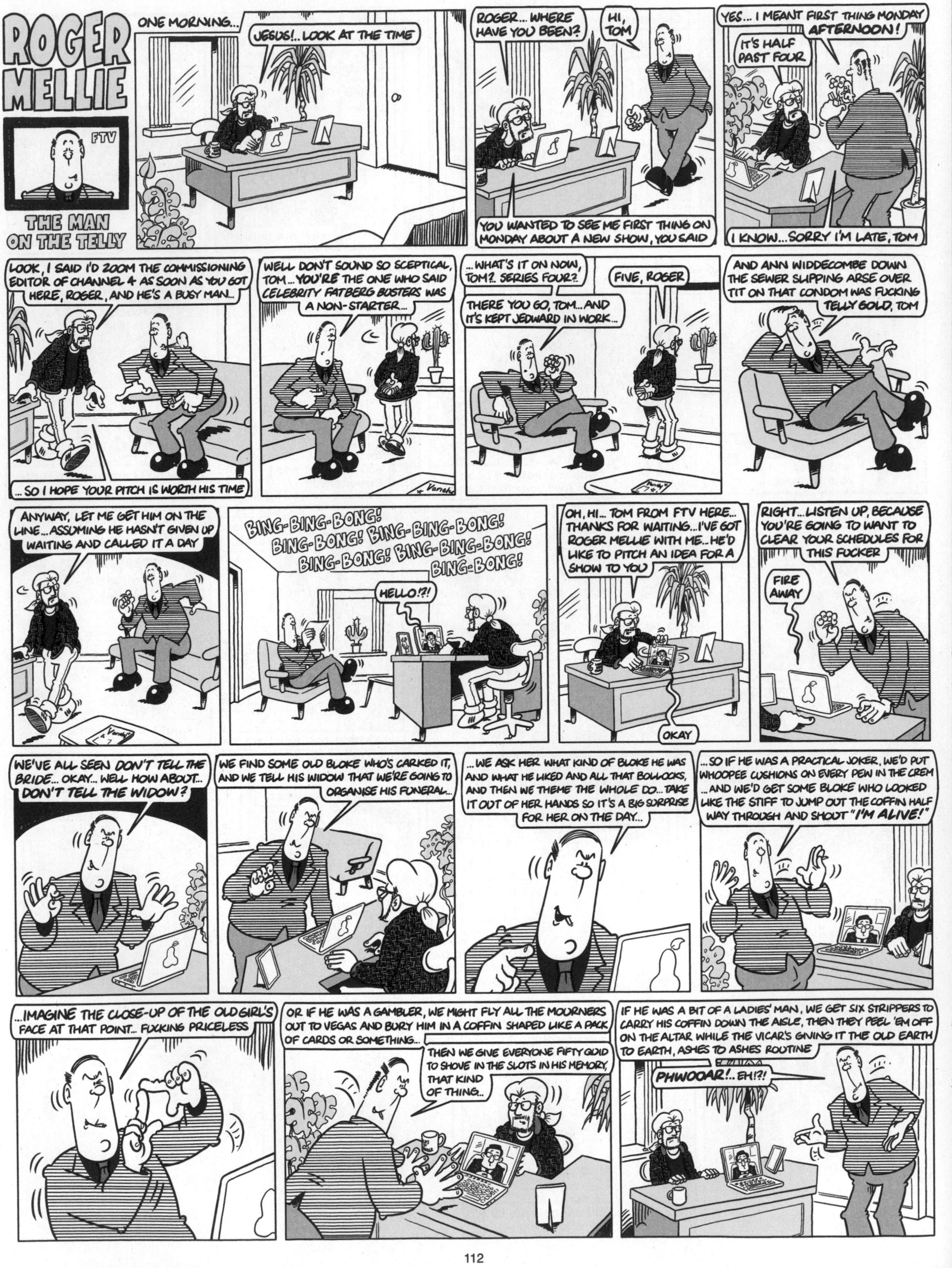
ROGER MELLIE
FTV
THE MAN ON THE TELLY
ONE MORNING...
JESUS!.. LOOK AT THE TIME
ROGER... WHERE HAVE YOU BEEN?
HI, TOM
YOU WANTED TO SEE ME FIRST THING ON MONDAY ABOUT A NEW SHOW, YOU SAID
YES... I MEANT FIRST THING MONDAY AFTERNOON!
IT'S HALF PAST FOUR
I KNOW... SORRY I'M LATE, TOM
LOOK, I SAID I'D ZOOM THE COMMISSIONING EDITOR OF CHANNEL 4 AS SOON AS YOU GOT HERE, ROGER, AND HE'S A BUSY MAN...
...SO I HOPE YOUR PITCH IS WORTH HIS TIME
WELL DON'T SOUND SO SCEPTICAL, TOM... YOU'RE THE ONE WHO SAID CELEBRITY FATBERG BUSTERS WAS A NON-STARTER...
...WHAT'S IT ON NOW, TOM?.. SERIES FOUR?
FIVE, ROGER
THERE YOU GO, TOM... AND IT'S KEPT JEDWARD IN WORK...
AND ANN WIDDECOMBE DOWN THE SEWER SLIPPING ARSE OVER TIT ON THAT CONDOM WAS FUCKING TELLY GOLD, TOM
ANYWAY, LET ME GET HIM ON THE LINE... ASSUMING HE HASN'T GIVEN UP WAITING AND CALLED IT A DAY
BING-BING-BONG! BING-BONG! BING-BING-BONG! BING-BONG! BING-BING-BONG! BING-BONG!
HELLO!?!
OH, HI... TOM FROM FTV HERE... THANKS FOR WAITING... I'VE GOT ROGER MELLIE WITH ME... HE'D LIKE TO PITCH AN IDEA FOR A SHOW TO YOU
OKAY
RIGHT... LISTEN UP, BECAUSE YOU'RE GOING TO WANT TO CLEAR YOUR SCHEDULES FOR THIS FUCKER
FIRE AWAY
WE'VE ALL SEEN DON'T TELL THE BRIDE... OKAY... WELL HOW ABOUT... DON'T TELL THE WIDOW?
WE FIND SOME OLD BLOKE WHO'S CARKED IT, AND WE TELL HIS WIDOW THAT WE'RE GOING TO ORGANISE HIS FUNERAL...
...WE ASK HER WHAT KIND OF BLOKE HE WAS AND WHAT HE LIKED AND ALL THAT BOLLOCKS, AND THEN WE THEME THE WHOLE DO... TAKE IT OUT OF HER HANDS SO IT'S A BIG SURPRISE FOR HER ON THE DAY...
...SO IF HE WAS A PRACTICAL JOKER, WE'D PUT WHOOPEE CUSHIONS ON EVERY PEW IN THE CREM ...AND WE'D GET SOME BLOKE WHO LOOKED LIKE THE STIFF TO JUMP OUT THE COFFIN HALF WAY THROUGH AND SHOUT "I'M ALIVE!"
...IMAGINE THE CLOSE-UP OF THE OLD GIRL'S FACE AT THAT POINT... FUCKING PRICELESS
OR IF HE WAS A GAMBLER, WE MIGHT FLY ALL THE MOURNERS OUT TO VEGAS AND BURY HIM IN A COFFIN SHAPED LIKE A PACK OF CARDS OR SOMETHING...
THEN WE GIVE EVERYONE FIFTY QUID TO SHOVE IN THE SLOTS IN HIS MEMORY, THAT KIND OF THING...
IF HE WAS A BIT OF A LADIES' MAN, WE GET SIX STRIPPERS TO CARRY HIS COFFIN DOWN THE AISLE, THEN THEY PEEL 'EM OFF ON THE ALTAR WHILE THE VICAR'S GIVING IT THE OLD EARTH TO EARTH, ASHES TO ASHES ROUTINE
PHWOOAR!.. EH!?!

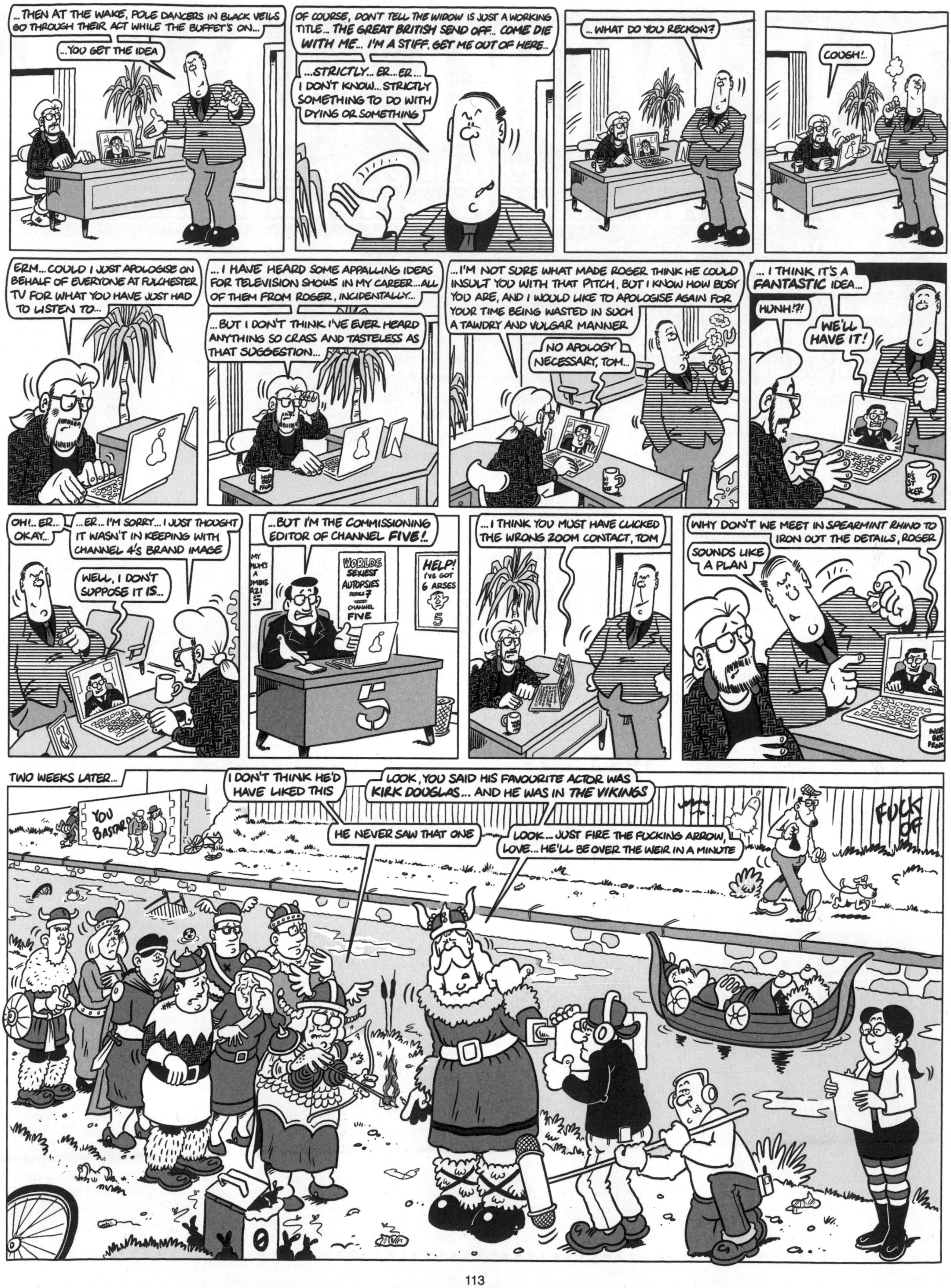

...THEN AT THE WAKE, POLE DANCERS IN BLACK VEILS GO THROUGH THEIR ACT WHILE THE BUFFET'S ON...
...YOU GET THE IDEA
OF COURSE, DON'T TELL THE WIDOW IS JUST A WORKING TITLE... THE GREAT BRITISH SEND OFF... COME DIE WITH ME... I'M A STIFF, GET ME OUT OF HERE...
...STRICTLY... ER... ER... I DON'T KNOW... STRICTLY SOMETHING TO DO WITH DYING OR SOMETHING
...WHAT DO YOU RECKON?
COUGH!..
ERM... COULD I JUST APOLOGISE ON BEHALF OF EVERYONE AT FULCHESTER TV FOR WHAT YOU HAVE JUST HAD TO LISTEN TO...
...I HAVE HEARD SOME APPALLING IDEAS FOR TELEVISION SHOWS IN MY CAREER... ALL OF THEM FROM ROGER, INCIDENTALLY...
...BUT I DON'T THINK I'VE EVER HEARD ANYTHING SO CRASS AND TASTELESS AS THAT SUGGESTION...
...I'M NOT SURE WHAT MADE ROGER THINK HE COULD INSULT YOU WITH THAT PITCH, BUT I KNOW HOW BUSY YOU ARE, AND I WOULD LIKE TO APOLOGISE AGAIN FOR YOUR TIME BEING WASTED IN SUCH A TAWDRY AND VULGAR MANNER
NO APOLOGY NECESSARY, TOM...
...I THINK IT'S A FANTASTIC IDEA...
HUNH!?!
WE'LL HAVE IT!
OH!.. ER... OKAY...
...ER... I'M SORRY... I JUST THOUGHT IT WASN'T IN KEEPING WITH CHANNEL 4'S BRAND IMAGE
WELL, I DON'T SUPPOSE IT IS...
...BUT I'M THE COMMISSIONING EDITOR OF CHANNEL FIVE!..
WORLDS SEXIEST AUTOPSIES SERIES 7 CHANNEL FIVE
HELP! I'VE GOT 6 ARSES 5
...I THINK YOU MUST HAVE CLICKED THE WRONG ZOOM CONTACT, TOM
WHY DON'T WE MEET IN SPEARMINT RHINO TO IRON OUT THE DETAILS, ROGER
SOUNDS LIKE A PLAN
TWO WEEKS LATER...
I DON'T THINK HE'D HAVE LIKED THIS
HE NEVER SAW THAT ONE
LOOK, YOU SAID HIS FAVOURITE ACTOR WAS KIRK DOUGLAS... AND HE WAS IN THE VIKINGS
LOOK... JUST FIRE THE FUCKING ARROW, LOVE... HE'LL BE OVER THE WEIR IN A MINUTE
YOU BASTAR
FUCK OF

THE WOKE HAVE LI[...]

"The self-righteous snowflake brigade have sabotaged my every career move," fumes so-penniless Lanford

FOR MONTHS, a pandemic has been rampaging through our green and pleasant land; a vile and merciless plague that destroys lives, wrecks businesses and rents families in twain.

A plague of WOKENESS.

A dangerous, mutant strain of political correctness, 'wokeness' can infect anyone – man, woman or child – stripping them of their Great British Values and transforming them into a dead-eyed Marxist replicant whose sole aim in life is to dismantle centuries-old traditions such as sexism, racism and homophobia. Despite the heroic actions of free-thinking firebrands such as **ANDREW NEIL**, **SARAH VINE** and **IAN BROWN** out of the Stone Roses, the Wokerati 'Thought Police' continue to burrow deeper and deeper into British society, spreading their sinister Orwellian tentacles through every nook and cranny of our lives.

And no one knows this better than **LANFORD PEDALBIN**.

If it ain't woke...: Pedalbin believe[...] Wokerati made his life a living h[...]

Morbidly obese Driffield bachelor Lanford has lost more than TWENTY jobs over the past 12 months, all because the spiteful PC-crazed Woke Brigade have conspired against him.

"Every time I find gainful employment, I am immediately 'cancelled' by my snowflake employers simply for being a heterosexual white male who loves my country," sighs the patriotic convicted sex offender. "I've watched it happen to all my heroes – great men like Laurence Fox, Toby Young and Oswald Mosley. And now it's happening to me, over and over again, like some kind of Stalinist *Groundhog Day*."

In this exclusive interview, so-unmarried Lanford, 62, lays bare the true horrors of this cancer of wokeness that is eating into the

EXCLUSIVE!

heart of Broken Britain, and he demonstrates how easily it can strip an innocent man of his honour, dignity and regular income.

Cra-vat's Not Fair!

Lanford's Orwellian 'woke' nightmare began back in June last year, when he managed to find his first job in decades.

"I'd been on the nash for forty-odd years due to an extremely rare and undetectable health condition that prevents me from doing literally any sort of work whatsoever. I won't bore you with the details, but it's definitely a real thing and I definitely suffer from it. However, someone must have dobbed me in about the cash-in-hand window cleaning I do sometimes, when I'm feeling up to it, because one day the dole gave me an ultimatum: *accept the first job they could find me or have my income cut off.* I chose the former, and the very next day I started work as a vending machine re-stocker at a local frozen foods factory.

> *My 'old fashioned' British values were out of sync with the company's ultra-woke Trotskyite groupthink*

Vend for yourself: Pedalbin's accessorising landed him in hot water with new employers.

It was my first day on the job, so I decided I would dress to impress. Eschewing the overalls I'd been issued with, I donned a smart three-piece suit and my favourite tie – a strikingly beautiful nylon number decorated with Union Jack flags. What better way to win over my new colleagues, I thought, than showing my love for my country via the medium of a themed neck accessory?

I could not have been more wrong.

handshake

Just three hours into my first day, I was summoned to my supervisor's office. I assumed she'd called me in to give me a firm handshake and a warm welcome, but instead I stood there gobsmacked as she and the Head of HR told me they were letting me go. I couldn't believe my ears. These jumped-up snowflakes were so 'offended' by my Union Jack tie that they were actually FIRING me on the spot! You literally couldn't make it up – which proves that I haven't.

Of course, they knew that sacking me for wearing a patriotic tie would never stand up in court, so they were forced to invent a tissue of lies to support my dismissal. They droned on about the 'official reason' for my dismissal – a simple misunderstanding that had occurred earlier in the day, involving me accidentally touching a female employee several times on her buttocks and breasts whilst reaching for a mug in the kitchen. But I knew the truth: my 'old fashioned' British values were out of sync with the company's ultra-woke Trotskyite groupthink.

I left the factory with my head held high, my tie fluttering proudly in the afternoon breeze. I thought of the other heroic figures who have faced cancellation at the hands of the snowflake brigade – Jeremy Clarkson, Nigel Farage, the banjo player out of Mumford & Sons – and I am not ashamed to say that I wept right there in the parking lot. I vowed that never again would I let this plague of wokeness stop me from achieving my dreams."

FT ME BROKE!

Right Royal Fuss Over Nothing

Lanford dusted himself off from his horrifying experience at the hands of the Wokerati, and got straight back to work.

" The nash soon found me another gig, working as a lavatory technician at a nearby DIY superstore. I couldn't wait to get started, as I was beginning to feel the pinch what with my dole cheques being cut off and my local offie hiking up the price of white cider.

Recalling the misunderstanding at my previous job, I decided it would be best to bring in my own tea mug this time, and I chose my absolute favourite: a smashing Royal Family souvenir cup, with the smiling face of HRH Prince Andrew on it.

Andrew has recently become the latest casualty of the Woke Brigade – an innocent man whose reputation has been dragged through the mud, whilst a free pass has been given to the *genuine* rotten branch of the Windsor family tree: Meghan Markle. Honestly, don't get me started on Meghan – she really gets my back up. I can't put my finger on it, but there's something about her that doesn't sit right with me.

retriever

Anyroad, two days passed without incident and I felt happy and confident that I was settling into my new workplace with ease.

And then, on the third day, disaster struck.

I was dealing with a particularly troublesome blockage in the gents' lavs, when my boss stormed in with

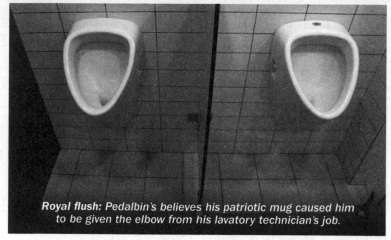
Royal flush: Pedalbin's believes his patriotic mug caused him to be given the elbow from his lavatory technician's job.

a face like thunder. I listened in stunned shock as he handed me a P45 and insisted I leave the premises immediately.

I felt physically sick to my stomach. This monarchy-loathing leftist had obviously spotted my Royal Family mug in the kitchen, and decided it didn't quite 'chime' with his anti-free-speech company policy. Of course, he wouldn't *dare* say that out loud – he claimed he was dismissing me due to various reports of a man who looked remarkably similar to me rummaging through the tills and removing a few measly fifty pound notes – but I knew the truth.

I was manhandled onto the street by security guards and told never to darken the shop's door again. As I trudged back to my bedsit, I reflected on just how deeply infested this once-great country had become by the pitiless plague of wokeness.

And I never got my mug back either. **"**

Read 'em and Weep

Over the months that followed, Lanford was let go from job after job due to his steadfast refusal to bow to the self-righteous ultra-leftist Woke Brigade.

" I got a gig emptying the bins in the local park, but I was fired within a week, simply for telling a group of female joggers that Covid-19 was a hoax," chuckles Lanford, hollowly. "The council claimed it was because my penis had accidentally slipped out of my trousers and waggled itself at the women as I spoke to them – but I knew the truth. Apparently, it's now a sackable offence to *express an opinion*. Welcome to Britain, 2021.

Re-Markle-able: Lanford believes certain royals are being persecuted while others, like Meghan, are given a free pass.

At my next job as a primary school janitor, I made the mistake of telling a colleague that I didn't entirely agree with the Black Lives Matter protests. Clearly he was a card-carrying wokeist because later that day, I was 'mysteriously' given the boot after I slipped on some empty white cider bottles and was discovered unconscious in the maintenance cupboard.

Again and again it happened: East Yorkshire's shady cabal of woke employers simply couldn't bear to see a free-thinking individual like myself succeed. In March of this year, however, after being sacked from 19 different jobs on the trot, I finally found what I thought was my dream gig.

oldie

The nash sorted me a part time stint unclogging the fat fryer at a local chip shop. Now, I love a chippy tea, and the part-time hours meant I still had plenty of time to pursue my hobbies, which include watching documentaries about German military history and making lively contributions to the *Mail Online's* comments section. I was on cloud nine as I headed in for my first day: I had found the perfect job.

Little did I know, the Wokerati were poised to strike yet again.

During my second week on the job, I nipped to the loo for a shit. I'd had tripe the night before, so I knew I might be in there a while, and as such, I took some reading material in with me. I brought in three excellent and informative publications – the latest issue of *The Spectator* magazine, Richard Littlejohn's hilarious *To Hell In A Handcart*, and *The Purple Revolution* by Britain's most successful party leader ever, Nigel Farage.

gate bridge

An hour or so later, having semi-successfully voided my bowels, I headed back to work. Just as I was getting stuck into the congealed fat build-up in fryer number two, though, the restaurant's owner, Mr Barraclough, asked if he could speak to me in private. I wondered what it could possibly be about, and then my blood ran cold as I realised: *I'd left my reading material in the cubicle.*

My vaguely right-of-centre literary tastes had clearly been uncovered and the anti-free-speech woke patrol couldn't have that, could they? With a sinking feeling, I sensed I was in for the chop – and I wasn't wrong. Mr Barraclough was too cowardly to address the real reason for my unjust dismissal, instead spouting a litany of false allegations that included everything from drinking on the job, stealing money from the till, making 'unsolicited advances' towards female colleagues and – most preposterously – doodling National Socialist insignia on customers' chip wrapping paper. I had to laugh as he showed me several hours of CCTV footage that had been cleverly doctored to make it look like I had actually done all these things. The lengths these woke bullies will go to simply beggars belief.

So here I sit: unemployed, flat broke, under house arrest and on the Sex Offenders Register – all because I refused to fall into line with the fanatical censorship laws of the snowflake Thought Police. I didn't ask to become a martyr: it's a role that has been thrust upon me. I can only hope that sharing my experience will open people's eyes to the true horrors of Britain's REAL pandemic: *Wokeness.* **"**

> **He claimed he was dismissing me due to various reports of a man who looked remarkably similar to me rummaging through the tills and removing a few measly fifty pound notes – but I knew the truth.**

NEXT WEEK: *Lanford is given a TEN YEAR prison sentence for simply stating that he is proud to be English whilst accidentally robbing a petrol station.*

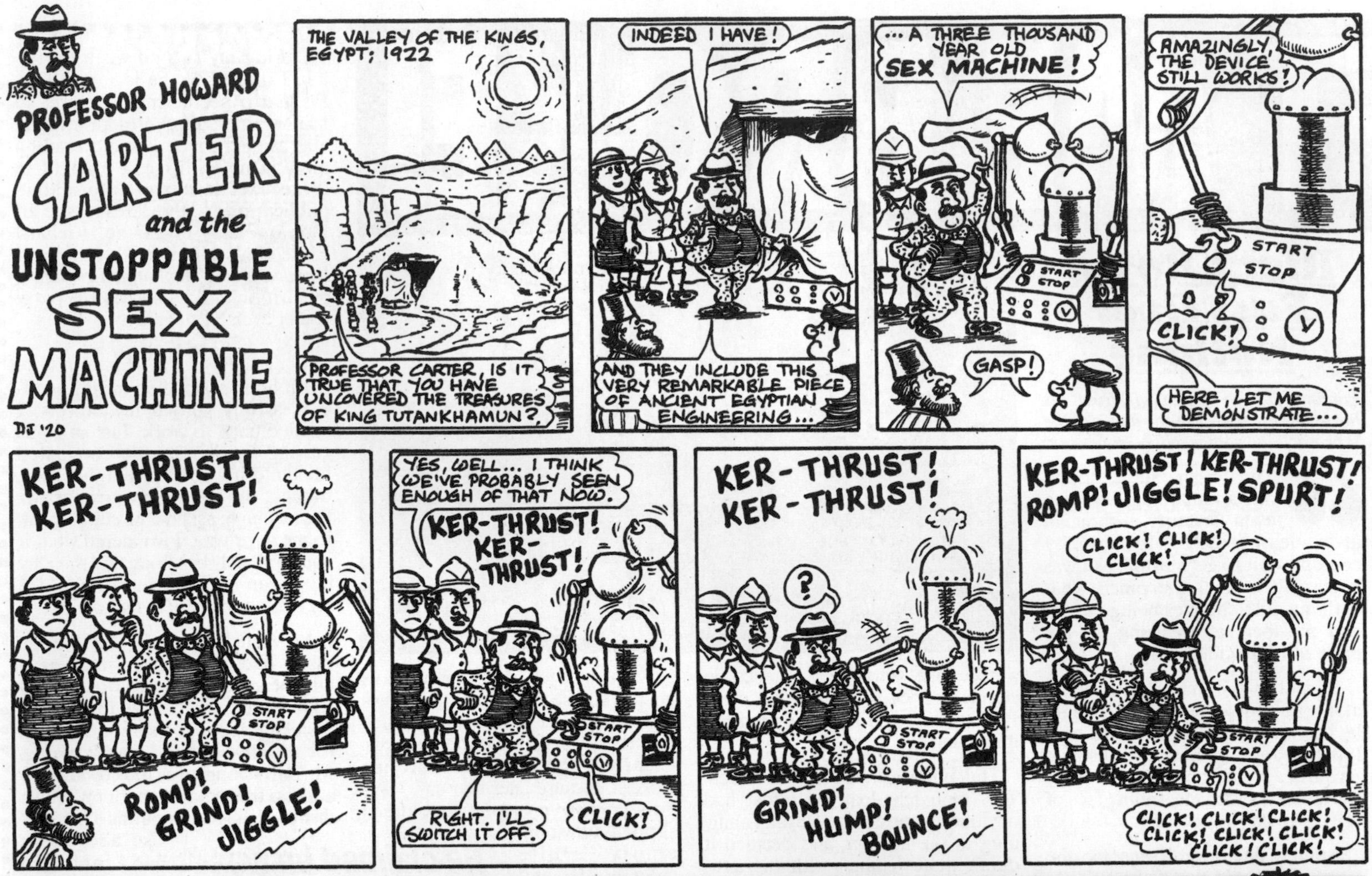
PROFESSOR HOWARD
CARTER
and the
UNSTOPPABLE
SEX
MACHINE
DJ '20
THE VALLEY OF THE KINGS, EGYPT; 1922
PROFESSOR CARTER, IS IT TRUE THAT YOU HAVE UNCOVERED THE TREASURES OF KING TUTANKHAMUN?
INDEED I HAVE!
AND THEY INCLUDE THIS VERY REMARKABLE PIECE OF ANCIENT EGYPTIAN ENGINEERING...
...A THREE THOUSAND YEAR OLD SEX MACHINE!
START
STOP
GASP!
AMAZINGLY, THE DEVICE STILL WORKS!
START
STOP
CLICK!
HERE, LET ME DEMONSTRATE...
KER-THRUST! KER-THRUST!
START
STOP
ROMP! GRIND! JIGGLE!
YES, WELL... I THINK WE'VE PROBABLY SEEN ENOUGH OF THAT NOW.
KER-THRUST! KER-THRUST!
START
STOP
RIGHT. I'LL SWITCH IT OFF.
CLICK!
KER-THRUST! KER-THRUST!
?
START
STOP
GRIND! HUMP! BOUNCE!
KER-THRUST! KER-THRUST! ROMP! JIGGLE! SPURT!
CLICK! CLICK! CLICK!
START
STOP
CLICK! CLICK! CLICK! CLICK! CLICK! CLICK! CLICK! CLICK!

STARS OF STAGE AND SCREAM!

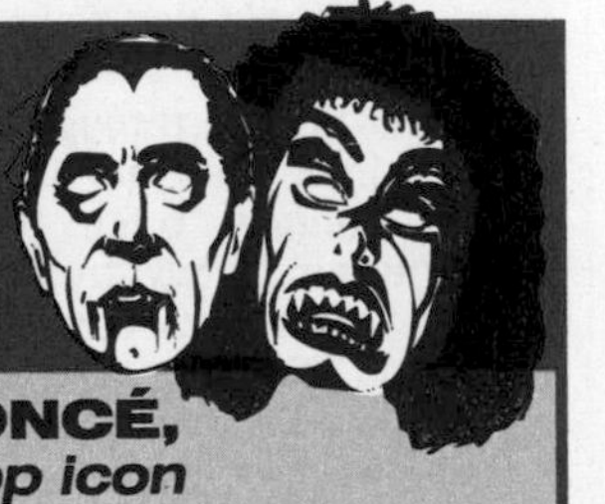

COME OCTOBER 31ST, every single person on Earth loves donning their scariest costume and going out 'Trick or Treating'. And by this logic, it stands to reason that showbiz A-Listers are no exception. So we rounded up some of our favourite celebrities and asked them one simple question: *What sort of ghastly ghoul or spooky spectre do* **YOU** *dress up as for Halloween?*

SUE BARKER,
national treasure

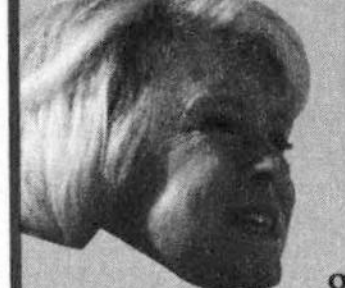

I don't usually bother with Trick or Treating. But if I do go, I'll go as Leatherface out of *Texas Chainsaw Massacre*. It's a right laugh and it shits the local kids up something rotten. I'll typically cut some eye-holes in a slice of supermarket ham or turkey for the cannibalistic human face mask. Then I'll chuck on a ketchup-spattered suit and pirouette wildly through the streets, revving a leaf blower and howling psychotically until my neighbours give me sufficient Haribos to make me fuck off.

LAURENCE FOX,
free speech advocate and twat

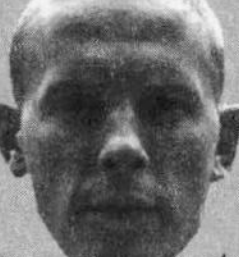

This October 31st, I'll be going Trick or Treating as the one thing the PC-crazed liberal elite fear most: a straight white male who dares to speak his mind. The Trotskyite woke mob will scream and cower behind their sofas as I materialise on their doorsteps as a heterosexual Caucasian man who is unafraid to exercise his right to free speech. And I won't have to pay a penny for the costume either – which is a bit of a bonus as the TV work has dried up a bit since I started acting the cunt on Twitter.

JEREMY CLARKSON,
petrolhead presenter

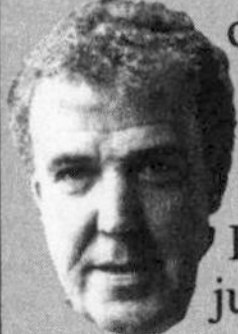

I love Trick or Treat, and on Halloween, I go knocking on my neighbours' doors in Chipping Norton dressed as Frankenstein's monster. I'm the right build, so I just put on my gardening trousers, a donkey jacket and some diver's boots and I'm away. A couple of the wheel nuts from one of my Lamborghini Gallardo Spyders sellotaped to each side of my neck completes the look. Then I'll knock on the doors of my neighbours, like Rebekah Brooks, David Cameron and Alex James, and ask them for some Haribos. The trouble is, if they haven't got any, I have a tendency to lose it and punch them in the face rather than do ghostly tapping on their windows or throwing bog roll in their trees.

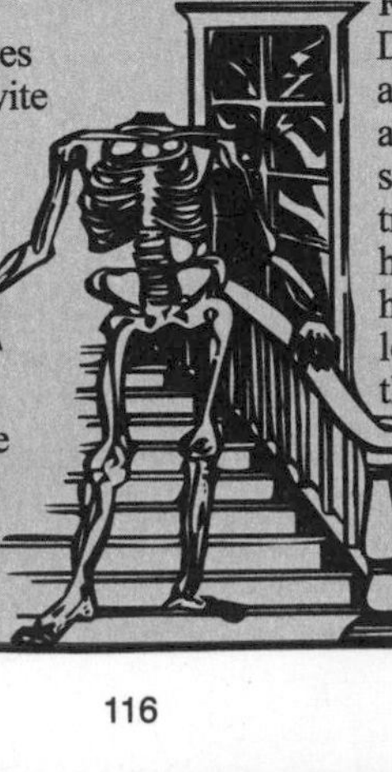

BEYONCÉ,
US pop icon

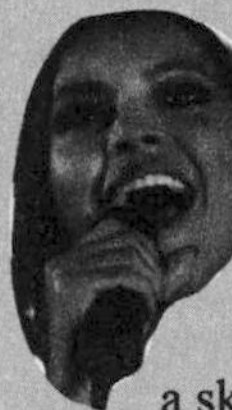

I always go Trick or Treating dressed as Bubble off of *Big Brother 2*. It's not scary in any way; in fact, he's rather jolly and friendly. But I just find it's a bit more original than going as a skellington or a Dracula or what have you. The costume's a piece of piss, too: Burberry bucket hat, Stone Island jacket, stick your tongue out a lot. Simples. The only problem is that no-one in Beverly Hills has ever heard of Bubble off of *Big Brother 2*, so I end up getting fuck-all Haribos.

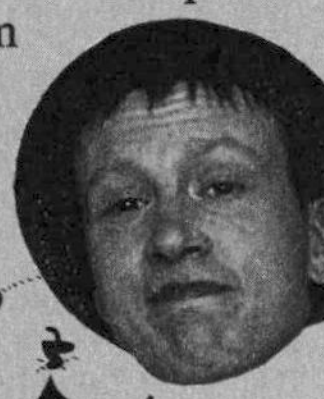

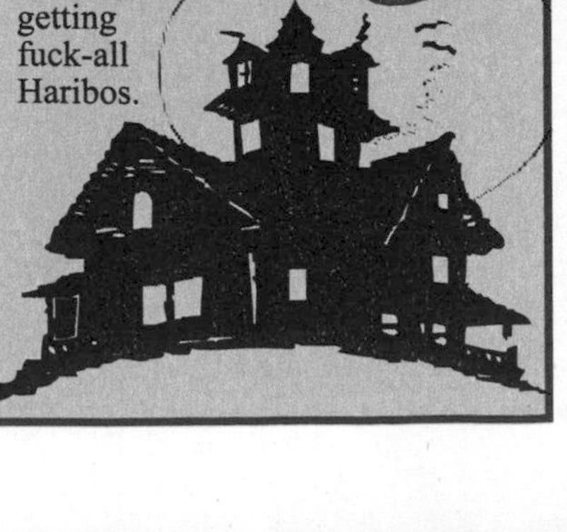

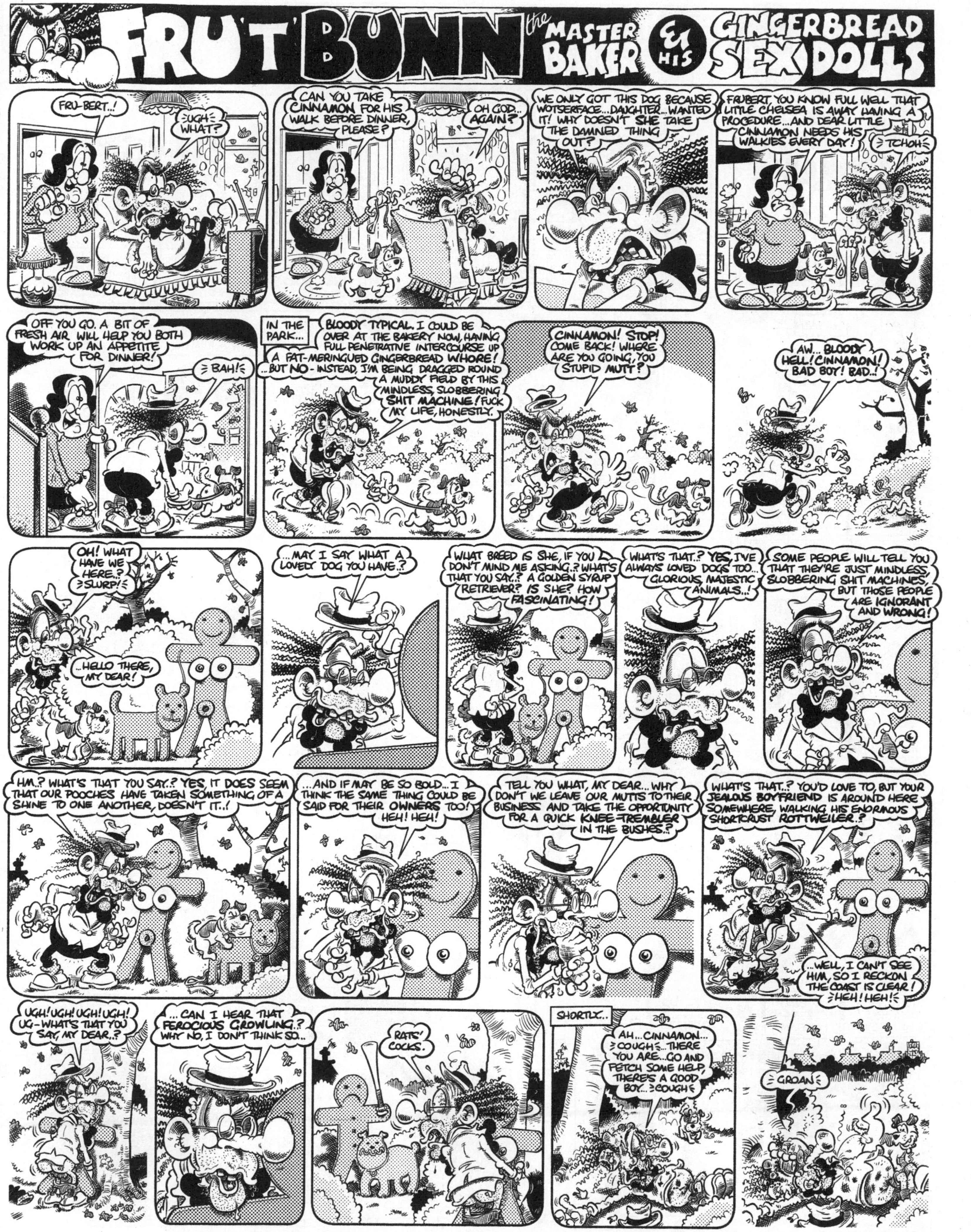

FRU'T BUNN the MASTER BAKER & HIS GINGERBREAD SEX DOLLS
FRU-BERT..!
UGH WHAT?
CAN YOU TAKE CINNAMON FOR HIS WALK BEFORE DINNER, PLEASE?
OH GOD... AGAIN?
WE ONLY GOT THIS DOG BECAUSE WOTSERFACE... DAUGHTER... WANTED IT! WHY DOESN'T SHE TAKE THE DAMNED THING OUT?
FRUBERT, YOU KNOW FULL WELL THAT LITTLE CHELSEA IS AWAY HAVING A PROCEDURE... AND DEAR LITTLE CINNAMON NEEDS HIS WALKIES EVERY DAY!
TCHOH
OFF YOU GO. A BIT OF FRESH AIR WILL HELP YOU BOTH WORK UP AN APPETITE FOR DINNER!
BAH!
IN THE PARK...
BLOODY TYPICAL. I COULD BE OVER AT THE BAKERY NOW, HAVING FULL PENETRATIVE INTERCOURSE UP A FAT-MERINGUED GINGERBREAD WHORE! ...BUT NO - INSTEAD, I'M BEING DRAGGED ROUND A MUDDY FIELD BY THIS MINDLESS, SLOBBERING SHIT MACHINE! FUCK MY LIFE, HONESTLY.
CINNAMON! STOP! COME BACK! WHERE ARE YOU GOING, YOU STUPID MUTT?
AW... BLOODY HELL! CINNAMON! BAD BOY! BAD..!
OH! WHAT HAVE WE HERE..? SLURP!
...HELLO THERE, MY DEAR!
...MAY I SAY WHAT A LOVELY DOG YOU HAVE..?
WHAT BREED IS SHE, IF YOU DON'T MIND ME ASKING..? WHAT'S THAT YOU SAY..? A GOLDEN SYRUP RETRIEVER? IS SHE? HOW FASCINATING!
WHAT'S THAT..? YES, I'VE ALWAYS LOVED DOGS TOO... GLORIOUS, MAJESTIC ANIMALS..!
SOME PEOPLE WILL TELL YOU THAT THEY'RE JUST MINDLESS, SLOBBERING SHIT MACHINES, BUT THOSE PEOPLE ARE IGNORANT AND WRONG!
HM..? WHAT'S THAT YOU SAY..? YES, IT DOES SEEM THAT OUR POOCHES HAVE TAKEN SOMETHING OF A SHINE TO ONE ANOTHER, DOESN'T IT..!
...AND IF MAY BE SO BOLD... I THINK THE SAME THING COULD BE SAID FOR THEIR OWNERS TOO! HEH! HEH!
TELL YOU WHAT, MY DEAR... WHY DON'T WE LEAVE OUR MUTTS TO THEIR BUSINESS AND TAKE THE OPPORTUNITY FOR A QUICK KNEE-TREMBLER IN THE BUSHES..?
WHAT'S THAT..? YOU'D LOVE TO, BUT YOUR JEALOUS BOYFRIEND IS AROUND HERE SOMEWHERE, WALKING HIS ENORMOUS SHORTCRUST ROTTWEILER..?
...WELL, I CAN'T SEE HIM, SO I RECKON THE COAST IS CLEAR! HEH! HEH!
UGH! UGH! UGH! UGH! UG- WHAT'S THAT YOU SAY, MY DEAR..?
...CAN I HEAR THAT FEROCIOUS GROWLING..? WHY NO, I DON'T THINK SO...
RATS' COCKS.
SHORTLY...
AH... CINNAMON... COUGH... THERE YOU ARE... GO AND FETCH SOME HELP, THERE'S A GOOD BOY... COUGH
GROAN

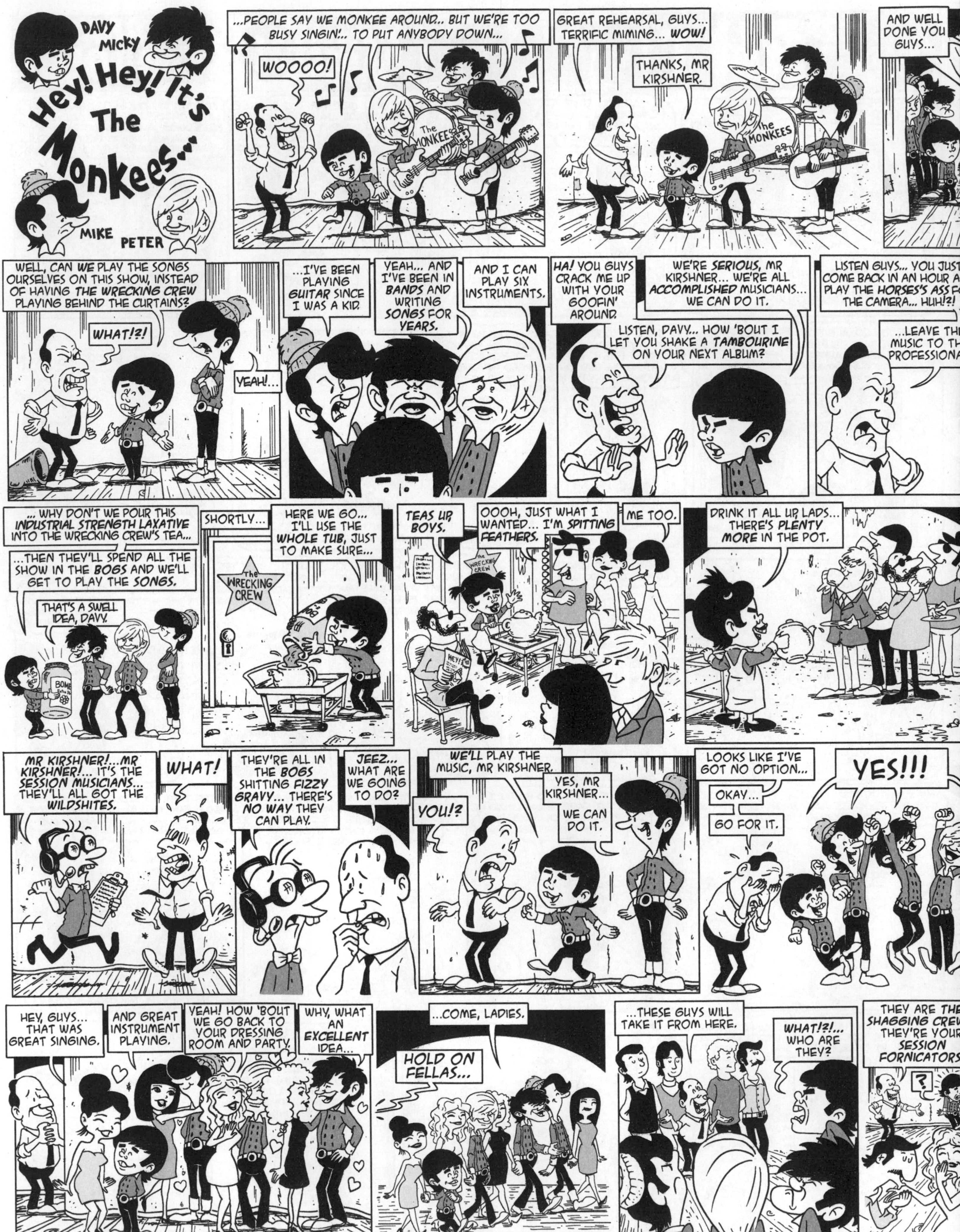

DAVY
MICKY
Hey! Hey! It's The Monkees...
MIKE
PETER
...PEOPLE SAY WE MONKEE AROUND... BUT WE'RE TOO BUSY SINGIN'... TO PUT ANYBODY DOWN...
WOOOO!
The MONKEES
GREAT REHEARSAL, GUYS... TERRIFIC MIMING... WOW!
THANKS, MR KIRSHNER.
The MONKEES
AND WELL DONE YOU GUYS...
WELL, CAN WE PLAY THE SONGS OURSELVES ON THIS SHOW, INSTEAD OF HAVING THE WRECKING CREW PLAYING BEHIND THE CURTAINS?
WHAT!?!
YEAH!...
...I'VE BEEN PLAYING GUITAR SINCE I WAS A KID.
YEAH... AND I'VE BEEN IN BANDS AND WRITING SONGS FOR YEARS.
AND I CAN PLAY SIX INSTRUMENTS.
HA! YOU GUYS CRACK ME UP WITH YOUR GOOFIN' AROUND.
WE'RE SERIOUS, MR KIRSHNER... WE'RE ALL ACCOMPLISHED MUSICIANS... WE CAN DO IT.
LISTEN, DAVY... HOW 'BOUT I LET YOU SHAKE A TAMBOURINE ON YOUR NEXT ALBUM?
LISTEN GUYS... YOU JUST COME BACK IN AN HOUR A PLAY THE HORSES'S ASS F THE CAMERA... HUH!?!
...LEAVE TH MUSIC TO TH PROFESSIONA
... WHY DON'T WE POUR THIS INDUSTRIAL STRENGTH LAXATIVE INTO THE WRECKING CREW'S TEA...
...THEN THEY'LL SPEND ALL THE SHOW IN THE BOGS AND WE'LL GET TO PLAY THE SONGS.
THAT'S A SWELL IDEA, DAVY.
SHORTLY...
HERE WE GO... I'LL USE THE WHOLE TUB, JUST TO MAKE SURE...
The WRECKING CREW
TEAS UP, BOYS.
OOOH, JUST WHAT I WANTED... I'M SPITTING FEATHERS.
ME TOO.
The WRECKING CREW
HEY!
DRINK IT ALL UP, LADS... THERE'S PLENTY MORE IN THE POT.
MR KIRSHNER!...MR KIRSHNER!... IT'S THE SESSION MUSICIANS... THEY'LL ALL GOT THE WILDSHITES.
WHAT!
THEY'RE ALL IN THE BOGS SHITTING FIZZY GRAVY... THERE'S NO WAY THEY CAN PLAY.
JEEZ... WHAT ARE WE GOING TO DO?
WE'LL PLAY THE MUSIC, MR KIRSHNER.
YOU!?
YES, MR KIRSHNER...
WE CAN DO IT.
LOOKS LIKE I'VE GOT NO OPTION...
OKAY...
GO FOR IT.
YES!!!
HEY, GUYS... THAT WAS GREAT SINGING.
AND GREAT INSTRUMENT PLAYING.
YEAH! HOW 'BOUT WE GO BACK TO YOUR DRESSING ROOM AND PARTY.
WHY, WHAT AN EXCELLENT IDEA...
...COME, LADIES.
HOLD ON FELLAS...
...THESE GUYS WILL TAKE IT FROM HERE.
WHAT!?!... WHO ARE THEY?
THEY ARE THE SHAGGING CREW THEY'RE YOUR SESSION FORNICATORS
?

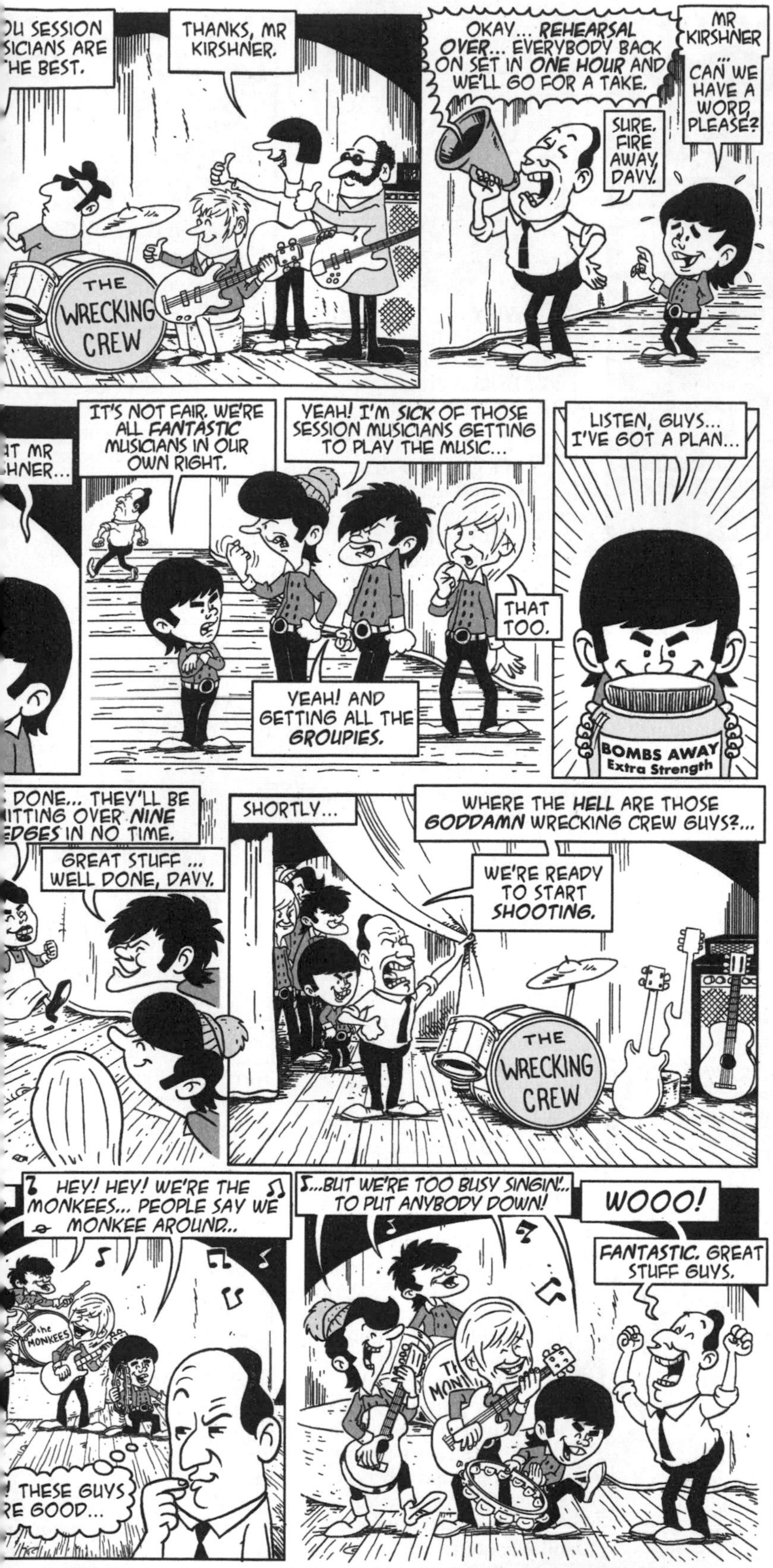
OU SESSION
SICIANS ARE
HE BEST.
THANKS, MR KIRSHNER.
OKAY... REHEARSAL OVER... EVERYBODY BACK ON SET IN ONE HOUR AND WE'LL GO FOR A TAKE.
MR KIRSHNER
CAN WE HAVE A WORD, PLEASE?
SURE. FIRE AWAY, DAVY.
THE WRECKING CREW
T MR
HNER...
IT'S NOT FAIR. WE'RE ALL FANTASTIC MUSICIANS IN OUR OWN RIGHT.
YEAH! I'M SICK OF THOSE SESSION MUSICIANS GETTING TO PLAY THE MUSIC...
LISTEN, GUYS... I'VE GOT A PLAN...
THAT TOO.
YEAH! AND GETTING ALL THE GROUPIES.
BOMBS AWAY Extra Strength
DONE... THEY'LL BE
ITTING OVER NINE
EDGES IN NO TIME.
GREAT STUFF ... WELL DONE, DAVY.
SHORTLY...
WHERE THE HELL ARE THOSE GODDAMN WRECKING CREW GUYS?...
WE'RE READY TO START SHOOTING.
THE WRECKING CREW
HEY! HEY! WE'RE THE MONKEES... PEOPLE SAY WE MONKEE AROUND..
...BUT WE'RE TOO BUSY SINGIN'.. TO PUT ANYBODY DOWN!
WOOO!
FANTASTIC. GREAT STUFF GUYS.
THESE GUYS
E GOOD...
?
THIS WAY, LADIES.
OKAY, BOYS. BACK ON SET IN FIVE MINUTES TO FILM THE BATMAN AND ROBIN SCENE.
RATS' COCKS!

WALKEN DISASTER

ZANY Hollywood A-lister *Christopher Walken* has announced plans to take a year out of acting in order to fulfil a lifelong dream - *to destroy America's tech capital Silicon Valley!*

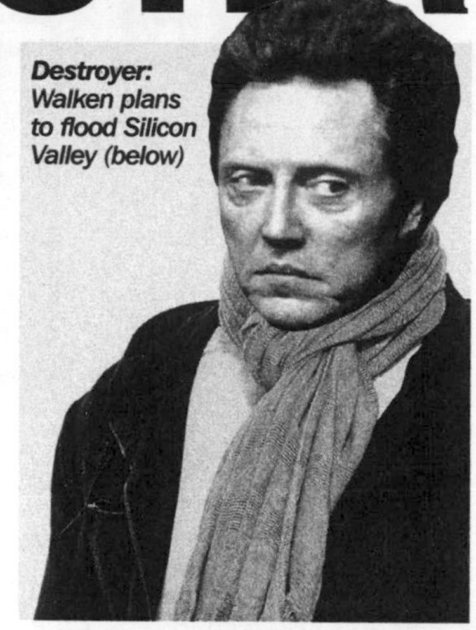

Destroyer: Walken plans to flood Silicon Valley (below)

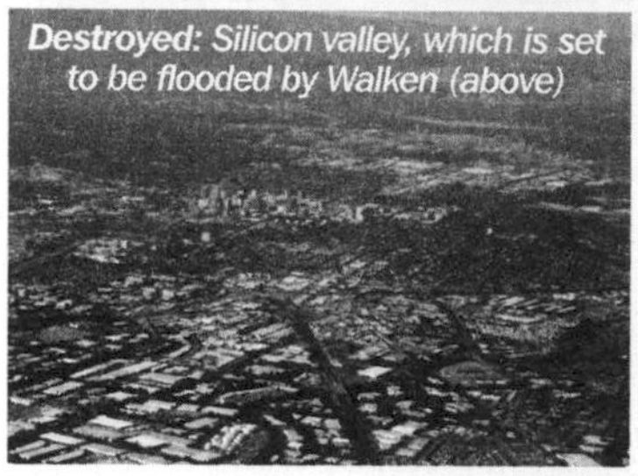

Destroyed: Silicon valley, which is set to be flooded by Walken (above)

Walken originally came up with his project thirty years ago, but he couldn't pursue his ambitious plan due to filming commitments. But when his latest film *Wild Mountain Thyme* went into post production in 2020, the New York born actor decided that it was now or never.

"I'm not getting any younger," he told *Variety* magazine. "And if I'm ever going to destroy the centre of computer technology, I think I'd better get on with it."

underground

Walken outlined his plans for the destruction of the northern California-based tech area, which involve planting underground explosive devices beneath several lakes near the San Andreas fault.

"Boom! When they go off, the ground will sink, the valley will be under 200 feet of water and I'll have ticked another thing off my bucket list," he said.

overground

And it won't just be an act of mindless destruction, because Walken intends to flood the epicentre of computer research and development for charity.

"I've asked all my Hollywood friends and neighbours to sponsor me," he said. "And so far, I've got $125 dollars pledged."

Killjoy environmentalists had initially condemned Walken's plans to destroy thousands of square miles of land by sinking it below a lake, saying that it would have a detrimental impact on the wildlife of the area. But they were brought on side when he said that half the money raised would go to 'green charities'.

wombling

To make the project even more exciting, Walken has invited superspy James Bond to get sponsors and try to stop him performing his environmentally catastrophic act! And ever up for excitement, the philanderous British secret agent has risen to the challenge.

But with the charitable act of destruction set for spring 2022, there is now just one stumbling block… *James Bond himself.*

Roger Moore had originally been the number one choice, but he has refused to take part, citing concerns over some of the stunts. The suave actor famously vowed never to take part in charity events again after spraining his ankle whilst running over the back of some alligators as part of Comic Relief in 2003.

Also, not-being-alive commitments mean that Moore will be unlikely to take part.

free

Another late Bond who turned down Walken's request was Moore's predecessor Sean Connery, who said that he has stepped back from charity work since his death in 2020.

"He was only too happy to pretend to bed a string of beauties in the 60s and 70s for pay, but when it's for charity, it seems it's a different story," Walken said.

to be wild

The current Bond, Daniel Craig has said that *No Time to Die* will see him drink a Martini, shaken, not stirred, for the final time. But Walken has hopes that the gritty five-times Bond actor will don the tuxedo for a good cause one last time.

"I'm waiting to hear from his agent," he said.

"Meanwhile, if anyone would like to sponsor me in this act of meglomaniacal destruction, they can visit my Justgiving page at JustGiving/CWalken/SiliconValley and make a pledge," he added.

Letterbocks

Viz Comic, P.O. Box 841 Whitley Bay, NE26 9EQ : letters@viz.co.uk

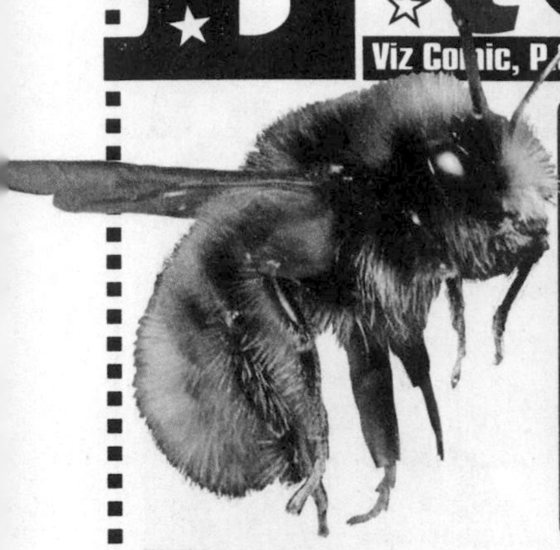

STAR LETTER

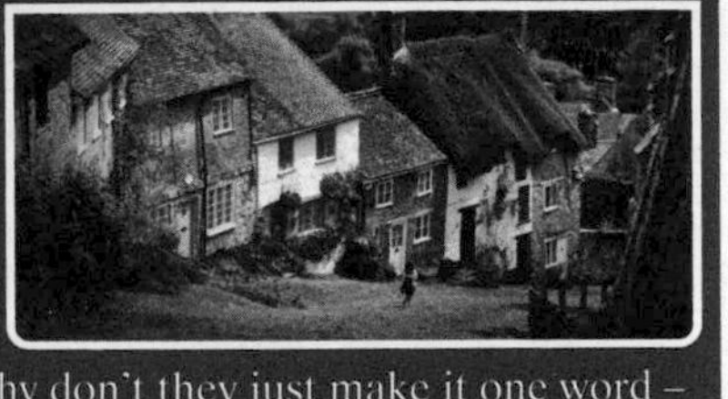

WHY is it that the word 'quintessentially' is always followed by the word 'British'? Can anything else be quintessential, or quintessentially something? If not, why don't they just make it one word – *quintessentiallybritish?*

F Baumgartner, Leeds

ALBERT Einstein reckoned that if all bees died out, humans would follow just four years later. Well I don't even get through a jar of honey a year, so I just need to stock up fifty jars and I'm set for life, thank you very much. And they say he was a genius? Fucking drama queen more like.

D Williams, Donegal

YOUNG people today just don't appreciate the 14th century crop rotation systems. They're all too busy on their X-boxes, watching those podcast things and using modern agricultural methodology.

David Slade, Stevenage

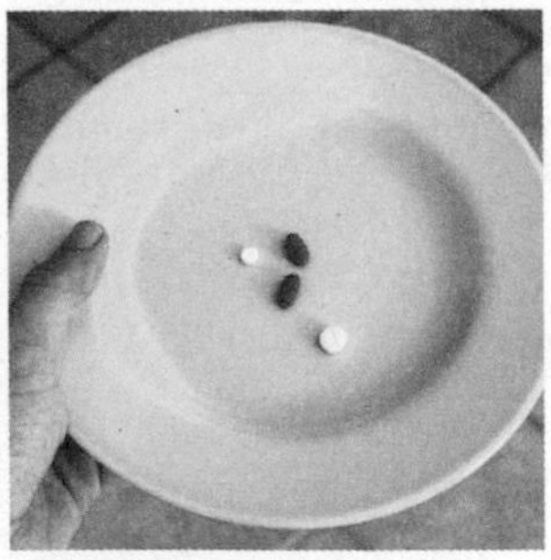

SCIENTISTS say that in the future, all meals will be in the form of a pill. Let's hope they are right, and they don't develop them in the form of a suppository. I think that would make dining out a most unpleasant experience.

Umberto Coaltit, Hull

WELL done Dyson for giving customers free postage on your hair products. You wouldn't want to take the piss by adding on £3 postage after charging £400 for a pair of fucking hair tongs.

Eldon Furse, Leeds

CAN the super-attractive, dark haired lady, late 30s, white T-shirt, skin-tight stonewash jeans, pushing her trolley on the way out of Morrison's in Bolton last Sunday at approximately 10.15am, please take note. If you are going to look that fucking gorgeous without seemingly trying, you're going to get perverted, sexist bastards like me under your spell, completely fixated on your arse. It's really, really unfair what you did. I'm the victim here. Same time next week?

R Williams, Bolton

I'VE SEEN a number of adverts recently for a new kind of toothbrush in which the claim was made that the product was invented by a well known dentist. I must confess that I can't think of a single well known dentist, and I doubt whether any of your readers can. In fact, I don't even know what my own dentist is called, although I recall that the hygienist has got a cracking arse.

Gunther Lunch, Penryn

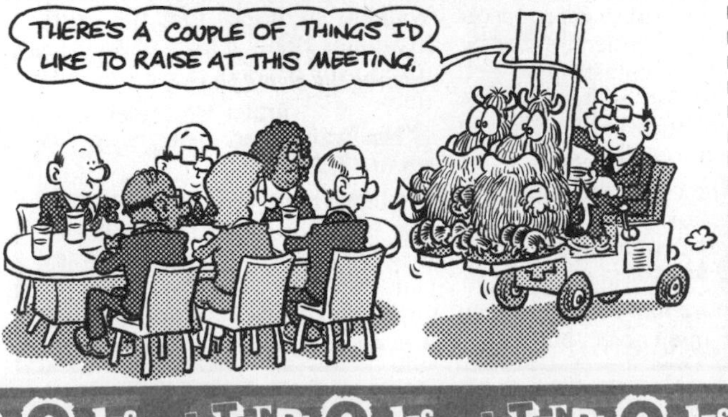
THERE'S A COUPLE OF THINGS I'D LIKE TO RAISE AT THIS MEETING.

VACUUM advertisers should remember that demonstrating your device with a trophy wife cleaning a sparsely furnished room with 300 square feet of flat white carpet just doesn't cut it. How about adding a touch of realism with a puffing, overweight, fat-arsed 40-something attempting to hoover around piles of magazines, DVD's, scattered toys, a lazy husband, two kids addicted to video games and a dog basket that smells like an old gusset.

Harriet Jumpjet, Scarborough

I'VE heard the song *Baker Street* hundreds of times, and yet I still have no idea what it's about. There's someone 'winding their way down on down Baker Street,' then a saxophone comes along and distracts the listener.

Neil Renton, Edinburgh

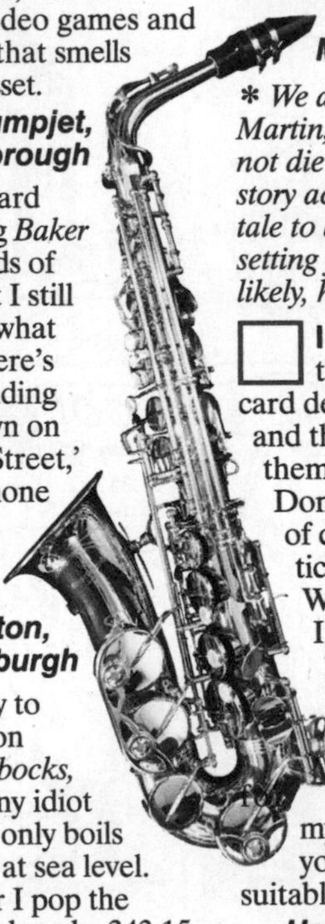

IN reply to Thanston Crabb (*Letterbocks, page 98*), as any idiot knows, water only boils at 373 Kelvin at sea level. But whenever I pop the kettle on, it's done by 343.15 Kelvin, making 1000°C about 3.71 times the temperature of boiling water. So Mr Crabb can piss right off.

Tenzing Norgay, Everest

IN all the nature programmes I've watched, I have never seen a lion having a shite. Come on, Attenborough. Pull your finger out and film the King of the Jungle laying a cable.

Markington Scales, Barnsley

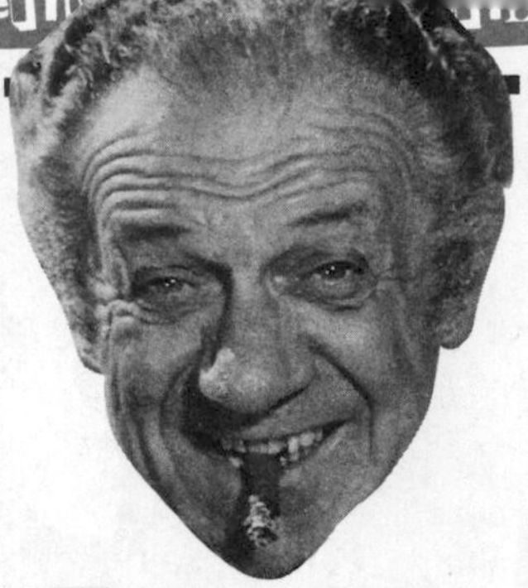

WHY don't men laugh like Sid James any more? Come on fellas. Let's make Britain great again with that dirty laugh.

C Hawtrey, Deal

MY grandad first started lighting his farts for a laugh during WWII. But with over 800,000 farts successfully lit over 30 years, he had no idea of the impending peril. One Christmas, while wearing wooly underpants, a gift from my granny, he lit a fart and set his pubes on fire. The flames quickly spread to his underpants and it was the shock of this which caused a second fart which ignited. The increased heat caused a backdraft up his ringpiece, all his guts blew up and he died.

Martin Lavin, Reddish

* *We are sorry for your loss, Martin, but your grandad did not die in vain, as this tragic story acts as a cautionary tale to anyone thinking about setting fire to his – or less likely, her – flatus.*

I JUST discovered that my NatWest debit card details had been stolen, and that somebody used them fraudulently to buy a Dominos pizza, £75 worth of clothes from Next and tickets to Chessington World of Adventure. I'm sure there's a *Two Ronnies* style punchline about the type of person the police are looking but comedy isn't my forte. Could any of your readers suggest a suitable quip?

Hector Golightly, Wells

ACCORDING to the bible, if your right arm causes you to sin, then you should cut it off. But it seems to me that it probably wouldn't take long to learn to sin with your left hand instead. In fact I strongly suspect that it's another part of the body entirely that's at the root of the problem. I'd like to see the Archbishop of Canterbury explain that one.

Phil Kitching, Isle of Jura

TOP

OYSTERCATCHERS. Avoi hunger by learning to catch mussels and clams too.

John Owens, Glasgo

SAVE money on energy bills by turning your TV and radio off every time Martin Lewis comes on.

Keith Robson, ema

UNSURE whether to buy shampoo for normal hair, greasy hair or damaged hair? Go for damaged. If it turns out to be the wrong choice, the first wash will be so injurious to your hair that thereafter it will be the correct product.

Micky Bullock, Londo

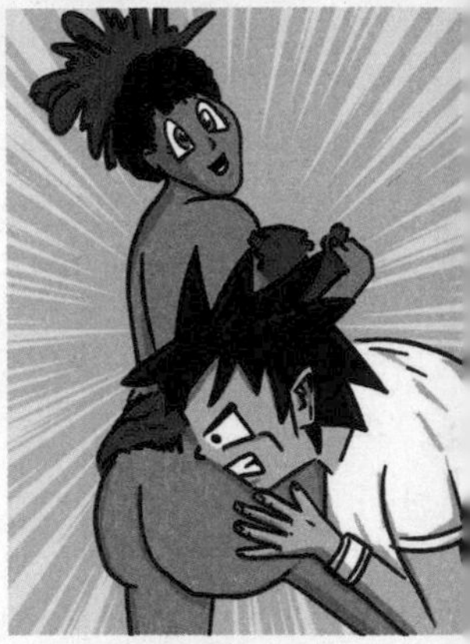

I BIG fan Manga and especial artist Akira Toriyama I like very much. I wonder, can you send me his signed photograph as make me very happy. If not possible, how bout that picture of bloke kissing that bird's arse with all big eyes and spiky hair? Thanks you.

Satoru Nakajima, Kyoto

MY neighbour has one child, but I've got two. You couldn't make it up!

Dominic Twose, L'ton Spa

* *Have you got more children than your neighbour like Mr Twose? Or are you're more like his neighbour and have fewer? Perhaps, incredibly, you have exactly the same number as each other. Write in and let us know.*

I'M not one to hanker after 'the good old days', but I find it very sad that you hardly ever hear of animals escaping from zoos any more. Come on keepers Give us all a trip down memory lane and some much-needed excitement in these uncertain times by accidentally leaving the odd cage door unlocked.

Dave Dunmall, High Halstow

COVERING bread with Factor 50 suncream before popping it in the toaster will prevent toast from burning.
Michael Thompson, Wales

DUNG beetles. A Ferrero Rocher makes an ideal shitball to roll back to your house with the added bonus that your insect neighbours will think you're a 'cut above.'
D Williams, Donegal

KEEP a bugle in your toilet. Then, if any flatulence is audible through the door, you will be able to avoid unnecessary embarrassment by claiming that you were simply practising the bugle while ensconced on the throne.
D Cooper, Malta

FOOL friends into thinking you're a builder by standing in their kitchen, pissing into a bucket.
David Craik, HULL

TURN a cup of ordinary instant coffee into 'barista-style' Americano by stirring in an egg-cup full of soot when you've drunk half.
Mark Glover, Coventry

AN ORDINARY can of deodorant doubles as an excellent air horn for libraries.
Will West, Bognor Regis

TIPS
toptips@viz.co.uk

MEDICAL students are given the boiling of an egg as an example of protein denaturation, whereby in boiling water, egg albumen changes from clear liquid to opaque semi-solid. However, I'll bet the average male medical student has probably never boiled a fucking egg in his life, but he will have spent the best part of 5 years of medical school knocking one out in the bath like Stevie Nicks' tambourine. So a better example of protein denaturation would be the floaty aftermath of bath time self abuse. Come on, top universities. Make your examples more relatable to your fee-paying students.
Professor Bobby Helmet, Fulchester University

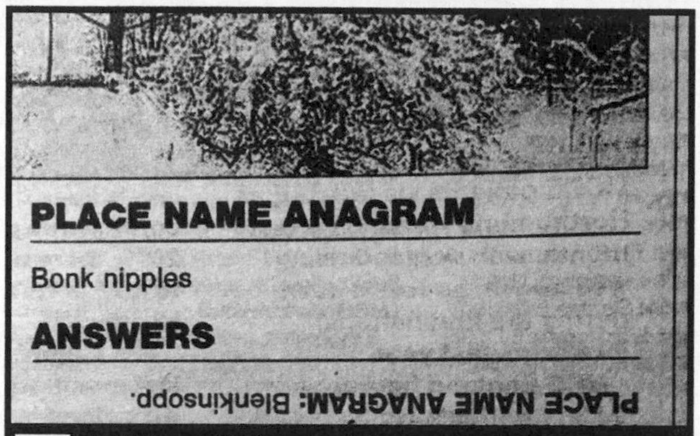
PLACE NAME ANAGRAM

Bonk nipples

ANSWERS

PLACE NAME ANAGRAM: Blenkinsopp.

I WAS appalled to see this abomination in the *Hexham Courant* recently. This quaint market town is not ready for such smut.
Sarah E Hall, Jesmond

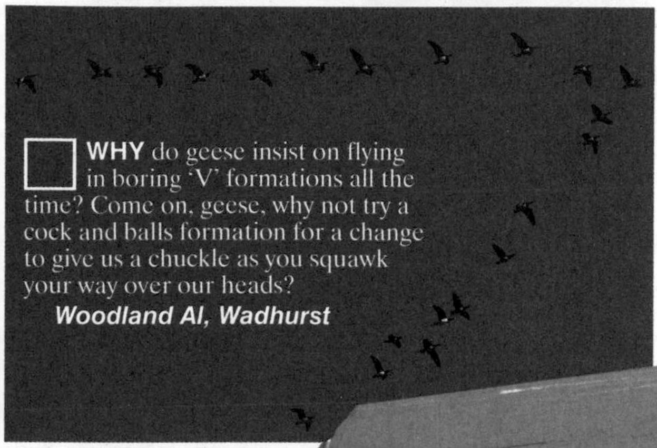

WHY do geese insist on flying in boring 'V' formations all the time? Come on, geese, why not try a cock and balls formation for a change to give us a chuckle as you squawk your way over our heads?
Woodland Al, Wadhurst

I'VE just bought a cheese and pickle sandwich from the Co-op which was labelled as 'limited edition'. Can any other reader beat this for a pitiful attempt at massively over-hyping a humble commodity food item?
Adrian Newth, Stratford upon Avon

WHY is there never a Sudoku puzzle in the *Oban Times* any more? I used to enjoy the challenge and would like to know whether there are any plans to reintroduce it.
Phil Kitching, Isle of Jura

** We're not sure, Mr Kitching. You would probably be better advised writing to the Oban Times, as it would be a decision for the newspaper's editor. Alternatively, if the editor would like to write to us and tell us if they have any plans to bring back the Sudoku puzzle section, we can let any Oban Times readers who also read Viz know one way or the other.*

I KEEP seeing Facebook memes about how glamorous 40s Hollywood actress Hedy Lamarr invented WiFi or something. But I have to say, if my experience with computer printers is anything to go by, she really didn't do a very good job, did she?
Dennis Sisterson, Alnwick

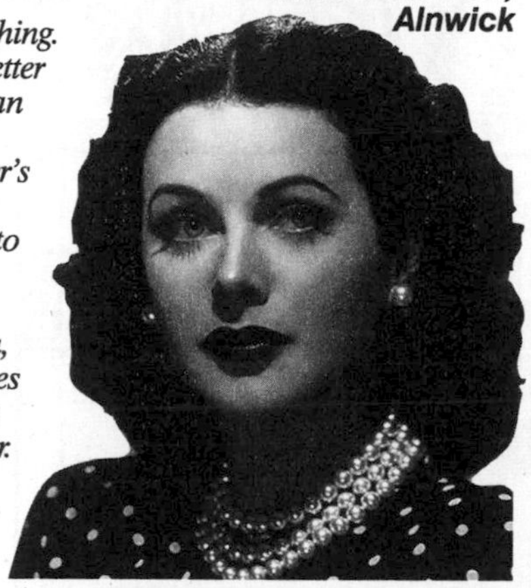

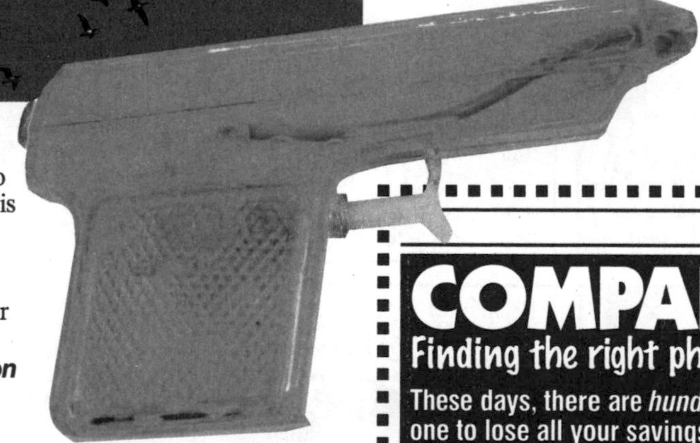

I AM sick and tired of TV chefs telling viewers "ask your butcher to do it." All I hear these days is "can you fillet this for me?" "can you bone that?" and "can I have some twine?" No, no and no. Just buy your meat and fuck off.
Toby the Butcher, Swindon

BY now, I must have watched dozens of episodes of *Would I Lie To You?* and surely the answer has to be 'yes.' Misrepresentation is endemic on the show.
Ali Wood, L'ton Spa

AS we approach the summer months, I'm reminded that there are few things in life as satisfying as squirting someone who has expressly asked not to be squirted with a water pistol. Already I've been asked politely to leave the undertakers, thrown out of Aldi twice and lost my job as a marriage guidance counsellor.
Johnny T, Kirkcaldy

I WAS in Lyme Regis recently and there was a sign that read 'Do Not Feed Me', accompanied by a photo of a scrawny seagull. That's all well and good, but there were literally thousands of the fuckers flying about, and they all looked the same. How was I meant to know which was the one in the photo?
Rupert Deering, Dulwich

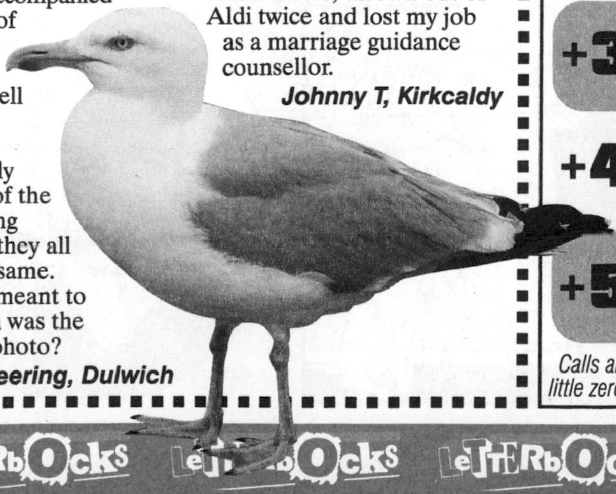

FRAUDULENT ADVICE LINES

COMPARE the SWINDLE.com

Finding the right phone scam for YOU in a confusing market!

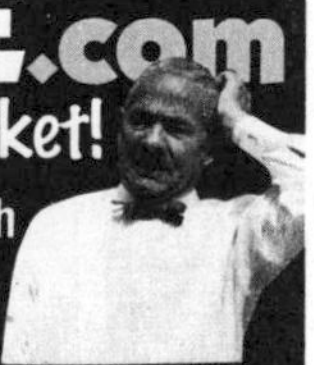

These days, there are *hundreds* of phone scams to fall for, and choosing which one to lose all your savings to can be a headache. ComparetheSwindle.com does the hard work for you, so you can get taken in by the right scam for you.

Just call **01 811 8055** *and add the number for the deception you require...*

+1 A bank you don't have an account with alerts you to ask for confirmation of your PIN number to accept a payment from a Mr Fuchyuova

+2 Automated call from "Postal Firm" needing your credit card details to book a delivery slot for a package that you didn't order.

+3 IT help desk detected a pc virus on your ipad and advises you to download their 'anti-spyware' software which will trawl your hard drive looking for your passwords.

+4 Insurance company rings asking for your bank details as you have been awarded £2000 in compensation for a car accident that you can't remember having.

+5 Automated voice says your Amazon Prime account will be renewed for £79 per month, unless you press 1 to cancel and connect you to a £5.99/min premium rate line.

"I'm as gullible as they come and I used to lose money to scammers right, left and centre. But after using ComparetheSwindle.com, I lost the lot to somebody saying that I was due a tax rebate and saved myself hours."
Edna Foolable, Penge

"My phone never stops ringing with scammers. But through Compare-theSwindle, I lost my savings to a robotic voice that said illegal activity had been detected on my broadband, and I would be cut off unless I pressed 1 and followed the instructions."
Arthur Molecules, Luton

All our call handlers are professionally trained boiler room scammers with at least 5-years experience stealing peoples' life savings.

Calls are advertised at 99p/min, but are actually charged at £99/min because if you look, there are two tiny, little zeros after the 99, and your telephone providers aren't going to do anything because they get half of that.

GOOD MORNING, RICKY!
MORNING, MISTER ROBIN!
HELLO, SMOKIE!
GOOD DAY TO YOU.
MORNING, MISTER GERVAIS!
GOOD MORNING, WRIGGLES!
MORNING, CROW!
CAW!
SWOOP
RICKY GERVAIS
HE TALKS TO THE ANIMALS
PBRAINEY
NOT NOW, BUDDY. I'LL TAKE YOU FOR A WALK LATER, THERE'S A GOOD BOY.
IT'S SUNDAY MORNING. REMEMBER OUR AGREE-MENT?
F'KIN 'ELL.
AND SO...
ONE OF THE CENTRAL BELIEFS OF CHRISTIANITY IS THAT JESUS WILL RETURN IN GLORY!
MORNING.
MORNING.
THE GOSPELS DO NOT TELL US WHEN HE WILL RETURN...
...WE DO KNOW THAT ONE DAY HE WILL RETURN, AND THE END WILL COME!
THANK YOU, LORD!
PRAISE BE TO GOD!
IT DOESN'T MATTER WHEN HE WILL RETURN BUT WHAT WE DO WITH OUR LIVES!
SO EMBARRASING. EVERY F'KIN WEEK.
SOON...
BODY OF CHRIST.
NOT FOR ME, MATE. FOR HIM.
I'M AFRAID THAT IT'S NOT POSSIBLE FOR A DOG TO RECEIVE THE BLESSED SACRAMENTS.
OKAY, GIVE IT TO ME AND I'LL GIVE IT TO HIM LATER.
LATER...
'ERE YOU ARE, THEN.
DO IT PROPERLY.
SIGH. BODY OF CHRIST.
AMEN.
I DON'T KNOW HOW YOU CAN EAT THAT STUFF.
NOW, HOW ABOUT SOME DIN-DINS?

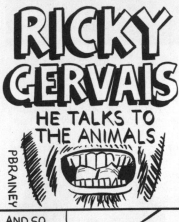

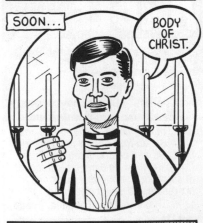

IS THIS A LIGHTSABER I SEE BEFORE ME?

New adaptation of Macbeth to be set in space, or the future, or both

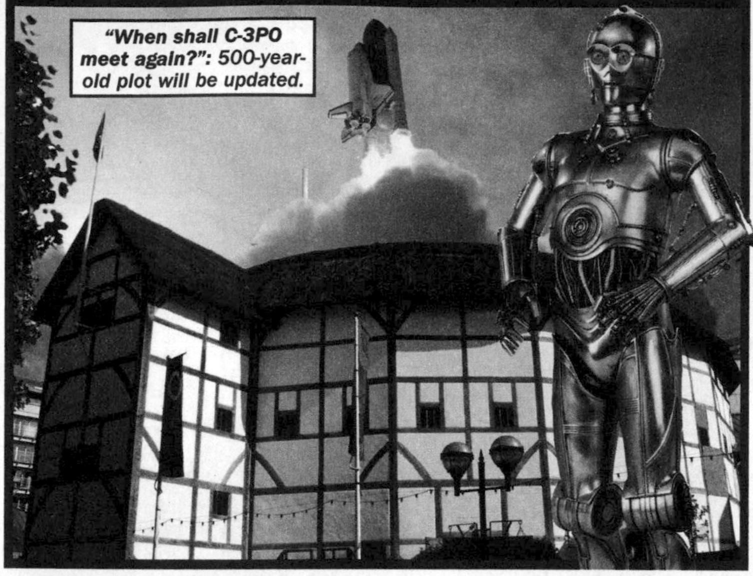

"When shall C-3PO meet again?": 500-year-old plot will be updated.

THE ROYAL Shakespeare Company has announced that their next season will feature a bold, new adaptation of *Macbeth* which will see the story take place in space, or 2000 years into the future, or possibly both.

"I think that, in many ways, William Shakespeare would have approved of this new twist on his work," said RSC Director Hector Popkiss. "His story of ambition, guilt and prophecy lends itself perfectly to being set in outer space in the year 3999, or perhaps on another planet."

"When the bard penned his famous plays, it was the olden days and they didn't have science, so he didn't understand space as a potential setting for his works," he continued. "Consequently, every one of his plays is set on earth."

rocket

It is thought that the new adaptation will be set on some sort of rocket on the edge of a black hole leading into an inter-dimensional space-wormhole.

"We haven't got it nailed down, concept-wise," said Popkiss. "But there will be rockets, tele-porters, ray guns, aliens and everything you would expect. And Lady Macbeth is probably going to be one of those sexy androids in a skin-tight silver suit, with her who was the posh robot in Solo doing the voice. And everyone might be floating around weightless."

iceberg

In addition to androids and hover cars, Popkiss revealed that there will also be some futuristic

EXCLUSIVE!

twists to Shakespeare's plot, first written in 1606. In the original play, Macbeth kills Duncan by running him through with a sword, but the RSC's 2021 version will see the king dispatched in a very different way, being zapped by a 'lightsaber' at the climax of a tense *Return of the Jedi*-style duel.

But although the look of the play will be brand new, the dialogue will still be incomprehensible. "We're sticking with the original script with all the old-fashioned words that nobody understands," said Popkiss.

"The mismatch between the technological sci-fi setting, all up in space and in the future and stuff, and all that 'thee', 'thou' and 'forsooth' bollocks should make for an interesting adaptation," he added.

little gem

Popkiss last hit the headlines in 2019, when his controversial adaptation of *Hamlet* – starring 84-year-old Darth Vader actor Dave Prowse in the title role and set in a giant 'Death Star' orbiting the planet Denmark – set a new record for poor ticket sales at the RSC.

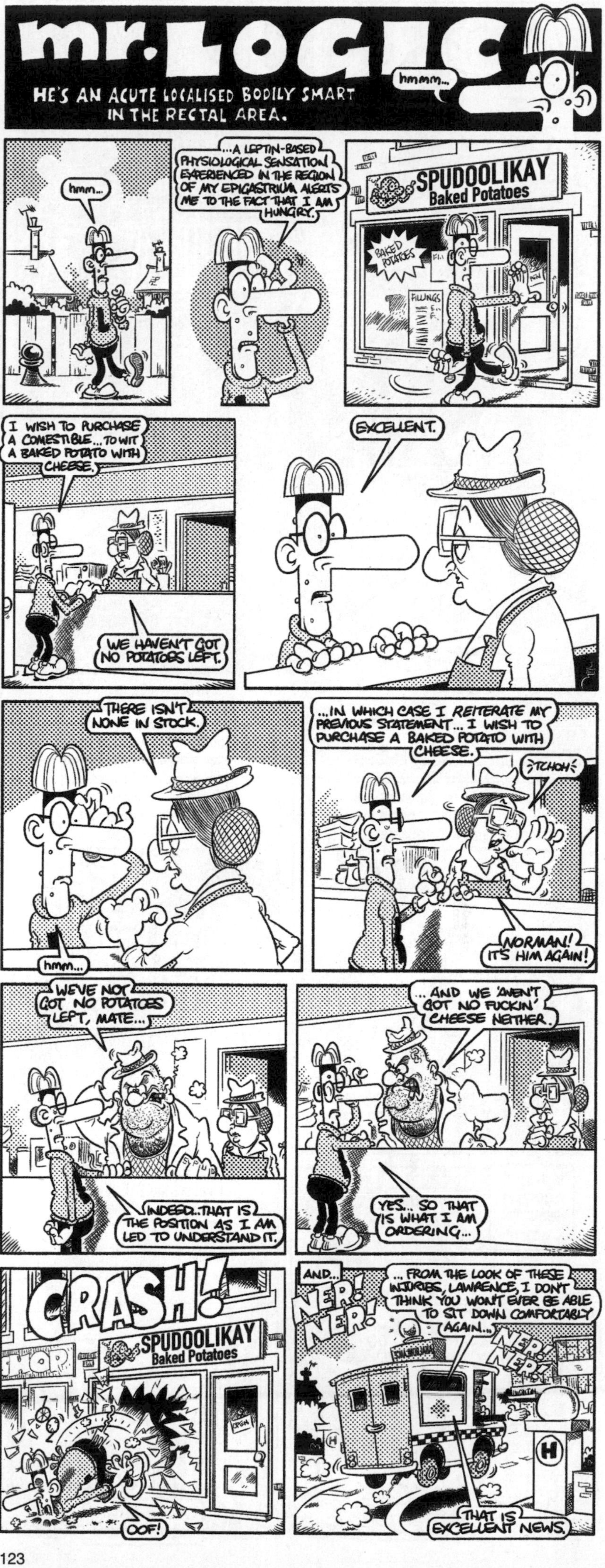

mr. LOGIC
hmmm...
HE'S AN ACUTE LOCALISED BODILY SMART IN THE RECTAL AREA.
hmm...
...A LEPTIN-BASED PHYSIOLOGICAL SENSATION EXPERIENCED IN THE REGION OF MY EPIGASTRIUM ALERTS ME TO THE FACT THAT I AM HUNGRY.
SPUDOOLIKAY Baked Potatoes
BAKED POTATOES
FILLINGS
I WISH TO PURCHASE A COMESTIBLE... TO WIT A BAKED POTATO WITH CHEESE.
WE HAVEN'T GOT NO POTATOES LEFT.
EXCELLENT.
THERE ISN'T NONE IN STOCK.
hmm...
...IN WHICH CASE I REITERATE MY PREVIOUS STATEMENT... I WISH TO PURCHASE A BAKED POTATO WITH CHEESE.
TCHOH
NORMAN! IT'S HIM AGAIN!
WE'VE NOT GOT NO POTATOES LEFT, MATE...
INDEED... THAT IS THE POSITION AS I AM LED TO UNDERSTAND IT.
...AND WE 'AVEN'T GOT NO FUCKIN' CHEESE NEITHER.
YES... SO THAT IS WHAT I AM ORDERING...
CRASH!
SPUDOOLIKAY Baked Potatoes
OOF!
AND...
NER! NER!
...FROM THE LOOK OF THESE INJURIES, LAWRENCE, I DON'T THINK YOU WON'T EVER BE ABLE TO SIT DOWN COMFORTABLY AGAIN...
NER! NER!
THAT IS EXCELLENT NEWS.

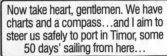

ADRIFT!

APRIL 28th 1789, 30 nautical miles south of the island of Tofua in the Southern Pacific Ocean...

Following a mutiny aboard HMS Bounty, Captain William Bligh and a few loyal crewmates are cast adrift in the ship's launch to take their chances...

Now take heart, gentlemen. We have charts and a compass...and I aim to steer us safely to port in Timor, some 50 days' sailing from here...

...And although we have rations for only five days, we shall eat frugally. With God's help, a fair wind and stout hearts, we will make it back to England and watch Fletcher Christian and his mutinous crew of scurvy dogs dance from the yardarm.

Hoorah!

Mr Fryer... take stock of our provisions.

Aye aye, Captain.

Five pounds of hard tack... three pounds of biltong... three pounds of dried pork... a keg of rum and 4 gallons of water, Captain...

There aren't any nuts in there, are there? I can't eat nuts... or anything that's got nuts in it. I'm allergic.

No, Mr Ledward... would to God that there *were* a few nuts.

Or even if it's been made in the same place as nuts. That's enough.

It is a pitiful amount of food, gentlemen... which we will have to ration severely... but I know you will bear the privations with fortitude...

Each soul on board shall receive one quarter pint of water per day, along with two ounces of hard tack and one ounce of dried meat.

Is there a vegetarian alternative, Captain?

What!?!

A vegetarian alternative... I don't eat meat.

Vegetarian!?! But you had fish last night.

Yes, well I eat fish.

Well you're not a vegetarian then.

Well, anyway, could I have four ounces of hard tack a day and no biltong, Captain?

What!?! No, that's not fair...

...just because you've decided not to eat meat doesn't mean we have to give up half *our* hard tack...

...I like a bit of hard tack with my biltong.

Me too.

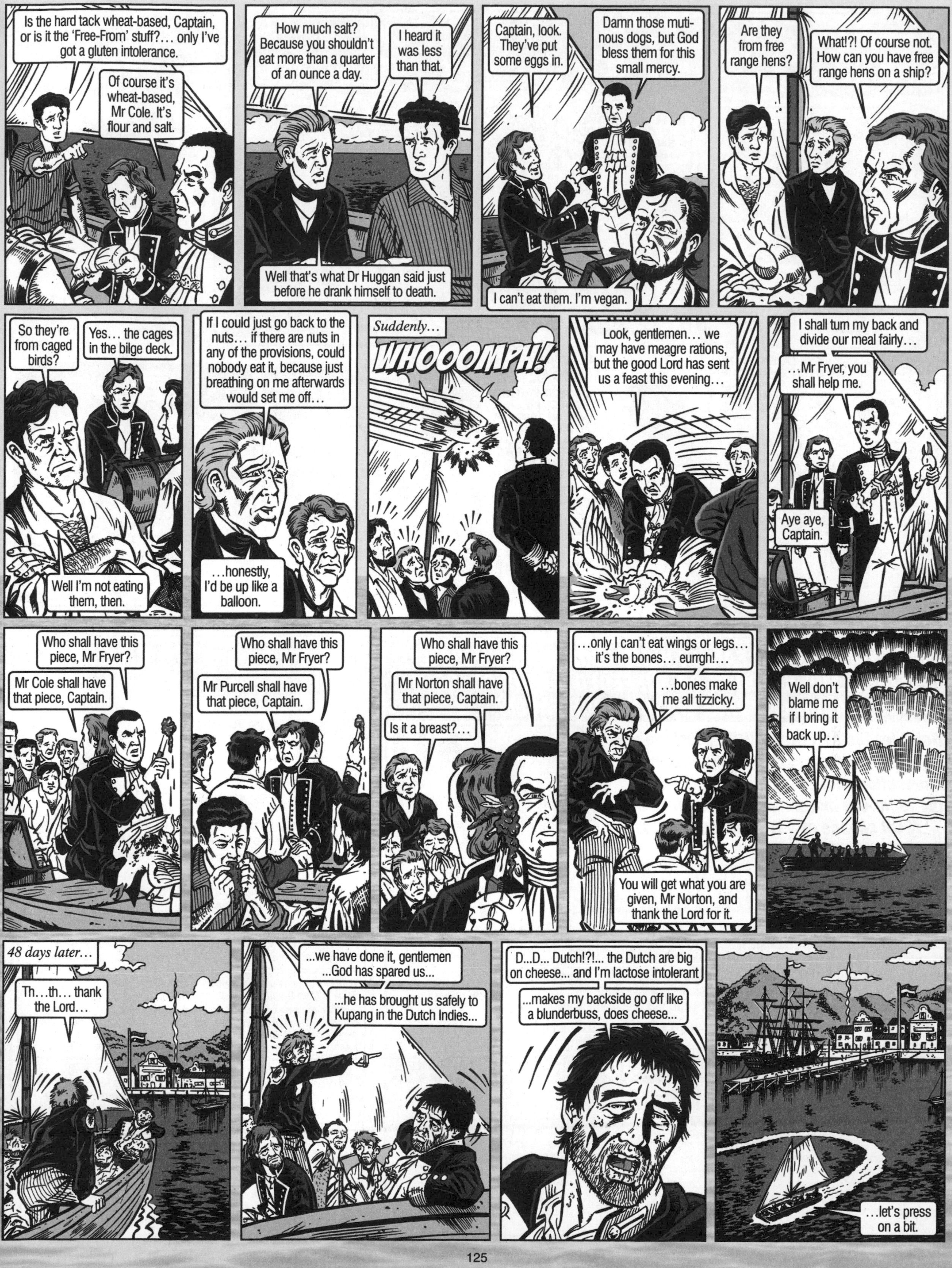

Is the hard tack wheat-based, Captain, or is it the 'Free-From' stuff?... only I've got a gluten intolerance.
Of course it's wheat-based, Mr Cole. It's flour and salt.
How much salt? Because you shouldn't eat more than a quarter of an ounce a day.
I heard it was less than that.
Well that's what Dr Huggan said just before he drank himself to death.
Captain, look. They've put some eggs in.
Damn those mutinous dogs, but God bless them for this small mercy.
I can't eat them. I'm vegan.
Are they from free range hens?
What!?! Of course not. How can you have free range hens on a ship?
So they're from caged birds?
Yes... the cages in the bilge deck.
Well I'm not eating them, then.
If I could just go back to the nuts... if there are nuts in any of the provisions, could nobody eat it, because just breathing on me afterwards would set me off...
...honestly, I'd be up like a balloon.
Suddenly...
WHOOOOMPH!
Look, gentlemen... we may have meagre rations, but the good Lord has sent us a feast this evening...
I shall turn my back and divide our meal fairly...
...Mr Fryer, you shall help me.
Aye aye, Captain.
Who shall have this piece, Mr Fryer?
Mr Cole shall have that piece, Captain.
Who shall have this piece, Mr Fryer?
Mr Purcell shall have that piece, Captain.
Who shall have this piece, Mr Fryer?
Mr Norton shall have that piece, Captain.
Is it a breast?...
...only I can't eat wings or legs... it's the bones... eurrgh!...
...bones make me all tizzicky.
You will get what you are given, Mr Norton, and thank the Lord for it.
Well don't blame me if I bring it back up...
48 days later...
Th...th... thank the Lord...
...we have done it, gentlemen ...God has spared us...
...he has brought us safely to Kupang in the Dutch Indies...
D...D... Dutch!?!... the Dutch are big on cheese... and I'm lactose intolerant
...makes my backside go off like a blunderbuss, does cheese...
...let's press on a bit.

FARMER PALMER
PIG SHIT
OOH! AAARGH!
...WOD IZZ ID, PAW..?
OOH! MOY GUTZ IZ DERRIBLE, JETHRO..! OI'VE GOD A SHOODIN' BAIN IN MOY INNARDZ, OI DO!
SHALL I CALL EE AN AMBULANCE, PAW..?
OOH AAR, ZUN...! OI THINK OI NEEDS T'GED TO THEY OZZBIDAL!
OOH! AAR! OOH! AAR!
SHORTLY...
WE'VE CARRIED OUT SOME TESTS AND YOUR FATHER HAS A SEVERELY ENLARGED PROSTATE.
OOH AAR..?
GROAN!
...HE NEEDS A TRANSURETHRAL RESECTION.. IT'S QUITE A SIMPLE PROCEDURE, AND WE CAN TAKE HIM INTO THEATRE TO DO IT STRAIGHT AWAY.
JAMBION!
SO...
SCALPEL
SCALPEL...
RETRACTORS...
OI!
GET ORF MOY GLAAND!

SUBCONSCIOUS LITIGATION SOLUTIONS

HAVE YOU HAD A DREAM IN WHICH YOU WERE UNJUSTLY FIRED, MIS-SOLD PPI OR SUFFERED A WORKPLACE ACCIDENT THAT WASN'T YOUR FAULT?

Don't let the fact that YOUR ill fortune was merely a succession of images and sensations occurring involuntarily during the rapid-eye movement stage of sleep affect YOUR chance of a WHOPPING PAYOUT!

WHY WAIT?! Call DREAM-INJURY-LAWYERS-4-U this instant!!

CONTACT

DREAM-INJURY-LAWYERS-4-U

DREAM-INJURY-LAWYERS-4-U are the UK's top unconscious brain activity law firm. Our crack team of oneirological litigation experts works tirelessly around the clock to wrangle **HUGE** payouts from confused HR departments across the country. So, if you've had a dream or nightmare in which something bad has happened to you that was definitely **NOT** your fault, get in touch with us today.

But wait – there's more!! Call ***DREAM-INJURY-LAWYERS-4-U*** right now and you will have a dream about receiving a **FREE PEN** just for enquiring!*

**Dream will occur within 3-6 weeks of enquiry. Free pen will exist only in applicant's unconscious mind.*

But don't just take OUR word for it...

"My line manager made an inappropriate joke about my weight during an employee appraisal he was giving me in a dream. I called ***Dream-Injury-Lawyers-4-U*** *the moment I woke up and they got £5,000 compensation out of him despite the fact he had literally no idea what they were on about."*
Mr G Freud, Barnet

"I had a terrible nightmare in which a drone went haywire on the Amazon factory floor and knocked some boxes onto me, spraining my shoulder. ***Dream-Injury-Lawyers-4-U*** *forced Jeff Bezos to cough up a nine grand payout for me. I don't even work at Amazon!"*
Mrs B Jung, Essex

"After watching Inception *last week, I had a dream within a dream within a dream in which I was unfairly sacked from my job for being the victim of an Internet phishing scam whilst falling off a ladder in the workplace. Dream-Injury-Lawyers-4-U wrangled £12,500 out of Leonardo DiCaprio to cover what my recuperation costs would have been if any of this had actually happened. Thank you,* ***Dream-Injury-Lawyers-4-U!!****"*
Mr C Nolan, Hollywood

WOMANISER TIME-SAVING ACCESSORIES

LOTHARIOS. Are you receiving TOO MUCH female attention? Are you CONSTANTLY badgered by lust-crazed ladies? Are you finding it difficult to get ANYTHING done? If YOU desperately need help beating off the women, then why not try W. Beatty's patented...

SHITTY STICK™ Female Attention Deterrent

NOW ONLY £200

The W. Beatty Shitty Stick™ has been voted 'No.1 Female Deterrent On The Market' SIX years running by *Philanderer Monthly* magazine.

Hand crafted from Devonshire oak, and hand-slathered with 100% organic excrement*, the **Shitty Stick™** provides today's busy seducer with a welcome break from perpetual pleas for sexual intercourse.

* Choose from horse, cow or dog

HOW DOES IT WORK?!

- *As you spot the approaching lust-consumed female(s), withdraw your W. Beatty* ***Shitty Stick™*** *from the belt holster.*
- *When the lust-consumed female(s) are within* ***ONE METRE****, simply wave the* ***Shitty Stick™*** *frantically in their direction.*
- *When they have run away, simply replace the* ***Shitty Stick™*** *in its holster and go about your non-sexual business.*
- *Don't let relentless requests for coitus stop YOU achieving your personal and professional goals. Start beating off women with a* ***Shitty Stick™ TODAY!***

"I've famously had penetrative intercourse with up to 3000 women. If it weren't for my trusty ***Shitty Stick™****, I would have been forced to make love to many, many more, and consequently I would not have had time to get my singing career off the ground. I owe the* ***Shitty Stick™*** *everything."*
Mick H, Manchester

"At the height of my Noughties fame, I was knobby-wobbing ninety-winety different birdy-wirdies a month. Thanks to the ***Shitty Stick™*** *I was able to take the occasional breather from this hecticy-wecticy schedule in order to appear in some of the TV programmes ever made. Thank-you-y, wank-you-y,* ***Shitty Stick™****!"*
Russell B, Essex

WWW.WBEATTYSHITTYSTICK.COM

FOR FOX SAKE

Hunt saboteurs forced to rethink in light of report

THE LEAGUE Against Cruel Sports won a victory in 2005 when the then Labour government introduced a ban on hunting wild animals with dogs. But nearly 20 years on, that might turn out to be a hollow victory in light of a new scientific report which shows that foxes actually *enjoy* being hunted.

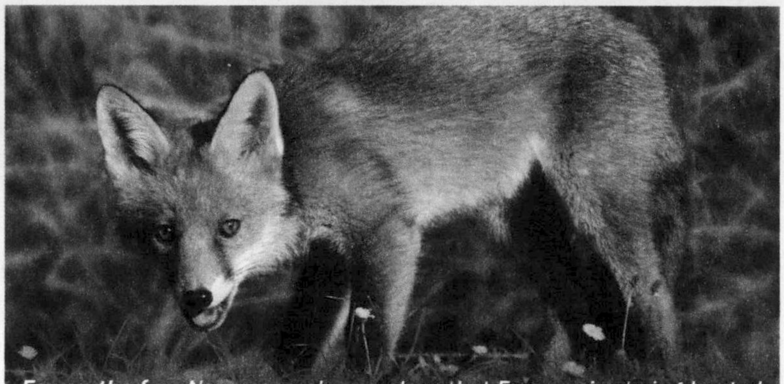

Fox on the fun: New research may show that Foxes enjoy being hunted.

According to scientists from the Royal Agricultural University, hunt saboteurs have deprived the red-coloured dogs of excitement, and have condemned them to dull, uneventful lives rummaging through wheelie bins.

"We needed to recreate the conditions of a hunt in order to test the hypothesis that foxes enjoyed it," said Dr Trimble Bowes-Lyon, head of the Cotswolds-based university's Hunting Research Group.

"For scientific research purposes, myself and twenty non-scientist friends mounted horses and chased a fox with forty dogs for about seven miles around the Gloucestershire countryside," he continued.

The animal was eventually caught and torn to pieces on a trading estate on the outskirts of Cirencester. After recovering part of its head from one of the dogs' mouths, Dr Bowes-Lyon took a blood sample for analysis back at his laboratory.

"The findings were remarkable," he said. "The adrenalin levels in the fox's blood were through the roof, almost ten times higher than when a fox is at rest," he continued.

"Adrenalin is the hormone which makes us feel excited. Humans have elevated adrenalin levels when playing high energy computer games, or watching our favourite soccer team win a match – all the things that make us feel really good."

"The fox's adrenalin levels were on a par with those of a human riding the Oblivion roller coaster at Alton Towers. We can only imagine the whale of a time that fox was having being chased across the fields by that pack of dogs. He wouldn't have missed it for the world."

experiment

Over the following weeks, Dr Bowes-Lyon and his friends repeated the experiment to verify their findings, but they ran into a series of experimental errors.

"On the second run of the experiment, there was nothing left of the fox when we got there, so we were unable to yield any data" he said.

"On a subsequent run, the fox was eaten, but we were able to sample the blood round the dogs' mouths," he continued. "However, the pack had also torn a cat to pieces during the experiment, and so the results were inconclusive."

data

The team were undeterred and vowed to continue their work. "Good science requires repetition of data so that we can identify outliers and get statistically reliable data," said Dr Bowes-Lyon.

"We'll probably have to run the experiment every other Sunday during the summer and also on bank holidays and boxing day."

spock

But the research project, due to be published in the scientific journal Equus et Canis, has not been without controversy, and each run of the empirical trial has attracted protesters.

"I understand that people may be opposed to hunting, and they have every right to protest peacefully," said Dr Bowes-Lyon. "But when the scruffy, long-haired troublemakers start standing in the way of science, I feel justified in hitting them with my riding crop," he added.

A Hunting You *SHALL* Go!

with VIZ lawyer Quercus Petraea

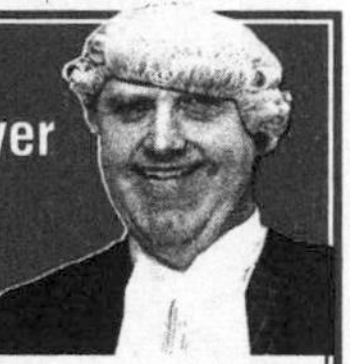

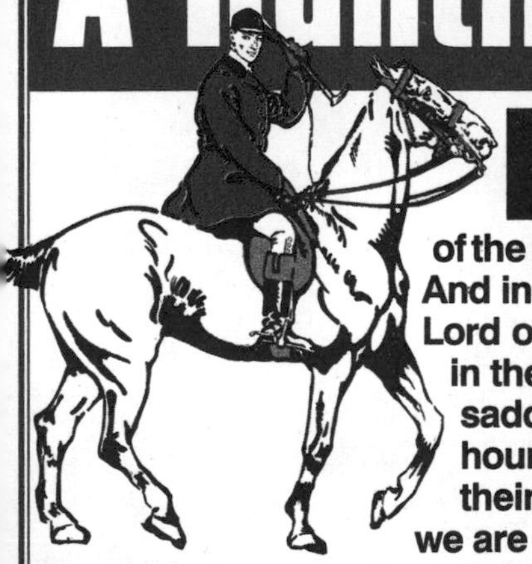

IT'S NOW almost two decades since killjoy politicians voted to BAN one of the most popular sports in Britain. And in that time, nobody – be they a Lord of the manor or a humble man in the street – has been allowed to saddle up their horses, call their hounds to heel and ride across their estate in pursuit of a fox. And we are all the poorer for it.

But all is not lost. The vagaries of the British legal system mean that the law is peppered with inconsistencies. If you know what you are doing, these can be exploited to allow you and your friends – be they landed gentry or factory workers living Gateshead – to pursue this time-honoured tradition.

Here, *Viz* lawyer QUERCUS PETRAEA gives a rundown of the loopholes in the law. *Tally Ho! The hunt is on.*

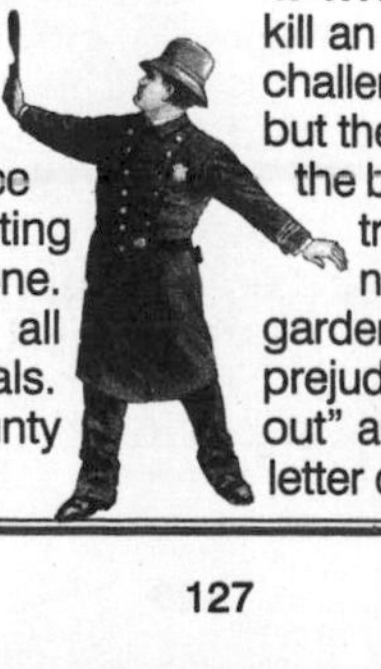

1. THE BIGGEST loophole you can exploit is the fact that the police invariably have other things to do. So saddle your horses, a-hunting you will go, and nine times out of ten the filth will leave you alone. And remember, a typical hunting party includes people from all walks of life, from Dukes and millionaire industrialists to minor royals. Rest assured, if you can include the Chief Constable of your county amongst your number, you can enjoy your pastime with impunity.

2. THE LAW as it stands does not allow the hunting of wild animals with dogs. However, it does not prevent anyone getting pissed up on sherry and riding across the countryside with 40 dogs for the fun of it. Your dogs may "accidentally" pick up the scent of a fox, chase it and tear it to shreds, but as long as this was not the purpose of your outing, no crime has been committed. Make sure your party includes a lawyer who can explain this to anyone who challenges you, and also threaten to "sue them for defamation of character till their arse bleeds" if they say otherwise.

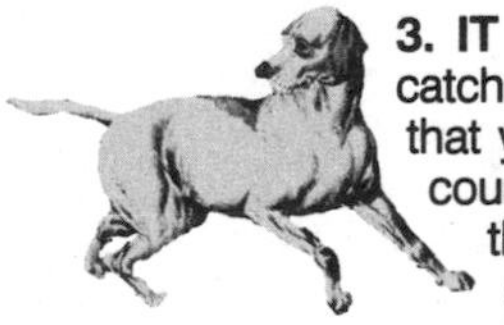

3. IT IS THE SPECIFIC mention of dogs in the law that catches many people out. So tell anyone who challenges you that you are simply enjoying an innocent ride through the countryside in your red coat, and that the 40 dogs ripping the fox to pieces are not yours. Since the requirement to register ownership of a dog was abandoned in 1987, nobody will be able to prove otherwise. Make sure your party includes a couple of enormous thugs on a quad bike who, whilst not explicitly threatening troublemakers with physical violence, will let them know that it is certainly on the cards.

4. WHILST HUNTING with dogs is a criminal offence, it is not an offence to kill an animal with a bird, so always take a bird of prey along on your hunt. If challenged, say you are chasing the fox, perfectly legally, but the kill will be made by the bird. You may not arrive with the bird before the fox is torn apart, but as long as you have tried, that is deemed acceptable in law. You do not even need a real bird – a plastic eagle, of the sort available from garden centres – will suffice. If challenged, simply say "without prejudice, I unintentionally picked up the wrong bird before coming out" and you will be in the clear legally. You may be obeying the letter of the law, rather than the spirit, but so fucking what.

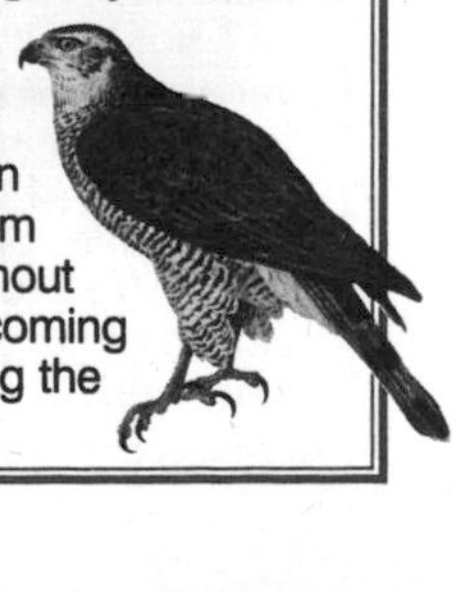

HUNT FOR A STAR

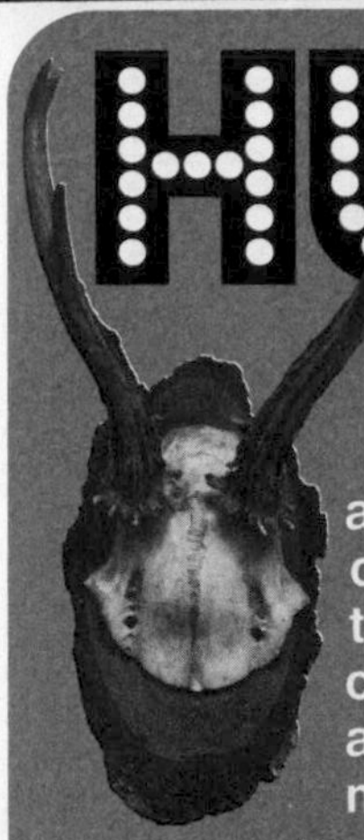
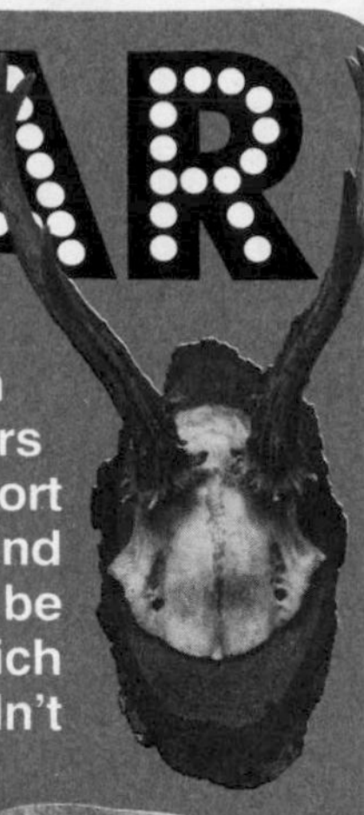

IT'S EVERYONE'S dream to take a gun and kill a large wild beast. The thrill of seeing a fully grown white rhinoceros in mid-charge drop to its knees as your rifle cracks from the safety of a reinforced Toyota Landcruiser is one we would all savour, and the stars are no different. But in this age of 'wokeness' and social media, killing a wild animal for sport could well be a career-ender for any celebrity. Photographs of the star sitting grinning behind their lifeless quarry would quickly circulate on Twitter, and before long, contracts would be cancelled, shows pulled, and the unlucky celeb 'flamed'. So we asked ten top stars which animal they would hypothetically like to kill, and what method they would use, if it wouldn't mean instant career suicide.

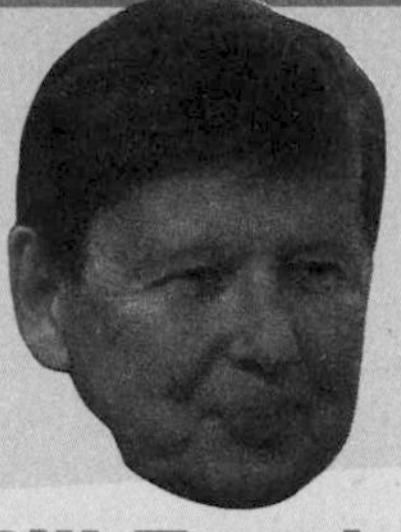

Bill Turnbull

former BBC Breakfast presenter

I THINK I would side with the Duke of Edinburgh and bag myself a tiger. I've got nothing against tigers, in fact I think they are a magnificent, proud beast, the true king of the Asiatic jungle. But they look too much like enormous wasps for my liking, and I can't stand those poisonous little fuckers as they attack my bee-hives.

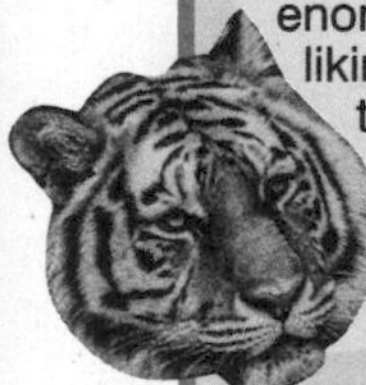

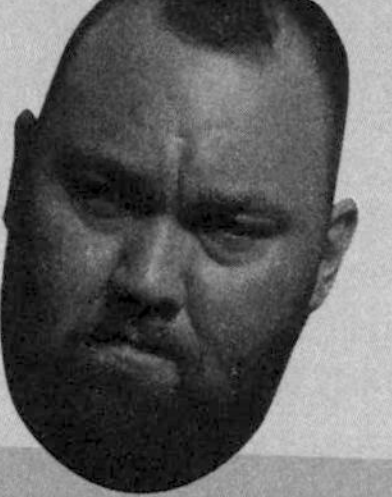

Hafþór Júlíus Björnsson

GoT 'The Mountain' actor

MY MOTTO is 'Go big, or go home.' So if I were to kill a beast, I'd like to harpoon a blue whale. But if I was restricted to hunting on land, then it would have to be an elephant. I don't know if it would be an Indian Elephant or an African elephant as I don't know which one is the bigger of the two. I've never actually seen one, as there are no elephants at all in Iceland.

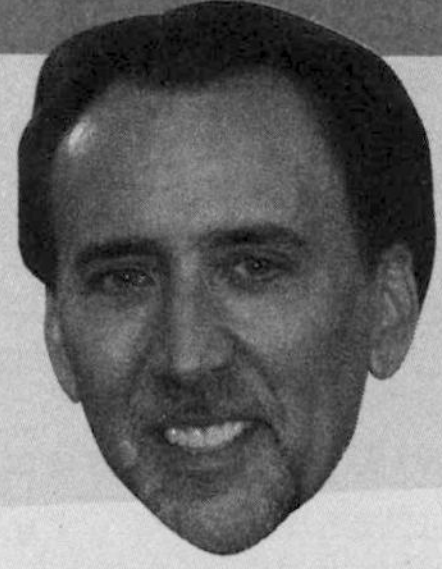

Nicholas Cage

straight-to-DVD actor

I'M NOT a very good shot, so the likes of a lion or a tiger would be no good, because if I just wounded it in the shoulder or something, it might come after me and tear me to pieces. So I'd go for a herbivore, like a gazelle or a zebra; something which wouldn't come after me if I didn't kill it outright, but just limp off into the bush to die.

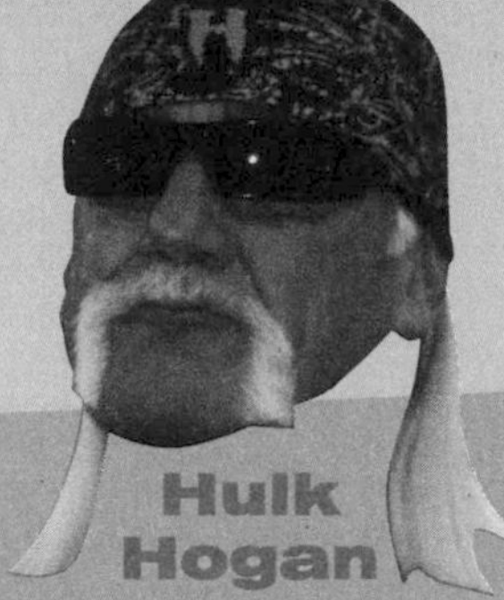

Hulk Hogan

former wrestler

I'VE ALWAYS dreamt about hunting a grizzly bear, but when push came to shove, I don't think I would be able to pull the trigger to kill one of these magnificent beasts. Instead, I think I'd just get right up in its face and 'trash talk' it for twenty minutes before hitting it across the back with a flimsy folding chair made of lightweight aluminium.

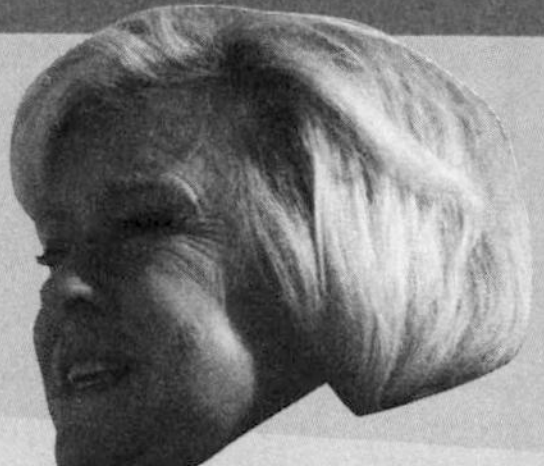

Sue Barker

former GB tennis No 1

THE QUEEN Mum once shot and killed a rhinoceros whilst on safari in Africa. According to her biographer, the episode 'broke her heart.' Her majesty was a wonderful, empathetic woman with the common touch, and if killing a rhinoceros broke her heart, it would likely break mine, too. So I'd whack a giraffe or a brace of gnus instead.

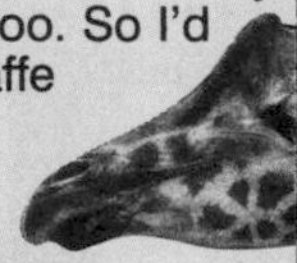

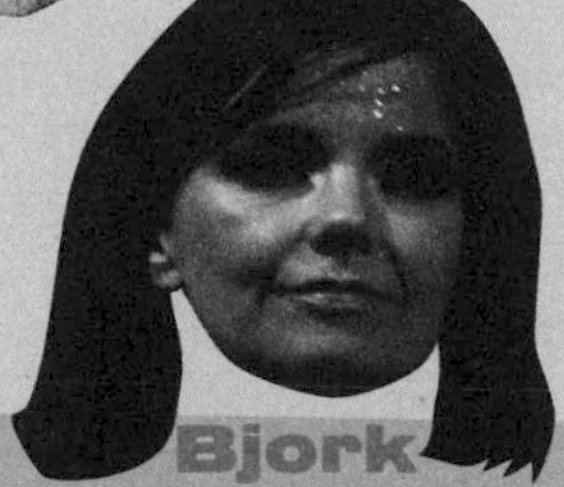

Bjork

Icelandic popstrel

BACK IN 1996, I got right into trouble for attacking a reporter who welcomed me to Bangkok airport, and I've more or less kept my head down since then. Apart from in 2008, when I really laid into a photographer at Aukland airport in New Zealand. So if I got the chance to hunt an animal, I'd probably get someone to dress up a bear as a photographer, and then bang its head against a concrete floor in an airport until security intervened.

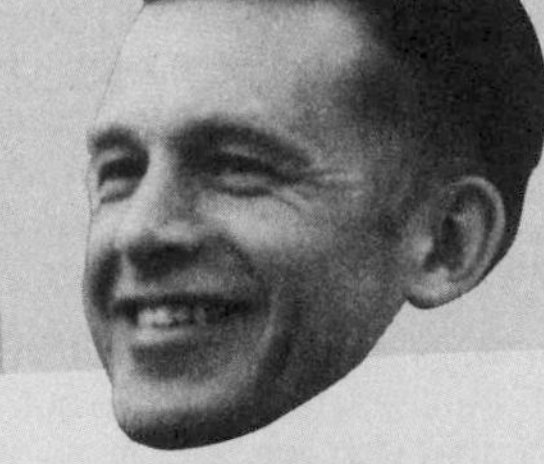

Chris Packham

TV naturist

ANDEAN Condors are magnificent beasts, with the largest wingspan of any living bird at ten foot six. To catch one, I'd build a camouflaged hide baited with a dead calf. When the condor came down to investigate, I'd poke my hands out from my concealed hiding place and grab it. Then I'd either strangle it or kill it with a rock.

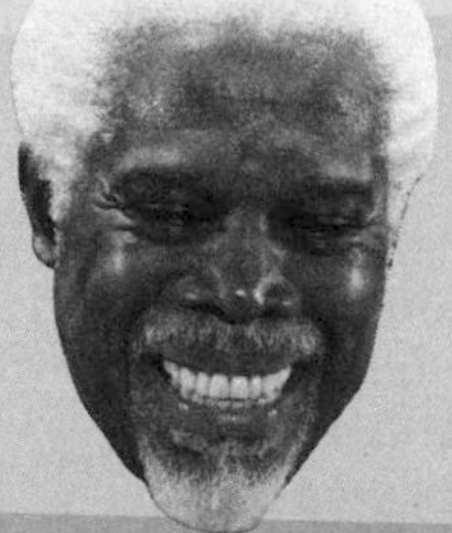

Billy Ocean

pop singer

WITH A surname like mine, you might expect me to suggest killing a *Jaws*-style shark by dropping a high-pressure gas cannister into its mouth and then exploding it with a deadly, pinpoint rifle shot. However, 'Ocean' is just a stage name that I took from a football team in Trinidad and Tobago; I'm really called Les Charles, so I think I'd rather just run over a load of badgers with a steam roller.

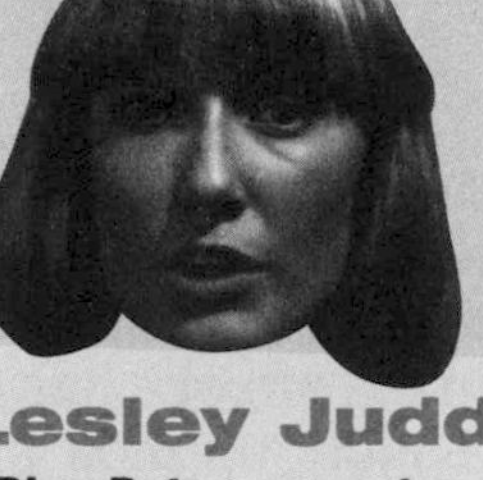

Lesley Judd

Blue Peter presenter

WHEN I was little, my favourite bit in a Tarzan film was always when Johnny Weissmuller or Ron Ely wrestled an alligator, spinning over and over in the water before stabbing it to death with a knife. Sadly, even though Biddy Baxter suggested it once during a Special Assignment to Chester Zoo, I never got to stab an alligator while I was on *Blue Peter*, because the BBC couldn't sort out the insurance.

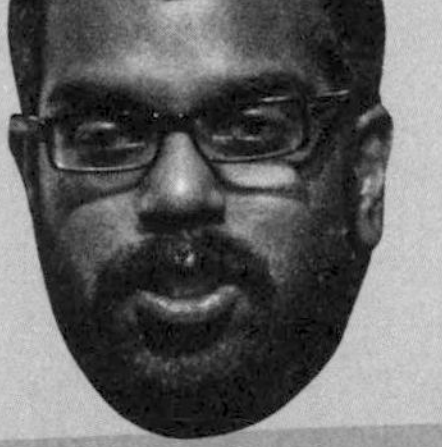

Romesh Ranganathan

TV funnyman

IT'S NOT something I've ever really thought about, but I'd use a mousetrap – baited with a sparrow instead of cheese – to catch a tarantula. If the trap didn't kill it outright, I'd hold it in a bucket of water until it drownded, if it's possible to drown spiders, which I think it is.

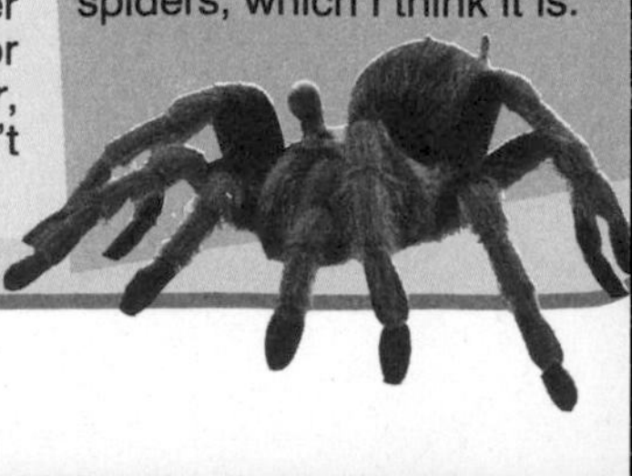

GET THE HUNTING HORN!

Hunting Pink is surefire way to bag a fox

Hounds of love: Huntsmen have long known the attraction that hunting pink holds for women.

FORGET candlelit dinners for two, weekends in Paris or bunches of flowers from the 24-hour garage – if you want to win a woman's heart, take her *hunting!* Because according to one scientist, nothing is more guaranteed to send a woman weak at the knees than the sight of a man in full hunting pink, riding with a pack of hounds.

"When a woman sees a man chasing after a fox, she desires him sexually. And there is nothing she can do about it," says Dr Trimble Bowes-Lyon, head of the Royal Agricultural University's Hunting research group. "These desires are hard-wired into women's brains."

"We have done experiments where we have taken three hunky male models dressed as a huntsman, a fireman and that Richard Gere *Officer and a Gentleman* costume, and put them in a room with 100 women," he said.

"87% of the women had sex with the one dressed as a huntsman."

THE FOXIEST STORIES ARE IN YOUR #1 VIZ

"Believe me, take up hunting and it won't only be the saboteurs you'll be beating off with a riding crop," he said.

huntsmen

The exact reason why women find huntsmen so sexually attractive isn't known, but Bowes-Lyon believes it could be a primeval response going all the way back to dinosaur times when human beings lived in caves.

"Perhaps the Neanderthal settlements where our primitive ancestors lived were plagued with foxes going through the bins," he continued. "Any man who put on the skin of a red deer and chased the foxes away would provide protection, and would therefore be a desirable mate."

"But whatever the reason, it's definitely a thing," he added.

tarantulii

And it is for this reason that Bowes-Lyon believes the 2005 ban on hunting with dogs may have repercussions on our own population, as well as that of foxes.

"The ill thought-out bloodsports ban will reduce the attraction felt by women towards men, and I don't need to tell you what that might mean," he told us.

"The government need to reverse this decision immediately, or we could be looking at the extinction of our species," he added.

NEVER MIND THE JORROCKS

TALLY HO! You can be the Master of Foxhounds in our Bloody Great Fox Hunting Competition!

IF YOU thought fox hunting was just for toffs, the landed gentry and sons of Roxy Music singers, then think again. Because whoever you are, **YOU** could be the master of your own hunt in our fantastic competition. We're giving away a fantastic Fox Hunt Starter Kit, including a red coat, a bottle of sherry, a trumpet, a horse and forty dogs, to the winner of this competition!

To win this fantastic prize, simply work out the answer to this hunting conundrum:

A HUNTING PARTY *set out with riders, walkers and dogs. There were twice as many dogs as horses and twice as many riders as people walking. Of the riders, 25% were sat two-to-a-horse. The hunt failed to catch a fox, but the dogs tore apart half as many cats as there were people walking as they ran through some gardens. If four horses had more than one rider, how many legs were involved in the hunt? Oh, and we forgot, but a quarter of all the four-legged animals only had 3 legs. And one of the Whippers-in had lost a leg after falling into the mechanism of an escalator.*

VIZ FOX HUNTING COMPETITION

There were .... legs involved in the hunt.

Name ....

Address ....

Chest measurement for the jacket .... ins

In case of a tie, simply answer this tiebreak question in 12 words or less: I think it would be really great to see a small animal torn limb from limb by some dogs whilst it's still alive because...

PLEASE NOTE. The horse in the prize may not be suitable for riding due to age, and the 40 dogs may represent a variety of breeds depending on what is available at the animal rescue centre on the day.

GRIN AND "BEAR

NOTHING goes smoothly all the time, and our best laid plans can often go awry. If you are a shopkeeper, an IT technician or road sweeper, things going belly-up is an annoying inconvenience at worst. But if you are a big game hunter, it could be the last thing that goes wrong in your life.

Unluckiest hunter keeps laughing through his tears

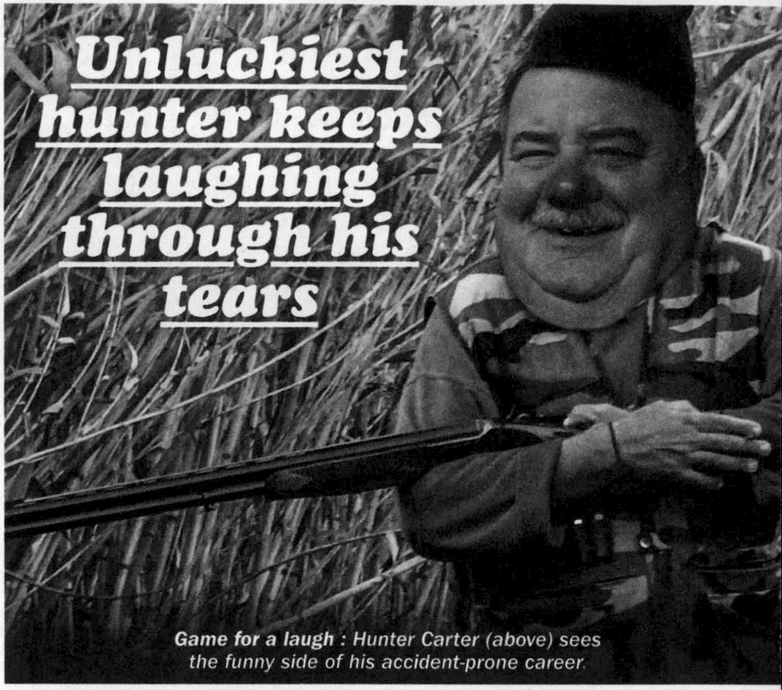

Game for a laugh : Hunter Carter (above) sees the funny side of his accident-prone career.

And nobody knows this better than freelance poacher CARTER BEESWAX. For the 58-year-old elephant-gun-for-hire has been on the receiving end of more animal attacks than many people have had hot dinners. And now he is putting down his rifle and picking up his pen to write his hilarious memoirs – *It Shouldn't Happen to a Big Game Hunter*.

The book is still in preparation, as Beeswax 'tests the market' to see if there will be any interest in another humorous careers-based autobiography. But he believes that if he can get half a dozen friends to agree to buy a copy, they would in turn get their friends to buy one, and before long, the Nottingham-based animal bagger would have a Christmas bestseller capable of knocking Adam Kay's *This is Going to Hurt* off its usual number 1 spot.

Busby Bear-keley

When Carter goes out to poach an animal, most of the time it's a case of Bang! Bang! Job done. But not always, as he discovered when hunting bears in the northern forests of Canada.

"I got a phone call from a bloke in the army telling me they needed another load of busby hats for the guards at Buckingham Palace, and he commissioned me to get them a dozen black bear skins. That sort of job is bread and butter work to a hunter like me, and after settling on a price of £25 per pelt, I was on the next plane to British Columbia.

I'd been camping in the woods for a couple of days and had already bagged 10 of the buggers, so I was looking forward to shooting another couple before getting back home and pocketing my cash. But it's at times like that when complacency sets in, and in my excitement, I made a bit of a cock-up.

I spotted a big female eating some berries in a clearing, and I sneaked forward to get a better shot. But as I looked behind me, I suddenly noticed that I had somehow got myself between her and her cubs. It was a schoolboy mistake, one they warn you about in Bear Hunting 101, and I had made it. It was a real facepalm moment. 'Doh! I thought to myself as the half-ton female leapt on top of me and started ripping away at my back with her razor sharp claws.

VIZ ALWAYS PROVIDES BANG FOR YOUR BUCK!

It was such a daft thing to do, and I had to chuckle to myself as she sank her teeth into my skull in her maternally protective frenzy.

blood

I'd lost nearly half the blood in my body, but by some miracle I survived and managed to call for help. I could see the paramedics from the air ambulance trying to keep their faces straight when they found out what I had done. Honestly, talk about stupid!

And the doctors at the hospital in Bannf were even worse, ribbing me every time they came to change my wound dressings and administer more morphine. They even gave me a card with a picture of Yogi Bear on it saying "You won't make that boo-boo again!" Honestly, I felt a right plonker.

And to make matters worse, I'd lost the 10 skins that I'd already collected, so when I finally got back home, I didn't even get my £300."

Just One Horn-etto

Actors often say that you should never work with children or animals, and Carter says that the old adage is even more true in the big-game-hunting business, especially the bit about animals. And since you can't avoid them in your working day, bloopers are par for the course.

"I remember this one time I was in Mozambique, poaching some rhinos for a billionaire. He'd heard that their horns could be ground up and used as aphrodisiacs, so he'd sent me to get a couple. I thought it was a load of nonsense, but he was paying me £200, so I was going to keep my feelings to myself.

Now people are always going on about rhinos being rare, but there are still quite a few knocking about if you know where to look for them. And I'd spotted one with the longest horn I'd ever seen, eating some spiky leaves off a bush. They've got very poor eyesight, but a great sense of smell and this huge beast picked up my scent and came charging towards me.

I'd been in this predicament many times before and it was no big deal. A bullet between the eyes usually shows them who is boss, so I aimed my rifle and pulled the trigger.

But nothing happened! I had to laugh, as my gun had jammed! Of all the times to fail me, it had to pick this one! Luckily, I saw the funny side, and chuckling at my misfortune, I turned on my heels and ran. But although they are big, rhinos are pretty quick, and I knew it would soon be right up my arse.

enormous

And I was right. The enormous beast shoved its horn right up my backside and tossed me a full 20 feet into the air. As I spun like a rag doll, bleeding from the massive wound in my anus, I couldn't help thinking how embarrassing this was going to be at the hospital. I landed with a sickening thud on the savannah, tears of laughter streaming from my eyes.

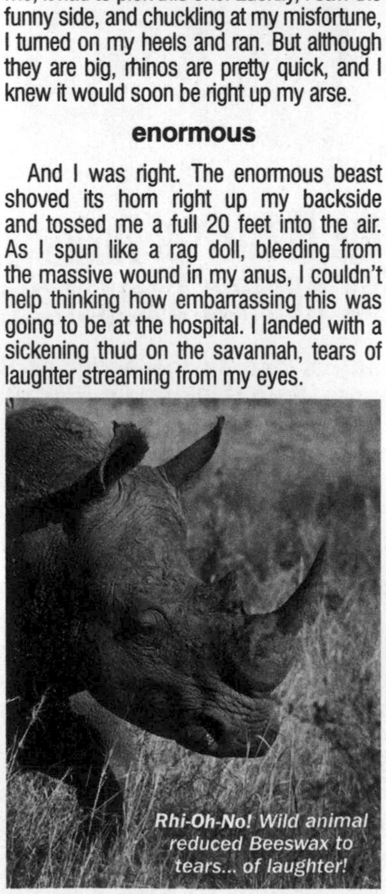

Rhi-Oh-No! Wild animal reduced Beeswax to tears... of laughter!

And I was right. I was rushed, re faced, to Maputo hospital where doctor asked me what had happened. The clearly didn't believe me when I told ther about my jammed gun, as they were a chuckling away. One of them asked me i was wearing a loose-fitting dressing gow when it happened, which reduced th entire staff, and me, to tears of laughte Chuckling away, they managed to stop th internal bleeding and put me on the ward.

The next two months were some o the funniest I can remember. One of th doctors who examined my wound wou say "Yes, Mr Beeswax... I'll give yo bottom the thumbs up!" every time h examined me. The whole ward, includin myself, would fall about laughing.

I never got to take a rhino horn back t the UK, so that promised £200 fee neve came my way. But I think I had £200 worth of laughs out of the affair."

Mane Attraction

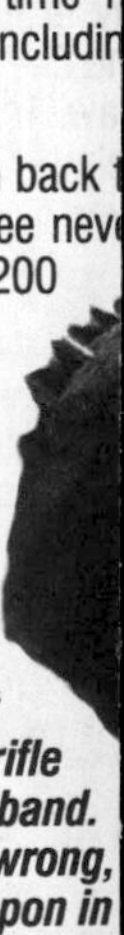

In the Big Game game, it is important to have the right equipment – binoculars, knife, rifle and a hat with a leopard skin band. But as things will often go wrong, perhaps the most important weapon in hunter's armoury is a sense of humour.

"I think the biggest laugh I have ever ha on the job was when I was on the plair in Botswana. My client was a woman fro Nottingham who was doing up a big, pos house had asked me to get a lion's head t go over her fireplace. Money seemed to b

' IT!

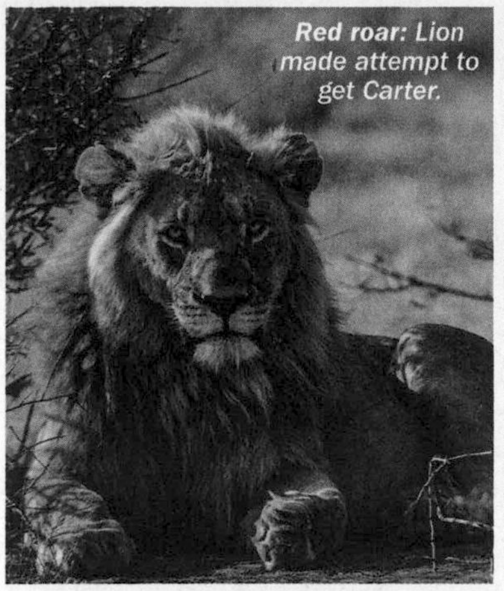

Red roar: Lion made attempt to get Carter.

› object, because when I told her it would ›st £150, she said yes without haggling. ›e next day saw me tooled up and out on ›e veldt in search of my quarry.

Lions are bread and butter work to the ›ofessional hunter – Fly out. Bang! Fly ›me – so I wasn't expecting much fun › this job. How wrong I was.

I spotted a lion with a huge mane which ›ould look lovely on the woman from ›ttingham's wall, and I aimed my gun. ›ut before I could fire, I inadvertently trod › a twig. It snapped and the lion looked ›y way. I rolled my eyes. It was going to › one of those days!

trigger

The big cat started heading my way and ›fted my rifle, aiming between his eyes. ›ith my mind already wondering what ›would spend my £175 on, I pulled the ›gger. The little 'click!' let me know that I ›d forgotten to load my gun. Once again, ›reased up with laughter at the thought what my mates at the pub would have say when this got back to them.

The lion was now coming at me full ›eed, so I dried my eyes and popped a ›uple of bullets in the chamber. They I re- ›ned and pulled the trigger – *Bang! Bang!*

My amusement turned to hysterics as ›e beast hurtled towards me unharmed. ›on't know whether I was shaking with ›ughter so much from my earlier howler, whether it was just bad luck, but I'd ›issed my target. Honestly, sometimes I ›uldn't hit a barn door if I was standing ›xt to it, and today was one of those ›ys. I doubled up with laughter.

But the lion soon wiped the smile off ›y face, quite literally, as it took my lips ›d cheek off with a swipe of its massive ›aw. There's not a lot you can do when ›ing attacked by a lion, but I couldn't ›en do that as I was in fits of hysterics.

Luckily some people from a nearby village saw what was happening and scared the lion away. One of my arms had been torn off, but one of the men stemmed the bleeding whilst another called for help. They were proper taking the piss out of me all the time, but I took it in good spirit and laughed along with them.

Boycey

I was rushed into the intensive care ward of Gaborone hospital and given 23 pints of blood. When they heard about how I had missed a lion at point-blank range, the doctors were in stitches… but not as many as I was… 650 in total, including 200 to put my face back on. What a Wally I felt!

When I was discharged 3 months later, the staff presented me with a cuddly toy lion… with a target painted on its backside! Honestly, what a bunch of jokers."

NEXT WEEK: "The laughs were on me when a pack of hyenas closed in and I realised I'd left my rifle in the jeep."

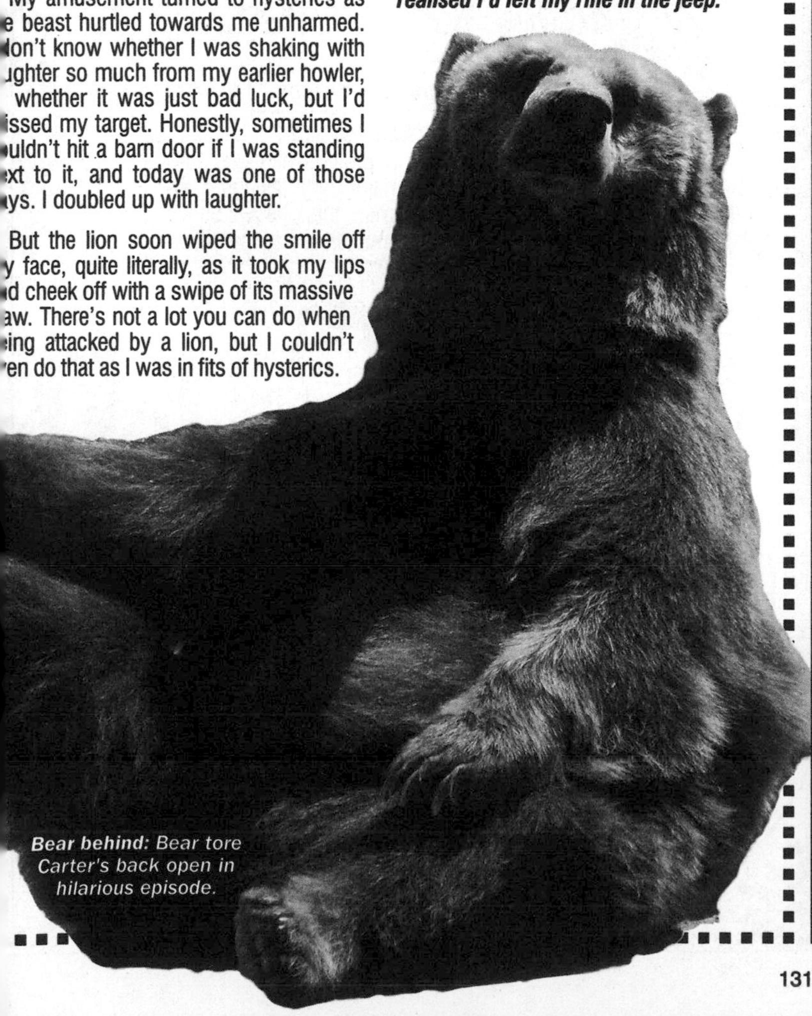

Bear behind: Bear tore Carter's back open in hilarious episode.

FOX AWAY!

Hunting ban could see red dogs rule the Earth

FOR MILLENNIA, the delicate balance of species on our planet has been stable, with populations kept under control by the invisible hand of Mother Nature. And Britain's foxhunters have played an important role in maintaining this equilibrium, keeping the number of these dog-like creatures at natural levels by getting pissed and chasing them on horses.

But all that could be set to change. Because one scientist believes that the ban on hunting with dogs imposed in 2005 could lead to an explosion in the fox population. And he warns that we are sleepwalking into an environmental catastrophe that will make climate change and global warming seem trivial by comparison.

"The number of foxes in the UK is set to explode very quickly," warned Dr Trimble Bowes-Lyon, head of the Royal Agricultural University's Hunting Research Group. "There are around 430,000 of these vulpine pests in Britain at the moment, and they can produce litters of up to 8 cubs a year as many as six times during their lifetime," he told *Horse and Hound* magazine.

"We have run some very complex computer modelling which horrifyingly showed that, left unchecked, there could be 240 duodecillion foxes in the UK by 2030," he scaremongered. "To put that figure into perspective, that's more than 40 decillion foxes – enough to fill the Albert Hall countless millions of billions times over – for every man, woman and child in the country."

catastrophe

Dr Trimble believes that in order to avert this impending catastrophe, the numbers of these animals must be controlled before it's too late.

FOXCLUSIVE!

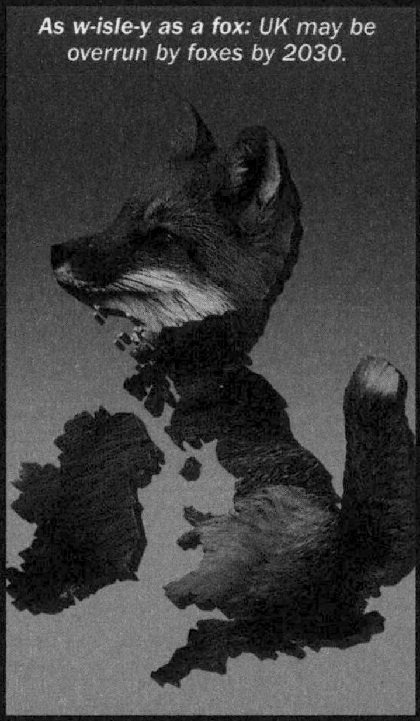

As w-isle-y as a fox: UK may be overrun by foxes by 2030.

"We are looking at a situation where people will be afraid to leave their houses because of the sheer number of foxes on the streets if we don't reduce their numbers," he said. "Babies will be nibbled in their cots and chickens will be snatched from their battery farms to be eaten alive. It's a nightmare scenario that simply doesn't bear thinking about."

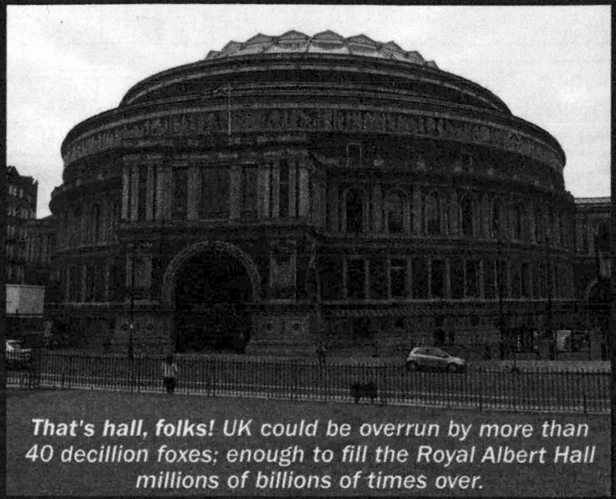

That's hall, folks! UK could be overrun by more than 40 decillion foxes; enough to fill the Royal Albert Hall millions of billions of times over.

"The best way, and indeed the only practical way, to keep fox numbers under control is to chase them on horseback with a pack of dogs," he added. "Preferably whilst dressed up like the bloke off a Johnnie Walker bottle, all pissed up and blowing a little trumpet."

"No oiks," Dr Bowes-Lyon added.

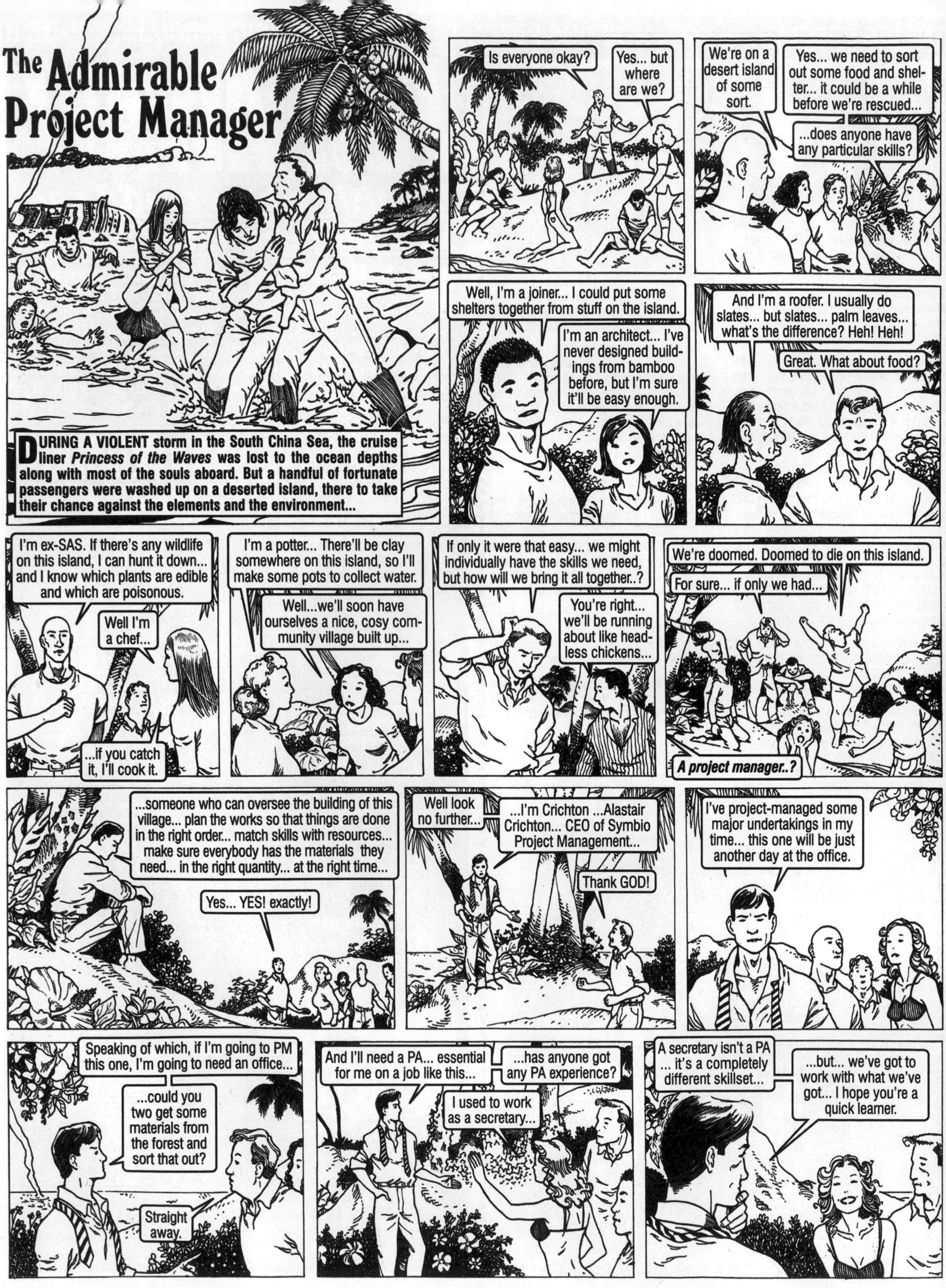

The Admirable Project Manager
DURING A VIOLENT storm in the South China Sea, the cruise liner *Princess of the Waves* was lost to the ocean depths along with most of the souls aboard. But a handful of fortunate passengers were washed up on a deserted island, there to take their chance against the elements and the environment...
Is everyone okay?
Yes... but where are we?
We're on a desert island of some sort.
Yes... we need to sort out some food and shelter... it could be a while before we're rescued...
...does anyone have any particular skills?
Well, I'm a joiner... I could put some shelters together from stuff on the island.
I'm an architect... I've never designed buildings from bamboo before, but I'm sure it'll be easy enough.
And I'm a roofer. I usually do slates... but slates... palm leaves... what's the difference? Heh! Heh!
Great. What about food?
I'm ex-SAS. If there's any wildlife on this island, I can hunt it down... and I know which plants are edible and which are poisonous.
Well I'm a chef...
...if you catch it, I'll cook it.
I'm a potter... There'll be clay somewhere on this island, so I'll make some pots to collect water.
Well...we'll soon have ourselves a nice, cosy community village built up...
If only it were that easy... we might individually have the skills we need, but how will we bring it all together..?
You're right... we'll be running about like headless chickens...
We're doomed. Doomed to die on this island.
For sure... if only we had...
A project manager..?
...someone who can oversee the building of this village... plan the works so that things are done in the right order... match skills with resources... make sure everybody has the materials they need... in the right quantity... at the right time...
Yes... YES! exactly!
Well look no further...
...I'm Crichton ...Alastair Crichton... CEO of Symbio Project Management...
Thank GOD!
I've project-managed some major undertakings in my time... this one will be just another day at the office.
Speaking of which, if I'm going to PM this one, I'm going to need an office...
...could you two get some materials from the forest and sort that out?
Straight away.
And I'll need a PA... essential for me on a job like this...
...has anyone got any PA experience?
I used to work as a secretary...
A secretary isn't a PA ... it's a completely different skillset...
...but... we've got to work with what we've got... I hope you're a quick learner.

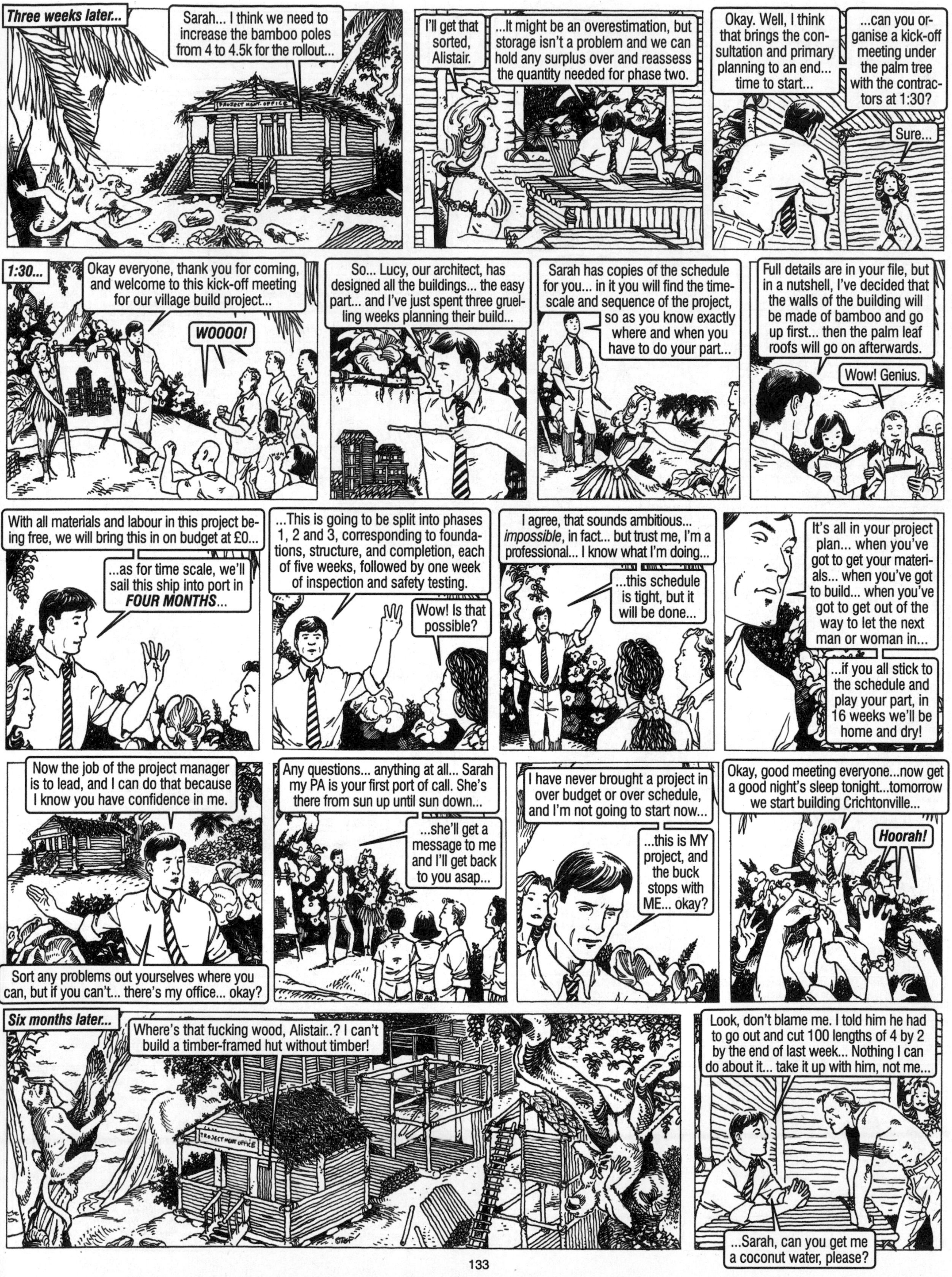

Three weeks later...
Sarah... I think we need to increase the bamboo poles from 4 to 4.5k for the rollout...
PROJECT MGMT. OFFICE
I'll get that sorted, Alistair.
...It might be an overestimation, but storage isn't a problem and we can hold any surplus over and reassess the quantity needed for phase two.
Okay. Well, I think that brings the consultation and primary planning to an end... time to start...
...can you organise a kick-off meeting under the palm tree with the contractors at 1:30?
Sure...
1:30...
Okay everyone, thank you for coming, and welcome to this kick-off meeting for our village build project...
WOOOO!
So... Lucy, our architect, has designed all the buildings... the easy part... and I've just spent three gruelling weeks planning their build...
Sarah has copies of the schedule for you... in it you will find the timescale and sequence of the project,
so as you know exactly where and when you have to do your part...
Full details are in your file, but in a nutshell, I've decided that the walls of the building will be made of bamboo and go up first... then the palm leaf roofs will go on afterwards.
Wow! Genius.
With all materials and labour in this project being free, we will bring this in on budget at £0...
...as for time scale, we'll sail this ship into port in FOUR MONTHS...
...This is going to be split into phases 1, 2 and 3, corresponding to foundations, structure, and completion, each of five weeks, followed by one week of inspection and safety testing.
Wow! Is that possible?
I agree, that sounds ambitious... impossible, in fact... but trust me, I'm a professional... I know what I'm doing...
...this schedule is tight, but it will be done...
It's all in your project plan... when you've got to get your materials... when you've got to build... when you've got to get out of the way to let the next man or woman in...
...if you all stick to the schedule and play your part, in 16 weeks we'll be home and dry!
Now the job of the project manager is to lead, and I can do that because I know you have confidence in me.
Sort any problems out yourselves where you can, but if you can't... there's my office... okay?
Any questions... anything at all... Sarah my PA is your first port of call. She's there from sun up until sun down...
...she'll get a message to me and I'll get back to you asap...
I have never brought a project in over budget or over schedule, and I'm not going to start now...
...this is MY project, and the buck stops with ME... okay?
Okay, good meeting everyone...now get a good night's sleep tonight...tomorrow we start building Crichtonville...
Hoorah!
Six months later...
Where's that fucking wood, Alistair..? I can't build a timber-framed hut without timber!
PROJECT MGMT OFFICE
Look, don't blame me. I told him he had to go out and cut 100 lengths of 4 by 2 by the end of last week... Nothing I can do about it... take it up with him, not me...
...Sarah, can you get me a coconut water, please?

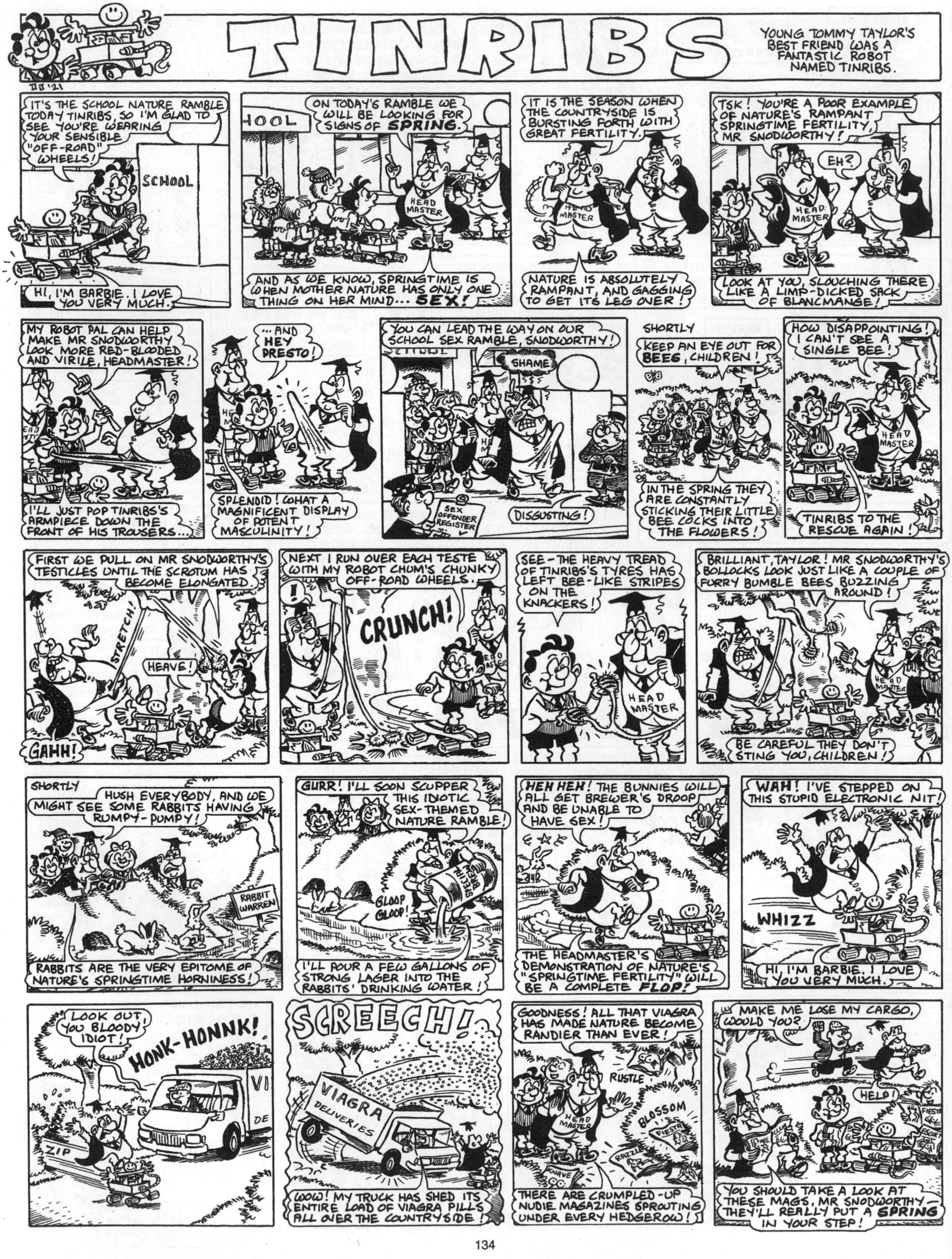
TINRIBS
YOUNG TOMMY TAYLOR'S BEST FRIEND WAS A FANTASTIC ROBOT NAMED TINRIBS.
IT'S THE SCHOOL NATURE RAMBLE TODAY TINRIBS, SO I'M GLAD TO SEE YOU'RE WEARING YOUR SENSIBLE "OFF-ROAD" WHEELS!
SCHOOL
HI, I'M BARBIE. I LOVE YOU VERY MUCH.
ON TODAY'S RAMBLE WE WILL BE LOOKING FOR SIGNS OF SPRING.
HOOL
HEAD MASTER
AND AS WE KNOW, SPRINGTIME IS WHEN MOTHER NATURE HAS ONLY ONE THING ON HER MIND... SEX!
IT IS THE SEASON WHEN THE COUNTRYSIDE IS BURSTING FORTH WITH GREAT FERTILITY.
HEAD MASTER
NATURE IS ABSOLUTELY RAMPANT, AND GAGGING TO GET ITS LEG OVER!
TSK! YOU'RE A POOR EXAMPLE OF NATURE'S RAMPANT SPRINGTIME FERTILITY, MR SNODWORTHY!
EH?
HEAD MASTER
LOOK AT YOU, SLOUCHING THERE LIKE A LIMP-DICKED SACK OF BLANCMANGE!
MY ROBOT PAL CAN HELP MAKE MR SNODWORTHY LOOK MORE RED-BLOODED AND VIRILE, HEADMASTER!
I'LL JUST POP TINRIBS'S ARMPIECE DOWN THE FRONT OF HIS TROUSERS...
...AND HEY PRESTO!
SPLENDID! WHAT A MAGNIFICENT DISPLAY OF POTENT MASCULINITY!
YOU CAN LEAD THE WAY ON OUR SCHOOL SEX RAMBLE, SNODWORTHY!
SHAME
SEX OFFENDER REGISTER
DISGUSTING!
SHORTLY
KEEP AN EYE OUT FOR BEES, CHILDREN!
IN THE SPRING THEY ARE CONSTANTLY STICKING THEIR LITTLE BEE COCKS INTO THE FLOWERS!
HOW DISAPPOINTING! I CAN'T SEE A SINGLE BEE!
HEAD MASTER
TINRIBS TO THE RESCUE AGAIN!
FIRST WE PULL ON MR SNODWORTHY'S TESTICLES UNTIL THE SCROTUM HAS BECOME ELONGATED.
STRETCH!
HEAVE!
GAHH!
NEXT I RUN OVER EACH TESTE WITH MY ROBOT CHUM'S CHUNKY OFF-ROAD WHEELS.
!
CRUNCH!
SEE - THE HEAVY TREAD OF TINRIBS'S TYRES HAS LEFT BEE-LIKE STRIPES ON THE KNACKERS!
HEAD MASTER
BRILLIANT, TAYLOR! MR SNODWORTHY'S BOLLOCKS LOOK JUST LIKE A COUPLE OF FURRY BUMBLE BEES BUZZING AROUND!
BE CAREFUL THEY DON'T STING YOU, CHILDREN!
SHORTLY
HUSH EVERYBODY, AND WE MIGHT SEE SOME RABBITS HAVING RUMPY-PUMPY!
RABBIT WARREN
RABBITS ARE THE VERY EPITOME OF NATURE'S SPRINGTIME HORNINESS!
GURR! I'LL SOON SCUPPER THIS IDIOTIC SEX-THEMED NATURE RAMBLE!
GLOOP GLOOP!
I'LL POUR A FEW GALLONS OF STRONG LAGER INTO THE RABBITS' DRINKING WATER!
HEH HEH! THE BUNNIES WILL ALL GET BREWER'S DROOP AND BE UNABLE TO HAVE SEX!
THE HEADMASTER'S DEMONSTRATION OF NATURE'S "SPRINGTIME FERTILITY" WILL BE A COMPLETE FLOP!
WAH! I'VE STEPPED ON THIS STUPID ELECTRONIC NIT!
WHIZZ
HI, I'M BARBIE. I LOVE YOU VERY MUCH.
LOOK OUT, YOU BLOODY IDIOT!
HONK-HONNK!
ZIP
SCREECH!
VIAGRA DELIVERIES
WOW! MY TRUCK HAS SHED ITS ENTIRE LOAD OF VIAGRA PILLS ALL OVER THE COUNTRYSIDE!
GOODNESS! ALL THAT VIAGRA HAS MADE NATURE BECOME RANDIER THAN EVER!
RUSTLE
BLOSSOM
HEAD MASTER
FIESTA
RAZZLE
KNAVE
THERE ARE CRUMPLED-UP NUDIE MAGAZINES SPROUTING UNDER EVERY HEDGEROW!
MAKE ME LOSE MY CARGO, WOULD YOU?
HELP!
YOU SHOULD TAKE A LOOK AT THESE MAGS, MR SNODWORTHY - THEY'LL REALLY PUT A SPRING IN YOUR STEP!

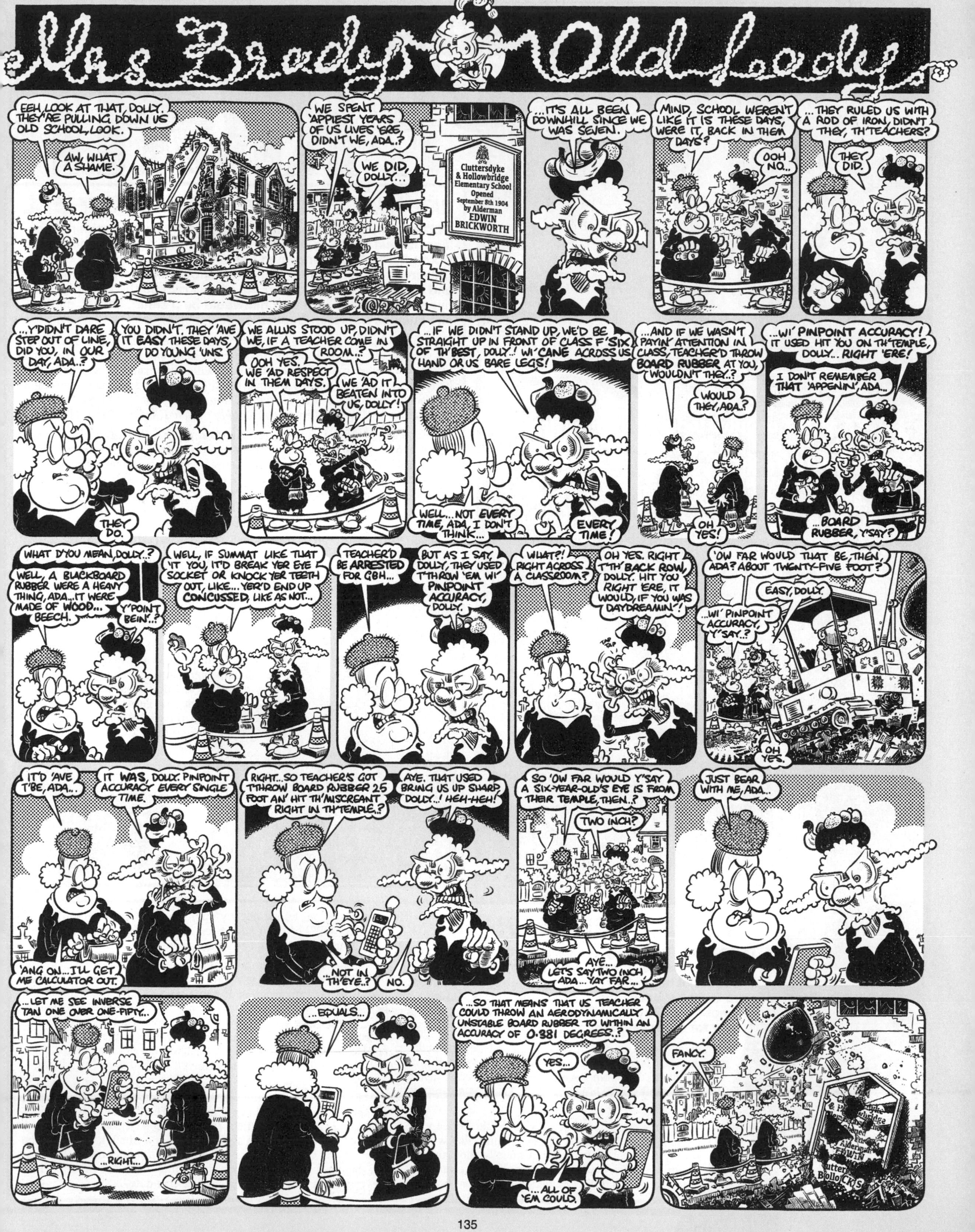
Mrs Brady Old Lady
EEH, LOOK AT THAT, DOLLY. THEY'RE PULLING DOWN US OLD SCHOOL, LOOK.
AW, WHAT A SHAME.
WE SPENT 'APPIEST YEARS OF US LIVES 'ERE, DIDN'T WE, ADA..?
WE DID, DOLLY...
Cluttersdyke & Hollowbridge Elementary School Opened September 8th 1904 by Alderman EDWIN BRICKWORTH
...IT'S ALL BEEN DOWNHILL SINCE WE WAS SEVEN.
MIND, SCHOOL WEREN'T LIKE IT IS THESE DAYS, WERE IT, BACK IN THEM DAYS?
OOH NO...
...THEY RULED US WITH A ROD OF IRON, DIDN'T THEY, TH'TEACHERS?
THEY DID.
...Y'DIDN'T DARE STEP OUT OF LINE, DID YOU, IN OUR DAY, ADA..?
YOU DIDN'T. THEY 'AVE IT EASY THESE DAYS, DO YOUNG 'UNS.
THEY DO.
WE ALLUS STOOD UP, DIDN'T WE, IF A TEACHER COME IN ROOM..?
OOH YES. WE 'AD RESPECT IN THEM DAYS.
WE 'AD IT BEATEN INTO US, DOLLY!
...IF WE DIDN'T STAND UP, WE'D BE STRAIGHT UP IN FRONT OF CLASS F'SIX OF TH'BEST, DOLLY..! WI' CANE ACROSS US HAND OR US' BARE LEGS!
WELL... NOT EVERY TIME, ADA, I DON'T THINK...
EVERY TIME!
...AND IF WE WASN'T PAYIN' ATTENTION IN CLASS, TEACHER'D THROW BOARD RUBBER AT YOU, WOULDN'T THEY..?
WOULD THEY, ADA..?
OH YES!
...WI' PINPOINT ACCURACY! IT USED HIT YOU ON TH'TEMPLE, DOLLY... RIGHT 'ERE!
I DON'T REMEMBER THAT 'APPENIN', ADA...
...BOARD RUBBER, Y'SAY?
WHAT D'YOU MEAN, DOLLY..?
WELL, A BLACKBOARD RUBBER WERE A HEAVY THING, ADA... IT WERE MADE OF WOOD... BEECH.
Y'POINT BEIN'..?
WELL, IF SUMMAT LIKE THAT 'IT YOU, IT'D BREAK YER EYE SOCKET OR KNOCK YER TEETH OUT, LIKE... YER'D END UP CONCUSSED, LIKE AS NOT...
TEACHER'D BE ARRESTED FOR GBH...
BUT AS I SAY, DOLLY, THEY USED T'THROW 'EM WI' PINPOINT ACCURACY, DOLLY.
WHAT?! RIGHT ACROSS A CLASSROOM?
OH YES. RIGHT T'TH'BACK ROW, DOLLY. HIT YOU RIGHT 'ERE IT WOULD, IF YOU WAS DAYDREAMIN'!
TAP TAP
'OW FAR WOULD THAT BE, THEN, ADA? ABOUT TWENTY-FIVE FOOT?
EASY, DOLLY.
...WI' PINPOINT ACCURACY, Y'SAY..?
OH YES.
IT'D 'AVE T'BE, ADA...
IT WAS, DOLLY. PINPOINT ACCURACY EVERY SINGLE TIME.
'ANG ON... I'LL GET ME CALCULATOR OUT.
RIGHT... SO TEACHER'S GOT T'THROW BOARD RUBBER 25 FOOT AN' HIT TH'MISCREANT RIGHT IN TH'TEMPLE..?
AYE. THAT USED BRING US UP SHARP, DOLLY..! HEH-HEH!
...NOT IN TH'EYE..?
NO.
SO 'OW FAR WOULD Y'SAY A SIX-YEAR-OLD'S EYE IS FROM THEIR TEMPLE, THEN..?
TWO INCH?
AYE... LET'S SAY TWO INCH, ADA... 'YAY FAR...
JUST BEAR WITH ME, ADA...
...LET ME SEE INVERSE TAN ONE OVER ONE-FIFTY...
...RIGHT...
...EQUALS...
...SO THAT MEANS THAT US TEACHER COULD THROW AN AERODYNAMICALLY UNSTABLE BOARD RUBBER TO WITHIN AN ACCURACY OF 0.381 DEGREES..?
YES...
...ALL OF 'EM COULD.
FANCY.

Our online dating expert teaches Y

SWIPE RIGHT!

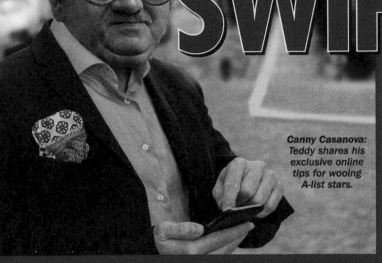

Canny Casanova: Teddy shares his exclusive online tips for wooing A-list stars.

ASK MOST couples todays how they first met, and they will no longer tell you "at work," "through friends," or "at the discotheque." They'll simply answer with one word: *"online."*

Just a decade ago, Internet dating was the domain of only the most pathetic and miserable members of the human species. But here in 2021, every self-respecting singleton is a confirmed user of one of the hundreds of dating 'apps' out there - Tinder, Hinge, Bumble, OKCupid and UniformDating.com. Just ask TEDDY FISHPASTE.

For the past nine years, the self-styled Don Juan of Ashington has been active on a whopping **FORTY-TWO** different dating applications and websites. And in that time he has personally connected with literally **HALF-DOZENS** of women. But ask the jobless lothario exactly how many lusty trysts he's enjoyed as a result of these digital dalliances, and he remains tight-lipped. "I don't kiss and tell," coos the Pegswood-based bachelor, with a wink.

However, when we pressed him for an actual, concrete figure - making it clear that this article would not go ahead unless he provided one - Teddy was more forthcoming. "Technically, I haven't got as far as a first date yet," he confirmed.

"But that's only because I like to keep my options open and play the field. I'm single - and I'm looking to mingle!" the involuntarily celibate Casanova quipped.

For a bit of hypothetical fun, we asked Teddy to talk us through how he might woo five top A-List stars this Valentine's Day. From how to select the right dating app and profile photo, through to what gift to bring the lucky lady, and where to wine and dine her, medically obese Teddy was only too happy to share his wealth of amorous experience. "If you want your favourite celeb to 'swipe right' on you this February 14th, then simply follow my step-by-step guide to erotic success," chuckles the 64-year-old probable virgin.

DATE 1: *VICTORIA COREN-MITCHELL*

TEDDY SAYS: "Step one with online dating is to consider which 'app' is best suited to the kind of woman you'd like to meet. Coren-Mitchell is a renowned brainbox, having studied at Oxford University and presented high-brow shows like *Only Connect* and *Have I Got News For You*. As such, I reckon the best place to hypothetically hook up with her would be a smug, liberal, elitist site such as *Guardian Soulmates*.

In the online dating game, first impressions are everything - so it's vital to get your profile picture just right. In order to catch Coren-Mitchell's eye among hundreds of other suitors, I would stage a selfie that made me appear suitably bookish and clever - perhaps wearing thick, Coke-bottle specs and perusing an intellectual tome like *A Brief History of Time* by Stephen Hawkings, *Crime and Punishment* by Dostoyevsky or *You Couldn't Make It Up* by Richard Littlejohn.

Once Coren-Mitchell had swiped right on my nerdy profile pic, it would be time to drop her a message. The sultry presenter is married to panel show funnyman David Mitchell, so a good sense of humour is clearly important to her. With that in mind, I would fire off a few devastatingly witty ripostes, such as: 'Hi Victoria, I hope we can *Only Connect* soon!' with a winking emoji underneath. Or perhaps 'Hi Victoria... *Have I Got Dick Pics For You!*' below a cheeky, unsolicited snap of my penis.

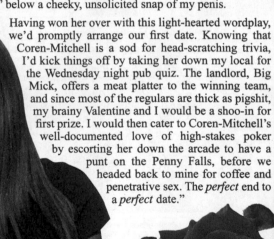

Having won her over with this light-hearted wordplay, we'd promptly arrange our first date. Knowing that Coren-Mitchell is a sod for head-scratching trivia, I'd kick things off by taking her down my local for the Wednesday night pub quiz. The landlord, Big Mick, offers a meat platter to the winning team, and since most of the regulars are thick as pigshit, my brainy Valentine and I would be a shoo-in for first prize. I would then cater to Coren-Mitchell's well-documented love of high-stakes poker by escorting her down the arcade to have a punt on the Penny Falls, before we headed back to mine for coffee and penetrative sex. The *perfect* end to a *perfect* date."

DATE 2: *KIM KARDASHIAN*

TEDDY SAYS: "Busty reality star Kim is every red-blooded male's dream woman. What's more, if rumours of her split from hip-hop hubby Kanye West are to be believed, she's also newly single. So she'll almost certainly be scouring the dating apps this year for a bit of no-strings Valentine's fun.

Knowing that Kim is a busy woman, with several multi-million dollar businesses to run, I wouldn't waste her time with small talk. I'd simply send her a direct message saying 'Fancy a drink on February 14th?' alongside a carefully chosen - and tastefully lit - dick pic.

Dick pics are a fantastic way to break the ice on a dating app: a charmingly cheeky gesture that women simply cannot resist. I've sent literally thousands of them over the years, and I've never once failed to get a message back. Granted, most of them say stuff like, 'Hang on, let me get my microscope,' 'Are you Mark Francois MP?' or 'You have been blocked from contacting this user.' But they still count as interactions.

So, once I'd shot Kim a few choice pics of my chopper, it'd be time to fly her over to Pegswood for our first date. As a top A-Lister, Kim is used to stepping out at glitzy events such as the launch of a new designer perfume, or the opening of a Hollywood blockbuster. So I would make sure to lay out the metaphorical red carpet for our Valentine's soiree. For an Ashington-style 'perfume launch,' we'd head to the car park of The Dog & Switchblade, where a friend of mine sells knock-off bottles of Chanel No. 5 from the boot of his Mazda.

Once we'd done the rounds there, and Kim had got a few pics for her Instagram, I would whisk her straight off to a swanky 'film premiere' - i.e. the unveiling of my mate Dave and his wife Sheila's latest home-made scud flick, *Dave and Sheila Shagging 4*. After hobnobbing with the film's stars (Dave and Sheila), we'd cap the evening off with a romantic moonlit knee-trembler on the beach at Newbiggin, before it was time for Kim to catch her flight back to Beverly Hills. The *perfect* end to a *perfect* date."

how to woo the stars this Valentine's Day

DATE 3: GILLIAN ANDERSON

TEDDY SAYS: "Foxy Gillian has been raising male pulses since the nineties, when she sashayed onto our screens as Agent Dana Scully in *The X-Files*. But as one of the most in-demand stars in Hollywood, attracting her attention on Tinder would require hard work - and serious research.

A quick squiz at Anderson's Wikipedia page tells me that she does a fair bit of charity work for animal rights and environmental organisations. To show that I, too, care deeply about all creatures great and small, I would post a profile pic of myself alongside my beloved Bullmastiff, Rocky, making sure to angle the camera away from his missing eye and ear which he lost in a car park dog fight I entered him in last month. To demonstrate my love of the great outdoors, I would also include a photo of myself on one of my many late-night rambles through some local woodlands, making sure to digitally remove the steamed-up Vauxhall Astra I am peering into.

Once Gillian had swiped right - and I'd broken the ice with a few dozen dick pics - I would suggest we met up in the flesh. As a hugely recognisable celebrity, Anderson would probably not want to spend Valentine's Day getting pestered for autographs in the streets of Ashington, so I would propose a quiet, romantic night in. I'd bring round a few tins and a Fray Bentos chicken'n'bacon pie, and then, with a cheeky wink, I'd suggest that we raid Gillian's extensive costume cupboard for some saucy 'cosplay' action.

To kick things off, we'd act out *The X-Files*, with me playing Mulder to her Scully, before moving on to some kinky role play from *The Fall* - Gillian as steely DS Gibson, grilling me as I portrayed Jamie Dornan's hunky serial killer. Finally, Gillian would don her 'Iron Lady' bouffant wig and powder blue trouser suit from *The Crown*, and I would enjoy penetrative intercourse with her whilst dressed as Denis Thatcher. The *perfect* end to a *perfect* date."

DATE 4: PIPPA MIDDLETON

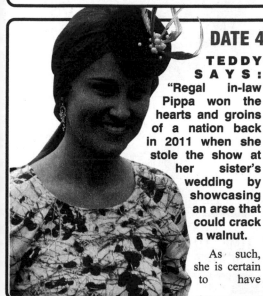

TEDDY SAYS: "Regal in-law Pippa won the hearts and groins of a nation back in 2011 when she stole the show at her sister's wedding by showcasing an arse that could crack a walnut.

As such, she is certain to have her fair share of hypothetical online wooers, all clamouring frantically for her attention. I would distinguish myself from the pack by tweaking my dating app profile to subtly mirror Pippa's interests. Since she is a keen swimmer and runner, I would list my hobbies as 'swimming and running'. Since she has had two long-term relationships with hedge fund managers, I would list my profession as 'hedge fund manager.' And since she resides on a 10,000 acre estate near Loch Ness, I would show my deep love for Scotland by donning a bright orange wig and 'See You Jimmy' hat in my photo.

Her attention grabbed, the firm-buttocked nearly-royal would swipe right and demand to meet me in person. Having popped over a WeTransfer link to my latest batch of dick pics, I'd suggest a romantic February 14th rendezvous, and Pippa would be quick to accept.

However, as the acclaimed author of a bestselling book about party planning, Ms Middleton would definitely not be impressed by your bog-standard dinner-and-a-movie-style date. I would be forced to think well outside the amorous box in order to impress her, and I would do this by suggesting we try the quirky new romance trend of 'Alphabet Dating'!

This unique concept involves proposing various zany date ideas, each beginning with a different letter of the alphabet. So, for instance, I'd start by whisking Pippa off to an aquarium, ant farm or abattoir, before heading to a bookies, burlesque show or bowling alley, and so on. Pippa would be stirred into a lustful frenzy by this charming and original Valentine's itinerary - so much so that it would probably strike 'Knee Trembler O'Clock' before we even made it to the carvery, campsite or crematorium! The *perfect* end to a *perfect* date."

DATE 5: IVANKA TRUMP

TEDDY SAYS: "She's best known as the daughter of former US President Donald Trump, but sultry Ivanka is a highly successful entrepreneuse in her own right. Stepping out of her father's shadow, she has forged an impressive career in her own right as Executive Vice President of the Trump Organization, co-star of Donald Trump's *The Apprentice*, and presidential adviser to Donald Trump. It's safe to assume, then, that the non-nepotist beauty puts business firmly before pleasure and as such, I would make my first contact with her not via a dating app, but on the employment-oriented social media hub 'LinkedIn.'

Fabricating an impressive online work history - including 'Chief Executive of Google,' 'CFO of Facebook' and 'Founder of the Trump Organization', I would contact Ivanka to see if she wanted to 'touch base' for a 'market-focused networking ideas interface' at The Dog & Switchblade on Valentine's Day. Wowed by my fictional CV and grasp of business jargon, not to mention a 6GB zip-file of dick pics, the svelte impresario would be quick to accept.

I've heard it said that a first date is a lot like a job interview (although, having no experience of either, I can't be 100% sure if this is true). At any rate, I would treat my February 14th rendezvous with Ivanka very much as if it was a high-stakes audition for her approval. I would dress in my smartest attire - the petrol green TX Maxx suit I wear for court appearances - and upon greeting the sexy exec, I would offer a firm handshake and maintain eye contact at all times, even when she went to the toilet.

Since Ivanka's business brain is hard-wired to the boardroom environment, she would no doubt ply me with tough, *Apprentice*-style questions throughout the date, and I would give as good as I got. In response to 'What are your strengths and weaknesses?' I would tell her my strengths were 'PowerPoint presentations and sex', and my weaknesses were 'beautiful women'. And when she asked 'Where do you see yourself in five years?' I'd shoot her a cheeky wink and whisper: 'In your bed, Ms Trump...'

By the time we'd polished off Big Mick's Valentine's Meal Deal (trout tikka masala and chips, plus a half-bottle of finest Libyan Merlot), the busty billionairess would be putty in my hands, and after splitting the bill, we'd sneak straight out to the car park hand-in-hand to enjoy penetrative intercourse behind the bins. The *perfect* end to a *perfect* date."

NEXT WEEK: *"The Perfect End To A Perfect Steak & Blowjob Day": Teddy offers his tips on how to woo five more sexy A-List stars on March 14th'*

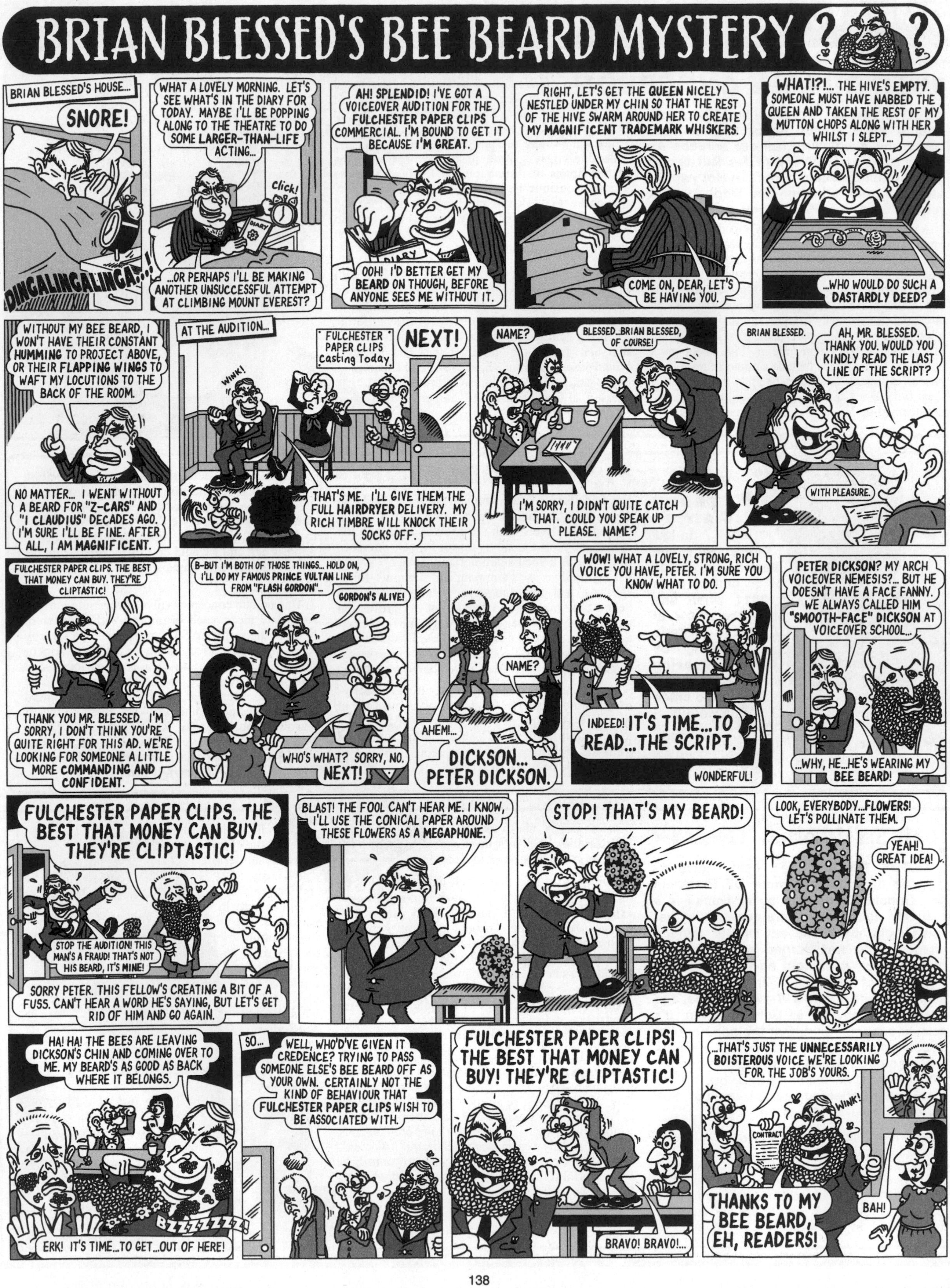
BRIAN BLESSED'S BEE BEARD MYSTERY
BRIAN BLESSED'S HOUSE...
SNORE!
DINGALINGALINGA...!
WHAT A LOVELY MORNING. LET'S SEE WHAT'S IN THE DIARY FOR TODAY. MAYBE I'LL BE POPPING ALONG TO THE THEATRE TO DO SOME LARGER-THAN-LIFE ACTING...
Click!
DIARY
...OR PERHAPS I'LL BE MAKING ANOTHER UNSUCCESSFUL ATTEMPT AT CLIMBING MOUNT EVEREST?
AH! SPLENDID! I'VE GOT A VOICEOVER AUDITION FOR THE FULCHESTER PAPER CLIPS COMMERCIAL. I'M BOUND TO GET IT BECAUSE I'M GREAT.
OOH! I'D BETTER GET MY BEARD ON THOUGH, BEFORE ANYONE SEES ME WITHOUT IT.
RIGHT, LET'S GET THE QUEEN NICELY NESTLED UNDER MY CHIN SO THAT THE REST OF THE HIVE SWARM AROUND HER TO CREATE MY MAGNIFICENT TRADEMARK WHISKERS.
COME ON, DEAR, LET'S BE HAVING YOU.
WHAT!?!... THE HIVE'S EMPTY. SOMEONE MUST HAVE NABBED THE QUEEN AND TAKEN THE REST OF MY MUTTON CHOPS ALONG WITH HER WHILST I SLEPT...
...WHO WOULD DO SUCH A DASTARDLY DEED?
WITHOUT MY BEE BEARD, I WON'T HAVE THEIR CONSTANT HUMMING TO PROJECT ABOVE, OR THEIR FLAPPING WINGS TO WAFT MY LOCUTIONS TO THE BACK OF THE ROOM.
NO MATTER... I WENT WITHOUT A BEARD FOR "Z-CARS" AND "I CLAUDIUS" DECADES AGO. I'M SURE I'LL BE FINE. AFTER ALL, I AM MAGNIFICENT.
AT THE AUDITION...
FULCHESTER PAPER CLIPS Casting Today
NEXT!
WINK!
THAT'S ME. I'LL GIVE THEM THE FULL HAIRDRYER DELIVERY. MY RICH TIMBRE WILL KNOCK THEIR SOCKS OFF.
NAME?
BLESSED...BRIAN BLESSED, OF COURSE!
I'M SORRY, I DIDN'T QUITE CATCH THAT. COULD YOU SPEAK UP PLEASE. NAME?
BRIAN BLESSED.
AH, MR. BLESSED. THANK YOU. WOULD YOU KINDLY READ THE LAST LINE OF THE SCRIPT?
WITH PLEASURE.
FULCHESTER PAPER CLIPS. THE BEST THAT MONEY CAN BUY. THEY'RE CLIPTASTIC!
THANK YOU MR. BLESSED. I'M SORRY, I DON'T THINK YOU'RE QUITE RIGHT FOR THIS AD. WE'RE LOOKING FOR SOMEONE A LITTLE MORE COMMANDING AND CONFIDENT.
B-BUT I'M BOTH OF THOSE THINGS... HOLD ON, I'LL DO MY FAMOUS PRINCE VULTAN LINE FROM "FLASH GORDON"...
GORDON'S ALIVE!
WHO'S WHAT? SORRY, NO. NEXT!
NAME?
AHEM!...
DICKSON... PETER DICKSON.
WOW! WHAT A LOVELY, STRONG, RICH VOICE YOU HAVE, PETER. I'M SURE YOU KNOW WHAT TO DO.
INDEED! IT'S TIME...TO READ...THE SCRIPT.
WONDERFUL!
PETER DICKSON? MY ARCH VOICEOVER NEMESIS?... BUT HE DOESN'T HAVE A FACE FANNY. WE ALWAYS CALLED HIM "SMOOTH-FACE" DICKSON AT VOICEOVER SCHOOL...
...WHY, HE...HE'S WEARING MY BEE BEARD!
FULCHESTER PAPER CLIPS. THE BEST THAT MONEY CAN BUY. THEY'RE CLIPTASTIC!
STOP THE AUDITION! THIS MAN'S A FRAUD! THAT'S NOT HIS BEARD, IT'S MINE!
SORRY PETER. THIS FELLOW'S CREATING A BIT OF A FUSS. CAN'T HEAR A WORD HE'S SAYING, BUT LET'S GET RID OF HIM AND GO AGAIN.
BLAST! THE FOOL CAN'T HEAR ME. I KNOW, I'LL USE THE CONICAL PAPER AROUND THESE FLOWERS AS A MEGAPHONE.
STOP! THAT'S MY BEARD!
LOOK, EVERYBODY...FLOWERS! LET'S POLLINATE THEM.
YEAH! GREAT IDEA!
HA! HA! THE BEES ARE LEAVING DICKSON'S CHIN AND COMING OVER TO ME. MY BEARD'S AS GOOD AS BACK WHERE IT BELONGS.
BZZZZZZZZ!
ERK! IT'S TIME...TO GET...OUT OF HERE!
SO...
WELL, WHO'D'VE GIVEN IT CREDENCE? TRYING TO PASS SOMEONE ELSE'S BEE BEARD OFF AS YOUR OWN. CERTAINLY NOT THE KIND OF BEHAVIOUR THAT FULCHESTER PAPER CLIPS WISH TO BE ASSOCIATED WITH.
FULCHESTER PAPER CLIPS! THE BEST THAT MONEY CAN BUY! THEY'RE CLIPTASTIC!
BRAVO! BRAVO!...
...THAT'S JUST THE UNNECESSARILY BOISTEROUS VOICE WE'RE LOOKING FOR. THE JOB'S YOURS.
CONTRACT
WINK!
THANKS TO MY BEE BEARD, EH, READERS!
BAH!

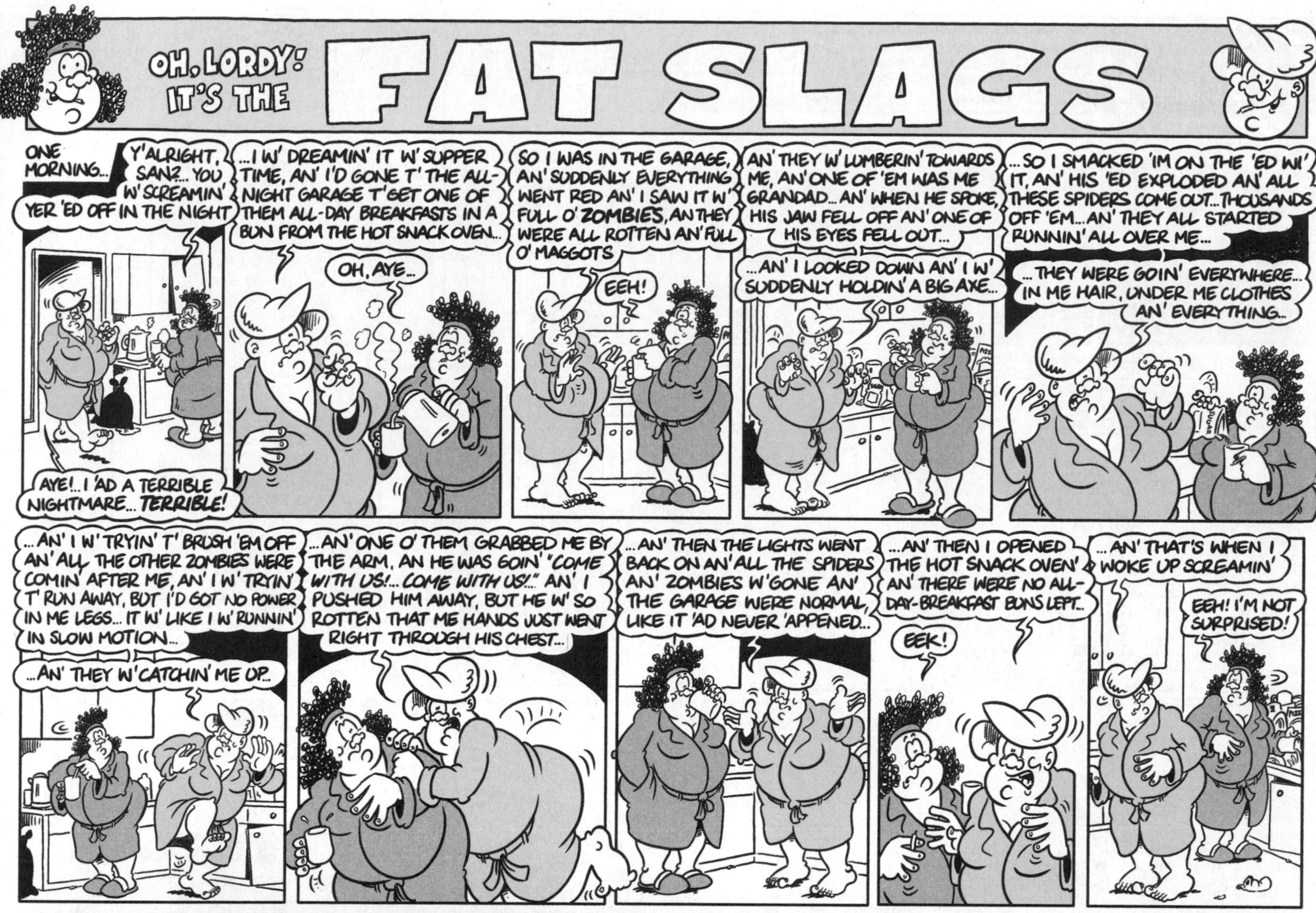
OH, LORDY! IT'S THE
FAT SLAGS
ONE MORNING...
Y'ALRIGHT, SANZ... YOU W' SCREAMIN' YER 'ED OFF IN THE NIGHT
AYE!.. I 'AD A TERRIBLE NIGHTMARE... TERRIBLE!
...I W' DREAMIN' IT W' SUPPER TIME, AN' I'D GONE T' THE ALL-NIGHT GARAGE T' GET ONE OF THEM ALL-DAY BREAKFASTS IN A BUN FROM THE HOT SNACK OVEN...
OH, AYE..
SO I WAS IN THE GARAGE, AN' SUDDENLY EVERYTHING WENT RED AN' I SAW IT W' FULL O' ZOMBIES, AN THEY WERE ALL ROTTEN AN' FULL O' MAGGOTS
EEH!
AN' THEY W' LUMBERIN' TOWARDS ME, AN' ONE OF 'EM WAS ME GRANDAD... AN' WHEN HE SPOKE, HIS JAW FELL OFF AN' ONE OF HIS EYES FELL OUT...
...AN' I LOOKED DOWN AN' I W' SUDDENLY HOLDIN' A BIG AXE...
...SO I SMACKED 'IM ON THE 'ED WI' IT, AN' HIS 'ED EXPLODED AN' ALL THESE SPIDERS COME OUT... THOUSANDS OFF 'EM... AN' THEY ALL STARTED RUNNIN' ALL OVER ME...
...THEY WERE GOIN' EVERYWHERE... IN ME HAIR, UNDER ME CLOTHES AN' EVERYTHING..
...AN' I W' TRYIN' T' BRUSH 'EM OFF AN' ALL THE OTHER ZOMBIES WERE COMIN' AFTER ME, AN' I W' TRYIN' T' RUN AWAY, BUT I'D GOT NO POWER IN ME LEGS... IT W' LIKE I W' RUNNIN' IN SLOW MOTION...
...AN' THEY W' CATCHIN' ME UP...
...AN' ONE O' THEM GRABBED ME BY THE ARM, AN HE WAS GOIN' "COME WITH US!... COME WITH US!" AN' I PUSHED HIM AWAY, BUT HE W' SO ROTTEN THAT ME HANDS JUST WENT RIGHT THROUGH HIS CHEST...
...AN' THEN THE LIGHTS WENT BACK ON AN' ALL THE SPIDERS AN' ZOMBIES W' GONE AN' THE GARAGE WERE NORMAL, LIKE IT 'AD NEVER 'APPENED...
...AN' THEN I OPENED THE HOT SNACK OVEN' AN' THERE WERE NO ALL-DAY-BREAKFAST BUNS LEFT..
EEK!
...AN' THAT'S WHEN I WOKE UP SCREAMIN'
EEH! I'M NOT SURPRISED!

Len's Jackpot Find as Easy as ABC!

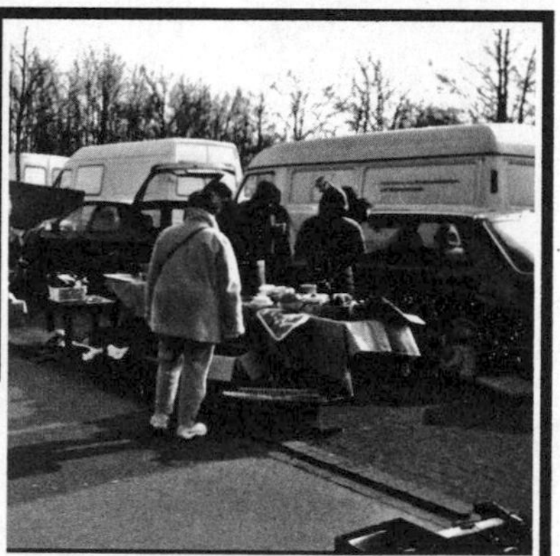

Bootiful: Boot sale (right) not wholey dissimilar to one that turned up Len's treasure

Car Boot sale gives up rare Pop collectible

A CAR BOOT sale punter in Goole got a pleasant surprise last weekend when a £2 impulse buy turned out to be the bloke out of ABC.

Len Barrow, a centre lathe turner, had gone to the car boot sale in Aldi's car park to look for a pair of garden shears, never intending to buy a frontman from an 80s new romantic group.

"I go to the boots most Sundays," said the retired gas fitter. "And I have to say, I've got an eye for a bargain."

dusty

Postman Len was rummaging through a box of souvenir eggcups, broken toys and Mantovani LPs' when he spotted what he thought was a dusty manequin propped up against one of the pasting tables.

"It looked pretty chipped and battered but I just had a funny feeling about it," he said.

"I'd already bought a box set of The Jewel In The Crown on VHS

EXCLUSIVE!

that set me back a fiver. So when the stallholder said he wanted three quid for the manequin, I had to think carefully."

william

Fortunately, binman Len managed to haggle the stallholder down to £2 as it was in a poor state, and he left the sale with his haul.

"I intended to clean it up as soon as I got home," he said. "But Dancing On Ice was just about to start, so I propped it up in the hall and left it."

damon

A series of jobs around the house, followed by a week in his sister's caravan meant that it was nearly a fortnight before shoe salesman Len got round to his task.

"As soon as the weather picked up, I took the 'shop dummy' in the yard and chucked a load of water from the washing up bowl over it," he said. "Then I started on the face with a rag made from an old pair of pants."

But as he worked, the bus driver got a surprise. "I was just scraping a stubborn bit of birdlime off the nose when it started singing The Look Of Love. I was flabbergasted," he said.

"I have to admit, I thought it was the lead singer of Heaven 17 at first, but I looked him up in a 1982 Smash Hits annual and saw it was definitely him out of ABC."

"I asked him to sing The Look Of Love again," said greengrocer Len. "But he started singing another one of his hits which I didn't recognise."

one tree

Pop swot Paul Morley described lab technician Len's find as remarkable. "In their day, ABC were massive, so two quid for the lead singer is a real bargain," he told us.

"Pop memorabilia is a particularly lucrative market at the moment, and the bloke out of ABC would make a desirable addition to any eighties obsessive's collection."

But Len has his own plans for his once-in-a-lifetime find: "When I've finished cleaning him up, I'm going to take him to a specialist auction," he said. "With all the work I've done, I reckon I could get as much as ten quid for him. Seven or eight, easy."

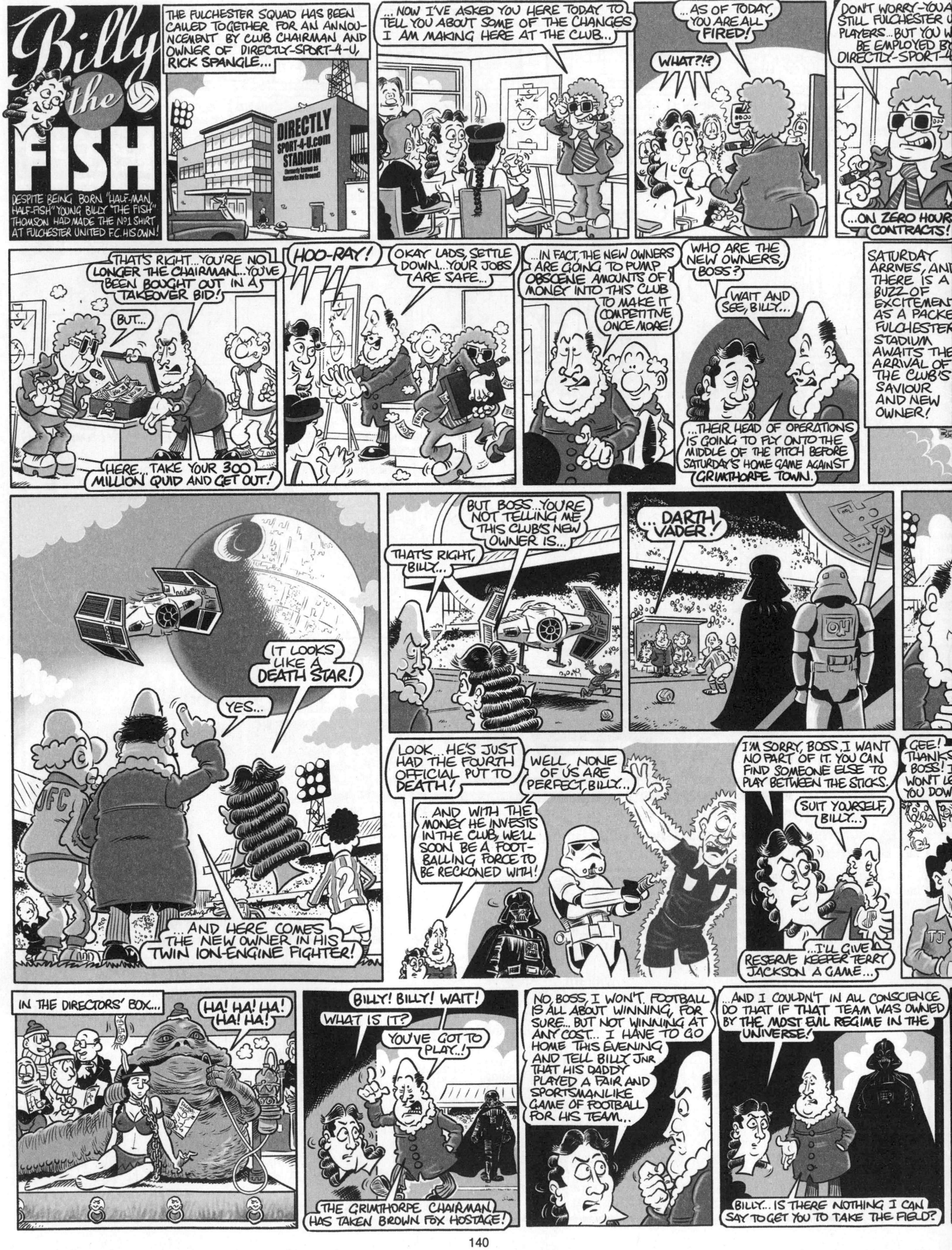
Billy the FISH
DESPITE BEING BORN "HALF-MAN, HALF-FISH" YOUNG BILLY "THE FISH" THOMSON HAD MADE THE No1 SHIRT AT FULCHESTER UNITED F.C. HIS OWN!
THE FULCHESTER SQUAD HAS BEEN CALLED TOGETHER FOR AN ANNOUNCEMENT BY CLUB CHAIRMAN AND OWNER OF DIRECTLY-SPORT-4-U, RICK SPANGLE...
DIRECTLY SPORT-4-U.com STADIUM
...NOW I'VE ASKED YOU HERE TODAY TO TELL YOU ABOUT SOME OF THE CHANGES I AM MAKING HERE AT THE CLUB...
...AS OF TODAY, YOU ARE ALL FIRED!
WHAT?!?
DON'T WORRY-YOU A STILL FULCHESTER U PLAYERS...BUT YOU W BE EMPLOYED BY DIRECTLY-SPORT-4
...ON ZERO HOUR CONTRACTS!
THAT'S RIGHT...YOU'RE NO LONGER THE CHAIRMAN...YOU'VE BEEN BOUGHT OUT IN A TAKEOVER BID!
BUT...
HERE...TAKE YOUR 300 MILLION QUID AND GET OUT!
HOO-RAY!
OKAY LADS, SETTLE DOWN...YOUR JOBS ARE SAFE...
...IN FACT, THE NEW OWNERS ARE GOING TO PUMP OBSCENE AMOUNTS OF MONEY INTO THIS CLUB TO MAKE IT COMPETITIVE ONCE MORE!
WHO ARE THE NEW OWNERS, BOSS?
WAIT AND SEE, BILLY...
...THEIR HEAD OF OPERATIONS IS GOING TO FLY ONTO THE MIDDLE OF THE PITCH BEFORE SATURDAY'S HOME GAME AGAINST GRIMTHORPE TOWN.
SATURDAY ARRIVES, AND THERE IS A BUZZ OF EXCITEMENT AS A PACKE FULCHESTER STADIUM AWAITS THE ARRIVAL OF THE CLUB'S SAVIOUR AND NEW OWNER!
IT LOOKS LIKE A DEATH STAR!
YES...
...AND HERE COMES THE NEW OWNER IN HIS TWIN ION-ENGINE FIGHTER!
BUT BOSS...YOU'RE NOT TELLING ME THIS CLUB'S NEW OWNER IS...
THAT'S RIGHT, BILLY...
...DARTH VADER!
LOOK...HE'S JUST HAD THE FOURTH OFFICIAL PUT TO DEATH!
WELL, NONE OF US ARE PERFECT, BILLY...
...AND WITH THE MONEY HE INVESTS IN THE CLUB, WE'LL SOON BE A FOOTBALLING FORCE TO BE RECKONED WITH!
I'M SORRY, BOSS, I WANT NO PART OF IT. YOU CAN FIND SOMEONE ELSE TO PLAY BETWEEN THE STICKS.
SUIT YOURSELF, BILLY...
...I'LL GIVE RESERVE KEEPER TERRY JACKSON A GAME...
GEE! THANKS BOSS! I WON'T LE YOU DOW
IN THE DIRECTORS' BOX...
HA! HA! HA! HA! HA!
BILLY! BILLY! WAIT!
WHAT IS IT?
YOU'VE GOT TO PLAY..!
THE GRIMTHORPE CHAIRMAN HAS TAKEN BROWN FOX HOSTAGE!
NO, BOSS, I WON'T. FOOTBALL IS ALL ABOUT WINNING, FOR SURE...BUT NOT WINNING AT ANY COST... I HAVE TO GO HOME THIS EVENING AND TELL BILLY JNR THAT HIS DADDY PLAYED A FAIR AND SPORTSMANLIKE GAME OF FOOTBALL FOR HIS TEAM...
...AND I COULDN'T IN ALL CONSCIENCE DO THAT IF THAT TEAM WAS OWNED BY THE MOST EVIL REGIME IN THE UNIVERSE!
BILLY...IS THERE NOTHING I CAN SAY TO GET YOU TO TAKE THE FIELD?

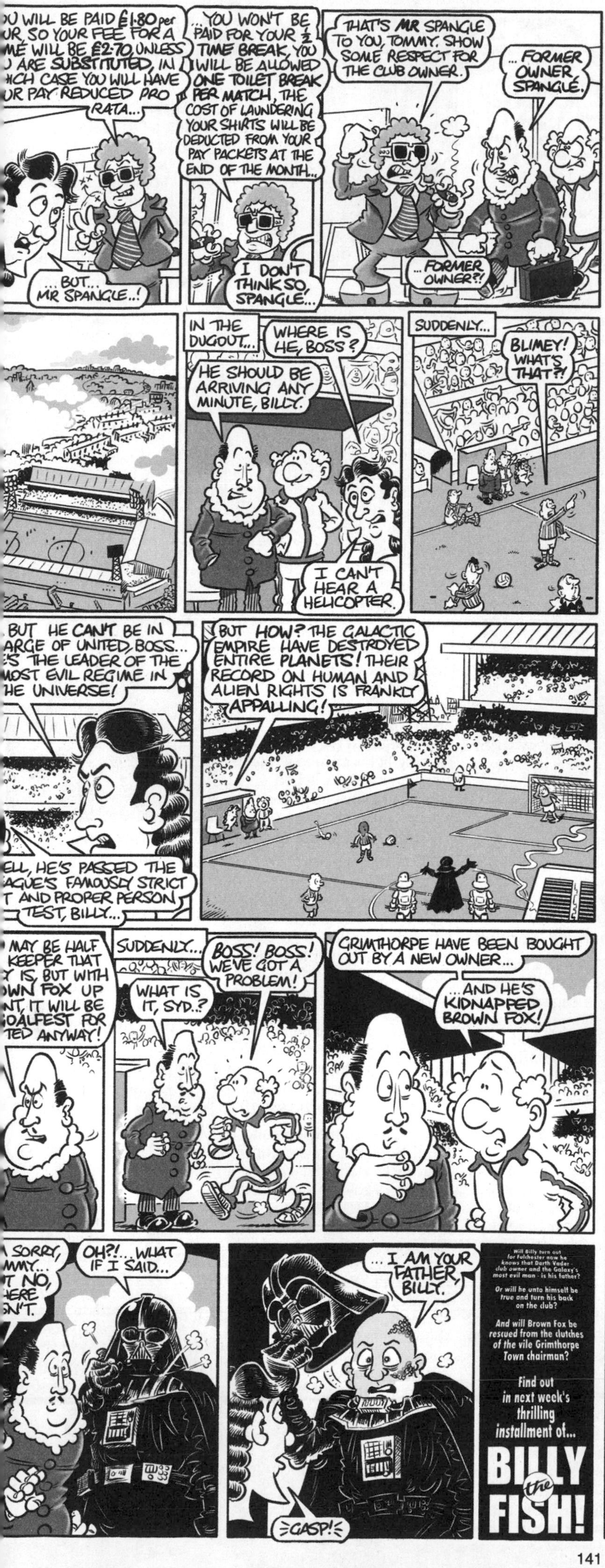
U WILL BE PAID £1.80 per UR, SO YOUR FEE FOR A ME WILL BE £2.70, UNLESS U ARE SUBSTITUTED, IN ICH CASE YOU WILL HAVE UR PAY REDUCED PRO RATA…
BUT… MR SPANGLE..!
…YOU WON'T BE PAID FOR YOUR ½ TIME BREAK, YOU WILL BE ALLOWED ONE TOILET BREAK PER MATCH, THE COST OF LAUNDERING YOUR SHIRTS WILL BE DEDUCTED FROM YOUR PAY PACKETS AT THE END OF THE MONTH…
I DON'T THINK SO, SPANGLE…
THAT'S MR SPANGLE TO YOU, TOMMY. SHOW SOME RESPECT FOR THE CLUB OWNER.
…FORMER OWNER SPANGLE.
…FORMER OWNER?!
IN THE DUGOUT…
WHERE IS HE, BOSS?
HE SHOULD BE ARRIVING ANY MINUTE, BILLY.
I CAN'T HEAR A HELICOPTER.
SUDDENLY…
BLIMEY! WHAT'S THAT?!
BUT HE CAN'T BE IN ARGE OF UNITED, BOSS… 'S THE LEADER OF THE MOST EVIL REGIME IN HE UNIVERSE!
ELL, HE'S PASSED THE AGUE'S FAMOUSLY STRICT T AND PROPER PERSON TEST, BILLY…
BUT HOW? THE GALACTIC EMPIRE HAVE DESTROYED ENTIRE PLANETS! THEIR RECORD ON HUMAN AND ALIEN RIGHTS IS FRANKLY APPALLING!
MAY BE HALF KEEPER THAT Y IS, BUT WITH OWN FOX UP NT, IT WILL BE OALFEST FOR TED ANYWAY!
SUDDENLY…
BOSS! BOSS! WE'VE GOT A PROBLEM!
WHAT IS IT, SYD..?
GRIMTHORPE HAVE BEEN BOUGHT OUT BY A NEW OWNER…
…AND HE'S KIDNAPPED BROWN FOX!
SORRY, MMY… T NO, HERE N'T.
OH?!…WHAT IF I SAID…
…I AM YOUR FATHER, BILLY.
GASP!
Will Billy turn out for Fulchester now he knows that Darth Vader - club owner and the Galaxy's most evil man - is his father?
Or will he unto himself be true and turn his back on the club?
And will Brown Fox be rescued from the clutches of the vile Grimthorpe Town chairman?
Find out in next week's thrilling installment of…
BILLY the FISH!

TRAFALGAR TREE DISASTER

LONDONERS were appalled this morning to discover that instead of their usual gift of a giant Christmas tree, the people of Norway had given Britain's capital city a SELECTION BOX.

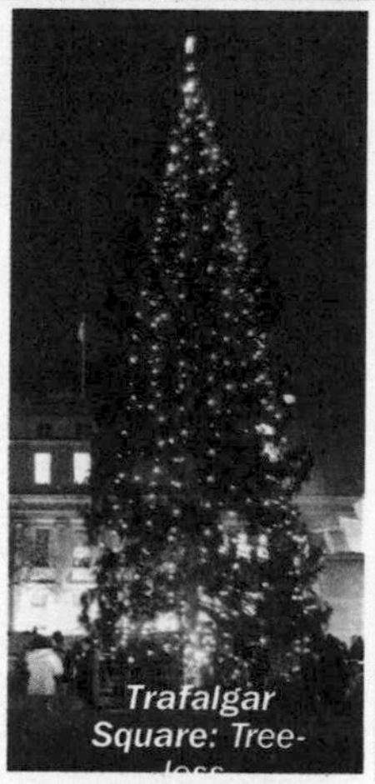
Trafalgar Square: Tree-

The Scandinavian nation has, for the past 74 years, supplied a mighty 20 metre fir tree to stand in Trafalgar Square, as a gesture of thanks for the UK's assistance during World War II.

However, this year the evergreen giant has been replaced by a £2.99 Cadbury's chocolate selection box.

"We're trying to make the best of it," said London's Mayor, Sadiq Khan. "But we're all really, really disappointed."

giant

"When the police told me a selection box had appeared in place of the usual tree, I thought they meant a giant one, which would have been something," he said. "But it's just a normal-sized selection box."

And talking to reporters, Khan found it hard to conceal his disappointment. "It's not even the *good* selection box, the one with Dairy Milk *and* Dairy Milk Caramel. And a Picnic," he said. "It's the one down from that, with stuff like a Fudge and a Chomp. It's hard not to take it as an insult, to be honest."

Speaking from his embassy in Belgrave Square, Norwegian Ambassador to the UK Per Egil Silvaag, told reporters that he was extremely sorry, but said that it had been a difficult and busy year.

"We meant to get round to it but things caught up with us and, before you know it, it's Christmas Eve," he said. "So I nipped to an all night garage in the New Kent Road and got a selection box."

And in Westminster, the government was playing down the affair in an attempt to prevent a diplomatic incident from developing.

needleina

"Everyone loves chocolate, and it makes a nice surprise not to get another boring old tree from our friends in Norway like every year," the Prime Minister told the house to cries of "Here! Here!" from his backbenchers.

Old-Age Pensioners - Welcome to

NEWTON HOUSE

The world's only Gravity-Free Retirement Home

All over the earth, pensioners are subject to the force of gravity, pulling them towards the centre of the earth. Well… not exactly everywhere! The residents of Newton House Retirement Home enjoy the benefits of WEIGHTLESSNESS 24 hours a day. And YOU can join them.

Newton House caters for 100 elderly residents in a cheerful, gravity-free setting. Guests can float around the day lounge, library or gardens without the worry of falling and breaking a hip. That's the peace of mind that living outside a gravitational field can give.

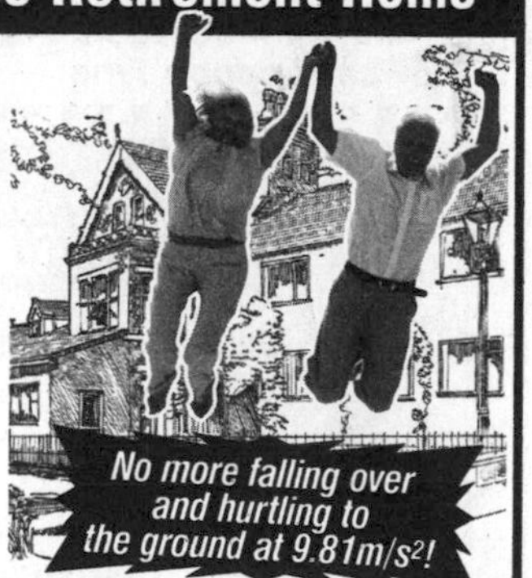
No more falling over and hurtling to the ground at 9.81m/s²!

How is Newton House Gravity Free?
We DON'T KNOW!… *IT JUST IS!*

Scientists are unable to explain why Newton House is not subject to the same laws of physics as every other retirement home in the world. But it is, *and that's that!*

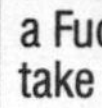
"I fell down the stairs last year. At any other retirement home this would probably have been curtains for me, but at Newton House I simply floated harmlessly to the bottom."
Ada Tizzard, 98

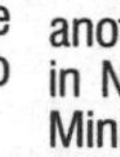
"Life at Newton House is wonderful. The only downside was that the pieces of my jigsaw puzzles kept floating away, but I got round that by sticking velcro onto the back of them."
Mable Syrup, 97

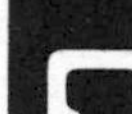
"I weighed 30 stone before I moved into Newton House and my knees were playing me up no end. Now I tip the scales at 0st 0lb and my joints have never felt better."
Ted Snurgle, 89

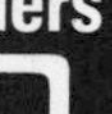
"It's out of this fucking world!"
Cmdr. Chris Hadfield

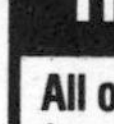
"I couldn't get up my stairs at home without a stairlift. At Newton House, I just lean forwards at 45°, give a little push and fly effortlessly to the top."
Edna Portcullis, 102

01-811-8055

Call now for a brochure or to arrange a visit. Please be aware that you may suffer dizziness, headaches and sickness until you become accustomed to the lack of gravitational pull.

LetteRbOCCks

Viz Comic, P.O. Box 841 Whitley Bay, NE26 9EQ : letters@viz.co.uk

STAR LETTER

I ALWAYS get actors Derek Jacobi and Bernard Cribbins mixed up, so I use their initials to remember them as a Disc Jockey and a Bin Collector respectively. This system worked fine until my wife pointed out that neither of them had played characters with those jobs in any films or TV shows, and now I'm more confused than I was before.

Derek Ballesteros, Meols

COULD the IT technicians at Adobe please remove the window that keeps popping up saying "InDesign unexpectedly quit"? I know it's fucking quit because everything disappears off my screen and I have to start it up again. And it happens so often, it's not actually that unexpected.

Hector Plantpots, Goole

AFTER I took a couple of Imodiums this morning, I read on the packet that they were about two years past their Use-by date. I wonder if any pharmacists amongst your readership could tell me whether I will shit myself faster or slower or not at all? *Andrew McGuigan, Newcastle upon Tyne*

I'M currently having a shit in the Yorkshire Wolds village of Fridaythorpe, but it's a Thursday! You couldn't make it up.

Jack, York

IF you ask me, Laurel and Hardy set a terrible example, what with their constant bickering and sudden outbursts of physical violence. No wonder knife crime is out of control.

TC Rusling, Cottingham

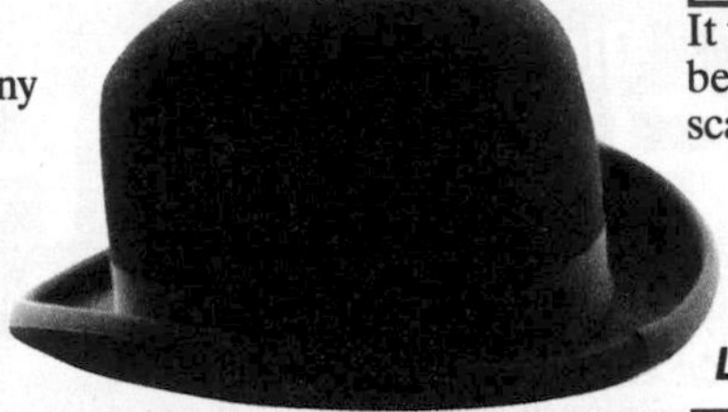

IF I were a spy captured by the Americans and they tried to break me by hanging me upside down in a shipping container and playing frenetic music like Norwegian black metal or hardcore Goa trance at a deafening volume for hours on end, I would be fine, as I am a fan of both Norwegian black metal and hardcore Goa trance. Better luck next time, CIA goons.

Double Oh Bawsack, Melbourne

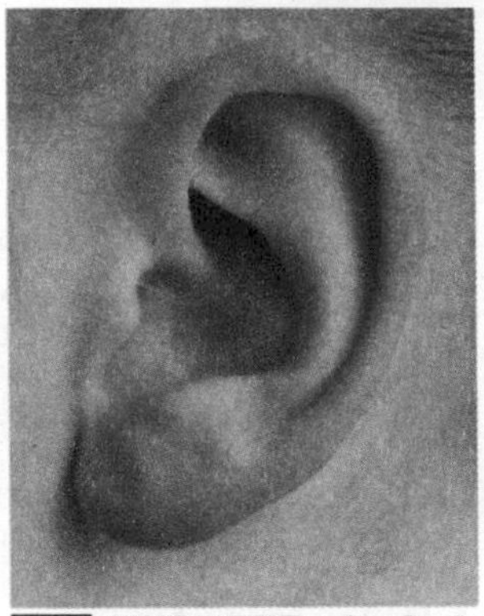

I WONDER why God only gave us two ears. It would have been a lot better if we had a few more scattered all over our bodies like a Dolby Surround Sound system. I bet he's probably kicking himself, but it's too late now.

Lenny Sherman, London

WHEN I was a kid, all our fruit and veg came in paper bags and we carried our shopping home in cardboard boxes, and the environmental boffins at the time all bellyached like fuck because we were killing all the trees. Then someone invented plastic and they seemed perfectly happy. Now they suddenly want all the plastic banned and a return to paper and cardboard. I'm beginning to think these twats don't know what the fuck they want. They can't just change the rules every 40-odd years and expect us all to fall for it.

Mark Brook, Paignton

WHAT is it with box sets recapping the story at the start of every episode? Nobody starts watching a series half way in, and if they do, that's their problem and they can fuck off.

Bjorn Scandinoir, Lund

BULLS are always keen to promote their image of being the macho tough guys of the farmyard. So I was astonished to come across one of these animals nibbling grass, buttercups and daisies, presumably thinking nobody was watching. It certainly reacted quite angrily to my jeering, and although I ultimately ended up having to run for my life, I think it's just proof of the embarrassment the bull felt for being so soft.

Phil Kitching, Isle of Jura

WITH the effects of transport on climate change, I'm at a loss to think why there's been no investment in teleporting. From what I've seen, all that's required is a chair with flashing lights around it and a few funny high pitched noises, and you can get to wherever you like instantly.

Harry Highpants, Luton

WHY on earth do American drill sergeants insist on telling their soldiers to march "left, left, left, right, left"? Surely having to do two little skips between steps puts them at a disadvantage against any enemy troops that use the more conventional marching tactic of following each left step with a right one.

Magnus Mbanu, Peterborough

I'M sure the pop band Boney M are counting their lucky stars that Tsar Nicholas's adviser was called Rasputin. Had he been called something else, like Igor, then his name would not have rhymed in the song. *Ra! Ra! Igor, Lover of the Russian Queen* doesn't scan and sounds ridiculous, and I suspect the song would not have gone on to become the hit it was.

Dr Jack Svenska, Bristol

142

TOP

TAKE a leaf out of criminals' books by replying "No comment" to all of your wife's questions about whether you've been sleeping with her sister.

Kevin Caswell-Jones, Wrexham

CYCLE lanes make ideal rush-hour waiting areas for works' vans that have to stop to pick up a colleague, or perhaps for the driver to nip to the shop to buy *The Daily Star* and a can of Monster energy drink.

Thomas ONeill, Glasgow

LIVEN up dull snooker matches by getting the referee to officiate in a

I WISH newspapers would stop referring to George Galloway as a 'maverick' or a 'firebrand.' He's just a bald twat in a hat. I'm sure the tabloids would happily print that, and the broadsheets could put an asterisk instead of the 'a' or something.

Brampton Crumpets, Derby

MY next door neighbour is called Pat and has a black and white cat. Unfortunately the similarities end there, as he works at the council and never seems to leave for work until after 9:00am. However, I did think the aforementioned facts were enough to scrape a letter together for *Viz*, so here you go. Do I win £5?

Willy Balls, Banbury

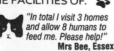

This cat is only fed by 4 homes... With YOUR help, he could eat at 5

Help cats live, eat and sleep in 3 or 4 houses without the different homeowners realising.

Join the Cats Over-Protection Society today. SIGN HERE ✿

Ms / Mrs / Miss / Rev _____
ADDRESS _____

POSTCODE _____

Just £100 could provide enough cat toys for 1 animal for a whole month.
I enclose cash / cheque for:
£100 £500 £1000 £10,000
and please debit my account the same amount every month.

☑ We are Britain's leading charity devoted to cosseting and the quite unnecessary fussing over of a popular pet that DOESN'T REALLY NEED YOUR HELP.

☑ Since our foundation we have helped to suitably house cats that have SEVERAL HOMES THAT THEY ALREADY TOTALLY ABUSE THE FACILITIES OF.

"In total I visit 3 homes and allow 8 humans to feed me. Please help!"
Mrs Bee, Essex

"Send money NOW! Dreamies don't grow on fucking trees, you stupid old pricks!"
Dig, Aberdeen

"Yes – carry on helping us – and fuck you very much you utter, utter twats"
Mr Whiskers, Herts

Cats Over-Protection Society

Overindulging the Feline Species Since 1870

Bernie Clifton-style ostrich costume. Every time a player takes too long on a shot, the ostrich can bite his bottom as he bends over the table.
J Sausages, Manchester

GENTLEMEN. Sick and tired of emptying the dishwasher? Simply rattle the cutlery basket and put it on again. Your wife will never know.
R Browntrousers, Bolton

TV ADVERTISERS. Slowed down, minor key piano renditions of well-known pop songs set to slow-motion footage of horses galloping along beaches does not invoke feelings of identity in as many viewers as you might like to think.
Dave, Guildford

MOTORISTS. Economically 'pimp your ride' by replacing the boring black dust caps on your tyre valves with white ones from used toothpaste tubes.
Viola Golfer, Wrexham

PUBLIC toilet roll dispenser makers. Do some calculations to ensure that the force needed to extract the bum roll from your wall mounted device is less than the tensile strength of the perforated paper within it.
Max Hold, Biggleswade

TIPS

toptips@ .uk

A POP-up advert on my computer for a Japanese kitchen knife claims it 'cuts everything like butter.' So margarine, soft cheese and lard won't be a problem, but what if I want to cut something harder like vegetables or meat? They really haven't thought it through.
James Tycroes, Tycroes

SIMULATION theory states that we are likely living in a computer simulation of reality. Well, whoever programmed me certainly put in a lot of wanking. If they are reading this, I'd just like to say thanks.
Pete Beat, Newcastle

I SEE that much-loved actor Ben Dover has been passed over again in the New Year's Honours list with not so much as a lowly MBE, even though his Member is something the British Empire should be rightly proud of. After decades of selfless service to adult entertainment, he deserves more respect.
NY London-Paris, Munich

WHILE I sympathise with Mr. London-Paris *(previous letter)* regarding Ben Dover fully deserving a public honour, I also fear that his investiture could cause untold embarrassment to His Majesty the King. What if Mr. Dover were to arrive wearing a top hat and his birthday suit rather than a morning suit? And what if he were to sport his trademark erection throughout the ceremony and then achieve a 'pop shot upon receiving his award? No thank-you. His Majesty deserves better than that.
P Muzik, Luton

IF Lionel Richie thinks Sunday mornings are easy, I wish he'd been round my house this morning when I woke up with a pounding headache and realised that I had shit the bed after a rake of ales the night before.
Grant B Warner, New Zealand

I ACCIDENTALLY boiled some soup the other day and as far as I can tell the flavour wasn't impaired. What other lies are the likes of Crosse and Blackwell telling us?
Eldon Furse, Leeds

OVER the years, computers have had parallel ports, USB ports, HDMI ports and too many other ports to remember. Yet we're still waiting for a computer to come with a fleshlight-style sex port on the side of it. Come on Apple, stop dicking around with USB-C and give the public what they really want.
Calvin Graham, Philly

ON page 121, Markington Scales complained that he'd never seen footage of a lion taking a shite. I can tell him that if he would like to perform a YouTube search for "lion taking a shite", he would be pleasantly surprised.
Alwyne Kennedy, email

WHY don't football linesmen have two flags each? That way, they could communicate with the referee and each other by semaphore, and it would save all the running over to confer with his linesman that the referee has to do.
TC Rusling, Cottingham

THE Australian flag includes a Union Jack in its design, and if Scotland leaves the UK, presumably St Andrew's Cross would disappear from our flag. That would leave us Aussies with only St George's Cross and the Cross of St Patrick in the top left hand corner, and from a design perspective, I don't think this would have sufficient weight visually. Sovereignty is an important principle, but so is design, and I would ask that all Scottish people consider our flag's composition before making any decisions about your nation's future.
Simon Sandall, Brisbane

I FIND it really embarrassing when people in films start to cry. The events they get so upset about aren't even real, so why they don't they act professionally and pull themselves together?
Forfar Five, East Fife

I RECENTLY received an email promoting a tablet which it claimed, could allow me to have harder erections. I don't wish to sound ungrateful, but I'd prefer it if they had a product that make erections easier rather than more difficult.
G Hasselback-Potatoes, Penryn

COULD I just warn your readers that when fashion-expert-turned-TV-chef Gok Wan says "use whichever mushrooms you can find," I think he means from a supermarket. I've been in the outside toilet for three days now, which, ironically, is where I found the toadstools I used.
Tom Flannery, Derby

ENCHANTED SLIMMING AIDS

It's the cake slice Weight Watchers tried to BAN!

Would YOU like to eat as much cake as you like without counting the calories? Now you CAN with the fantastic

CALORIE GONE CAKE SLICE!

We don't know how it works... IT JUST DOES!

This fantastic innovation actually ***REMOVES ALL CALORIES*** as it cuts through a cake, leaving your slice - whatever the size - completely ***CALORIE FREE!***

*"I tried everything to lose weight and nothing worked. Then I bought myself a **Calorie Gone cake slice** and the pounds just fell off."* **Mrs B, Essex**

*"I eat 10 black forest gateaus a day, cutting them with my **Calorie Gone cake slice**, and I can still get into my wedding dress."* **Mrs L, Hull**

*"I bought a **Calorie Gone cake slice**, and now I'm happy to be photographed sideways on, pulling out the waistband on my old trousers."* **Mr F, Luton**

Cut with standard cake slice ***680 cal***

Cut with Calorie Gone cake slice ***0 cal***

Order yours TODAY from www.caloriegonecakeslice.org

Antiques Roadshow
It's a Ming..
Of course.
May I just stop you for a second my son?
Hello Bishop, it's Reverend Jones, and you can shove God's Cook up your fat wife's hairy arse! Bye.
As I was saying, it's a Minging vase and isn't worth shit. But thank you for showing it to us Reverend.

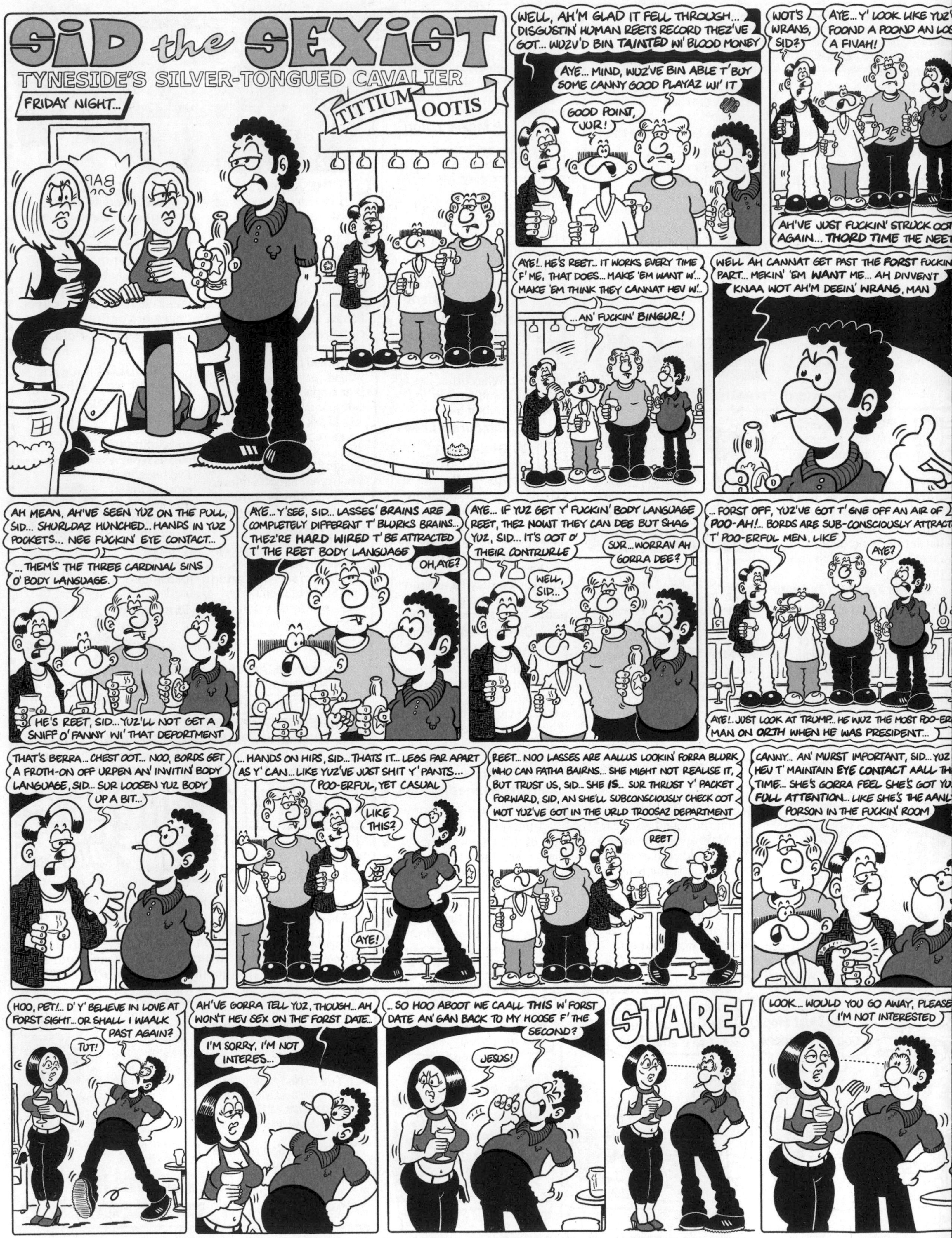

SID the SEXIST
TYNESIDE'S SILVER-TONGUED CAVALIER
FRIDAY NIGHT...
TITTIUM
OOTIS
WELL, AH'M GLAD IT FELL THROUGH... DISGUSTIN' HUMAN REETS RECORD THEZ'VE GOT... WUZV'D BIN TAINTED WI' BLOOD MONEY
AYE... MIND, WUZ'VE BIN ABLE T' BUY SOME CANNY GOOD PLAYAZ WI' IT
GOOD POINT, JUR!
WOT'S WRANG, SID?
AYE... Y' LOOK LIKE YUZ'
FOOND A POOND AN LOS
A FIVAH!
AH'VE JUST FUCKIN' STRUCK OOT
AGAIN... THORD TIME THE NEET
AYE!.. HE'S REET... IT WORKS EVERY TIME F' ME, THAT DOES... MAKE 'EM WANT W'... MAKE 'EM THINK THEY CANNAT HEV W'...
...AN' FUCKIN' BINGUR!
WELL AH CANNAT GET PAST THE FORST FUCKIN
PART... MEKIN' 'EM WANT ME... AH DIVVEN'T KNAA WOT AH'M DEEIN' WRANG, MAN
AH MEAN, AH'VE SEEN YUZ ON THE PULL, SID... SHURLDAZ HUNCHED... HANDS IN YUZ POCKETS... NEE FUCKIN' EYE CONTACT...
...THEM'S THE THREE CARDINAL SINS O' BODY LANGUAGE.
HE'S REET, SID... YUZ'LL NOT GET A SNIFF O' FANNY WI' THAT DEPORTMENT
AYE... Y'SEE, SID... LASSES' BRAINS ARE COMPLETELY DIFFERENT T' BLURKS BRAINS... THEZ'RE HARD WIRED T' BE ATTRACTED T' THE REET BODY LANGUAGE
OH, AYE?
AYE... IF YUZ GET Y' FUCKIN' BODY LANGUAGE REET, THEZ NOWT THEY CAN DEE BUT SHAG YUZ, SID... IT'S OOT O' THEIR CONTRURLE
SUR... WORRAV AH GORRA DEE?
WELL, SID...
...FORST OFF, YUZ'VE GOT T' GIVE OFF AN AIR OF
POO-AH!.. BORDS ARE SUB-CONSCIOUSLY ATTRACT
T' POO-ERFUL MEN, LIKE
AYE?
AYE!.. JUST LOOK AT TRUMP... HE WUZ THE MOST POO-ER
MAN ON ORTH WHEN HE WAS PRESIDENT...
THAT'S BERRA... CHEST OOT... NOO, BORDS GET A FROTH-ON OFF URPEN AN' INVITIN' BODY LANGUAGE, SID... SUR LOOSEN YUZ BODY UP A BIT...
...HANDS ON HIPS, SID... THATS IT... LEGS FAR APART AS Y' CAN... LIKE YUZ'VE JUST SHIT Y' PANTS...
POO-ERFUL, YET CASUAL
LIKE THIS?
AYE!
REET... NOO LASSES ARE AALUS LOOKIN' FORRA BLURK WHO CAN FATHA BAIRNS... SHE MIGHT NOT REALISE IT, BUT TRUST US, SID... SHE IS... SUR THRUST Y' PACKET FORWARD, SID, AN SHE'LL SUBCONSCIOUSLY CHECK OOT WOT YUZ'VE GOT IN THE URLD TROOSAZ DEPARTMENT
REET
CANNY... AN' MURST IMPORTANT, SID... YUZ
HEV T' MAINTAIN EYE CONTACT AALL TH
TIME... SHE'S GORRA FEEL SHE'S GOT YU
FULL ATTENTION... LIKE SHE'S THE AAL
PORSON IN THE FUCKIN' ROOM
HOO, PET!.. D' Y' BELIEVE IN LOVE AT FORST SIGHT... OR SHALL I WAALK PAST AGAIN?
TUT!
AH'VE GORRA TELL YUZ, THOUGH... AH WON'T HEV SEX ON THE FORST DATE...
I'M SORRY, I'M NOT INTERES...
...SO HOO ABOOT WE CAALL THIS W' FORST DATE AN' GAN BACK TO MY HOOSE F' THE SECOND?
JESUS!
STARE!
LOOK... WOULD YOU GO AWAY, PLEASE
I'M NOT INTERESTED

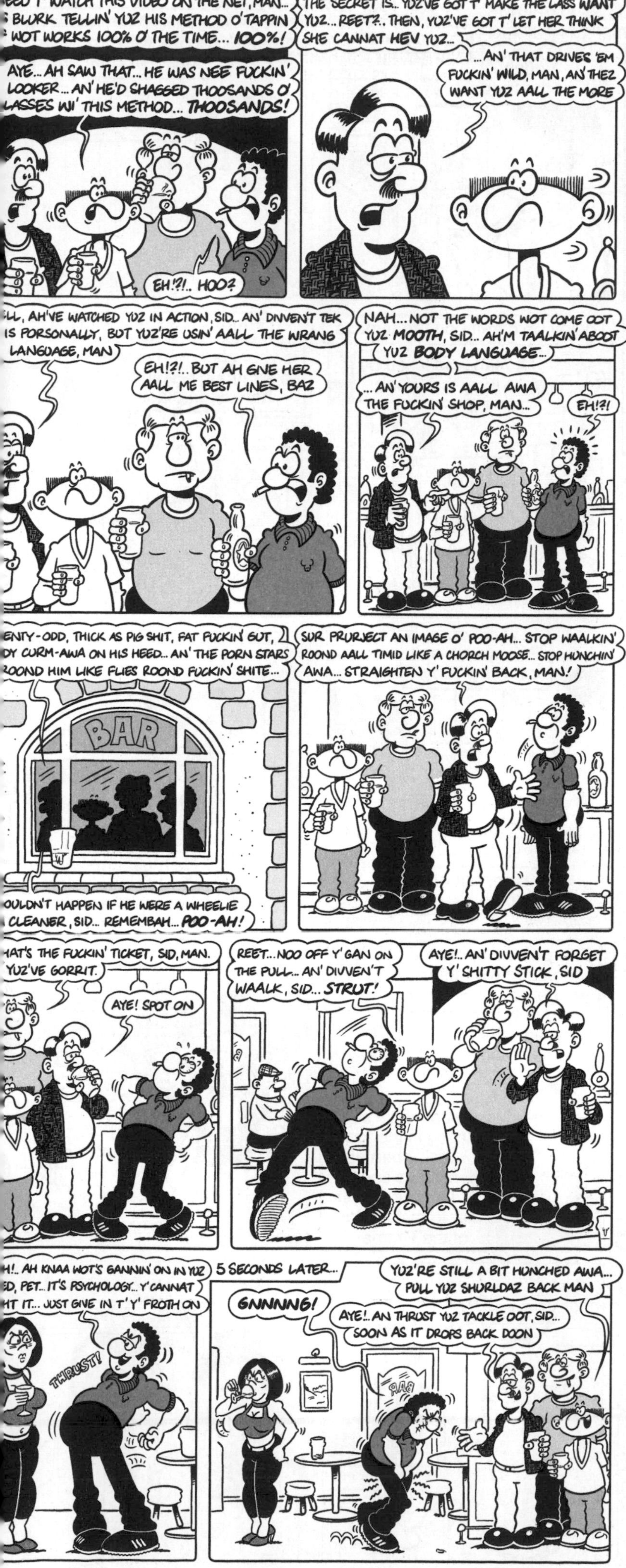
EED T' WATCH THIS VIDEO ON THE NET, MAN... S BLURK TELLIN' YUZ HIS METHOD O' TAPPIN WOT WORKS 100% O' THE TIME... 100%!
AYE... AH SAW THAT... HE WAS NEE FUCKIN' LOOKER... AN' HE'D SHAGGED THOOSANDS O' LASSES WI' THIS METHOD... THOOSANDS!
EH!?!.. HOO?
THE SECRET IS... YUZ'VE GOT T' MAKE THE LASS WANT YUZ... REET?.. THEN, YUZ'VE GOT T' LET HER THINK SHE CANNAT HEV YUZ...
...AN' THAT DRIVES 'EM FUCKIN' WILD, MAN, AN' THEZ WANT YUZ AALL THE MORE
LL, AH'VE WATCHED YUZ IN ACTION, SID... AN' DIVVEN'T TEK IS PORSONALLY, BUT YUZ'RE USIN' AALL THE WRANG LANGUAGE, MAN
EH!?!.. BUT AH GIVE HER AALL ME BEST LINES, BAZ
NAH... NOT THE WORDS WOT COME OOT YUZ MOOTH, SID... AH'M TAALKIN' ABOOT YUZ BODY LANGUAGE...
...AN' YOURS IS AALL AWA THE FUCKIN' SHOP, MAN...
EH!?!
ENTY-ODD, THICK AS PIG SHIT, FAT FUCKIN' GUT, DY CURM-AWA ON HIS HEED... AN' THE PORN STARS ROOND HIM LIKE FLIES ROOND FUCKIN' SHITE...
BAR
OULDN'T HAPPEN IF HE WERE A WHEELIE CLEANER, SID... REMEMBAH... POO-AH!
SUR PRURJECT AN IMAGE O' POO-AH... STOP WAALKIN' ROOND AALL TIMID LIKE A CHORCH MOOSE... STOP HUNCHIN' AWA... STRAIGHTEN Y' FUCKIN' BACK, MAN!
HAT'S THE FUCKIN' TICKET, SID, MAN. YUZ'VE GORRIT.
AYE! SPOT ON
REET... NOO OFF Y' GAN ON THE PULL... AN' DIVVEN'T WAALK, SID... STRUT!
AYE!.. AN' DIVVEN'T FORGET Y' SHITTY STICK, SID
H!.. AH KNAA WOT'S GANNIN' ON IN YUZ ED, PET... IT'S PSYCHOLOGY... Y' CANNAT HT IT... JUST GIVE IN T' Y' FROTH ON
THRUST!
5 SECONDS LATER...
GNNNNG!
YUZ'RE STILL A BIT HUNCHED AWA... PULL YUZ SHURLDAZ BACK MAN
AYE!.. AN THRUST YUZ TACKLE OOT, SID... SOON AS IT DROPS BACK DOON

OH! OH! HEAVEN!

MANY NAMES have been put in the frame to replace Daniel Craig as the next James Bond – Tom Hardy, James Norton and Idris Elba to name but a few. But the one which stands out as the hot favourite is none other than the late SIR ROGER MOORE, who is tipped to re-don the superspy's tuxedo after a 35-year hiatus.

Moore tipped to don tuxedo a second time!

The much-loved actor played the British secret agent seven times, and was last seen dangling from the Golden Gate Bridge while battling with super-villain Christopher Walken in the 1985 thrill-fest *A View to a Kill*, before passing his 007 licence to Timothy Dalton for 1987's *The Living Daylights*.

Other actors have taken on the role since, portraying Bond variously as brooding, gritty and suave. But many fans have longed for a return to the fun-packed days of the Moore era, which saw Bond run over a bunch of crocodiles, dump wheelchair-bound nemesis Ernst Blofeld down a chimney stack, and defuse a nuclear bomb whilst dressed as a circus clown.

"There's no getting away from it, Moore starred in some of the most successful Bond films ever made," said producer Cubby Broccoli. "We've spoken to Roger's agent about coming back, and we'll wait and see what happens."

current

If Moore does replace current 007 Daniel Craig, it will be the first time a deceased actor has played the part in the franchise's 50-year history. But Broccoli, who himself died in 1996, thinks that shouldn't be a problem. "I know Roger isn't around any longer, and that may affect a few of the shooting schedules," he said. "But we'll cross that bridge when we come to it."

Many former Bonds both dead and alive welcomed the news that Sir Roger could make a long-awaited comeback to the iconic role. "Actors are very neurotic people, but even we will admit he was the best Bond," said Pierce Brosnan, who is still alive and played the part four times between 1995 and 2002. And six-times Bond Sean Connery, who died last year, agreed. "It is a great opportunity for a great actor," he said.

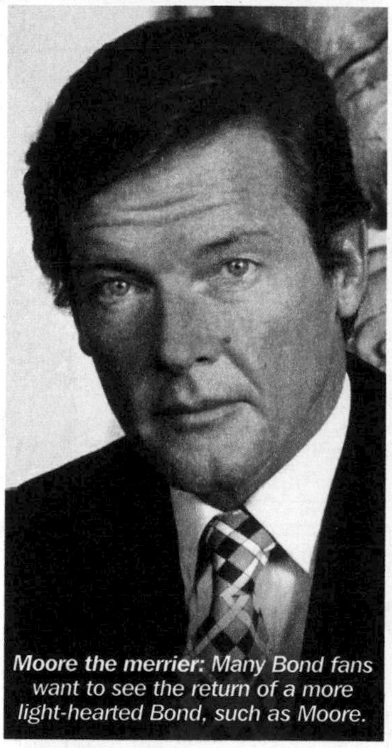

Moore the merrier: Many Bond fans want to see the return of a more light-hearted Bond, such as Moore.

But not everyone agrees that casting a dead star in such a famous role is a good idea. "I died in 1964 after just three films were made," said writer Ian Fleming, who created the Bond character before his death. "As such, I only ever saw Sean Connery play 007 on screen, and he was alive at the time."

sultana

"I'd even been dead for three years before David Niven played Bond in Casino Royale, so I never even saw that, even though it's not really counted as a proper 007 film, except in pub quizzes."

"I'm not sure that a dead actor would be able to bring the necessary life to the character that the role requires," Fleming added, spelling his words out via a moving glass on *Most Haunted* presenter Yvette Fielding's coffee table.

Foodie Bollocks

"Can I take your order?"

"I doubt it, let's see."

"What on this menu has been *foraged*?"

"Er, everything?"

"Oh yes, they're definitely in the fridge."

"Even the steaks?"

"*Foraged.* *Foraged.*"

"*Hello*? Harvested in the wild, from the local environment?"

"Ohhhh. None of it."

"Wow."

"That is literally indefensible."

"What would you say if I told you I could *forage* a Michelin-quality menu within walking distance of this table in less than an hour?"

"I'd say be careful on the bypass."

"A man was killed by a lorry last week."

THE BROWN DOG

SIZZLIN' GRILL 2 FOR 1
KIDS EAT FREE

"Food is risk, deal with it!"

"Is your chef even *aware* a sourcing revolution has taken place?"

"I'll go and ask."

"Mention Tove Blomquist."

"If he isn't following Blomquist he's in the wrong job!"

"Bloke on table ten..."

"What about him?"

PING!

"*Absolute* cunt."

"He says he isn't following Toby –"

"*Tove.*"

"Tove, but he'll look into it."

FORAGE AGAINST THE MACHINE

"He *must* check-out Tove's small plate pop-up *side-hustle* on Borough Market."

"Tove's family are *Royal bankers* dating back to mediaeval times, but foraging is his *passion.*"

"He took a sabbatical just before the crash, and he's lived his dream ever since!"

"His main dining concept *Kfö* is a minimalist canteen on a volcanic island 200 miles off Norway."

"All they serve is a lichen found on the rocky shoreline, pickled."

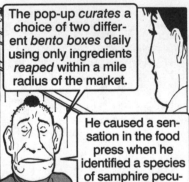

"The pop-up *curates* a choice of two different *bento boxes* daily using only ingredients *reaped* within a mile radius of the market."

"He caused a sensation in the food press when he identified a species of samphire peculiar to that stretch of the Thames –"

"- It's *incredibly* bitter and tough."

"So... Can I take your order?"

"Actually, I'll pass."

"The *edgy* cuisine I crave is right outside that door!"

"Fuckin' crank."

"What – what is he doing?"

"Ow!"

"*Ow!*"

"*Oww!!*"

"I think he's eating a thistle."

STREF

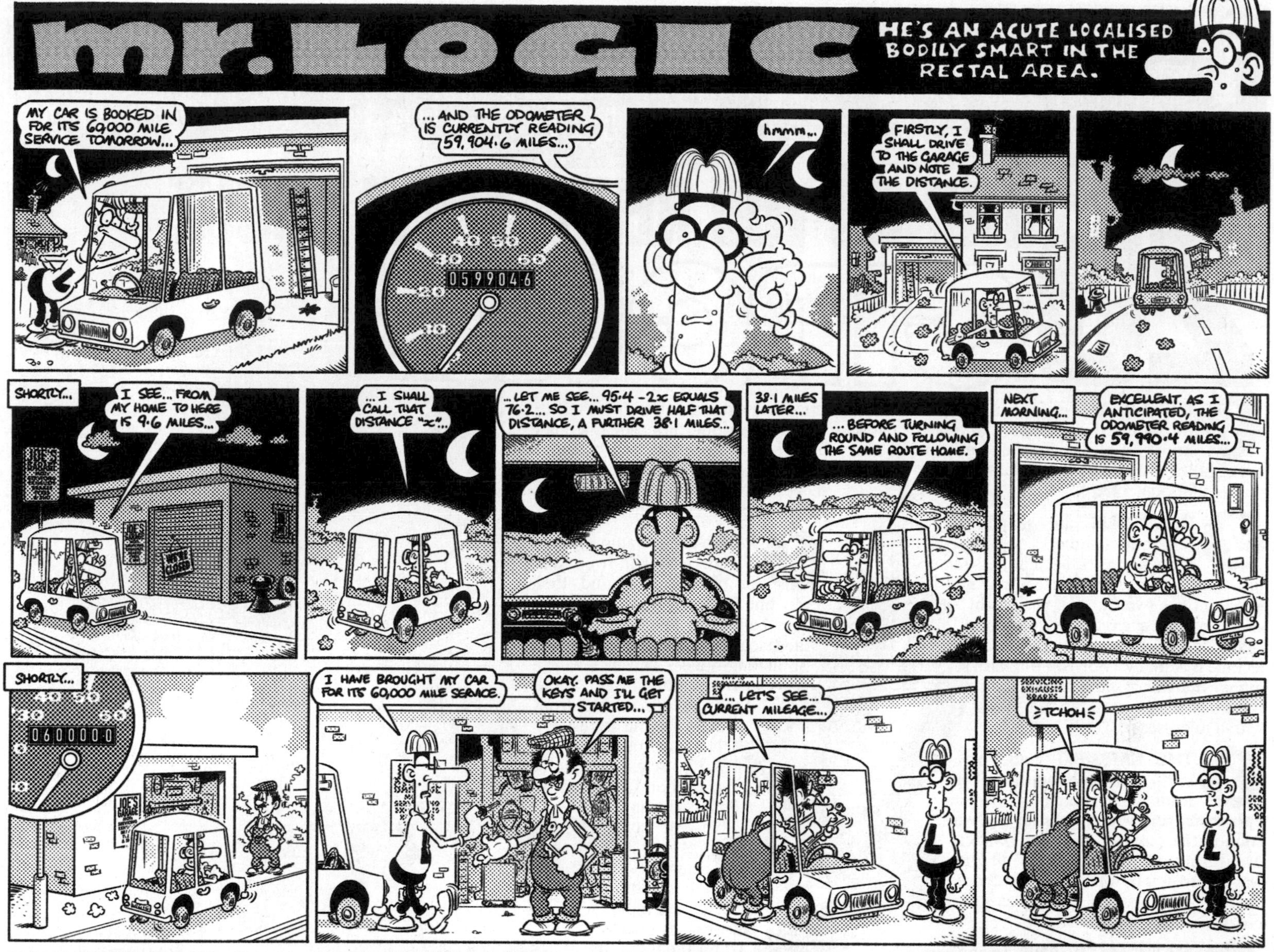
MR. LOGIC
HE'S AN ACUTE LOCALISED BODILY SMART IN THE RECTAL AREA.
MY CAR IS BOOKED IN FOR ITS 60,000 MILE SERVICE TOMORROW...
...AND THE ODOMETER IS CURRENTLY READING 59,904.6 MILES...
0599046
hmmm...
FIRSTLY, I SHALL DRIVE TO THE GARAGE AND NOTE THE DISTANCE.
SHORTLY...
I SEE... FROM MY HOME TO HERE IS 9.6 MILES...
WE'RE CLOSED
...I SHALL CALL THAT DISTANCE "x"...
...LET ME SEE... 95.4 - 2x EQUALS 76.2... SO I MUST DRIVE HALF THAT DISTANCE, A FURTHER 38.1 MILES...
38.1 MILES LATER...
...BEFORE TURNING ROUND AND FOLLOWING THE SAME ROUTE HOME.
NEXT MORNING...
EXCELLENT. AS I ANTICIPATED, THE ODOMETER READING IS 59,990.4 MILES...
SHORTLY...
0600000
JOE'S GARAGE
I HAVE BROUGHT MY CAR FOR ITS 60,000 MILE SERVICE.
OKAY. PASS ME THE KEYS AND I'LL GET STARTED...
...LET'S SEE... CURRENT MILEAGE...
TCHOH

Royal Thumbs Down for Oranges

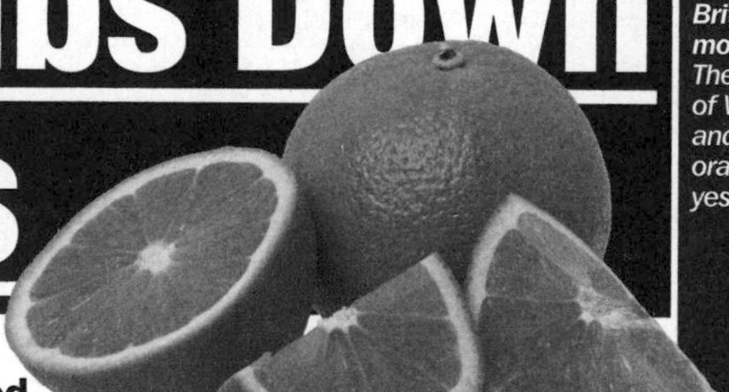

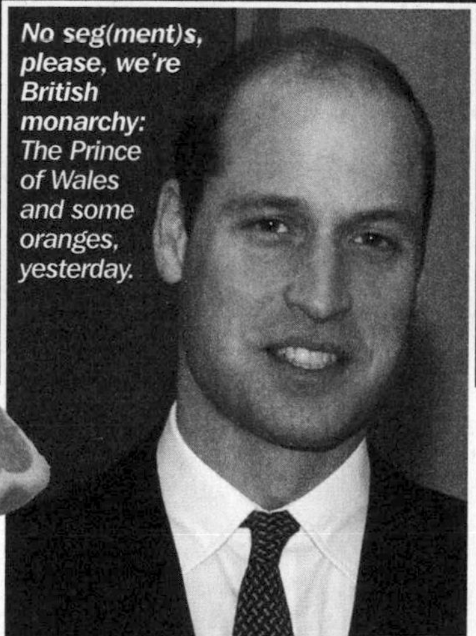
No seg(ment)s, please, we're British monarchy: The Prince of Wales and some oranges, yesterday.

BUCKINGHAM Palace stunned the world's press this week when they announced that Prince William, the Prince of Wales, has *never eaten an orange!*

In the statement, the Prince, who is first in line to the throne, said he has at no time in his life eaten one of the chromatically named fruits, although he stressed that he was well aware that they were extremely popular.

gratitude

He went on to express his gratitude to greengrocers across the country for providing oranges for people who did enjoy them.

"It is rather ironic that the Duke has never eaten an orange when you consider that King William III liked them so much that he named himself Willam of Orange after them," said

EXCLUSIVE!

BBC Royal Correspondent Nicholas Witchell, who Prince Charles once called a 'dreadful little man.'

"When His Royal Highness accedes to the throne, we shall probably have to call him William *not* of Orange," he quipped.

latitude

The news came as a blow to orange importers in the UK, who have had a difficult year due to the Covid pandemic. "Having a member of the Royal family say that they love oranges would have given our industry a much-

Monarch -in-Waiting a Stranger to Citrus Fruit favourites

needed boost," said Hector Golightly, president of the UK Consortium of Orange Importers. "So to have the first in line to the throne say he doesn't like them is a hammer blow."

In response, Palace officials said that the Duke has nothing against citrus fruit and often enjoyed lemons and limes in alcoholic drinks.

burning man

They also stressed that the consortium had misrepresented the Prince, and clarified his remarks. "His Royal Highness at no time said he did not like oranges. He simply said that he had never had one, so he wouldn't actually know," the Palace added.

THEY'RE everywhere we look – in our homes, in our gardens and in the sky. They run our cars and our washing machines, but probably not our fridges. They've been around – quite literally – since the universe began. They come in all different sizes, from smaller than a penny to as big as a circus ring... but only one shape. They're CIRCLES, and our lives would be very different without them. You may think you know your way around these ultimate curved shapes. But do you really? Here are...

25 THINGS YOU NEVER KNEW ABOUT CIRCLES

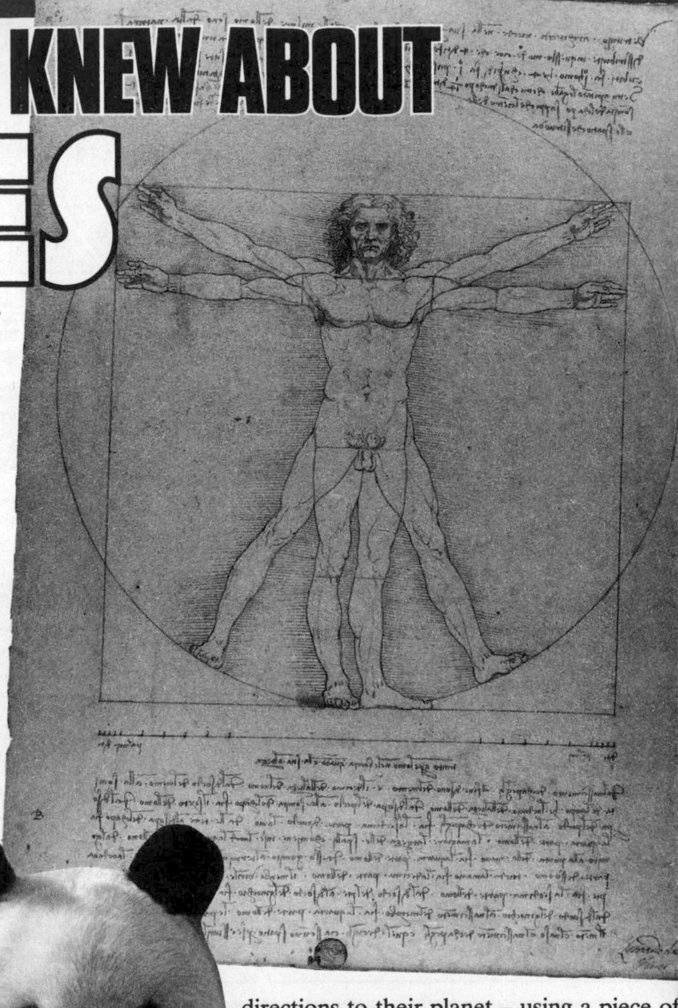

1 THE AREA of a circle is equal to πr^2, so you would think the area of a larger circle would be bigger. But believe it or not, the area of the big circle is exactly the same as the smaller one... πr^2!

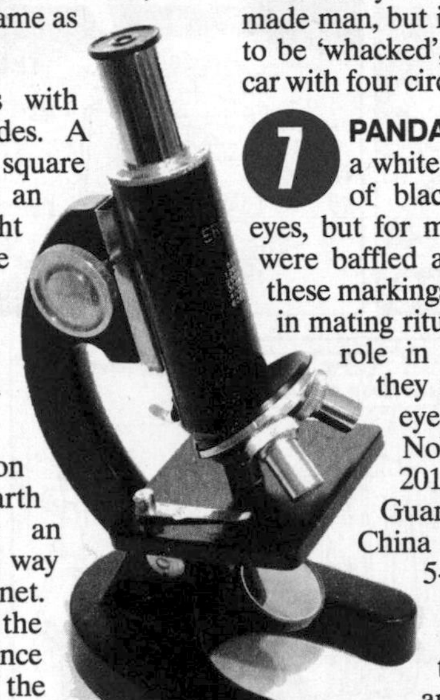

2 POLYGONS are shapes with different numbers of sides. A triangle has three sides, a square has four, a pentagon has five and an icosagon has twenty. And you might suppose that a circle has just one side... *but you'd be wrong.* Because a circle is actually a polygon with an *infinite number of sides*, it's just that the sides are too small to see, even with a microscope.

3 THE LARGEST circle on earth is actually on the earth itself. The equator is an enormous ring which goes all the way round the middle of the planet. Measuring 40,075 kilometres all the way round, it is by fantastic coincidence exactly the same length as the circumference of the earth.

4 MATHEMATICIANS draw a circle by taking a graph with x and y axes, and plotting all the points $(x(k),y(k))$ for K, sitting on a circle, C, of radius r. Joining these points together gives a complete circle. Or they may plot the formula $x^2 + y^2 + Dx + Ey + F = 0$, where D, E and F are integers that are coefficients of the x and y values. Normal people use a pair of compasses or draw round a plate.

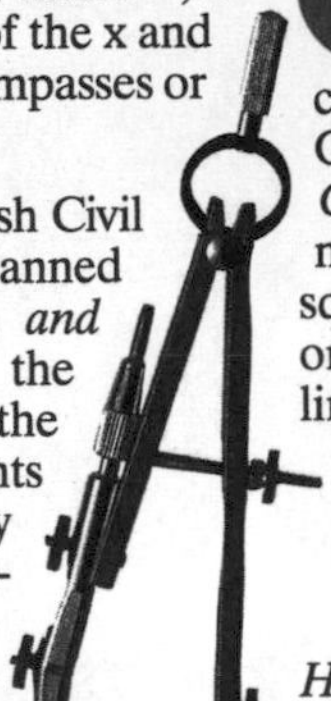

5 AFTER his victory in the English Civil War, Oliver Cromwell banned Christmas, theatre, dancing... *and circles.* The bonkers Puritan deemed the single-sided shapes to be the work of the Devil, and threatened severe punishments for anyone caught with a circle of any sort. However, after his second-in-command Thomas Fairfax pointed out that Cromwell's New Model Army were nicknamed The Roundheads on account of their circle-shaped helmets, the red-faced Lord Protector of the Commonwealth of England was forced to hastily scrap his new rule.

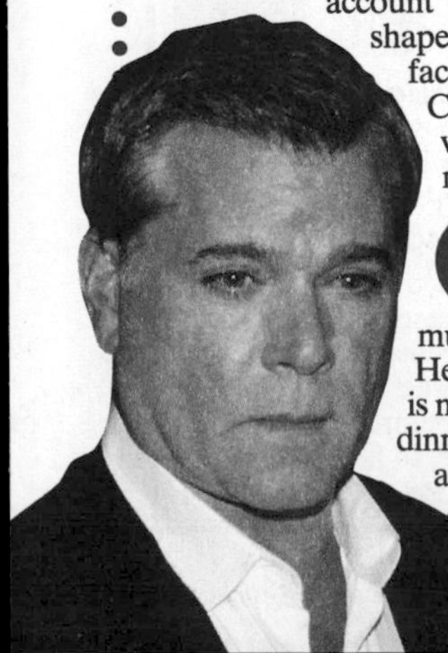

6 MARTIN Scorsese's 1990 gangster epic *Goodfellas* makes much use of circles. When Henry Hill, played by Ray Liotta, is making pasta sauce for a family dinner, he mixes the ingredients in a pan which is circular. Later in the film, when Joe Pesci's character Tommy DeVito believes he is going to a ceremony where he will become a made man, but is actually being taken to be 'whacked', he is driven off in a car with four circular wheels.

7 PANDA bears famously have a white face with two circles of black fur around their eyes, but for many years, biologists were baffled as to the purpose of these markings: Were they involved in mating rituals? Did they have a role in camouflage? Could they reduce attacks from eye-infecting parasites? Nobody knew. Then in 2015, scientists from Guangzhou University in China began a 5-year study of over 350 pandas in the wild in an attempt to answer this question. Unfortunately, the data collected was inconclusive, leaving them just as baffled as before.

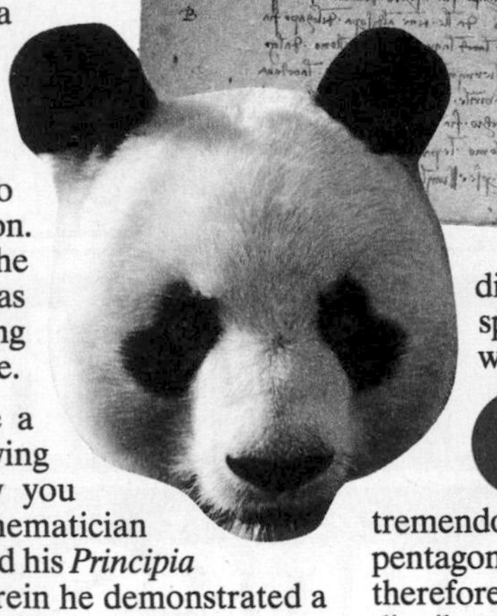

8 "YOU can't square a circle," so the saying goes. But actually you can. In 1696, German mathematician Gottfried Leibniz published his *Principia Circulus ut Quadrata*, wherein he demonstrated a mathematical proof of how to turn a circle into a square. It involved plotting four equidistant points on the circumference of a circle, drawing straight lines between them, and then rubbing out the curved bits.

9 SOME of the greatest works of art involve circles, including *The Haywain Triptych* by Hieronymus Bosch, *The Head of Medusa* by Caravaggio, and that one by Leonardo da Vinci of that bloke stood in the Billy Bollocks with four arms and four legs.

10 CROP circles are large, circular areas of flattened vegetation in agricultural fields, often interlinked and forming complicated geometrical patterns. Although they have the appearance of having been made by a bored farmer using a plank of wood and a piece of string, a lot of evidence points to these mysterious symbols being extraterrestrial in origin. Alien beings are thought to regularly visit our planet and make these marks – coded directions to their planet – using a piece of space string and a plank made of a type of wood not found on earth.

11 FROM SOAP bubbles to sea urchins to planets, nature loves circles. This is down to them having tremendous strength. Unlike triangles, squares and pentagons, circles have no corners or edges and therefore no weak spots, with all forces being distributed evenly throughout the shape. In laboratory tests, circles have been shown to be approximately 150 times stronger than steel.

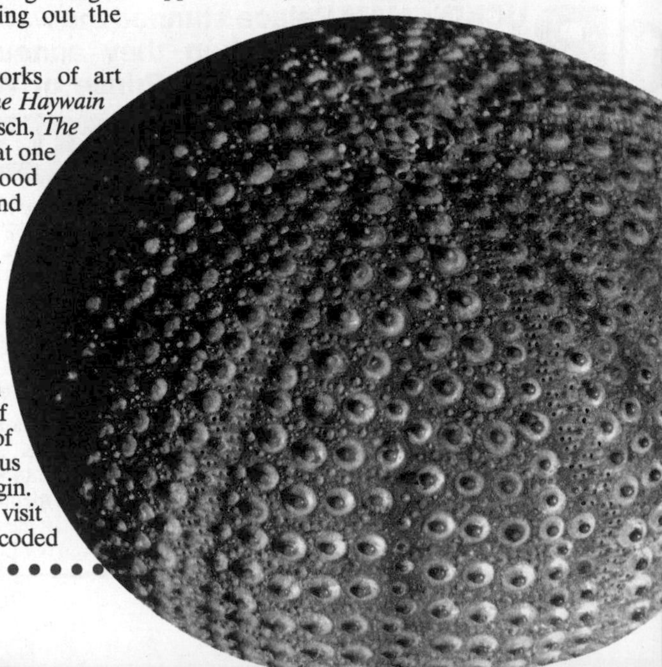

12 **HOWEVER,** circles are not nature's answer to everything, because although they have strength, they do not pack together efficiently. If bees made their honeycombs circular, there would be large gaps between them which would waste hive space and collect dust. So instead, bees store their honey in combs that are made up of hexagons – a kind of six-sided circle.

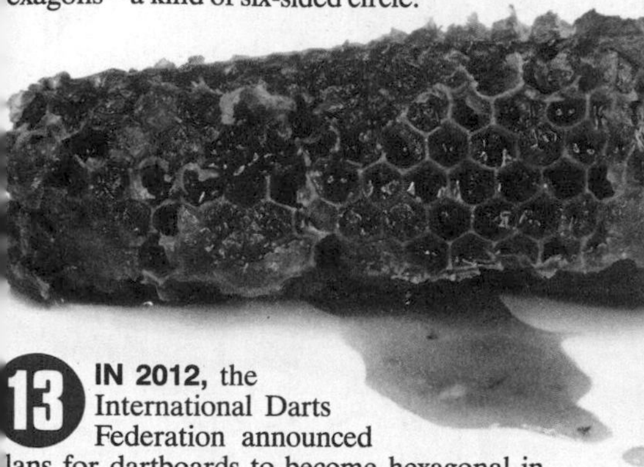

13 **IN 2012,** the International Darts Federation announced plans for dartboards to become hexagonal in shape. Taking a leaf out of the honeybee's book, it was thought that pubs could fit more hexagonal boards than circular ones onto the same area of wall, leading to more people being able to play, and increasing the popularity of the game. However, professional darts players found the new boards with their 6-sided bullseye 'confusing and distracting', and after a delegation of players – led by the late Eric 'swan's neck' Bristow and Phil 'the power' Taylor – picketed the IDF headquarters in Geneva, the plans were dropped.

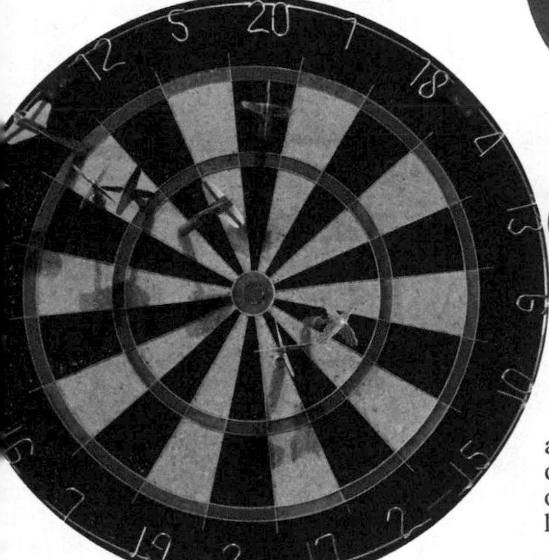

14 **IN THE** Disney epic *The Lion King*, Elton John sings about *The Circle of Life*, which tells how all living things continue their existence in a never-ending cycle. However, scientists believe that life is more like a finite straight line than a circle. "We get born, then at some point in the next 100 years we die, and that's it. To call life a circle is 'not even wrong'," says *Bad Science* author Dr Ben Goldacre.

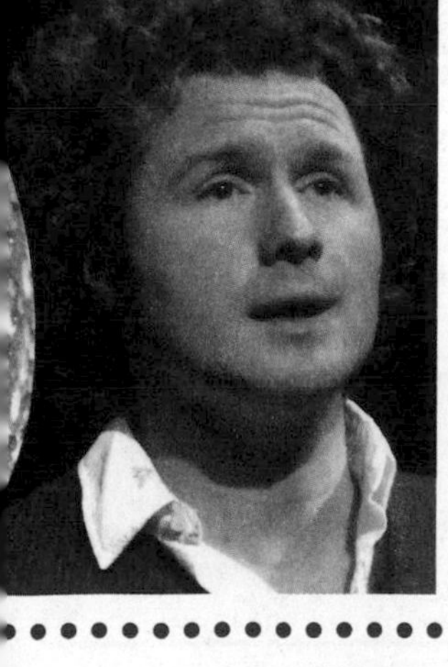

15 **CIRCULAR** things can be cut into a maximum of 360 parts. Each of these parts is called a degree, and is about the size of a slice of Daim Bar cake in the Ikea restaurant.

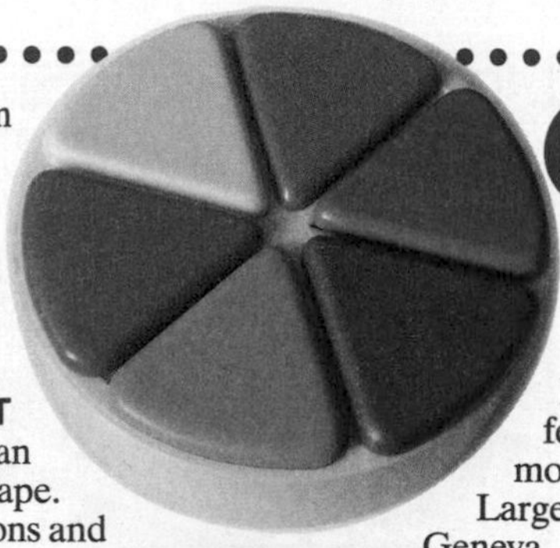

16 **THE SMALLEST** things known to man are circular in shape. "Atoms are circular. And protons and neutrons that make them up are circles as well. And they are made of circular quarks and mesons. I don't know what *they're* made of, but my money's on them fuckers being round as well," said BBC *Science Now* presenter Dr Adam Rutherford.

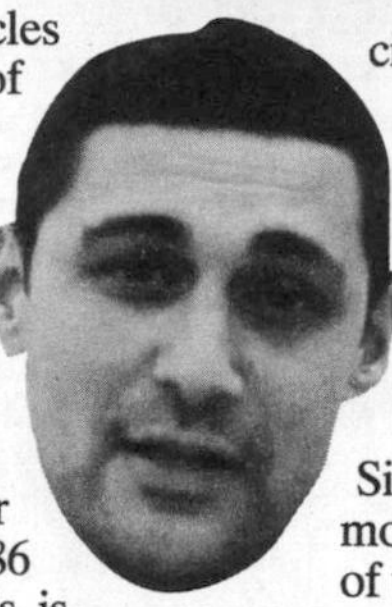

17 **THE COUNTRY** with the largest number of circles per capita is Monaco, with 986 round things for every resident. This is due to the principality's small population of just over 39,000, coupled with the large number of coins, gambling chips and sports car wheels found in the sovereign microstate.

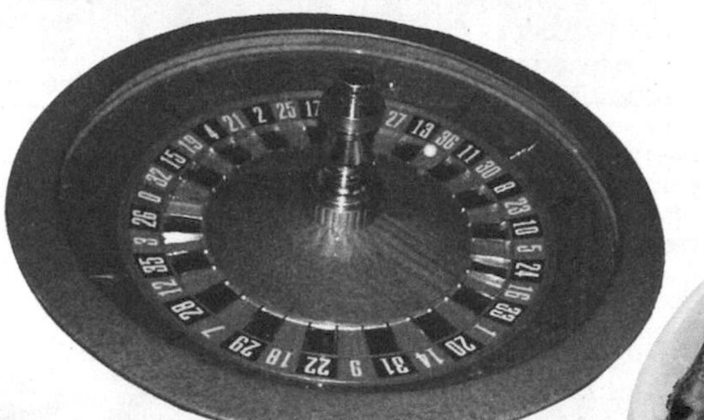

18 **COMPUTERS** today run every aspect of our lives, but without circles they simply would not work. That's because these complex machines operate on binary code, a system that uses a series of ones… and *zeros* – a kind of circle.

19 **ACCORDING** to JRR Tolkien, the doors of Hobbit holes were circular. But hinges rely on two pieces of metal pivoting about a straight pin, and so would not function on a round door. In stories filled with dragons, wizards and rings of invisibility, a hinged circular door is for many a leap of the imagination too far.

20 **THE CIRCULAR** windows on ships are known as portholes, and have only about 78% of the area of a square window of the same height and width. Whereas this would be a problem in a house, it is of little consequence out at sea as there is nothing to look at.

21 **WHEN** the Romans came to Britain, they criss-crossed the country with a network of straight roads joining towns together with circular roundabouts at their intersections. However, they quickly realised that we march on the left over here, causing problems on the roundabouts. "The Latin occupiers never quite got the hang of which way to go round, what lane to use, or when to signal, and they gave up and fucked off after 367 years," says Cambridge classicist Dr Mary Beard.

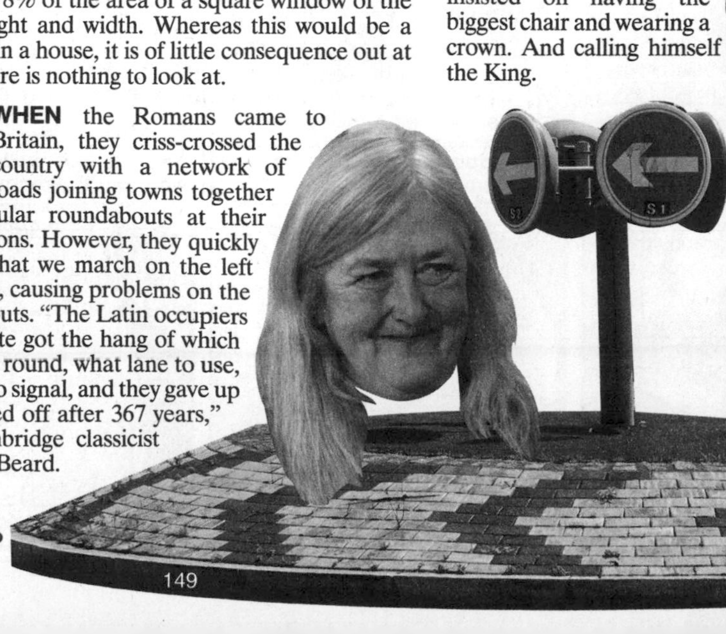

22 **YOU MIGHT** think that the most expensive circle in the world would be a solid gold ring of size Z+6, large enough to fit the finger of somebody like wrestler Andre the Giant or Richard Kiel who played Jaws in the Bond films. But not for the first time in this feature, you would be wrong. The most expensive circle in the world is the Large Hadron Collider at CERN in Geneva. With a circumference of 27km, the circular steel tube cost a staggering €3.1 billion (£2.8 billion) to construct.

23 **IF BOFFINS** at CERN had decided to build the Large Hadron Collider out of solid gold, the project would have cost an even more staggering €4.9 × 10^{17} (£3.8 × 10^{17}) – so expensive that if the world's three richest people – Jeff Bezos, Bill Gates, and Simply Red's Mick Hucknall – pooled all their money, they would still only be able to buy a 2° slice of the 24-carat collider.

24 **IF CHEFS** made a pizza the size of the Large Hadron Collider, there would not be enough cheese in the world to sprinkle on top of it. Rather than a Margherita or a Quattro Formaggi, they would have to prepare a Marinara - a more traditional cheese-free pizza, popular in Naples and northern Italy.

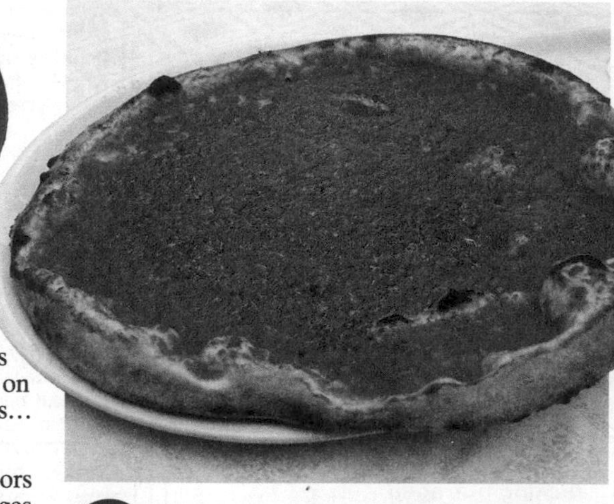

25 **THE 'HEAD** of the table' is traditionally the place where the most important person is seated. King Arthur famously had a circular table to show that all at his court were equal, and that no one person was more distinguished than any other. It was a noble gesture, but spoiled by the fact that when seated at it, he insisted on having the biggest chair and wearing a crown. And calling himself the King.

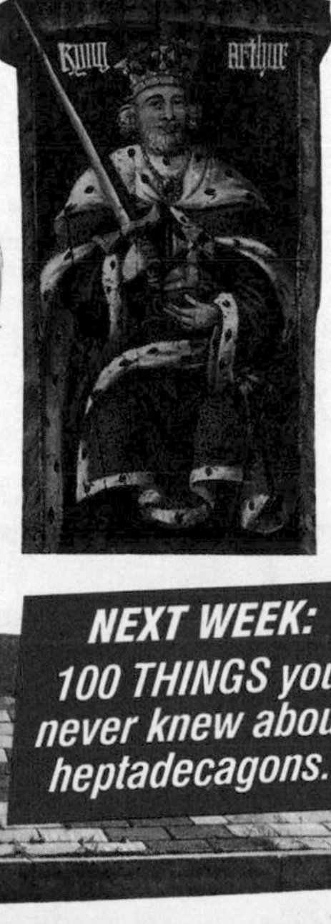

NEXT WEEK:* 100 THINGS *you never knew about heptadecagons.

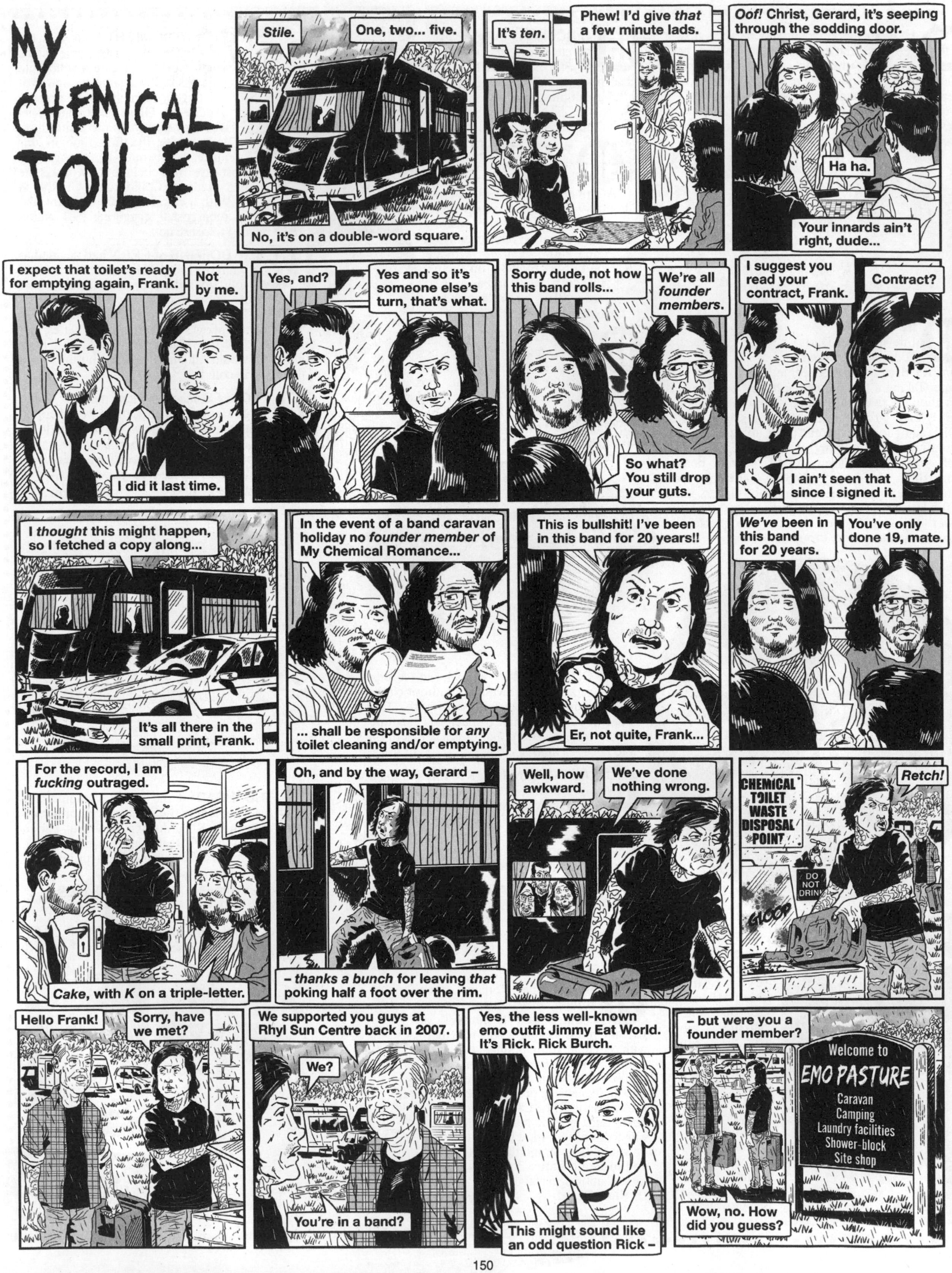
MY CHEMICAL TOILET
Stile.
One, two... five.
No, it's on a double-word square.
It's *ten*.
Phew! I'd give *that* a few minute lads.
Oof! Christ, Gerard, it's seeping through the sodding door.
Ha ha.
Your innards ain't right, dude...
I expect that toilet's ready for emptying again, Frank.
Not by me.
I did it last time.
Yes, and?
Yes and so it's someone else's turn, that's what.
Sorry dude, not how this band rolls...
We're all *founder members*.
So what? You still drop your guts.
I suggest you read your contract, Frank.
Contract?
I ain't seen that since I signed it.
I *thought* this might happen, so I fetched a copy along...
It's all there in the small print, Frank.
In the event of a band caravan holiday no *founder member* of My Chemical Romance...
... shall be responsible for *any* toilet cleaning and/or emptying.
This is bullshit! I've been in this band for 20 years!!
Er, not quite, Frank...
We've been in this band for 20 years.
You've only done 19, mate.
For the record, I am *fucking* outraged.
Cake, with *K* on a triple-letter.
Oh, and by the way, Gerard –
– *thanks a bunch* for leaving *that* poking half a foot over the rim.
Well, how awkward.
We've done nothing wrong.
CHEMICAL TOILET WASTE DISPOSAL POINT
Retch!
DO NOT DRINK
GLOOP
Hello Frank!
Sorry, have we met?
We supported you guys at Rhyl Sun Centre back in 2007.
We?
You're in a band?
Yes, the less well-known emo outfit Jimmy Eat World. It's Rick. Rick Burch.
This might sound like an odd question Rick –
– but were you a founder member?
Welcome to EMO PASTURE
Caravan
Camping
Laundry facilities
Shower-block
Site shop
Wow, no. How did you guess?

MAJOR MISUNDERSTANDING
THANK YOU FOR TAKING PART, EVERYBODY!
CHILDRENS EASTER FANCY DRESS CONTEST
VILLAGE HALL
ALL YOUR COSTUMES HAVE BEEN SPLENDID!
LOOK MUMMY, I'M A BUNNY RABBIT HOPPING ALONG!
BOING! BOING! BOING!
BE CAREFUL, DANIEL...
BOING!
CRACK!
SHIT!
DANIEL!
IS HE OK?. THAT WAS A HELL OF A KNOCK!
OH GOD, HE'S UNCONSCIOUS!
I'M CALLING AN AMBULANCE!
COULDN'T YOU HAVE BEEN MORE CAREFUL WITH THAT GREAT BIG LOG?!
I'M SORRY MISSUS, BUT HE RAN STRAIGHT INTO IT...
I CAN ASSURE YOU, MADAM, THE RSPCA WILL NOT BE THE SLIGHTEST BIT INTERESTED IN YOUR CALL.
THESE CREATURES ARE CLASSED AS VERMIN.
THE COUNTRYSIDE ISN'T THE CUDDLY, FLUFFY, BEATRIX POTTER WORLD OF YOUR IMAGINATION.
HELLO, YES. AMBULANCE PLEASE...
YOU CAN'T BE SENTIMENTAL ABOUT PESTS.
IF THE FARMERS DIDN'T KEEP THEIR POPULATION DOWN, ALL THE CROPS WOULD BE DECIMATED.
AND WHERE WOULD YOU GET THE CARROTS AND LETTUCE FOR YOUR OH-SO-ETHICAL VEGAN DIET THEN?
THAT ONE IS STILL ALIVE, BY THE LOOKS OF IT.
YOU SHOULD FINISH IT OFF WITH A SPADE.
DJ '21

A DOG FOR A DAY

IMAGINE waking up one morning and looking in the mirror to find you have of turned into a dog. At some point in our lives, each and every one of us has wondered what it would be like to be canine for 24 hours, and anyone who says they haven't is either lying or is already a dog. We've "hounded" up *(rounded up)* four of our fave A-Listers to ask them one simple question – if you were *A Dog For A Day,* what sort of dog would you be and what would you do if you were *A Dog For A Day?*

JAMES MARTIN, telly gastronome

I RARELY mention it, but I was born and raised in God's Own County – Yorkshire! So if I could be any sort of *Dog For A Day*, I'd definitely be a Yorkshire Terrier. I'd spend my 24 hours as a pooch proudly yapping on about how Yorkshire is the best place on Earth, all from the comfort of my kennel in Hampshire. Then, if I had any time left on the canine clock, I'd chase some cyclists into a ditch.

MICHAEL McINTYRE, inexplicably popular comedian

IF I WAS *A Dog For A Day*, the first thing I'd do is eat as much white food as I could – flour, sugar, coconut, feta cheese, that sort of stuff. And then I'd spend the rest of the day shitting all over the pavements near my house. Consequently, when I returned to human form, I would see my own white dog shit everywhere, and bingo: I'd have the basis for a phenomenally successful and groundbreaking new stand-up routine about how you actually DO see white dog shit these days.

TOBY YOUNG, utter twat

MY STAG DO was famously only attended by four people, so if I was *A Dog For A Day* I'd take advantage of briefly being Man's Best Friend by throwing another bachelor party where everyone invited actually turned up. Me and my legions of new chums would have a great time at all the classic stag locations – the Go-Kart track, the paintball centre, the strip club. Although, being a dog I probably wouldn't be allowed into any of those places. So we'd have to do more dog-friendly activities instead, such as chasing squirrels, retrieving sticks or rolling in cow shit.

JK GALBRAITH, deceased economist

BACK WHEN I was alive, I clocked in at a whopping 6 foot 9 inches tall. So if I was *A Dog For A Day*, I think I'd like to try being the smallest kind of dog possible, perhaps one of them Chihuahuas. I'd spend my day walking around looking at people's ankles, doing tiny little shits the size of AA batteries and rattling about inside Paris Hilton's handbag, enjoying my newfound minuscule stature until the clock struck midnight and I shot back up to my tall, human, deceased self again.

AUTO BREAKERS DAYS OUT

THE UK's BEST AUTHENTICALLY GRIMY HERITAGE PARK

SCRAPYARD LAND

OPEN TO PUBLIC AND TRADE

Immerse yourself in the sights, sounds and smells of one of the last fully working SEVENTIES-style vehicle scrap yards...

VINTAGE "ROOF-ON ROOF" AUTO-WRECK ACTION!

KIDS GO FREE!

- ✔ **Smash as many windows as you like!** *Choose from a wide selection of mallets, hammers & jemmys* ***FREE*** *on arrival!*
- ✔ **Kids scrap-play zone** – *see if your child can climb to the top of cars haphazardly piled in a heap!*
- ✔ **Genuine greasy caff on site!** *Scalding hot tea with 17 sugars served in handcrafted oil-fingered styrofoam cups. BIG doorstep butties containing sausage* of indeterminate quality.*

*fried in your choice of diesel or 4-star leaded.

OUR GUARANTEE:
Your vehicle crushed within 1hr of parking up. includes DVLA online destruction certificate

CARS ★ VANS ★
BUSES ★ LORRIES
WE'VE GOT THE LOT TO SMASH UP!
4 STAR SCRAP & SALVAGE
N. Wales Ind. Est, Fflint, Ffflintshire, N.Wales

Postman PLOD THE MISERABLE BASTARD

JESUS! NOBODY SENDS BIRTHDAY CARDS WITH MONEY IN THESE DAYS ...FUCKIN' BANK TRANSFERS

AND THE INTERNET'S DONE FOR JAZZ MAGS AN' ALL... NONE OF THEM FUCKERS TO NICK...

THE ONLY PERK WE GET THESE DAYS IS JUMPING THE FUCKIN' QUEUE AT THE SUPERMARKET

DING! DONG

NOW... HOW ABOUT ONE WITH YOU BENDING OVER TO PICK IT UP WITH YOUR TITS FALLING OUT, EH!?! ...GIVE A BIT BACK TO THE KEY WORKERS

SLAM! MISERABLE FUCKER

SHORTLY... OOH...AIRMAIL... GREAT STUFF!

DING! DONG!

MORNING, LOVE... LETTER FROM SPAIN!

OOH!..THAT'LL BE FROM MY SISTER IN MALAGA

WELL, EITHER WAY, I CAN'T HAND IT OVER TILL YOU GIVE ME THE DUTY ON IT. EEEH! THEY DIDN'T PUT THAT ON THE SIDE OF THE RUDDY BUS

HEH! HEH!.. NICE LITTLE BREXIT DIVIDEND, THERE

SHORTLY... KNOCK! KNOCK! KNOCK!

CLINK! CLINK!

MORNING, LOVE... POST...

OOH, THANK YOU

...AND HERE'S THE BOT OF MILK YOU ASKED M GET FOR YOU... EH DID MIL

KNOCK! KNOCK!

MORNING, LOVE... POST... AND HERE'S THE BOTTLE OF MILK YOU ASKED ME TO GET FOR YOU

EH!?!

WHAT!?! YOU'VE JUST GIVE IT ME EH!?!.. NO, LOVE...THAT WERE YESTERDAY IT WERE YESTERDAY

NO!..NO IT WERE...

EEH!?!.. THAT'S WORRYING, THAT IS... DON'T WORRY, LOVE, WE ALL GET A BIT PUGGLED AT TIMES... ANYWAY... THAT'LL BE A TENNER

A TENNER!?!.. IT WERE ONLY A F YESTER

AYE...BUT IT'S GONE UP, LOVE... BREXIT

EEH!..MAN A

...IT'S GOT YOUR FUCKING NAME ON IT! EH!?! WHAT THE FUCK!?!

DON'T BOTHER, PLOD...YOU'RE GONE! THE COMPLAINTS HAVE BEEN COMING IN ALL DAY... SEXUAL HARASSMENT... CUSTOMS FRAUD... OBTAINING MONEY UNDER FALSE PRETENCES...

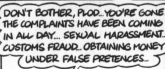

THE ROYAL MAIL, PLOD... ROYAL... WE'RE A REPUTABLE AND HIGHLY TRUSTED COMPANY ... THERE'S NO PLACE FOR THE LIKES OF YOU

AYE!.. WELL YOU CAN GO FUCK YERSELF ...POSTIES HAVE KEPT THE COUNTRY GOING THROUGH THIS PANDEMIC!.. DELIVERY SERVICES ARE THE BACK- -BONE OF SOCIETY...

THE COUNTRY NEEDS US, I'LL NOT LET THE PEOPLE I'LL GET ANOTHER JOB KEEP THE COUNTRY'S WHEELS C COMMERCE TURNING

RCEL, LOVE
OOH, LOVELY... DO I HAVE TO SIGN FOR IT?
OOH, NO... COVID AN' ALL THAT... I'VE JUST GOT TO TAKE A PICTURE TO SHOW IT'S BEEN DELIVERED
THERE WE GO...
CLICK!
GREAT
GPO
UBLE IS, THERE'S CUSTOMS TO PAY ON TERS FROM ABROAD NOW... A FIVER!
EEH, NO... THAT'S NOT RIGHT
IT IS, LOVE... BREXIT... NO POINT MOANING... YOU VOTED FOR IT
NO! I DIDN'T...
I VOTED TO STAY IN!
DID, LOVE... 'BRING ME A TLE OF MILK TOMORROW, IE' YOU SAID
EEH!.. I CAN'T REMEMBER THAT
WELL, YOU DID... THAT'LL BE A FIVER, LOVE
EEH!
BACK AT THE DEPOT...
PLOD... COULD YOU POP INTO MY OFFICE FOR A SECOND?
I KNOW YOU'VE FINISHED YOUR SHIFT, BUT THERE'S JUST ONE MORE LETTER TO DELIVER IF YOU DON'T MIND...
WELL, I DO
LOOKS LIKE A P45 TO ME... AND... WAIT A MINUTE...
BOSS
BLIMEY!.. WHERE'S MY IPHONE 11?..
...IT WAS SUPPOSED TO BE HERE BY LUNCHTIME
IPHONE 11?.. FOR FUCK'S SAKE...
P
pdp
...COULD HE NOT HAVE GOT THE 11-PRO, THE FUCKING CHEAP BASTARD

Ask the AB of C

YOUR theological enquiries answered by the Archbishop of Canterbury, JUSTIN WELBY

Dear AB of C, **I LENT** my neighbour my lawn mower last week, and he returned it with a crack in the grass collection box that wasn't there when I lent it to him. He never said anything and I found my heart full of dark, vengeful thoughts towards him. I know the Bible says that I should forgive him not seven times, but seventy times seven, but I don't want to lend it to him 490 times only for him to bring it back knackered. What should I do?

Len Mastiff, Tring

∗ *The Lord is very hot on forgiveness and you have a duty to pardon your neighbour's trespasses. Having said that, your neighbour has a duty to confess the sin of cracking your grass box and seek forgiveness. Since there is no contrition on his part, you are under no theological obligation to forgive him. Why don't you simply refuse to lend it to him in future? After all, it is said 'neither a borrower nor a lender be,' which I think comes from the Bible, perhaps Proverbs or something. But even if it doesn't, it's the kind of thing that's in there.*

Dear AB of C, **I MOVED** into a house by the River Ouse in York earlier this year, and to my dismay I found the insurance premium was sky high because the property was on a flood plain. I contacted the brokers and told them that God promised never to send another flood after the Noah incident, and even sent a rainbow as token of that everlasting covenant. But they still wanted a £600 excess on top to cover flood damage. I wonder if you could get in touch and assure them that God has promised not to send any more floods. It's with Admiral Homecare, and the policy number is AD65184/008/JC.

Edna Beagles, York

∗ *I think you have slightly misunderstood the Bible, Mrs Beagles. When the Lord promised to give up on the whole flood-sending business, he was talking about deluges of a Biblical proportion that wipeth all living things from the face of the earth. There has only been one of those and there certainly won't be any more. But He never said anything about a river bursting its banks and coming a couple of foot up your living room wall, so I'd pay the premium if I were you. Having said that, £600 is a little steep, so shop around. Alternatively, you could pray, asking the Lord to keep the waters down, but don't forget to do it every night or else your 'heavenly policy' may be invalidated.*

Dear AB of C, **I'VE GOT** one of those Nespresso coffee machines that makes lovely coffee, but for the past week it has been on the blink. It's out of guarantee, but our local small electricals repair shop want £60 just to look at it. And that's before parts. Are there any saints that look after small electricals who I could pray to and ask if they could fix it?

Doreen Pug, Bolton

∗ *I'm afraid we don't do saints, Doreen; you're thinking of the Catholic church, and converting to Catholicism would seem a bit of a drastic move to save £60. Perhaps you have a Catholic friend who could pray to the patron saint of small electricals and ask for a vicarious repair on your behalf. If not, you have nothing to lose by asking God to miraculously fix it, but to be honest, it's not really the kind of thing He does. I'd try checking the fuse and descaling it before you pray for its repair, and if the Lord decides in His wisdom not to intercede, then pop it down to the shop.*

Dear AB of C, **I WAS** always taught that God made all creatures, from the mightiest to the lowliest, and I was also led to believe He loved every one of us. So why did He make a virus that rips across the globe, killing the most vulnerable people in society in their hundreds of thousands? And why, when it looked like we were finally getting things under control with a vaccine does He start making all these variants of the bloody thing that are more deadly and more transmissible? I don't understand it.

Stan Terrier, London

∗ *Oh, sorry, Mr Terrier, I think I just heard the doorbell.*

*Have **YOU** got a theological question you would like answering? Write to the **AB of C, c/o Viz Comic, PO Box 841, Whitley Bay, NE26 9EQ.** But remember to keep your questions nice and simple - nothing too tricky about starving children, pandemics or earthquakes in parts of the world where the poor sods haven't got a pot to piss in.*

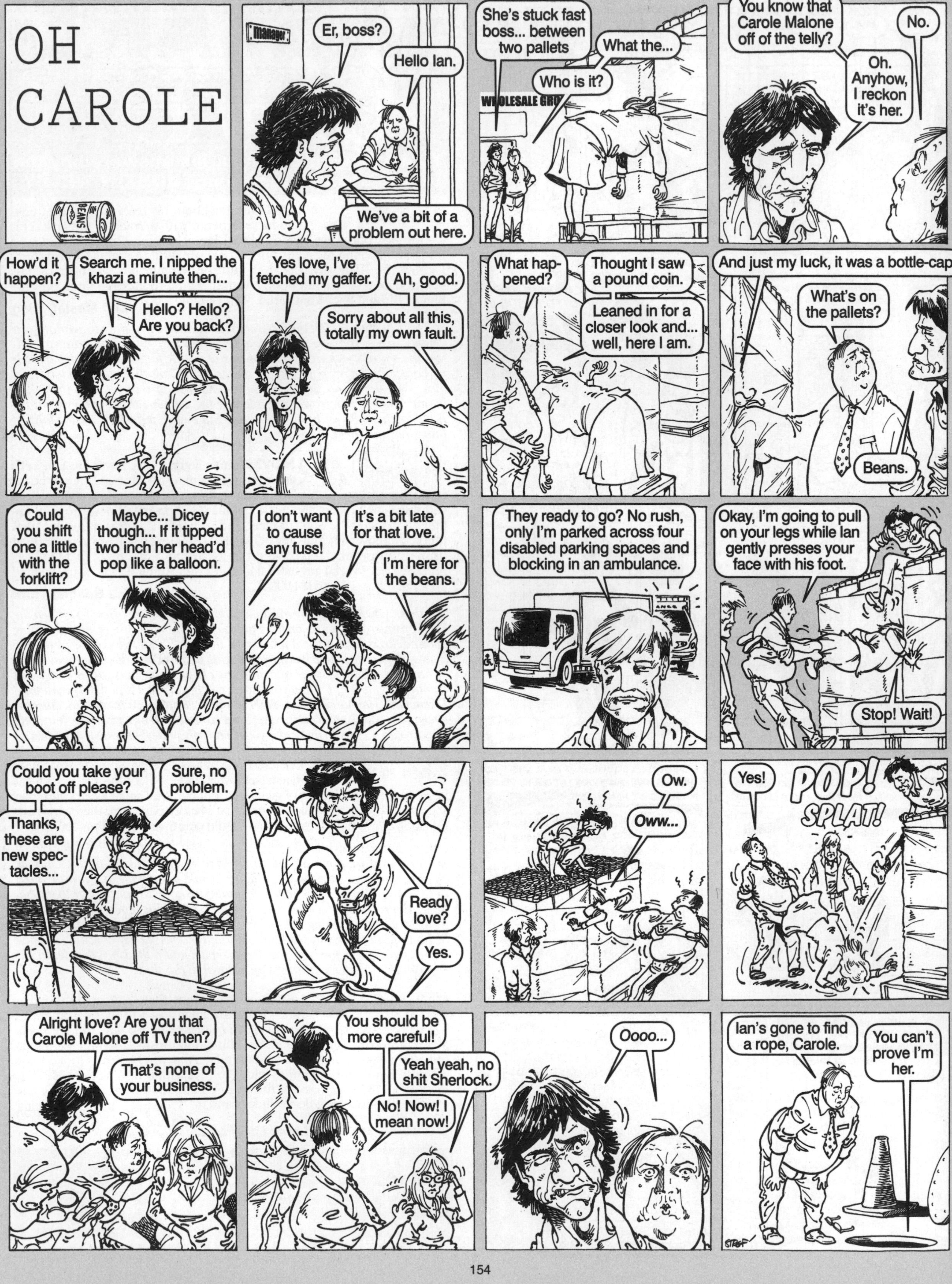
OH CAROLE
BEANS
Manager
Er, boss?
Hello Ian.
We've a bit of a problem out here.
She's stuck fast boss... between two pallets
What the...
Who is it?
WHOLESALE GRO
You know that Carole Malone off of the telly?
No.
Oh. Anyhow, I reckon it's her.
How'd it happen?
Search me. I nipped the khazi a minute then...
Hello? Hello? Are you back?
Yes love, I've fetched my gaffer.
Ah, good.
Sorry about all this, totally my own fault.
What happened?
Thought I saw a pound coin.
Leaned in for a closer look and... well, here I am.
And just my luck, it was a bottle-cap!
What's on the pallets?
Beans.
Could you shift one a little with the forklift?
Maybe... Dicey though... If it tipped two inch her head'd pop like a balloon.
I don't want to cause any fuss!
It's a bit late for that love.
I'm here for the beans.
They ready to go? No rush, only I'm parked across four disabled parking spaces and blocking in an ambulance.
Okay, I'm going to pull on your legs while Ian gently presses your face with his foot.
Stop! Wait!
Could you take your boot off please?
Sure, no problem.
Thanks, these are new spectacles...
Ready love?
Yes.
Ow.
Oww...
Yes!
POP!
SPLAT!
Alright love? Are you that Carole Malone off TV then?
That's none of your business.
You should be more careful!
Yeah yeah, no shit Sherlock.
No! Now! I mean now!
Oooo...
Ian's gone to find a rope, Carole.
You can't prove I'm her.

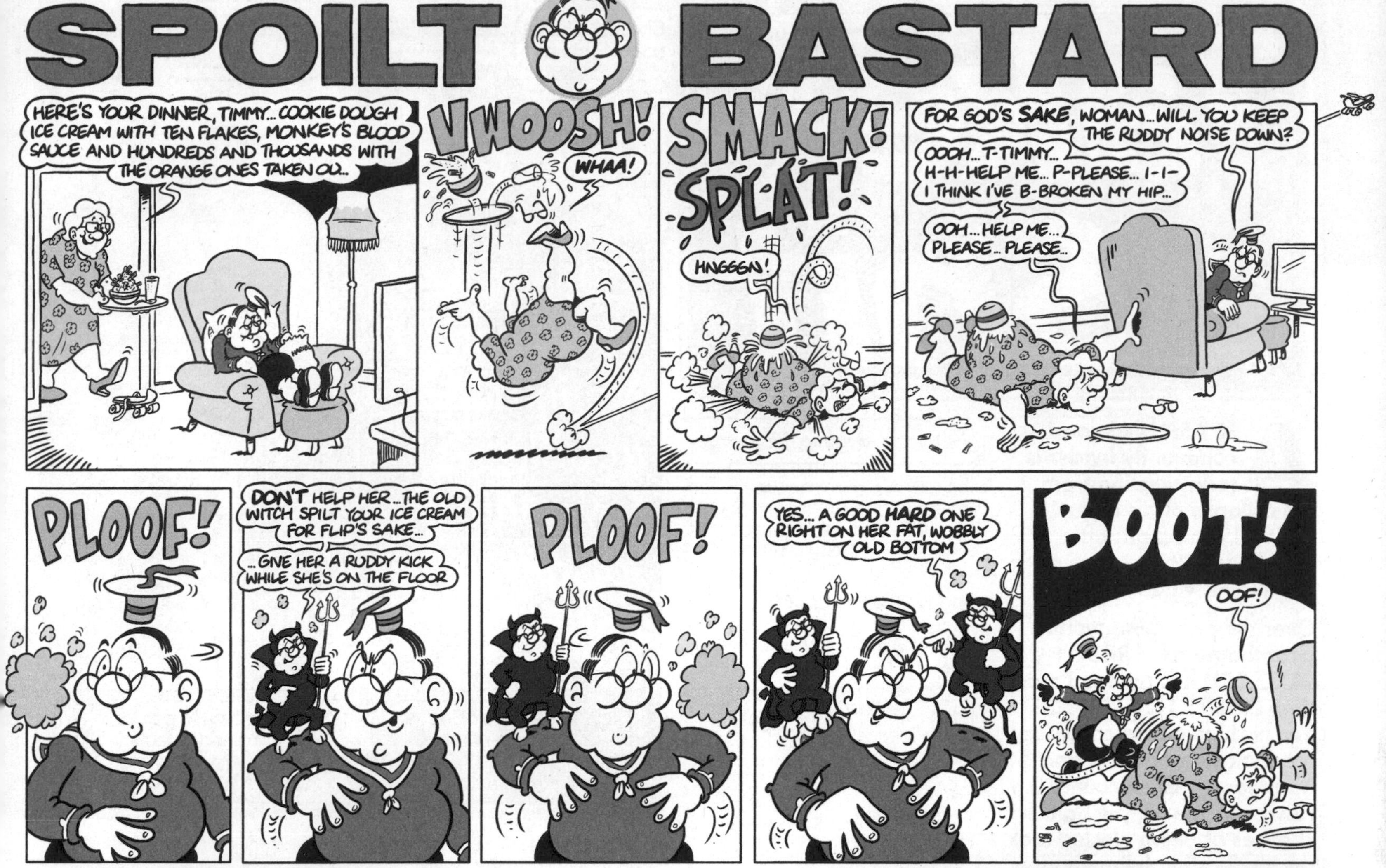
SPOILT BASTARD
HERE'S YOUR DINNER, TIMMY... COOKIE DOUGH ICE CREAM WITH TEN FLAKES, MONKEY'S BLOOD SAUCE AND HUNDREDS AND THOUSANDS WITH THE ORANGE ONES TAKEN OU..
VWOOSH!
WHAA!
SMACK!
SPLAT!
HNGGGN!
FOR GOD'S SAKE, WOMAN... WILL YOU KEEP THE RUDDY NOISE DOWN?
OOOH... T-TIMMY...
H-H-HELP ME... P-PLEASE... I-I-
I THINK I'VE B-BROKEN MY HIP...
OOH... HELP ME... PLEASE... PLEASE...
PLOOF!
DON'T HELP HER... THE OLD WITCH SPILT YOUR ICE CREAM FOR FLIP'S SAKE...
...GIVE HER A RUDDY KICK WHILE SHE'S ON THE FLOOR
PLOOF!
YES... A GOOD HARD ONE RIGHT ON HER FAT, WOBBLY OLD BOTTOM
BOOT!
OOF!

BATTLE OF AGINCOURT ENDS

POLICE in Northern France got a shock this week when they arrested a man who was still fighting the BATTLE OF AGINCOURT.

Responding to reports of a strangely dressed figure seen acting oddly in woods near Calais, gendarmes searched the area for several hours before spotting the man hiding behind a tree.

"He was brandishing some sort of weapon, so I ordered him to lay down his arms," said Chief Gendarme Didier LeBac. "He shouted something in reply, and I could tell he was English, but it was a strange dialect that I couldn't understand."

The man refused to comply with the Chief's commands, and brandished what appeared to be a longbow, causing officers to take cover behind trees.

After giving his name as Thomas Dutton, the man continued shouting to the confused police, ordering them to pledge allegiance to King Henry V.

Due to the presence of the longbow, the situation was classed as an armed siege and as things began to escalate, a police negotiator was brought in from Calais. A dialogue was struck up, and the situation calmed slightly.

EXCLUSIVE!

It emerged that Dutton had been patrolling the woods since the afternoon of St Crispin's Day 1415, and was seemingly unaware that the battle had been over for some 600 years. When M LeBac informed Dutton that their countries were now at peace, he accused him of being a 'Gaulish deceiver' and a 'hedge-born cox-comb', and said he would only take orders from his commanding officer.

elderly

After some brief research, the officer in command of Dutton's wing of the army at the time of the battle was identified as Sir Thomas Camoys of Trotton in Sussex. The elderly peer, who retired from the army in 1421, was contacted by Sussex constabulary and immediately agreed to travel to France and order his soldier to lay down his longbow.

"It was a very moving moment," said LeBac. "As Sir Thomas approached, Monsieur Dutton dropped to one knee and laid his longbow on the ground, saying 'my Liege', at which point the peer bade him 'arise'."

The longbowman was clearly relieved to learn that the battle was finally over, and the two men stood chatting for a few minutes, discussing stories of the battle. After a few minutes, they shook hands, at which point Mr Dutton was taken into custody by French police.

henry

Further research revealed that English King Henry V gave the command to disarm at 6pm on the day of the battle, October 25th 1415, but the messenger he sent to inform Dutton had died of an 'unspecified ague' on the way.

Police questioned the veteran archer for several hours, and he confessed that in the absence of an order to cease, he had continued to 'do his duty', spending the intervening 600 years 'loosing his shafts' at the French. He was asked about an incident in 1826, when a farmer from Fruges was hit in the thigh with an arrow, and another in 1968 when an arrow took off a postman's hat.

Dutton admitted culpability, but it was decided that no good would be served by prosecuting the Hundred Years War veteran and, after accepting a caution for behaviour likely to cause a breach of the peace, he was allowed to return home.

Merry St. Crispin's, War is Over: Battle of Agincourt 606 years ago, yesterday.

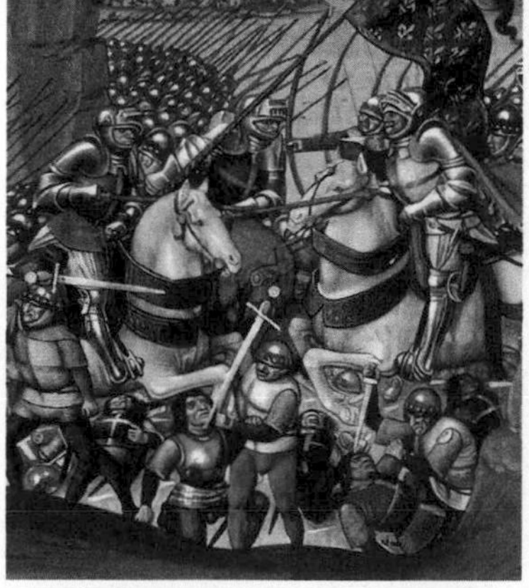

But Dutton's joy at seeing England again was short-lived. On arriving back, he discovered that the Nottinghamshire village of his birth had been wiped out in the second Great Plague of 1665, and that interest on an unpaid bill for a bushel of pig feed meant he now owes local landowner, the 12th Earl of Portland, £16 billion.

Take a Shit VIDEO

WINNER MAGAZINE OF THE YEAR ~Take a Shit Magazine of the Year Awards

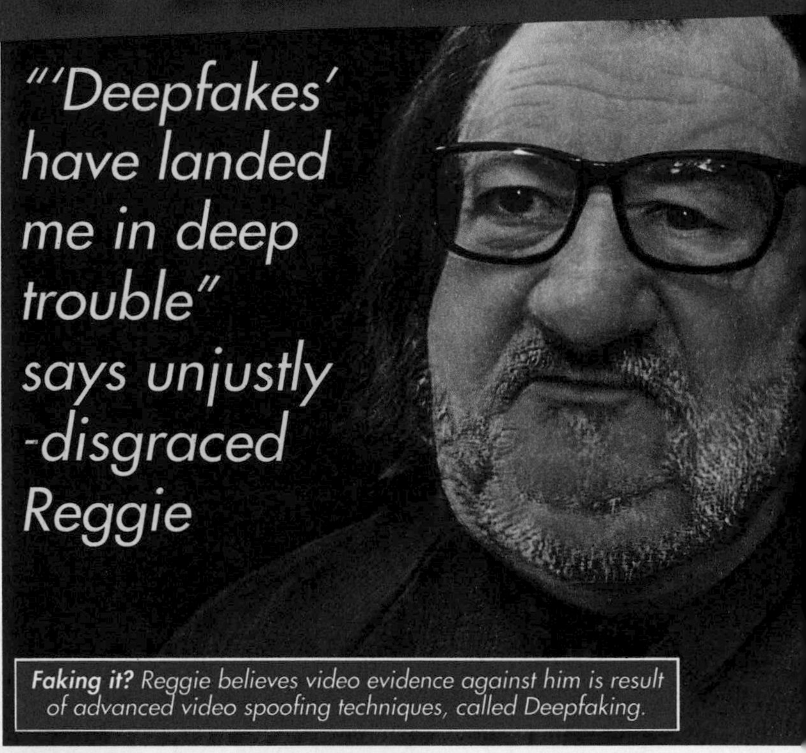

"'Deepfakes' have landed me in deep trouble" says unjustly-disgraced Reggie

Faking it? *Reggie believes video evidence against him is result of advanced video spoofing techniques, called Deepfaking.*

AN ASPIRING local community leader is today reeling from the collapse of his debut political campaign, after he fell victim to a series of 'deepfake' video hoaxes.

Over the past three months, Grantham-based REGGIE JAYCLOTH has pumped more than EIGHTY-FIVE POUNDS into his high profile candidacy for chairman of the Belton & Manthorpe parish council. However, the 61-year-old's chances of being elected look decidedly slim, following the release of cleverly doctored mobile phone and CCTV footage in which Reggie's face has been digitally transposed onto various figures undertaking sordid CRIMINAL activities.

"My shameless opponents will stoop to anything to besmirch my reputation," says thrice-convicted sex offender Reggie. *"Many of my political heroes have already been exposed to 'deepfake' smear tactics – Donald Trump, Vladimir Putin, Kim Jong-un – so I suppose it was only a matter of time before my cowardly electoral rivals employed similar strategies on me."*

The quality of 'deepfakes' (digitally manipulated videos in which one person's likeness is switched for another's) is progressing at an alarming speeds – so much so that it is becoming increasingly difficult even for experts to distinguish the real from the fabricated.

"It's astounding and terrifying," confirms quadruple divorcee Reggie. "To look at these hyper-realistic videos, you would genuinely think it was me doing all these sickening things. But it's not – and I'll take a lie detector test any time to prove it."

When we informed Reggie that we had access to a lie detector, he explained that it would be useless, as he has a medical condition which makes him sweat profusely and his heart rate increase when asked questions. "It would come out looking like I'd failed the test because of this condition, even though I'd passed," he informed us.

As told to ***Vaginia Discharge***

Here, speaking exclusively to *Viz*, Reggie tells his full, barely credible story for the first time, in the hope of clearing his name. "If it weren't for these vicious deepfake hoaxes, I could have been the next Martin Luther King, JFK or Laurence Fox", sighs the 26-stone bachelor. "But if just one fresh-faced political hopeful takes heed of my tragic tale and avoids becoming the next victim of synthetic media propaganda, then it will all have been worth it."

SHAM THEFT AUTO

Jobless Jaycloth's deepfake debacle began back in April, when he made the decision to run for local government.

"I'd been an active attendee at parish council meetings for many years, and as a firm believer in government accountability, I always make sure to watch the monthly assemblies on Zoom and chip in with helpful comments and advice for the councillors.

But recently I'd become sick to the back teeth of the increasingly draconian regulations the board was imposing. At the behest of their chairman – a thoroughly unpleasant ex-copper named Alan – the council talked constantly about cracking down on harmless activities like dog fighting, outdoor drinking and woodland-based group sex. I don't indulge in any of these pastimes myself, but as a staunch liberal I see no reason why the good people of Grantham should not do so if they so wish.

To look at these hyper-realistic videos, you would genuinely think it was me doing all these sickening things.

After one meeting in which Alan mooted the chillingly Orwellian concept of an *on-the-spot fine* for anyone caught light-heartedly masturbating in public, I decided enough was enough. I launched into a rambunctious half-hour monologue about this council's catalogue of past failures, culminating with the declaration that I – Reggie Jaycloth – intended to throw my own hat in the ring in the forthcoming council elections.

When I finished speaking, I was surprised to see the meeting continuing as usual, with nobody paying a blind bit of attention to me. It was only then I noticed that I had been 'muted' by Alan, presumably for some of the more lively comments I made about immigrants earlier in the meeting. Yet again the man in the street had been shut out of the elitist political debate. As I clicked 'Leave meeting,' I was more determined than ever to topple Alan's totalitarian dictatorship by being elected chairman myself.

I began penning my manifesto the very next day, deciding that my candidacy would revolve around making the streets of Belton and Manthorpe safer. I would be tough on crime, and tough on the *causes* of crime. As a successful second-hand car stereo salesman, I pride myself on earning an honest wage, and nothing sickens me more than those who break the law to line their pockets.

However, just as I finished drafting the opening paragraph, my doorbell rang. I answered it to find two policemen stood on the doorstep. It was a stroke of luck, I thought. Here were two real-life bobbies whose brains I could pick about how best to crack down on criminal wrong-doing! But the luck quickly changed as the pair proceeded to tell me they were actually here to place me **UNDER ARREST**.

When I asked what on earth for, they showed me a video that had been sent to them anonymously the previous evening. Recorded on a mobile phone from an upstairs window, it showed a man who bore a startling resemblance to myself wandering down a deserted street in the dead of night, smashing several car windows and yanking the stereos out of the dashboards.

My blood ran cold as I realised what had happened. I'd read an article on Facebook earlier that week about 'deepfake' videos and how they were being used to smear politicians, making them appear to say or do things they hadn't. After my announcement the previous evening, Alan had obviously hired a crack team of digital hackers to scupper my crime-focused campaign by grafting an image of my face onto the body of a common thief. I tried to explain this to the fuckwitted filth, but they simply wouldn't listen. The stack of car stereos in my garage – which I had bulk-bought legally, but sadly mislaid the receipts for – only compounded their 'evidence.'

NASTY!

Lay-by the book: Reggie believes he was unscrupulously deepfaked into a dirty online 'dogging' movie.

I was hit with a whopping fine and given thirty days community service. I knew that as an outspoken outsider with little to no political experience, the liberal elite would do everything they could to shut my candidacy down before it could build up a head of steam.

But not for one second did I imagine they would go to lengths as sinister and despicable as these. "

CAN'T STOOL ME TWICE

Shrugging off his first setback at the hands of deepfake hoax technology, Reggie pushed ahead with his campaign to be elected parish council chairman.

" Once I'd finished my stint scrubbing graffiti off the local underpass, I decided it was time to relaunch my campaign at a grassroots level. Holed up in his decadent ivory tower – a two-bedroomed mid-terrace mansion off the A607, Alan had clearly lost touch with the common people. My candidacy would revolve around regaining the public's trust and connecting with them personally, in a way that Alan has never been able to throughout his merciless reign of terror.

Donning my smartest suit, I spent the entire day pounding the pavements of Belton, chatting with its salt of the earth residents. Every single person I spoke to me told me they were sick to death of living in Alan's oppressive one-party state. As the day wore on, I shook hands, I kissed babies and I kicked a football with local youths. Little by little I sensed I was restoring the public's faith in local government.

When I got home that evening, I cracked open a few bottles of celebratory white cider and toasted myself for a job well done. I felt I had won the hearts, minds and trust of my would-be electorate.

Clean break: Jaycloth was made to scrub local underpass as part of community service.

Unfortunately, my celebrations were short-lived. A knock on the door an hour later revealed the same pair of cock-witted policemen who'd wrongfully arrested me a few weeks earlier. This time, the duo spouted a pathetic tissue of lies about me 'vandalising public property.'

I laughed long and loud at this preposterous accusation – but then, one of the rozzers pulled out an iPad and showed me some CCTV footage he claimed had been recorded earlier that day.

It appeared to show a man who strongly resembled me drinking heavily and ranting to himself as he staggered around the local precinct. Fast-forwarding through several hours of this, the footage then followed my digital doppelganger as he stumbled three streets over, and proceeded to drop his trousers, before **DEFECATING** violently outside the front door of Alan's house.

It would be the understatement of the century to say that I couldn't believe what I was seeing. Clearly, this was another spiteful, politically motivated deepfake, but the quality of it was *remarkable*. My face had been superimposed so perfectly that even my own mother would have sworn it was me in the video, shitting on Alan's front step.

I had to hand it to the parish council's shady cabal of cyber terrorists: *they were good. Real good.*

I knew full well I had countless alibis to prove my innocence, since I'd spent the day knocking on doors and talking to voters. But I also knew full well that if Alan's team could deepfake me into looking like I'd done a shit on his doormat, they could do the same – or worse – to my beloved electorate. Not wanting to risk the reputations of hundreds of innocent Grantham residents, I selflessly accepted the 200 hour community service slap on the wrist, vowing never again to let myself fall foul of this kind of sinister digital manipulation.

Little did I know, Alan's dastardly deepfake squadron were already plotting their biggest hoax yet... "

SEX, LIES & VIDEO-FAKE

From Bill Clinton to Silvio Berlusconi, politicians and sex scandals go hand

> ### I had to hand it to the parish council's shady cabal of cyber terrorists: they were good. Real good.

in hand. But so-loyal Reggie was certain that his rock solid seventh marriage could handle anything his corrupt opponents could throw at it.

" My beloved fifth wife Carol is the light of my life. Or at least she was – until my political rivals' unscrupulous deepfake propaganda got to her.

The parish council elections were due to kick-off on Monday morning, with voting taking place at the Manthorpe Town Hall. Now, I'd missed out on valuable campaigning hours due to my 200 hours community for 'curling one out' on Alan's doorstep. I've done finger quotes around 'curling one out' because, obviously, I never did anything of the sort – my face was just deepfaked onto whoever did. That's the truth, and as I've explained, a lie detector test would be inconclusive due to my medical condition.

Anyroad, I planned to head to the venue early with Carol, both of us dressed up to the nines, to do a bit of last-minute flesh-pressing in my attempt to topple Alan's tyrannical autocracy.

I leapt out of bed to brush my teeth and sink an invigorating can of white cider, all ready for what should have been the proudest day of my life. But when I came back to the bedroom to get dressed, I found Carol staring at her laptop with a face like thunder. 'What the ruddy hell is this, Reg?' she fumed. Although truth be told she didn't say 'ruddy' – she said a word that is simply too rude to print here – *effing!* (ie. fucking).

I glanced at the screen, and my stomach dropped into my shoes. It was an adult site called 'PornHub' and the video Carol was watching was entitled 'Wild dogging sesh in Manthorpe Woods.' Right in front of me, in breathtaking high definition, was what appeared to be **ME**, enjoying full penetrative intercourse with the barmaid from my local pub, whilst a crowd of sick perverts masturbated frantically around us.

Now, let me be very clear, dogging – or indeed any kind of public group

sex – is not something I am interested in. Simple as, end of. You can check my internet history if you want proof. I don't mean right now, by the way. I'm just saying, theoretically, you're welcome to check it so long as you give me a day or so's notice.

But as I watched the sordid video, I understood why Carol was so angry. *It was the most convincing deepfake I'd ever seen.*

The technology Alan's team were using had progressed so rapidly that they had not only perfectly replicated my face – they had also replicated my *body*, right down to the thick, matted hair on my shoulders, and the 'Tommy Robinson for PM' tattoo on my arse. They had even deepfaked Carol's Seat Alhambra – numberplate and all – over the car 'I' was shagging inside. Most sinister of all, they'd deepfaked my cock to look much smaller than it really is.

Carol had been sent the video by a friend, and had fallen hook, line and sinker for the cunningly manipulated hoax. Clearly, my parish political rivals thought that if they could dislodge the trusty bedrock of my marriage, they could topple my entire campaign. *And they were right.*

I tried to explain everything to Carol, but she called me every unprintable name under the sun and ordered me out of the house for good. I was so upset, I forgot all about the election, and Alan subsequently got voted back in as chairman for the next four years.

Now, as I sit here in my bedsit, my tears soaking into the divorce papers Carol has just sent me, I realise that the grubby world of politics is no place for a decent man like myself. My reputation – like my marriage – is in tatters, and may never recover. So, the next time you have fun with a face-swapping 'app' or chuckle at a YouTube video of Nicolas Cage superimposed over Gregg Wallace, just remember: *deepfakes can ruin lives.* "

NEXT WEEK: *Reggie decides to run for President of the United States of America, only for Joe Biden's team to deepfake him into a video of a man selling knock-off sportswear outside a Sedgebrook pub car park*

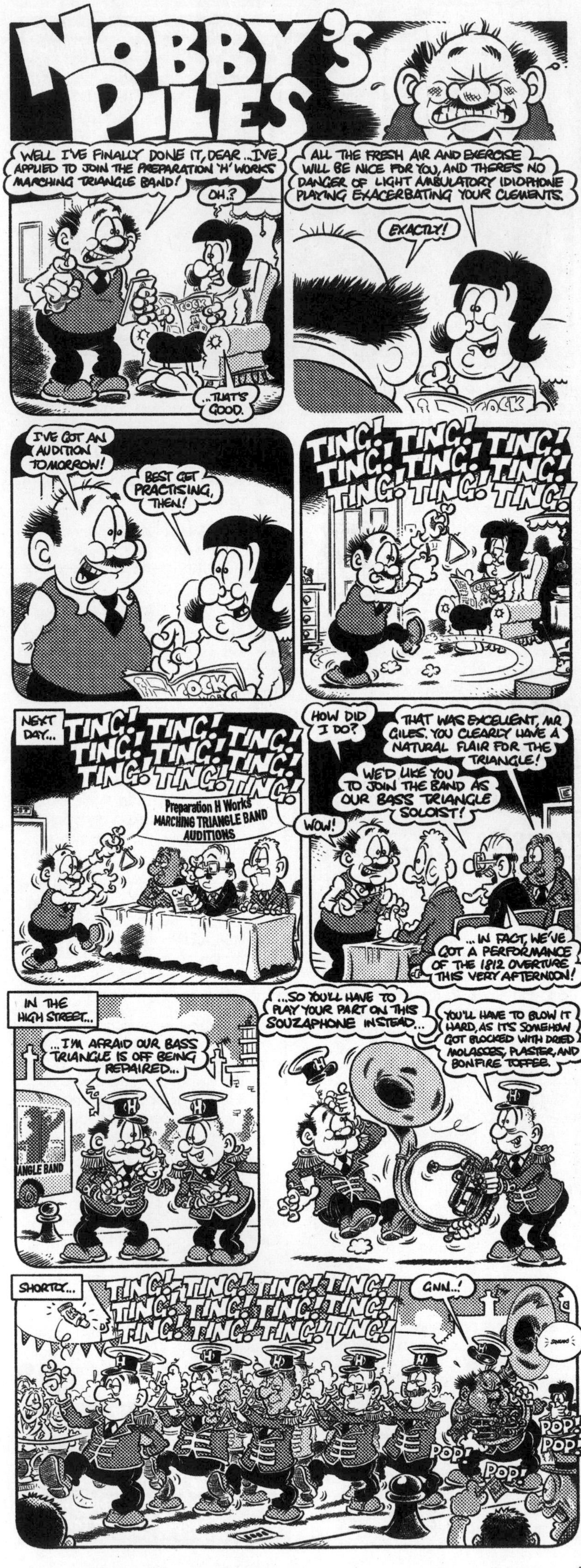
NOBBY'S PILES
WELL I'VE FINALLY DONE IT, DEAR.. I'VE APPLIED TO JOIN THE PREPARATION 'H' WORKS MARCHING TRIANGLE BAND!
OH.?
ALL THE FRESH AIR AND EXERCISE WILL BE NICE FOR YOU, AND THERE'S NO DANGER OF LIGHT AMBULATORY IDIOPHONE PLAYING EXACERBATING YOUR CLEMENTS.
EXACTLY!
...THAT'S GOOD.
I'VE GOT AN AUDITION TOMORROW!
BEST GET PRACTISING, THEN!
TING! TING! TING! TING! TING! TING! TING! TING! TING!
NEXT DAY...
TING! TING! TING! TING! TING! TING! TING! TING! TING!
Preparation H Works MARCHING TRIANGLE BAND AUDITIONS
HOW DID I DO?
THAT WAS EXCELLENT, MR GILES. YOU CLEARLY HAVE A NATURAL FLAIR FOR THE TRIANGLE!
WE'D LIKE YOU TO JOIN THE BAND AS OUR BASS TRIANGLE SOLOIST!
WOW!
...IN FACT, WE'VE GOT A PERFORMANCE OF THE 1812 OVERTURE THIS VERY AFTERNOON!
IN THE HIGH STREET...
...I'M AFRAID OUR BASS TRIANGLE IS OFF BEING REPAIRED...
...SO YOU'LL HAVE TO PLAY YOUR PART ON THIS SOUZAPHONE INSTEAD...
YOU'LL HAVE TO BLOW IT HARD, AS IT'S SOMEHOW GOT BLOCKED WITH DRIED MOLASSES, PLASTER, AND BONFIRE TOFFEE.
SHORTLY...
TING! TING! TING! TING! TING! TING! TING! TING! TING! TING! TING! TING!
GNN..!
POP! POP! POP! POP!

DAZED DONOVAN IN ALASKA FLASHBACK FIASCO

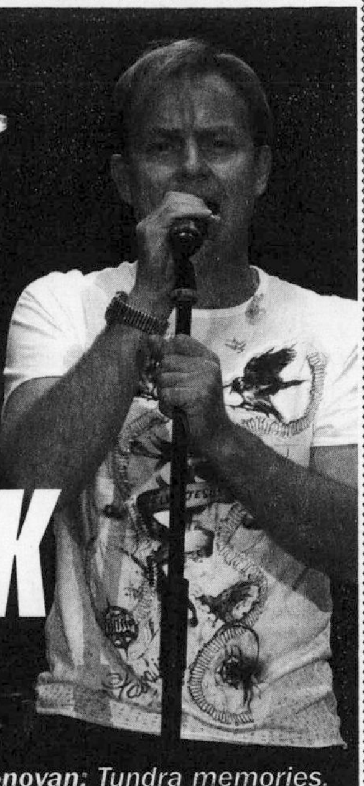
Donovan: *Tundra memories.*

THIS YEAR'S prestigious Pride of Britain awards ceremony was last night disrupted after host Jason Donovan experienced a flashback to a past life as a nineteenth century Alaskan fur-trader.

EXCLUSIVE!

The lavish ceremony at the Grosvenor House Hotel had been underway for forty minutes, and the former *Neighbours* star was mid way through presenting a trophy to a man who had jumped into a canal to save a pensioner, when he suddenly fell silent and gazed blankly into the camera while clutching at his hair.

Fellow presenter Carol Vorderman immediately saw something was wrong and stepped forward to finish presenting the award. After a short pause, the Aussie songster shook himself from his trance and offered an explanation as to what had happened.

"I don't…I'm…sorry, everyone. I just…I just had a flashback to when I was a fur-trader in 1850s Alaska," the *Too Many Broken Hearts* singer told the invited audience.

"I don't know where you guys stand on reincarnation, but I've just briefly regressed into one of my immutable soul's previous vessels," he continued. "It was really something, I can tell you."

herring

The former heartthrob, who was once on-screen romantically linked with Kylie Minogue, went on to relay in vivid detail the content of his flashback, speaking evocatively of the scent of dried herring on the Anchorage dockside, the scratchy-yet-warm feel of the enormous seal fur mittens he wore, and the thrill of bartering thirty bear pelts for an enormous iron cooking pot.

With the audience growing restless, Donovan, who boasts 4 number 1 singles and 3 platinum albums, elaborated on his family life on the windswept tundra north of the Bering Strait, giving potted biographies of his wife and each of his fourteen children, as well as the names of all thirty dogs in his sleigh team.

lee

After 25 minutes, the *Especially For You* singer stopped his musings and continued with the ceremony. But due to the tight scheduling of the evening, many of the winners were bumped from the running order, including brave cabbie Ron Brylcream, who had travelled from Inverness to receive an award after rescuing a dog from a bonfire.

"Don't get me wrong, it's all very interesting hearing about igloo construction techniques and overland trade routes from Greenland," Brylcream told *The Daily Express*. "But I've achieved literally one thing in my life and it was this award. Now I'm not even going to get it," he complained.

grobbelaar

TV historian Mark Lawson put Donovan's time-jump experience in context: "While incidents like this aren't exactly an everyday occurrence, this isn't the first time this kind of thing has happened," he told the *Radio Times*. "Older viewers may remember Eamonn Andrews flashing back to his time as Prefect of Ilyria during Eddie Large's *This Is Your Life*."

"And more recently there was Denise Van Outen interrupting the final episode of *The Big Breakfast* to tell viewers she'd just realised she's the reincarnation of Cardinal Wolsey," he added.

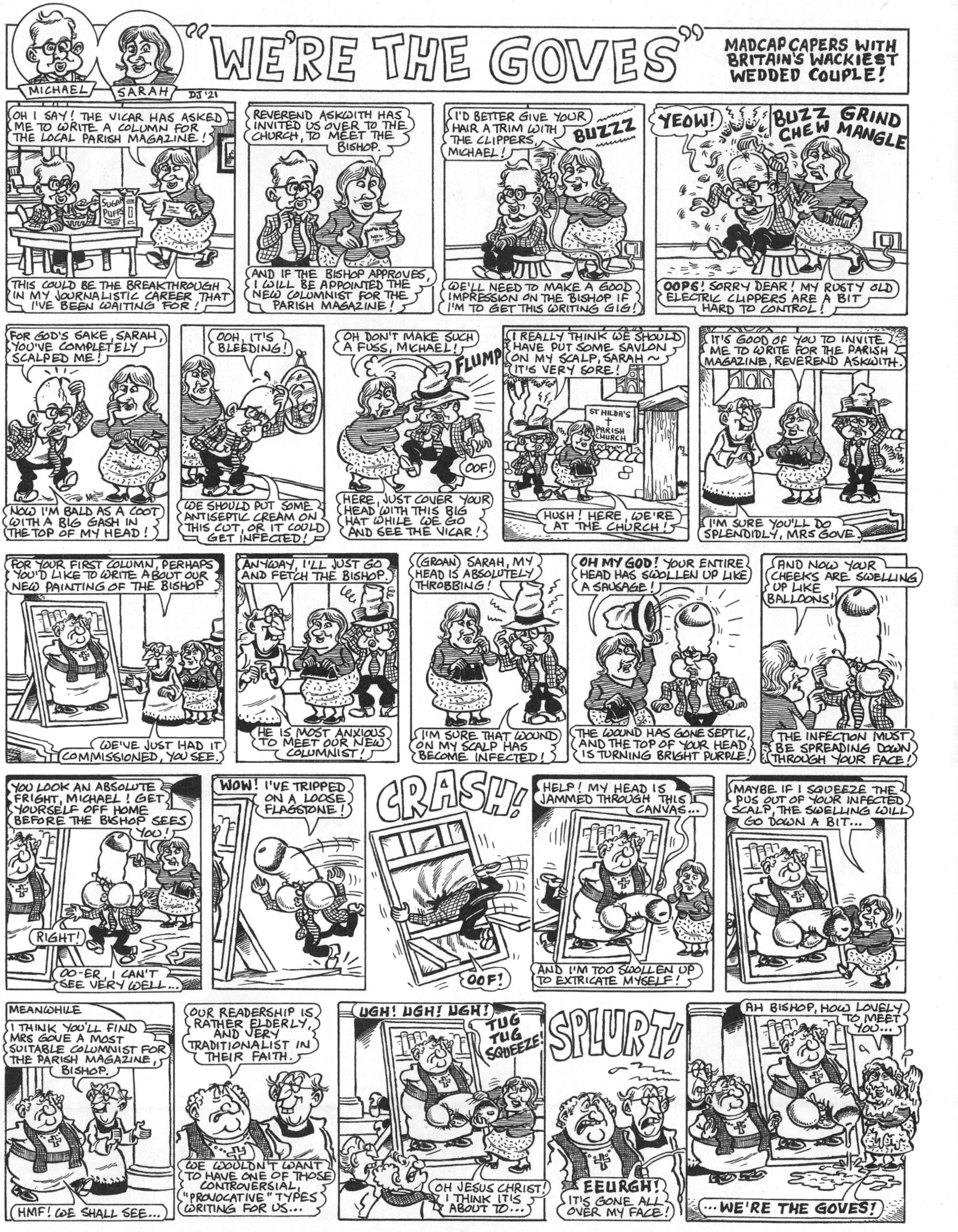

MICHAEL
SARAH
DJ '21
"WE'RE THE GOVES"
MADCAP CAPERS WITH BRITAIN'S WACKIEST WEDDED COUPLE!
OH I SAY! THE VICAR HAS ASKED ME TO WRITE A COLUMN FOR THE LOCAL PARISH MAGAZINE!
SUGAR PUFFS
THIS COULD BE THE BREAKTHROUGH IN MY JOURNALISTIC CAREER THAT I'VE BEEN WAITING FOR!
REVEREND ASKWITH HAS INVITED US OVER TO THE CHURCH, TO MEET THE BISHOP.
AND IF THE BISHOP APPROVES, I WILL BE APPOINTED THE NEW COLUMNIST FOR THE PARISH MAGAZINE!
I'D BETTER GIVE YOUR HAIR A TRIM WITH THE CLIPPERS, MICHAEL!
BUZZZ
WE'LL NEED TO MAKE A GOOD IMPRESSION ON THE BISHOP IF I'M TO GET THIS WRITING GIG!
YEOW!
BUZZ GRIND CHEW MANGLE
OOPS! SORRY DEAR! MY RUSTY OLD ELECTRIC CLIPPERS ARE A BIT HARD TO CONTROL!
FOR GOD'S SAKE, SARAH, YOU'VE COMPLETELY SCALPED ME!
NOW I'M BALD AS A COOT WITH A BIG GASH IN THE TOP OF MY HEAD!
OOH, IT'S BLEEDING!
WE SHOULD PUT SOME ANTISEPTIC CREAM ON THIS CUT, OR IT COULD GET INFECTED!
OH DON'T MAKE SUCH A FUSS, MICHAEL!
FLUMP
OOF!
HERE, JUST COVER YOUR HEAD WITH THIS BIG HAT WHILE WE GO AND SEE THE VICAR!
I REALLY THINK WE SHOULD HAVE PUT SOME SAVLON ON MY SCALP, SARAH ~ IT'S VERY SORE!
ST HILDA'S PARISH CHURCH
HUSH! HERE, WE'RE AT THE CHURCH!
IT'S GOOD OF YOU TO INVITE ME TO WRITE FOR THE PARISH MAGAZINE, REVEREND ASKWITH.
I'M SURE YOU'LL DO SPLENDIDLY, MRS GOVE.
FOR YOUR FIRST COLUMN, PERHAPS YOU'D LIKE TO WRITE ABOUT OUR NEW PAINTING OF THE BISHOP
WE'VE JUST HAD IT COMMISSIONED, YOU SEE.
ANYWAY, I'LL JUST GO AND FETCH THE BISHOP.
HE IS MOST ANXIOUS TO MEET OUR NEW COLUMNIST!
(GROAN) SARAH, MY HEAD IS ABSOLUTELY THROBBING!
I'M SURE THAT WOUND ON MY SCALP HAS BECOME INFECTED!
OH MY GOD! YOUR ENTIRE HEAD HAS SWOLLEN UP LIKE A SAUSAGE!
THE WOUND HAS GONE SEPTIC, AND THE TOP OF YOUR HEAD IS TURNING BRIGHT PURPLE!
AND NOW YOUR CHEEKS ARE SWELLING UP LIKE BALLOONS!
THE INFECTION MUST BE SPREADING DOWN THROUGH YOUR FACE!
YOU LOOK AN ABSOLUTE FRIGHT, MICHAEL! GET YOURSELF OFF HOME BEFORE THE BISHOP SEES YOU!
RIGHT!
OO-ER, I CAN'T SEE VERY WELL...
WOW! I'VE TRIPPED ON A LOOSE FLAGSTONE!
CRASH!
OOF!
HELP! MY HEAD IS JAMMED THROUGH THIS CANVAS...
AND I'M TOO SWOLLEN UP TO EXTRICATE MYSELF!
MAYBE IF I SQUEEZE THE PUS OUT OF YOUR INFECTED SCALP, THE SWELLING WILL GO DOWN A BIT...
MEANWHILE
I THINK YOU'LL FIND MRS GOVE A MOST SUITABLE COLUMNIST FOR THE PARISH MAGAZINE, BISHOP.
HMF! WE SHALL SEE...
OUR READERSHIP IS RATHER ELDERLY, AND VERY TRADITIONALIST IN THEIR FAITH.
WE WOULDN'T WANT TO HAVE ONE OF THOSE CONTROVERSIAL, "PROVOCATIVE" TYPES WRITING FOR US...
UGH! UGH! UGH!
TUG TUG SQUEEZE!
OH JESUS CHRIST! I THINK IT'S ABOUT TO...
SPLURT!
EEURGH!
IT'S GONE ALL OVER MY FACE!
AH BISHOP, HOW LOVELY TO MEET YOU...
...WE'RE THE GOVES!

JACK BLACK AND THE Bilderberg Mystery
The Christmas holidays were here at last, and young Jack Black and his dog Silver were staying with Aunt Meg at her Bilderberg Group golfing hotel in the Cotswold village of Castlecombover…
There you are, Herr Strauss… room 23 on the second floor.
Danke.
What's going on, Aunt Meg? The hotel is full of sinister men…
Yes, Jack. They're all members of the Bilderberg Group. They've come to my hotel for their annual Christmas dinner.
The Bilderberg Group!?! Who are they?
They're a shadowy group of world leaders who regularly meet in secret in order to discuss financial matters, Jack.
Really!?… that all sounds very suspicious, if you ask me.
Well suspicious or not, the hotel is nice and full, Jack…
…and what they discuss while they are having dinner is up to them.
STAFF ONLY KITCHEN
I've hired Miss Hawthorn from the village to help you wait at the table tonight.
Hmm! Okay, Aunt Meg… but something's not right.
That night, Jack listened carefully as he and Miss Hawthorn served Christmas dinner to the Bilderberg diners…
…but this year I turned over 18.3 billion… 5 billion up on last year.
Well how did you achieve that, Gerhardt?
I simply split my company in two wholly-owned subsidiary companies, each of which loaned half of their assets to the other, meaning neither made a profit on paper…
I say!… so a zero tax bill.
Indeed.
You made a mistake there, Gerhardt. If you had written the debts off immediately on both of the companies, they would have made theoretical losses of around 9 billion, and you would have been eligable for a 3 billion tax rebate.
Ha!… Next year, Nikolas… next year.
This is a beautiful hotel, my dear… have you worked here long?
Oh, no, sir, I run the wool shop in the village… The owner asked me if I would help out tonight.
And what about you, young man? Are you just working here for the evening?
No. My Aunt Meg is the owner of Labumum House.
Ah! Indeed.
Well, if you are going to inherit this wonderful place, have your Aunt leave it to you in a trust fund of which you are both executor and sole beneficiary…
…that way you can liquidate the assets to a company which you create and are sole director of without it being subject to capital gains tax.
Speaking of which, Charles, how did the sale of your estate go?
Splendidly… I sold it to one of my companies and rented it back to myself via an intermediate shell company, defaulted on the payments and claimed on the insurance…
…I ended up getting twice the market value in cash… and I still own the place.
That's genius, Charles.
I'll introduce you to the man who devised the scheme.
CLAP! CLAP! CLAP!

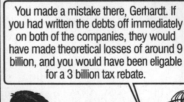

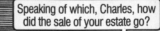

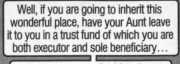

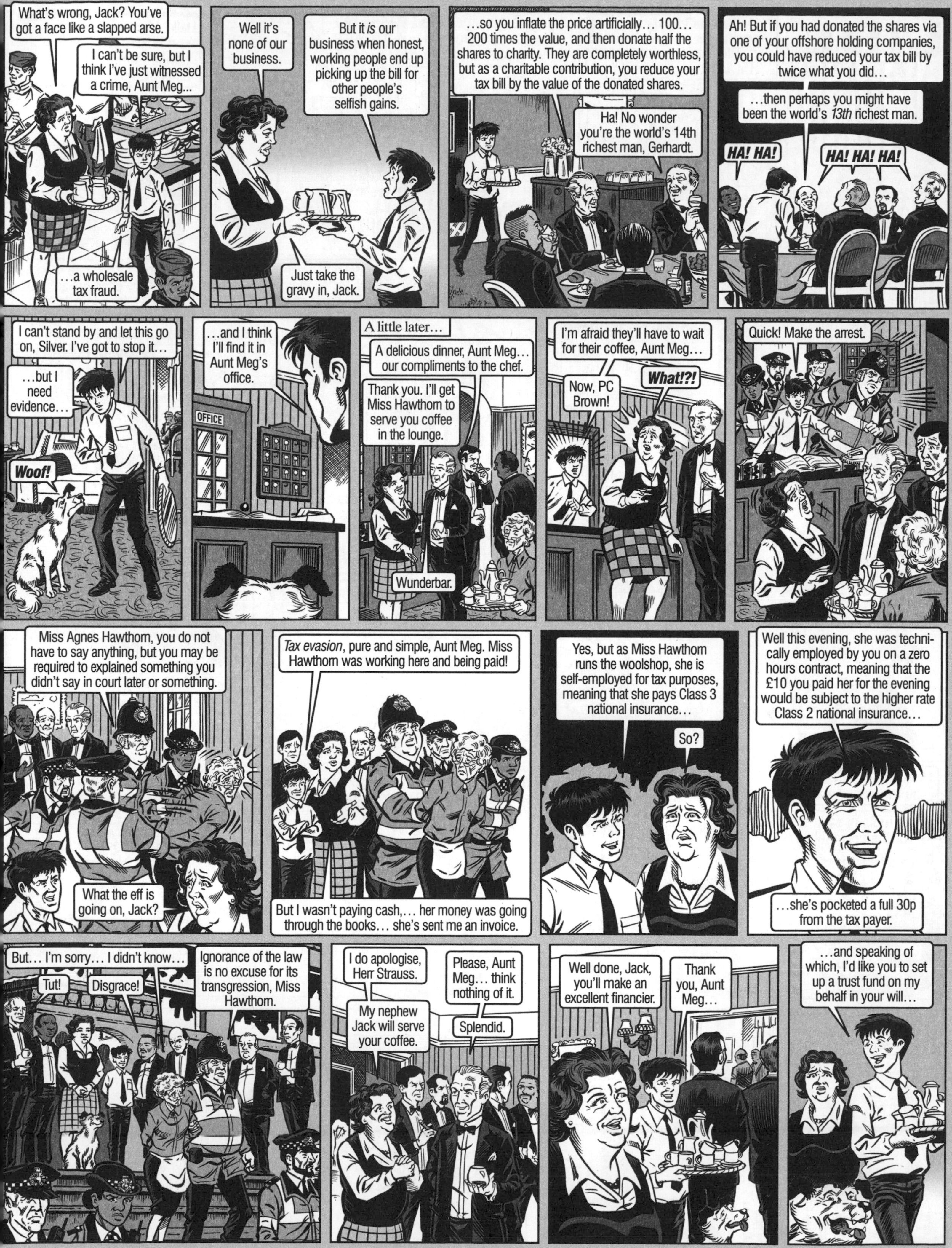

What's wrong, Jack? You've got a face like a slapped arse.
I can't be sure, but I think I've just witnessed a crime, Aunt Meg...
...a wholesale tax fraud.
Well it's none of our business.
But it *is* our business when honest, working people end up picking up the bill for other people's selfish gains.
Just take the gravy in, Jack.
...so you inflate the price artificially... 100... 200 times the value, and then donate half the shares to charity. They are completely worthless, but as a charitable contribution, you reduce your tax bill by the value of the donated shares.
Ha! No wonder you're the world's 14th richest man, Gerhardt.
Ah! But if you had donated the shares via one of your offshore holding companies, you could have reduced your tax bill by twice what you did...
...then perhaps you might have been the world's *13th* richest man.
HA! HA!
HA! HA! HA!
I can't stand by and let this go on, Silver. I've got to stop it...
...but I need evidence...
Woof!
...and I think I'll find it in Aunt Meg's office.
OFFICE
A little later...
A delicious dinner, Aunt Meg... our compliments to the chef.
Thank you. I'll get Miss Hawthorn to serve you coffee in the lounge.
Wunderbar.
I'm afraid they'll have to wait for their coffee, Aunt Meg...
Now, PC Brown!
What!?!
Quick! Make the arrest.
Miss Agnes Hawthorn, you do not have to say anything, but you may be required to explained something you didn't say in court later or something.
What the eff is going on, Jack?
Tax evasion, pure and simple, Aunt Meg. Miss Hawthorn was working here and being paid!
But I wasn't paying cash,... her money was going through the books... she's sent me an invoice.
Yes, but as Miss Hawthorn runs the woolshop, she is self-employed for tax purposes, meaning that she pays Class 3 national insurance...
So?
Well this evening, she was technically employed by you on a zero hours contract, meaning that the £10 you paid her for the evening would be subject to the higher rate Class 2 national insurance...
...she's pocketed a full 30p from the tax payer.
But... I'm sorry... I didn't know...
Tut!
Disgrace!
Ignorance of the law is no excuse for its transgression, Miss Hawthorn.
I do apologise, Herr Strauss.
My nephew Jack will serve your coffee.
Please, Aunt Meg... think nothing of it.
Splendid.
Well done, Jack, you'll make an excellent financier.
Thank you, Aunt Meg...
...and speaking of which, I'd like you to set up a trust fund on my behalf in your will...

The End

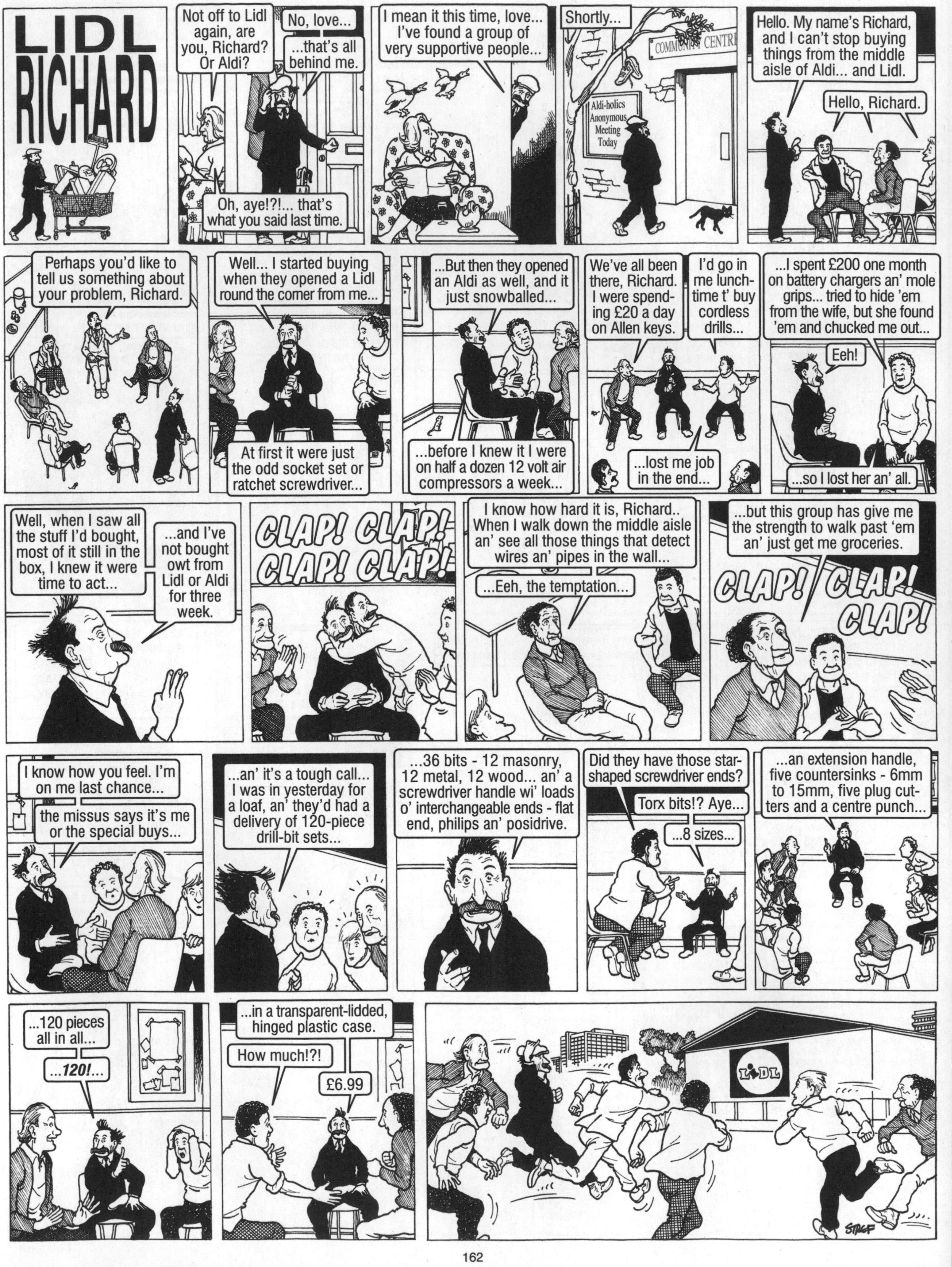
LIDL RICHARD
Not off to Lidl again, are you, Richard? Or Aldi?
No, love...
...that's all behind me.
Oh, aye!?!... that's what you said last time.
I mean it this time, love... I've found a group of very supportive people...
Shortly...
COMMUNITY CENTRE
Aldi-holics Anonymous Meeting Today
Hello. My name's Richard, and I can't stop buying things from the middle aisle of Aldi... and Lidl.
Hello, Richard.
Perhaps you'd like to tell us something about your problem, Richard.
Well... I started buying when they opened a Lidl round the corner from me...
At first it were just the odd socket set or ratchet screwdriver...
...But then they opened an Aldi as well, and it just snowballed...
...before I knew it I were on half a dozen 12 volt air compressors a week...
We've all been there, Richard. I were spending £20 a day on Allen keys.
I'd go in me lunch-time t' buy cordless drills...
...lost me job in the end...
...I spent £200 one month on battery chargers an' mole grips... tried to hide 'em from the wife, but she found 'em and chucked me out...
Eeh!
...so I lost her an' all.
Well, when I saw all the stuff I'd bought, most of it still in the box, I knew it were time to act...
...and I've not bought owt from Lidl or Aldi for three week.
CLAP! CLAP! CLAP! CLAP!
I know how hard it is, Richard.. When I walk down the middle aisle an' see all those things that detect wires an' pipes in the wall...
...Eeh, the temptation...
...but this group has give me the strength to walk past 'em an' just get me groceries.
CLAP! CLAP! CLAP!
I know how you feel. I'm on me last chance...
the missus says it's me or the special buys...
...an' it's a tough call... I was in yesterday for a loaf, an' they'd had a delivery of 120-piece drill-bit sets...
...36 bits - 12 masonry, 12 metal, 12 wood... an' a screwdriver handle wi' loads o' interchangeable ends - flat end, philips an' posidrive.
Did they have those star-shaped screwdriver ends?
Torx bits!? Aye...
...8 sizes...
...an extension handle, five countersinks - 6mm to 15mm, five plug cutters and a centre punch...
...120 pieces all in all...
...120!...
...in a transparent-lidded, hinged plastic case.
How much!?!
£6.99
LIDL
STRGF

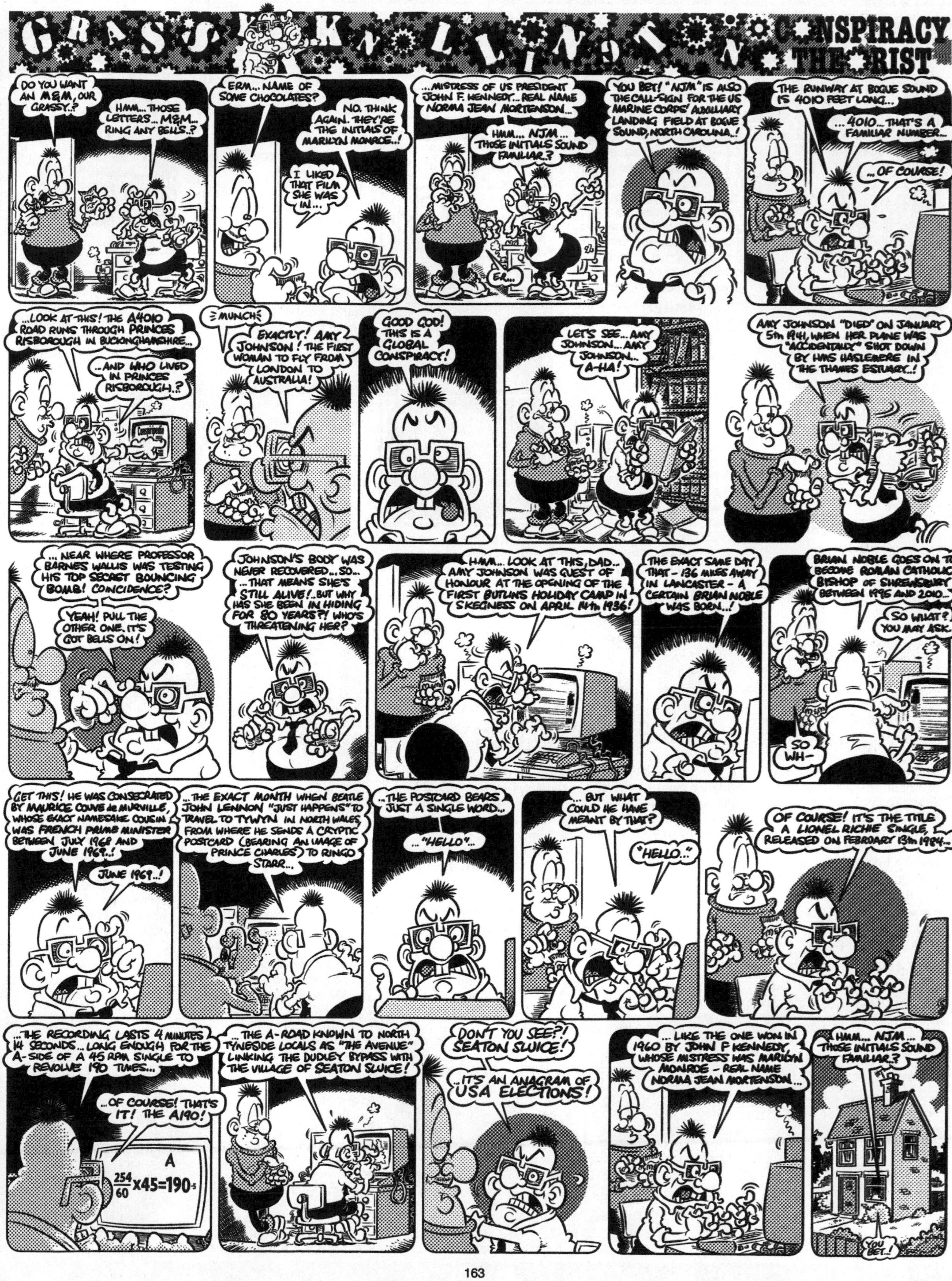
GRASSY KNOLLINGTON
CONSPIRACY THEORIST
DO YOU WANT AN M&M, OUR GRASSY..?
HMM... THOSE LETTERS... M&M... RING ANY BELLS..?
ERM... NAME OF SOME CHOCOLATES?
NO. THINK AGAIN. THEY'RE THE INITIALS OF MARILYN MONROE..!
I LIKED THAT FILM SHE WAS IN...
...MISTRESS OF US PRESIDENT JOHN F. KENNEDY... REAL NAME NORMA JEAN MORTENSON...
HMM... NJM... THOSE INITIALS SOUND FAMILIAR..?
ER...
YOU BET! "NJM" IS ALSO THE CALL-SIGN FOR THE US MARINE CORPS' AUXILIARY LANDING FIELD AT BOGUE SOUND, NORTH CAROLINA..!
THE RUNWAY AT BOGUE SOUND IS 4010 FEET LONG...
...4010... THAT'S A FAMILIAR NUMBER...
...OF COURSE!
...LOOK AT THIS! THE A4010 ROAD RUNS THROUGH PRINCES RISBOROUGH IN BUCKINGHAMSHIRE...
...AND WHO LIVED IN PRINCES RISBOROUGH..?
MUNCH
EXACTLY! AMY JOHNSON! THE FIRST WOMAN TO FLY FROM LONDON TO AUSTRALIA!
GOOD GOD! THIS IS A GLOBAL CONSPIRACY!
LET'S SEE... AMY JOHNSON... AMY JOHNSON... A-HA!
AMY JOHNSON "DIED" ON JANUARY 5th 1941, WHEN HER PLANE WAS "ACCIDENTALLY" SHOT DOWN BY HMS HASLEMERE IN THE THAMES ESTUARY..!
... NEAR WHERE PROFESSOR BARNES WALLIS WAS TESTING HIS TOP SECRET BOUNCING BOMB! COINCIDENCE?
YEAH! PULL THE OTHER ONE. IT'S GOT BELLS ON!
JOHNSON'S BODY WAS NEVER RECOVERED... SO... ...THAT MEANS SHE'S STILL ALIVE!.. BUT WHY HAS SHE BEEN IN HIDING FOR 80 YEARS?! WHO'S THREATENING HER?
HMM... LOOK AT THIS, DAD... AMY JOHNSON WAS GUEST OF HONOUR AT THE OPENING OF THE FIRST BUTLINS HOLIDAY CAMP IN SKEGNESS ON APRIL 14th 1936!
THE EXACT SAME DAY THAT - 136 MILES AWAY IN LANCASTER - A CERTAIN BRIAN NOBLE WAS BORN...!
BRIAN NOBLE GOES ON TO BECOME ROMAN CATHOLIC BISHOP OF SHREWSBURY BETWEEN 1995 AND 2010...
SO WHAT? YOU MAY ASK.
SO WH-
GET THIS! HE WAS CONSECRATED BY MAURICE COUVE de MURVILLE, WHOSE EXACT NAMESAKE COUSIN WAS FRENCH PRIME MINISTER BETWEEN JULY 1968 AND JUNE 1969..!
JUNE 1969..!
...THE EXACT MONTH WHEN BEATLE JOHN LENNON "JUST HAPPENS" TO TRAVEL TO TYWYN IN NORTH WALES, FROM WHERE HE SENDS A CRYPTIC POSTCARD (BEARING AN IMAGE OF PRINCE CHARLES) TO RINGO STARR...
...THE POSTCARD BEARS JUST A SINGLE WORD...
..."HELLO"...
... BUT WHAT COULD HE HAVE MEANT BY THAT?
"HELLO..."
OF COURSE! IT'S THE TITLE A LIONEL RICHIE SINGLE, RELEASED ON FEBRUARY 13th 1984...
...THE RECORDING LASTS 4 MINUTES 14 SECONDS... LONG ENOUGH FOR THE A-SIDE OF A 45 RPM SINGLE TO REVOLVE 190 TIMES...
...OF COURSE! THAT'S IT! THE A190!
A
254/60 X45=190.5
... THE A-ROAD KNOWN TO NORTH TYNESIDE LOCALS AS "THE AVENUE" LINKING THE DUDLEY BYPASS WITH THE VILLAGE OF SEATON SLUICE!
DON'T YOU SEE?! SEATON SLUICE!
...IT'S AN ANAGRAM OF USA ELECTIONS!
... LIKE THE ONE WON IN 1960 BY JOHN F KENNEDY, WHOSE MISTRESS WAS MARILYN MONROE - REAL NAME NORMA JEAN MORTENSON...
HMM... NJM... THOSE INITIALS SOUND FAMILIAR..?
YOU BET..!

LETTERBOCKS

Viz Comic, P.O. Box 841 Whitley Bay, NE26 9EQ : letters@viz.co.uk

I GOT arrested for stealing a load of sports trainers from a van last month, and in my defence, I cleverly asked the court to decide who the real criminals were – me, or the global sportswear giants with their tax evasion schemes and their sweatshops in third world countries. They decided it was me and I got 200 hours community service and a £350 fine.

Ian Webb, Bury St Edmunds

I'M sick of baldies shaving their heads and strutting round pretending they are hard as fuck, like some Jason Statham character. If they really were hard, they would grow a ridiculous combover, or wear a wig and fight anyone who laughed at them in the pub.

Tubby Tanks, Oundle

I'VE just watched a Harry Potter film where a right bossy woman tried taking over Hogwarts School of Witchcraft and Wizardry. I don't know why they didn't all just magic her to fuck off. It would have saved a lot of pissing and farting about.

Eric Dumbledor, email

THE bare-faced cheek of these Italians, expecting us to learn the names of all their silly pasta shapes. Do they know all the different species of turkey dinosaur? Or all the Monster Munch monsters? I somehow doubt it.

Robert White, Whitehaven

APPARENTLY, there are more cyclists on our roads than ever before. So it doesn't take a genius to realise that the noticeable increase in potholes and the deterioration of our road surfaces must therefore be down to them. It's about time the government levied a 'Road Fund Licence' charge on these two-wheeled vandals to discourage them from causing further damage, and get them back into their cars or onto public transport.

T. ONeill, Glasgow

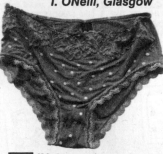

IN the movies, disgruntled wives often hold up a pair of women's knickers and ask, "who's underwear is this?" I couldn't identify my wife's own pants, let alone those of all the people I may, or may not, have had the pants off of.

Mat (One T), Leith

STAR LETTER

DOES anyone know what electric eels were called before electricity was discovered? I'd google it myself, but I'm in prison on a terrorism charge after calling Priti Patel "Vinegar Tits" on Twitter.

Leo Stitch, Belmarsh

THESE days, everyone is always banging on about Covid vaccines. But what if the entire human race was enslaved by a race of genetically-engineered robot super-spiders? That's a far bigger worry if you ask me, and you can't vaccinate against something like that happening.

Ben Nunn, Caterham

WE were told that after Brexit we could make our own laws. What a load of bollocks. I passed a law to make it legal for me to drive at 80mph back from the pub and what happened? I got nicked before they loaded me into the ambulance. Yet more Brexit lies.

Rigsby, email

PEOPLE say that if you drink raw egg whites, it increases the volume of your ejaculate. But frankly, I prefer mine silent in case the noise it makes is a like a swanee whistle, or an old-time car horn.

Brian Saxby, Chicago

I DON'T know if you've noticed, but your magazine is only a small slip on a Qwerty keyboard away from *Via* magazine, a "small, attractive magazine with a clear gospel message". Anyway, I was a bit hammered last night and those god-botherers now know the story of why one of my friends is referred to as 'Ol' Onion Dick'.

Shenkin Arsecandle, Llareggub

WHENEVER me and my missus go out, I'll go for a piss wherever we are and never think twice about the toilets. Yet when she goes, she comes back and says, "Those toilets are a disgrace," every time without fail. I can only conclude that women are dirtier than men and need to learn our superior toilet hygiene.

Dave Heeley, Walsall

HAS anyone ever got really close to a bear to see if they smell bad? I reckon they are right whiffy, but I would like to know for sure.

Richard Devereux, Hereford

* *Have you ever been close enough to a bear to know what it smelt like? Perhaps you are a zoo keeper somewhere, and spend a lot of time around these ursine monsters. Maybe you are a ringmaster in one of those cruel circuses where they make bears dance and occasionally catch a whiff as they waltz past. Or perhaps you were attacked by a grizzly bear in the wilds of Canada and survived against all the odds. Write in and let us know what they smelt like.*

CLIFTON ROCKS RAILWAY.

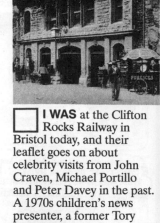

I WAS at the Clifton Rocks Railway in Bristol today, and their leaflet goes on about celebrity visits from John Craven, Michael Portillo and Peter Davey in the past. A 1970s children's news presenter, a former Tory MP who lost a safe seat, and somebody I've never heard of are such modest visitors to boast about that I felt rather sorry for them. I wonder if there are any better stars who could lend their weight to this tourist attraction.

Hubert Dentrisangle, Hull

* *Well, let's hope so, Mr Dentrisangle. Are you a higher quality celebrity than those mentioned? ie. Are you any kind of celebrity at all? If so, have you ever visited – or do you plan on visiting – the Clifton Rocks Railway in Bristol? Write in with your endorsement of this attraction and we'll pass it on.*

ON September 17th 1973, I fell off my bike and hurt my leg. Unfortunately there was no social media back then, so I'm telling everyone about it now.

Clivey, Exeter

THE theme tune from *Champion The Wonder Horse* clearly states "Like a mighty cannonball he seems to fly, You'll hear about him everywhere you go." Well, I was in Ipswich last week, and nobody mentioned him.

Michael Radcliffe, Colchester

NANA NANA
NANA NANA
NANA NANA
NANA NANA
BATNAN
HAND OVER ALL YOUR CASH... OR ELSE!
AHEM. NOT SO FAST, YOUNG MAN...
I SAID "NOT SO FAST, YOUNG MAN."
DON'T PRETEND YOU CAN'T HEAR ME...
BLUSH!
YOU'RE NOT SO BIG THAT I CAN'T PUT YOU OVER MY KNEE, YOU KNOW!
NOW, WHY DON'T YOU PUT THAT SILLY KNIFE AWAY WHILE I SHOW YOU SOME PICTURES OF MY GRAND-CHILDREN?
W-WHAT?!? GRANDKIDS? OH NO! NO WAY!!
I-I'M GETTING OUT OF HERE. YOU'RE CRAZY!
SPIN!
OH NO, YOU DON'T...
...NOT WHILE I'VE GOT MY NANCHUKS ON ME!
LOB!
THWUMP!
HONESTLY, LOOK HOW YOU'RE DRESSED FOR THIS WEATHER. YOU'LL CATCH YOURSELF A DEATH, YOU SILLY BILLY...
KNIT! KNIT! KNIT! KNIT! KNIT! KNIT!
AND SO, LATER...
SO, HOW'D IT GO?
GROAN... DON'T ASK, BOSS.

SOAP SOUP

***This week's top soup-related Soap plots with TV soap soup watcher* Baxter Campbell.**

Coronation Street
There's an awkward dilemma for Roy this week when he has to decide on the café's Soup of the Day. Should it be ***Cream of Tomato*** or ***French Onion***? His decision doesn't go down well with Carla.

Emmerdale
The relationship between Marlon and Rhona is tested when the pair go out for a meal in a restaurant. Against Marlon's advice, Rhona chooses the ***oxtail*** soup as a starter... and ends up feeling too full to eat her main course.

Pobol Y Cwm
Garry finds himself in hot water when a group of English tourists arrive at Y Deri. Trying to be hospitable, he writes '***Soup***' on the menu blackboard instead of '***Cawl***,' only to find his regulars are none too pleased.

Doctors
Zara treats a man suffering from an allergic reaction to shellfish. She suspects it is due to a prawn vol-au-vent, but when Jimmi spots an empty tin of ***clam chowder*** on the seat of the man's car, his worst fears are about to be realised.

Hollyoaks
After Goldie leaves Nana's ***broccoli and stilton*** soup on the hob for too long, Mercedes goes out to buy a new soup pan at Price Slice. Little does she realise that Silas is hiding behind a dogshit bin in the folly, with revenge on his mind.

EastEnders
Tensions escalate between Ben and Ian when Ben returns to the garage unexpectedly one lunchtime to find Ian wanking into his ***cup-a-soup***.

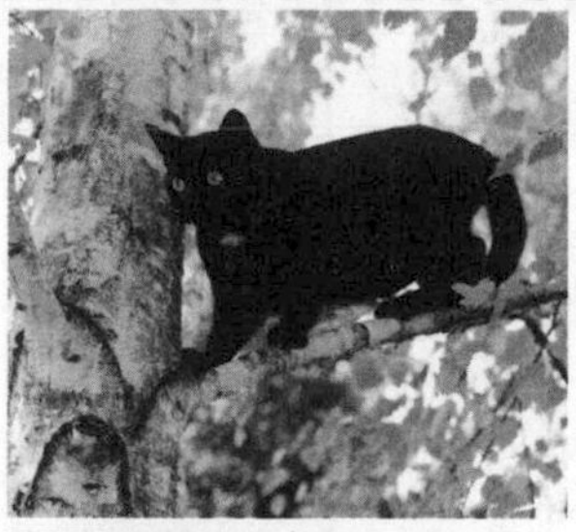

WHY do people call the fire brigade when a cat gets stuck up a height? Any fucker can spray a hosepipe up a tree.
Micky Bullock, Bristol

IF it doesn't have a cat in a zoot suit on double bass and an octopus wearing a beret on the drums, it's just not a proper 1940s cartoon animal jazz band in my opinion.
Gareth Randall, Colchester

I AM currently thirsty, but I also need a piss. Would any scientists like to explain how that is possible?
Ian Thompson, N'berland

I HAVE recently been watching the original *Hawaii 5-0* series, and I was astounded how many times across 279 episodes Commander Steve McGarrett had to tell Detective Sergeant Danny "Danno" Williams to "Book 'em Danno!" after they had apprehended a criminal. I can't help but think that if Commander McGarrett had gone to the trouble of employing a competent Detective Sergeant who didn't need reminding of basic police procedure every single time they caught a villain, then the crime rate in Hawaii would have been vastly reduced.
Tommy Tank, L'borough

TOP TIPS

TV viewers. Pretend you live in your favourite soap opera by imagining getting a doctor's appointment the same day, and a police officer being arsed to come to your house for any and every minor incident.
Eldon Furse, Leeds

BOXERS. Place a dog toy inside each of your gloves to create a squeak every time you land a punch. This will confuse your opponent and give you an extra advantage. For extra effect, use toys with differing squeaks.
Brian Brains, Braintree

RECEDING hairline? Shave your eyebrows off and paint them back on further up your forehead, thus reducing the space between brow and hairline. As your hairline continues to recede, simply rub off the brows and paint them on a little higher.
Yammy Fitzgibbon, Mid Yell

NAIL a banana to the inside of your front and back doors as a useful reminder of where the exits are. Then, in case of fire, simply follow the banana.
Glen Hattersley, Stockport

CONFOUND over-zealous law enforcement officers by walking around with your body attached to the negative terminal of a car battery. In the event of being tasered, not only are you rendered invulnerable to the electricity, but the battery is charged up at the same time.
Simon Measures, Dover

EXPERIENCE what it feels like to touch a dolphin without the expense of a trip to Mexico by playing with an aubergine in the bath.
Orla Trimmings, Dunstable

toptips@viz.co.uk

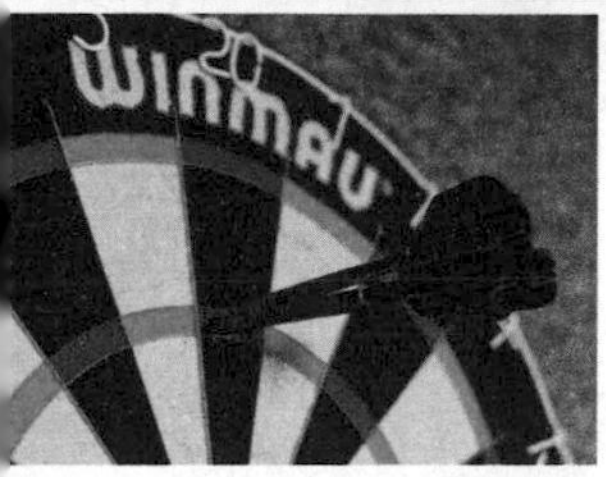

CYCLISTS can practise on an exercise bike, rowers can practise on a rowing machine, and even tennis players can practise on a swingball. But there's nothing for us dart players. We have to practise on an actual dart board.
D Williams, Donegal

IF masturbation is nothing to be ashamed of, why do people talk about someone being 'caught' doing it rather than 'interrupted'? Three times in as many weeks, for Heaven's sake.
R R Rasputin, email

I THINK the thing that has given me the most satisfaction was smashing Slug Barwell in the face during a French lesson. No wonder they say school days are the happiest days of your life.
Dominic Twose, Leamington Spa

IN a global water crisis, it is downright irresponsible that councils leave rivers running all of the time. Imagine how much water we could save if we just turned them off and only used them when needed?
Arthur Rytis, Newcastle

RIVERS and lakes are described as 'freshwater' in geography. Yet when I drank a gallon of water from the river after my drinking water supply ran out while camping, I got severe diarrhoea and a rotten fever. Fresh my arse.
Lew, Bristol

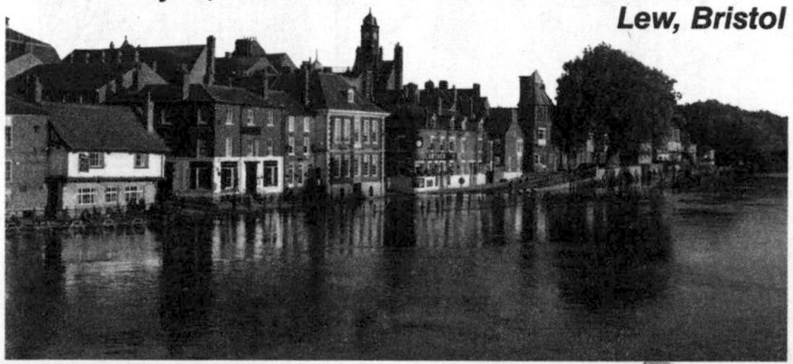

The Moral Maze — *This Week...* Would YOU eat a sandwich made by Hitler?

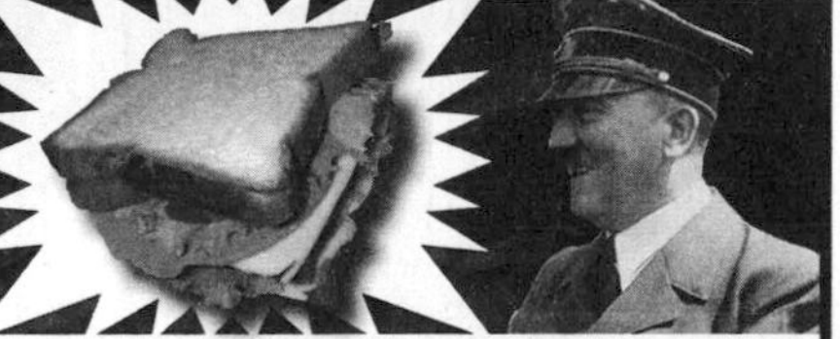

IT'S APRIL 1945, and you are a soldier with the Allied Forces in Berlin, fighting against the nazi menace. You burst into Hitler's bunker to find that the Führer has shot himself in the head and then set himself on fire. However, before committing these two final acts, he has made himself a sandwich, which now sits on the countertop in the bunker kitchen. Battle weary, you haven't eaten in 24 hours. Hitler's girlfriend Eva Braun is dead, and his SS guards aren't hungry, so the sandwich is going spare. The question you have to ask yourself is this: *Knowing that it was made by the world's most evil man, could you in all conscience eat that sandwich?* We went on the street to see what *YOU* would do.

"**I WOULD** definitely not eat it, no matter how hungry I was. He was the most evil man who has ever lived and I want nothing to do with him or his sandwiches, thank-you very much."
Edna Wholegrain, Croydon

"**I CAN'T** see anything wrong with tucking into it. Just because I ate the Fuhrer's sandwich doesn't mean I agree with his politics or condone his actions. I don't ask how the staff at McDonald's vote when I order a Big Mac and fries."
Stan Ballsup, Surrey

"**NO,** I wouldn't eat it. I would be worried that if I did, and it was delicious, then when people asked me what I thought about Hitler, I would have to answer honestly – that he was an evil monster, but he made a lovely sandwich. That's not a position I would like to find myself in."
Dennis Marbles, Quorn

"**I WOULD** definitely eat it. If I didn't, there would always be a chance that 'Hitler's Sandwich' would become a shrine for neo-nazis around the world. We must avoid that at all costs."
Brian Waxcandle, Dover

"**BEFORE** I ate it, I would ask around to see if there was another sandwich made by somebody slightly less evil, such as Mussolini or Emperor Hirohito. If there wasn't, then reluctantly I would eat it, but I wouldn't enjoy it at all."
Len Gallstones, Deal

"**I WOULDN'T** eat it because the only things I like in sandwiches are ham, corned beef and chicken. From what I understand, Hitler was a vegetarian, so I would leave his evil rabbit-food sandwich where it was."
Ernest Ballsover, Goole

Mobile Dick

I do *so* enjoy eating out alone.

About... half-eight.

Either put down that bloody phone or I'm leaving.

There, see? Isn't it nice to be back in the room?

PING

Yes...

I thought we could drive to the coast Saturday.

PING

Put it down!

Turn off your notifications!

It pinged! You heard!

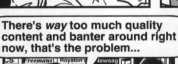

But I might miss something important.

Were those pings important?

Fairly! I've been tagged into a clip of a cockatoo rapping along with Kanye West!

Could we have the bill please?

Just... gone ten to nine.

He's paying.

The coast, yeah, sure, great...

Eventually

Come back!

I'm sorry!

There's *way* too much quality content and banter around right now, that's the problem...

PING

I'll *definitely* mute my notifications next time we come out, *honest!*

For a few hours...

Two at least...

Unless there's, you know, a *twitterstorm* or something...

This bloody thing ain't the boss of me!

No sirree...

SCREEEEEEECH!

TEN TON TRUCK CO.

Soon

...and so we come together in the sight of our Lord to remember Dick...

PING

Johnny Fartpants
He's the Boy with a Bum Like THUNDER!
OH NO!
BANKSY'S DONE ONE OF OF HIS GRAFFITTIS ON THE BLOODY GARAGE DOOR.
THAT'S GOING TO TAKE AGES TO SCRUB OFF!
NOT NECESSARILY...! FIRST I'LL EAT A POUND OF THEM SHINY METAL BALLS YOU USED TO GET ON CAKES...
GOLP!
...THEN THREE CANS OF MY OWN SPECIAL COCKTAIL OF CRESTA, BICARBONATE OF SODA, AND TINNED TURNIP WATER...
SLOOP!
... AND THEN A GOOD TEN MINUTES OF BOUNCING ON MY POGO STICK TO MIX IT ALL UP PROPERLY...
AND...
HERE WE GO... PLEASE STAND CLEAR OF THE BUTTOCKS...
3...2...1...
BLARP!
SQUONK!
OOPS!
HMM... YOU'VE FOLLOWED THROUGH, JOHNNY, AND COVERED THE GARAGE DOOR IN LIQUID FEESHUS!
...STILL, IT'S BETTER THAN A BANKSY, I SUPPOSE.

THROUGH THE LOOKING GLASS

YOUR theological queries about mirrored surfaces, answered by the Archbishop of Canterbury, DR JUSTIN WELBY

Dear AB of C,

IN THE Bible, it says God made man in His own image. So, does this mean that He invented mirrors before He invented men?

Agnes Secret-Side, Sheam

The AB of C says: *"Not necessarily, Agnes. God may well have invented some other sort of reflective object first – such as water, teaspoons or the back of a CD – and then used that to look upon His own mighty countenance and sketch a blueprint from which to create man. But don't forget, God is three people in one, so He could simply have looked at one of His other forms, such as Jesus or the Holy Ghost, and created man from that description. But on the other hand, yes, He could well have invented mirrors first and invented man that way, as you suggest. Although, come to think of it, if He had of done that our hands would be on the wrong arms. Either way, it is not for us to question the ways of the Lord."*

Dear AB of C,

IT STRUCK me recently that evil people always seem to have trouble with reflective surfaces. For instance, there was Narcissus, who drowned after staring at his own image in a lake; Dracula, who couldn't see himself in a looking glass; and Medusa, who would turn to stone if she caught a glimpse of her own reflection. Since godlessness and the inability to use a mirror properly seem to go hand in hand, I was wondering if the church might consider setting up some sort of 'mirror test' whenever they suspect somebody of being a heathen.

Edith Rosesin-Thesnow, Ackford

The AB of C says: *"You might well be onto something there, Edith. And as well as all the examples you mention, there's also Robert De Niro in Taxi Driver, who looked in the mirror and asked 'Are you talkin' to me?' before going on a murderous rampage through the streets of New York. I'll make sure to bring up your idea of a 'mirror test' for potential heathens at the next General Synod. Depending on what the other archbishops reckon, we could probably get this concept fast-tracked and greenlit by January."*

Dear AB of C,

MY HUSBAND broke a mirror a month ago and was thus condemned to endure seven years' bad luck. The trouble is, he's 95 and not very well, and I was wondering, if he pegs it in a year as I suspect he will, will the seven years' bad luck carry over into the afterlife? I'd hate to think of my husband constantly stepping on Lego, losing his keys and getting piles for his first six years in Heaven.

Dolly Janitor-Oflunacy, Hosterly

The AB of C says: *"Rest assured Dolly, the concept of 'bad luck' simply does not exist in Heaven. Up in the ethereal realm of Paradise, only good things happen to you. Consequently, if you step on a Lego, it will be one of those flat, non-knobbly pieces, such as a roof tile or a window pane, and you don't even need keys because there's no such thing as crime and nobody locks their doors. As for piles, he'll be sitting around on a fluffy cloud for eternity, so there's no worries there. And if your husband has led a sinful life and is destined for Hell, then stepping on the odd bit of Lego and losing his keys will be the least of his problems when he's having his skin flayed ceaselessly from his body by Lucifer's grotesque hordes. So there's no cause to fret on that count, either."*

Have YOU got a query about mirrors, looking glasses, speculums or any other kind of reflective surface that is also in some way connected to the Anglican faith? Why not write in to: Through The Looking Glass, c/o The AB of C, Viz Comic, PO Box 841, Whitley Bay, NE26 9EQ

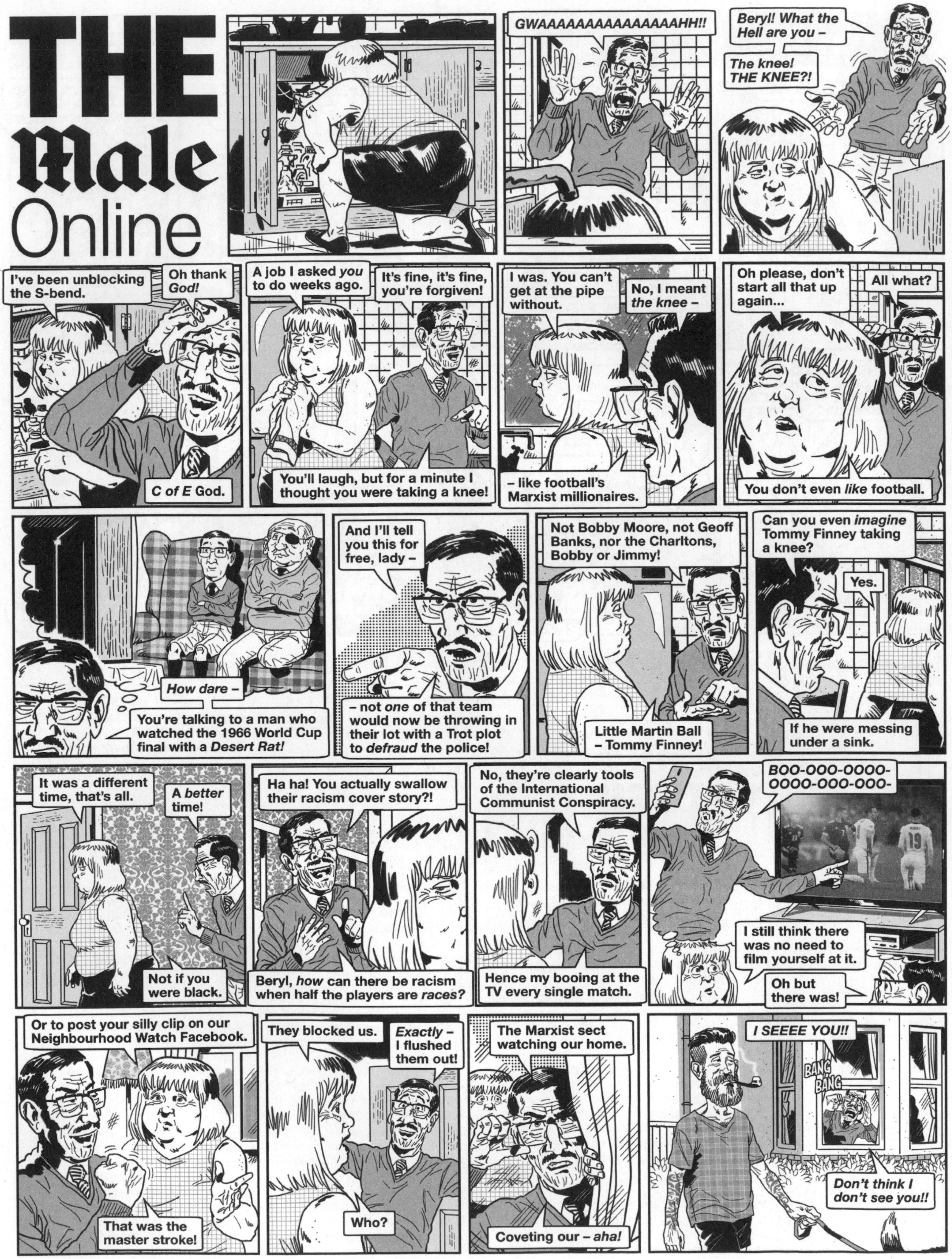
THE
Male
Online
GWAAAAAAAAAAAAAAAAH!!
Beryl! What the Hell are you –
The knee! THE KNEE?!
I've been unblocking the S-bend.
Oh thank God!
C of E God.
A job I asked you to do weeks ago.
It's fine, it's fine, you're forgiven!
You'll laugh, but for a minute I thought you were taking a knee!
I was. You can't get at the pipe without.
No, I meant the knee –
– like football's Marxist millionaires.
Oh please, don't start all that up again...
All what?
You don't even like football.
How dare –
You're talking to a man who watched the 1966 World Cup final with a Desert Rat!
And I'll tell you this for free, lady –
– not one of that team would now be throwing in their lot with a Trot plot to defraud the police!
Not Bobby Moore, not Geoff Banks, nor the Charltons, Bobby or Jimmy!
Little Martin Ball – Tommy Finney!
Can you even imagine Tommy Finney taking a knee?
Yes.
If he were messing under a sink.
It was a different time, that's all.
A better time!
Not if you were black.
Ha ha! You actually swallow their racism cover story?!
Beryl, how can there be racism when half the players are races?
No, they're clearly tools of the International Communist Conspiracy.
Hence my booing at the TV every single match.
BOO-OOO-OOOO-OOOO-OOO-OOO-
I still think there was no need to film yourself at it.
Oh but there was!
Or to post your silly clip on our Neighbourhood Watch Facebook.
That was the master stroke!
They blocked us.
Exactly – I flushed them out!
Who?
The Marxist sect watching our home.
Coveting our – aha!
I SEEEE YOU!!
BANG BANG
Don't think I don't see you!!

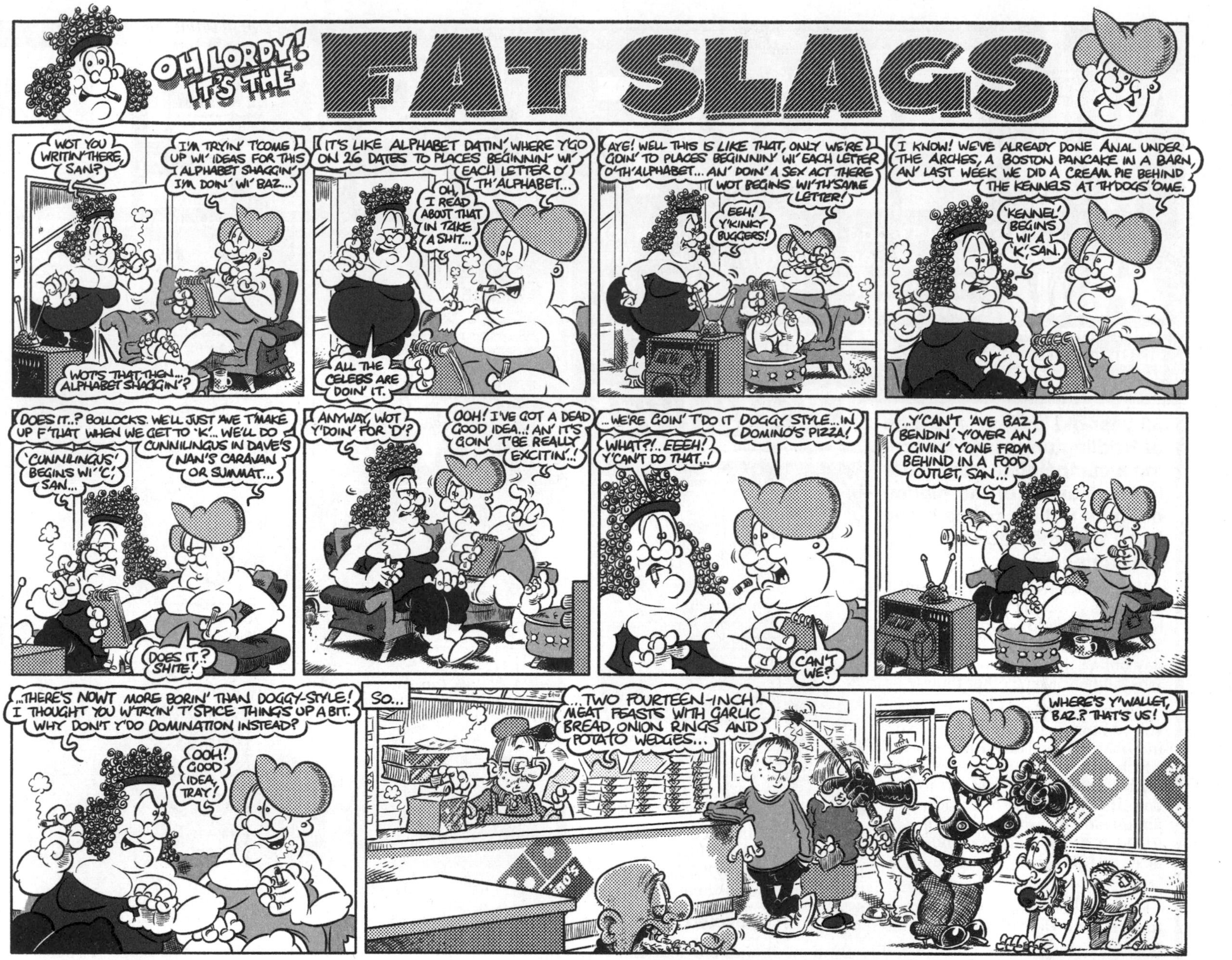
OH LORDY! IT'S THE
FAT SLAGS
WOT YOU WRITIN' THERE, SAN?
I'M TRYIN' T'COME UP WI' IDEAS FOR THIS ALPHABET SHAGGIN' I'M DOIN' WI' BAZ...
WOT'S THAT, THEN... ALPHABET SHAGGIN'?
IT'S LIKE ALPHABET DATIN', WHERE Y'GO ON 26 DATES TO PLACES BEGINNIN' WI' EACH LETTER O' TH'ALPHABET...
OH, I READ ABOUT THAT IN TAKE A SHIT...
ALL THE CELEBS ARE DOIN' IT.
AYE! WELL THIS IS LIKE THAT, ONLY WE'RE GOIN' TO PLACES BEGINNIN' WI' EACH LETTER O' TH'ALPHABET... AN' DOIN' A SEX ACT THERE WOT BEGINS WI' TH'SAME LETTER!
EEH! Y'KINKY BUGGERS!
I KNOW! WE'VE ALREADY DONE ANAL UNDER THE ARCHES, A BOSTON PANCAKE IN A BARN, AN' LAST WEEK WE DID A CREAM PIE BEHIND THE KENNELS AT TH'DOGS' 'OME.
'KENNEL' BEGINS WI' A 'K', SAN.
DOES IT..? BOLLOCKS. WE'LL JUST 'AVE T'MAKE UP F'THAT WHEN WE GET TO 'K'... WE'LL DO CUNNILINGUS IN DAVE'S NAN'S CARAVAN OR SUMMAT...
'CUNNILINGUS' BEGINS WI' 'C', SAN...
DOES IT? SHITE!
ANYWAY, WOT Y'DOIN' FOR 'D'?
OOH! I'VE GOT A DEAD GOOD IDEA..! AN' IT'S GOIN' T'BE REALLY EXCITIN'..!
...WE'RE GOIN' T'DO IT DOGGY STYLE... IN DOMINO'S PIZZA!
WHAT?!.. EEEH! Y'CAN'T DO THAT...!
CAN'T WE?
...Y'CAN'T 'AVE BAZ BENDIN' Y'OVER AN' GIVIN' Y'ONE FROM BEHIND IN A FOOD OUTLET, SAN..!
...THERE'S NOWT MORE BORIN' THAN DOGGY-STYLE! I THOUGHT YOU W'TRYIN' T'SPICE THINGS UP A BIT. WHY DON'T Y'DO DOMINATION INSTEAD?
OOH! GOOD IDEA, TRAY!
SO...
...TWO FOURTEEN-INCH MEAT FEASTS WITH GARLIC BREAD, ONION RINGS AND POTATO WEDGES...
WHERE'S Y'WALLET, BAZ..? THAT'S US!

GRAZED EXPECTATIONS

Minister's call to bring back scabs

THE government today announced plans to bring back loose, gravelled surfaces on playgrounds, along with smooth, slippy soles on children's shoes, in an attempt to put a halt to what many ministers believe is a 'softening up' of today's youth.

Secretary of State for the Environment, Food and Rural Affairs George Eustace introduced a Private Members' Bill which would see coarse gravel replace the rubber crumb which has been a feature of adventure playgrounds since the early 80s.

smooth

If passed, the new law would also compel shoe manufacturers to use extremely smooth plastic on the soles of all children's shoes, in place of the heavily treaded rubber typically used today.

"Like every other boy in my class, I had almost permanent scabs on my knees throughout my childhood," the member for Cambourne and Redruth told Parliament. "I spent many hours picking bits of gravel out of my ripped flesh. It was character building and it made me the man I am today."

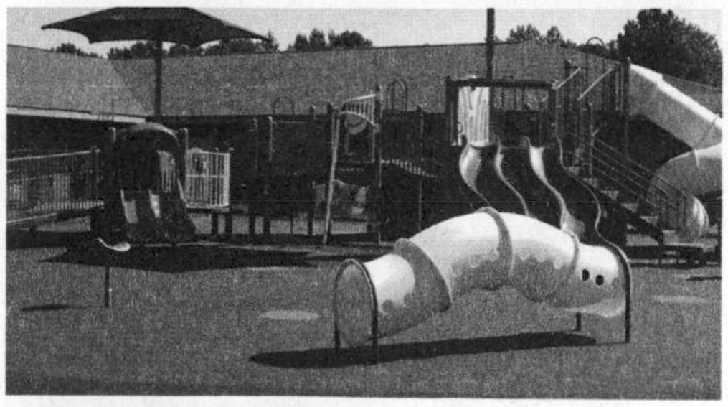

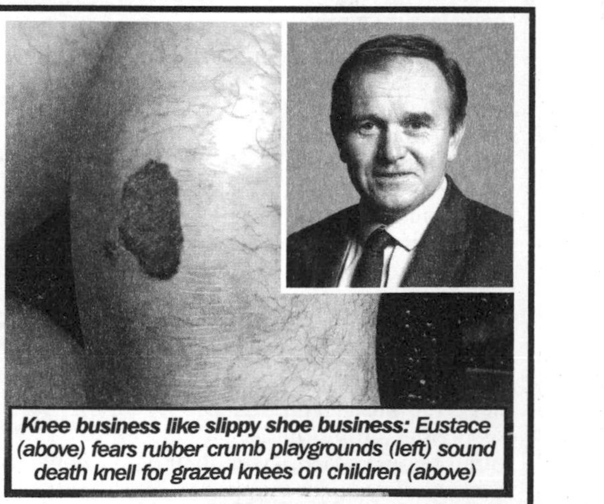

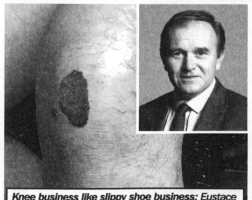

Knee business like slippy shoe business: Eustace (above) fears rubber crumb playgrounds (left) sound death knell for grazed knees on children (above)

The former UKIP member said that losing one's footing whilst running and skidding along sharp gravel in short trousers was a 'rite of passage' for all schoolboys. "The Gravel and Slippy Shoes Bill would ensure this right would not be denied to our children," he said.

wanted

The bill passed its first reading despite opposition from Labour, who said it was a step in the wrong direction. "Any child jumping from a swing or being thrown from a fast moving roundabout has the right to land on a soft surface without their knees and palms being ripped to shreds," said shadow Foreign Secretary Lisa Nandy. "If anything, we should be moving towards even softer playground surfacing, like bubble wrap."

However, in the second chamber, the Lords added a series of amendments to the bill, including a requirement for all grazed knees to be swabbed with neat Dettol and covered with a plaster that is too small and comes off after getting in the bath.

WEB OF DECEIT

AN EAST COAST odd-job man has been left thousands of pounds out of pocket after falling victim to a heartless computer con. And to make matters even worse, the incident saw the scammers get away scot free and the victim taken to court, charged, and placed on the Sex Offenders Register.

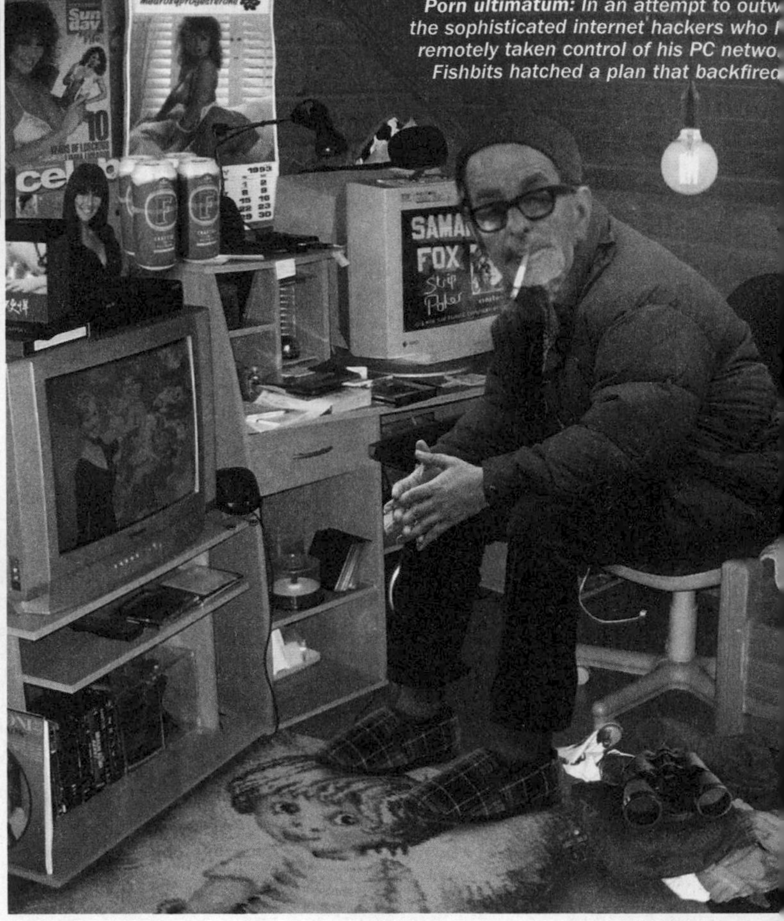

Porn ultimatum: In an attempt to outw the sophisticated internet hackers who I remotely taken control of his PC netwo Fishbits hatched a plan that backfired

EXCLUSIVE!

52-year-old *Hilton Fishbits* of Bridlington is now launching a campaign to warn other internet users of the hidden dangers lurking online in the hope that they don't fall into the same trap.

"I'd been working for the council, but I was given the tin tack in October," Fishbits told the *Bridlington Oxter and Lisk*. "So I was spending all day online in my bedsit, looking for jobs, and also some other things."

"My work at the town hall had involved mending broken office chairs in the accounts department, work which often took me late into the night when the staff had left for the day. But there was a bit of a misunderstanding with a woman who found a hidden camera under her desk, so I was given the heave-ho."

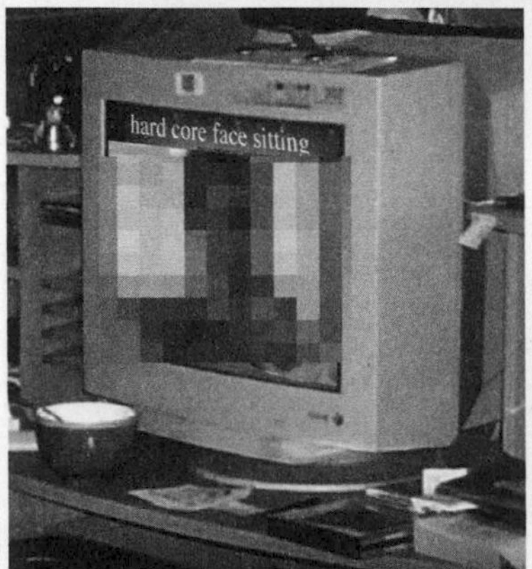

hard core face sitting

PC gone mad: *Innocent Hilton's computer was taken over and floodedwith hardcore filth by XXX-rated scammers.*

triggered

Fishbits believes it was this enforced leave that triggered the unfortunate series of events which eventually left him a sitting target for heartless scammers.

"I was browsing the internet, looking for a job one day, and I'd clearly typed something in wrong because a message popped up saying 'Did you mean 'facesitting images'?'

"I wasn't sure what it meant, so I clicked 'yes', and before I knew it there were thousands of images on my screen of people sitting on other people's faces - with their bare bottoms."

> **"I couldn't believe my eyes as I scrolled through page after page of obscene photographs, feeling sick as I clicked on each of them in turn"**

"I couldn't believe my eyes as I scrolled through page after page of obscene photographs, feeling sick as I clicked on each of them in turn."

rodneyed

Despite Fishbits's trusting nature, he began to suspect that his computer might have been hacked.

"I thought it best to take a screenshot as evidence," he said. "But I must have pressed the wrong button or something, because, before I knew it, I had downloaded 3,500 of the images onto my hard drive, saved them, and placed them in a secure folder."

boycied

By now, it was too late and the scammers had Fishbits firmly in their grasp. "I was worried they might lock up my computer remotely and delete the evidence, so I decided the best thing was to print off all the images," he said.

Scammers often lure their victims into a false sense of security by demanding small amounts to begin with, later increasing the amounts, so Fishbits thought spending £120 on printer paper and ink cartridges would be money well spent.

uncle alberted

Once the evidence was safely printed off, Fishbits realised he needed to contact the appropriate authorities to alert them to the sinister scam. But not trusting the police after a previous misunderstanding about a two-way mirror in the ladies' toilets at work, he decided to entrust his evidence to a woman who worked in the accounts department at the council.

"I knew her from when I worked there, so I decided to send the pictures I had printed off to her at home for safekeeping, as she seemed reliable and trustworthy," he said.

"She's also got a cracking arse, but that has nothing to do with this," he added.

> **"It dawned on me she was probably at work, so I popped in through a downstairs window to leave a note"**

Even at this stage, Fishbits took every precaution to stay one step ahead of the scammers and, worried that his indecent images might get lost in the post, he decided to post them to her individually, in batches of three or four each day.

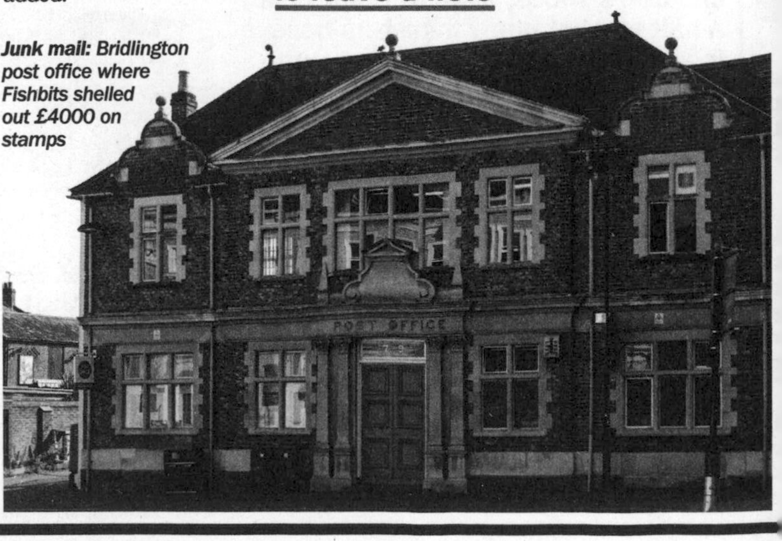

POST OFFICE

Junk mail: **Bridlington post office where Fishbits shelled out £4000 on stamps**

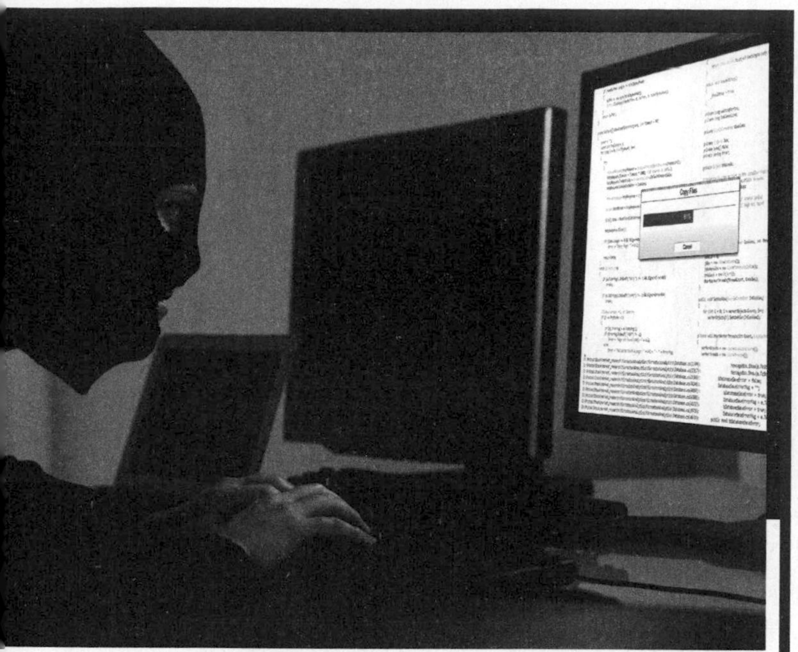

Brid handyman tangles with sinister internet scammers

Scammers are never satisfied with the amounts of money they take from their victims, so Fishbits thought the £4,000 he spent on stamps and envelopes could actually be a saving in the long run.

> **I'd photoshopped our faces on out of courtesy to the innocent people in the photos**

Fishbits decided that he should warn the woman from accounts about his course of action. "I realised I hadn't actually told her I was going to entrust her with these offensive photos, so I popped round to her house one morning to let her know," he said.

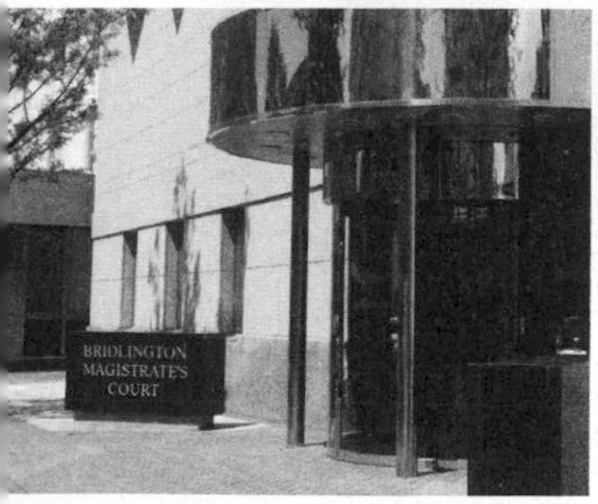
BRIDLINGTON
MAGISTRATE'S
COURT

"She didn't answer when I knocked, and it dawned on me that she was probably at work. So I popped in through a downstairs window in order to leave her a note," he added.

"I think I must have passed out or something because the next thing I knew the police were knocking at the door. I thought they had come to tell me they had caught the scammers, even though I hadn't yet reported the crime. But to my horror, they arrested me!"

Fishbits was taken to Bridlington Police station, where he was charged with breaking and entering and attempting to install a secret camera in a shower. He was also treated for the effects of toxic fumes after sniffing the seat fabric of an armchair for several hours.

When detectives searched Fishbits's flat, they found almost 3,500 printed indecent images with his and the woman from accounts's faces photoshopped on, along with 3,500 envelopes and first class stamps.

"I'd photoshopped our faces on out of courtesy to the innocent people in the photos," he said. "After all, I was the one being scammed, and there was no reason to drag the reputations of thousands more victims through the mud."

delboyed

In court, Bridlington magistrates refused to believe Fishbits's version of events, and placed him on the Sex Offenders' Register, in addition ordering him to perform 250 hours of community service.

But despite his wrongful conviction - compounded by seeing the true scammers get away Scot free - Fishbits nevertheless remains upbeat. "I've been branded a sex offender and left thousands out of pocket as a result of this escapade, so it was certainly a hard lesson for me to learn, and I certainly won't be scammed again," he said.

"Not unless I accidentally click on something dodgy and download it by mistake when I'm searching for something else that's not dodgy, and then accidentally end up photoshopping it and sending it to someone else, such as that bird with the nice arse at the council, also by mistake," he added. "The thing is, it's so easily done."

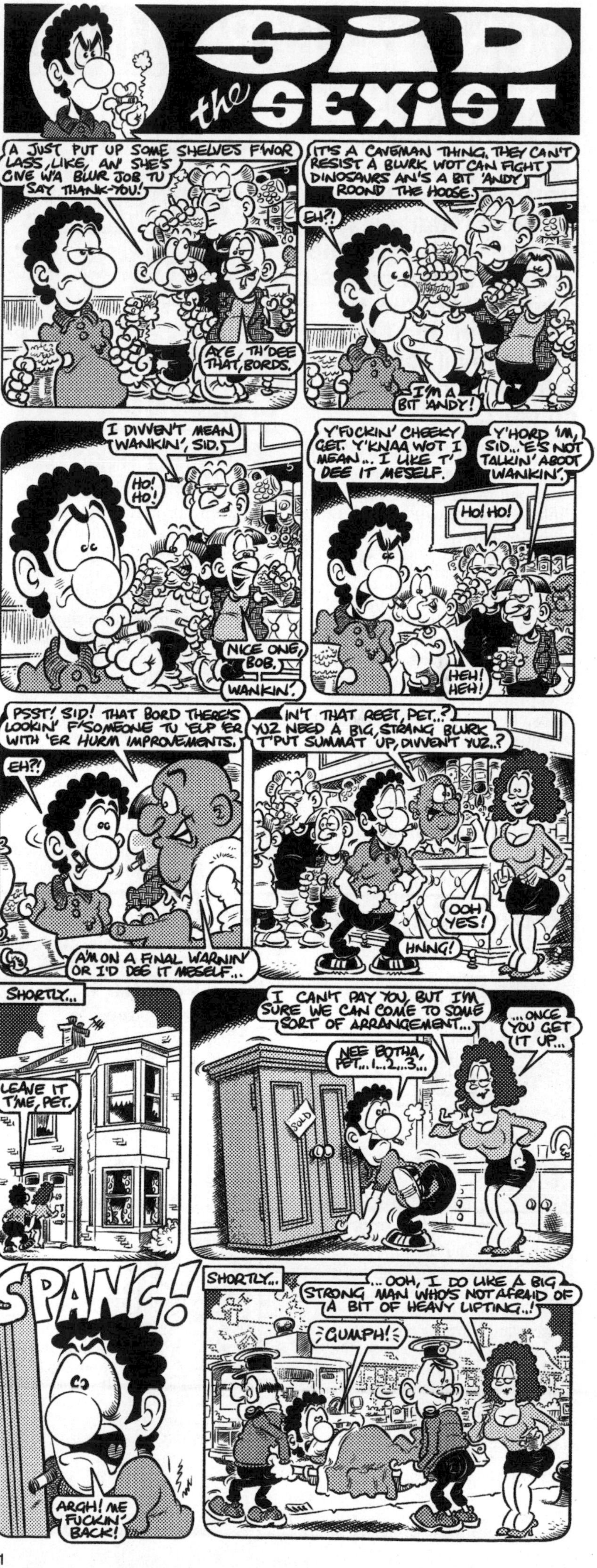
SID the SEXIST
A JUST PUT UP SOME SHELVES F'WOR LASS, LIKE, AN' SHE'S GIVE W'A BLUR JOB TU SAY THANK-YOU!
AYE, TH'DEE THAT, BORDS.
IT'S A CAVEMAN THING. THEY CAN'T RESIST A BLURK WOT CAN FIGHT DINOSAURS AN'S A BIT 'ANDY ROOND THE HOOSE.
EH?!
I'M A BIT 'ANDY!
I DIVVEN'T MEAN WANKIN', SID.
HO! HO!
NICE ONE, BOB.
WANKIN'.
Y'FUCKIN' CHEEKY GET. Y'KNAA WOT I MEAN... I LIKE T' DEE IT MESELF.
Y'HORD 'IM, SID... 'E'S NOT TALKIN' ABOOT WANKIN'.
HO! HO!
HEH! HEH!
PSST! SID! THAT BORD THERE'S LOOKIN' F'SOMEONE TU 'ELP 'ER WITH 'ER HURM IMPROVEMENTS.
EH?!
A'M ON A FINAL WARNIN' OR I'D DEE IT MESELF...
IN'T THAT REET, PET..? YUZ NEED A BIG, STRANG BLURK T'PUT SUMMAT UP, DIVVEN'T YUZ..?
OOH YES!
HNNG!
SHORTLY...
LEAVE IT T'ME, PET.
I CAN'T PAY YOU, BUT I'M SURE WE CAN COME TO SOME SORT OF ARRANGEMENT...
NEE BOTHA, PET... 1... 2... 3...
...ONCE YOU GET IT UP...
SOLD
SPANG!
ARGH! ME FUCKIN' BACK!
SHORTLY...
...OOH, I DO LIKE A BIG STRONG MAN WHO'S NOT AFRAID OF A BIT OF HEAVY LIFTING..!
GUMPH!

TONY PARSEHOLE

Bye Bye Prince P, Prince P Goodbye! (also Les off the Rollers)

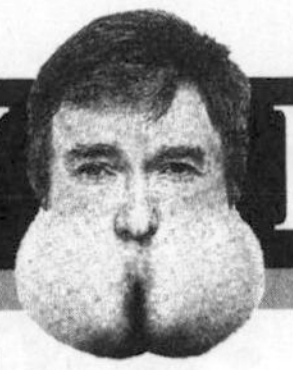

WHEN I heard the news that HRH (that stands for His Royal Highness, so thats three words) The Duke of Edinburgh had died, I wept. I wept and I wept and I wept. I wept royal tears of grief for the Queen's consort.

Her Majesty the Queen's consort.

And just at the exact moment I stopped wepting over Prince Philip, I heard the news that Les McKeown out of the Bay City Rollers had died, and I wept again. I wept again and I wept again and I wept again.

For fate had taken these two iconic men off the face of our globe just days apart. Two men, a duke and a troubador, who had never met, yet shared so much (subs check if they ever met actually dont bother).

Both were royalty: Philip - a prince of Great Britain and Northern Ireland, Les - a prince of pop.

They both hailed from Scotland: Philip from Edinburgh, Les from Bay City.

They both proudly displayed their Scotchness in their dress: Philip - a Balmoral kilt and tweed jacket, Les - a tartan stripe down the side of his Oxford bags.

And both men liked to shoot: Philip - tigers, deer and pheasants. Les - one of his fans with an air-gun in 1975 (subs check I think it was him but might have been one of the others actually dont bother you cant libel the dead).

Yet, though these two men were very similar, they were yet so very different.

HRH (three words dont forget) the Duke of Edinburgh was loved by us all. Born plain old Prince

Philip of Greece and Denmark, he rose to the second highest position in the land, that of husband to HRH (three words again) Queen Elizabeth the second.

And it was a position that carried a great weight of responsibility. A weight that he bore stoically.

A weight that he bore steadfastly.

A weight that he bore uncomplainingly.

And it is a position that none of us would envy, for we would not do the job with the same stoicism.

We would not do the job with the same steadfastness.

We would not do the job with the same uncomplainicty.

Yes, he was occasionally gaffe-prone (2 wds even though its got a hyfen). And yes, he was often racist. And yes he was usually short-tempered (hyfen again). But we loved him for it (actually drop that bit about loving him for being racist that looks bad her from the times got knacked for that).

We loved him for the first and third ones.

And if there is one other man who bore his own duties with the same uncomplaining, steadfast stoicism as did HRH Prince Philip, that man is/was Les McKeown.

Les was born in (subs check town) in (subs check year), the son of a (subs check what dad did for living) and a (subs check what mum did for living).

And from those humble beginnings he rose to be the lead singer of the most successful band the world has ever seen.

As the front man of The Bay City Rollers, he spoke for a generation and had the world at his there that's 500 words. Inv enc.

Don't flag me down
WOOP WOOP
POLI
POLICE
POLICE
POL

MEDDLESOME RATBAG
DJ '21
SEX SHOP
!!
ADULT XXX
NOW OPEN
QUALITY TIMBER
SEX S
TOOLS
NOW OPEN
SCUTTLE
BANG! HAMMER!
SEX
HAMMER! BANG!
HOME FOR POOR INNOCENT ORPHANS
SEX
OME FOR OR INNOCENT ORPHANS
SEX SHOP
ADUL XXX
COUNCIL
SEX SHOP
CLOSED DOWN BY ORDER
SHORTLY
NEW BUSINESS
SWEET SHOP
!!
ORPHANS WELCOME!
NOW OPEN
AND
HOME FOR EXTREMELY DIABETIC ORPHANS WHO WILL DIE IF THEY GO NEAR SWEETS
NEW BUSINE
SWEET SH
COUNCIL
NOW OPEN

ALL THE CELEBRITY NEWS & GOSSIP

PIERCE DORGAN

He was truly The Duke of Edinburgh of Hearts

WE WILL ALL remember where we were when we heard the news of the tragic death of the Duke of Edinburgh. I was in the Noma Restaurant in Copenhagen, one of the most exclusive and difficult eateries in the world to get into.

I was having dinner with a few close friends, including - but not limited to - ***Idris Elba***, ***Kit Harrington***, ***Uma Thurman***, ***Harry Styles***, ***Scarlett Johanssen***, ***Jean-Paul Gaultier***, ***Normski*** and ***Kim Källström***.

I was inconsolable. The Duke of Edinburgh, or Philip, as he was to me, actually Phil, was a great, great friend. Indeed, I was so upset that I couldn't finish my meal. Most people would have forced it down because it is such a difficult restaurant to get into and the food's so expensive. But the cost was nothing to me and I can get in any time.

"I'm so, so sorry, Piers. I know what a good friend he was to you," said ***Sofia Vergara*** who was dining with me, as was ***Elizabeth Moss***, ***Bjorn Borg***, ***Sofie Gråbøl***, ***Dennis Waterman***, ***JK Rowling***, ***Lars Mikkelsen***, ***The Barron Knights*** and ***Lionel Messi***. I could see the tears welling up in all their eyes at my grief.

But *my* tears were mainly for the Queen. To lose one's spouse is always a blow, but to lose one's spouse in such a time of national emergency makes it all the worse. And now, in the midst of her grief, I knew her Majesty would be charged with selecting the 30 lucky guests to be invited to Windsor Castle for the exclusive funeral.

Naturally I knew that I would be first on her list. But knowing intimately how the monarchy works, I also knew that an army of advisers and private secretaries would be telling her Majesty that the Duke's family should take precedence. Of course, the Queen would argue with them, saying I am her rock and she wanted me there, and there would be a stand-off. To save her this further aggravation, I decided to contact her Majesty immediately and diplomatically inform her I was unable to attend the funeral.

My absence would be a double blow to her, of course, but I knew it was the right course of action. I decided to tell her a completely believable story, that I was playing golf with ***Jack Nicholson***, ***Morgan Freeman***, ***Freddie "Parrot Face" Davis*** and ***Alice Cooper*** in Beverly Hills that day.

The Duke and me at a gathering of lots of my famous friends

I took out one of my phones - I have many, since there isn't enough memory on one phone to hold all my celebrity contacts, including ***Nelly Furtado***, ***Billy Bob Thornton***, ***Lewis Hamilton***, ***Professor Jonathan Van-Tam***, ***Rufus Wainwright***, ***Irene Handl*** and ***Lizz Truss***.

I sent the text to her Majesty, simply signing it 'Piers'. I didn't need to put 'Morgan' after it, as we are such good friends.

My pudding arrived, a chocolate ganache with sugared mint leaves and lingonberry coulis. It looked delicious but I couldn't eat it, even though it cost nearly £70 - the most expensive dessert on the menu by miles. In fact, I was so upset, I called it a night, and I was given a lift home by ***Phil Collins***, ***Bill Gates*** and ***Kamala Harris***.

I am nothing if not a man of the people, and the following Saturday I joined the nation as I watched the funeral on my Samsung QP98R-8K 98" TV in my £15million London mansion. My heart broke as I watched her Majesty the Queen sitting alone in St George's Chapel, a widescreen, ultra-high definition picture of grief. I wondered how much of that grief was for the loss of her husband of 73 years, and how much was for the fact that I was not beside her at the funeral.

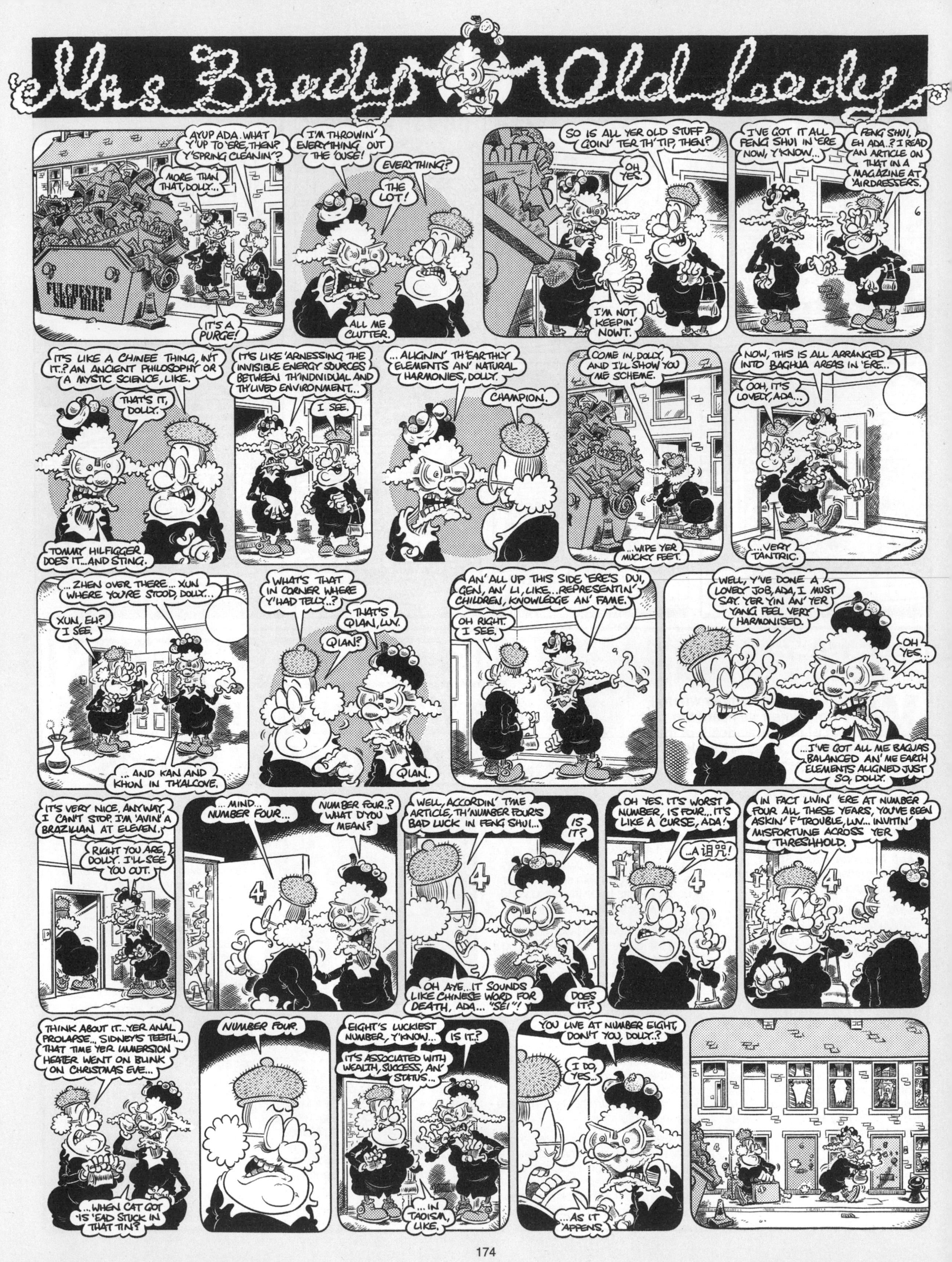
Mrs Brady Old Lady
AYUP ADA. WHAT Y'UP TO 'ERE, THEN? Y'SPRING CLEANIN'?
MORE THAN THAT, DOLLY...
FULCHESTER SKIP HIRE
IT'S A PURGE!
I'M THROWIN' EVERYTHING OUT THE 'OUSE!
EVERYTHING?
THE LOT!
ALL ME CLUTTER.
SO IS ALL YER OLD STUFF GOIN' TER TH' TIP, THEN?
OH YES.
I'M NOT KEEPIN' NOWT.
I'VE GOT IT ALL FENG SHUI IN 'ERE NOW, Y'KNOW...
FENG SHUI, EH ADA..? I READ AN ARTICLE ON THAT IN A MAGAZINE AT 'AIRDRESSERS.
IT'S LIKE A CHINEE THING, IN'T IT..? AN ANCIENT PHILOSOPHY OR A MYSTIC SCIENCE, LIKE.
THAT'S IT, DOLLY.
TOMMY HILFIGGER DOES IT... AND STING.
IT'S LIKE 'ARNESSING THE INVISIBLE ENERGY SOURCES BETWEEN TH'INDIVIDUAL AND TH'LIVED ENVIRONMENT...
I SEE.
...ALIGNIN' TH'EARTHLY ELEMENTS AN' NATURAL HARMONIES, DOLLY.
CHAMPION.
COME IN, DOLLY, AND I'LL SHOW YOU ME SCHEME.
...WIPE YER MUCKY FEET.
NOW, THIS IS ALL ARRANGED INTO BAGHUA AREAS IN 'ERE...
OOH, IT'S LOVELY, ADA...
...VERY TANTRIC.
...ZHEN OVER THERE... XUN WHERE YOU'RE STOOD, DOLLY...
XUN, EH? I SEE.
...AND KAN AND KHON IN TH'ALCOVE.
WHAT'S THAT IN CORNER WHERE Y'HAD TELLY..?
THAT'S QIAN, LUV.
QIAN?
QIAN.
AN' ALL UP THIS SIDE 'ERE'S DUI, GEN, AN' LI, LIKE... REPRESENTIN' CHILDREN, KNOWLEDGE AN' FAME.
OH RIGHT. I SEE.
WELL, Y'VE DONE A LOVELY JOB, ADA, I MUST SAY. YER YIN AN' YER YANG FEEL VERY HARMONISED.
OH YES...
...I'VE GOT ALL ME BAGUAS BALANCED AN' ME EARTH ELEMENTS ALIGNED JUST SO, DOLLY.
IT'S VERY NICE, ANYWAY. I CAN'T STOP. I'M 'AVIN' A BRAZILIAN AT ELEVEN.
RIGHT YOU ARE, DOLLY. I'LL SEE YOU OUT.
...MIND... NUMBER FOUR...
NUMBER FOUR..? WHAT D'YOU MEAN?
WELL, ACCORDIN' T'ME ARTICLE, TH'NUMBER FOUR'S BAD LUCK IN FENG SHUI...
IS IT?
OH AYE... IT SOUNDS LIKE CHINESE WORD FOR DEATH, ADA... "SEI"!
DOES IT?
OH YES. IT'S WORST NUMBER, IS FOUR... IT'S LIKE A 'CURSE, ADA!
...A 诅咒!
IN FACT LIVIN' 'ERE AT NUMBER FOUR ALL THESE YEARS, YOU'VE BEEN ASKIN' F'TROUBLE, LUV... INVITIN' MISFORTUNE ACROSS YER THRESHHOLD.
THINK ABOUT IT... YER ANAL PROLAPSE... SIDNEY'S TEETH... THAT TIME YER IMMERSION HEATER WENT ON BLINK ON CHRISTMAS EVE...
...WHEN CAT GOT 'IS 'EAD STUCK IN THAT TIN?
NUMBER FOUR.
EIGHT'S LUCKIEST NUMBER, Y'KNOW...
IS IT..?
IT'S ASSOCIATED WITH WEALTH, SUCCESS, AN' STATUS...
...IN TAOISM, LIKE.
YOU LIVE AT NUMBER EIGHT, DON'T YOU, DOLLY..?
I DO, YES...
...AS IT 'APPENS.

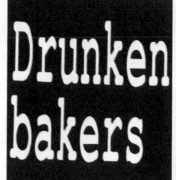

Drunken bakers

"Have you seen them pasty bastards up the road's window?"

"All decked-out with Halloween shite..."

"We should –"

"No."

"We shouldn't."

"You don't even know what it was I was going to say."

"I do."

"Say the same every year."

"Soon as you clock their fuckin' window."

Oh, oh, we should do something for Halloween.

We're missing a trick, them kiddies all love Halloween.

The little twats.

"So? We should."

"We have."

"Every sodding time."

"Like that big fuckin' meringue you had us make for the window."

"Good idea that. Meringue *do* look like ghosts."

"That one didn't. Fucker spread out and burnt."

"Looked like a pile of shit."

HAUNTid Meringes

WOOOO!

50P

"It was *me* said we should've had another crack at it."

"We probably would have. If we'd had another 400 eggs."

"Then it was fuckin' *vampire tarts*..."

"Was it?"

Bakewell with a set of plastic fangs baked into the mix.

"We got rid of a few."

"We got rid of the lot."

"Ate all we could and the rest went down the drain out back."

"Tasted good though."

"Aye, bakewell tart *does* taste good."

"Even better without a lump of half-melted plastic in it."

"But kids don't want bakewell tart any road."

"I wanted bakewell tart when I was a kid."

"Same here, but times change. We're relics, pal."

"I'm going for a walk."

FIFTYPEEPASTY

HAPPY HALLOWEEN!

GHOSTLY GOODIES!

SPOOKY SPECIALS! 2 STEAK PASTIES FOR 99P!

FULCHESTER PARK

MOOR AT OWN RISK

Later

KER

HALOWEEN

ZOMBEE BISKITS

BLOOD DONUTS

"Well, we've fuck all to lose."

"You're not wrong."

175

BACK IN 2020, Covid-19 began its relentless journey across the planet, causing untold death and misery, and turning everyone's lives upside down. Nobody had ever seen the like of this disease before. But that is not to say that the current pandemic is a unique and unprecedented event. Throughout history, invisible organisms have brought disease and pestilence to countless people across the globe and, lacking the scientific knowledge that we enjoy today, our predecessors suffered more than we are suffering now.

So how exactly were our ancestors' lives affected by these unseen pathogens that cut them down in their millions? Let's go back in time to the year 1348, and pay a visit to a typical English village in the grip of the Black Death, to see...

Who's Who and What's What in a **Medieval Plague Village**

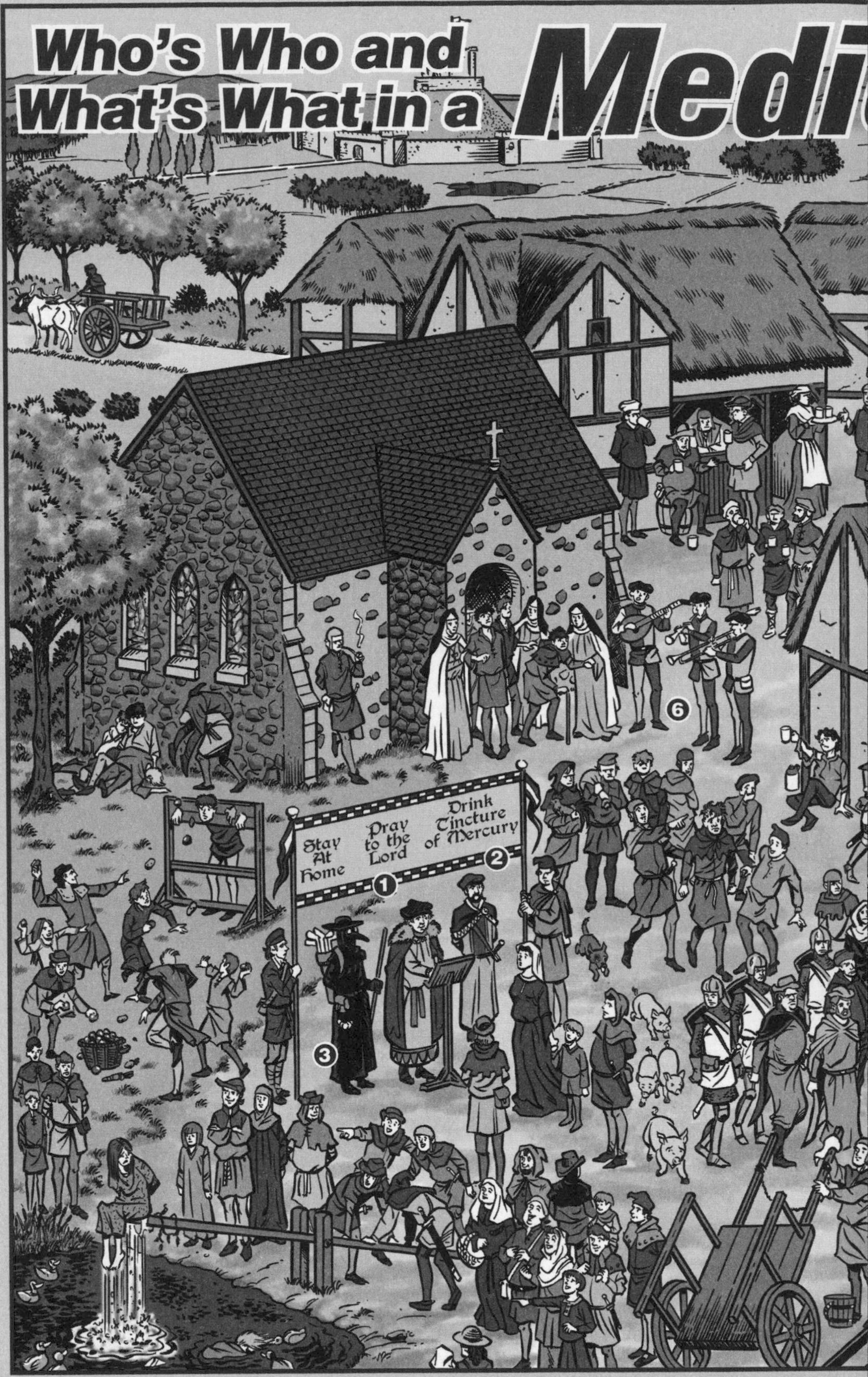

Who's Who and What's What in a Medi
Stay At Home
Pray to the Lord
Drink Tincture of Mercury
1
2
3
6

1. The Lord of the Manor

THIS was the man to whom the villagers looked as a natural leader to take charge and steer them through their troubled times. Each day he would make a proclamation on the green, announcing how many people had been gathered unto the Lord's arms in the previous 24 hours. He would also tell them that he "misspoke" in his proclamation the previous day, when said that peasants could gather in groups of 6 in their huts. What he actually meant was in groups of no more than 4, and only in the garden.

2. The Keeper of the Purse

THIS man was tasked with collecting taxes and tithes from the villagers for the Lord of the Manor. During times of plague, it was his job to secure his master's income whilst also slowing the spread of the disease. At the daily proclamations, he would tell villagers to work from home if they could, and advised farm workers to tend the fields only if they didn't have enormous black swellings under their arms and blood coming out the corners of their eyes.

3. The Village Physician

THE man charged with the health of the village stood beside the Lord of the Manor each day to tell the populace how the disease was progressing, before heading out for a round of golf. He would press home the message of how to contain the disease: *Stay at Home, Pray to the Lord, Drink Tincture of Mercury*. And he would keep spirits high by telling villagers that the search for a cure was going ahead apace, and that a nosegay of aromatic herbs that would protect against the Black Death would probably be available by Christmas 1349.

4. Pedlars

JUST like in a modern pandemic, medieval traders faced strict controls on what they could sell and when they could open for business. Markets were temporarily suspended and villagers had their movements restricted. As a result, travelling sellers became important figures during the Black Death lockdown, delivering their wares direct to the peasants' doorsteps, or leaving them in a safe place or with a neighbour if the residents were out. In today's pandemic, deliverymen and women take mobile phone photographs of delivered packages in lieu of signatures, something their medieval counterparts couldn't do, as modern 5G-capable digital cameraphones were still 500 years away, and nobody except priests could write their own name.

5. Flagellants

ALMOST everyone living through the Black Death believed that the disease was sent from God as a punishment for men's sins. Flagellants believed that if they wandered from village to village whilst whipping themselves, God would look upon their self-mortification as atonement, and take the plague away. Indeed such was their altruism and selflessness, that many peasants would show their gratitude by standing outside their huts at 8 o'clock on a Thursday night and "Clapping for Flagellants"

6. Charity Performers

IT'S hard to imagine now, but centuries befor the founding of our modern, well-funded National Health Service, infirmaries depended on public donations for their upkeep. Here, a band of minstrels are performing their latest charity madrigal to raise much-needed funds to pay for a new Bubonic Plague Unit "that therein infirm people and strangers might receive remedy of their health and necessity"

val Plague Village?

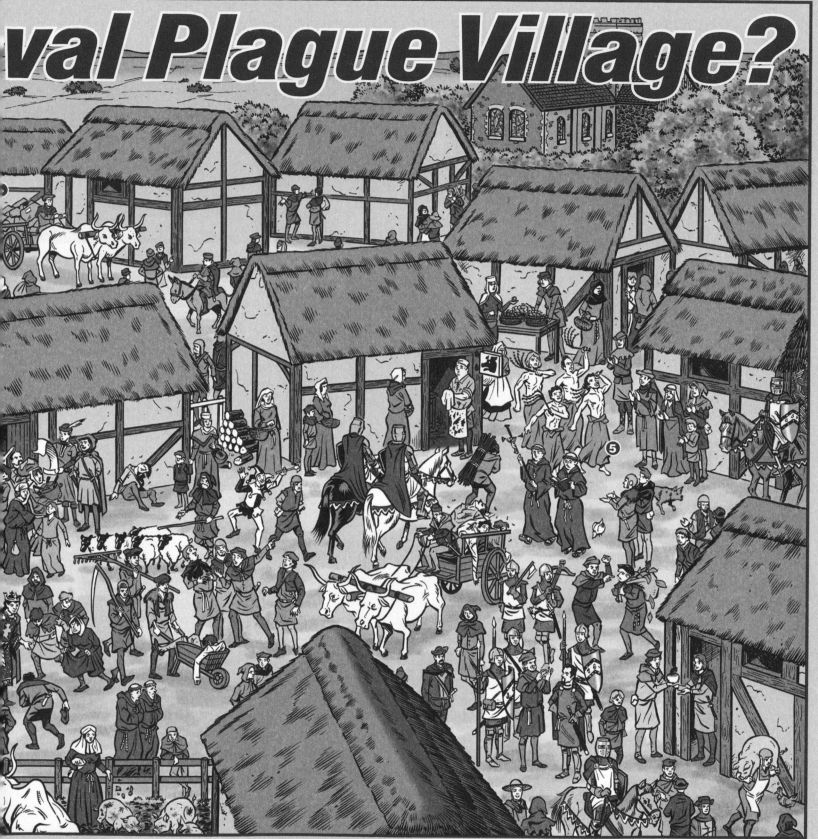

Royal Visitor

...ENTURIES ago it was believed that being touched ...a member of the royal family could cure deadly ...eases such as the plague. Here, the current heir ...the throne, The Black Prince, is enjoying a royal ...alkabout', shaking hands with the local peasants ...d asking them what they do for a living, and if they ...ve come far from their rude dwellings.

an You Spot...?

● A good neighbour dropping a turnip off at the hut of the ...age's oldest resident, who at 38 is taking no chances ...d social distancing.

● Furloughed workers, who now receive 80% of a turnip ...ch day instead of a full one.

● A man in the stocks being punished for breaking lockdown rules by taking ale at the brewer's hut without an accompanying substantial bowl of pottage.

● A woman being dipped in the pond on the village 'ducking stool' for attempting to buy three crab-apples when there was a two-crab-apples-per-customer limit.

● A man who has been dobbed in by his neighbour for breaking the 'rule of six', trying to explain to the village sheriff that it was not his fault as he is unable to count to more than four.

● A group of women queuing outside a shop, standing 2 perches apart.

● A man being ridiculed by his mates for suggesting that the Black Death was caused by rat fleas,

rather than the conjunction of three planets in the heavens and a bloody star in the eastern sky.

● A man being ridiculed by his mates because his wife has given him a haircut even more ridiculous than the ones men of that era usually had.

● A villager wiping the handles of his cart with a sanitising hand gel made of goose fat, lavender and urine.

● A man being berated by a neighbour for stockpiling dock leaves to use as toilet paper.

● A village elder breaking the curfew by driving an ox cart to a neighbouring hamlet, where he has a second hut.

● A man sitting outside the pub, telling anyone who will listen that the Black Death is a hoax, perpetuated by the village elders to take everyone's mind off the famine.

WITH HIS matinee idol good looks, taste for the high life and rock'n'roll lifestyle, Northern Irish footballer George Best was often called "the fifth Beatle." But his namesake – Liverpudlian drummer Pete Best – could also lay legitimate claim to that title after his two-and-a-half years playing with the Fab Four in Hamburg just before the group hit the 60s big time. Well now it's time to climb aboard a Viz Magical Mystery Tour of head-to-head contests to discover just which of this Fab Two is the best Best. Scores will be awarded, and at the end they'll be added together so that – in the words of the group's "Best"-selling 1965 double-A-side with *Daytripper* – *We Can Work It Out*.

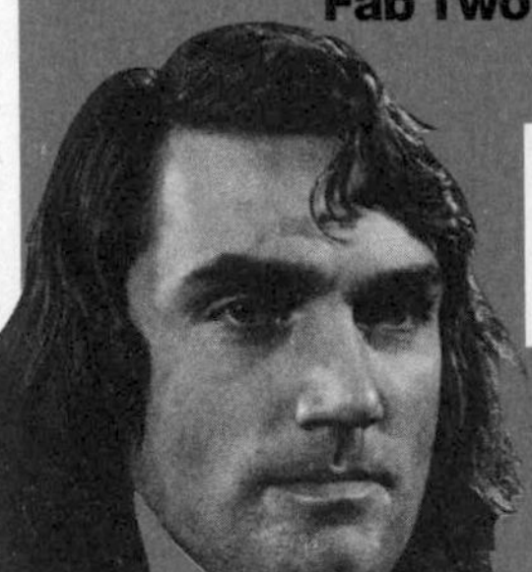

BEST vs BEST

WHO'S THE FIFTH-EST BEATLE?

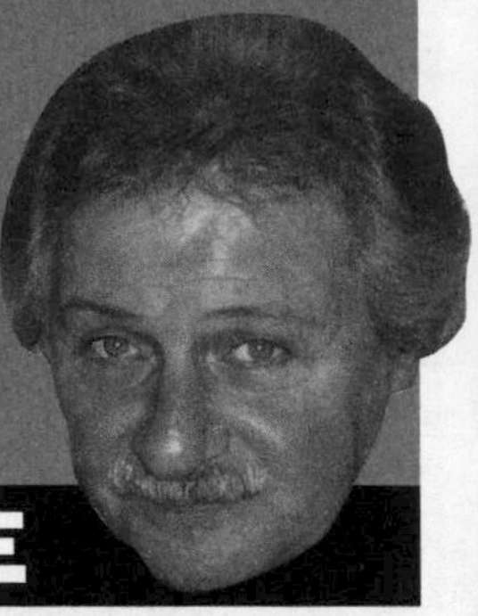

GEORGE	ROUNDS	PETE

NAME

BORN on May 22nd 1946, the future footballing whizzkid's parents – Richard and Anne Best – had him christened George, the name with which he went on to find worldwide fame. However, his official birth certificate reveals that he was originally called *Ronald Samuel* Best, with his name only changed to its final form when he was a couple of weeks old. Although this mix-up doesn't affect his surname in any way, it leaves a question mark hanging in the air, meaning that – unlike during Man Utd's 1970 FA Cup fifth round match against Northampton Town, when George slammed SIX past goalie Kim Book in the space of 90 minutes – he doesn't score quite as spectacularly in this opening round as he might have hoped.

8 — 9

PETE BEST – later to find modest fame as the Beatles' first drummer and the nearly man of pop – was born in Madras, India, on November 24th 1941. Originally called Randolph Peter *Scanland*, his surname was changed when he was a toddler after his war-widow mother Mona re-married army PT instructor Johnny Best. Although you might suppose that this surname-change would mean Pete, like George, loses marks in this round, you would be wrong. That's because Pete was replaced as Beatles drummer in 1962 by Ringo Starr – who was born Richard Starkey *and therefore retains neither his original Christian name or surname*. As a result, it's a promising start for the erstwhile Fabs percussionist.

TOP OF THE POPS APPEARANCES

BACK IN 1965, when the Rolling Stones performed their current single – *The Last Time* – on *Top of the Pops*, cameras picked out a familiar figure dancing in the studio audience. It was then 19-year-old Manchester United star George Best, taking a break from his first full season at Old Trafford to catch up on the latest hit parade sounds. But if you look carefully, the title of this round is Top of the Pops *appearances. It's a plural.* And a cursory Google search shows that in the 42 years that the show was on the air, Red Devil George only made his way onto the screen *once*.

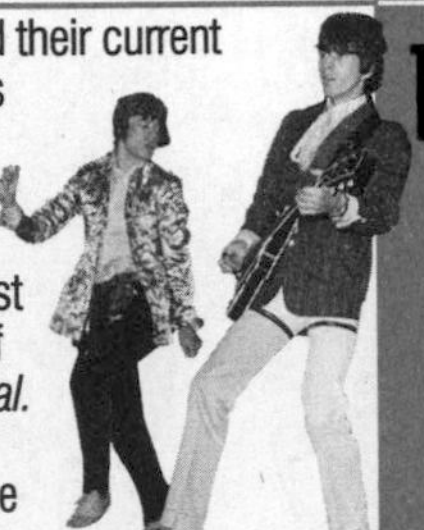

4 — 5

PETE FAMOUSLY left the Fab Four just before they began their meteoric rise to international pop stardom, and thus never played with the group on any of their *TOTP* performances. But that doesn't necessarily mean that he didn't make numerous appearances on the iconic Thursday night charts rundown. Because down the years, countless groups played on the show who had members wearing masks or other heavy makeup to disguise their true identity, including the Wombles, Kiss, and those one-hit wonders who dressed up as astronauts with space helmets on. In these performances, literally *anybody* could have been playing the drums ... including Pete Best!

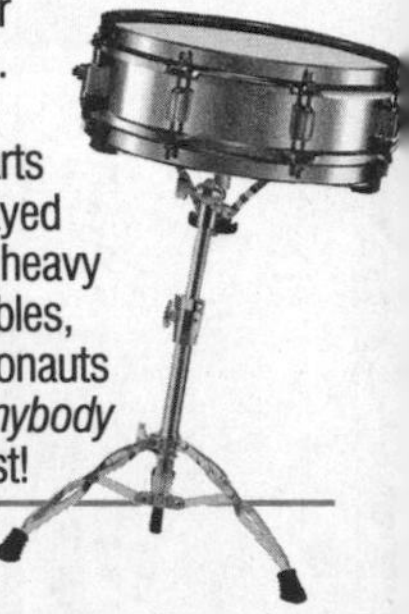

TV AND FILM ACTING CREDITS

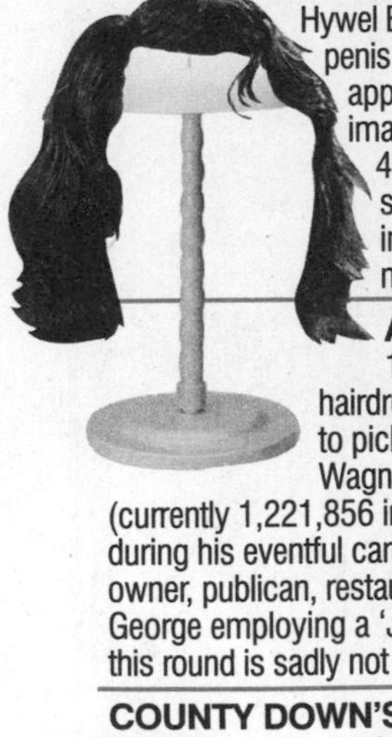

IN THE 1971 British sex comedy *Percy*, which starred Hywel Bennett as Edwin Anthony, a man who has a penis transplant following an accident, winger George appeared in a cameo role as himself. So you might imagine that, just like out on the pitch in one of his 470 appearances for Manchester United, he would score impressively in this round. However, the imdb film website lists him as "uncredited" in the movie. So it's no marks.

0 — 1

A LOOK THROUGH Pete's short-ish imdb listing shows a few Beatles-related documentaries in which he has appeared in his capacity as the Fab Four's callously discarded nearly man, but he has yet to make his *acting* debut on screen in a TV or movie drama. But all is not lost, as Pete's niece – actress Leanne Best – has an extensive list of on-screen credits in everything from *Line of Duty* to *Star Wars, Doctors* and *Casualty*. As a result, it's a single token point for the ex-Garston Jobcentre manager and bread delivery driver.

HAIRDOS

A PICTURE on the web shows George in 1969, having hairspray applied by his "personal hairdresser" Malcolm Wagner, so you might expect him to pick up a good score in this round. However, in 2010 Wagner wrote his autobiography *George Best & Me* (currently 1,221,856 in the Amazon bestsellers list), which revealed that during his eventful career, he had also worked as a musician, nightclub owner, publican, restaurateur, chop-house manager and pilot. With George employing a 'Jack-of-all-trades' to shape his barnet, his score in this round is sadly not as luxuriant as we might have expected.

4 — 6

BACK IN the early 60s, the Beatles became famous at least partly thanks to their trademark 'mop-top' hairdos, developed by German photographers Astrid Kirchherr and Jurgen Vollmer. The revolutionary style involved trimming the back and sides to a medium length, while the fringe was cut pudding-bowl-style across the forehead, just above the eyebrows. Whilst Pete was playing drums with the group at around this time, his curly hair did not suit being trimmed in the new style as it went all like a bog brush, so he was unable to join in with his bandmates' hair fashion.

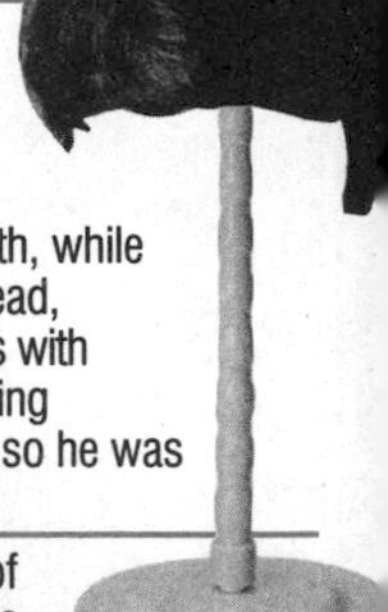

PROPERTY PRICES OF THINGS NAMED AFTER THEM

COUNTY DOWN'S City air terminal was renamed 'George Best Airport' in memory of the late footballer back in 2006. Unfortunately, the 500-acre site is not currently for sale, so we don't know how much it is worth. In the absence of this information, we have to assign it the current average value of a typical Belfast residential property; £140,750.

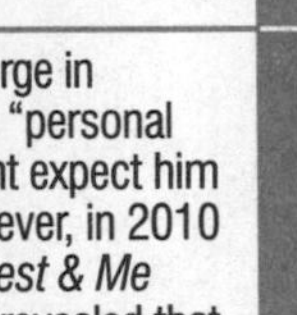

5 — 7

IN 2011, a residential street in the West Derby area of Liverpool was named in honour of the one time Beatles tub-thumper. At the time of going to press, properties for sale on Pete Best Drive, including 4 and 5-bedroom detached houses, some of which appear to have horribly low ceilings, are commanding an asking price of around £550,000.

LOVE LIFE

THROUGHOUT his career, George made as many headlines for his riotous sex life as he did for his time on the football pitch. Squiring a succession of Miss Worlds, busty actresses and glamorous models, he often missed training due to being in the fart sack with three or even four women. Indeed, at the height of his fame, it is believed that he once bedded (fucked) seven different women in a 24-hour period, a professional footballing record that stands to this day.

10 — 2

IN 1963, Pete wed his sweetheart Kathy, and the pair – who have two daughters and four grandchildren – have remained happily married ever since.

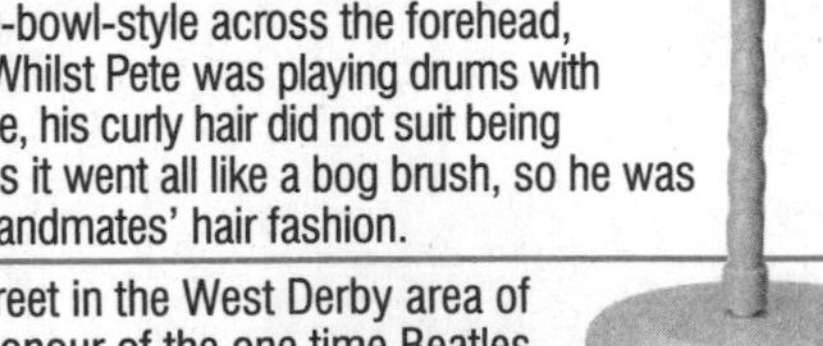

HOW DID THEY DO?

ALTHOUGH he famously never made it into the finals of a top football tournament, Good Time George lifts the *Viz* Fifth Beatle Cup for being the Best of the Bests! He may have spent half his Old Trafford career with a number 8 on his shirt, but today he's in with a bullet at Number One in the Fab Five Hit Parade!

36 — 35

IT'S BEEN a Long and Winding Road – a song written and recorded a good 8 years after he was thrown out of the group – for Pete, but he's finally reached the end of this particular Magical Mystery Tour. He can stick his drumsticks where the sun don't shine, because statistics don't lie. He's the worst of the Bests.

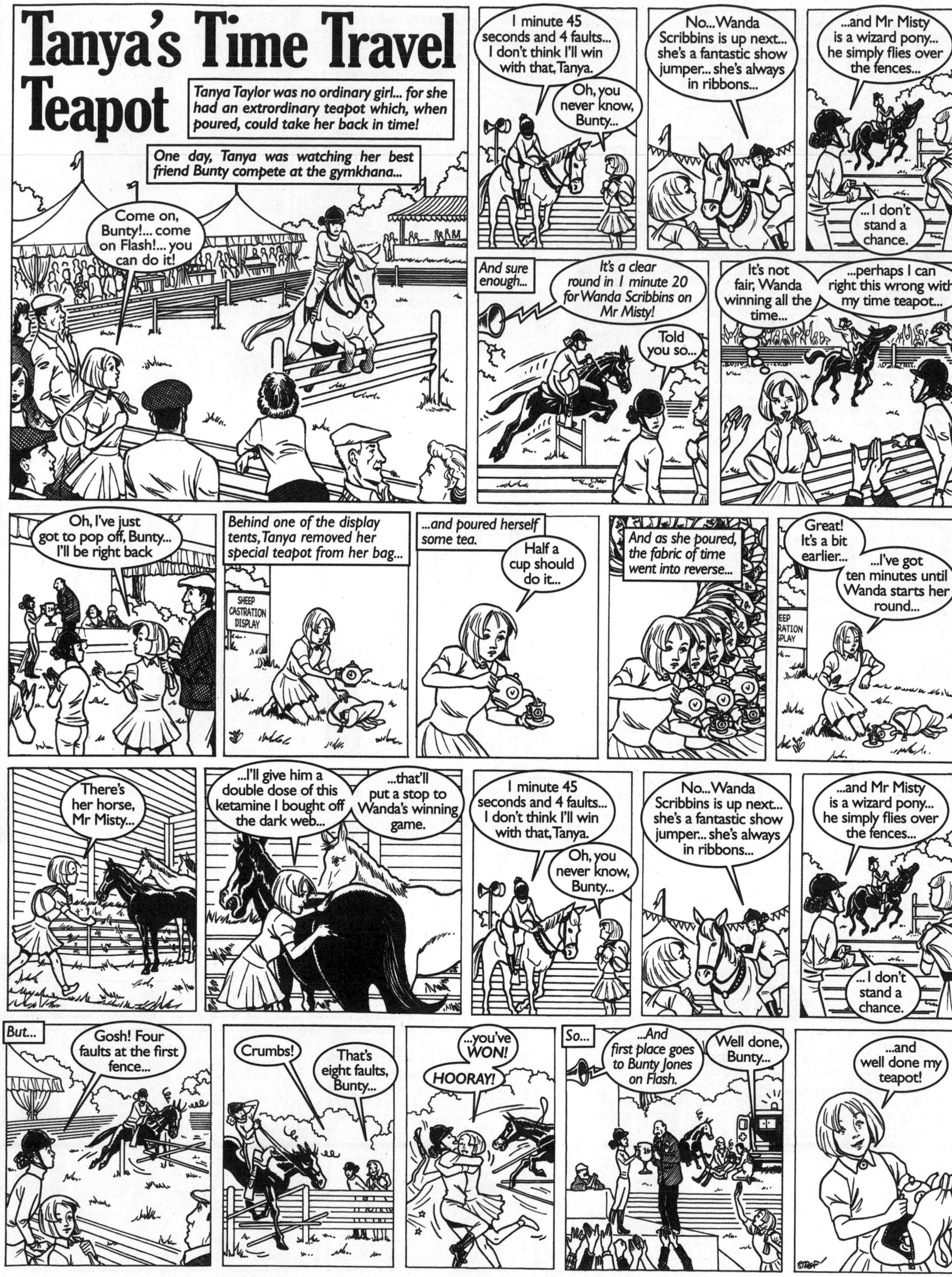

Tanya's Time Travel Teapot
Tanya Taylor was no ordinary girl... for she had an extrordinary teapot which, when poured, could take her back in time!
One day, Tanya was watching her best friend Bunty compete at the gymkhana...
Come on, Bunty!... come on Flash!... you can do it!
1 minute 45 seconds and 4 faults... I don't think I'll win with that, Tanya.
Oh, you never know, Bunty...
No... Wanda Scribbins is up next... she's a fantastic show jumper... she's always in ribbons...
...and Mr Misty is a wizard pony... he simply flies over the fences...
...I don't stand a chance.
And sure enough...
It's a clear round in 1 minute 20 for Wanda Scribbins on Mr Misty!
Told you so...
It's not fair, Wanda winning all the time...
...perhaps I can right this wrong with my time teapot...
Oh, I've just got to pop off, Bunty... I'll be right back
Behind one of the display tents, Tanya removed her special teapot from her bag...
SHEEP CASTRATION DISPLAY
...and poured herself some tea.
Half a cup should do it...
And as she poured, the fabric of time went into reverse...
Great! It's a bit earlier...
...I've got ten minutes until Wanda starts her round...
There's her horse, Mr Misty...
...I'll give him a double dose of this ketamine I bought off the dark web...
...that'll put a stop to Wanda's winning game.
1 minute 45 seconds and 4 faults... I don't think I'll win with that, Tanya.
Oh, you never know, Bunty...
No... Wanda Scribbins is up next... she's a fantastic show jumper... she's always in ribbons...
...and Mr Misty is a wizard pony... he simply flies over the fences...
...I don't stand a chance.
But...
Gosh! Four faults at the first fence...
Crumbs!
That's eight faults, Bunty...
...you've WON!
HOORAY!
So...
...And first place goes to Bunty Jones on Flash.
Well done, Bunty...
...and well done my teapot!

Science meets Religion in this High-Octane Adventure of Speed and Theology!

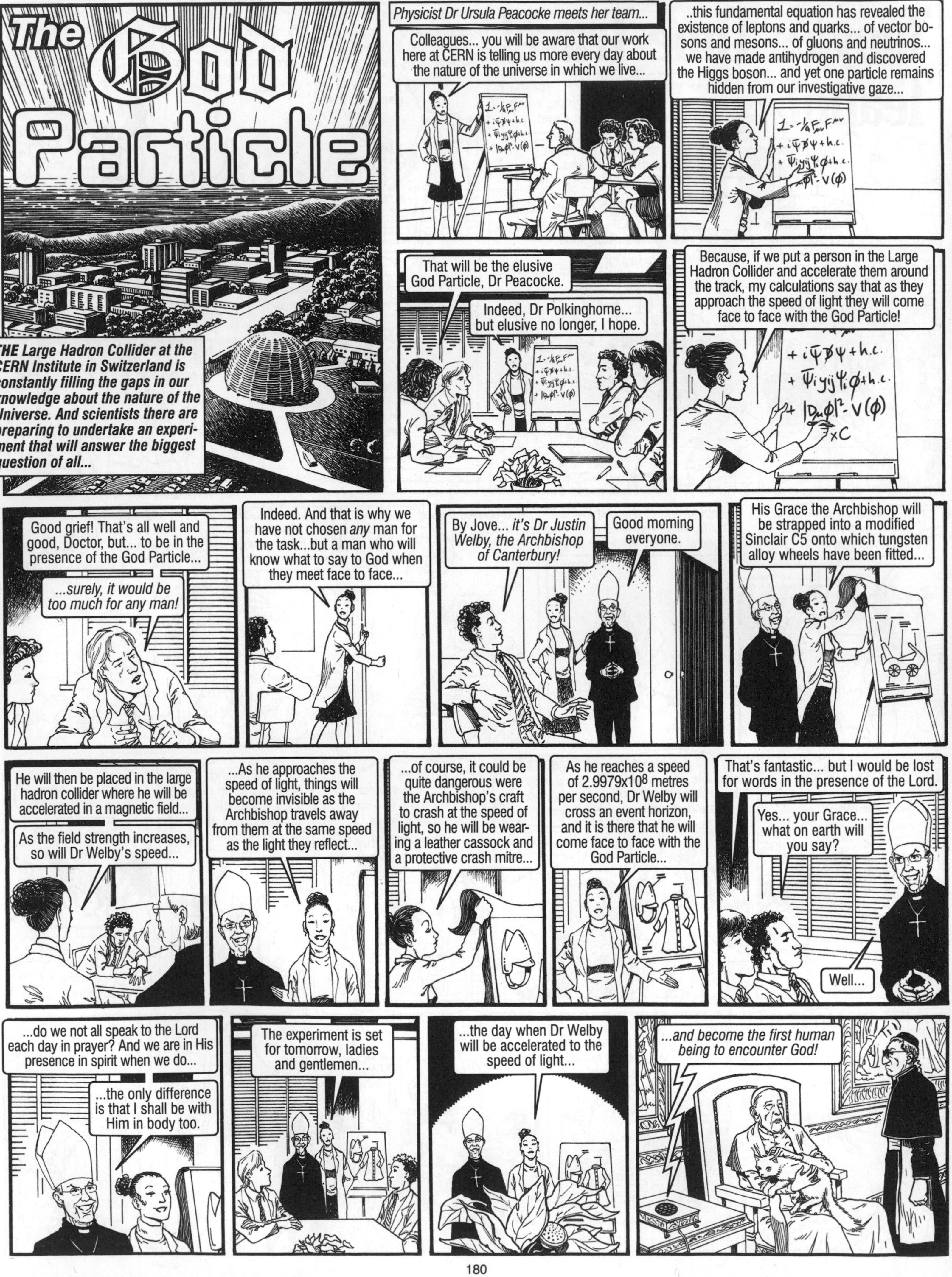
The God Particle
THE Large Hadron Collider at the CERN Institute in Switzerland is constantly filling the gaps in our knowledge about the nature of the Universe. And scientists there are preparing to undertake an experiment that will answer the biggest question of all...
Physicist Dr Ursula Peacocke meets her team...
Colleagues... you will be aware that our work here at CERN is telling us more every day about the nature of the universe in which we live...
..this fundamental equation has revealed the existence of leptons and quarks... of vector bosons and mesons... of gluons and neutrinos... we have made antihydrogen and discovered the Higgs boson... and yet one particle remains hidden from our investigative gaze...
That will be the elusive God Particle, Dr Peacocke.
Indeed, Dr Polkinghorne... but elusive no longer, I hope.
Because, if we put a person in the Large Hadron Collider and accelerate them around the track, my calculations say that as they approach the speed of light they will come face to face with the God Particle!
Good grief! That's all well and good, Doctor, but... to be in the presence of the God Particle...
...surely, it would be too much for any man!
Indeed. And that is why we have not chosen any man for the task...but a man who will know what to say to God when they meet face to face...
By Jove... it's Dr Justin Welby, the Archbishop of Canterbury!
Good morning everyone.
His Grace the Archbishop will be strapped into a modified Sinclair C5 onto which tungsten alloy wheels have been fitted...
He will then be placed in the large hadron collider where he will be accelerated in a magnetic field...
As the field strength increases, so will Dr Welby's speed...
...As he approaches the speed of light, things will become invisible as the Archbishop travels away from them at the same speed as the light they reflect...
...of course, it could be quite dangerous were the Archbishop's craft to crash at the speed of light, so he will be wearing a leather cassock and a protective crash mitre...
As he reaches a speed of 2.9979x10⁸ metres per second, Dr Welby will cross an event horizon, and it is there that he will come face to face with the God Particle...
That's fantastic... but I would be lost for words in the presence of the Lord.
Yes... your Grace... what on earth will you say?
Well...
...do we not all speak to the Lord each day in prayer? And we are in His presence in spirit when we do...
...the only difference is that I shall be with Him in body too.
The experiment is set for tomorrow, ladies and gentlemen...
...the day when Dr Welby will be accelerated to the speed of light...
...and become the first human being to encounter God!

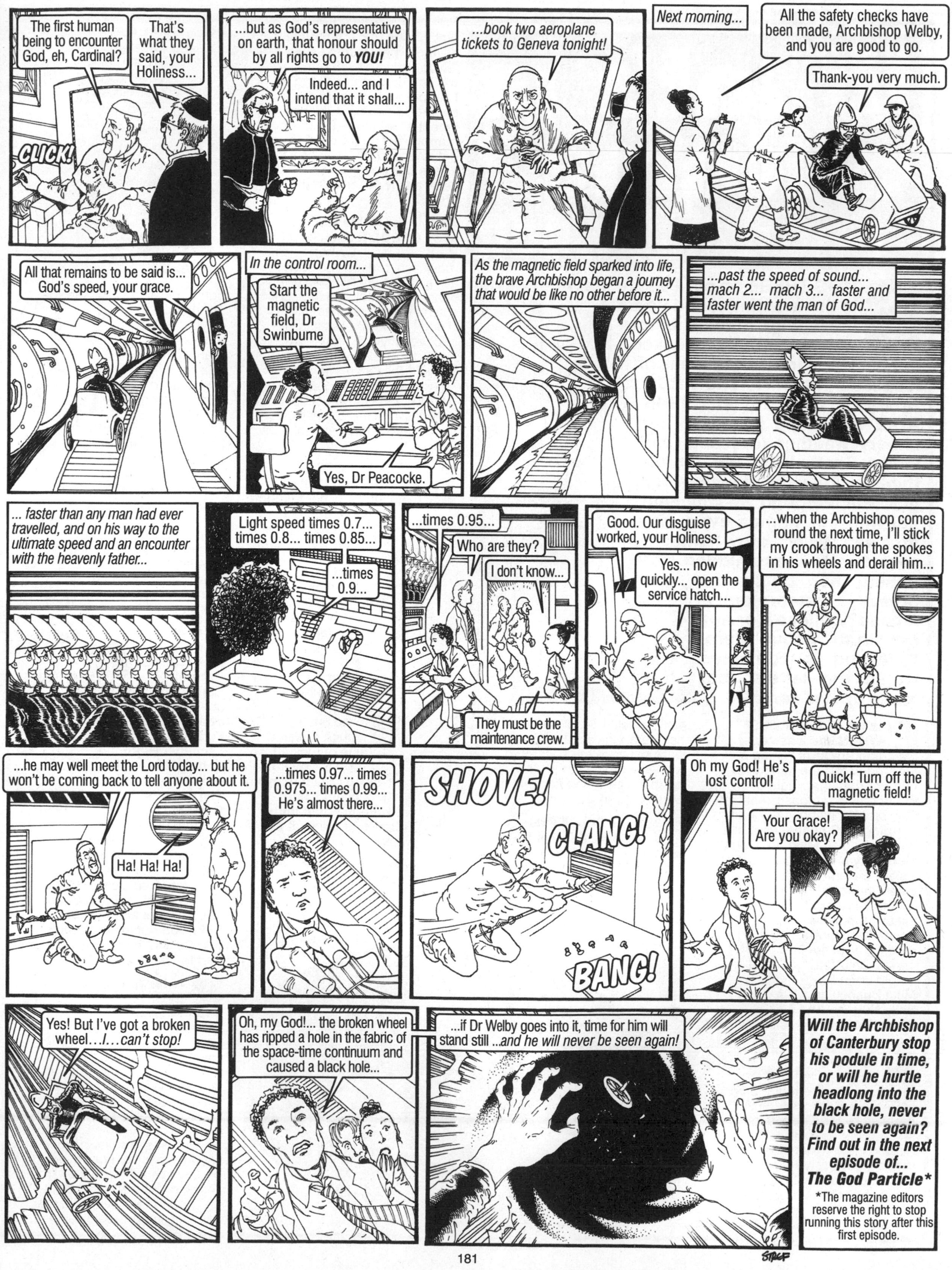
The first human being to encounter God, eh, Cardinal?
That's what they said, your Holiness...
CLICK!
...but as God's representative on earth, that honour should by all rights go to *YOU!*
Indeed... and I intend that it shall...
...book two aeroplane tickets to Geneva tonight!
Next morning...
All the safety checks have been made, Archbishop Welby, and you are good to go.
Thank-you very much.
All that remains to be said is... God's speed, your grace.
In the control room...
Start the magnetic field, Dr Swinburne
Yes, Dr Peacocke.
As the magnetic field sparked into life, the brave Archbishop began a journey that would be like no other before it...
...past the speed of sound... mach 2... mach 3... faster and faster went the man of God...
... faster than any man had ever travelled, and on his way to the ultimate speed and an encounter with the heavenly father...
Light speed times 0.7... times 0.8... times 0.85...
...times 0.9...
...times 0.95...
Who are they?
I don't know...
They must be the maintenance crew.
Good. Our disguise worked, your Holiness.
Yes... now quickly... open the service hatch...
...when the Archbishop comes round the next time, I'll stick my crook through the spokes in his wheels and derail him...
...he may well meet the Lord today... but he won't be coming back to tell anyone about it.
Ha! Ha! Ha!
...times 0.97... times 0.975... times 0.99... He's almost there...
SHOVE!
CLANG!
BANG!
Oh my God! He's lost control!
Quick! Turn off the magnetic field!
Your Grace! Are you okay?
Yes! But I've got a broken wheel... *I... can't stop!*
Oh, my God!... the broken wheel has ripped a hole in the fabric of the space-time continuum and caused a black hole...
...if Dr Welby goes into it, time for him will stand still *...and he will never be seen again!*
Will the Archbishop of Canterbury stop his podule in time, or will he hurtle headlong into the black hole, never to be seen again? Find out in the next episode of... The God Particle*
*The magazine editors reserve the right to stop running this story after this first episode.
STRCF

What's in a Name?
~Carol Kirkwood

SHE'S THERE on our TV screens when we rise in the mornings, and us Brits don't step outside before we've carefully checked out her warm fronts and areas of localised pressure. She's *BBC Breakfast* iso-barmaid **CAROL KIRKWOOD**, and thanks to her cheery weather forecasts and smiley Scottish demeanour, we think we know what makes her tick. But although we welcome her into our homes every day, do we *really* know what secrets she keeps hidden behind her bright and breezy meteorological facade? Believe it or not, the truth about Carol Kirkwood is contained within the letters that make up her name!

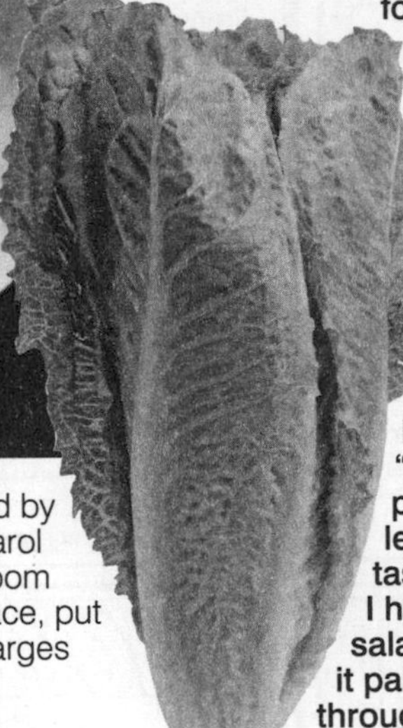

C is for CLAIRVOYANT
WHEN she was very young, Carol visited a fairground fortune teller who told her that she would grow up to become a famous breakfast telly star. Amazingly, her early morning BBC colleagues Dan Walker, Louise Minchin, Naga Munchety and Charlie Stayt also visited the same fortune teller on the same day … and all received exactly the same spookily accurate reading from her crystal ball! And so did John Kay, Mike Bushell and Sally Nugent. And Steph McGovern.

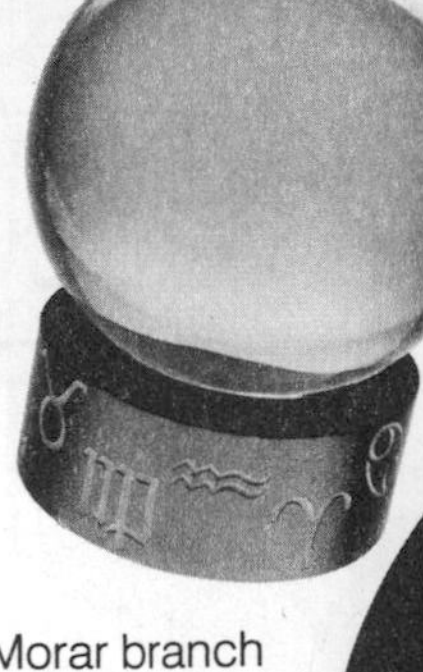

A is for ALIBI
IN 1984, violent armed robbers raided the Morar branch of Barclays Bank, threatening cashiers by firing a sawn-off shotgun into the ceiling before making off with more than £30,000 in cash. Several witnesses identified Carol as the trigger-happy thief toting the gun, and Inverness-shire police put out a warrant for her arrest. However, a signed statement provided by her mum, claiming that Carol was upstairs tidying her room when the robbery took place, put her in the clear and all charges were dropped.

R is for ROULETTE
KIRKWOOD has spent years working on a foolproof Roulette system to beat the Las Vegas casinos. "I only bet on the even numbers, and every time an odd number comes up I double my previous stake and add a dollar," she told ITV money saving expert Martin Lewis. "Eventually an even number will come up, and as long as I keep doubling my previous stake and adding a dollar every time the ball lands on an odd number, I'm guaranteed to come out on top in the end. As long as the ball doesn't land on the zero, and it doesn't do that very often."

O is for OSMOSIS
CAROL'S favourite physical process is Osmosis – the movement of water molecules from a dilute solution into a concentrated solution through a semi-permeable membrane. "I don't know why, but it really captured my imagination when I was doing science at school," she told TalkRadio's Martin Kelner. "Having said that, I couldn't stand diffusion – the movement of solute particles from an area of higher concentration to an area of lower concentration."

L is for LETTUCE
SALAD-FAN Carol says that Lettuce is her favourite food, and she claims to chomp her way through at least TEN of the crispy, Vitamin K-rich, leafy green salad-staples every single day. She told Radio Northampton's Bernie Keith: "The only problem is, lettuce doesn't taste of fuck all, so I have to cover it in salad cream to make it palatable. I get through about thirty bottles of the stuff every week."

K is for KNUCKLE-DUSTER
BACK in 1990, when Kirkwood was living in Cheshire, she was arrested and questioned by local police after a Macclesfield bank clerk was kidnapped, tied up and beaten viciously with a knuckle-duster in an attempt to extract the combination numbers for his branch's safe. Although the man – who lost fourteen teeth and suffered a fractured skull and broken jaw in the attack – later identified Kirkwood as his assailant, even picking her out of an identity parade, all charges were dropped after Carol's mother signed an affidavit stating that her daughter had been 200 miles away, tidying her room at home when the crime was committed.

I is for ICE Cube
BELIEVE it or not, Carol's childhood sweetheart at Fort William's Lochaber High School was NWA rapper Ice Cube. The *Straight Outta Compton* bad boy – who later went on to pen songs including *Fuck tha Police* and *Bop Gun (One Nation)* – was on an exchange visit from George Washington High School in South Central Los Angeles and asked Kirkwood out after meeting her at a Ceilidh, where the pair took part in *The Pride of Erin Waltz*.

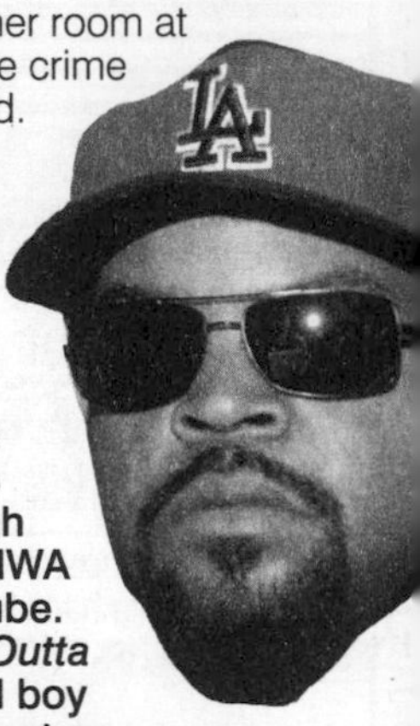

R is for RAINBOWS
DESPITE having spent her TV career out and about reporting on UK weather from Land's End and John O'Groats, Carol has never seen a rainbow. "Every time one appears, I always seem to be looking in the wrong direction or I can't find my glasses or my hat's fallen down in front of my eyes or something," she told Radio Cornwall's David White. "And believe it or not, I even missed seeing the rainbow in *The Wizard of Oz*, because I'd got up to go to the toilet at the exact moment it appeared on screen."

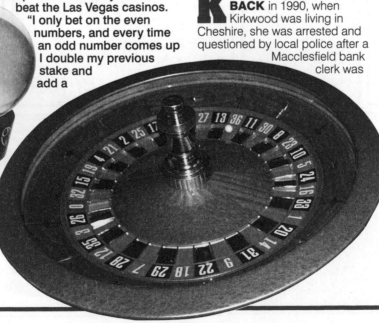

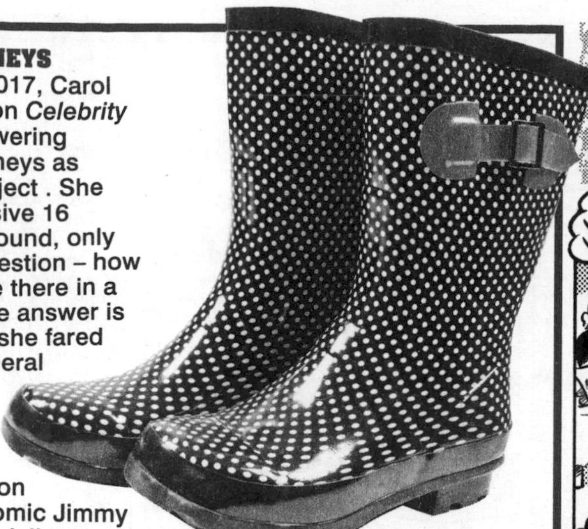

K is for KIDNEYS

BACK in 2017, Carol appeared on *Celebrity Mastermind*, answering questions on Kidneys as her specialist subject . She scored an impressive 16 points in the first round, only passing on one question – how many nephrons are there in a mouse's kidney (the answer is 12,500). However, she fared less well in the General Knowledge round, scoring no points after passing on all 18 questions. The episode was won by Northern Irish comic Jimmy Cricket, whose specialist subject was Liver.

W is for WELLINGTONS

CAROL travels all over the country to make her live *BBC Breakfast* weather forecasts from different places every morning. And the one thing she always remembers to take on location with her is a pair of Wellington boots. "They're them expensive neoprene ones to keep my toes warm if I'm stood in a puddle, and I've got them a size bigger than my feet, so they fit me even if I've got thick socks on," she told Radio London's Jo Good. "The viewers at home never see them because we only use a little lens on the camera."

O is for OSIRIS

FEW VIEWERS who tune in to watch Carol on breakfast telly realise that – like many BBC weather forecasters – she worships Osiris, the Ancient Egyptian God of the Afterlife. At midnight on Midsummer's Day each year, Carol – along with Tomasz Shafernaker, Darren Bett, Sarah Keith-Lucas and Helen Willetts – strips naked and performs a series of bizarre rituals on Salisbury Plain in his honour, culminating in a bloodthirsty sacrifice of thirteen white oxen.

O is for OUIJA Board

PERHAPS Carol's most frightening moment came during a live Halloween broadcast in 1998, when she appeared to accidentally raise the spirit of Victorian murderer Jack the Ripper whilst using a ouija board to forecast the weather. The glass in her hand seemed to have a mind of its own, and started spelling out a series of revolting threats against a number of BBC stars, including a promise to "slit Dave LeeTravis from gizzard to bollocks". It was later revealed that the terrifying happening had been an elaborate "Gotcha" set-up by *Late Late Breakfast Show* funnyman Noel Edmonds.

D is for DNA

IN 2006, DNA evidence suggested to Glasgow cops that Carol had been present at a brutal gangland killing in the city's East End. Grisly remains found in meat processing plant machinery led forensics experts to believe that at least three men had been murdered and butchered to hide their identities, with their carcasses processed as sausagemeat. Although experts said bloody fingerprints on the control levers of a slaughterhouse mincing machine matched Kirkwood's, the case was dropped after her mum told cops she was at home tidying her room when the grisly massacre took place.

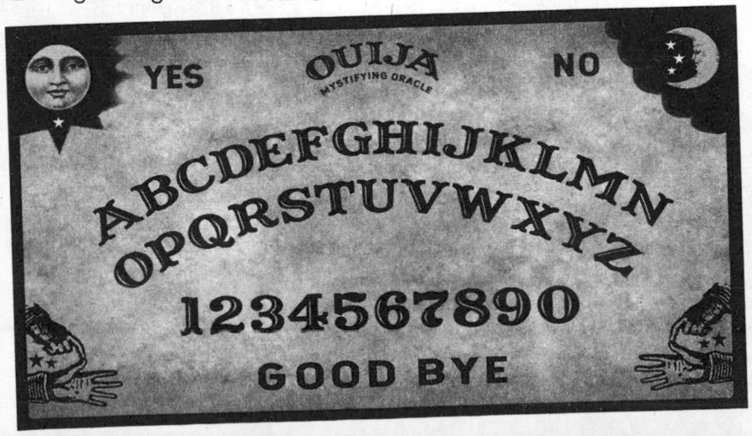

YES
OUIJA
MYSTIFYING ORACLE
NO
ABCDEFGHIJKLMN
OPQRSTUVWXYZ
1234567890
GOOD BYE

NEXT WEEK: It's All in the Name 10-page pullout special – **His Royal Highness King Charles Philip Arthur George Mountbatten-Windsor**

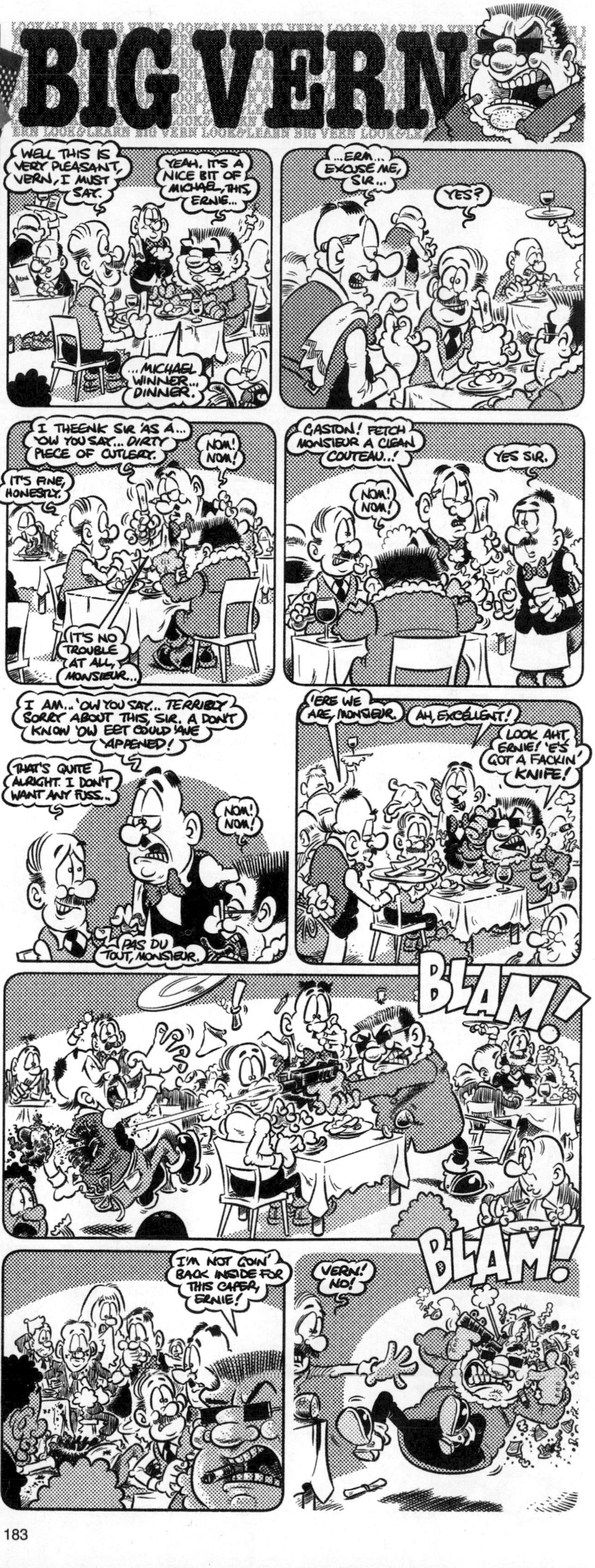

BIG VERN
WELL THIS IS VERY PLEASANT, VERN, I MUST SAY.
YEAH. IT'S A NICE BIT OF MICHAEL, THIS, ERNIE...
...MICHAEL WINNER... DINNER.
...ERM... EXCUSE ME, SIR...
YES?
I THEENK SIR 'AS A... 'OW YOU SAY... DIRTY PIECE OF CUTLERY.
NOM! NOM!
IT'S FINE, HONESTLY.
IT'S NO TROUBLE AT ALL, MONSIEUR...
GASTON! FETCH MONSIEUR A CLEAN COUTEAU..!
NOM! NOM!
YES SIR.
I AM... 'OW YOU SAY... TERRIBLY SORRY ABOUT THIS, SIR. A DON'T KNOW 'OW EET COULD 'AVE 'APPENED!
THAT'S QUITE ALRIGHT. I DON'T WANT ANY FUSS..
NOM! NOM!
PAS DU TOUT, MONSIEUR.
'ERE WE ARE, MONSIEUR.
AH, EXCELLENT!
LOOK AHT, ERNIE! 'E'S GOT A FACKIN' KNIFE!
BLAM!
I'M NOT GOIN' BACK INSIDE FOR THIS CAPER, ERNIE!
BLAM!
VERN! NO!

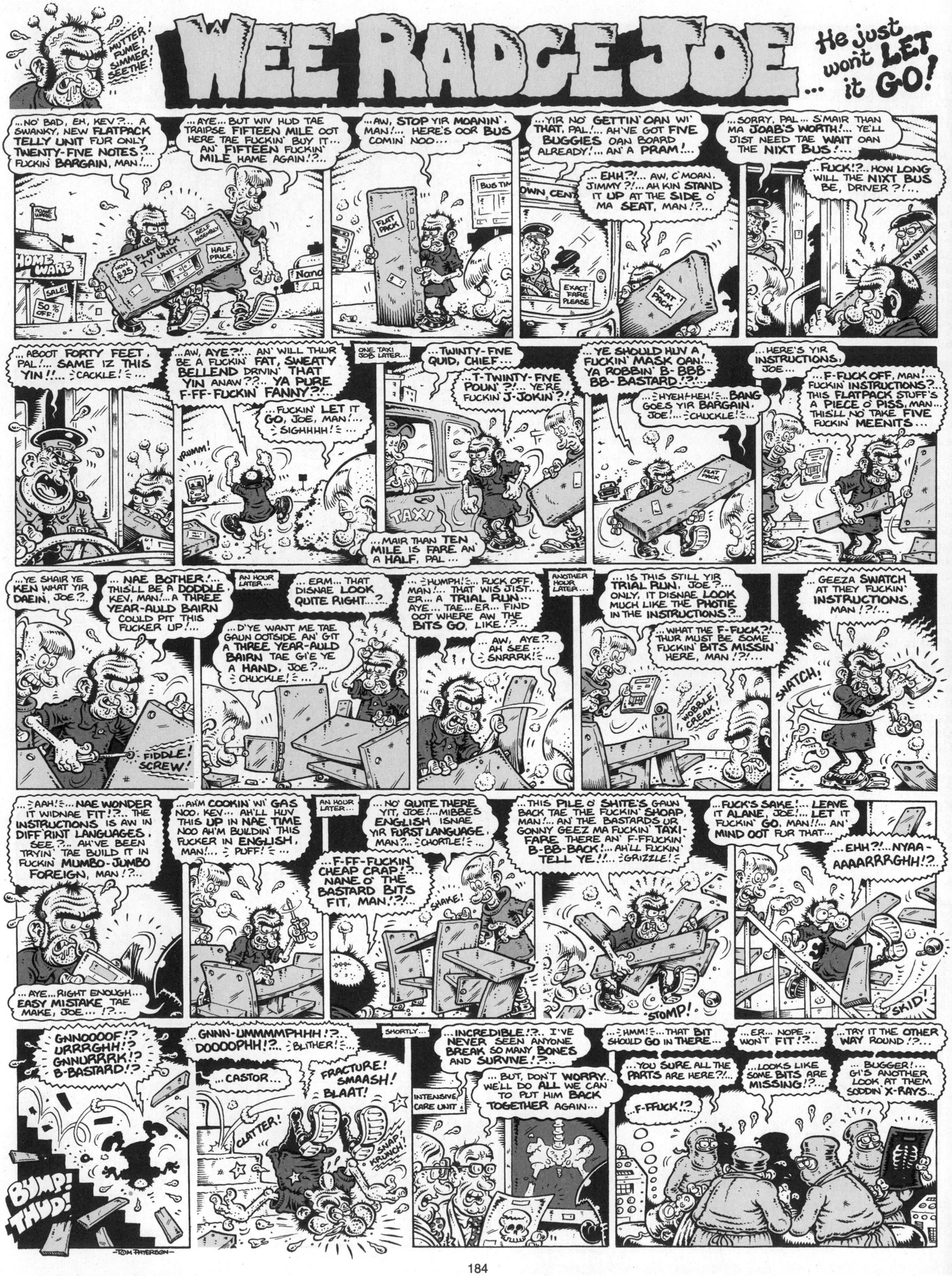
MUTTER! FUME! SIMMER! SEETHE!
WEE RADGE JOE
... He just wont LET it GO!
...NO' BAD, EH, KEV?... A SWANKY, NEW FLATPACK TELLY UNIT FUR ONLY TWENTY-FIVE NOTES?... FUCKIN' BARGAIN, MAN!...
HOME WARE
HOME WARE
SALE!
50% OFF!
NOW £25
FLATPACK TV UNIT
SELF ASSEMBLY
HALF PRICE!
...AYE... BUT WIV HUD TAE TRAIPSE FIFTEEN MILE OOT HERE TAE FUCKIN' BUY IT... AN' FIFTEEN FUCKIN' MILE HAME AGAIN!?...
Nando
...AW, STOP YIR MOANIN', MAN!... HERE'S OOR BUS COMIN' NOO...
FLAT PACK
BUS TIM
...YIR NO' GETTIN' OAN WI' THAT, PAL!... AH'VE GOT FIVE BUGGIES OAN BOARD ALREADY!... AN' A PRAM!...
...EHH?!... AW, C'MOAN, JIMMY?!... AH KIN STAND IT UP AT THE SIDE O' MA SEAT, MAN!?...
OWN CENT
EXACT FARE PLEASE
FLAT PACK
...SORRY, PAL... S'MAIR THAN MA JOAB'S WORTH!... YE'LL JIST NEED TAE WAIT OAN THE NIXT BUS!...
...FUCK!?... HOW LONG WILL THE NIXT BUS BE, DRIVER?!...
TV UNIT
...ABOOT FORTY FEET, PAL!... SAME IZ THIS YIN!!... CACKLE!...
...AW, AYE?!... AN' WILL THUR BE A FUCKIN' FAT, SWEATY BELLEND DRIVIN' THAT YIN ANAW??... YA PURE F-FF-FUCKIN' FANNY?!...
VRUMM!
...FUCKIN' LET IT GO, JOE, MAN!... SIGHHHH!...
ONE TAXI JOB LATER...
...TWINTY-FIVE QUID, CHIEF...
...T-TWINTY-FIVE POUN'?!... YE'RE FUCKIN' J-JOKIN'?!
TAXI
...MAIR THAN TEN MILE IS FARE AN' A HALF, PAL...
...YE SHOULD HUV A FUCKIN' MASK OAN, YA ROBBIN' B-BBB-BB-BASTARD!?!...
...HYEH-HEH!... BANG GOES YIR BARGAIN, JOE!... CHUCKLE!...
FLAT PACK
...HERE'S YIR INSTRUCTIONS, JOE...
...F-FUCK OFF, MAN!... FUCKIN' INSTRUCTIONS?... THIS FLATPACK STUFF'S A PIECE O' PISS, MAN... THIS'LL NO' TAKE FIVE FUCKIN' MEENITS...
...YE SHAIR YE KEN WHAT YIR DAEIN, JOE?...
...NAE BOTHER!... THIS'LL BE A DODDLE, KEV, MAN!... A THREE YEAR-AULD BAIRN COULD PIT THIS FUCKER UP!...
FIDDLE! SCREW!
AN HOUR LATER...
...ERM... THAT DISNAE LOOK QUITE RIGHT...?
...D'YE WANT ME TAE GAUN OOTSIDE AN' GIT A THREE YEAR-AULD BAIRN TAE GI'E YE A HAND, JOE?... CHUCKLE!...
...HUMPH!... FUCK OFF, MAN!... THAT WIS JIST... ER... A TRIAL RUN... AYE... TAE... ER... FIND OOT WHERE AW THE BITS GO, LIKE!?...
...AW, AYE?... AH SEE... SNRRRK!...
ANOTHER HOUR LATER...
...IS THIS STILL YIR TRIAL RUN, JOE?... ONLY, IT DISNAE LOOK MUCH LIKE THE PHOTIE IN THE INSTRUCTIONS?...
...WHAT THE F-FUCK?!... THUR MUST BE SOME FUCKIN' BITS MISSIN' HERE, MAN!?!...
WOBBLE! CREAK!
...GEEZA SWATCH AT THEY FUCKIN' INSTRUCTIONS, MAN!?!...
SNATCH!
...AAH!... NAE WONDER IT WIDNAE FIT!?... THE INSTRUCTIONS IS AW IN DIFF'RINT LANGUAGES, SEE?... AH'VE BEEN TRYIN' TAE BUILD IT IN FUCKIN' MUMBO-JUMBO FOREIGN, MAN!?...
...AYE... RIGHT ENOUGH... EASY MISTAKE TAE MAKE, JOE...!?...
...AH'M COOKIN' WI' GAS NOO, KEV... AH'LL HUV THIS UP IN NAE TIME NOO AH'M BUILDIN' THIS FUCKER IN ENGLISH, MAN!... PUFF!...
AN HOUR LATER...
...NO' QUITE THERE YIT, JOE!... MIBBES ENGLISH ISNAE YIR FURST LANGUAGE, MAN?... CHORTLE!...
...F-FF-FUCKIN' CHEAP CRAP!?... NANE O' THE BASTARD BITS FIT, MAN!?!...
SHAKE!
...THIS PILE O' SHITE'S GAUN BACK TAE THE FUCKIN' SHOAP, MAN!... AN' THE BASTARDS UR GONNY GEEZ MA FUCKIN' TAXI-FARE THERE AN' F-FFUCKIN' B-BB-BACK!... AH'LL FUCKIN' TELL YE!!... GRIZZLE!...
STOMP!
...FUCK'S SAKE!... LEAVE IT ALANE, JOE!... LET IT FUCKIN' GO, MAN!!... AN' MIND OOT FUR THAT...
...EHH?!... NYAA-AAAARRRGHH!?
SKID!
...GNNOOOOF!?... URRRGHH!?... GNNURRRRK!?... B-BASTARD!?
BUMP! THUD!
...GNNN-UMMMMPHHH!?... DOOOOPHH!?... BLITHER!...
...CASTOR...
FRACTURE! SMAASH! BLAAT!
CLATTER!
SNAP! KRUNCH!
SHORTLY...
INTENSIVE CARE UNIT
...INCREDIBLE!?... I'VE NEVER SEEN ANYONE BREAK SO MANY BONES AND SURVIVE!?...
...BUT, DON'T WORRY... WE'LL DO ALL WE CAN TO PUT HIM BACK TOGETHER AGAIN...
...HMM!... THAT BIT SHOULD GO IN THERE...
...YOU SURE ALL THE PARTS ARE HERE?!...
...F-FFUCK!?
...ER... NOPE... WON'T FIT!?...
...LOOKS LIKE SOME BITS ARE MISSING!?...
...TRY IT THE OTHER WAY ROUND!?...
...BUGGER!... GI'S ANOTHER LOOK AT THEM SODDIN' X-RAYS...
-TOM PATERSON-

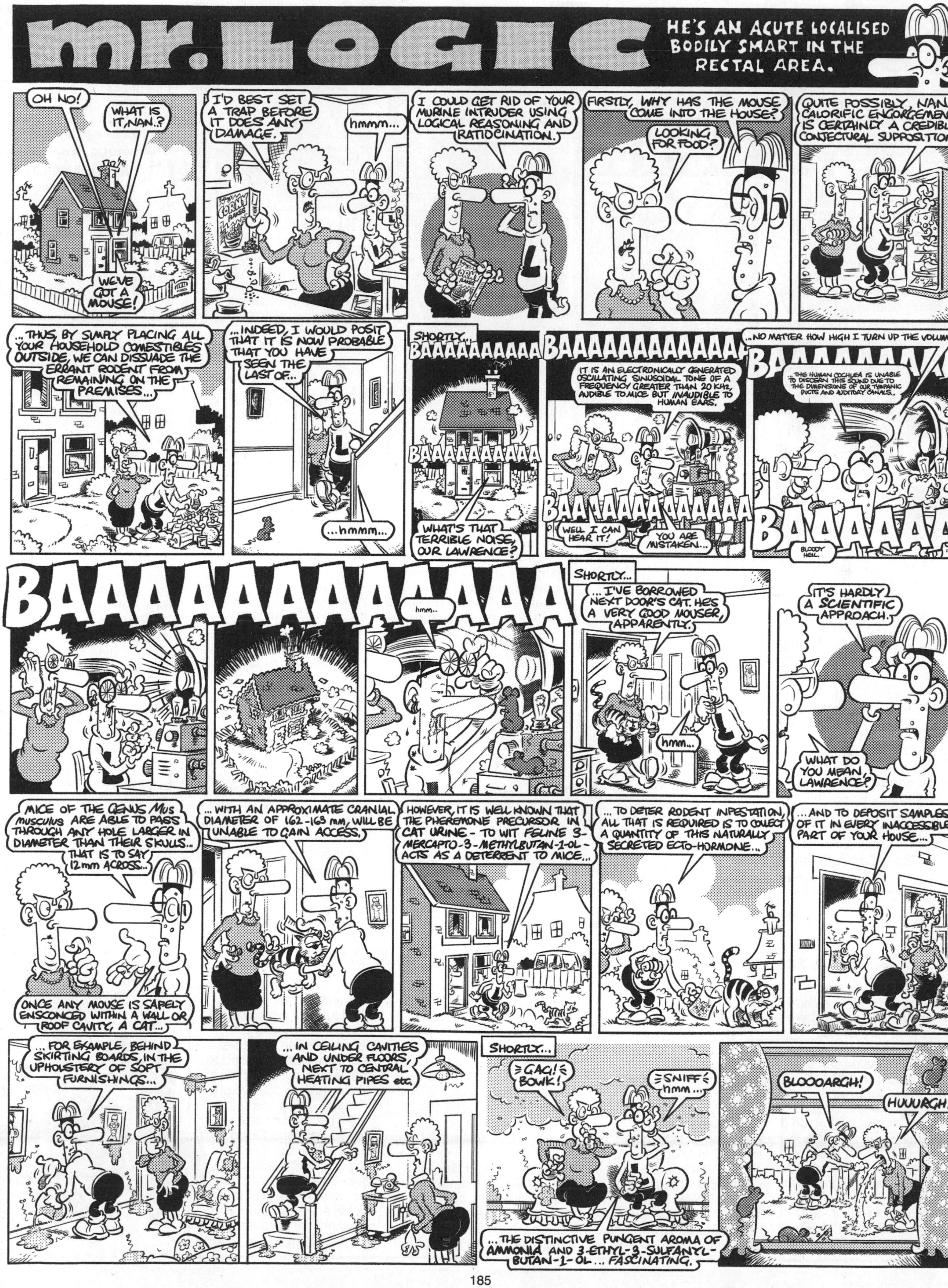
mr. LOGIC
HE'S AN ACUTE LOCALISED BODILY SMART IN THE RECTAL AREA.
OH NO!
WHAT IS IT, NAN..?
WE'VE GOT A MOUSE!
I'D BEST SET A TRAP BEFORE IT DOES ANY DAMAGE.
hmmm...
CORNY FLAKES
I COULD GET RID OF YOUR MURINE INTRUDER USING LOGICAL REASONING AND RATIOCINATION.
FIRSTLY, WHY HAS THE MOUSE COME INTO THE HOUSE?
LOOKING FOR FOOD?
QUITE POSSIBLY, NAN... CALORIFIC ENGORGEMENT IS CERTAINLY A CREDIBLE CONJECTURAL SUPPOSITION...
...THUS, BY SIMPLY PLACING ALL YOUR HOUSEHOLD COMESTIBLES OUTSIDE, WE CAN DISSUADE THE ERRANT RODENT FROM REMAINING ON THE PREMISES...
...INDEED, I WOULD POSIT THAT IT IS NOW PROBABLE THAT YOU HAVE SEEN THE LAST OF...
...hmmm...
SHORTLY...
BAAAAAAAAAAA
BAAAAAAAAAAA
WHAT'S THAT TERRIBLE NOISE, OUR LAWRENCE?
BAAAAAAAAAAAAA
IT IS AN ELECTRONICALLY GENERATED OSCILLATING SINUSOIDAL TONE OF A FREQUENCY GREATER THAN 20 KHz, AUDIBLE TO MICE BUT INAUDIBLE TO HUMAN EARS.
BAAAAAAAAAAAAA
WELL I CAN HEAR IT!
YOU ARE MISTAKEN...
...NO MATTER HOW HIGH I TURN UP THE VOLUME...
BAAAAAAAAA
...THE HUMAN COCHLEA IS UNABLE TO DISCERN THIS SOUND DUE TO THE DIMENSIONS OF OUR TYMPANIC DUCTS AND AUDITORY CANALS...
BAAAAAA
BLOODY HELL.
BAAAAAAAAAAAA
hmm...
SHORTLY...
...I'VE BORROWED NEXT DOOR'S CAT. HE'S A VERY GOOD MOUSER, APPARENTLY.
hmm...
IT'S HARDLY A SCIENTIFIC APPROACH.
WHAT DO YOU MEAN, LAWRENCE?
MICE OF THE GENUS Mus musculus ARE ABLE TO PASS THROUGH ANY HOLE LARGER IN DIAMETER THAN THEIR SKULLS... THAT IS TO SAY 12mm ACROSS...
ONCE ANY MOUSE IS SAFELY ENSCONCED WITHIN A WALL OR ROOF CAVITY, A CAT...
...WITH AN APPROXIMATE CRANIAL DIAMETER OF 162-163 mm, WILL BE UNABLE TO GAIN ACCESS.
HOWEVER, IT IS WELL KNOWN THAT THE PHEREMONE PRECURSOR IN CAT URINE - TO WIT FELINE 3-MERCAPTO-3-METHYLBUTAN-1-OL - ACTS AS A DETERRENT TO MICE...
...TO DETER RODENT INFESTATION, ALL THAT IS REQUIRED IS TO COLLECT A QUANTITY OF THIS NATURALLY SECRETED ECTO-HORMONE...
...AND TO DEPOSIT SAMPLES OF IT IN EVERY INACCESSIBLE PART OF YOUR HOUSE...
...FOR EXAMPLE, BEHIND SKIRTING BOARDS, IN THE UPHOLSTERY OF SOFT FURNISHINGS...
...IN CEILING CAVITIES AND UNDER FLOORS, NEXT TO CENTRAL HEATING PIPES etc.
SHORTLY...
GAG! BOWK!
SNIFF hmm...
...THE DISTINCTIVE PUNGENT AROMA OF AMMONIA AND 3-ETHYL-3-SULFANYL-BUTAN-1-OL... FASCINATING.
BLOOOARGH!
HUUURGH!

Letterbocks

Viz Comic, P.O. Box 841 Whitley Bay, NE26 9EQ   letters@viz.co.uk

I WOULDN'T consider myself a vaccine sceptic, but before I had the jab I would often win at least a fiver every time I bought some scratchcards. But since I've had my second jab, I've bought 20 scratchies and haven't won a sausage. So there has to be something going on that the government is hiding from us.

Graham Flintoft, Gatesheed

IN HIS song *Maggie May*, Rod Stewart suggests that he should either go back to school, or alternatively, steal his daddy's cue and make a living out of playing pool. Far be it from me to piss on Rod's parade, but I would strongly advise he returns to full time education, as the fact that he doesn't even own a cue suggests he is probably shit at the game. And if I'm wrong, the most I've ever seen a pool player win is another game of pool. If any other oversexed 1970s crooners require career advice, please feel free to share my contact details.

Kevin Caswell-Jones, Wrexham

STAR LETTER

I WAS thinking about the use of the word 'costume' when applied to swimming clothes. Clothes complement a person, whereas a costume suggests clothing that makes you look like something that you aren't. Which is a relief, as it means that most of the men on the beach down here yesterday aren't actually fat, sunburnt baldies with big tits in real life.

Nigel Nice-Norks, Bournemouth

I JUST picked up a cat while completely naked. I doubt Tom Cruise will do that in *Mission:Impossible 7*.

Will Preston, Wapping

DO you know if you can get tennis elbow from telling yourself off too much? And by telling yourself off I mean wanking.

Richard, Whittington

＊ *That's an interesting question, Richard. Whilst it is well-documented that masturbation causes hairs to grow on your palms, insanity and blindness, does it also cause tennis elbow? Perhaps there is a doctor reading this who could tell us. Or perhaps you have been diagnosed with tennis elbow despite not playing the game and spending most of your time wanking.*

I WAS rather surprised to see a mouse confronting my cat with a meat cleaver the other day, but not half as surprised as my cat, whose eyes momentarily popped out of his head whilst he simultaneously made the sound of a vintage car horn.

Belinda, Carlisle

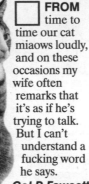

FROM time to time our cat miaows loudly, and on these occasions my wife often remarks that it's as if he's trying to talk. But I can't understand a fucking word he says.

Col P Fawcett, Durham

WHY IS it that whenever whales come ashore, there are always people trying to push them back into the sea? I feel sorry for the things, constantly having to swim about all day. Leave them alone and let them have a bit of a lie down on the beach, I say.

Terry Refurbed, Cromer

HAVING recently seen what I thought was a UFO, I was very excited to be visited by two men in black a few days later. Imagine my disappointment when I realised that they weren't interested in my sighting, but were in fact two High Court Enforcement Officers collecting a debt for an old veterinary bill in relation to my ex-wife's cockapoo, which I hadn't known she'd put in my name.

John, Rendlesham

DRESS for the job you want not the job you have, or so they say. Well I'm a builder who wants to be a ballet dancer, and not wearing a helmet on site is against the rules, and that's before all the mockery over the tutu.

A builder, Bexhill-on-Sea

THE UK national debt now stands at over £2 trillion, but if every adult in the UK paid a mere £41,000 each, we could wipe it out in a stroke. Where's our sense of pulling together as a nation?

J R-Mogg, Westminster

AMERICANS talk about "shit going down" like it's a bad thing. Well, I'd rather my shit went down every time, rather than have to hack at a monster log with an old breadknife in order to flush it.

Andy B, Alfreton

MICHAEL Radcliffe (*Letterbocks page 164*) should listen more carefully to the theme tune to *Champion the Wonder Horse* when he complains that nobody was talking about the animal when he visited Ipswich. "You'll hear about him everywhere you go," the song informs us, 'you'll' being a contraction of '*you will*,' i.e. at some point in the future. It even goes on to say "The time will come when everyone will know the name of *Champion the Wonder Horse*," implying once again, that this will be the case at some point in the future with no specific timescale described. Mr Radcliffe simply needs to keep visiting Ipswich, and they will have heard of *Champion the Wonder Horse* eventually.

Clarkson Isacock, email

I'VE ABSOLUTELY no proof, but I reckon most of the *Antiques Roadshow* experts piss in the hotel shower when they're on location. The filthy bastards.

J Brown, Edinburgh

WHILST walking past a load of ducks in my local park the other day, I accidentally did a trouser cough that sounded exactly like one of them quacking. I was astonished when one of them stopped what he was doing, looked me in the eye and quacked back at me. I felt just like Dr. Doolittle.

Andy, Trowbridge

Grandmas *Almost* Say the Funniest Things about Cocks

DURING the war, my grandma worked in a dildo factory, and naturally, there was some very bawdy humour among the girls on the production line due to the nature of their work. Each member of staff was issued with a phallus-shaped 'clock card' which was obviously a source of amusement. After she'd had a few sherries at Christmas, we would ask our grandma to tell us the term that she used for 'clocking in' and 'clocking off. Unfortunately, she had no sense humour at all and simply referred to it as 'punching in' and 'punching out'.

Doris Antimony, Leeds

MY GRANDMA used to work for a company that was formed as a result of the merger of two local businesses - Barry Cock and Jimmy Balls. When they merged they decided to shorten the name of the new business to incorporate just the surnames. My grandma always had a cheeky sense of humour and so we'd often go round to see her and ask her to tell us the name of the company she used to work for. We'd all be in hysterics anticipating what she was going to say. Unfortunately, after she left the company 30 years ago she became a nun and had taken a vow of silence, so we never got to hear her say it.

Terry Bismuth, Otley

IN HER younger days, my granny was a member of her local rowing club, and in the back of her boat was the person who used to steer and shout commands at the rowers. This one person was unusually big for the role, but they were incredibly effective compared to the smaller one who they alternated with. We used to love asking our grandma to tell us which of the two she preferred – emphasising that in her answer she must use the shortened form of the term that designates the person who sits in the stern. Unfortunately, she was completely deaf and couldn't hear our question, so we never heard her say it.

Terry Chromium, Derby

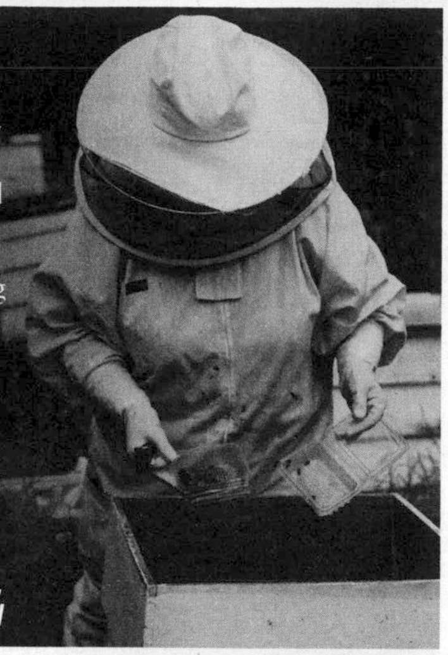

MODERN bees should be ashamed of themselves. Back in the 70s, there were hardly any rules governing what sorts of shit farmers could spray at them, and they just got on with the job of making honey and ruining picnics. Nowadays, despite having new, safe chemicals governed by strict environmental laws, this snowflake generation of bees just drop dead at the slightest whiff of anything they don't like. Pathetic.

T Paper, Wibbly on the Wold

ON THE Friday edition of the ITV game show *Blockbusters*, all the audience members would join together and do the hand jive during the closing credits. It was a little bit of fun to end the week's run of shows. As *Blockbusters* is no longer on TV, perhaps *Question Time* could pick up the baton and do the same. Personally, I need anything to cheer me up after that parade of cunts.

Joel, email

IT'S HIGH time pop stars were banned from using the word 'yeah' in their lyrics when the correct word is 'yes'. And don't tell me its origins can be traced all the way back to the Old English word 'gēa' or some such shit, because everyone knows 'yeah' was invented by the fucking Beatles in order to boost the sale of their so-called records.

Farquar Bismarc, Hackney

KIDS THESE days think they've got it made with everything being all remote-controlled and user-friendly. Well when I was a kid, I used to change the channels on my 20" Ferguson colour TV by poking the buttons with an old snooker cue just so I didn't have to get out of bed. Beat that, you spotty bunch of sods.

Stu Mandry, Droitwich Spa

I'VE NEVER watched the film *A Clockwork Orange* but I bet it's pretty good. I wonder if any other readers haven't watched a film that they imagine is equally as good, or even shite.

Terry Farricker, Blackpool

** What's the best film you've never seen, and why did you like it? Or perhaps the best film you've never seen wasn't really your cup of tea. Write in and tell us either way.*

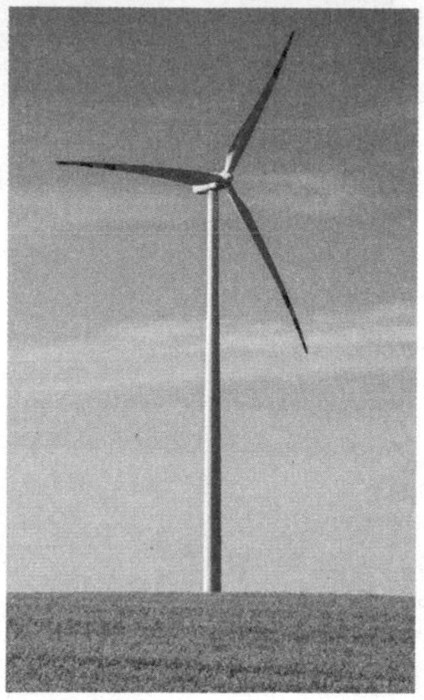

THERE has been all this talk about there not being enough wind to drive wind turbines recently. Why don't they put wind farms on the back of trucks and just drive to where it's windiest? I can recommend the car park at my local Tescos where the wind does tend to get up quite a bit, plus parking is free for 2 hours.

Nigel Quicksand, Bristol

I JUST watched the trailer for *Herbie Goes Bananas*, and I have to say whoever played the swanee whistle - just as Herbie hits a table and throws a chef from his bonnet who skims across a table whilst holding a large cake which ends up in Harvey Korman's face - got the timing absolutely bang on.

Buck, Buckland Dinham

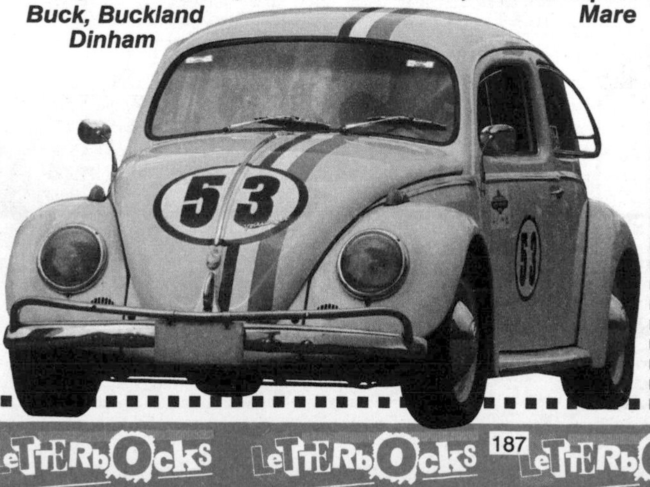

ALL THAT hue and cry about square pegs in round holes. Come on, it's not that difficult. Just make sure the square peg is appropriately smaller than the round hole and then it'll slip in quite easily.

T Waterman, Brighton

MR WATERMAN *(above)* is correct, although rather ambiguous in his description of an "appropriately smaller" square peg fitting into a round hole. To be more specific, any square peg whose side length is equal to or smaller than the diameter of the circular hole divided by the square root of 2, will fit.

Bulstrode Whitelock, London

I WAS always a big fan of Derek Acorah, but since he passed over to the spirit world we've not had a whisper out of him. I was convinced he ruffled the curtains the other day but it turned out it was just the cat. I do hope everything is okay and that he is not in some sort of trouble.

Shane Westley, Bristol

I DROPPED a guff on the grand pier in Weston-super-Mare that was so smelly that it started an argument with a family that was behind me. Can any of your readers top that?

Luke Newland, Bristol

I JUST found out the word 'flaccid' can also be quite legitimately be pronounced 'flak-sid'. This nice little factoid may be deployed the next time your wife or girlfriend uses the word to complain when you're pushing string.

Prince Asbo, Canterbury

WITH THE advent of such shower gel scents as 'Vanilla and Raspberry', it is very reassuring to know that, albeit for a very short time, my ringpiece smells like a Muller Fruit Corner.

Ian Baker, Weston-super-Mare

TOP TIPS

WHEN using a sweetener dispenser for a cup of tea or coffee, always make sure there is some liquid in the cup first, otherwise the sweetener could bounce out and land on the work surface or - worst case scenario - the floor.

Salohcin Rolyat, Blackpool

USHERS. Thoroughly try on your wedding suit prior to the big day to save the photographer 2 weeks of painstaking labour, photoshopping your bulging genitalia out of all the snaps.

Moose-knuckle, Newtown

KWIK fit. Remove any clocks from your waiting area so that customers are less able to see how kwik you aren't.

Nick Lyon, Penryn

LIVEN up a dull episode of *Celebrity MasterChef* by taking bets on which celeb will be wearing a blue plaster first.

The Owl, Northfields

BED and Mattress manufacturers. Stuck for ideas on how to advertise your products? Simply show some grown adults having a pillow fight – it's bound to fully explain all the numerous possible uses of your products.

Dick Scratcher, email

SACHETS of ketchup make ideal and inexpensive blood capsules for film makers on a budget. Likewise, brown sauce sachets are good to use as turd capsules if for any reason the film script requires scenes of someone farting and following through.

Djay-M, Cheshire

UK Government. Save the spiralling costs of HS2 by purchasing helicopters for each of the 50 potential users and handing them over 25 years from now.

Jack, Brum

toptips@viz.co.uk

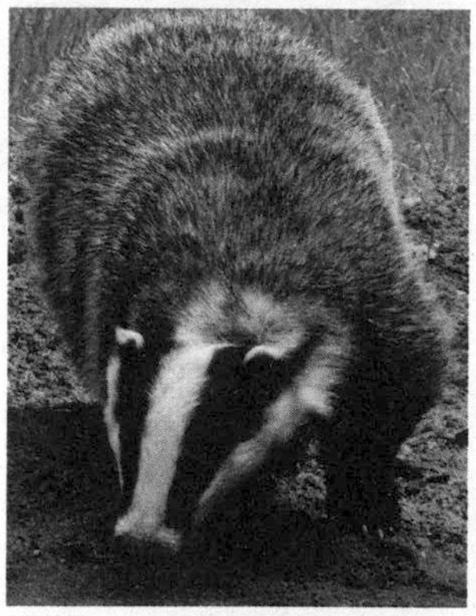

I ONCE hit a badger in my BMW 5-series, which completely fucked up the front grille and cost me over 1500 quid to get repaired. So I was overjoyed when I heard that the badger cull was to be extended.

Tom Noble, London

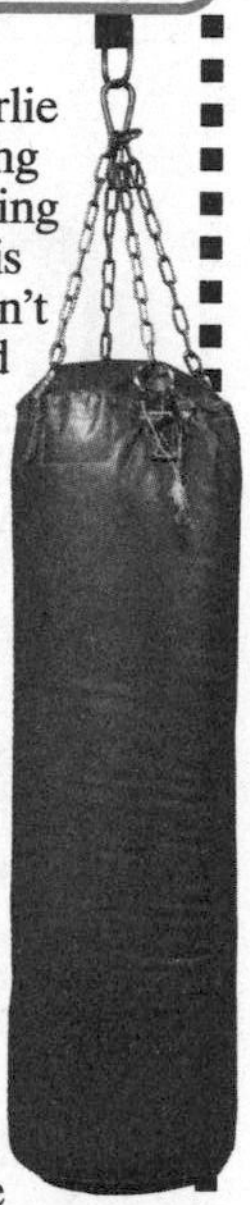

POP pundits described Charlie Watts as the stabilising force within the Rolling Stones. I just hope his untimely demise doesn't cause the rest of band to go off the rails.

Stuie, Bunny

IF THESE boxing coaches taught their charges the importance of compromise, forgiveness and reconciliation instead of pummelling a punchbag, then maybe they wouldn't be itching for a fight every time they got in the ring.

D Williams, Donegal

ARE YOU AGED OVER 50?...DO YOU STILL RIDE A SKATEBOARD? ...DO YOU WORRY ABOUT FALLING OFF?

SKATE 50+

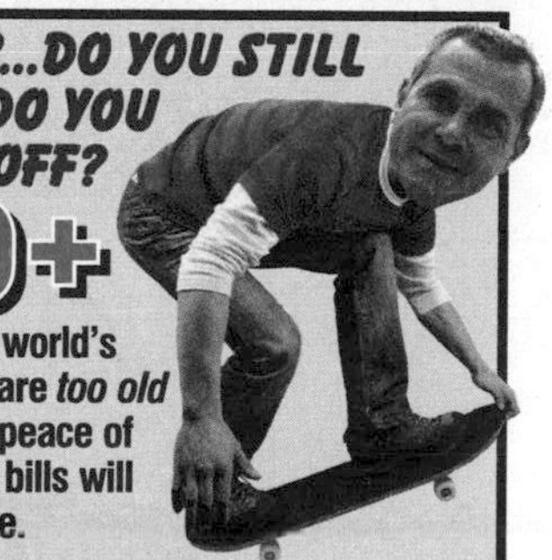

A Protection Plan with Skate50+, the world's leading insurers of people who really are *too old* to be skateboarding, will give you the peace of mind of knowing that all your medical bills will be covered if you take a bit of a tumble.

*"I was pulling some big air in a half-pipe when I came off and fractured my hip. **Skate50+** paid out £10,000 in medical bills and bought me a new zimmer frame."*

T Hawk, California

*"My balance isn't what it used to be, and I came off my board whilst grinding down the hand rail of some steps on my way to a bowls match. My **Skate50+** policy covered all my medical bills with enough left over to treat myself to a walk-in bath."*

B Margera, Pennsylvania

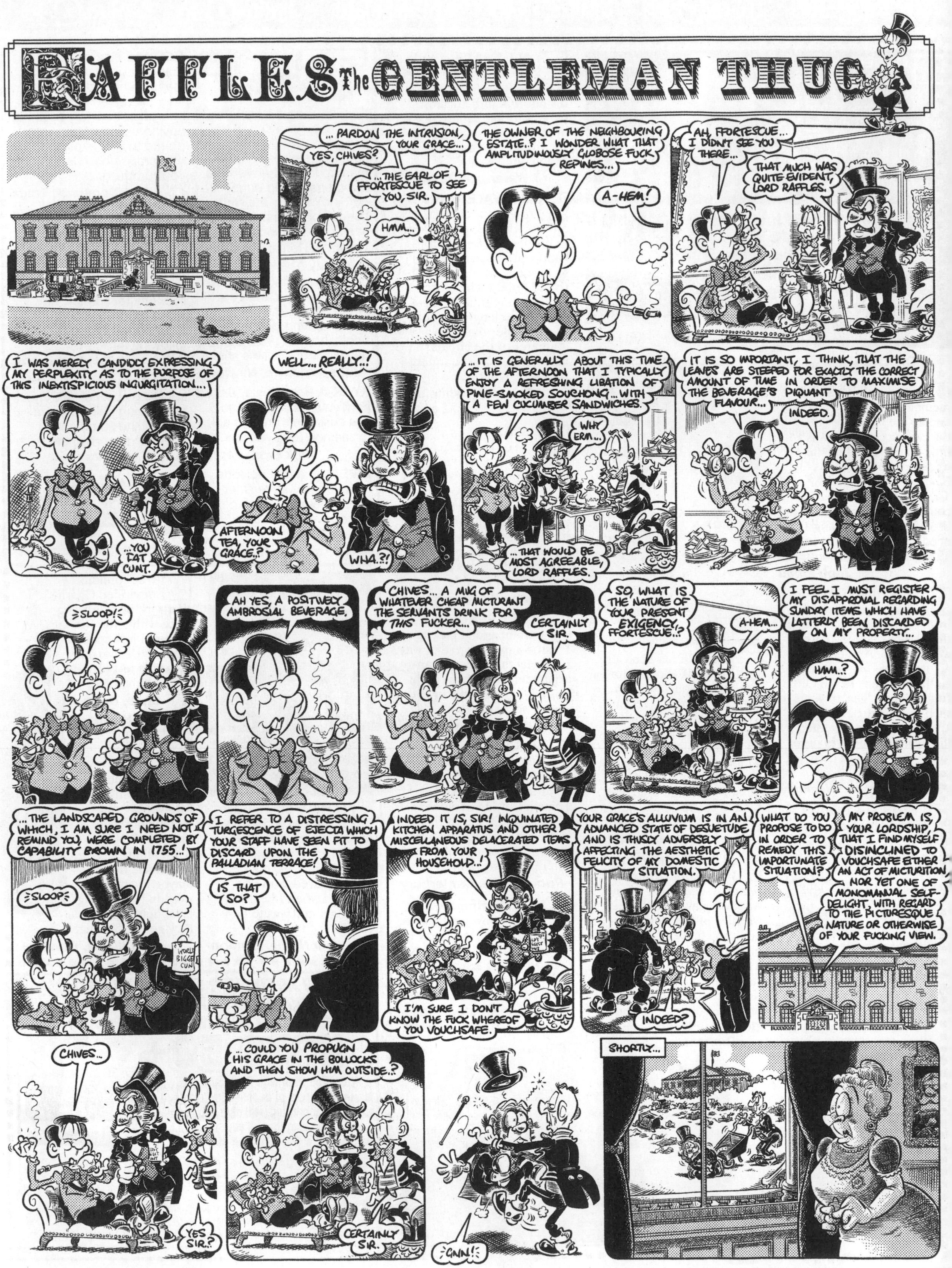
RAFFLES the GENTLEMAN THUG
...PARDON THE INTRUSION, YOUR GRACE...
YES, CHIVES?
...THE EARL OF FFORTESCUE TO SEE YOU, SIR.
HMM...
THE OWNER OF THE NEIGHBOURING ESTATE..? I WONDER WHAT THAT AMPLITUDINOUSLY GLOBOSE FUCK REPINES...
A-HEM!
AH, FFORTESCUE... I DIDN'T SEE YOU THERE...
THAT MUCH WAS QUITE EVIDENT, LORD RAFFLES.
I WAS MERELY CANDIDLY EXPRESSING MY PERPLEXITY AS TO THE PURPOSE OF THIS INEXTISPICIOUS INGURGITATION...
...YOU FAT CUNT.
WELL... REALLY..!
AFTERNOON TEA, YOUR GRACE..?
WHA..?!
...IT IS GENERALLY ABOUT THIS TIME OF THE AFTERNOON THAT I TYPICALLY ENJOY A REFRESHING LIBATION OF PINE-SMOKED SOUCHONG... WITH A FEW CUCUMBER SANDWICHES.
WHY ERM...
...THAT WOULD BE MOST AGREEABLE, LORD RAFFLES.
IT IS SO IMPORTANT, I THINK, THAT THE LEAVES ARE STEEPED FOR EXACTLY THE CORRECT AMOUNT OF TIME IN ORDER TO MAXIMISE THE BEVERAGE'S PIQUANT FLAVOUR...
INDEED.
SLOOP!
AH YES, A POSITIVELY AMBROSIAL BEVERAGE.
CHIVES... A MUG OF WHATEVER CHEAP MICTURANT THE SERVANTS DRINK FOR THIS FUCKER...
CERTAINLY SIR.
SO, WHAT IS THE NATURE OF YOUR PRESENT EXIGENCY, FFORTESCUE..?
A-HEM...
I FEEL I MUST REGISTER MY DISAPPROVAL REGARDING SUNDRY ITEMS WHICH HAVE LATTERLY BEEN DISCARDED ON MY PROPERTY...
HMM..?
...THE LANDSCAPED GROUNDS OF WHICH, I AM SURE I NEED NOT REMIND YOU, WERE COMPLETED BY CAPABILITY BROWN IN 1755..!
SLOOP
I REFER TO A DISTRESSING TURGESCENCE OF EJECTA WHICH YOUR STAFF HAVE SEEN FIT TO DISCARD UPON THE PALLADIAN TERRACE!
IS THAT SO?
INDEED IT IS, SIR! INQUINATED KITCHEN APPARATUS AND OTHER MISCELLANEOUS DELACERATED ITEMS FROM YOUR HOUSEHOLD..!
I'M SURE I DON'T KNOW THE FUCK WHEREOF YOU VOUCHSAFE.
YOUR GRACE'S ALLUVIUM IS IN AN ADVANCED STATE OF DESUETUDE AND IS THUSLY ADVERSELY AFFECTING THE AESTHETIC FELICITY OF MY DOMESTIC SITUATION.
INDEED?
WHAT DO YOU PROPOSE TO DO IN ORDER TO REMEDY THIS IMPORTUNATE SITUATION?
MY PROBLEM IS, YOUR LORDSHIP, THAT I FIND MYSELF DISINCLINED TO VOUCHSAFE EITHER AN ACT OF MICTURITION, NOR YET ONE OF MONOMANUAL SELF-DELIGHT, WITH REGARD TO THE PICTURESQUE NATURE OR OTHERWISE OF YOUR FUCKING VIEW.
CHIVES...
YES SIR..?
...COULD YOU PROPUGN HIS GRACE IN THE BOLLOCKS AND THEN SHOW HIM OUTSIDE..?
CERTAINLY SIR.
GNN!
SHORTLY...

SECOND CORNWALL TO OPEN IN SUMMER 2025

WITH Britons increasingly choosing UK holidays in preference to travelling abroad, the government yesterday gave the green light for a second Cornwall to be built in the south west.

Twice as nice: Second Cornwall will be built to take overflow of holidaymakers.

Cornwall has long been the most popular holiday destination in the UK, and as Britons anticipate another 'staycation' this year, holiday companies have reported that hotels, campsites and BnBs across the county are fully booked.

"The demand is clearly there for another Cornwall," says the *Independent*'s travel editor Simon Calder. "Will that do? Only I'm due on 5Live in a minute to talk about Britain's ageing railway stock, and then I've got to get over to BBC News because Matthew Amroliwala's doing a thing about caravanning."

UK tourism experts hope that the decision to build a second Cornwall will double the number of people able to book a well-earned break on the English Riviera.

"Each year, Cornwall sees over four million people flock to its theme parks, beaches and tea shops, with all the inevitable stress and strain that puts on local services," said Lord Mayor of Truro, Josiah Trevelwyn. "So another

EXCLUSIVE!

Cornwall is going to make life easier for we Cornish, and give our visitors a better holiday experience."

putting

The new county will be identical to the original province, with its own Bodmin Moor, its own Eden Project, and its own Lost Gardens of Heligan. And like its picturesque counterpart, Cornwall2 will be built on the side of Devon and have only one main road into it. Ministers hope that all the work will be completed in time for the beginning of the tourist season in September.

Because of the short timescale involved in the project, the government has dispensed with the time-consuming procedure of putting the scheme out to tender, and has instead handed construction contracts to a few trusted companies run by people who own pubs

in cabinet members' constituencies. But although ministers have said that building Cornwall2 will make the Great British Holiday great again, not everyone has greeted the news with enthusiasm.

robson

"There are already far too many cars driving around the existing Cornwall, polluting the atmosphere and creating noise. The last thing we need is another one adding to the existing problems," said anti-roads protestor Swampy.

Along with fellow campaigners, the veteran environmental activist, 48, intends to disrupt building work on the 1,369 square mile province when it begins in April.

"Well, it won't actually be me, as I have to be somewhere else that day, so I'll be sending another version of myself, Swampy2, to chain himself to the earth-moving equipment," the scruffy bugger who could do with a bloody good wash and a haircut added.

CREAM TEA FOR TWO!

Scone industry eyes up post-Covid boom

EVERYONE loves a Cornish cream tea – a scone served with the jam under the cream. And a whole new county could instantly double demand for the traditional overpriced delicacy, turning south-west scone, cream and jam manufacturers into overnight billionaires. As holidaymakers prepare to flock to the brand new county in their thousands, bakers and tea-room proprietors could be set to cash-in big.

That's according to Dragons Den business guru Deborah Meaden, who says that if it plays its cards right, the New Cornish Riviera may well be about to experience a cream tea boom that will make the Stock Market 'Big Bang' of 1983 pale into insignificance.

"Horribly overpriced cream teas with the jam under the cream are a staple of the traditional Cornish tourism economy," she told us. "But Cornwall2 will be unable to serve mirror image cream teas," she warned.

Who wants to tea a billionaire?: Dragon's Den's Meaden yesterday.

"Because if the jam goes on top of the cream it's a Devon cream tea."

"If the tearoom proprietors of the new county are able to come up with an idiosyncratic local twist for a Cornish2 Cream Tea – perhaps putting the jam under the scone and the cream on top or vice versa, they'll cash in big."

But Meaden, who has made millions in the hospitality industry, had this warning. "If they get it wrong, perhaps putting the jam under the plate or with all the raisins in the cream rather than the scone, then it could spell disaster for the cream tea industry."

"It'll be a case of going, going scone," she added.

Flipping Hell!

REPORTS say that Cornwall2 will be identical in every way to the original county... except that it will be a *mirror image!* Anyone who has never been to Britain's southernmost county will not notice anything different in the new version. But for those familiar with Cornwall, Cornwall2 will seem a strange, *Alice Through the Looking Glass*-style world where nothing is quite the way it seems, where left is right, and vice versa. We've taken pictures of some of the county's most famous landmarks and, using computer technology, altered them to show you what they will look like in Cornwall2.

The Eden Project attracts over 1 million visitors per year...

...but will Cornwall2's Nede Project be quite such a hit?

St Michael's Mount is a picturesque island accessible at low tide...

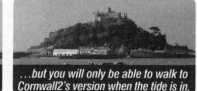
...but you will only be able to walk to Cornwall2's version when the tide is in.

Could this be the Beast of Bodmin Moor?...

...or is it the Beast of Bodmin Moor2?

THE SPACE WRAITH

Jobs set to join billionaire space tourism rush

HOT ON the heels of Richard Branson, Jeff Bezos and Elon Musk, Apple founder STEVE JOBS is the latest billionaire businessman to set his sights on a trip into space. The late tech boss, who died a decade ago at the age of 52, is understood to have ploughed more than $10 billion of his own fortune into developing a sophisticated rocket capable of carrying his ghost into low-earth orbit.

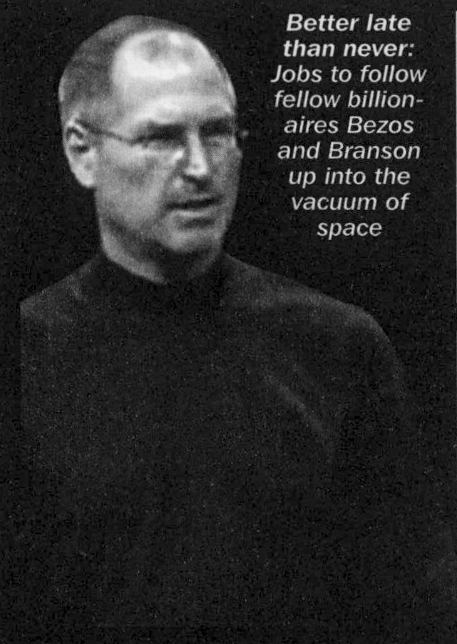

Better late than never: Jobs to follow fellow billionaires Bezos and Branson up into the vacuum of space

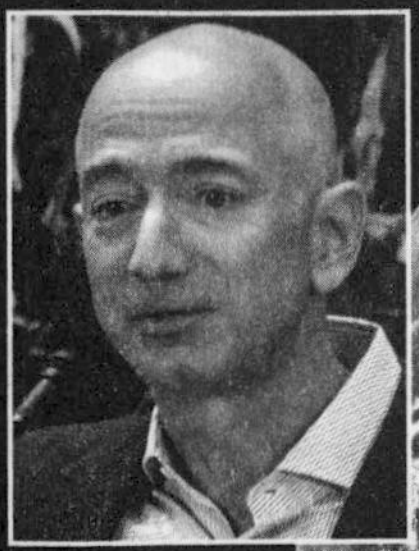

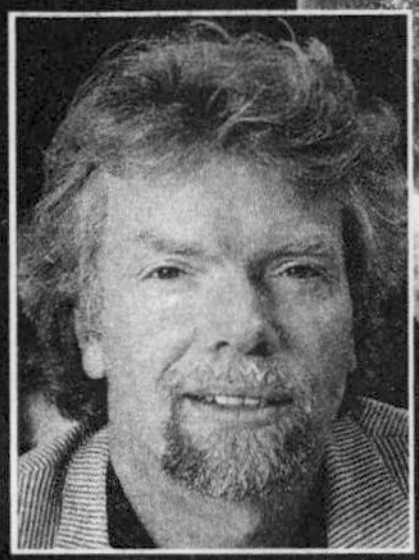

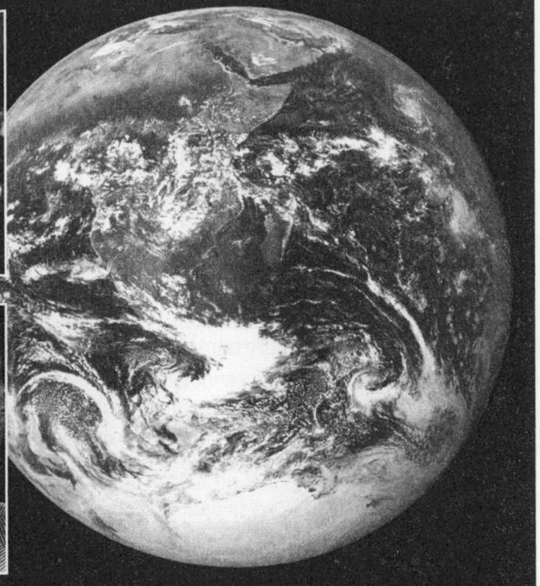

Speaking from a haunted grandfather clock at his state-of-the-art launch facility in the Mojave desert, Jobs told ESPN's Doris Stokes: "Other billionaires have had to overcome the force of gravity in order to get them out of the earth's atmosphere. But I calculate that the cost of lifting my weightless, see-through wraith up into space should be much less."

"I'm quids in," he said.

Communicating to reporters via a moving glass on a ouija board and a series of slow knocks on a table-top, the late tycoon outlined other advantages to his plan, including reduced risk of personal injury should his prototype liquid oxygen-fuelled rocket - dubbed 'Genesis I' - malfunction.

capsule

"Other billionaires have to make sure their capsules are airtight and equipped with high-tech life-support systems, failsafe parachutes and complex, gyroscopically controlled vertical landing capabilities," he said.

"That's not a problem for me, as I don't need to breathe when I'm up in the vacuum of space as I'm already dead, and even if my capsule explodes on the launchpad or plummets vertically into the ground at 1000mph, as a ghost I will suffer no injury whatsoever."

Jobs said he foresaw having no difficulty controlling his spaceship, using his 'poltergeist'-type powers to operate the complex flight-deck controls.

machine

"As a ghost, I can push vases off shelves, slam doors and turn the lights on and off," he said. "So I can't see any reason why I won't be able to operate the sophisticated fly-by-wire turbo-thrusters, solid rocket boosters and plasma engines that will keep my capsule on course to make its way up into the ionosphere and beyond."

"And even better, because I'm made of see-through ectoplasm, a sort of translucent spiritual vapour, I can fit in the works of the rocket round all the pipes and wires and stuff, so they won't have to put a dedicated command module on the top that looks like a bellend," he added.

...Who Wants to be a Millionaire in Space?

ELON Musk, Richard Branson and Bill Gates aren't the only business big-shots who are pissing their profits up the wall by blasting off into a really low bit of the infinite celestial cosmos. The lure of interplanetary adventure and the chance to float gravity-free for a couple of minutes is now proving irresistible to space-mad go-getters from all parts of the business world. We asked some of Britain's well-heeled bosses about their plans to journey to Infinity and beyond...

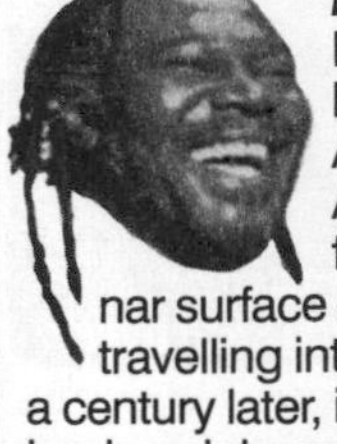

Levi Roots

I ALWAYS remember watching Neil Armstrong and Buzz Aldrin taking their first steps on the lunar surface and dreaming about travelling into space myself. Half a century later, it finally feels as if my boyhood dream of flying among the stars could finally be about to come true. If I got the chance to be a passenger on a flight into outer space, I would pop a jar of my famous Reggae Reggae Sauce, a frying pan and a picnic stove in my astronaut's backpack, and - during the 5 or so minutes of reduced gravity at the top of the rocket's flight parabola - I would cook up some of my famous Jerk Chicken Party Wraps, and Calypso Chicken Burgers for my fellow astronauts to enjoy. And I'd take my guitar and sing them that song I did on Dragon's Den.

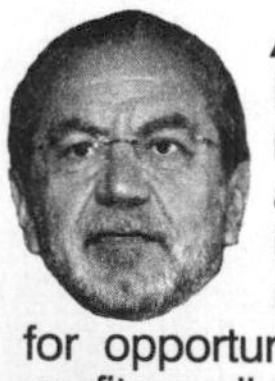

Alan Sugar

I WOULD take a hard-nosed, business-like approach to travelling into space - spending my flight time looking for opportunities to maximise the profits available during the trip. Before blast-off, I would get two teams of young business entrepreneurs to invent competing luxury space travel souvenirs, such as astronaut aftershave, gravity-free sparkling wine or sausages shaped like a rocket, which I would then attempt to sell to my fellow well-heeled passengers during the 5-minute weightless portion of the flight. Back in the boardroom after splashdown, I would reveal which team's products had proved the most profitable, and then I would fire a member of the losing team by pointing at them and making them go home in a taxi whilst wearing a very big scarf.

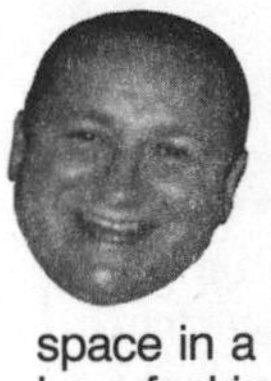

Mike Ashley

FUCK KNOWS how much I weigh these days, but it's a lot, I can tell you that. So if I wanted to blast myself up to space in a rocket, it would have to be a fucking big one. Mind, having said that, it says on the computer that I'm the 61st richest person in Britain, with the thick end of three billion quid in the fucking bank, so I could easy afford to build one. And if I did, I'd paint the words 'SPORTS DIRECT' up the side of the bastard, like on one of them massive fucking cups, and I'd take a shitload of cans up with me an' all and make a fucking day of it. And if I got to the moon, I'd rename it Earth Sattelite@SportsDirect.com and I'd put a big sign on the fucker so as everyone could read it from earth. And I'd probably buy Venus and Mars while I was at it.

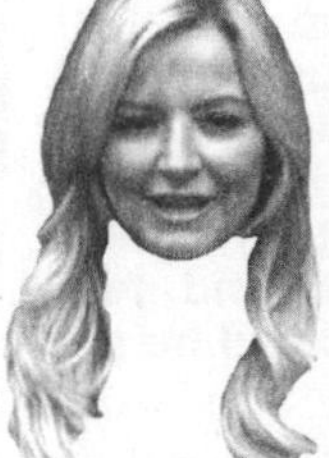

Michelle Mone

ALTHOUGH space tourism is currently the preserve of the very rich, it won't be long before the ordinary person in the street is able to afford pleasure trips up into the trackless vacuum of the cosmos. I would estimate that within the next ten years or so, a rocket flight to the Moon or Mars will cost about the same as a package holiday to the Costa Brava does now, making inter-stellar travel well within the budget of ordinary working families. And once women start blasting off and flying through the solar system, they're going to need comfortable lingerie that is suitable for weightless conditions. I would use my first spaceflight to try out a new Ultimo bra design, that lifts and separates your tits in zero-G.

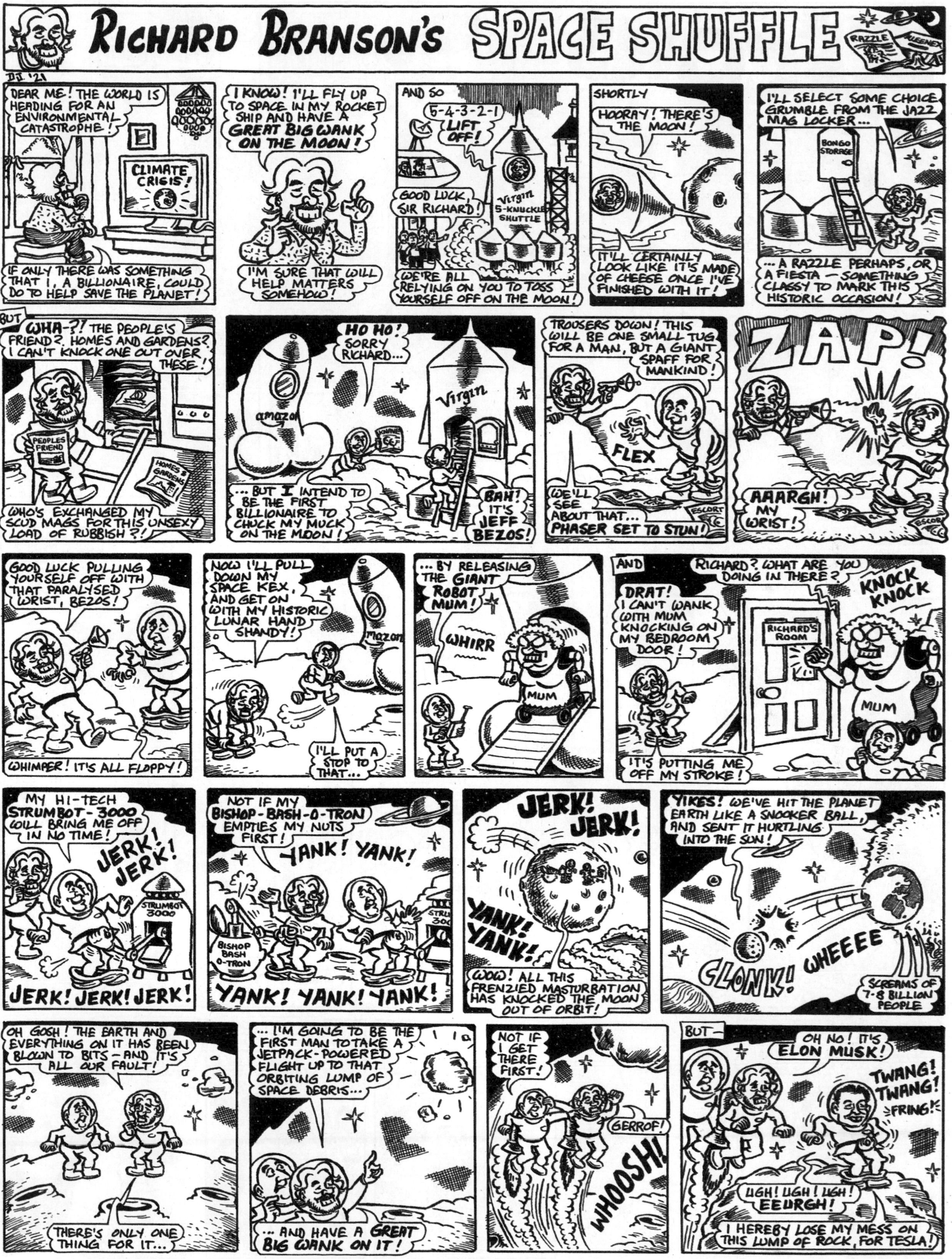
RICHARD BRANSON'S SPACE SHUFFLE
RAZZLE
KLEENEX
D.J. '21
DEAR ME! THE WORLD IS HEADING FOR AN ENVIRONMENTAL CATASTROPHE!
CLIMATE CRISIS!
IF ONLY THERE WAS SOMETHING THAT I, A BILLIONAIRE, COULD DO TO HELP SAVE THE PLANET!
I KNOW! I'LL FLY UP TO SPACE IN MY ROCKET SHIP AND HAVE A GREAT BIG WANK ON THE MOON!
I'M SURE THAT WILL HELP MATTERS SOMEHOW!
AND SO
5-4-3-2-1
LIFT OFF!
GOOD LUCK, SIR RICHARD!
Virgin 5-KNUCKLE SHUTTLE
WE'RE ALL RELYING ON YOU TO TOSS YOURSELF OFF ON THE MOON!
SHORTLY
HOORAY! THERE'S THE MOON!
IT'LL CERTAINLY LOOK LIKE IT'S MADE OF CHEESE ONCE I'VE FINISHED WITH IT!
I'LL SELECT SOME CHOICE GRUMBLE FROM THE JAZZ MAG LOCKER...
BONGO STORAGE
... A RAZZLE PERHAPS, OR A FIESTA — SOMETHING CLASSY TO MARK THIS HISTORIC OCCASION!
BUT
WHA-?! THE PEOPLE'S FRIEND?, HOMES AND GARDENS? I CAN'T KNOCK ONE OUT OVER THESE!
PEOPLES FRIEND
HOMES & GARDENS
WHO'S EXCHANGED MY SCUD MAGS FOR THIS UNSEXY LOAD OF RUBBISH?!
HO HO! SORRY RICHARD...
amazon
Virgin
... BUT I INTEND TO BE THE FIRST BILLIONAIRE TO CHUCK MY MUCK ON THE MOON!
BAH! IT'S JEFF BEZOS!
TROUSERS DOWN! THIS WILL BE ONE SMALL TUG FOR A MAN, BUT A GIANT SPAFF FOR MANKIND!
FLEX
WE'LL SEE ABOUT THAT... PHASER SET TO STUN!
ESCORT
ZAP!
AAARGH! MY WRIST!
ESCORT
GOOD LUCK PULLING YOURSELF OFF WITH THAT PARALYSED WRIST, BEZOS!
WHIMPER! IT'S ALL FLOPPY!
NOW I'LL PULL DOWN MY SPACE KEX, AND GET ON WITH MY HISTORIC LUNAR HAND SHANDY!
amazon
I'LL PUT A STOP TO THAT...
... BY RELEASING THE GIANT ROBOT MUM!
WHIRR
MUM
AND
RICHARD? WHAT ARE YOU DOING IN THERE?
KNOCK KNOCK
DRAT! I CAN'T WANK WITH MUM KNOCKING ON MY BEDROOM DOOR!
RICHARD'S ROOM
MUM
IT'S PUTTING ME OFF MY STROKE!
MY HI-TECH STRUMBOT-3000 WILL BRING ME OFF IN NO TIME!
JERK! JERK!
STRUMBOT 3000
JERK! JERK! JERK!
NOT IF MY BISHOP-BASH-O-TRON EMPTIES MY NUTS FIRST!
YANK! YANK!
BISHOP BASH O-TRON
YANK! YANK! YANK!
JERK! JERK!
YANK! YANK!
WOW! ALL THIS FRENZIED MASTURBATION HAS KNOCKED THE MOON OUT OF ORBIT!
YIKES! WE'VE HIT THE PLANET EARTH LIKE A SNOOKER BALL, AND SENT IT HURTLING INTO THE SUN!
CLONK! WHEEEE
SCREAMS OF 7.8 BILLION PEOPLE
OH GOSH! THE EARTH AND EVERYTHING ON IT HAS BEEN BLOWN TO BITS – AND IT'S ALL OUR FAULT!
THERE'S ONLY ONE THING FOR IT...
... I'M GOING TO BE THE FIRST MAN TO TAKE A JETPACK-POWERED FLIGHT UP TO THAT ORBITING LUMP OF SPACE DEBRIS...
... AND HAVE A GREAT BIG WANK ON IT!
NOT IF I GET THERE FIRST!
GERROF!
WHOOSH!
BUT—
OH NO! IT'S ELON MUSK!
TWANG! TWANG!
FRING!
UGH! UGH! UGH! EEURGH!
I HEREBY LOSE MY MESS ON THIS LUMP OF ROCK, FOR TESLA!

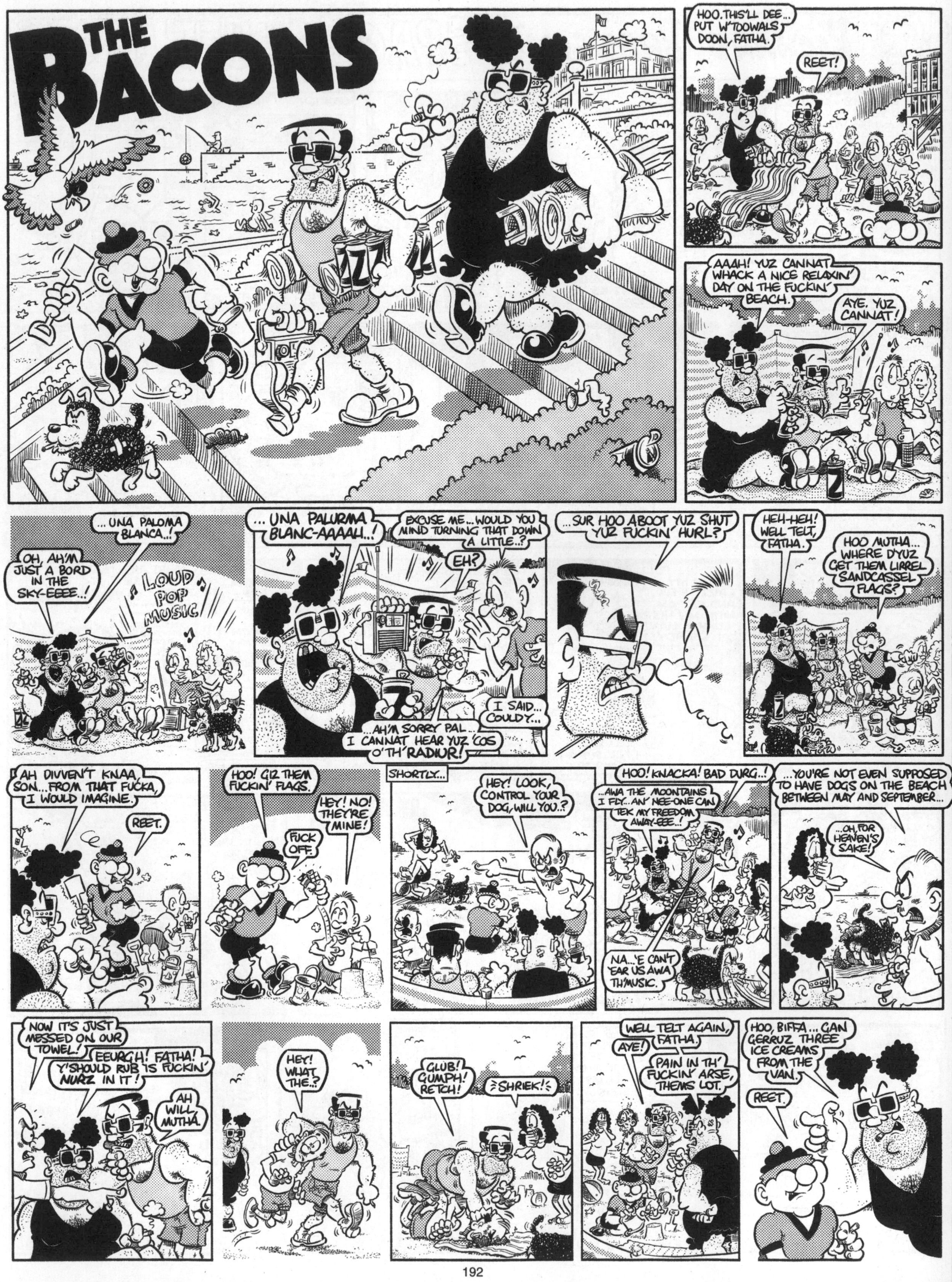
THE BACONS
HOO. THIS'LL DEE... PUT W'TOOWALS DOON, FATHA.
REET!
AAAH! YUZ CANNAT WHACK A NICE RELAXIN' DAY ON THE FUCKIN' BEACH.
AYE. YUZ CANNAT!
...UNA PALOMA BLANCA..!
OH, AH'M JUST A BORD IN THE SKY-EEEE..!
LOUD POP MUSIC
...UNA PALURMA BLANC-AAAAAH...!
EXCUSE ME... WOULD YOU MIND TURNING THAT DOWN A LITTLE..?
EH?
I SAID... COULDY...
...AH'M SORRY PAL... I CANNAT HEAR YUZ 'COS O'TH' RADIUR!
...SUR HOO ABOOT YUZ SHUT YUZ FUCKIN' HURL?
HEH-HEH! WELL TELT, FATHA.
HOO MUTHA... WHERE D'YUZ GET THEM LIRREL SANDCASSEL FLAGS?
AH DIVVEN'T KNAA, SON... FROM THAT FUCKA, I WOULD IMAGINE.
REET.
HOO! GIZ THEM FUCKIN' FLAGS.
HEY! NO! THEY'RE MINE!
FUCK OFF.
SHORTLY...
HEY! LOOK, CONTROL YOUR DOG, WILL YOU..?
HOO! KNACKA! BAD DURG..!
...AWA THE MOONTAINS I FLY... AN' NEE-ONE CAN TEK MY FREEDOM AWAY-EEE..!
NA... 'E CAN'T 'EAR US AWA TH'MUSIC.
...YOU'RE NOT EVEN SUPPOSED TO HAVE DOGS ON THE BEACH BETWEEN MAY AND SEPTEMBER...
...OH, FOR HEAVEN'S SAKE!
NOW IT'S JUST MESSED ON OUR TOWEL!
EEURGH! FATHA! Y'SHOULD RUB 'IS FUCKIN' NURZ IN IT!
AH WILL, MUTHA.
HEY! WHAT THE..?
GLUB! GUMPH! RETCH!
SHRIEK!
WELL TELT AGAIN, FATHA.
AYE!
PAIN IN TH' FUCKIN' ARSE, THEMS LOT.
HOO, BIFFA... GAN GERRUZ THREE ICE CREAMS FROM THE VAN.
REET.

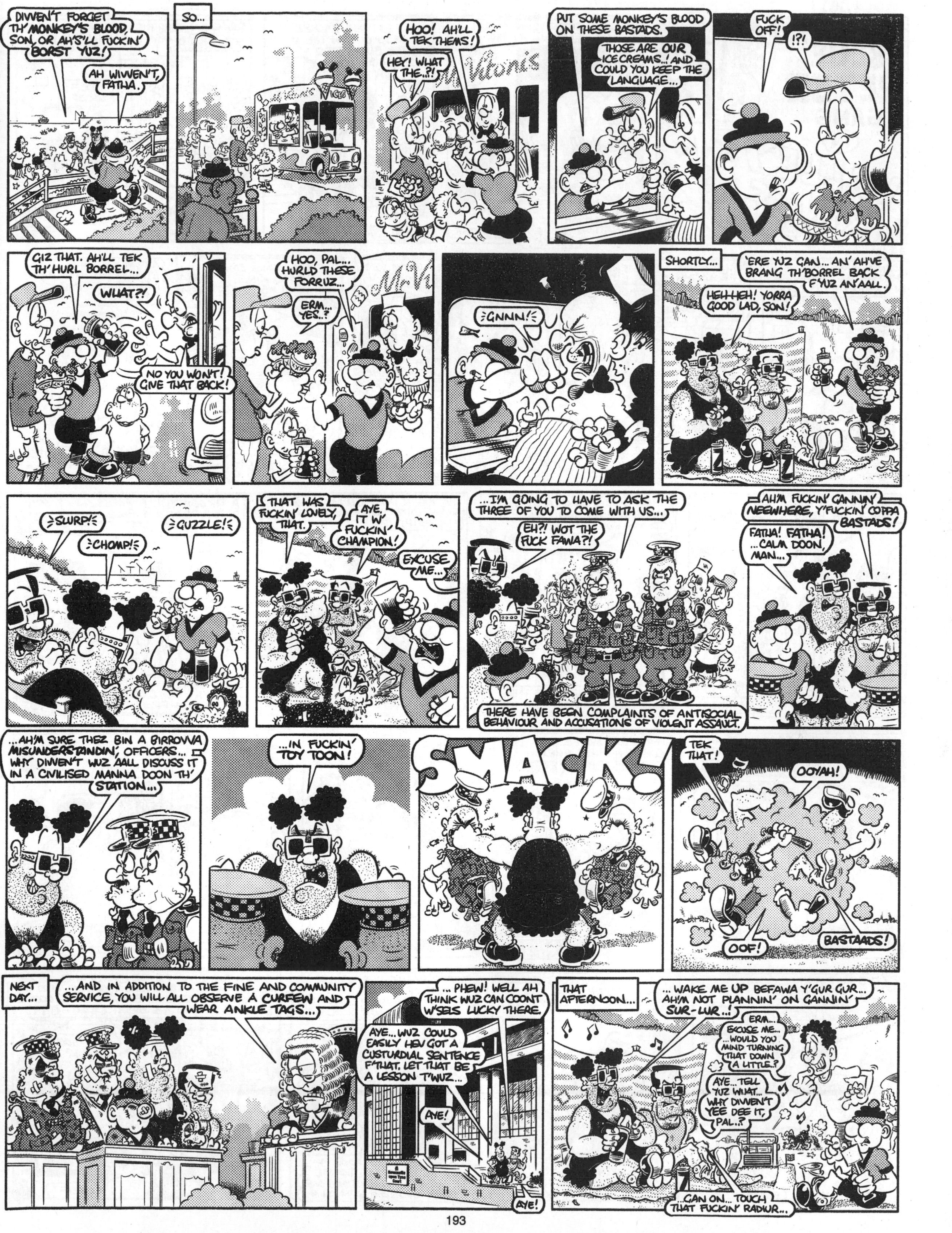
DIVVEN'T FORGET TH' MONKEY'S BLOOD, SON, OR AH'S'LL FUCKIN' BORST YUZ!
AH WIVVEN'T, FATHA.
SO...
HOO! AH'LL TEK THEMS!
HEY! WHAT THE..?!
PUT SOME MONKEY'S BLOOD ON THESE BASTADS.
THOSE ARE OUR ICE CREAMS..! AND COULD YOU KEEP THE LANGUAGE...
FUCK OFF!
!?!
GIZ THAT. AH'LL TEK TH' HURL BORREL...
WHAT?!
NO YOU WON'T! GIVE THAT BACK!
HOO, PAL... HURLD THESE FORRUZ...
ERM... YES..?
GNNN!
SHORTLY...
'ERE YUZ GAN... AN' AH'VE BRANG TH' BORREL BACK F'YUZ AN'AALL.
HEH-HEH! YORRA GOOD LAD, SON!
SLURP!
CHOMP!
GUZZLE!
THAT WAS FUCKIN' LOVELY, THAT.
AYE. IT W' FUCKIN' CHAMPION!
EXCUSE ME...
...I'M GOING TO HAVE TO ASK THE THREE OF YOU TO COME WITH US...
EH?! WOT THE FUCK FAWA?!
THERE HAVE BEEN COMPLAINTS OF ANTISOCIAL BEHAVIOUR AND ACCUSATIONS OF VIOLENT ASSAULT.
AH'M FUCKIN' GANNIN' NEEWHERE, Y'FUCKIN' COPPA BASTADS!
FATHA! FATHA! ...CALM DOON, MAN...
...AH'M SURE THEZ BIN A BIRROWA MISUNDERSTANDIN', OFFICERS... WHY DIVVEN'T WUZ AALL DISCUSS IT IN A CIVILISED MANNA DOON TH' STATION...
...IN FUCKIN' TOY TOON!
SMACK!
TEK THAT!
OOYAH!
OOF!
BASTAADS!
NEXT DAY...
...AND IN ADDITION TO THE FINE AND COMMUNITY SERVICE, YOU WILL ALL OBSERVE A CURFEW AND WEAR ANKLE TAGS...
...PHEW! WELL AH THINK WUZ CAN COONT W'SELS LUCKY THERE.
AYE...WUZ COULD EASILY HEV GOT A CUSTURDIAL SENTENCE F'THAT. LET THAT BE A LESSON T'WUZ...
AYE!
AYE!
THAT AFTERNOON...
...WAKE ME UP BEFAWA Y'GUR GUR... AH'M NOT PLANNIN' ON GANNIN' SUR-LUR..!
ERM... EXCUSE ME... ...WOULD YOU MIND TURNING THAT DOWN A LITTLE..?
AYE... TELL YUZ WHAT... WHY DIVVEN'T YEE DEE IT, PAL..?
...GAN ON... TOUCH THAT FUCKIN' RADIUR...

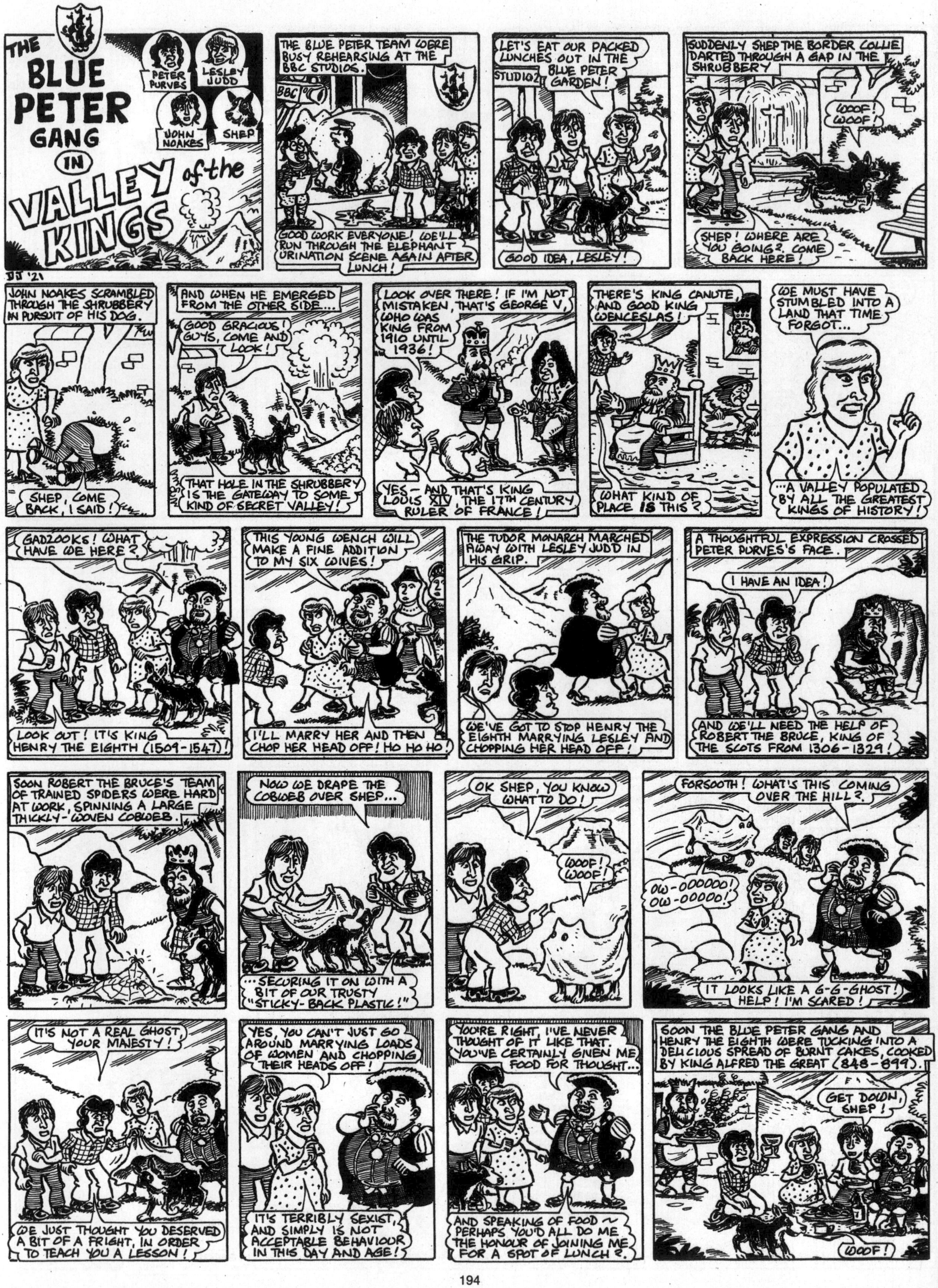
THE BLUE PETER GANG IN VALLEY of the KINGS
PETER PURVES
LESLEY JUDD
JOHN NOAKES
SHEP
DJ '21
THE BLUE PETER TEAM WERE BUSY REHEARSING AT THE BBC STUDIOS.
GOOD WORK EVERYONE! WE'LL RUN THROUGH THE ELEPHANT URINATION SCENE AGAIN AFTER LUNCH!
LET'S EAT OUR PACKED LUNCHES OUT IN THE BLUE PETER GARDEN!
STUDIO 2
GOOD IDEA, LESLEY!
SUDDENLY SHEP THE BORDER COLLIE DARTED THROUGH A GAP IN THE SHRUBBERY
WOOF! WOOF!
SHEP! WHERE ARE YOU GOING? COME BACK HERE!
JOHN NOAKES SCRAMBLED THROUGH THE SHRUBBERY IN PURSUIT OF HIS DOG.
SHEP, COME BACK, I SAID!
AND WHEN HE EMERGED FROM THE OTHER SIDE....
GOOD GRACIOUS! GUYS, COME AND LOOK!
THAT HOLE IN THE SHRUBBERY IS THE GATEWAY TO SOME KIND OF SECRET VALLEY!
LOOK OVER THERE! IF I'M NOT MISTAKEN, THAT'S GEORGE V, WHO WAS KING FROM 1910 UNTIL 1936!
YES – AND THAT'S KING LOUIS XIV THE 17TH CENTURY RULER OF FRANCE!
THERE'S KING CANUTE, AND GOOD KING WENCESLAS!
WHAT KIND OF PLACE IS THIS?
WE MUST HAVE STUMBLED INTO A LAND THAT TIME FORGOT...
...A VALLEY POPULATED BY ALL THE GREATEST KINGS OF HISTORY!
GADZOOKS! WHAT HAVE WE HERE?
LOOK OUT! IT'S KING HENRY THE EIGHTH (1509-1547)!
THIS YOUNG WENCH WILL MAKE A FINE ADDITION TO MY SIX WIVES!
I'LL MARRY HER AND THEN CHOP HER HEAD OFF! HO HO HO!
THE TUDOR MONARCH MARCHED AWAY WITH LESLEY JUDD IN HIS GRIP.
WE'VE GOT TO STOP HENRY THE EIGHTH MARRYING LESLEY AND CHOPPING HER HEAD OFF!
A THOUGHTFUL EXPRESSION CROSSED PETER PURVES'S FACE.
I HAVE AN IDEA!
AND WE'LL NEED THE HELP OF ROBERT THE BRUCE, KING OF THE SCOTS FROM 1306-1329!
SOON ROBERT THE BRUCE'S TEAM OF TRAINED SPIDERS WERE HARD AT WORK, SPINNING A LARGE THICKLY-WOVEN COBWEB.
NOW WE DRAPE THE COBWEB OVER SHEP...
...SECURING IT ON WITH A BIT OF OUR TRUSTY "STICKY-BACK PLASTIC!"
OK SHEP, YOU KNOW WHAT TO DO!
WOOF! WOOF!
FORSOOTH! WHAT'S THIS COMING OVER THE HILL?
OW-OOOOOO! OW-OOOOO!
IT LOOKS LIKE A G-G-GHOST! HELP! I'M SCARED!
IT'S NOT A REAL GHOST, YOUR MAJESTY!
WE JUST THOUGHT YOU DESERVED A BIT OF A FRIGHT, IN ORDER TO TEACH YOU A LESSON!
YES, YOU CAN'T JUST GO AROUND MARRYING LOADS OF WOMEN AND CHOPPING THEIR HEADS OFF!
IT'S TERRIBLY SEXIST, AND SIMPLY IS NOT ACCEPTABLE BEHAVIOUR IN THIS DAY AND AGE!
YOU'RE RIGHT, I'VE NEVER THOUGHT OF IT LIKE THAT. YOU'VE CERTAINLY GIVEN ME FOOD FOR THOUGHT...
AND SPEAKING OF FOOD ~ PERHAPS YOU'D ALL DO ME THE HONOUR OF JOINING ME FOR A SPOT OF LUNCH?
SOON THE BLUE PETER GANG AND HENRY THE EIGHTH WERE TUCKING INTO A DELICIOUS SPREAD OF BURNT CAKES, COOKED BY KING ALFRED THE GREAT (848-899).
GET DOWN, SHEP!
WOOF!

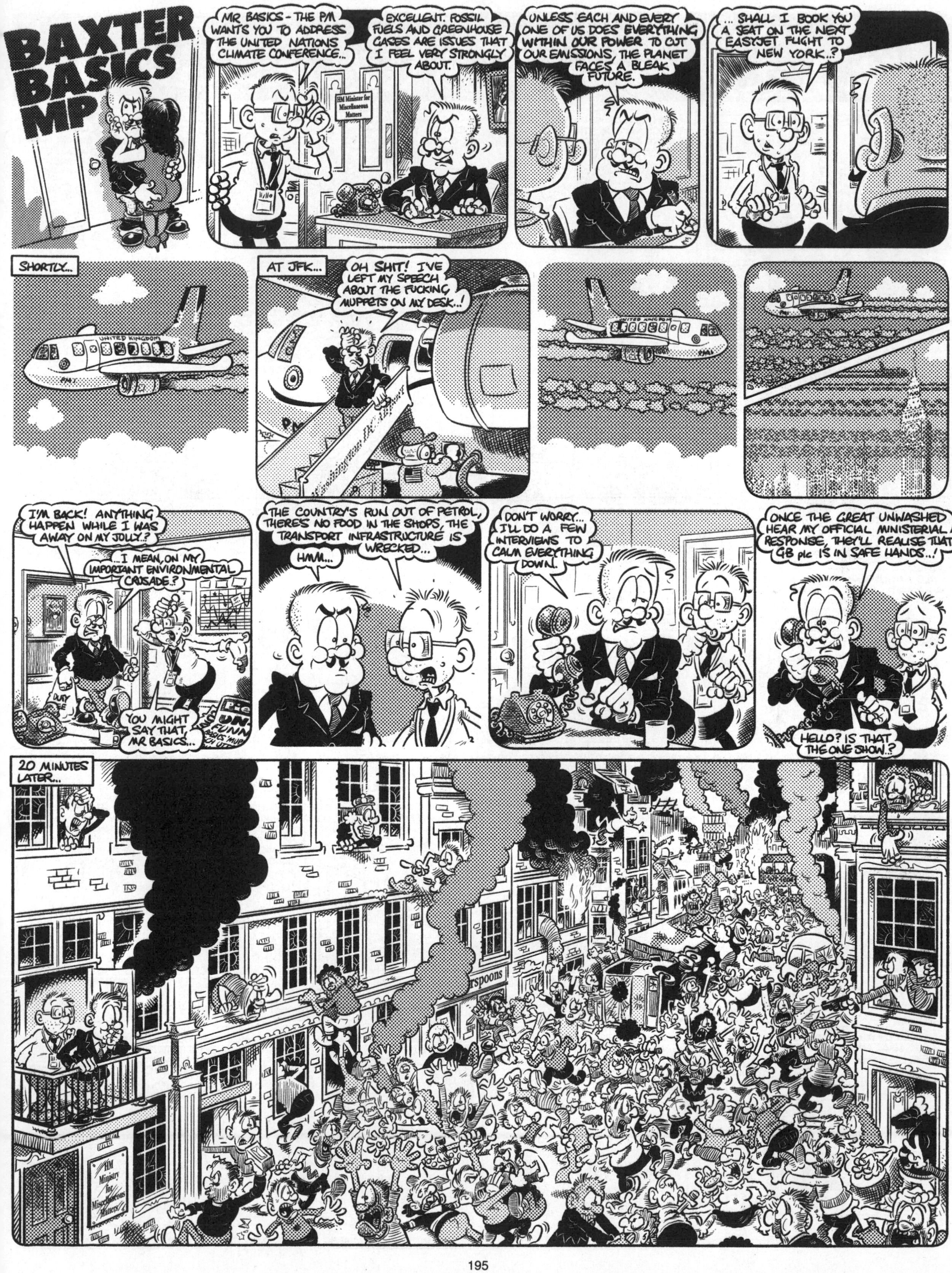
BAXTER BASICS MP
MR BASICS - THE PM WANTS YOU TO ADDRESS THE UNITED NATIONS CLIMATE CONFERENCE..
HM Minister for Miscellaneous Matters
EXCELLENT. FOSSIL FUELS AND GREENHOUSE GASES ARE ISSUES THAT I FEEL VERY STRONGLY ABOUT.
UNLESS EACH AND EVERY ONE OF US DOES EVERYTHING WITHIN OUR POWER TO CUT OUR EMISSIONS, THE PLANET FACES A BLEAK FUTURE.
... SHALL I BOOK YOU A SEAT ON THE NEXT EASYJET FLIGHT TO NEW YORK..?
SHORTLY..
UNITED KINGDOM
AT JFK...
OH SHIT! I'VE LEFT MY SPEECH ABOUT THE FUCKING MUPPETS ON MY DESK..!
I'M BACK! ANYTHING HAPPEN WHILE I WAS AWAY ON MY JOLLY..?
...I MEAN, ON MY IMPORTANT ENVIRONMENTAL CRUSADE..?
YOU MIGHT SAY THAT, MR BASICS...
THE COUNTRY'S RUN OUT OF PETROL, THERE'S NO FOOD IN THE SHOPS, THE TRANSPORT INFRASTRUCTURE IS WRECKED...
HMM...
DON'T WORRY... I'LL DO A FEW INTERVIEWS TO CALM EVERYTHING DOWN.
ONCE THE GREAT UNWASHED HEAR MY OFFICIAL MINISTERIAL RESPONSE, THEY'LL REALISE THAT GB plc IS IN SAFE HANDS...!
HELLO? IS THAT THE ONE SHOW..?
20 MINUTES LATER...
HM Ministry for Miscellaneous Matters

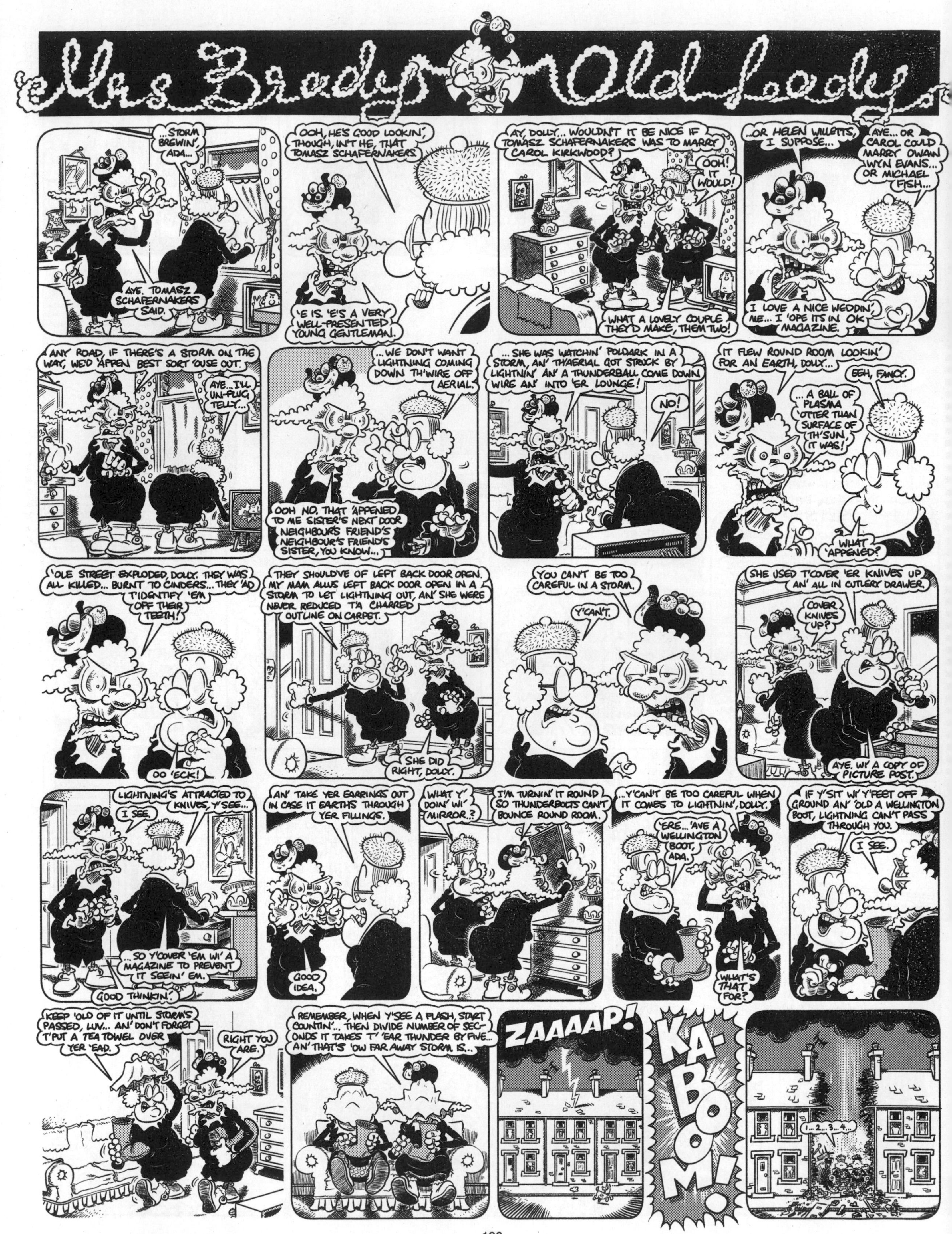
Mrs Brady Old Lady
...STORM BREWIN', ADA...
AYE. TOMASZ SCHAFERNAKERS SAID.
OOH, HE'S GOOD LOOKIN', THOUGH, IN'T HE, THAT TOMASZ SCHAFERNAKERS.
'E IS. 'E'S A VERY WELL-PRESENTED YOUNG GENTLEMAN.
AY, DOLLY... WOULDN'T IT BE NICE IF TOMASZ SCHAFERNAKERS WAS TO MARRY CAROL KIRKWOOD?
OOH! IT WOULD!
WHAT A LOVELY COUPLE THEY'D MAKE, THEM TWO!
...OR HELEN WILLETTS, I SUPPOSE...
AYE... OR CAROL COULD MARRY OWAIN WYN EVANS... OR MICHAEL FISH...
I LOVE A NICE WEDDIN', ME... I 'OPE ITS IN OK MAGAZINE.
ANY ROAD, IF THERE'S A STORM ON THE WAY, WE'D 'APPEN BEST SORT 'OUSE OUT.
AYE... I'LL UN-PLUG TELLY...
...WE DON'T WANT LIGHTNING COMING DOWN TH'WIRE OFF AERIAL.
OOH NO. THAT 'APPENED TO ME SISTER'S NEXT DOOR NEIGHBOUR'S FRIEND'S NEIGHBOUR'S FRIEND'S SISTER, YOU KNOW...
...SHE WAS WATCHIN' POLDARK IN A STORM, AN' TH'AERIAL GOT STRUCK BY LIGHTNIN' AN' A THUNDERBALL COME DOWN WIRE AN' INTO 'ER LOUNGE!
NO!
IT FLEW ROUND ROOM LOOKIN' FOR AN EARTH, DOLLY...
EEH, FANCY.
...A BALL OF PLASMA 'OTTER THAN SURFACE OF TH'SUN, IT WAS!
WHAT 'APPENED?
'OLE STREET EXPLODED, DOLLY. THEY WAS ALL KILLED... BURNT TO CINDERS... THEY 'AD T'IDENTIFY 'EM OFF THEIR TEETH!
OO 'ECK!
THEY SHOULD'VE OF LEFT BACK DOOR OPEN. MY MAM ALLUS LEFT BACK DOOR OPEN IN A STORM TO LET LIGHTNING OUT, AN' SHE WERE NEVER REDUCED T'A CHARRED OUTLINE ON CARPET.
SHE DID RIGHT, DOLLY.
YOU CAN'T BE TOO CAREFUL IN A STORM.
Y'CAN'T.
SHE USED T'COVER 'ER KNIVES UP AN' ALL IN CUTLERY DRAWER.
COVER KNIVES UP?
AYE. WI' A COPY OF PICTURE POST.
LIGHTNING'S ATTRACTED TO KNIVES, Y'SEE...
I SEE.
...SO Y'COVER 'EM WI' A MAGAZINE TO PREVENT IT SEEIN' EM.
GOOD THINKIN'.
AN' TAKE YER EARRINGS OUT IN CASE IT EARTHS THROUGH YER FILLINGS.
GOOD IDEA.
WHAT Y' DOIN' WI' MIRROR..?
I'M TURNIN' IT ROUND SO THUNDERBOLTS CAN'T BOUNCE ROUND ROOM.
...Y'CAN'T BE TOO CAREFUL WHEN IT COMES TO LIGHTNIN', DOLLY.
'ERE... 'AVE A WELLINGTON BOOT, ADA.
WHAT'S THAT FOR?
IF Y'SIT WI' Y'FEET OFF GROUND AN' 'OLD A WELLINGTON BOOT, LIGHTNING CAN'T PASS THROUGH YOU.
I SEE.
KEEP 'OLD OF IT UNTIL STORM'S PASSED, LUV... AN' DON'T FORGET T'PUT A TEA TOWEL OVER YER 'EAD.
RIGHT YOU ARE.
REMEMBER, WHEN Y'SEE A FLASH, START COUNTIN'... THEN DIVIDE NUMBER OF SECONDS IT TAKES T' 'EAR THUNDER BY FIVE... AN' THAT'S 'OW FAR AWAY STORM IS...
ZAAAAP!
KA-BOOM!
1...2...3...4...

MERRY CHRISTMAS AND A VICE-FREE NEW YEAR

IT'S a story as old as time. At midnight on December 31st, every man in Britain vows to give up masturbating. But chances are that by lunchtime on New Year's Day he has already fallen off the wagon and cracked a quick one out.

And now a new study by scientists at Bristol University tells us what we already know from bitter experience – refraining from wringing the bell is much harder than it appears. According to the boffins, if men want to give up, then they have a difficult task ahead of them.

"A man's body is full of hormones," explained the report's author Professor Kurt-Heinz Zuffle. "These chemicals course around in his bloodstream and give him powerful urges in the trouser department," he said. "These compulsions are so powerful that no-one can resist them."

The research from the Bristol team was based around experiments which involved leaving men in a locked room with a pornographic magazine and observing how long it was before they had one over the thumb.

"Most of the subjects were pulling the Pope's cap off within forty-five seconds of entering the room," said Professor Zuffle. "If we removed the bongo mag, our test subjects managed to keep their trousers up for about two minutes on average, before dropping them and feeding the ducks."

Self-abuse in men has long been known to cause blindness, feebleness of mind and severe tennis elbow. And since the Coronavirus pandemic has led to many men working from home, it is estimated that around 30 working hours per male employee per week are lost due to onanism, costing the economy untold billions of pounds ever year.

"It will be all but impossible to eradicate playing chopsticks entirely," said Zuffle. "But if everyone could just hold out a bit longer, perhaps until the evening of New Year's Day, then the country will be moving in the right direction."

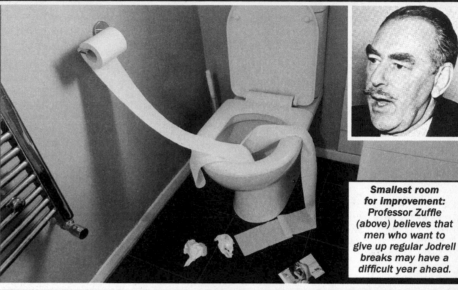

Smallest room for improvement: Professor Zuffle (above) believes that men who want to give up regular Jodrell breaks may have a difficult year ahead.

LADIES! Stop YOUR PARTNER masturbating for GOOD with the

Wank-no-More™ HAND SHANDY BRACELET

ting-a-ling-a-ling!

This innovative, yet stylish bracelet acts as an alert to let YOU know when your husband or boyfriend is up to no good.

The top quality chrome bells can be heard from any room in the house, and even outdoors up to 100m. It is fitted in seconds and is suitable for left- or right-handed onanists.

"My husband would regularly nip to the shed to 'do some woodwork', but after fitting him with a Wank-No-More Hand Shandy Bracelet, I knew exactly what the filthy pig was up to, and I was able to rush down there and whack him on the lid with a spoon."

Mrs B, Essex.

Only £12.99 Or if your hubby is ambidextrous, get TWO or just £20

Order *NOW* from wanknomorebracelet.co.uk

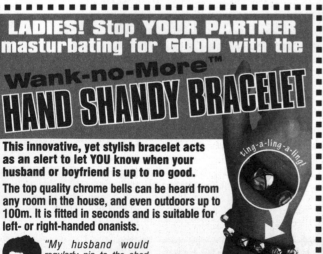

STOP TIPS

Here's Professor Zuffle's advice on how to resist the urge

1 Get up as soon as you wake up.

A man's sex hormones increase during sleep, and many men wake up in the morning with a bonk-on. The prevailing attitude is that it would be a shame to waste it and snuggle under the blankets for quick morning tug. But if you jump out of bed the minute you wake, like famously clean-living Scouts founder Lord Baden-Powell used to do, the hormones dissipate and the urge will recede.

2 Try not to think about sex

Nothing causes a man to want to engage in the monomanual vice more than thinking about you-know-what, and the average bloke thinks about it every seven minutes ... or even more. So spend your day pondering non-erotically charged subjects like football or gardening. If your mind does start to stray to thinking about people, don't think of them writhing naked on a bed – try to imagine them with stout, loose-fitting clothes on, in non-sexual situations, like at a chess championship or unblocking a sink.

3 Avoid masculine gatherings

When large groups of men get together, they experience a sense of masculinity and fraternity. This feeling is in response to their bodies increasing production of the hormone that makes them want to pull themselves off. So avoid situations where primarily men gather such as the tills at B&Q or petrol station forecourts.

4 Don't watch pornography

Research has shown that men who are watching pornography are up to 3 times more likely to interfere with themselves than those who are not. So if you get the urge to put an XXX-rated scud DVD on the telly, fight it. Instead, watch something completely un-erotic, such as a Formula 1 Grand Prix, an episode of *Terry and June*, or a 1970s *Confessions* film starring Bob Todd and Liz Smith.

5 Have a cold shower

Nothing depresses the urge to have a game of pocket billiards more than being freezing cold, so a chilly shower should quickly damp down any unwanted urges that may be making their presence felt. If you cannot take your showers cold, then be vigilant – if you feel your right hand wandering to the fruitbowl in the warm water, quickly reach for the cold tap with your left, or keep a toffee hammer handy to tap yourself on the Herman Gelmet.

BLAIR TODAY, GONE TOMORROW

LOOKING like Tony Blair is a problem that few of us face. Indeed only a handful of people in the country are mistaken for the former Prime Minister on a regular basis, being constantly stopped in the street and asked for their autograph, or having eggs thrown at them whilst being called a war criminal. But, for those few people, the problem of resembling the mad-eyed ex-Premier is very real.

If you look like Tony Blair, don't worry, because help is at hand. Here *Viz* life coach Braxton Hicks gives you a few tips on how to make 2021 the year when you look less like the New Labour PM.

Blair and Blair alike: Will your physical similarity to the former UK premier hold YOU back in the new year?

1 WEAR A HAT

BORN in 1953, Tony Blair is a *Baby Boomer*, a member of the first generation to eschew the wearing of hats. Indeed, in his 10 years as PM, he was rarely seen with anything atop his head. As a result, a simple act such as donning a trilby, a baseball cap or a woolly hat is a good first step to distancing yourself facially from the former premier.

2 GROW A MOUSTACHE

TONY BLAIR was famously clean shaven, never once experimenting with a beard or moustache whilst he was resident in Downing Street. As a consequence, any kind of facial hair you grow, be it a set of Dickensian mutton chops, a Hitler tache or a Sean Dyche disc-beard, will create a dissimilarity between you and Blair. And in the unlikely event that the former UN Middle East envoy suddenly stops shaving and starts sporting the same facial hairstyle as you, simply shave yours off.

3 PUT ON WEIGHT

APART from roly-poly Billy Bunter lookalike Boris Johnson, Prime Ministers tend to be trim figures. Their hectic schedule of meetings and appointments means that they are never sedentary for more than a few minutes at a time. Indeed, throughout his time as Premier, Tony Blair never went an ounce or two over a slim 11 stone, and since leaving office he still tips the scales at the same weight. So piling on the pounds - perhaps to 18 or 19 stone - means you will look markedly different from the svelte Blair. And the more weight you put on, the more dissimilar you will look.

4 DON'T WEAR A SUIT

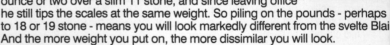

TONY Blair was always immaculately turned out in a Charles Tyrwhitt shirt, Kingsman and Drake tie, and an Armani suit. To avoid looking like him, it's best if you avoid these brands. In fact, you should avoid smart dress altogether. Nothing says "I'm not Tony Blair" better than tracksuit bottoms, over-engineered trainers and a football top.

5 DON'T SMILE

TONY BLAIR was one of the smiliest Prime Ministers this country has seen, and it's difficult to bring his face to mind without his trademark fixed grin. So when you are out and about, adopt a furrow-browed scowl, an expression that Tony never exhibited once in his premiership, and you will pass through the crowds unnoticed.

6 LEAVE YOUR WIFE

THIS may seem rather an extreme way of not looking like Tony Blair, but this advice only needs to be followed if your wife looks like your Doppelganger's missus, high-powered lawyer Cherie. Whilst the chances that anyone regularly being mistaken for Tony would be married to somebody regularly being mistaken for Cherie are extremely small, they are not impossible odds. If it is the case, then splitting up and marrying someone who looks like someone else - such as Keira Knightley, Scary Spice or Dame Edna Everage - would go a long way towards not being mistaken for the old New Labour PM.

***NEXT YEAR:** How to not look like Noel Edmond*

NEW YEAR'S BEZ-OLUTION

Manc icon vows to do more ironing in 2021

BEZ out of the Happy Mondays says he intends to start the new year as he means to go on... by doing more ironing. The drug-addled freaky dancer, 56, said he had even bought himself an iron in the January sales, so he will have no excuse for wearing wrinkly clothes in 2024.

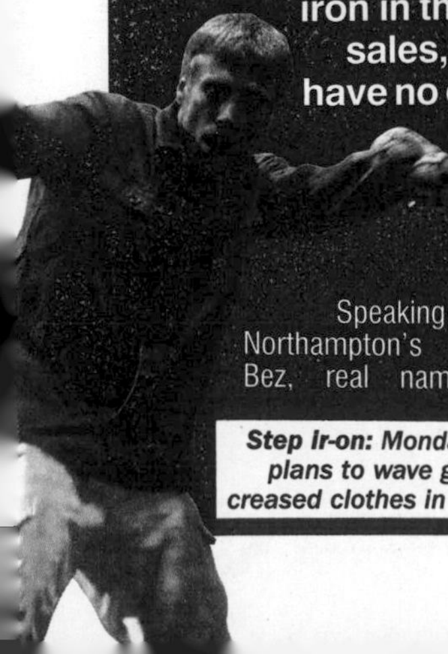

Speaking to BBC Radio Northampton's Bernie Keith, Bez, real name The Hon.

Berwick Bonham-Carter, explained how he treated himself to the brand new Tefal steam iron on impulse after spotting it on special offer whilst shopping at Manchester's Trafford Centre. *"It was in Currys and they had it reduced from forty pounds to nineteen ninety-nine because the box had been opened,"* he said. *"I'd been looking for a new iron because my last one got toffee on it, and I just went mad for it."*

"It's tons better than my old iron. It's even got a filter cartridge to prevent limescale build-up," the maracas virtuoso, who keeps bees and was declared bankrupt in 2005 and 2008, explained. *"Although Urmston where I live is a soft water area, so that's not really a problem."* —Reuters

Step ir-on: Mondays star Bez plans to wave goodbye to creased clothes in the new year.

NEW YEAR'S RAJ-OLUTIONS!

"The personal goal YOU set yourself in January speaks VOLUMES about why you've never brought your wife to orgasm" says telly shrink DR RAJ PERSAUD

WE all love the time-honoured tradition of NEW YEAR'S RESOLUTIONS. Every January 1st, each of us makes a solemn vow to take up something new, to give up something unhealthy, or to achieve some long-intended goal. But what you probably didn't know is that the Resolution YOU make at the beginning of each New Year says EVERYTHING THERE IS TO SAY about why you are unable to sexually satisfy your spouse!

That's according to small screen egghead DR RAJ PERSAUD, who

still occasionally gets on the telly. Says Dr Raj: *"If you're after concrete proof of why you have never once brought your wife to climax, you need look no further than the New Year's Resolution you plan on making this January."*

Here, Dr Raj examines a few of the most common New Year's promises we Brits make - and what they tell us about our truly dismal performance between the sheets.

JAN 1

NEW YEAR'S RAJ-OLUTION: TO GO VEGAN

Dr Raj says: "More and more people across the UK are choosing to cut out meat and dairy products from their diet in pursuit of a healthier lifestyle. It's not surprising, then, that 'Going Vegan' will be etched at the top of many men's New Year's Resolution lists this January. However, the luckless wives of these would-be plant-munchers are ALREADY on a strict 'meat-free' diet. That's because every single man who pledges to become a vegan in 2021 suffers from the embarrassing condition of *micropenis*. These acom-cocked unfortunates are unable to provide their better halves with carnal pleasure, so they shouldn't be surprised if their spouses start shopping around for new, and better-equipped, sexual partners."

CELEBRITY EXAMPLES: Boris Johnson MP, Dominic Raab MP, Mark Francois MP

NEW YEAR'S RAJ-OLUTION: GET PROMOTED AT WORK

Dr Raj says: "Climbing one step further up the career ladder is a common wish for millions of Brits at the start of each year. Whether they're butchers, bakers or candlestick-makers, millions of men will be firmly resolving to get promoted in 2021. But regrettably, the job market is not the only place where these hapless Casanovas are struggling to 'rise.' Because the average January promotion-seeker is chronically impotent – utterly incapable of achieving any degree of penile rigidity – and it'll be a cold day in Hell before he gives his joyless spouse anything approaching an orgasm."

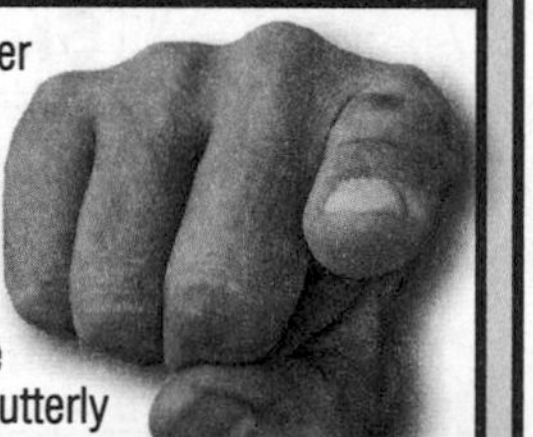

CELEBRITY EXAMPLES: Matt Hancock MP, Michael Gove MP, Gavin Williamson MP

NEW YEAR'S RAJ-OLUTION: TAKE UP A MUSICAL INSTRUMENT

Dr Raj says: "Self-improvement is a popular theme of many January resolutions, and there are always a few would-be Keith Moons, Acker Bilks or Jimi Hendrices who start the year by pledging to learn a musical instrument. Of course, mastering the guitar, piano, banjo or bassoon means countless hours of tedious, repetitive practice in the spare room... and sadly that's exactly what's going on in these would-be virtuosos's bedrooms, too. Fellas who resolve to master an instrument in 2021 are guaranteed to be dull, unimaginative lovers, capable of two minutes of silent, missionary position intercourse per month, leaving their frustrated missuses reaching for the Rampant Rabbit."

CELEBRITY EXAMPLES: Jacob Rees-Mogg MP, Rishi Sunak MP, Grant Shapps MP

NEW YEAR'S RAJ-OLUTION: SAVE SOME MONEY

Dr Raj says: "Vowing to tighten your purse strings ahead of the New Year suggests a dangerous predilection for blowing your wad far too soon. As such, there are no prizes for guessing which humiliating sexual issue plagues our January money-savers: *premature ejaculation*. These two-push Charlies are up and over like a pan of milk before their poor old spouses have even had time to switch the light off. They'll only have themselves to blame when they return home mid-February to find the missus gleefully getting a special delivery from the postie."

CELEBRITY EXAMPLES: Robert Jenrick MP, Brandon Lewis MP, Oliver Dowden MP

NEXT WEEK: Be My Pal-entine! Dr Persaud tells us why the type of chocolates YOU buy your loved one on February 14th speaks VOLUMES about which of your mates she is having it off with whilst you're at work.

HYPNOSIS-BASED NEW YEAR'S RESOLUTION SOLUTIONS

Lose pounds without going hungry? It can't be done! YES IT CAN!

Weight Loss Hypnosis

YOUR BRAIN can tell you that you are hungry even when your body does not need nourishment. Your cravings for food are all in the mind. My simple hypnosis techniques will retrain your brain and stop you feeling hungry.

The treatment is all online and costs just **£100**, and results are *GUARANTEED!* To find out how to sign up, read on...

But wait... you are suddenly feeling very sleepy...very sleepy. Your eyelids are becoming heavier and heavier... you are having trouble keeping them open... you're so very, very tired. But before you sleep... a deep, deep, dreamless sleep... you go to your computer... you're feeling so, so sleepy... the quiet, gentle hum of the computer lulls you into a slumber... you log into your internet banking account as you drift towards a relaxed sleep... you cannot keep your eyes open as you make a bank transfer of £100 into sort code 06-00-39 account number 018118055... you are almost fast asleep... you press Send... and you're gone... safe in a deep, deep sleep. When you wake, you will not remember anything about this advertisement.

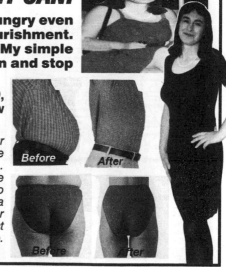

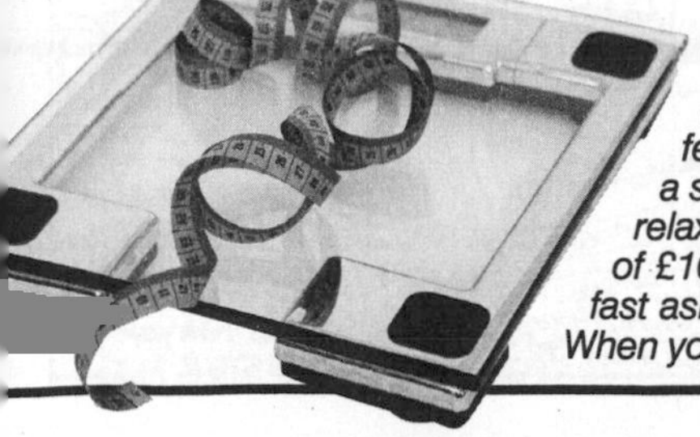

Before *After*
Before *After*

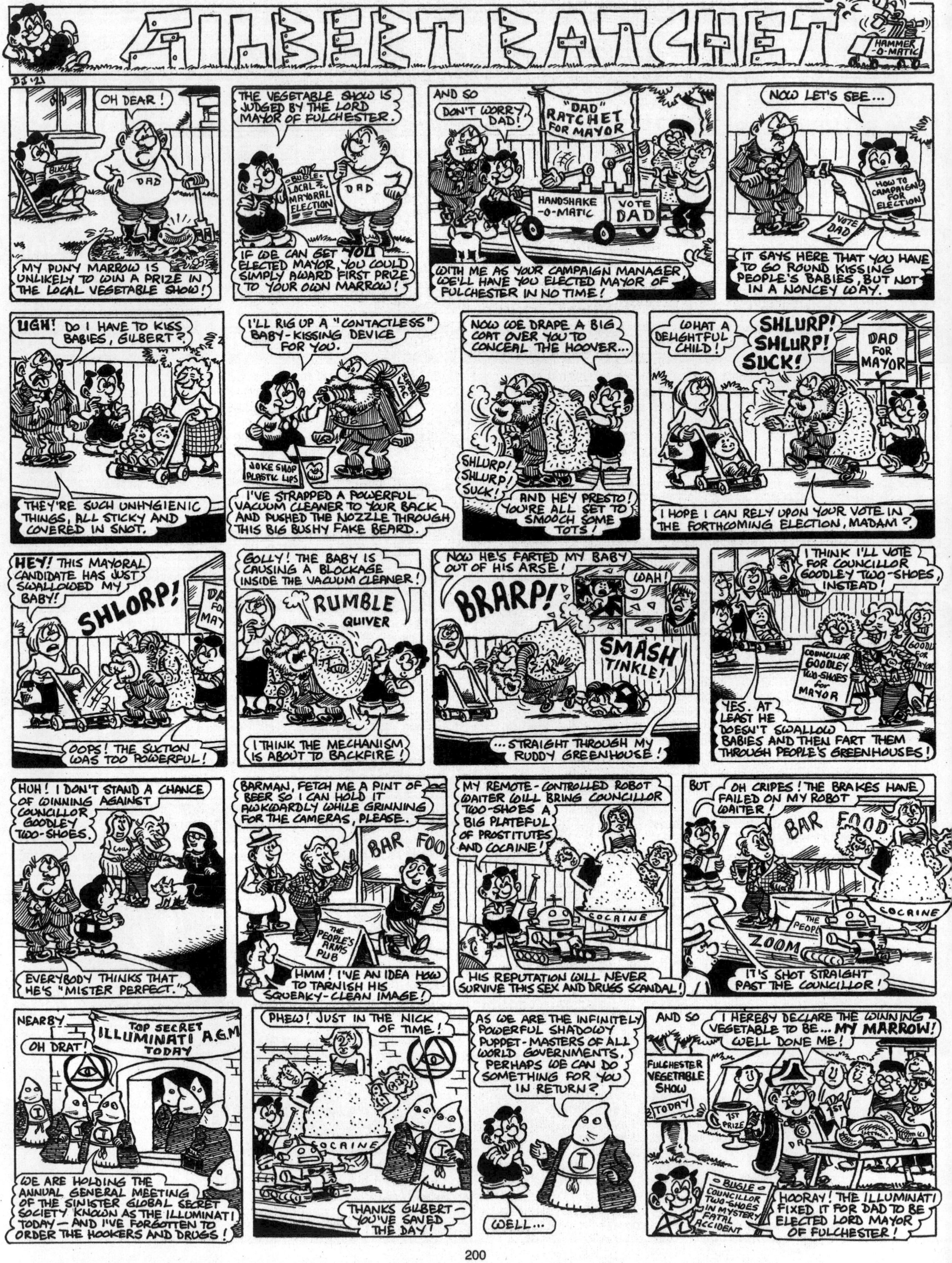
GILBERT RATCHET
HAMMER-O-MATIC
OH DEAR!
BUGLE
DAD
MY PUNY MARROW IS UNLIKELY TO WIN A PRIZE IN THE LOCAL VEGETABLE SHOW!
THE VEGETABLE SHOW IS JUDGED BY THE LORD MAYOR OF FULCHESTER.
BUGLE LOCAL MAYORAL ELECTION
IF WE CAN GET YOU ELECTED MAYOR, YOU COULD SIMPLY AWARD FIRST PRIZE TO YOUR OWN MARROW!
AND SO
DON'T WORRY, DAD!
"DAD" RATCHET FOR MAYOR
HANDSHAKE -O-MATIC
VOTE DAD
WITH ME AS YOUR CAMPAIGN MANAGER, WE'LL HAVE YOU ELECTED MAYOR OF FULCHESTER IN NO TIME!
NOW LET'S SEE...
HOW TO CAMPAIGN FOR ELECTION
VOTE DAD
IT SAYS HERE THAT YOU HAVE TO GO ROUND KISSING PEOPLE'S BABIES, BUT NOT IN A NONCEY WAY.
UGH! DO I HAVE TO KISS BABIES, GILBERT?
THEY'RE SUCH UNHYGIENIC THINGS, ALL STICKY AND COVERED IN SNOT.
I'LL RIG UP A "CONTACTLESS" BABY-KISSING DEVICE FOR YOU.
JOKE SHOP PLASTIC LIPS
I'VE STRAPPED A POWERFUL VACUUM CLEANER TO YOUR BACK AND PUSHED THE NOZZLE THROUGH THIS BIG BUSHY FAKE BEARD.
NOW WE DRAPE A BIG COAT OVER YOU TO CONCEAL THE HOOVER...
SHLURP! SHLURP! SUCK!
AND HEY PRESTO! YOU'RE ALL SET TO SMOOCH SOME TOTS!
WHAT A DELIGHTFUL CHILD!
SHLURP! SHLURP! SUCK!
DAD FOR MAYOR
I HOPE I CAN RELY UPON YOUR VOTE IN THE FORTHCOMING ELECTION, MADAM?
HEY! THIS MAYORAL CANDIDATE HAS JUST SWALLOWED MY BABY!
SHLORP!
OOPS! THE SUCTION WAS TOO POWERFUL!
GOLLY! THE BABY IS CAUSING A BLOCKAGE INSIDE THE VACUUM CLEANER!
RUMBLE
QUIVER
I THINK THE MECHANISM IS ABOUT TO BACKFIRE!
NOW HE'S FARTED MY BABY OUT OF HIS ARSE!
BRARP!
WAH!
SMASH
TINKLE!
...STRAIGHT THROUGH MY RUDDY GREENHOUSE!
I THINK I'LL VOTE FOR COUNCILLOR GOODLEY TWO-SHOES, INSTEAD!
COUNCILLOR GOODLEY TWO-SHOES for MAYOR
YES. AT LEAST HE DOESN'T SWALLOW BABIES AND THEN FART THEM THROUGH PEOPLE'S GREENHOUSES!
HUH! I DON'T STAND A CHANCE OF WINNING AGAINST COUNCILLOR GOODLEY TWO-SHOES.
EVERYBODY THINKS THAT HE'S "MISTER PERFECT."
BARMAN, FETCH ME A PINT OF BEER SO I CAN HOLD IT AWKWARDLY WHILE GRINNING FOR THE CAMERAS, PLEASE.
BAR
THE PEOPLE'S ARMS PUB
HMM! I'VE AN IDEA HOW TO TARNISH HIS SQUEAKY-CLEAN IMAGE!
MY REMOTE-CONTROLLED ROBOT WAITER WILL BRING COUNCILLOR TWO-SHOES A BIG PLATEFUL OF PROSTITUTES AND COCAINE!
COCAINE
HIS REPUTATION WILL NEVER SURVIVE THIS SEX AND DRUGS SCANDAL!
BUT
OH CRIPES! THE BRAKES HAVE FAILED ON MY ROBOT WAITER!
BAR FOOD
COCAINE
ZOOM
IT'S SHOT STRAIGHT PAST THE COUNCILLOR!
NEARBY
TOP SECRET ILLUMINATI A.G.M. TODAY
OH DRAT!
WE ARE HOLDING THE ANNUAL GENERAL MEETING OF THE SINISTER GLOBAL SECRET SOCIETY KNOWN AS THE ILLUMINATI TODAY — AND I'VE FORGOTTEN TO ORDER THE HOOKERS AND DRUGS!
PHEW! JUST IN THE NICK OF TIME!
COCAINE
THANKS GILBERT — YOU'VE SAVED THE DAY!
AS WE ARE THE INFINITELY POWERFUL SHADOWY PUPPET-MASTERS OF ALL WORLD GOVERNMENTS, PERHAPS WE CAN DO SOMETHING FOR YOU IN RETURN?
WELL...
AND SO
I HEREBY DECLARE THE WINNING VEGETABLE TO BE... MY MARROW! WELL DONE ME!
FULCHESTER VEGETABLE SHOW
TODAY
1ST PRIZE
BUGLE COUNCILLOR TWO-SHOES IN MYSTERY FATAL ACCIDENT
HOORAY! THE ILLUMINATI FIXED IT FOR DAD TO BE ELECTED LORD MAYOR OF FULCHESTER!

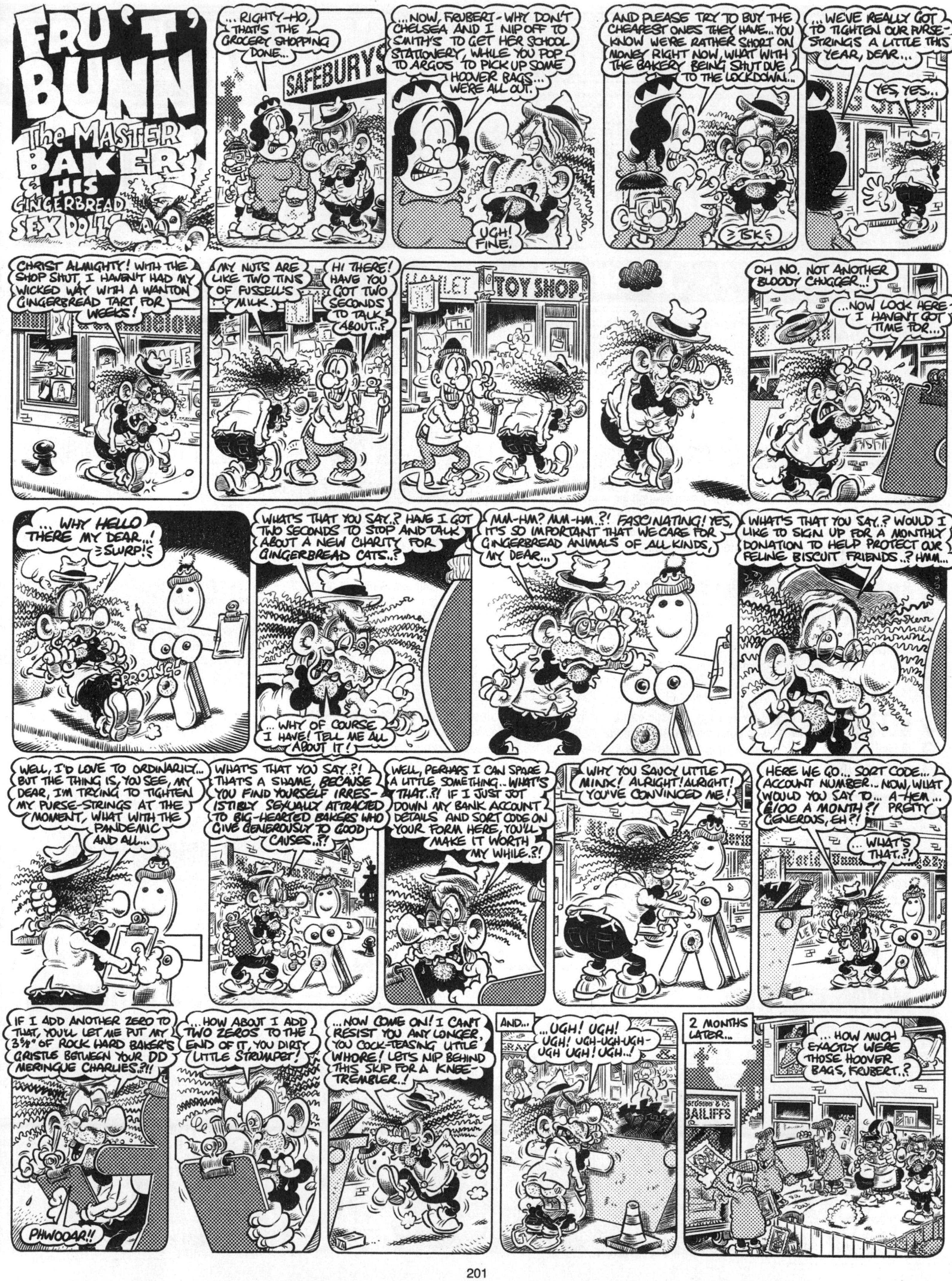
FRU 'T' BUNN
The MASTER BAKER & HIS GINGERBREAD SEX DOLLS
...RIGHTY-HO, THAT'S THE GROCERY SHOPPING DONE...
SAFEBURYS
...NOW, FRUBERT - WHY DON'T CHELSEA AND I NIP OFF TO SMITH'S TO GET HER SCHOOL STATIONERY, WHILE YOU POP TO ARGOS TO PICK UP SOME HOOVER BAGS... WE'RE ALL OUT.
UGH! FINE.
AND PLEASE TRY TO BUY THE CHEAPEST ONES THEY HAVE... YOU KNOW WE'RE RATHER SHORT ON MONEY RIGHT NOW, WHAT WITH THE BAKERY BEING SHUT DUE TO THE LOCKDOWN...
TSK
...WE'VE REALLY GOT TO TIGHTEN OUR PURSE-STRINGS A LITTLE THIS YEAR, DEAR...
YES, YES...
CHRIST ALMIGHTY! WITH THE SHOP SHUT, I HAVEN'T HAD MY WICKED WAY WITH A WANTON GINGERBREAD TART FOR WEEKS!
MY NUTS ARE LIKE TWO TINS OF FUSSELL'S MILK.
HI THERE! HAVE YOU GOT TWO SECONDS TO TALK ABOUT..?
TOY SHOP
OH NO, NOT ANOTHER BLOODY CHUGGER..!
...NOW LOOK HERE - I HAVEN'T GOT TIME FOR...
...WHY HELLO THERE MY DEAR..! SLURP!
SPROING!
WHAT'S THAT YOU SAY..? HAVE I GOT TWO SECONDS TO STOP AND TALK ABOUT A NEW CHARITY FOR GINGERBREAD CATS..?
...WHY OF COURSE I HAVE! TELL ME ALL ABOUT IT!
MM-HM? MM-HM..?! FASCINATING! YES, IT'S SO IMPORTANT THAT WE CARE FOR GINGERBREAD ANIMALS OF ALL KINDS, MY DEAR...
WHAT'S THAT YOU SAY..? WOULD I LIKE TO SIGN UP FOR A MONTHLY DONATION TO HELP PROTECT OUR FELINE BISCUIT FRIENDS..? HMM...
WELL, I'D LOVE TO ORDINARILY... BUT THE THING IS, YOU SEE, MY DEAR, I'M TRYING TO TIGHTEN MY PURSE-STRINGS AT THE MOMENT, WHAT WITH THE PANDEMIC AND ALL...
WHAT'S THAT YOU SAY..?! THAT'S A SHAME, BECAUSE YOU FIND YOURSELF IRRESISTIBLY SEXUALLY ATTRACTED TO BIG-HEARTED BAKERS WHO GIVE GENEROUSLY TO GOOD CAUSES..?!
WELL, PERHAPS I CAN SPARE A LITTLE SOMETHING... WHAT'S THAT..?! IF I JUST JOT DOWN MY BANK ACCOUNT DETAILS AND SORT CODE ON YOUR FORM HERE, YOU'LL MAKE IT WORTH MY WHILE..?!
WHY YOU SAUCY LITTLE MINX! ALRIGHT! ALRIGHT! YOU'VE CONVINCED ME!
HERE WE GO... SORT CODE... ACCOUNT NUMBER... NOW, WHAT WOULD YOU SAY TO... A-HEM... £100 A MONTH?! PRETTY GENEROUS, EH?!
...WHAT'S THAT..?!
IF I ADD ANOTHER ZERO TO THAT, YOU'LL LET ME PUT MY 3½" OF ROCK HARD BAKER'S GRISTLE BETWEEN YOUR DD MERINGUE CHARLIES..?!!
PHWOOAR!!
...HOW ABOUT I ADD TWO ZEROS TO THE END OF IT, YOU DIRTY LITTLE STRUMPET!
...NOW COME ON! I CAN'T RESIST YOU ANY LONGER, YOU COCK-TEASING LITTLE WHORE! LET'S NIP BEHIND THIS SKIP FOR A KNEE-TREMBLER..!
AND...
...UGH! UGH! UGH! UGH-UGH-UGH-UGH UGH! UGH..!
2 MONTHS LATER...
BAILIFFS
...HOW MUCH EXACTLY WERE THOSE HOOVER BAGS, FRUBERT..?

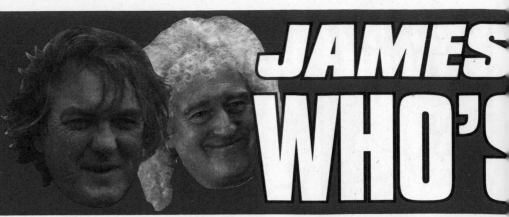

PRE-RAPHAELITE muse Christina Georgina Rossetti famously wrote: "There is but one May in the year." But she was talking out her fucking arse. That's because, as everyone knows, there are actually *three* Mays - car nut **JAMES**, Queen axe-man **BRIAN**, and maladroit failed PM **THERESA**. But which one is the best? It "may" be any one of them, so it's time for a 3-way contest to find out the definitive answer once and for all...

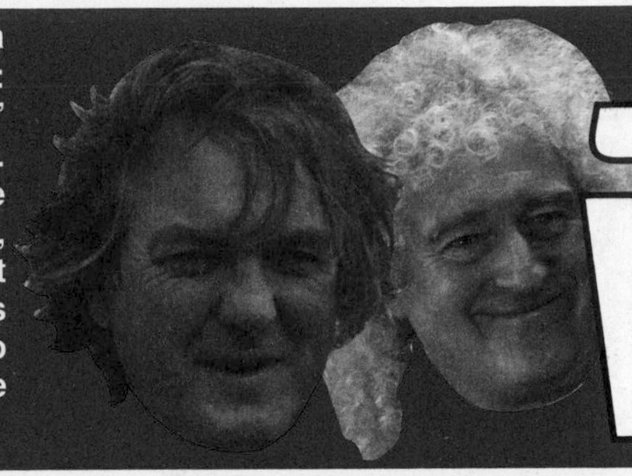

JAMES WHO'S

JAMES

ROUND 1

MUSICAL ABILITY

Despite making his name on *Top Gear* as one of thirsty filmcrew-walloper Jeremy Clarkson's motor-mad sidekicks, James originally studied *music* to degree level at Lancaster University, where he played the flute and piano. And those two instruments are not the only ones on which he can bang out a tune; back in 2015, he posted an internet video of himself practising *The British Grenadiers* on a descant recorder, a performance which was described by musicologist Miriam Nerval as "not always pleasing". Nevertheless, it's a solid opening movement for Captain Slow as he squeaks into an early lead.

Score 8

ROUND 2

YORKSHIRE-BUILT CARS

Although he spent his teenage years in the South Riding town of Rotherham, car-crazed honorary Tyke James seems never to have cemented his link to his northern homeland by buying himself a Yorkshire-built set of wheels. Indeed, a glance through the lengthy list of exotic jalopies he has owned down the years - everything from Swedish Saabs, Italian Alfa-Romeos and Japanese Toyotas to German Porsches, French Alpines and American Teslas - shows no evidence that he has ever shelled out for a motor manufactured in God's Own County.

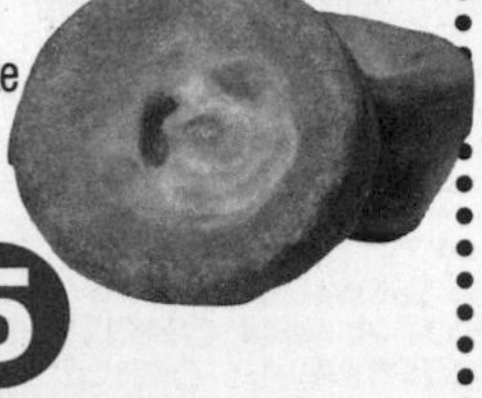

Score 5

ROUND 3

ASTEROID NOMENCLATURE

Situated somewhere between the Red Planet and Jupiter at an orbital inclination of 36.29962 degrees floats a spherical rock, 6.4km in diameter, known to astronomers as 2335 … or 'James'. This Mars-crossing asteroid was discovered by astronomer EF Helin on October 17th 1974 when the future *Top Gear* presenter was an 11-year-old schoolboy at Oakwood Comp, Rotherham. This means it is unlikely - though not *completely* impossible - that it was named after him, and his middling score in this round reflects this uncertainty.

Score 6

ROUND 4

GETTING FIRED

Early in his journalistic career, whilst working for *Autocar*, James was famously tasked with putting together the magazine's 1992 *Road Test Yearbook*. Each review in the glossy supplement began with a large red initial, and the cheeky hack surreptitiously arranged for these letters to spell out a foul-mouthed message, peppered with 4-letter words and disgusting obscenities not fit to be printed here. When his 'prank' was discovered by his bosses at the Haymarket Media Group, May was immediately dismissed.

Score 10

ROUND 5

PUB OWNERSHIP

In 2020, James shelled out for a share in the Royal Oak pub in Swallowcliffe, Wiltshire, so you might think that this would be a high-scoring round for him. However, since he owns only 50% of this charming, thatched establishment that boasts "a wonderful blend of 18th century architecture and stylish, modern interior design", we can only pour him a similar half measure of the available marks.

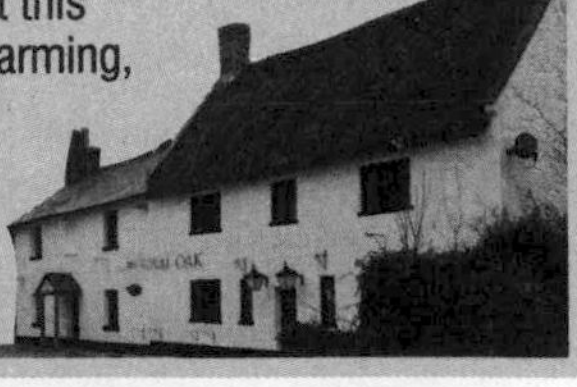

Score 5

ROUND 6

MAXIMUM ALTITUDE

Whilst filming his 2009 BBC documentary *James May at the Edge of Space*, the aviation-mad presenter flew up to the stratosphere in a Lockheed U2 spy plane. Achieving a maximum altitude of 70,000 feet, he became the fourth highest person in the world at that moment, only beaten by 2 astronauts on the International Space Station, and his US Air Force pilot, who was sitting on a cushion.

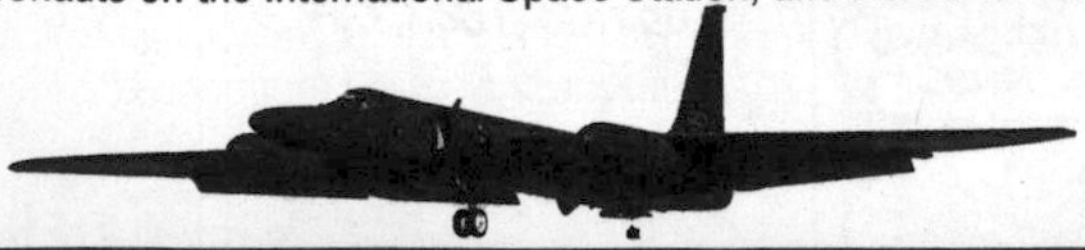

Score 9

B

MUSICAL ABILITY

As lead guitarist in one of the biggest-selling bands of all time, Brian has been lauded as one of rock's greatest virtuosos. Strumming his home-made electric guitar 'The Red Special', cobb together by the teenaged plank-spanker and his da using timber from an old fireplace, he has thrilled

YORKSHIRE-BUILT CARS

Rock guitaris are famed for their wild taste in exotic supercars, typically crashing Ferraris, Lamborghinis and Maserat into their swimming pools whilst ripped to the tits on drink, drugs and groupies. But Brian bucks this trend with his slightly more pedestrian taste in cars; 20 yea ago, he and Queen drummer Roger Taylor bought

ASTEROID NOMENCLATURE

Rc st are forever getting things named after them - roa sandwiches and airports to name but a few. Such honours come with the territory, along with gold discs, sex orgies and platform boots. But in 2008 the heavens-gazing Queen axeman received a

GETTING FIRED

In addition to his half-century-long day job as Queen's lead guitarist, PhD boffin Brian has maintained at least two other careers in parallel - as both a leading astrophysicist and a stereoscopic photographer. Happily for him - but sadly in terms of his scoring performance in this round - he doesn't appear to have been dismisse

PUB OWNERSHIP

Regulars at no-nonsense Barnsley pub The Strafford Arms nearly had a *Sheer Heart Attack* back in 2014, when Brian turned up in the snug in search of a bite to eat and a pint of bitter shandy. According to the local rag, after polishing off his meal the corkscrew-barneted Queen axem made time to chat and shake hands with the

MAXIMUM ALTITUDE

As a guest of the Red Arrov in 2011, Brian was taken on a pleasure flight in a Hawk T1A aerobatic jet. The official service ceilin for this aircraft is 44,500 feet, although it is not clear exactly how high Brian flew during his jaunt However, one thing we know for certain is that as part of the Queen's Golden Jubilee celebrations

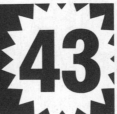

HOW DID THEY DO?

JAMES *Vroom! Beep! Beep!* Captain Slow puts thepedal to the metal and shifts into a turbo-charged top gear, burning rubber as he zooms from 0-43 in record time to take the chequered flag in this high-octane Mays Grand Prix.

43

BRIAN *He aren't th champions,* yet another round bites the dus But don't stop him now; with a flick of the wrist, Brian will dus himself down and carry on. As

BRIAN v THERESA
THE BEST MAY?

BRIAN

...ueen fans around the world and sold countless ...illions of records. Amazingly, however, music ...asn't his first love; he originally graduated from ...ondon University with a degree in Mathematics and ...hysics, and briefly considered ...acking it all in to study for a PhD in ...strology at Jodrell Bank. **Score 6**

...ensible Mazda MX5s from a Surrey-based main ...ealer, and he was recently papped whilst getting out ...f a stately AMG-Mercedes limo. However, back in the ...ghties, he purchased a 1952 Jowett Javelin saloon ...r as a present for his dad. Settling behind ...e wheel of this sedate, Bradford-built 52 ...P horseless carriage, Brian drops a cog and ...vertakes his rival Mays in this round. **Score 8**

...articularly special privilege when Main-belt ...steroid number 52665 was officially named ...rianmay' in his honour. However, he still has ...ome way to go before he matches his group's ...amboyant lead singer Freddie, who had a ...hole planet - 'Mercury' - named ...ter him. **Score 10**

...om any of these three ...bs for incompetence ...r misconduct, or ...en due to long ...rm illness or ...dundancy. **Score 4**

...ndlord, bar staff and other customers. However ...e article reporting the visit makes no mention of ...ulti-millionaire May putting his hand in his pocket ...actually *buy* the boozer during the course of his ...nchtime visit, so we can only assume that he ...dn't. **Score 4**

...ck in 2002, he played the National Anthem from ...e roof of Buckingham Palace, at a height of ...proximately 70 feet. **Score 6**

...e always says, *The Show ...ust Go On.* **38**

THERESA

MUSICAL ABILITY
Although she read Geography at Oxford University, Theresa May grew up in a musical household. Her father was a vicar, so they probably watched *Songs of Praise* on a Sunday night, and her love of a toe-tapping tune has manifested itself on numerous occasions throughout her political career. Visiting South Africa in 2018, she performed a weird and stilted R2-D2 jig whilst watching a school band. And she went on to repeat the humiliating spectacle on several subsequent occasions, culminating in a gangly-limbed, preying mantis-style shimmy to the podium at the Conservative party conference in Birmingham. **Score 4**

ROUND 1

YORKSHIRE-BUILT CARS
During her disastrous tenure as Prime Minister, Theresa was whisked from 10 Downing Street to her farce-prone official engagements in an armoured Jaguar XJ40. This bullet- and bomb-proof luxury limo, complete with a supercharged 5-litre, 450 horsepower V8 engine under its bonnet, was built at the Jaguar Land Rover factory in Castle Bromwich, West Midlands, approximately 73 miles from Yorkshire's most southerly point, Bondhay Dyke. As a result, the gangly ex-premier steers her way to yet another humiliating loss to add to her laughably catastrophic performance in the 2017 general election. **Score 3**

ROUND 2

ASTEROID NOMENCLATURE
Back in 1890, whilst peering through his telescope, Austrian star-gazer Johann Palisa spotted the 28km wide asteroid 'Theresia' for the first time. However, the Vienna Observatory director turned up his toes in 1925, *three decades* before Mrs May's dad even fucked her mum, meaning that the odds against it being the failed British premier that Johann had in mind when picking a name for his heavenly discovery are literally astronomical. Also, it's spelled different. **Score 1**

ROUND 3

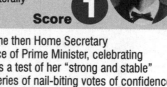

GETTING FIRED
Following David Cameron's Brexit referendum, the then Home Secretary found herself unexpectedly promoted to the office of Prime Minister, celebrating her appointment by triggering Article 50 and announcing a snap election as a test of her "strong and stable" leadership. Her resultant dramatically reduced Commons majority and a series of nail-biting votes of confidence eventually led to her resignation on May 24th 2019, meaning that she wasn't *technically* fired from her job. Just like her entire political career, this round is a substandard performance that ends in utter, humiliating failure. **Score 0**

ROUND 4

PUB OWNERSHIP
In 2017, after then Home Secretary May slashed police budgets by £413 million, *The Independent* reported that angry pub landlords in her Berkshire constituency were planning to ban her from all licensed premises in Maidenhead. With such bad blood between Theresa and her neighbourood boozers, it is just possible that she decided to shell out and build a pub of her own, perhaps adding a well-stocked bar to her garden shed to avoid the humiliation of being heaved onto the street by burly bouncers when trying to enjoy a few quiet pints and a bag of scratchings at her local. **Score 2**

ROUND 5

MAXIMUM ALTITUDE
BBC newsreader Sophie Raworth surprised viewers in 2019 when she announced: "Theresa May says she intends to go back to Brussels to negotiate her Brexit deal" over crackly black and white film footage of Spitfires taking off from Biggin Hill airfield during World War II. This was an unfortunate blooper from the BBC as PM May was not aboard any of the planes featured in the footage. And even if she were, the iconic Battle of Britain warplane's maximum flight altitude of 34,000 feet means, once again, it's a characteristically dismal performance for the gaffe-prone failed premier. **Score 3**

ROUND 6

THERESA
Theresa Mayday! Theresa Mayday! Just like her beloved No Deal Brexit, it's a humiliating catastrophe for the disaster-prone ex-PM. As she did with her parliamentary majority and her country's world standing, she's lost it in style. **13**

Next week:
SPRINGFIELD v HILL v BIN
Who's the best Dusty?

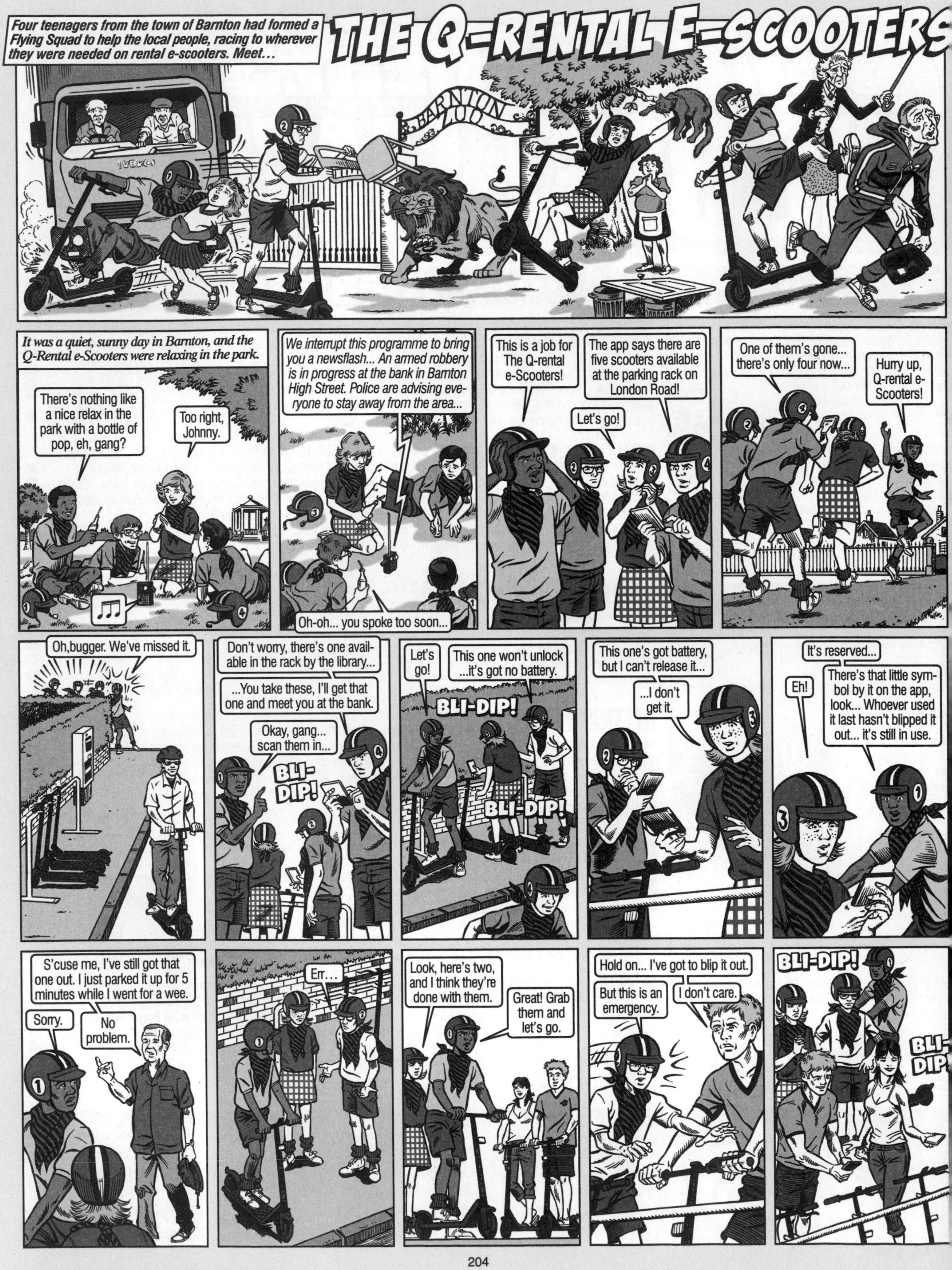
Four teenagers from the town of Barnton had formed a Flying Squad to help the local people, racing to wherever they were needed on rental e-scooters. Meet…
THE Q-RENTAL E-SCOOTERS
BARNTON ZOO
It was a quiet, sunny day in Barnton, and the Q-Rental e-Scooters were relaxing in the park.
There's nothing like a nice relax in the park with a bottle of pop, eh, gang?
Too right, Johnny.
We interrupt this programme to bring you a newsflash... An armed robbery is in progress at the bank in Barnton High Street. Police are advising everyone to stay away from the area...
Oh-oh... you spoke too soon...
This is a job for The Q-rental e-Scooters!
The app says there are five scooters available at the parking rack on London Road!
Let's go!
One of them's gone... there's only four now...
Hurry up, Q-rental e-Scooters!
Oh,bugger. We've missed it.
Don't worry, there's one available in the rack by the library...
...You take these, I'll get that one and meet you at the bank.
Okay, gang... scan them in...
BLI-DIP!
Let's go!
This one won't unlock ...it's got no battery.
BLI-DIP!
BLI-DIP!
This one's got battery, but I can't release it...
...I don't get it.
It's reserved...
Eh!
There's that little symbol by it on the app, look... Whoever used it last hasn't blipped it out... it's still in use.
S'cuse me, I've still got that one out. I just parked it up for 5 minutes while I went for a wee.
Sorry.
No problem.
Err…
Look, here's two, and I think they're done with them.
Great! Grab them and let's go.
Hold on... I've got to blip it out.
But this is an emergency.
I don't care.
BLI-DIP!
BLI-DIP

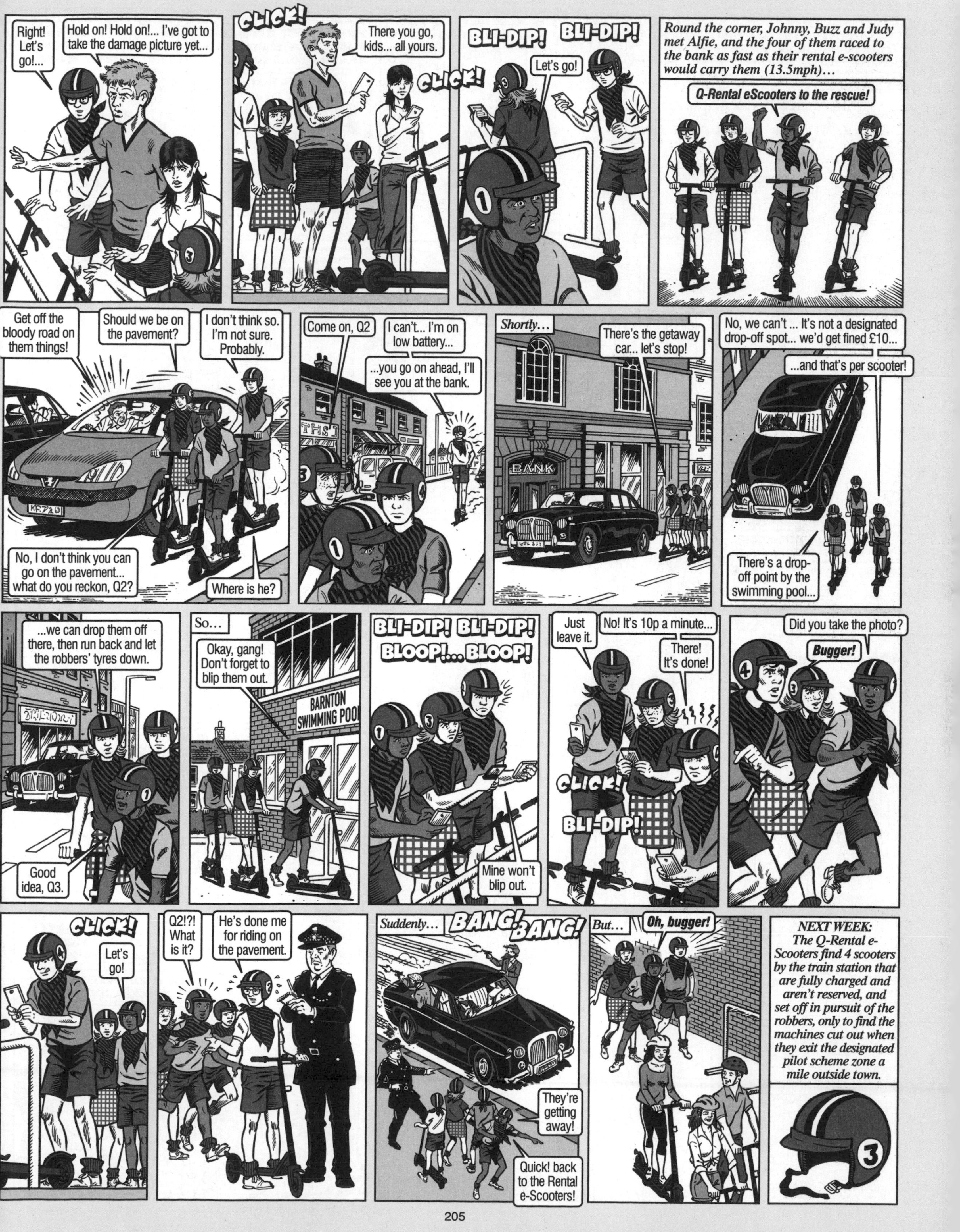

Right! Let's go!...
Hold on! Hold on!... I've got to take the damage picture yet...
CLICK!
There you go, kids... all yours.
CLICK!
BLI-DIP! BLI-DIP!
Let's go!
Round the corner, Johnny, Buzz and Judy met Alfie, and the four of them raced to the bank as fast as their rental e-scooters would carry them (13.5mph)…
Q-Rental eScooters to the rescue!
Get off the bloody road on them things!
Should we be on the pavement?
I don't think so. I'm not sure. Probably.
No, I don't think you can go on the pavement... what do you reckon, Q2?
Where is he?
Come on, Q2
I can't... I'm on low battery...
...you go on ahead, I'll see you at the bank.
Shortly…
There's the getaway car... let's stop!
BANK
No, we can't ... It's not a designated drop-off spot... we'd get fined £10...
...and that's per scooter!
There's a drop-off point by the swimming pool...
...we can drop them off there, then run back and let the robbers' tyres down.
Good idea, Q3.
So…
Okay, gang! Don't forget to blip them out.
BARNTON SWIMMING POO
BLI-DIP! BLI-DIP! BLOOP!... BLOOP!
Mine won't blip out.
Just leave it.
No! It's 10p a minute...
There! It's done!
CLICK!
BLI-DIP!
Did you take the photo?
Bugger!
CLICK!
Let's go!
Q2!?! What is it?
He's done me for riding on the pavement.
Suddenly…
BANG! BANG!
They're getting away!
Quick! back to the Rental e-Scooters!
But…
Oh, bugger!
NEXT WEEK:
The Q-Rental e-Scooters find 4 scooters by the train station that are fully charged and aren't reserved, and set off in pursuit of the robbers, only to find the machines cut out when they exit the designated pilot scheme zone a mile outside town.

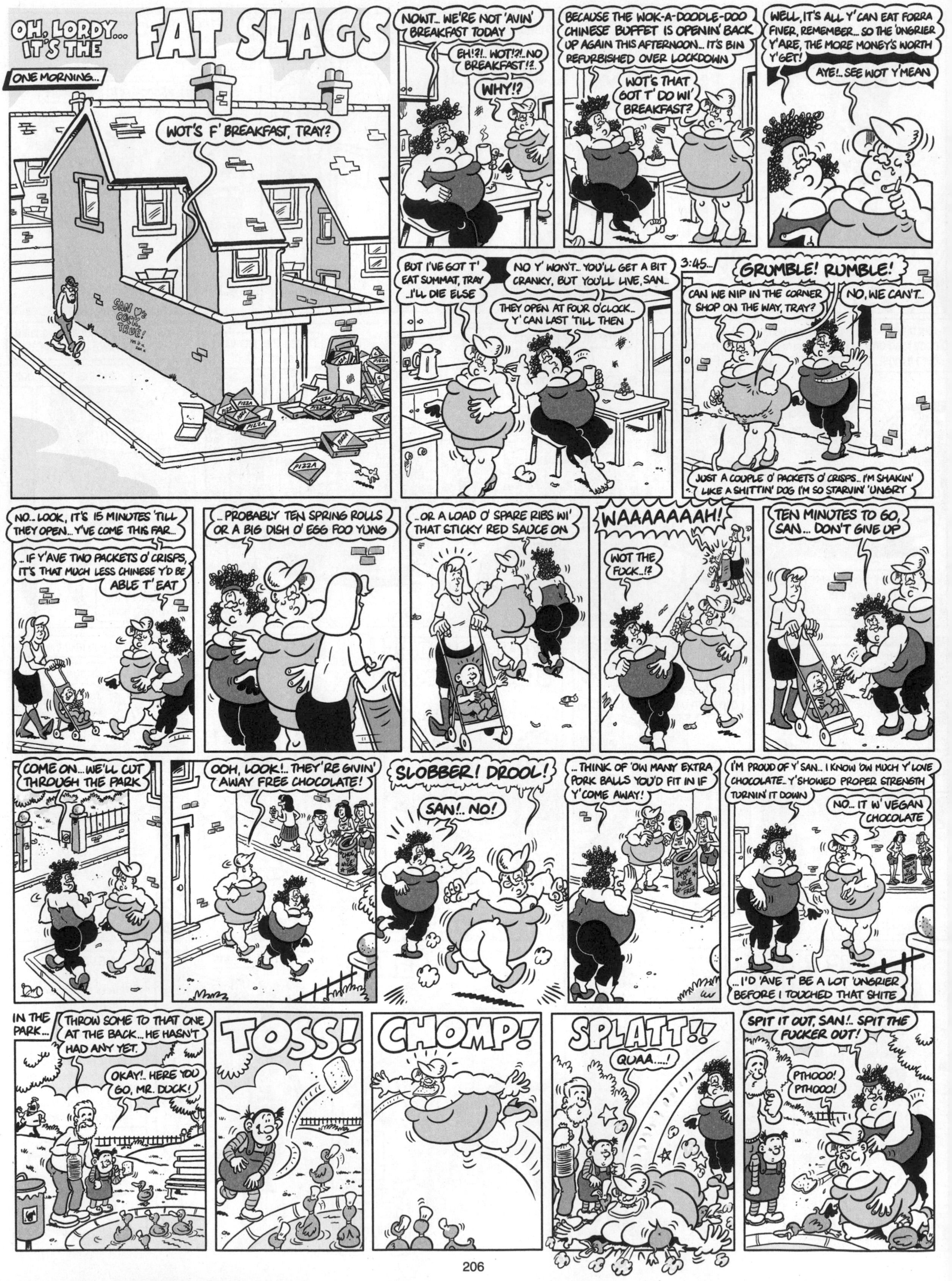
OH, LORDY... IT'S THE
FAT SLAGS
ONE MORNING...
WOT'S F' BREAKFAST, TRAY?
SAN ♥'s COCK TRUE!
NOWT... WE'RE NOT 'AVIN' BREAKFAST TODAY
EH!?!.. WOT!?!.. NO BREAKFAST!?..
WHY!?
BECAUSE THE WOK-A-DOODLE-DOO CHINESE BUFFET IS OPENIN' BACK UP AGAIN THIS AFTERNOON... IT'S BIN REFURBISHED OVER LOCKDOWN
WOT'S THAT GOT T' DO WI' BREAKFAST?
WELL, IT'S ALL Y' CAN EAT FORRA FIVER, REMEMBER... SO THE 'UNGRIER Y'ARE, THE MORE MONEY'S WORTH Y'GET!
AYE!.. SEE WOT Y'MEAN
BUT I'VE GOT T' EAT SUMMAT, TRAY ...I'LL DIE ELSE
NO Y' WON'T... YOU'LL GET A BIT CRANKY, BUT YOU'LL LIVE, SAN...
THEY OPEN AT FOUR O'CLOCK... Y' CAN LAST 'TILL THEN
3:45...
GRUMBLE! RUMBLE!
CAN WE NIP IN THE CORNER SHOP ON THE WAY, TRAY?
NO, WE CAN'T...
JUST A COUPLE O' PACKETS O' CRISPS... I'M SHAKIN' LIKE A SHITTIN' DOG I'M SO STARVIN' 'UNGRY
NO... LOOK, IT'S 15 MINUTES 'TILL THEY OPEN... Y'VE COME THIS FAR...
... IF Y'AVE TWO PACKETS O' CRISPS, IT'S THAT MUCH LESS CHINESE Y'D BE ABLE T' EAT
... PROBABLY TEN SPRING ROLLS OR A BIG DISH O' EGG FOO YUNG
...OR A LOAD O' SPARE RIBS WI' THAT STICKY RED SAUCE ON
WAAAAAAAH!
WOT THE FUCK...!?
TEN MINUTES TO GO, SAN... DON'T GIVE UP
COME ON... WE'LL CUT THROUGH THE PARK
OOH, LOOK!.. THEY'RE GIVIN' AWAY FREE CHOCOLATE!
CHOC O' NICE FREE
SLOBBER! DROOL!
SAN!.. NO!
... THINK OF 'OW MANY EXTRA PORK BALLS YOU'D FIT IN IF Y'COME AWAY!
I'M PROUD OF Y' SAN... I KNOW 'OW MUCH Y' LOVE CHOCOLATE... Y' SHOWED PROPER STRENGTH TURNIN' IT DOWN
NO... IT W' VEGAN CHOCOLATE
... I'D 'AVE T' BE A LOT 'UNGRIER BEFORE I TOUCHED THAT SHITE
IN THE PARK...
THROW SOME TO THAT ONE AT THE BACK... HE HASN'T HAD ANY YET.
OKAY!.. HERE YOU GO, MR. DUCK!
TOSS!
CHOMP!
SPLATT!!
QUAA....!
SPIT IT OUT, SAN!.. SPIT THE FUCKER OUT!
PTHOOO! PTHOOO!

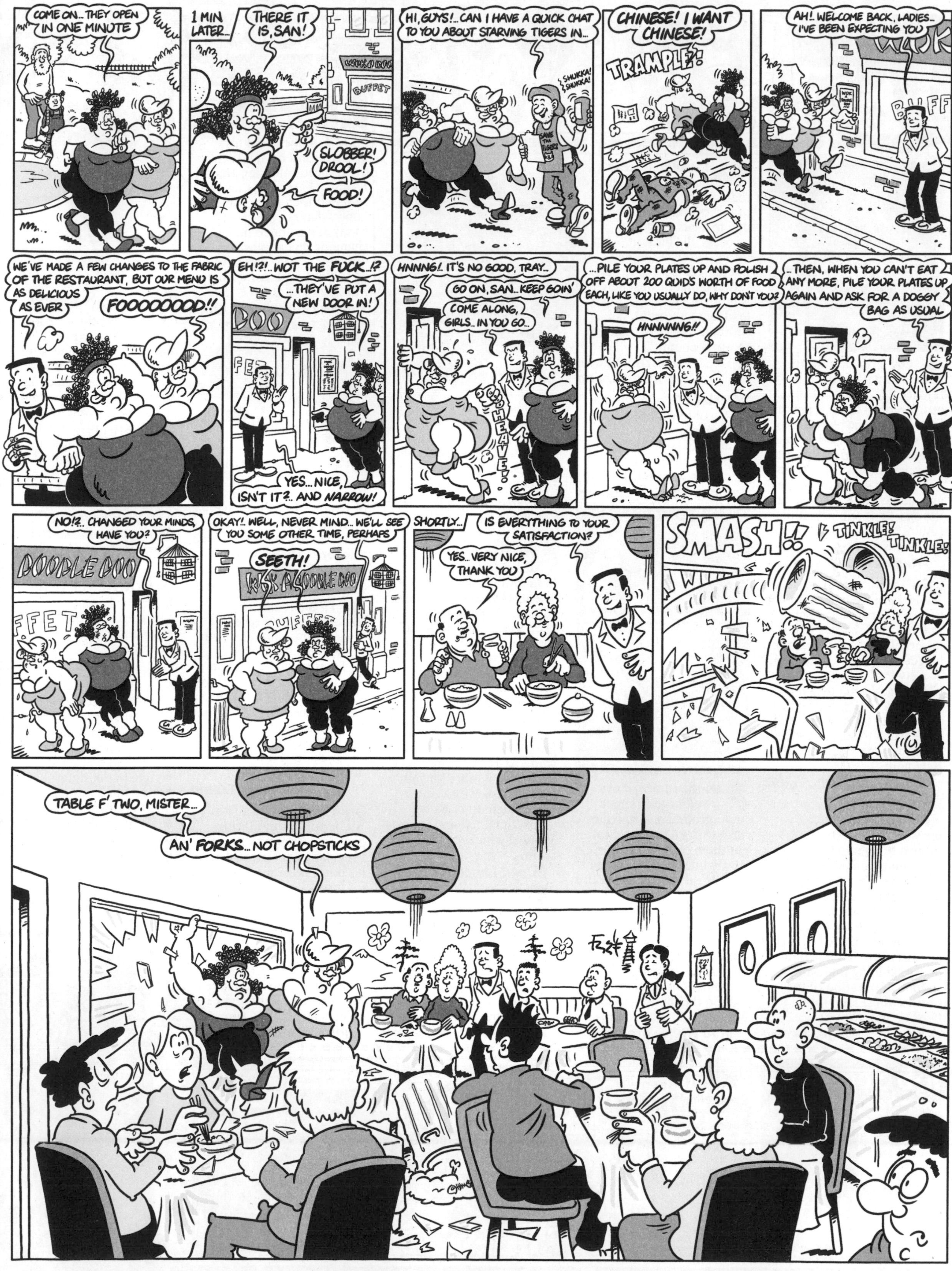
COME ON... THEY OPEN IN ONE MINUTE
1 MIN LATER...
THERE IT IS, SAN!
SLOBBER! DROOL!
FOOD!
HI, GUYS!... CAN I HAVE A QUICK CHAT TO YOU ABOUT STARVING TIGERS IN...
SHUKKA! SHUKKA!
SAVE THE TIGERS
CHINESE! I WANT CHINESE!
TRAMPLE!
AH!.. WELCOME BACK, LADIES... I'VE BEEN EXPECTING YOU
WE'VE MADE A FEW CHANGES TO THE FABRIC OF THE RESTAURANT, BUT OUR MENU IS AS DELICIOUS AS EVER
FOOOOOOOD!!
EH!?!.. WOT THE FUCK..!?
...THEY'VE PUT A NEW DOOR IN!
YES... NICE, ISN'T IT?.. AND NARROW!
HNNNG!.. IT'S NO GOOD, TRAY...
GO ON, SAN... KEEP GOIN'
COME ALONG, GIRLS... IN YOU GO...
HEAVE!
...PILE YOUR PLATES UP AND POLISH OFF ABOUT 200 QUID'S WORTH OF FOOD EACH, LIKE YOU USUALLY DO, WHY DON'T YOU?
HNNNNNG!!
...THEN, WHEN YOU CAN'T EAT ANY MORE, PILE YOUR PLATES UP AGAIN AND ASK FOR A DOGGY BAG AS USUAL
NO!?.. CHANGED YOUR MINDS, HAVE YOU?
DOODLE DOO
OKAY!.. WELL, NEVER MIND... WE'LL SEE YOU SOME OTHER TIME, PERHAPS
SEETH!
WOK A DOODLE DOO
SHORTLY...
IS EVERYTHING TO YOUR SATISFACTION?
YES... VERY NICE, THANK YOU
SMASH!!
TINKLE! TINKLE!
TABLE F' TWO, MISTER...
AN' FORKS... NOT CHOPSTICKS

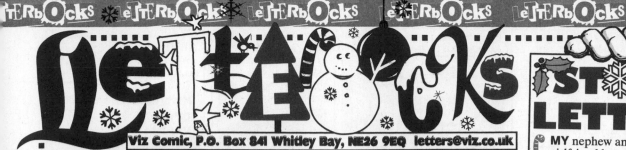

Letterbocks

Viz Comic, P.O. Box 841 Whitley Bay, NE26 9EQ letters@viz.co.uk

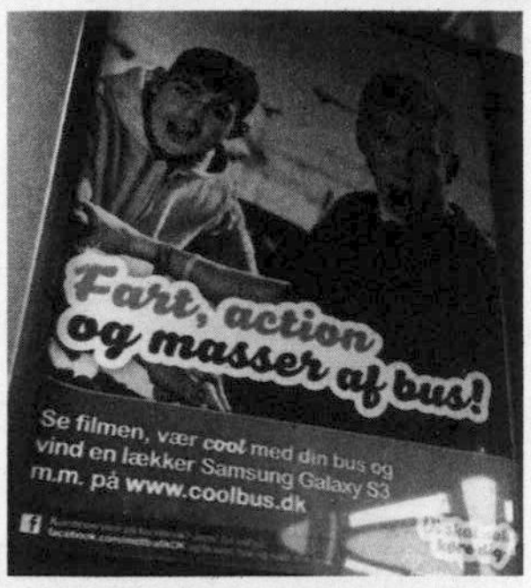
Fart, action og masser af bus!
Se filmen, vær cool med din bus og vind en lækker Samsung Galaxy S3 m.m. på www.coolbus.dk

ON a recent visit to Denmark I saw this remarkable poster inside a bus. Needless to say, I put my foot through the bus window and was hospitalised for a considerable amount of time. However, I was perfectly fine and I didn't even have to pay any medical bills because of the excellent public health system in Scandinavia. Do I win five Krone?

Reginald Chaos, email

IF, as we're told, variety is the spice of life, then it's hardly surprising that the British are such miserable fuckers when our biggest crisp manufacturers' Variety Pack always consists of boring old Ready Salted, Cheese & Onion and Salt & Vinegar. If Gary Lineker truly wants to sort out social injustices, maybe he should start here.

Micky Spudsworth, Luton

PERHAPS you or your readers could assist me with this question: Is there a threshold between a skidmark and a shit, and if there is, what is it and how might one measure it? This is important as the missus is claiming that I have shit my pants, but it is my assertion that it is only heavy skidding following a sudden application of the brakes whilst attempting to twist on nineteen.

S Minge, Jersey

I HAVE just read a news story which said there may be a shortage of turkeys this Christmas due to a lack of staff to 'process' the birds at farms. Surely if there is not enough people to kill turkeys, that means there is more of them about, leading to a surplus, not a shortage. So there's nothing to worry about.

Ian Thompson, Northumberland

MUTED trumpets may be old fashioned, but I still like them. And if the so-called 'woke' brigade try to stop me enjoying them, I'll give them what for.

Rodney Watts, W Drayton

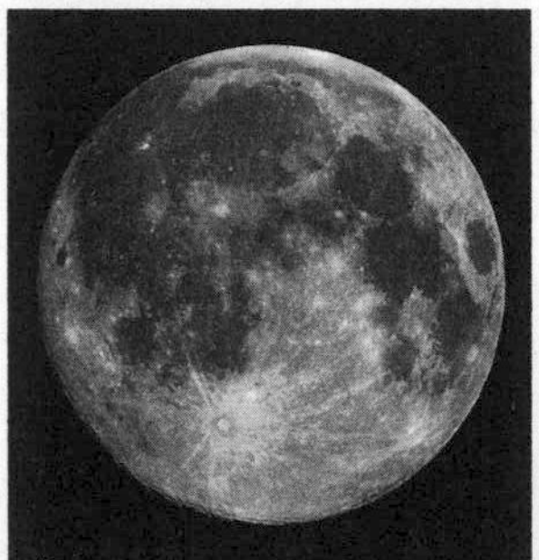

WHY are photos of the moon always in black and white? Come on NASA, take one in colour for once.

Brian Wigdrain, Plantpot

IN the future, if any workers get trapped underground and rescuers have to dig a borehole to get them out, rather than slowly hoisting them up in a cylindrical cage like they did with those Chilean miners, I think they should be fired up it like a big cannon. They could land in a massive net on the surface, with all clowns cheering and clapping. I'm sure it would lighten the mood for any onlooking anxious relatives.

Fat Al White, Wrenthorpe

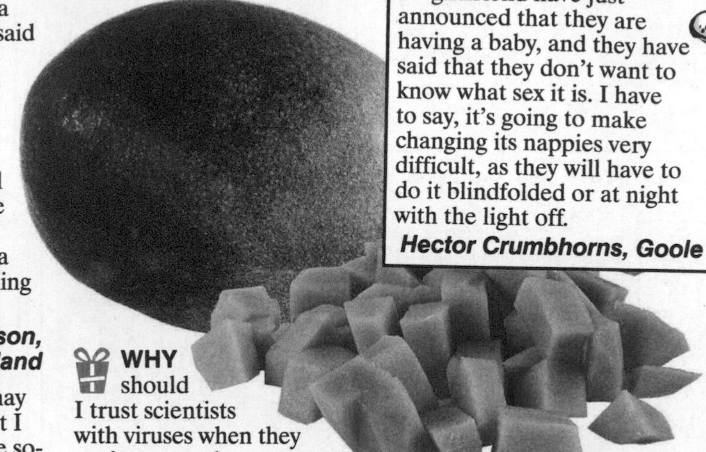

WHY should I trust scientists with viruses when they can't even make a mango with edible skin? Come on, scientists. If you can make smooth-skinned peaches, I'm sure you can make it possible to eat a mango like an apple.

Yarners, London

WITH reference to the above letter. I won't hold my breath waiting for scientists to make a mango with an edible skin. We've been waiting for decades for them to find cures for diseases, develop drought resistant plants and discover ever smaller sub-atomic particles. But no, that's too much to ask. They're all too busy swanning about their laboratories in their white coats like Lord Muck, calling each other Dr this, and Professor that, and giving each other Nobel prizes right, left and centre. Work-shy fuckers, the lot of them.

Hubert Lanceboil, Derby

HOW come you never see those man-powered trolleys with the seesaw-type mechanism on train tracks any more? They used to be in all the films. Come on, Hollywood. Bring them back and give us all a laugh in these difficult times.

Tony Steward, W Drayton

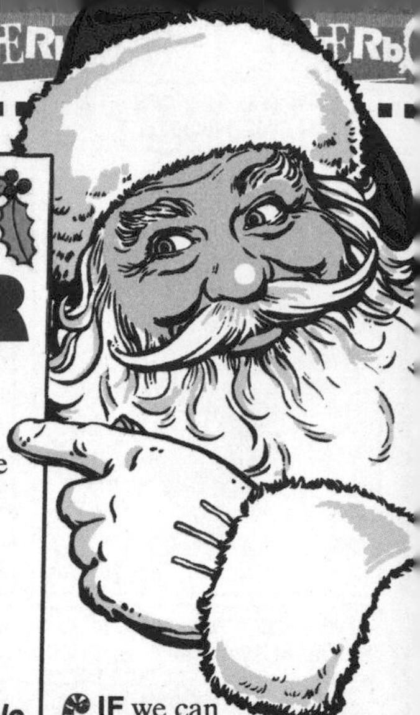

STAR LETTER

MY nephew and his girlfriend have just announced that they are having a baby, and they have said that they don't want to know what sex it is. I have to say, it's going to make changing its nappies very difficult, as they will have to do it blindfolded or at night with the light off.

Hector Crumbhorns, Goole

HAVE any other readers noticed that there are no emergency stop buttons or handles like they have on trains for passengers on aeroplanes? As usual it's one rule for rail passengers and another for the rest of us.

Col P Fawcett, Durham

IT'S become fashionable recently to view films and television shows from the past and find them problematic or 'unwoke.' However, it is not always the case. I rewatched a German porn film called *Nun Fuckers* yesterday which I first saw in the early 90s, and it was fucking great then, and it's fucking great now.

James Millar, Sutton

THEY say chocolate is poisonous for dogs. Now I may not be a dog, but I regularly eat chocolate and it's never done me any harm.

Mikery Stroudbarston, Worcester

I TRAINED our dog to lick my bollocks using Nutella as a treat. However, the other day he went too far and I had to tell my wife that I got caught up on some barbed wire.

Bob Coombs, email

IF we can have wind-up radios and torches, why can't we have other appliances that can be powered in the same way? I for one would like to survive the forthcoming winter of discontent with its gas, electricity and petrol shortages, so a wind-up cooker, TV and central heating would be great. James Dyson should earn his knighthood and get to work on it right away. What do we pay these 'so-called' scientists for?

T.ONeill, Glasgow

I KNOW a bloke called Jonny Foreigner… and he's English. It just goes to show anything is possible these days.

Ian Webb, Bury St Edmunds

GROWING up in the 1980s, my mum regularly put the fear of God into me with tales about catching rabies. I'm now a parent myself, but not once have I passed this irrational anxiety on to my own children. So come on, modern mums and dads. Let's bring back the good old-fashioned fear of rabies, and give the current snowflake generation something to really worry about.

Tom Muskett, Huddersfield

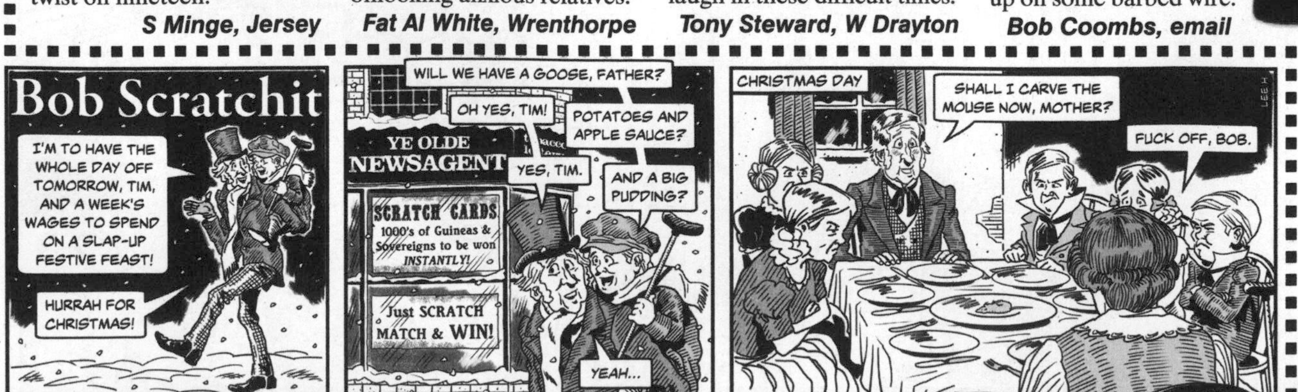
Bob Scratchit
I'M TO HAVE THE WHOLE DAY OFF TOMORROW, TIM, AND A WEEK'S WAGES TO SPEND ON A SLAP-UP FESTIVE FEAST!
HURRAH FOR CHRISTMAS!
WILL WE HAVE A GOOSE, FATHER?
OH YES, TIM!
POTATOES AND APPLE SAUCE?
YES, TIM.
AND A BIG PUDDING?
YE OLDE NEWSAGENT
SCRATCH CARDS 1000's of Guineas & Sovereigns to be won INSTANTLY!
Just SCRATCH MATCH & WIN!
YEAH...
CHRISTMAS DAY
SHALL I CARVE THE MOUSE NOW, MOTHER?
FUCK OFF, BOB.

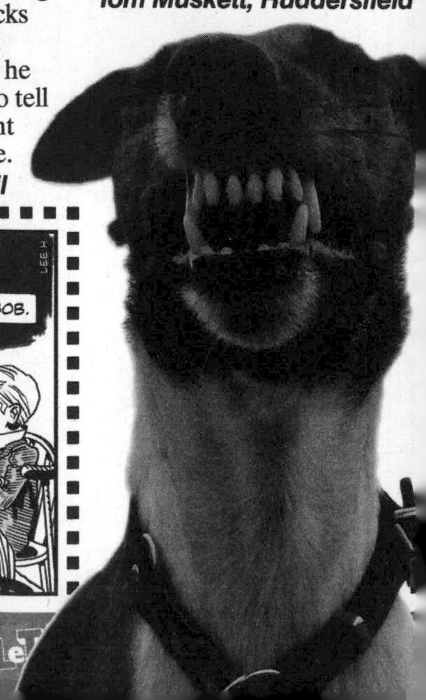

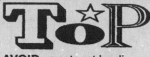

APPARENTLY, there are more people alive today than have ever lived in all of human history. It must therefore follow that there are more living people than there can possibly be ghosts. So I would suggest that ghosts are nothing to be scared of because we outnumber them, and quite frankly, they should stop all the rattling chains and woooing noises and wind their fucking necks in.

Dawn Chorus, Cornwall

I RECENTLY started writing a musical about Brenda Blethyn simply called *Brenda*. However, I had to stop because I realised that I know nothing about her, and in addition, I can't write music.

Michael Mathew, Watford

I RECKON I could easily be the Olympic 100 metres champion if I could be arsed. Do any other readers believe they could easily be world champion at something if only they could be arsed?

Ian Webb, Bury St Edmunds

** That's an interesting question to ask our readers, Mr Webb. What is it you would be best in the world at, but you just can't be arsed? Perhaps you would be the World Chess Champion if you could be bothered. Or maybe you can't be arsed to break the world high jump record. Or perhaps you have the world's best selling book of all time in your head, but you're just too apathetic to get it down on paper. Write in and let us know, if you can be arsed, of course.*

COME on, train drivers. It wouldn't hurt you to stop at a level crossing and let pedestrians and traffic pass for a change. Just once in a while.

D Williams, Donegal

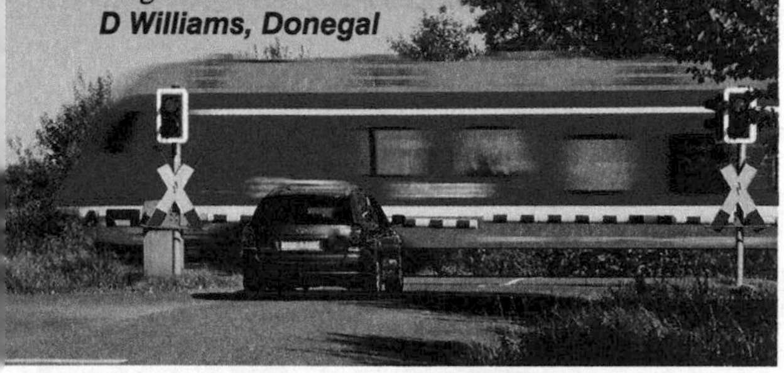

TOP TIPS

AVOID your toast landing butter side down by throwing it in a horizontal frisbee motion with the butter facing upwards.

Domingo, Little Oakley

FOOL your wife into having a threesome by getting her to sit on her left hand before wanking you off, so it feels to her like somebody else's wife is doing it.

Andrew McGuigan, Blaydon

PSYCHIC mediums. Save money on air conditioning by inviting ghosts to come among you in the hot summer months, bringing their sudden drops in temperature with them.

Dave Vicarage, Toad in the Hole

FILM makers. When making a 6-part drama, including a sex scene in the first two minutes of episode one ensures that people will watch every episode of the series to the very end. Well, it does me, anyway.

Tommy Nylander, Derby

WHEN buying a new car, always take your garage door to make sure the car will fit inside.

Michael Thompson, Wales

DEVIL Worshippers. Save money on heating bills by summoning the devil in the cold winter months, bringing the warmth from the fiery pit of Hell with him.

Dave Vicarage, Toad in the Hole

toptips@viz.co.uk

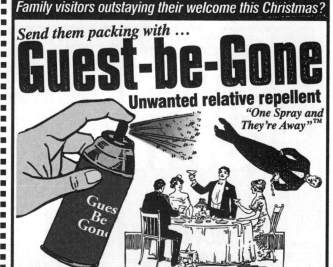

WHY are tigers endangered but lions aren't? I'd much rather have a lion skin rug in my living room than a tiger one. Those stripes wouldn't go with my curtains.

Greg Alam, Hanham

SPIDERS would have far more luck catching flies if they spun their webs over dog shit or across a cow's arse. There you go, spiders. You can thank me later.

D Attenborough, London

A LOT of hard working people in this country are struggling to make ends meet. Yet football clubs are rewarding their players by making them millionaires for kicking a football about each week, which doesn't seem fair. Why don't these clubs give one or two ordinary people a run-out for their team every Saturday and pay them in line with their professional players? It wouldn't disadvantage a team in a match if both sides did it, and a single 60-70 minute run-out for any Premier League side would set them up for life.

John Mason, email

IN the article *15 Things You Never Knew About Chess (page 92)*, you state there are only twelve possible opening moves in a game. This is bullshit, as each prawn could advance either one or two spaces forward, making a total of twenty moves - along with the four moves the knights could make. Furthermore, the white player may choose to just sack the whole thing off and surrender his king for his opening gambit, so he can do something more worthwhile with his time instead, like going to the pub or having a wank. So that's twenty-one moves.

Dave Sayers, Beverley

YOU can keep your Pyramids at Giza, your Great Walls of China and your Roman Colosseums. The humble ROAD is constantly overlooked when discussing great feats of engineering. They are the longest man-made structures on the planet but you don't see coachloads of tourists pulling up to have their picture taken with them. Maybe you should think about that next time you stop for a piss on the A303 on your way to Stonehenge.

D Williams, Donegal

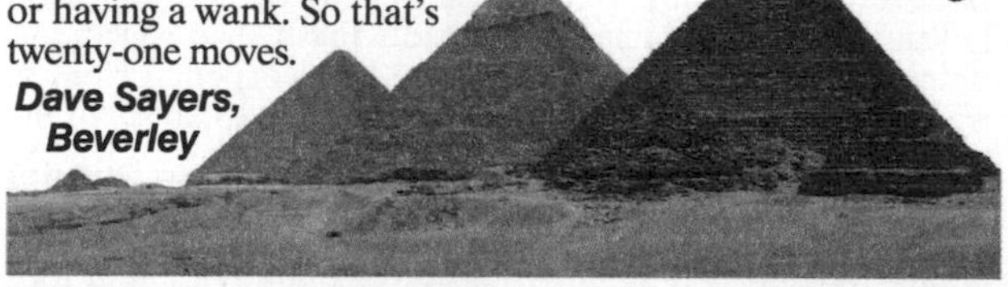

THE other day I attempted some humour by doing the old 'pull my finger' fart routine. However, I had forgotten that a few days earlier I had dislocated the finger that was to be pulled, and when my mate tugged it, I gave out an almighty scream, together with a much louder than normal fart. It left my mate genuinely stunned and horrified at the pain he'd caused me, and any humour was lost in the moment. I also got more than I'd bargained for, as I had to give my bum a wipe and, if truth be told, I probably should have changed my underpants too.

Ken, Barlow

WE have unisex toilets at my work, and while I was waiting for a free cubicle, a female colleague exited one declaring "that smell in there wasn't me." Correct me if I'm wrong, but any bloke would have proudly accepted full responsibility for the eye-watering stench that assaulted my olfactory senses. This gender equality thing is clearly nonsense.

Mike Tatham, St. Andrews

DOES anyone know if there is an emoji for a swollen scrotum? I can't find one on my iPhone and it's rather urgent.

Boody, Chesvegas

WHY do boxers take such long breaks between fights? In my local boozer last month, Wee Davie and Mad Mick went outside and knocked the shit out of each other all over some woman. And the very next week, it happened again. If they were professional boxers, the re-match would have been several months after.

Dr Doalot, ICU, Glasgow

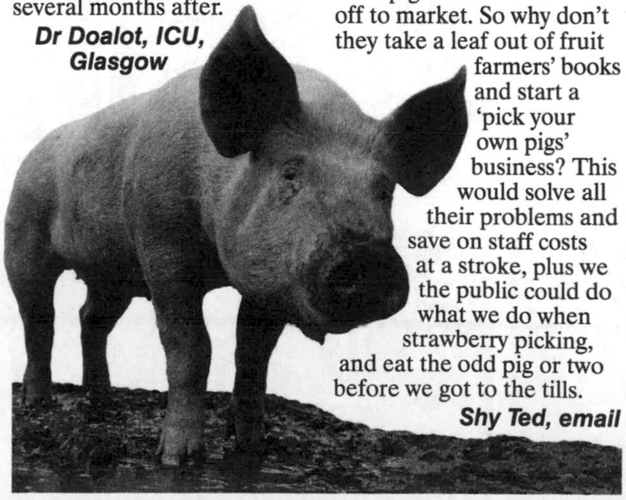

FARMERS are always complaining that they can't get enough slaughtermen to deal with their pigs and send them off to market. So why don't they take a leaf out of fruit farmers' books and start a 'pick your own pigs' business? This would solve all their problems and save on staff costs at a stroke, plus we the public could do what we do when strawberry picking, and eat the odd pig or two before we got to the tills.

Shy Ted, email

Have Your Say

LAST MONTH we heard *One Britain, One Nation* sung for the first time. This wonderful and inspiring anthem sings of Britain's place in the world as a shining example of fairness, tolerance and respect. The vast majority of us listened with a lump in our throat, and the Department of Education backed the song and suggested that it should be sung each morning in schools. Not surprisingly, your letters about it have come flooding in. Of course, there were a few unpatriotic nay-sayers who wrote in critical of this anthem to patriotism, and we put their traitorous missives straight in the fucking bin.

...**I THINK** *One Britain, One Nation* is a marvellous song. It tells of what a wonderful country we are, of our great democracy, and our tolerance and sense of fair play as a nation. In fact, rather than just school children singing it, I think we should all sing it every morning. Anyone found not singing it could be given a fine in the first instance, and if they continued to refuse, they could be sent to some sort of government-run camp for 'rehabilitation.'

Ada Ballsover, Bolsover

...**IT'S A** wonderful song that sings of our free, democratic nation, and everyone should be forced to sing it every morning. Schoolteachers could question their pupils about whether their parents sing it or not, and people could be encouraged to inform on their non-singing neigbours.

Doris Weasel, Stoke

...**BRITAIN** has been divided for too long, and singing this song every morning is a wonderful way to unite us. And I think that if all 60 million of us wore the same drab-looking uniform, this would help us once again celebrate the fact that we truly are One Nation.

Stan Gormless, Bude

...**A SONG** instilling pride in our nation is a wonderful thing, and we have many things of which to be proud. We invented the jet engine and discovered penicillin. We worked out the complex nature of DNA and led the way in producing the world's first Covid vaccine. I say "we" - I didn't play any part in these myself. I was expelled from school when I was thirteen for burning the library down and I've spent my adult life in and out of prison, but you get my point.

Eddie Burntoast, Carlisle

...**I THINK** it's a wonderful idea as there is nothing like a song to bring people together. I remember that sense of unity I felt at football matches in the 70s, singing *"You can stuff Derek Dougan up your arse"* along with my 50,000 fellow supporters. The Wolves fans didn't like it very much, but there will always be whingers.

Barry Cheeseminger, Birmingham

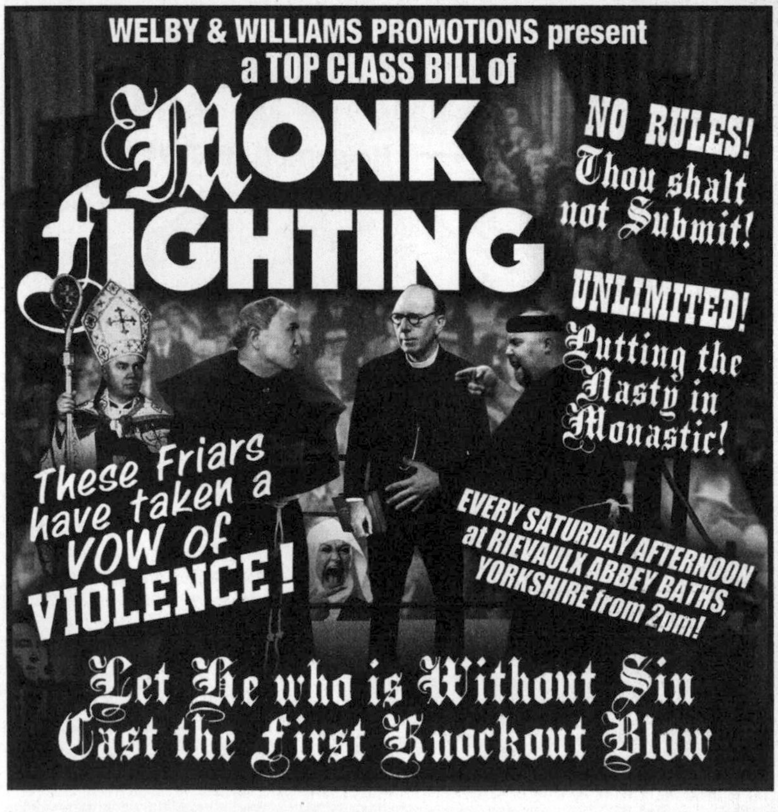

WELBY & WILLIAMS PROMOTIONS present
a TOP CLASS BILL of
MONK FIGHTING
NO RULES!
Thou shalt not Submit!
UNLIMITED!
Putting the Nasty in Monastic!
These Friars have taken a VOW of VIOLENCE!
EVERY SATURDAY AFTERNOON at RIEVAULX ABBEY BATHS, YORKSHIRE from 2pm!
Let He who is Without Sin Cast the First Knockout Blow

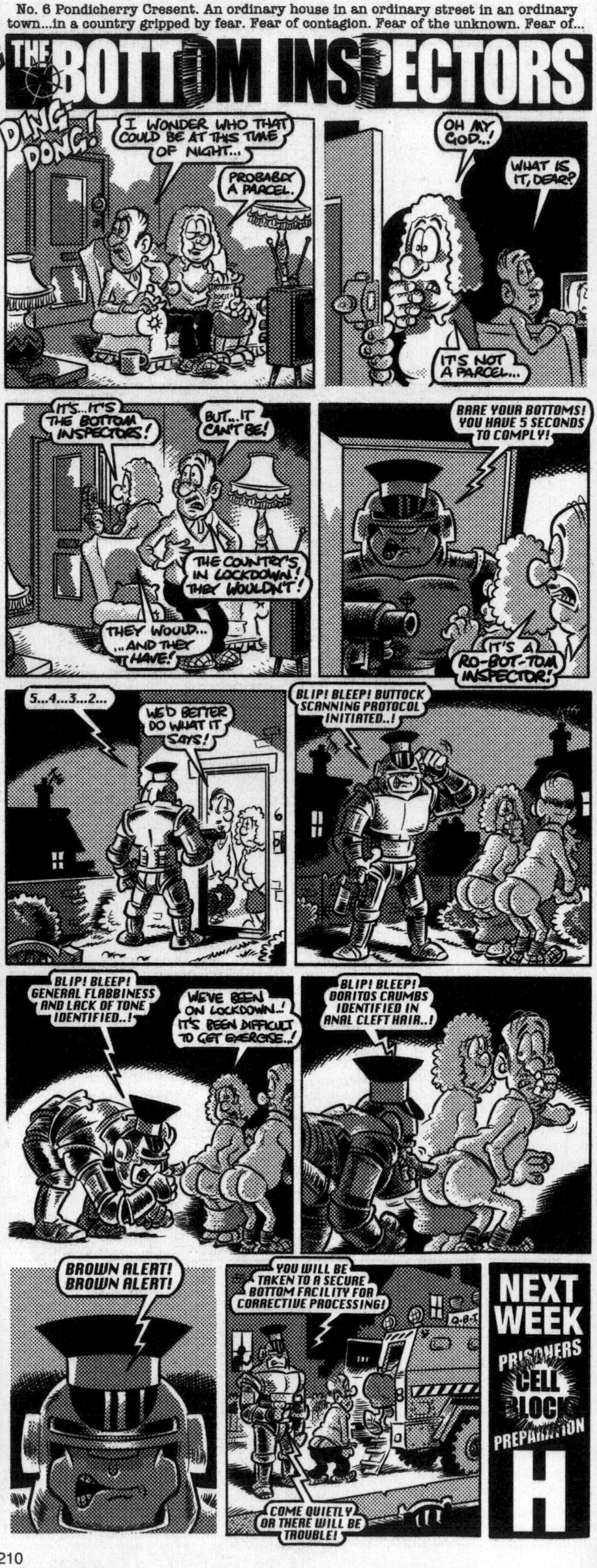

No. 6 Pondicherry Cresent. An ordinary house in an ordinary street in an ordinary town...in a country gripped by fear. Fear of contagion. Fear of the unknown. Fear of...
THE BOTTOM INSPECTORS
DING DONG!
I WONDER WHO THAT COULD BE AT THIS TIME OF NIGHT...
PROBABLY A PARCEL.
OH MY GOD..!
WHAT IS IT, DEAR?
IT'S NOT A PARCEL...
IT'S...IT'S THE BOTTOM INSPECTORS!
BUT...IT CAN'T BE!
THE COUNTRY'S IN LOCKDOWN! THEY WOULDN'T!
THEY WOULD... ...AND THEY HAVE!
BARE YOUR BOTTOMS! YOU HAVE 5 SECONDS TO COMPLY!
IT'S A RO-BOT-TOM INSPECTOR!
5...4...3...2...
WE'D BETTER DO WHAT IT SAYS!
BLIP! BLEEP! BUTTOCK SCANNING PROTOCOL INITIATED..!
BLIP! BLEEP! GENERAL FLABBINESS AND LACK OF TONE IDENTIFIED..!
WE'VE BEEN ON LOCKDOWN..! IT'S BEEN DIFFICULT TO GET EXERCISE..!
BLIP! BLEEP! DORITOS CRUMBS IDENTIFIED IN ANAL CLEFT HAIR..!
BROWN ALERT! BROWN ALERT!
YOU WILL BE TAKEN TO A SECURE BOTTOM FACILITY FOR CORRECTIVE PROCESSING!
COME QUIETLY OR THERE WILL BE TROUBLE!
NEXT WEEK
H

JOCKEY'S WHIPS

THE LIFE of a jockey is surely one of the most glamorous imaginable. Driving to racecourses the length and breadth of the land in order to dress up in a gaily-coloured clown costume with a big hat before sitting on a horse doing 50mph for ninety seconds. It's a lifestyle most of us can only dream of.

But that is not the half of it, according to one Wetherby-based jockey, who says the rewards of winning races are nothing compared to the perks of the job off the track.

Tip-top: Jockey Bismuth found plenty of riches off the turf.

Chips Were Down

Jonny Bismuth is a veteran of over 10,000 flat and steeplechase races, notching up 3 wins and 520 unseatings in his 8-year career.

"I remember one time going to get some chips for my dinner," he told the *Wetherby Avulsion and Fracture*. "I was the only customer in the shop and I was chatting with the woman serving me. When I told her I was a jockey, she asked me if I had any tips. *'Yes, never bet on the horses!'* I replied. It's what I always say in response to this question and it always brings the house down. The chip-shop woman chuckled. 'No, seriously,' she said. 'I'll make it worth your while.'

favourite

It just so happened that I was racing at Chepstow the following day, and the horse I was on - the firm favourite - was going to be nobbled with tranquilisers to let one of the back runners win. I gave her the name of the winner, which she wrote down on a piece of chip wrapping paper, and I told her to put everything she had on it and pay the tax first.

She looked me in the eye and said: 'Thanks for that. Now let me do something for you.' She was

Fries on the prize: Chippy tip led to bigger portions for Johnny.

EXCLUSIVE!

wearing one of those white trilby hats with a net at the back, and I thought she was going to take it off and shake her long, golden hair loose. But she didn't.

Nevertheless, I walked out of that shop with a bag of chips that was much bigger than the usual portion, with free batter bits, which they normally charge you 10 pence for. That was six years ago, and I get extra chips and free batter every time I go in that shop. You should see the envious looks on all the other customers' faces."

Flat Tip Pen

Jonny makes his living participating in horse races, but his insider knowledge means that he makes money betting on them too. And on one occasion, he won a little more than cash.

"It was one of my days off, and I'd gone into a bookies in Wetherby to put some money on a horse that had been given a dose of testosterone and thyroxine to give it an edge. I knew the information was reliable because it was me that gave it the injection that morning at the stable.

The bookie behind the counter recognised me and asked if I had any tips. He tried to sound as though he was joking, but I knew he wasn't. His face was a picture of seriousness when he opened his till and said that we could surely come to an arrangement. Selling information that could affect the betting odds of a race is illegal under

Jockey Club rules - the equivalent of insider trading. If I revealed the race was fixed in return for money, I would be breaking those rules, which I couldn't in all conscience do, and I told him so.

'Okay, let's take money out of the equation,' he said, putting a pile of small, bookies' biros on the counter. There must have been fifty of them at least, and I looked at them for a few seconds. 'There's more where they came from,' he said quietly.

polo

The upshot is, I walked out of that bookies with 100 little biros in my pocket. I felt a bit giddy at the thought that I would never need to buy a pen ever again."

Sick As A Carrot

The life of a jockey may be glamorous, but it is also hard work, and when Bismuth is not in the saddle, chances are he is in the race yard, grooming the horses or mucking out the stables.

"I remember once I was serving a two-week suspension for excessive use of the whip, so I'd been on yard duty for a fortnight. I don't mind mucking stables out, as it gives you time to reflect, and the yard owner lets you take as much manure as you like. It's no use to me as I live above a butcher's shop in Wetherby, but for some of the other lads who have gardens or allotments, it's just another great perk of the job.

I was looking forward to riding in my first race after my suspension the following day, so I was disappointed when my boss came over and said he wanted me to throw the race. 'I don't care what you do,' he told me. 'Stay in the stalls, refuse a fence, fall off. Anything, just don't come higher than fifth.'

sweat

Now, when every jockey mounts their steed, they intend to win the race. It goes against every fibre of their being not to give 100%, and I told my boss this. He shook his head slowly, then turned it in the direction of the feed shed.

'That's a pity,' he said, sadly. 'I'm going to have to throw that bag of horse carrots away, now.'

I looked and saw a 20 kilogramme bag of horse carrots leaning against the shed door. Horse carrots are sold as 'not for human consumption' but they are absolutely fine if you peel them properly and boil them for a bit longer, and my boss was implying that they were mine if I would throw the race.

I felt ashamed of myself as I took the horse carrots home that night. But I needn't have done because I didn't need to throw the race as I fell off completely by accident anyway. So I ended up with the carrots and a clear conscience."

NEXT WEEK: Jonny tells how his barber gave him 10% off a haircut and singe in return for the names of the horses that were going to be spiked with ketamine before the Grand National.

RICH AS CREASES

Professional gambler shares his tips on making it rich

A FOOL and his money are soon parted, so the saying goes. But Barton Creases would have to disagree. "I've still got all my money, and plenty more to boot," he says. For Creases has spent his life amassing a fortune plying his trade as a professional gambler.

And the Osset-based 56-year-old says he has never regretted cashing in his chips as a plumber for the high-rolling life of a chance-taker.

"I left school at 16 and started an apprenticeship as a plumber, but after three days, I knew that life wasn't for me and I jacked it in," he says. "And I'd always been a bit of a gambler at school – betting 50p on which teacher would come out the staffroom next, 20p on the outcome of a fight in the bike sheds, that sort of thing – so I thought *why not do it for a living?"*

Barton took his chance, and for the last 40 years has been living a life that many of us can only dream of, rubbing shoulders with the rich and famous at Wetherby Racecourse, the Casino Tropicana in Dewsbury, and Kinsley Greyhound Stadium.

"I made mistakes in the early days and lost big," Barton admits. "But like everything, practice makes perfect, and for the last couple of years I've been at the top of my gambling game."

And now Creases, who supplements his income with Universal Credit, is sharing the secrets of his glamorous lifestyle with *Viz* readers. Here, in his own words, are the dos and don'ts of the gamble game. "Take my advice and tip the odds in your favour!" he says.

The Casino

"NOTHING conjures up the romance and excitement of the gambler's life more than the casino. Whether you're sitting next to a spy at the roulette wheel in Monte Carlo Bay, or pushing pound coins into the slots in the High Rollerz in Wakefield, these glitzy palaces of risk and chance make easy pickings for the gambler if you follow a few simple rules.

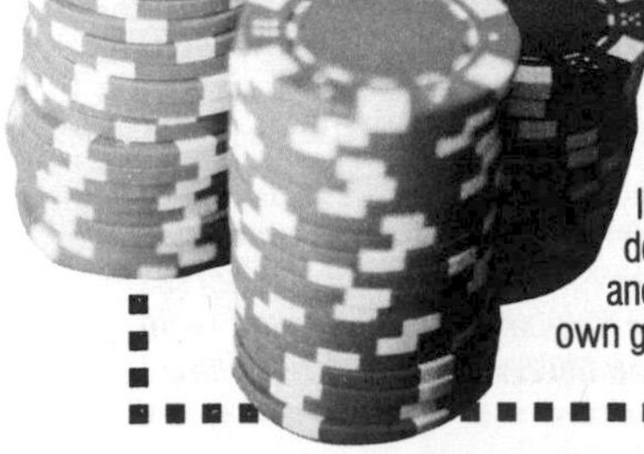

At the roulette wheel, don't just pick a colour and stick with it, watch for patterns emerging. The chance of the ball landing on the same colour five times in a row must be a thousand-to-one. If it drops on black four times, it's a thousand-to-one against the same thing happening on the next spin, so shove everything you have on red. Kerching! You'll be quids in! But try to be nonchalant about it. The management don't like it when punters start doing maths in their head and beating them at their own game.

If roulette isn't your thing, then there's easy money to pick up at the Black Jack table. The dealer has orders from the boss to twist on seventeen or under without exception, like a robot. You can use your brainpower to assess the situation and make a rational decision, so you are in the driving seat at every deal. If you go one higher and twist on eighteen or below, you'll beat the house every time, or at least you will in the long run. I don't quite understand the maths, but it's something to do with high card numbers being less likely to be dealt than lower ones, and I'm surprised the casinos haven't cottoned onto this. You may have to chase your losses a bit, possibly for a few months or years, but the numbers are on your side, so you're guaranteed to come out on top eventually."

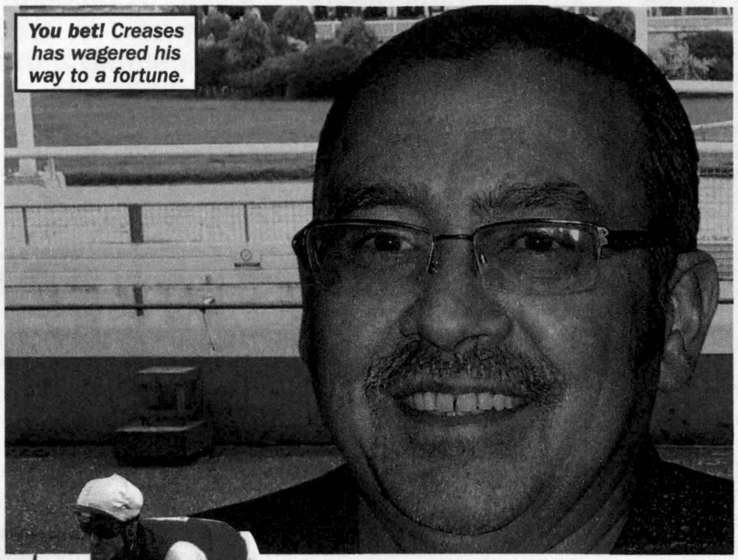

You bet! Creases has wagered his way to a fortune.

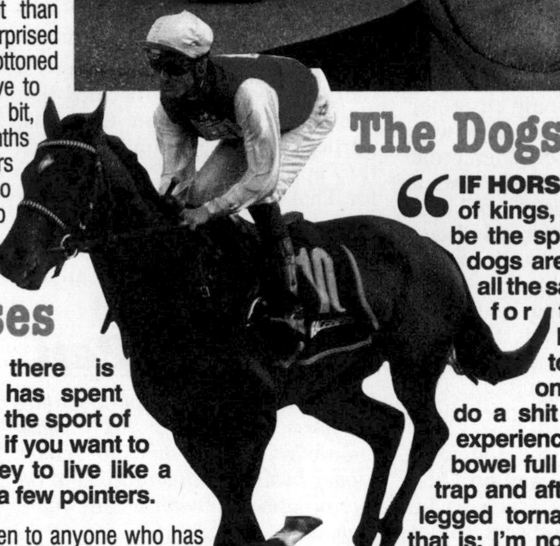

The Horses

"I DOUBT there is anyone who has spent more time studying the sport of kings than me. And if you want to make enough money to live like a king, then here are a few pointers.

First of all, don't listen to anyone who has a "red-hot tip" for you. Chances are, they'll be a bookie's runner who is simply trying to shorten the odds to get more fools to have a flutter on a no-hoper. Remember that everyone is out for themselves in this game, and if anyone is giving you tips on how to beat the bookies, they're taking you for a mug.

After betting on the nags for forty years, I've noticed that horses with a little white patch of fur between the eyes win much more often than those without, and I've concluded that running fast and having a white patch must be in the genes. It's simple science, and it works. So much so that many trainers paint one of the white marks in to make their horses go faster. Put everything you have on any horse with one of those markings and you'll go home happy.

Handicap stakes also offer the seasoned gambler a chance to coin it in. In these races, horses that have won a lot of prize money are disadvantaged with weights under their saddle. The more they have won, the heavier the weight – the idea being that all the runners have an equal chance of winning. So any nag that does an enormous big shit in the parade ring before the off automatically has the advantage and is worth putting your shirt on."

The Dogs

"IF HORSE RACING is the sport of kings, then dog racing must be the sport of princes, and as dogs are just like little horses, all the same rules apply, except for the one about shitting before a race. That is to say, put your money on any dog that *doesn't* do a shit before the off. In my experience, a greyhound with a bowel full of dog-eggs is out the trap and after the hare like a four-legged tornado. I'm not sure why that is; I'm not a biologist. But I *am* a professional gambler, and take my word for it, it's good advice.

Another thing to take into account is colour. The dogs in the UK follow a standard system of coat colours -red, blue, white, black, orange and black and white stripes for traps 1 to 6 respectively. Dogs can only see in black and white, so only the dog in the stripes will be visible to the pack, and this means he can't sneak up on the others, so is at a disadvantage.

Another reason to stay clear of the dog in trap 6, when you think about it, is that this dog is at another disadvantage because it has much further to run than all the others. I have to admit, I'm staggered that the bookies haven't spotted this flaw. In fact, the dog on the inside trap has got the upper paw on the other five, unless, of course, its bowels are empty. My golden rule is, work from the inside trap outwards, and bet on the first dog that hasn't had a shit unless it's the dog in trap 6, in which case bet on the dog in trap 1."

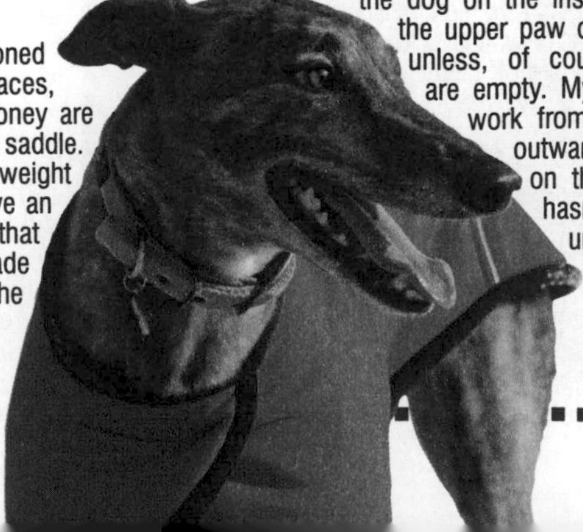

The Fruit Machines

“ADMITTEDLY, the bandits are not the most glamorous form of gambling. It's hard to imagine that Pussy Galore would have been so impressed by James Bond if he had been shovelling coins into a fruitie, rather than sitting at the roulette wheel in a tuxedo. But they do offer the chance to make some serious money if you know what you are doing.

What you have to remember is that the bandits are machines – highly sophisticated robotic machines with AI, but machines nevertheless – and as such, they will never be able to outsmart the human mind. If you are offered a chance to hold and nudge, here's a tip. By squatting down and looking up at the wheels, it is possible to see what the next turn will bring. This gives you a distinct advantage over the bandit. It staggers me that the manufacturers have not yet cottoned on to this flaw.

But the best tip I can give for the fruities is to be patient. Like when you eat a big meal, it's got to come out eventually, and the more you stuff your face, the sooner it's going to happen. And exactly the same is true of the bandits. Watch out for less experienced gamblers wasting their money, shovelling it in the slots until they are broke. When they go, they leave the machines with a bandit equivalent of the turtle's head, bursting to release their load. Just a pound or two from you will release the jackpot. If it doesn't, simply keep going… it will come eventually.”

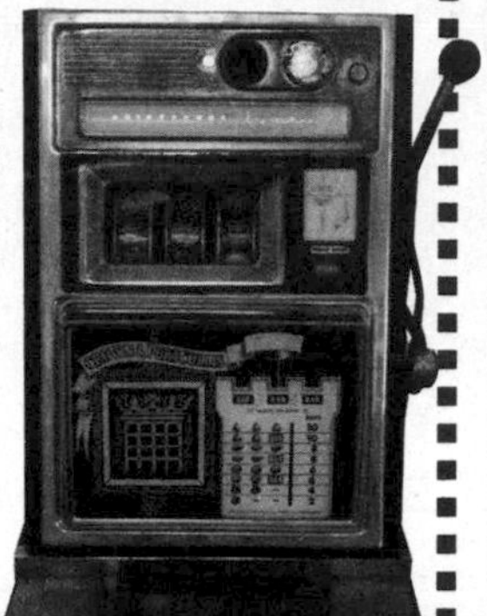

The Illegal Dog Fight

“ANIMAL RIGHTS enthusiasts would have you believe that getting two dogs to fight to the death for our entertainment is cruel beyond belief. But what they are forgetting is that these Covid-19 pandemic times have seen many horse and greyhound race meetings cancelled. Remember, the chancellor's furlough scheme does not stretch to professional gamblers, and we would otherwise lose our livelihoods if these fights did not continue. We should be clapping the dogfight organisers on a Thursday night.

As for gambling tips, I would say *avoid betting on either dog*, as very often neither animal makes it, in which case all bets are off, and trying to get your stake back off the 'bookie' is often quite a dangerous task. Wait until they bring out a badger before you put your hand in your pocket. Again, the animal rights loonies would say that getting a dog to tear a badger to pieces for sport is a little cruel, but don't forget that badgers are Britain's largest carnivores. In addition, they are no longer an endangered species, and they all have TB or some such disease. And the fight is simply nature in action, red in tooth and claw. And as the badger will have had all of these snapped off before the fight, put your money on the dog every time whatever odds they offer you.”

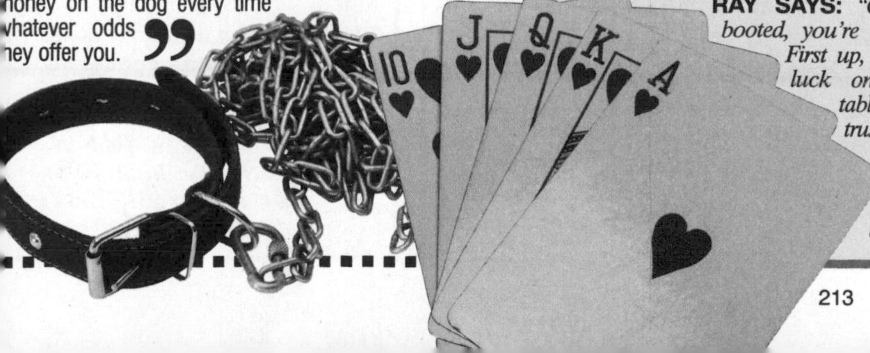
10
J
Q
K
A

HEDGE YOUR BETS

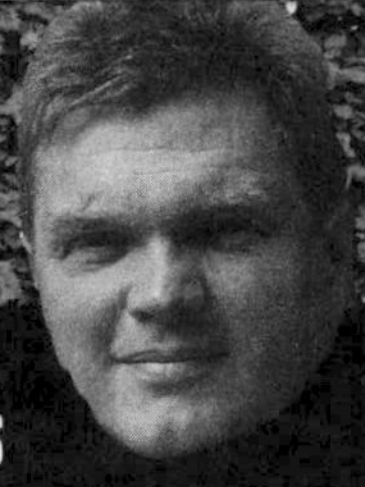

YOUR guide to gambling in the wilderness, with salad-averse TV woodsman RAY MEARS

BRITAIN is a nation of shopkeepers. And those shops are *betting shops*, because Britain is also a nation of gamblers. From Land's End to John O'Groats, every single one of us loves a flutter. But what if the unthinkable happened one day, and we took a wrong turning en route to our beloved local bookies and ended up lost in the woods? Trapped in such a hostile and merciless environment with no access to fruit machines, craps tables or roulette wheels, would we really be able to cope?

The simple answer is YES. Because we've teamed up with stocky survivalist RAY MEARS to show YOU how to forage your very own CASINO from the forest floor! So join Ray as he presents a step-by-step guide to sating YOUR ruinous gambling addiction using only the detritus from Mother Nature's bounty.

THE ATTIRE

RAY SAYS: *“Every self-respecting casino boasts a strict dress code, and your woodland gambling den should be no different. The good news is that making a dapper tuxedo from nature's harvest is both simple and fun. First, stitch a stylish jacket and trousers out of fallen leaves using a pine needle and bindweed 'thread.' Once finished, soak your trendy suit in crushed berries or faeces to turn it jet black. Accessorise with chic button mushroom or ladybird 'cufflinks' before stretching a dead bat around your neck as a bow-tie. And if you fancy whetting your whistle before you hit the tables, simply blend your very own wilderness cocktail using a mish-mash of the surrounding edible foodstuffs and drinkables. How about a buttercup and badger urine Martini - shaken, not stirred?”*

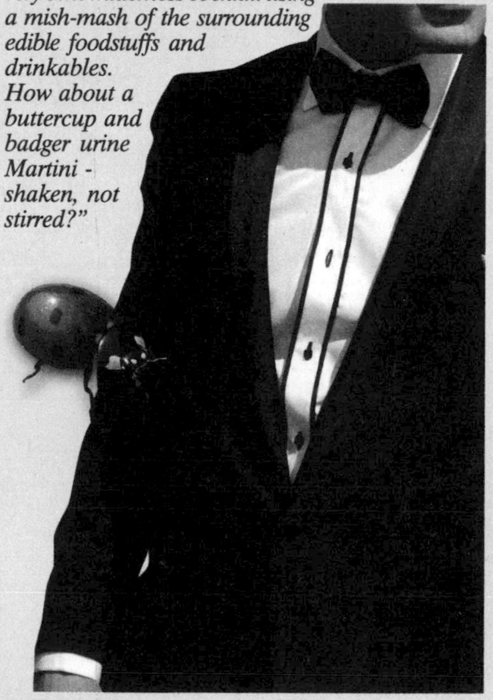

THE GAMES

RAY SAYS: *“Once suited and booted, you're ready to gamble. First up, why not try your luck on the Blackjack table? Using your trusty penknife, carve out a large D-shaped clump of green turf, and balance it on top of a nearby tree stump. If there aren't any tree stumps, simply use your penknife to cut down a tree. For your deck, trap 26 butterflies and pull their wings off. Hey presto! – 52 beautifully adorned playing cards! Daub the numbers and suits on them using squashed blackberries for spades and clubs, and redcurrants for hearts and diamonds – then get dealing! If you fancy a spin on the roulette wheel, simply locate one of the many cars that will have been abandoned in the woods following a dogging session, and remove a hubcap. Glue thin twigs around the edges with tree sap to create ridges, before adding red and black colouring with your leftover berries. A week-old rabbit dropping makes an ideal ball to be tossed in as you spin the wheel. Faites vos jeux!”*

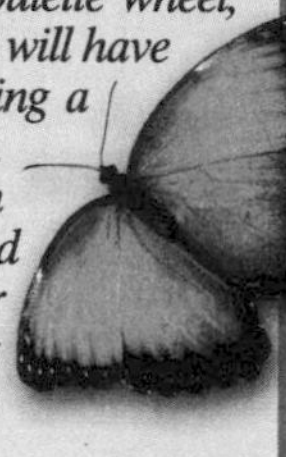

THE MONEY

RAY SAYS: *“Lost in the wilderness miles from human civilisation, paper notes and metal coins will be of little use to either you or your casino clientele. Instead, encourage your punters to bet with items that will aid survival in the great outdoors, such as food, water, shelter or dock leaves. If any of your clients suffer particularly heavy losses at the blackjack table or roulette hubcap, they may need a little Las Vegas-style 'encouragement' to settle their tab. In this eventuality, simply fix a large rock to a solid tree branch to create a rudimentary sledgehammer, perfect for kneecapping any overdue debtors. Additionally, four snails can be transformed into an effective knuckle duster by simply wrapping the molluscs' bodies around your fingers and using the shells to punch your late payer hard on the bridge of the nose until you either hear the bone splinter or he pays up. Or both.”*

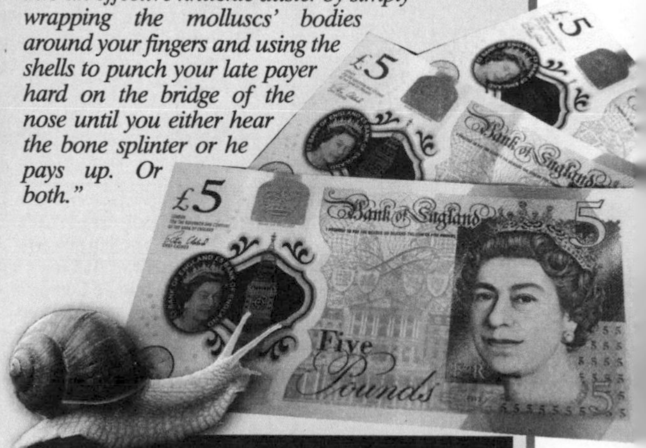
£5
Bank of England
Five Pounds

NEXT WEEK: 'SPACE YOUR BETS!' Professor Brian Cox explains how to remove the fingernails of anyone you find 'counting cards' in zero gravity.

ODDS 'N' GODS

YOUR theological gambling queries, answered by the Archbishop of Canterbury 'Honest' Justin Welby

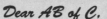

Dear AB of C,

I WAS flicking through the Bible the other day, and I came upon a passage in Exodus where God says, "You cannot see my face, for no man shall see me and live." It struck me that this would give God an unfair advantage during poker games as, since no one's allowed to look at Him, He would not have to perfect His 'poker face' in order to conceal the strength of His cards.

Martin Heathen, Bracknell

The AB of C says: God has no need to adopt a 'poker face', Martin, because He would never play poker. It's not just that He considers gambling a sin, although He probably does, but rather because card games aren't particularly enjoyable for Him, since He knows exactly what cards all the other players have, thus draining all elements of surprise and excitement from any game. This is also why God can't enjoy betting on sport of any kind. The Lord's all-knowing existence is one utterly devoid of wonder, joy or astonishment, and we therefore shouldn't be surprised when He occasionally gets wrathful and sends down a tidal wave or a global pandemic or Russell Brand.

Dear AB of C,

I'VE JUST had a corking little tip off a bloke in the pub about a horse running in the 3.15 at Chepstow. I've stuck the wife's jewellery on it at 25/1 and I was wondering if there was a particular patron saint I could pray to in order to make totally sure that it romps home in first place?

Derek Spivsworth, Margate

The AB of C says: I'm afraid you've got Anglicanism mixed up with Roman Catholicism, Derek. In the C of E, we have vague, non-specific, 'Jacks-of-all-saints' who are trained in general prayer answering. Catholics, on the other hand, have saints who are pigeon-holed into very specific areas. You could certainly try praying to Saint Cajetan, the RC patron saint of good fortune, but if I were you, I'd direct my pleas towards an Anglican saint instead, such as Margery Kempe or the Venerable Bede. They may not possess Cajetan's level of expertise in the field, but the advantage with them is that you will not burn in a lake of fire for all eternity for worshipping false idols. But it's your call.

Dear AB of C,

I'VE JUST won the jackpot on a fruit machine after three apples came up in a row. I'm £45 up, but I just wanted to check that God won't be angry over my win, as I imagine He takes rather a dim view of apples after what happened with Adam and Eve in the Garden of Eden. Do you think God would mind that I've benefited from this apple-based piece of good fortune?

Edith Peel-Sessions, Valhalla

The AB of C says: I think you're probably OK, Edith. The whole Garden of Eden thing was a long time ago and, crucially, it wasn't really the apple that was at fault – it was that foul serpent that did approacheth Adam and Eve and did eggeth them on to eat of it. If you had won with three snakes coming up in a row, God probably wouldn't be quite so forgiving, and would undoubtedly visit a plague of boils or frogs upon you and your family well into the fiftieth generation. But I reckon apples is fine. Go enjoy your £45, safe in the knowledge that God will almost certainly not punish you.

Have YOU got a question about betting, speculating or wagering for financial gain that is in some way linked to the Christian faith? Why not write in to: 'Odds 'n' Gods', c/o 'Honest' Justin Welby, Viz Comic, PO Box 841, Whitley Bay, NE26 9EQ.

BET Viz Presents

TOMMY 'BANANA' JOHNSON

HE'S GOT A BIG BANANA!

Tommy Banana Johnson is an in-cartoon betting strip where you can gamble on the outcome of the story. Start by placing a £5 stake on the first frame, then use your winnings as a stake on the next frame. Keep betting until the end of the cartoon for a jackpot win. Or if you feel your lucky streak is coming to an end, you can cash out at any time. Good luck, and remember — When the fun stops, stop reading!

I THINK I'LL GO TO THE PARK TODAY

AT THE PARK...

OH, DEAR! THIS PAINT IS STILL WET, AND IT LOOKS LIKE IT'S GOING TO RAIN

WET PAINT

"What's Tommy going to suggest the man uses his big banana as? Look at these odds, place your bets, and carry on reading..."

A large umbrella to protect the fence from rain	5/2
A giant hairdryer to dry the paint	7/4 fav
An enormous weather machine to stop the rain	50/1

PLACE YOUR BETS

HEY, MISTER!.. WHY NOT USE MY BANANA AS A GIANT HAIR DRYER TO DRY THE PAINT?

EH!?!

WINNER! A giant hairdryer to dry the paint

Well would you believe it! What are you going to do now? Cash out, or play on..?

CASH OUT / PLAY ON

PISS OFF! AND TAKE YOUR GIANT FRIGGIN' BANANA WITH YOU!

ALRIGHT. I'M GOING

LATER...

HAVE YOU SEEN MY LITTLE DOG ANYWHERE? HE'S GONE MISSING

"Here's a tricky one. What's Tommy going to suggest the man uses his big banana as this time? Do you feel lucky?..."

A giant net to catch his dog	5/1
A massive sonar machine to locate the animal	25/1
A large telescope to look for him	2/1 fav

PLACE YOUR BETS

NO, BUT WHY NOT USE MY BANANA AS A LARGE TELESCOPE TO LOOK FOR HIM?

UH!?

WINNER! A large telescope to look for him

Got it wrong? Bad luck. Got it right? Well done, my son. But what now?...

CASH OUT / PLAY ON

GO ON, FUCK OFF!

...BLOODY BANANA TELESCOPE

SHORTLY...

HEY, TOMMY!..

THAT BANANA IS JUST WHAT I'M LOOKING FOR. COULD I BORROW IT FOR A SECOND?

"Okay, we've come a long way. What's the bobby going to do with Tommy's big banana? Come on... you know the score..."

Stick it down his throat	12/1
Push it up his hog's eye	25/1
Shove it up his arse	evens fav

PLACE YOUR BETS

AAAGH! MY HOG'S EYE!

THAT SHOULD PUT A STOP TO YOUR BANANA PRANKS, EH, TOMMY! HO! HO! HO!

WINNER! Push it up his hog's eye

If you lost, please send your original £5 stake to: *Viz Comic In-Cartoon betting, PO Box 841, Whitley Bay, NE26 9EQ.* If you won or cashed out, write and tell us the value of your winnings and we will send you a cheque in the post. Viz Comic is not responsible for any items lost in the post, and a bloke in the pub told us that gambling debts aren't like normal debts in that they're not legally enforceable.

INCA-REDIBLE!

Essex punter's flutter unlocks age-old mystery

CALLS to ban fixed odds betting terminals have intensified after a machine in a Croydon betting shop paid out big when one surprised punter hit the jackpot... *and won The Secret of the Incas!*

OOH BETTY!
OOH BETTY!
BET NOW!
BET NOW!

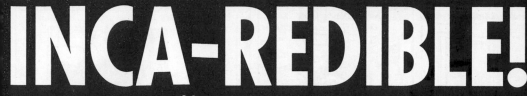

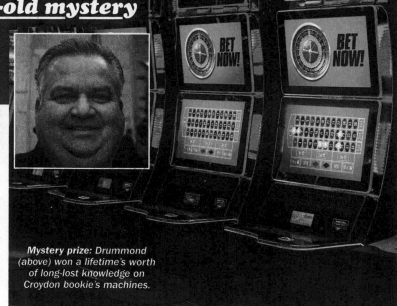

Mystery prize: *Drummond (above) won a lifetime's worth of long-lost knowledge on Croydon bookie's machines.*

Furloughed Essex telesales worker Aken Drummond was playing the machine in William Hill's when the incident took place. *"I was just passing time while I waited for the 2:30 from Haydock Park to start,"* said Aken. *"I'd put about fifteen quid in and won ten back so I was having quite a good session."*

"Then, when I put another quid in and hit the buttons, the screen went black for a second, before flashing up a message saying 'WINNER'. I was over the moon."

jack

Drummond thought he had hit the £200 jackpot and took off his hat to catch the cash as it came out. But his joy turned to surprise as, instead of the jingling cascade of coins he was expecting, the screen informed him that he had won the Secret of the Incas.

The 34-year-old father of two watched as the terminal displayed scrolling text detailing the reasons for the sudden collapse of the ancient South America civilisation in the 16th century, which has mystified scholars for more than 400 years.

"There was a lot of stuff flashing up about why the Incas died out, how some of their technological innovations really worked, where their sacred scrolls are to be found, that sort of thing," Drummond told reporters. "It was really interesting."

vera

Gambling watchdogs were quick to condemn the development. "This represents a new low for the betting industry," said Simon Cushioncover, chair of FlutterAnon. "For years we've been warning about the easy gratification offered by these enticing, gaudy machines."

"It was bad enough when it was a monetary prize on offer, but now they've started doling out the answers to perplexing, centuries-old conundra, I can only see the problem worsening."

spender

And it seems that the watchdog's fears may have been realised already, as Drummond admitted that he immediately put more money into the machine. "There was a bit about a Neo-Inca state being established in the mountains of Vilcabamba, but I didn't quite catch it," he said. "So I fed another thirty-five quid in trying to win again."

"I ended up forty quid down. I've no idea what I'm going to tell the wife. That was the electricity money," he added.

But a spokesman for FrutieBandit Ltd, the manufacturers of the machines, said the company stood by the decision to offer the answers to long sought-after questions as prizes. "We've got plans to introduce a machine where the players instantly win answers to riddles like *'What happened on the Marie Celeste?'* and *'Does Bigfoot really exist?'*," he said.

"If they accumulate enough of these credits, punters can cash them in for the secret of eternal life."

It's a fair BET you'll find the top Incan Empire EXCLUSIVES in your No.1 VIZ!

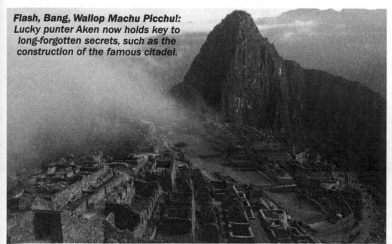

Flash, Bang, Wallop Machu Picchu!: *Lucky punter Aken now holds key to long-forgotten secrets, such as the construction of the famous citadel.*

FANCY A FLUTTER FROM THE OTHER SIDE?

BETDEAD
AFTERLIFE BOOKMAKERS

Don't let being DEAD stop you enjoying a little punt on the horses or putting a tenner on a footie match.

BETDEAD will take your bets, *whatever your state of existence!*

Simply leave all your money to us in your will, and we'll open an account for you to use on the other side. Then place your bets via our dedicated turf accountant mediums.

£
£
£
£
£

FREE £20 BET with every new account.

"I had a red hot tip on the Grand National, but I was knocked over by a bus the week before. Fortunately, I had left all my money to BetDead and I was able to stick a monkey on Mr Bojangles who romped home at 13/2"
Mr B, Essex

"I was disappointed to pop my clogs from a heart attack at the dogs after only three cards of a twelve-race meeting. Fortunately I'd left my money to BetDead and I was able to lose nearly a hundred quid on the last nine races."
Mr J, Fulchester

www.BetDeadAfterlifeGambling.com

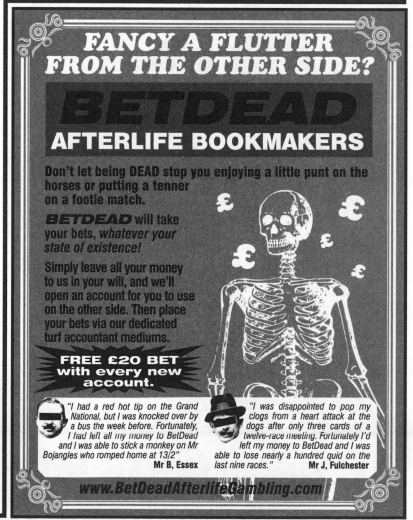

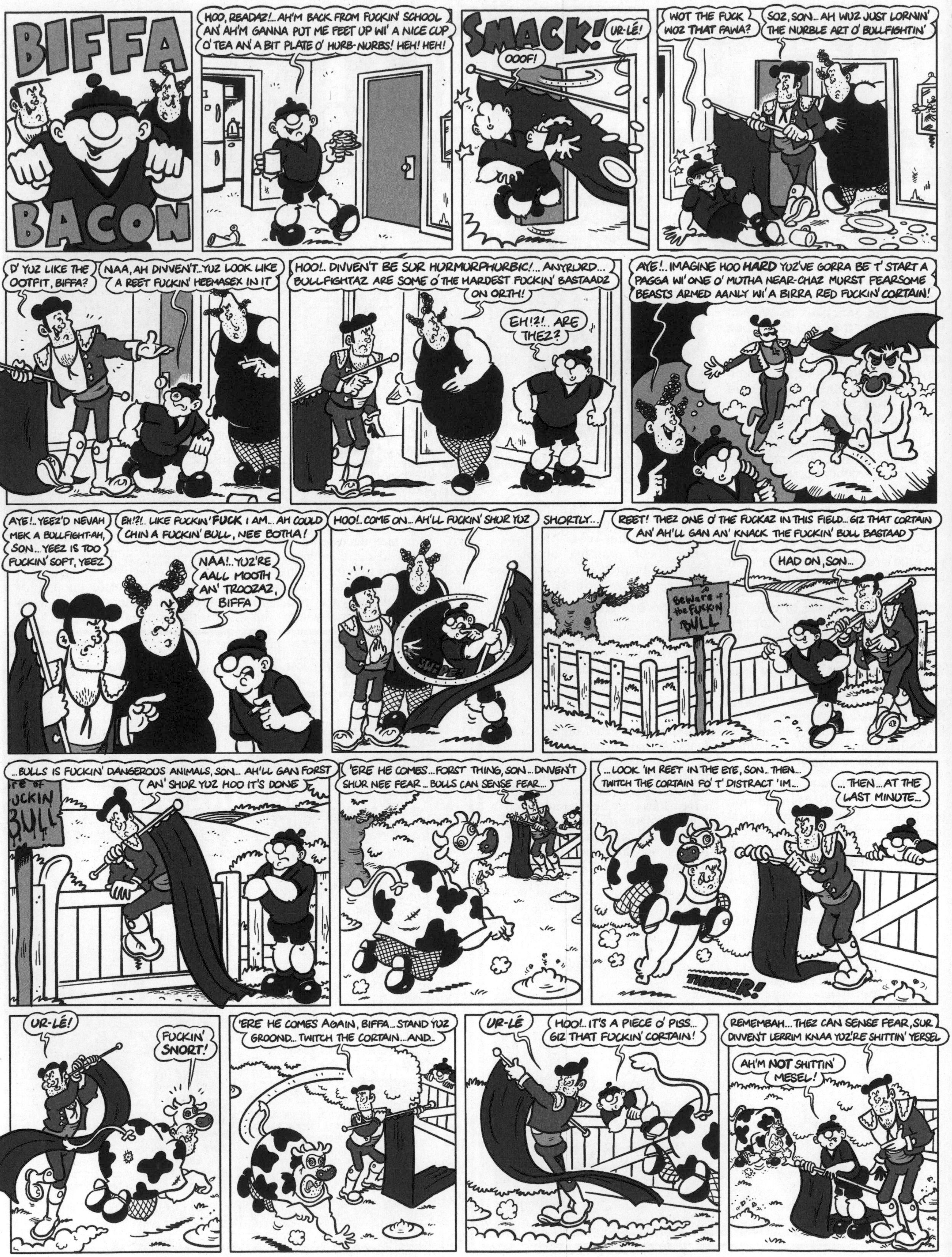
BIFFA BACON
HOO, READAZ!... AH'M BACK FROM FUCKIN' SCHOOL AN' AH'M GANNA PUT ME FEET UP WI' A NICE CUP O' TEA AN' A BIT PLATE O' HURB-NURBS! HEH! HEH!
SMACK!
UR-LÉ!
OOOF!
WOT THE FUCK WOZ THAT FAWA?
SOZ, SON... AH WUZ JUST LORNIN' THE NURBLE ART O' BULLFIGHTIN'
D' YUZ LIKE THE OOTFIT, BIFFA?
NAA, AH DIVVEN'T... YUZ LOOK LIKE A REET FUCKIN' HEEMASEX IN IT
HOO!.. DIVVEN'T BE SUR HURMURPHURBIC!... ANYRURD... BULLFIGHTAZ ARE SOME O' THE HARDEST FUCKIN' BASTAADZ ON ORTH!
EH!?!.. ARE THEZ?
AYE!.. IMAGINE HOO HARD YUZ'VE GORRA BE T' START A PAGGA WI' ONE O' MUTHA NEAR-CHAZ MURST FEARSOME BEASTS ARMED AANLY WI' A BIRRA RED FUCKIN' CORTAIN!
AYE!.. YEEZ'D NEVAH MEK A BULLFIGHT-AH, SON... YEEZ IS TOO FUCKIN' SOFT, YEEZ
EH!?!.. LIKE FUCKIN' FUCK I AM... AH COULD CHIN A FUCKIN' BULL, NEE BOTHA!
NAA!.. YUZ'RE AALL MOOTH AN' TROOZAZ, BIFFA
HOO!.. COME ON... AH'LL FUCKIN' SHUR YUZ
SWIPE!
SHORTLY...
REET! THEZ ONE O' THE FUCKAZ IN THIS FIELD... GIZ THAT CORTAIN AN' AH'LL GAN AN' KNACK THE FUCKIN' BULL BASTAAD
Beware of the FUCKIN BULL
HAD ON, SON...
...BULLS IS FUCKIN' DANGEROUS ANIMALS, SON... AH'LL GAN FORST AN' SHUR YUZ HOO IT'S DONE
'ERE HE COMES... FORST THING, SON... DIVVEN'T SHUR NEE FEAR... BULLS CAN SENSE FEAR...
...LOOK 'IM REET IN THE EYE, SON... THEN... TWITCH THE CORTAIN FO' T' DISTRACT 'IM...
...THEN... AT THE LAST MINUTE...
THUNDER!
UR-LÉ!
FUCKIN' SNORT!
'ERE HE COMES AGAIN, BIFFA... STAND YUZ GROOND... TWITCH THE CORTAIN... AND...
UR-LÉ
HOO!.. IT'S A PIECE O' PISS... GIZ THAT FUCKIN' CORTAIN!
REMEMBAH... THEZ CAN SENSE FEAR, SUR DIVVENT LERRIM KNAA YUZ'RE SHITTIN' YERSEL
AH'M NOT SHITTIN' MESEL!

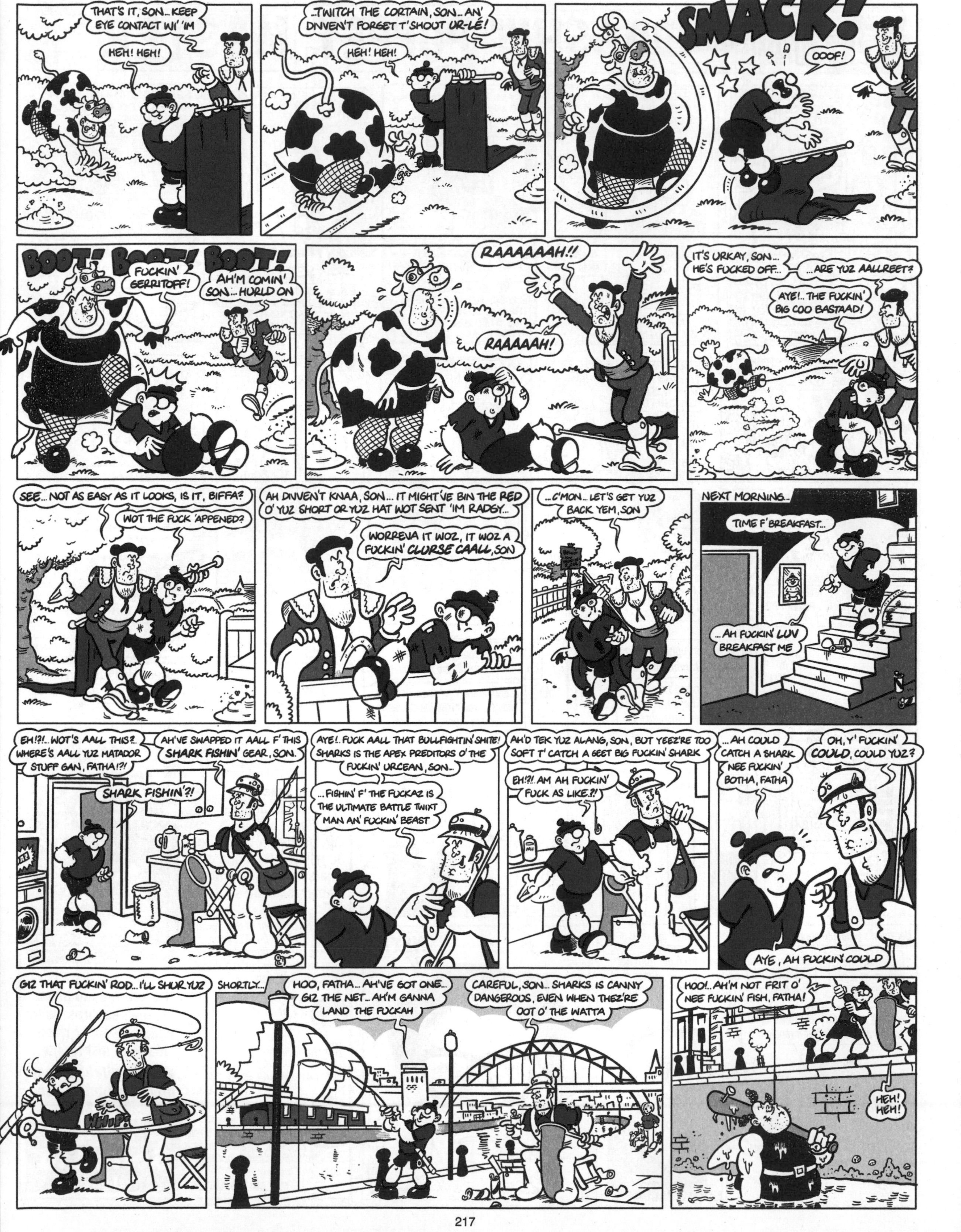
THAT'S IT, SON... KEEP EYE CONTACT WI' 'IM
HEH! HEH!
...TWITCH THE CORTAIN, SON... AN' DINVEN'T FORGET T' SHOUT UR-LÉ!
HEH! HEH!
SMACK!
OOOF!
BOOT! BOOT! BOOT!
FUCKIN' GERRITOFF!
AH'M COMIN' SON... HURLD ON
RAAAAAAH!!
RAAAAAH!
IT'S URKAY, SON... HE'S FUCKED OFF...
...ARE YUZ AALLREET?
AYE!.. THE FUCKIN' BIG COO BASTAAD!
SEE... NOT AS EASY AS IT LOOKS, IS IT, BIFFA?
WOT THE FUCK 'APPENED?
AH DINVEN'T KNAA, SON... IT MIGHT'VE BIN THE RED O' YUZ SHORT OR YUZ HAT WOT SENT 'IM RADGY...
WORREVA IT WOZ, IT WOZ A FUCKIN' CLURSE CAALL, SON
...C'MON... LET'S GET YUZ BACK YEM, SON
NEXT MORNING...
TIME F' BREAKFAST...
...AH FUCKIN' LUV BREAKFAST ME
EH!?!... WOT'S AALL THIS?.. WHERE'S AALL YUZ MATADOR STUFF GAN, FATHA!?!
AH'VE SWAPPED IT AALL F' THIS SHARK FISHIN' GEAR, SON.
SHARK FISHIN'?!
AYE!.. FUCK AALL THAT BULLFIGHTIN' SHITE! SHARKS IS THE APEX PREDITORS O' THE FUCKIN' URCEAN, SON...
...FISHIN' F' THE FUCKAZ IS THE ULTIMATE BATTLE TWIXT MAN AN' FUCKIN' BEAST
AH'D TEK YUZ ALANG, SON, BUT YEEZ'RE TOO SOFT T' CATCH A BEET BIG FUCKIN' SHARK
EH!?!.. AM AH FUCKIN' FUCK AS LIKE.?!
...AH COULD CATCH A SHARK NEE FUCKIN' BOTHA, FATHA
OH, Y' FUCKIN' COULD, COULD YUZ?
AYE, AH FUCKIN' COULD
GIZ THAT FUCKIN' ROD... I'LL SHUR YUZ
WHUP!
SHORTLY...
HOO, FATHA... AH'VE GOT ONE... GIZ THE NET... AH'M GANNA LAND THE FUCKAH
CAREFUL, SON... SHARKS IS CANNY DANGEROUS, EVEN WHEN THEZ'RE OOT O' THE WATTA
HOO!.. AH'M NOT FRIT O' NEE FUCKIN' FISH, FATHA!
HEH! HEH!

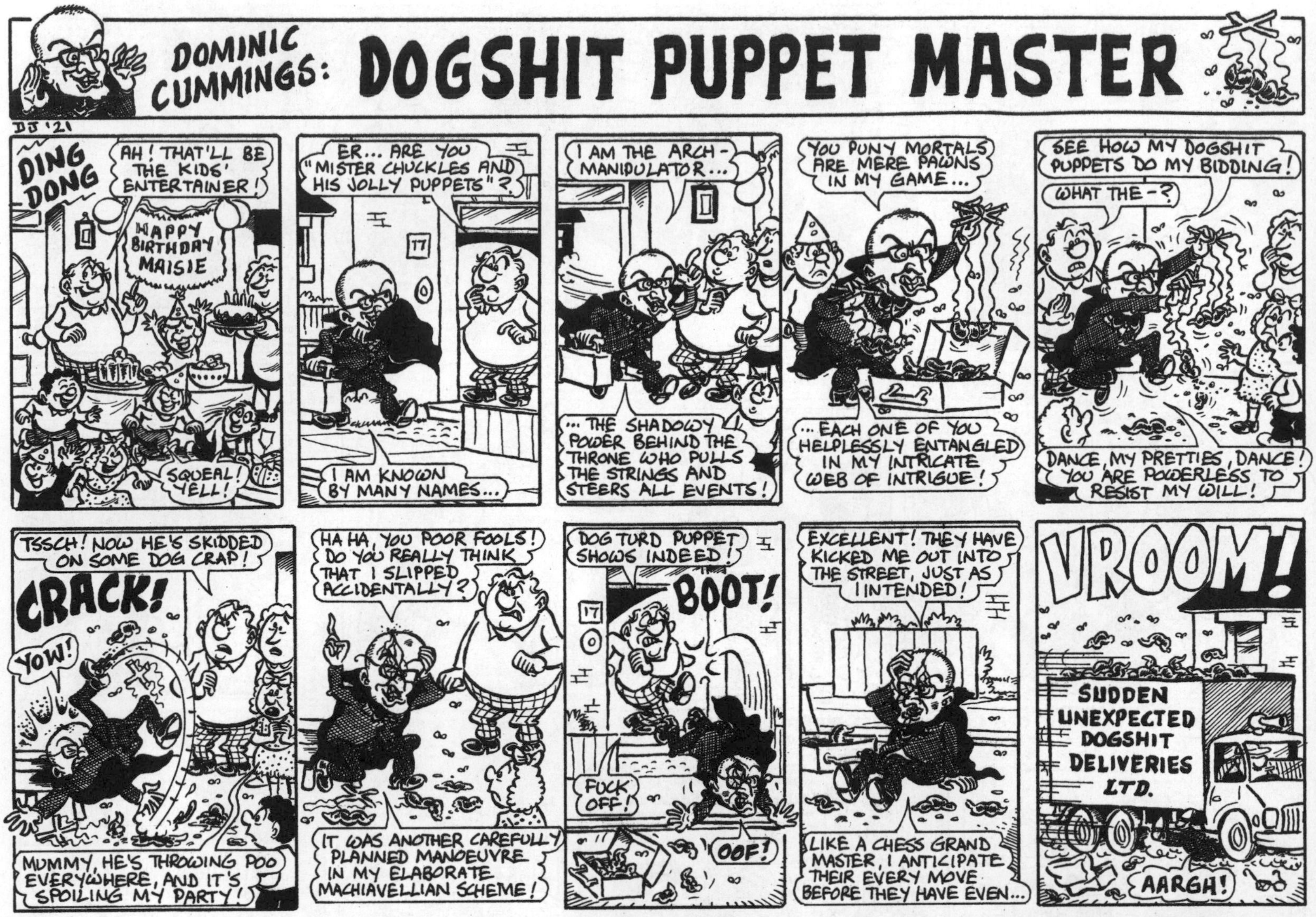
DOMINIC CUMMINGS: DOGSHIT PUPPET MASTER
DJ '21
DING DONG
AH! THAT'LL BE THE KIDS' ENTERTAINER!
HAPPY BIRTHDAY MAISIE
SQUEAL! YELL!
ER... ARE YOU "MISTER CHUCKLES AND HIS JOLLY PUPPETS"?
17
I AM KNOWN BY MANY NAMES...
I AM THE ARCH-MANIPULATOR...
...THE SHADOWY POWER BEHIND THE THRONE WHO PULLS THE STRINGS AND STEERS ALL EVENTS!
YOU PUNY MORTALS ARE MERE PAWNS IN MY GAME...
...EACH ONE OF YOU HELPLESSLY ENTANGLED IN MY INTRICATE WEB OF INTRIGUE!
SEE HOW MY DOGSHIT PUPPETS DO MY BIDDING!
WHAT THE -?
DANCE, MY PRETTIES, DANCE! YOU ARE POWERLESS TO RESIST MY WILL!
TSSCH! NOW HE'S SKIDDED ON SOME DOG CRAP!
CRACK!
YOW!
MUMMY, HE'S THROWING POO EVERYWHERE, AND IT'S SPOILING MY PARTY!
HA HA, YOU POOR FOOLS! DO YOU REALLY THINK THAT I SLIPPED ACCIDENTALLY?
IT WAS ANOTHER CAREFULLY PLANNED MANOEUVRE IN MY ELABORATE MACHIAVELLIAN SCHEME!
DOG TURD PUPPET SHOWS INDEED!
BOOT!
17
FUCK OFF!
OOF!
EXCELLENT! THEY HAVE KICKED ME OUT INTO THE STREET, JUST AS I INTENDED!
LIKE A CHESS GRAND MASTER, I ANTICIPATE THEIR EVERY MOVE BEFORE THEY HAVE EVEN...
VROOM!
SUDDEN UNEXPECTED DOGSHIT DELIVERIES LTD.
AARGH!

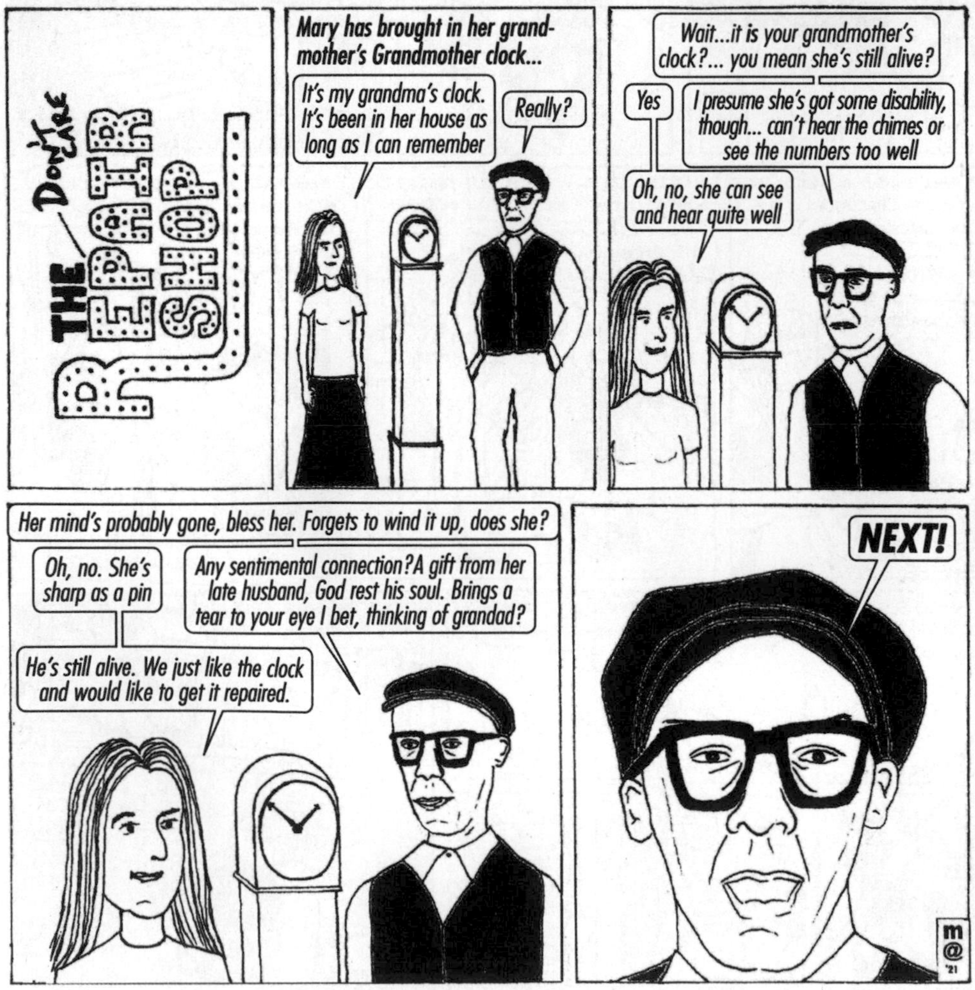
THE Don't Care REPAIR SHOP
Mary has brought in her grandmother's Grandmother clock...
It's my grandma's clock. It's been in her house as long as I can remember
Really?
Wait...it is your grandmother's clock?... you mean she's still alive?
Yes
I presume she's got some disability, though... can't hear the chimes or see the numbers too well
Oh, no, she can see and hear quite well
Her mind's probably gone, bless her. Forgets to wind it up, does she?
Oh, no. She's sharp as a pin
Any sentimental connection?A gift from her late husband, God rest his soul. Brings a tear to your eye I bet, thinking of grandad?
He's still alive. We just like the clock and would like to get it repaired.
NEXT!
m@ '21

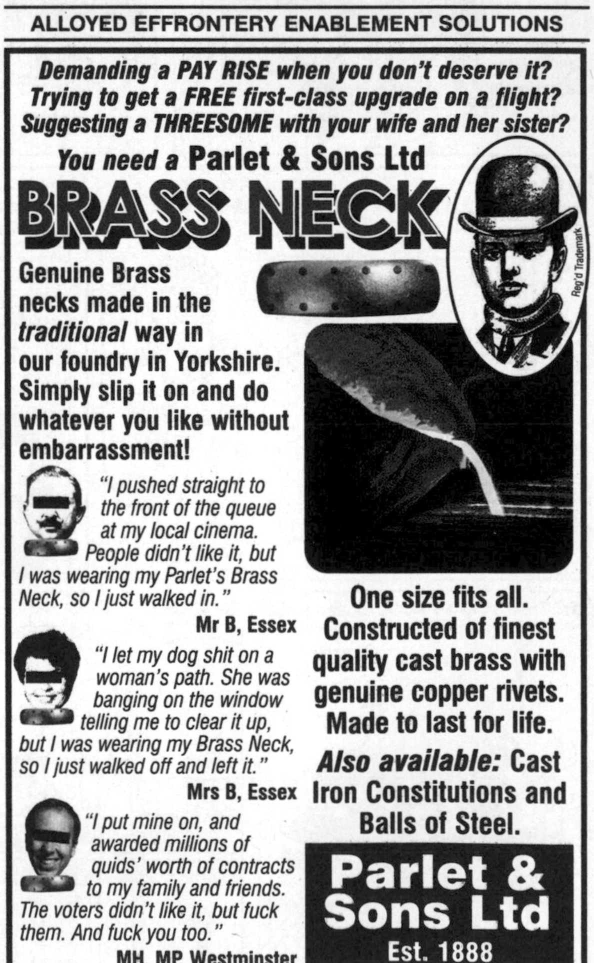
ALLOYED EFFRONTERY ENABLEMENT SOLUTIONS
Demanding a PAY RISE when you don't deserve it?
Trying to get a FREE first-class upgrade on a flight?
Suggesting a THREESOME with your wife and her sister?
You need a Parlet & Sons Ltd
BRASS NECK
Reg'd Trademark
Genuine Brass necks made in the traditional way in our foundry in Yorkshire. Simply slip it on and do whatever you like without embarrassment!
"I pushed straight to the front of the queue at my local cinema. People didn't like it, but I was wearing my Parlet's Brass Neck, so I just walked in."
Mr B, Essex
"I let my dog shit on a woman's path. She was banging on the window telling me to clear it up, but I was wearing my Brass Neck, so I just walked off and left it."
Mrs B, Essex
"I put mine on, and awarded millions of quids' worth of contracts to my family and friends. The voters didn't like it, but fuck them. And fuck you too."
MH, MP, Westminster
One size fits all. Constructed of finest quality cast brass with genuine copper rivets. Made to last for life.
Also available: Cast Iron Constitutions and Balls of Steel.
Parlet & Sons Ltd
Est. 1888

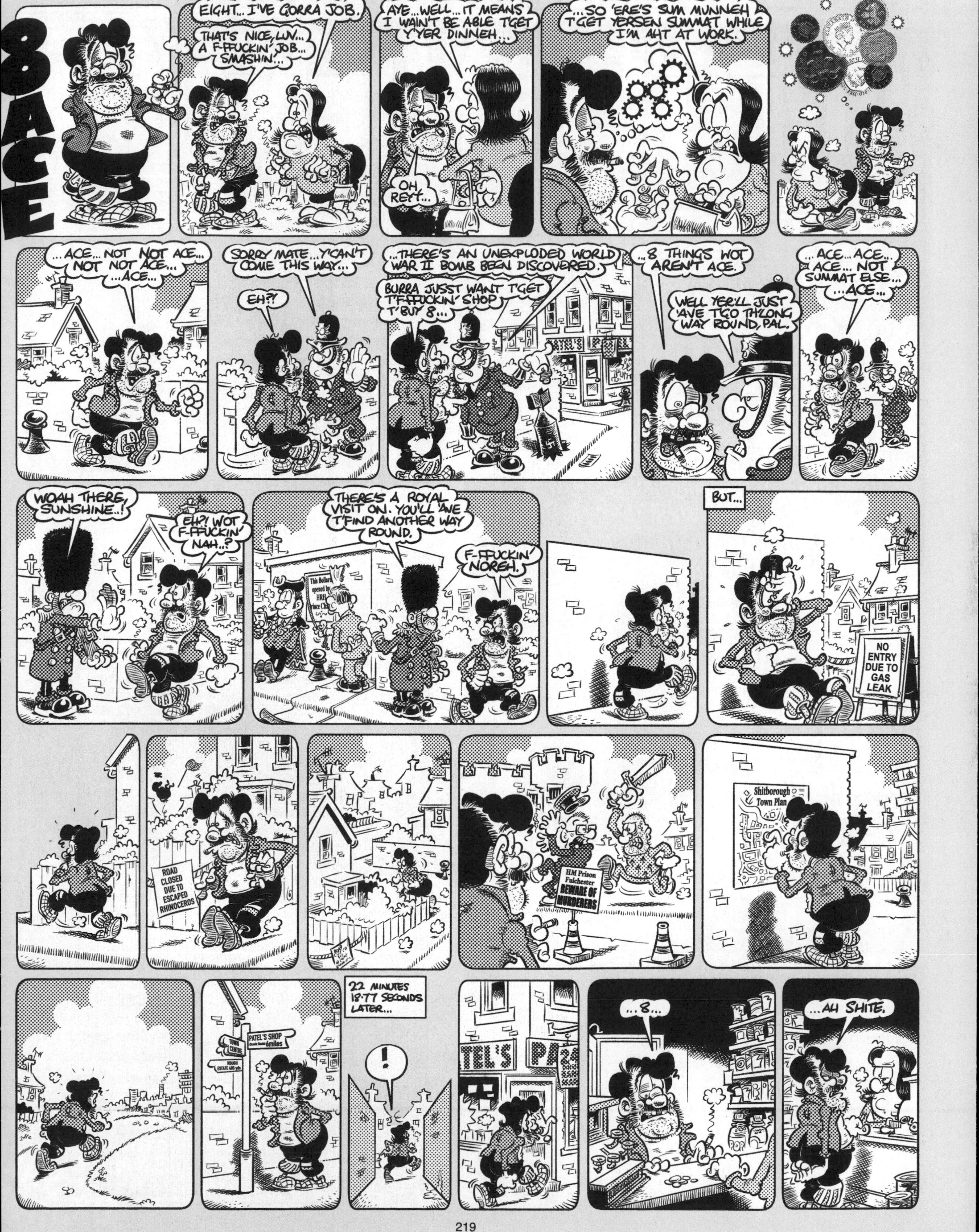
8 ACE
EIGHT... I'VE GORRA JOB.
THAT'S NICE, LUV... A F-FFUCKIN' JOB... SMASHIN'...
AYE... WELL... IT MEANS I WAIN'T BE ABLE T'GET Y'YER DINNEH...
OH REYT...
...SO 'ERE'S SUM MUNNEH T'GET YERSEN SUMMAT WHILE I'M AHT AT WORK.
...ACE... NOT NOT ACE... NOT NOT ACE... ...ACE...
SORRY MATE... Y'CAN'T COME THIS WAY...
EH?!
...THERE'S AN UNEXPLODED WORLD WAR II BOMB BEEN DISCOVERED.
BURRA JUSST WANT T'GET T'F-FFUCKIN' SHOP T'BUY 8...
...8 THINGS WOT AREN'T ACE.
WELL YER'LL JUST 'AVE T'GO TH'LONG WAY ROUND, PAL.
...ACE... ACE... ACE... NOT SUMMAT ELSE... ...ACE...
WOAH THERE, SUNSHINE..!
EH?! WOT F-FFUCKIN' NAH..?
THERE'S A ROYAL VISIT ON. YOU'LL 'AVE T'FIND ANOTHER WAY ROUND.
F-FFUCKIN' NOREH.
BUT...
NO ENTRY DUE TO GAS LEAK
ROAD CLOSED DUE TO ESCAPED RHINOCEROS
HM Prison Fulchester
BEWARE OF MURDERERS
Shitborough Town Plan
PATEL'S SHOP 6miles
TOWN CENTRE
22 MINUTES 18·77 SECONDS LATER...
!
...8...
...AH SHITE.

The Magazine that's ABCESS ALL AREAS

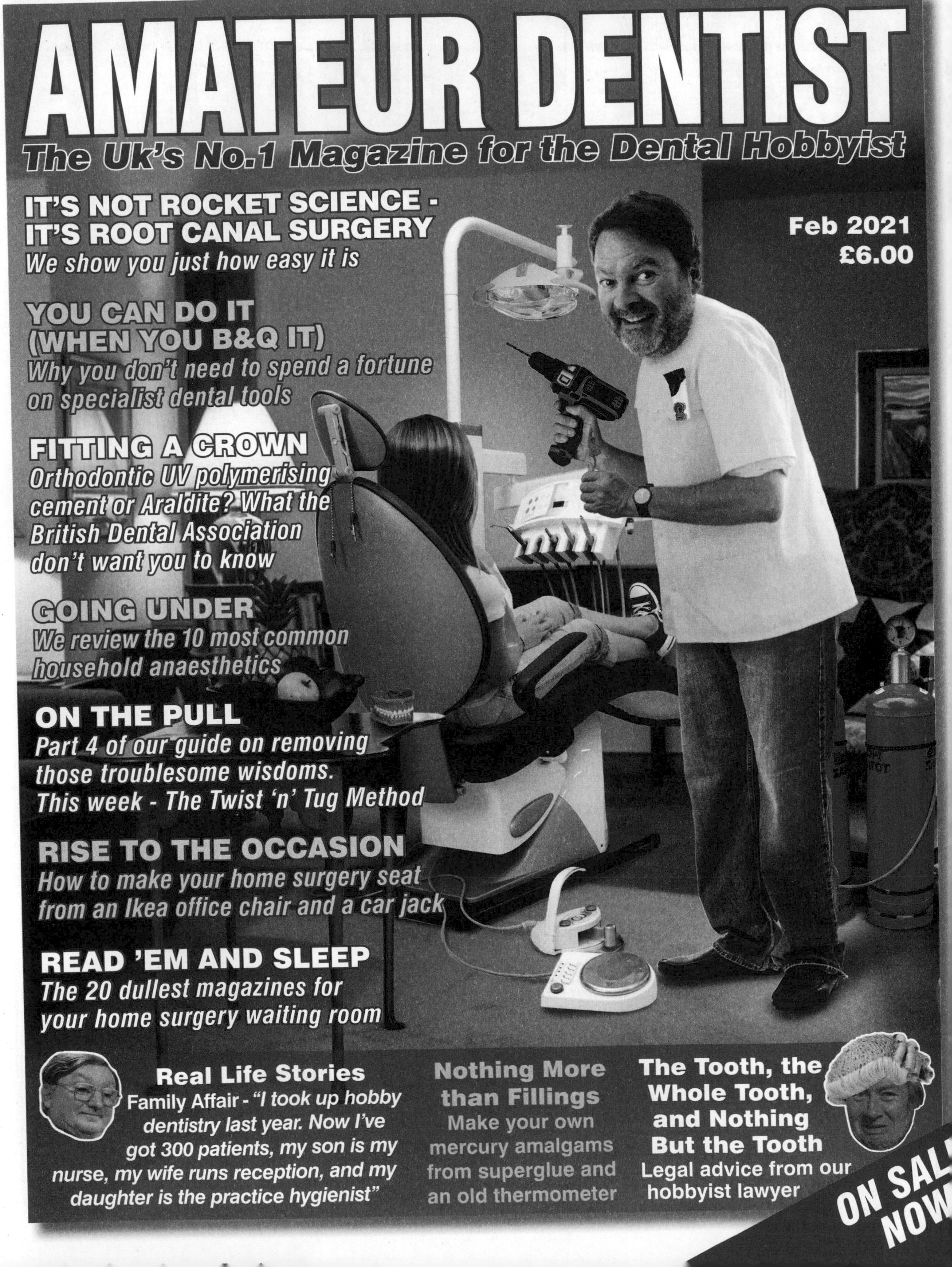

AMATEUR DENTIST
The Uk's No.1 Magazine for the Dental Hobbyist

Feb 2021
£6.00

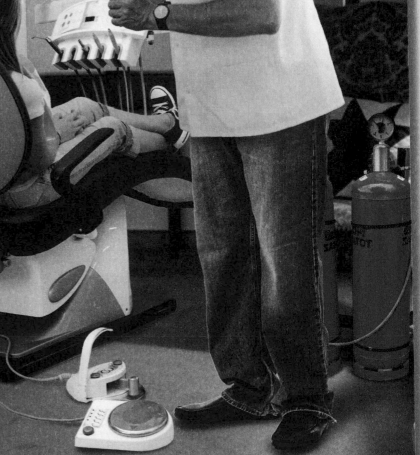

IT'S NOT ROCKET SCIENCE - IT'S ROOT CANAL SURGERY
We show you just how easy it is

YOU CAN DO IT (WHEN YOU B&Q IT)
Why you don't need to spend a fortune on specialist dental tools

FITTING A CROWN
Orthodontic UV polymerising cement or Araldite? What the British Dental Association don't want you to know

GOING UNDER
We review the 10 most common household anaesthetics

ON THE PULL
Part 4 of our guide on removing those troublesome wisdoms. This week - The Twist 'n' Tug Method

RISE TO THE OCCASION
How to make your home surgery seat from an Ikea office chair and a car jack

READ 'EM AND SLEEP
The 20 dullest magazines for your home surgery waiting room

Real Life Stories
Family Affair - "I took up hobby dentistry last year. Now I've got 300 patients, my son is my nurse, my wife runs reception, and my daughter is the practice hygienist"

Nothing More than Fillings
Make your own mercury amalgams from superglue and an old thermometer

The Tooth, the Whole Tooth, and Nothing But the Tooth
Legal advice from our hobbyist lawyer

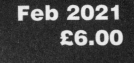

ON SALE NOW

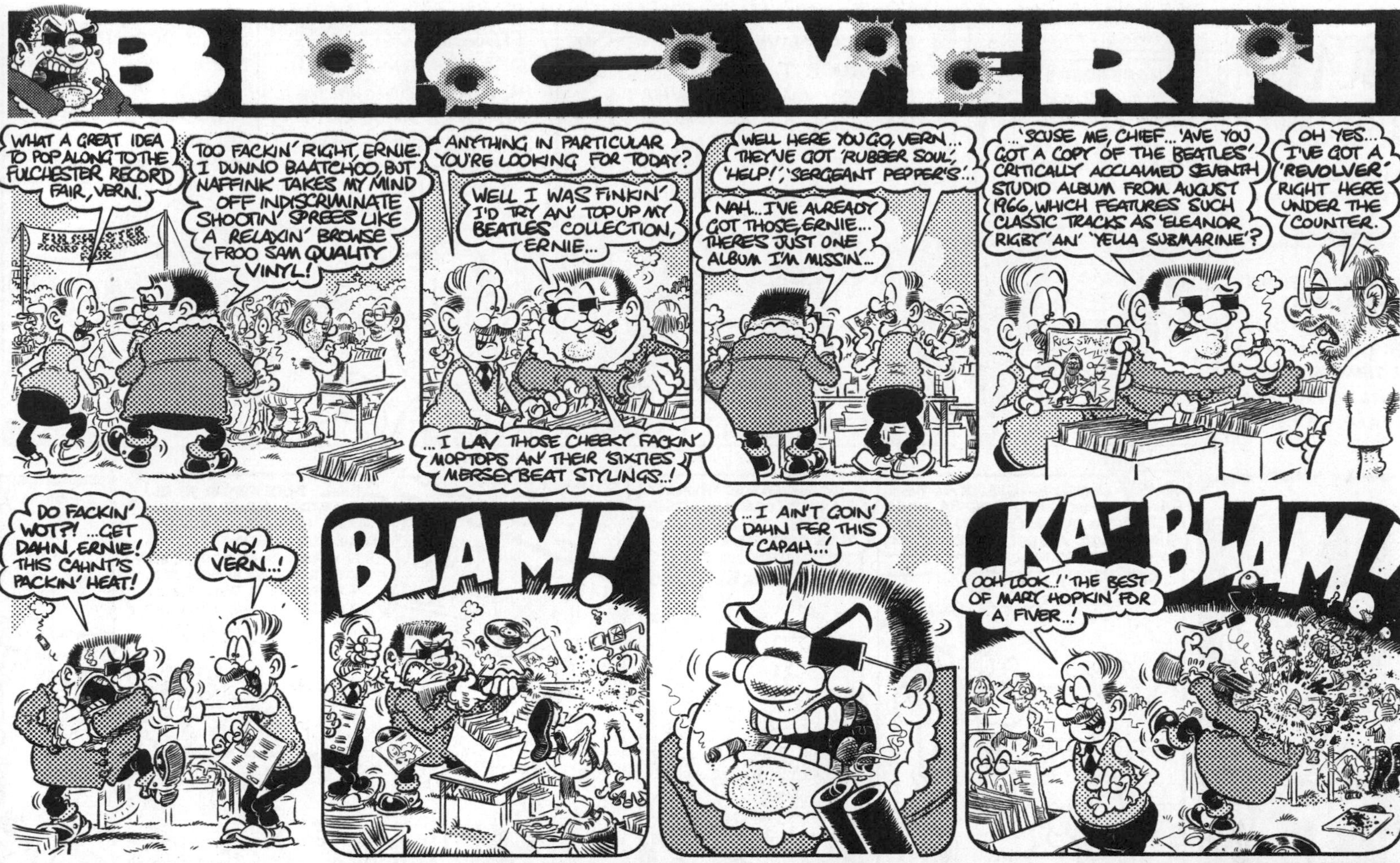

BIG VERN
WHAT A GREAT IDEA TO POP ALONG TO THE FULCHESTER RECORD FAIR, VERN.
TOO FACKIN' RIGHT, ERNIE. I DUNNO BAATCHOO, BUT NAFFINK TAKES MY MIND OFF INDISCRIMINATE SHOOTIN' SPREES LIKE A RELAXIN' BROWSE FROO SAM QUALITY VINYL!
ANYTHING IN PARTICULAR YOU'RE LOOKING FOR TODAY?
WELL I WAS FINKIN' I'D TRY AN' TOP UP MY BEATLES COLLECTION, ERNIE...
...I LAV THOSE CHEEKY FACKIN' MOPTOPS AN' THEIR SIXTIES MERSEYBEAT STYLINGS..!
WELL HERE YOU GO, VERN... THEY'VE GOT 'RUBBER SOUL', 'HELP!', 'SERGEANT PEPPER'S'...
NAH... I'VE ALREADY GOT THOSE, ERNIE... THERE'S JUST ONE ALBUM I'M MISSIN'...
...'SCUSE ME, CHIEF... 'AVE YOU GOT A COPY OF THE BEATLES' CRITICALLY ACCLAIMED SEVENTH STUDIO ALBUM FROM AUGUST 1966, WHICH FEATURES SUCH CLASSIC TRACKS AS 'ELEANOR RIGBY' AN' 'YELLA SUBMARINE'?
OH YES... I'VE GOT A 'REVOLVER' RIGHT HERE UNDER THE COUNTER.
DO FACKIN' WOT?! ...GET DAHN, ERNIE! THIS CAHNT'S PACKIN' HEAT!
NO! VERN..!
BLAM!
...I AIN'T GOIN' DAHN FER THIS CAPAH..!
KA-BLAM!
OOH LOOK..! 'THE BEST OF MARY HOPKIN' FOR A FIVER..!

ARE YOU A SOFT OR HARD SEXMAS CHOCAHOLIC?

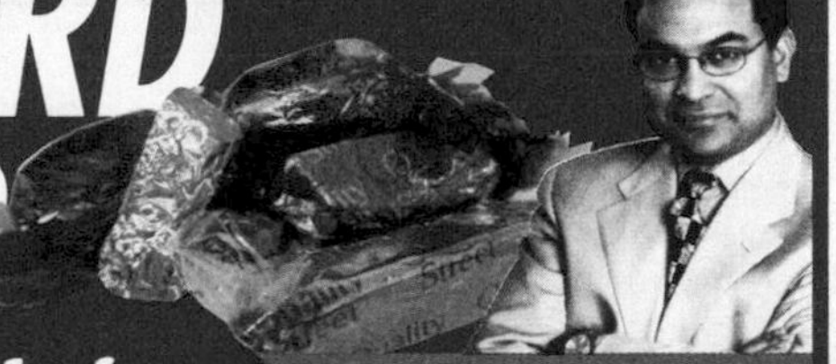

Your choice of Xmas choc reveals your innermost, darkest desires

with Dr Raj Persaud

WE ALL like to think of ourselves as wonderful lovers, able to bring our partners and ourselves to the height of sexual ecstasy. But whilst some of us can lay claim to being red-hot Casanovas, most of us are luke warm at best, and some individuals are complete flops between the sheets. Our abilities to satisfy our lovers vary wildly, and it is difficult to score our own performance with honesty.

But there are many things which, although completely disconnected from the sexual act, nevertheless give clues as to our ability to pleasure our partner. The colour of shirt you prefer to wear, the flavour of crisps you eat, or the type of television programme you like to watch - *all are powerful indicators about how good you are in bed.*

Indeed, there are so many different things which indicate how good a lover you are, that it is often difficult to decide which one of these pointers to rely on. But you don't need to think about it. That's because the type of Quality Street chocolate you prefer says a lot about the type of thing you think says a lot about how good a lover you are. And here, Dr Raj Persaud tells you what you can learn about what people think is indicative your sexual prowess when you pass the Quality Street tin round this Christmas...

The Hazelnut Caramel

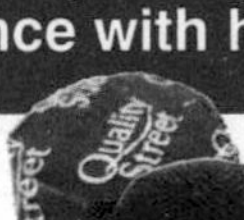

WITH its purple, shiny wrapper, this wedge-shaped *Hazelnut Caramel* is the most popular Quality Street in the tin, and people who plump for this particular sweet every time the lid comes off demonstrate they have little imagination. Consequently, they will believe that something very ordinary - like the type of pet you own or what car you drive - reveals what you are like in bed. Whether it's a horse indicating someone who can perform sexually for hours without tiring, or someone sexually shy and timid who drives a Nissan Micra, the *Hazelnut Caramel* reveals their inner psyche.

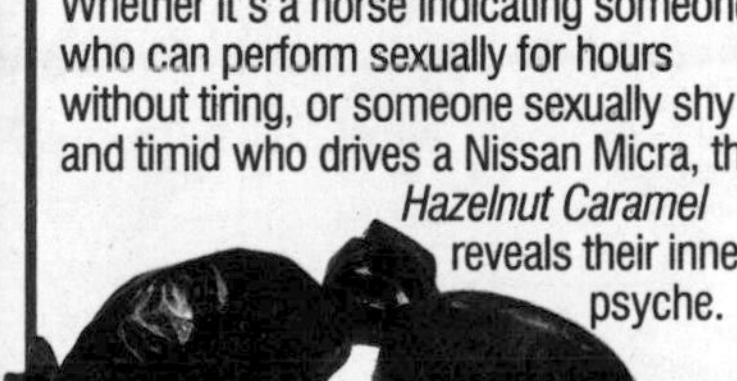

The Orange Chocolate Crunch

WITH its crunchy, citrus-flavoured centre, the *Orange Chocolate Crunch* surprises anyone who may have expected a softer-textured cream. So although they may not realise it, those who count this as their favourite Quality Street like surprises, and are turned off by anything run-of-the-mill. Therefore, it comes as no surprise that their lovemaking skills are a reflection of something out of the ordinary, such as which ice-based sport they prefer. Be it the ice hockey lover who is fast and rough between the sheets, or the slower, more tender lovers who like ice-dancing, their love of the *Orange Chocolate Crunch* speaks volumes.

The Toffee Penny

PERHAPS the dullest Quality Street in the tin, the *Toffee Penny*, is the favourite of only the most conservative of people. Not for them the excitement of the strawberry delight or caramel swirl, indicative of thrill-seekers who believe the type of dangerous sport you like says a lot about what you are like in bed. The lover of the *Toffee Penny* is more likely to believe your sexual inclinations are revealed by your more standard choices, such as your choice of footwear, or the colour of your front door.

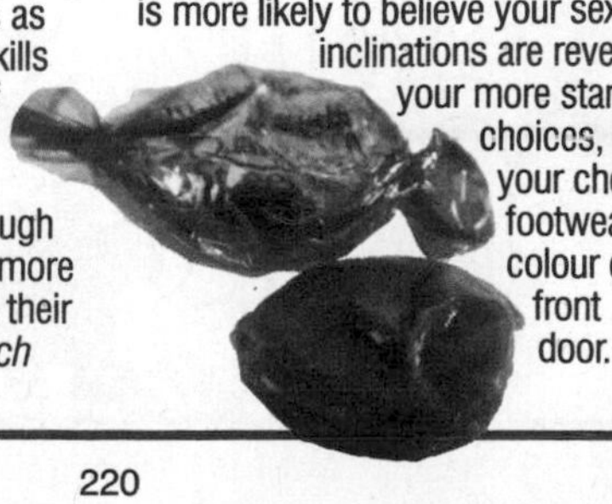

The Coconut Eclair

SOFT, yet with a little more texture than a plain soft-centre, the *Coconut Eclair* is the most exotic flavour in the Quality Street tin. And those who deem it their favourite like to try something new and are not afraid to make a decision when faced with a choice. For this reason, the *Coconut Eclair* lovers are likely to believe that your choice of Cadbury's Roses divulges your innermost sexual thoughts.

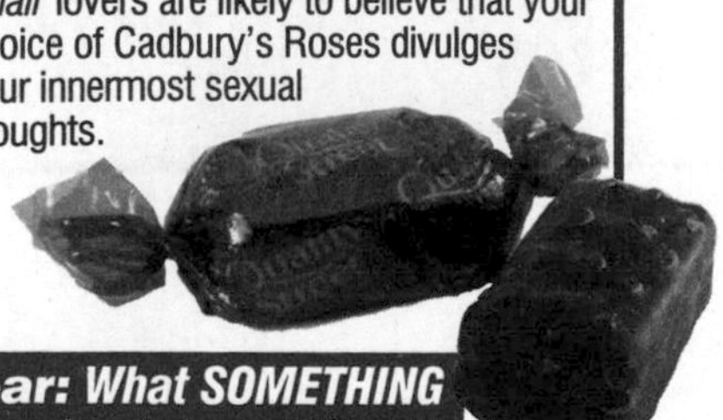

Next Year: ***What SOMETHING ELSE says about something or other to do with you and sex.***

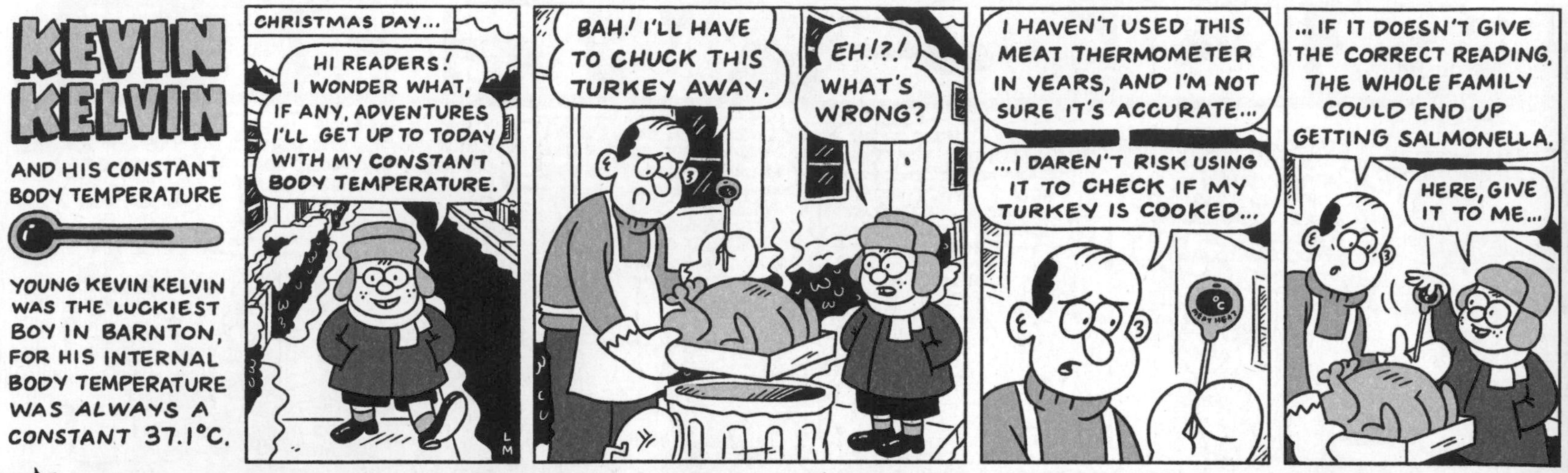
KEVIN KELVIN
AND HIS CONSTANT BODY TEMPERATURE
YOUNG KEVIN KELVIN WAS THE LUCKIEST BOY IN BARNTON, FOR HIS INTERNAL BODY TEMPERATURE WAS ALWAYS A CONSTANT 37.1°C.
CHRISTMAS DAY...
HI READERS! I WONDER WHAT, IF ANY, ADVENTURES I'LL GET UP TO TODAY WITH MY CONSTANT BODY TEMPERATURE.
BAH! I'LL HAVE TO CHUCK THIS TURKEY AWAY.
EH!?! WHAT'S WRONG?
I HAVEN'T USED THIS MEAT THERMOMETER IN YEARS, AND I'M NOT SURE IT'S ACCURATE...
...I DAREN'T RISK USING IT TO CHECK IF MY TURKEY IS COOKED...
...IF IT DOESN'T GIVE THE CORRECT READING, THE WHOLE FAMILY COULD END UP GETTING SALMONELLA.
HERE, GIVE IT TO ME...

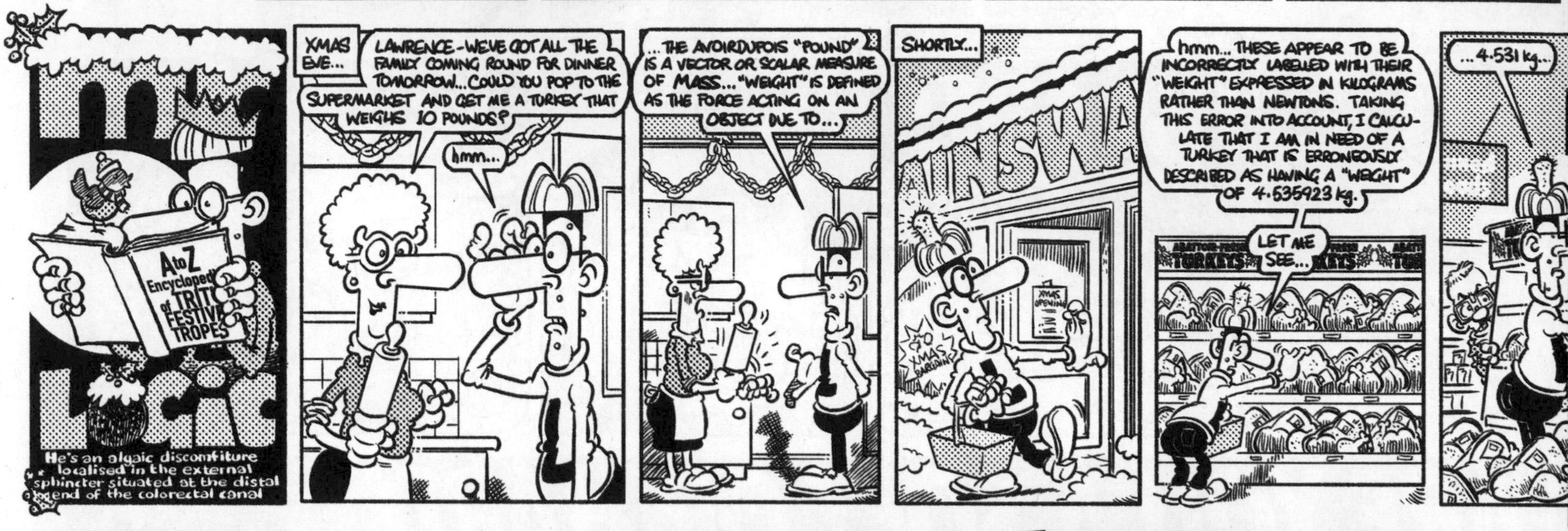
A to Z Encyclopedia of TRITE FESTIVE TROPES
He's an algaic discomfiture localised in the external sphincter situated at the distal end of the colorectal canal
XMAS EVE...
LAWRENCE - WE'VE GOT ALL THE FAMILY COMING ROUND FOR DINNER TOMORROW... COULD YOU POP TO THE SUPERMARKET AND GET ME A TURKEY THAT WEIGHS 10 POUNDS?
hmm...
...THE AVOIRDUPOIS "POUND" IS A VECTOR OR SCALAR MEASURE OF MASS... "WEIGHT" IS DEFINED AS THE FORCE ACTING ON AN OBJECT DUE TO...
SHORTLY...
hmm... THESE APPEAR TO BE INCORRECTLY LABELLED WITH THEIR "WEIGHT" EXPRESSED IN KILOGRAMS RATHER THAN NEWTONS. TAKING THIS ERROR INTO ACCOUNT, I CALCULATE THAT I AM IN NEED OF A TURKEY THAT IS ERRONEOUSLY DESCRIBED AS HAVING A "WEIGHT" OF 4.535923 kg.
LET ME SEE...
...4.531 kg...

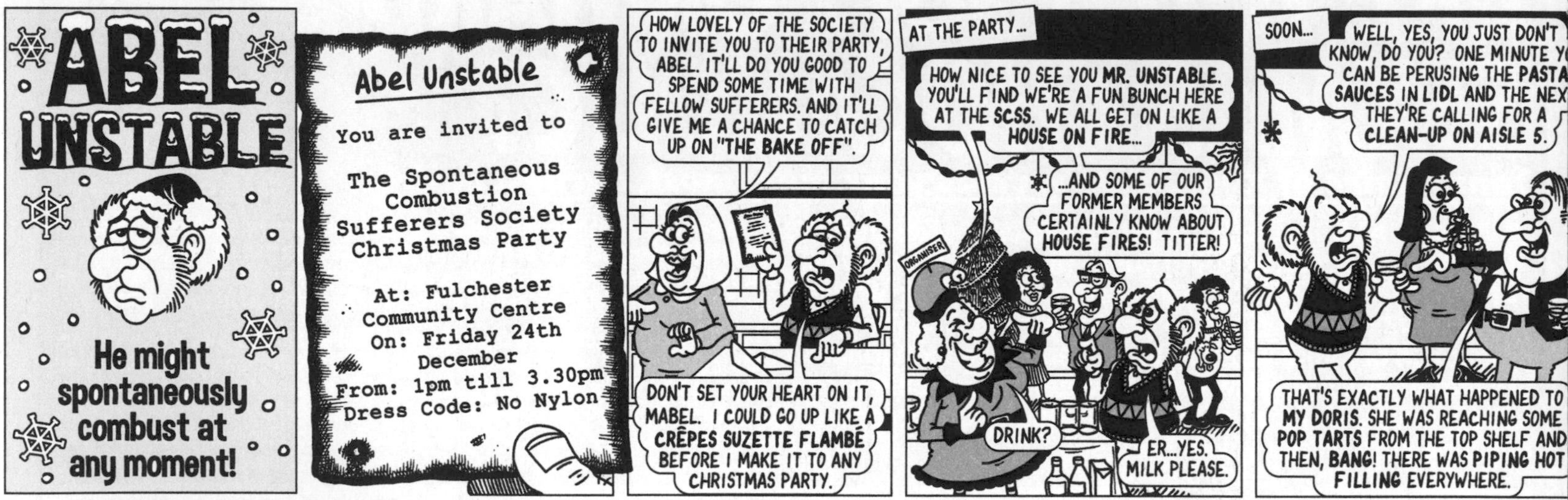
ABEL UNSTABLE
He might spontaneously combust at any moment!
Abel Unstable
You are invited to
The Spontaneous Combustion Sufferers Society Christmas Party
At: Fulchester Community Centre
On: Friday 24th December
From: 1pm till 3.30pm
Dress Code: No Nylon
HOW LOVELY OF THE SOCIETY TO INVITE YOU TO THEIR PARTY, ABEL. IT'LL DO YOU GOOD TO SPEND SOME TIME WITH FELLOW SUFFERERS. AND IT'LL GIVE ME A CHANCE TO CATCH UP ON "THE BAKE OFF".
DON'T SET YOUR HEART ON IT, MABEL. I COULD GO UP LIKE A CRÊPES SUZETTE FLAMBÉ BEFORE I MAKE IT TO ANY CHRISTMAS PARTY.
AT THE PARTY...
HOW NICE TO SEE YOU MR. UNSTABLE. YOU'LL FIND WE'RE A FUN BUNCH HERE AT THE SCSS. WE ALL GET ON LIKE A HOUSE ON FIRE...
...AND SOME OF OUR FORMER MEMBERS CERTAINLY KNOW ABOUT HOUSE FIRES! TITTER!
ORGANISER
DRINK?
ER...YES. MILK PLEASE.
SOON...
WELL, YES, YOU JUST DON'T KNOW, DO YOU? ONE MINUTE YO CAN BE PERUSING THE PASTA SAUCES IN LIDL AND THE NEX THEY'RE CALLING FOR A CLEAN-UP ON AISLE 5.
THAT'S EXACTLY WHAT HAPPENED TO MY DORIS. SHE WAS REACHING SOME POP TARTS FROM THE TOP SHELF AND THEN, BANG! THERE WAS PIPING HOT FILLING EVERYWHERE.

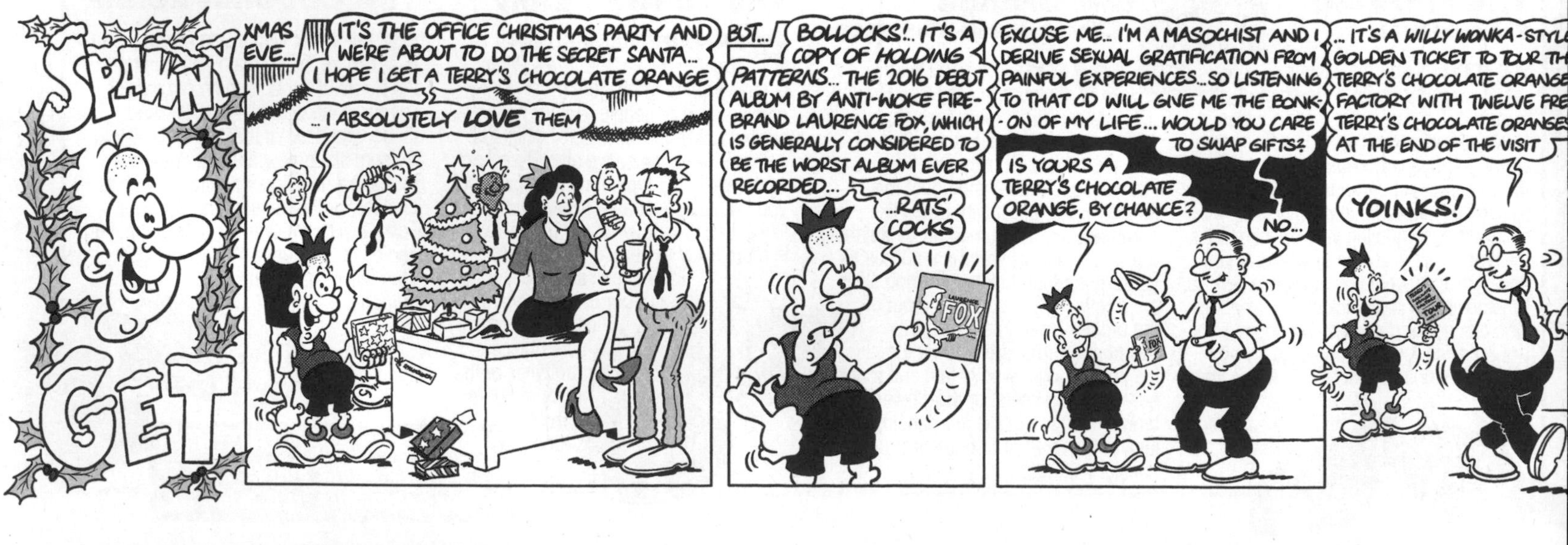
SPAWNY GET
XMAS EVE...
IT'S THE OFFICE CHRISTMAS PARTY AND WE'RE ABOUT TO DO THE SECRET SANTA... I HOPE I GET A TERRY'S CHOCOLATE ORANGE
...I ABSOLUTELY LOVE THEM
BUT...
BOLLOCKS!.. IT'S A COPY OF HOLDING PATTERNS... THE 2016 DEBUT ALBUM BY ANTI-WOKE FIRE-BRAND LAURENCE FOX, WHICH IS GENERALLY CONSIDERED TO BE THE WORST ALBUM EVER RECORDED...
...RATS' COCKS
FOX
EXCUSE ME... I'M A MASOCHIST AND I DERIVE SEXUAL GRATIFICATION FROM PAINFUL EXPERIENCES...SO LISTENING TO THAT CD WILL GIVE ME THE BONK-ON OF MY LIFE... WOULD YOU CARE TO SWAP GIFTS?
IS YOURS A TERRY'S CHOCOLATE ORANGE, BY CHANCE?
NO...
...IT'S A WILLY WONKA-STYL GOLDEN TICKET TO TOUR TH TERRY'S CHOCOLATE ORANGE FACTORY WITH TWELVE FRE TERRY'S CHOCOLATE ORANGE AT THE END OF THE VISIT
YOINKS!

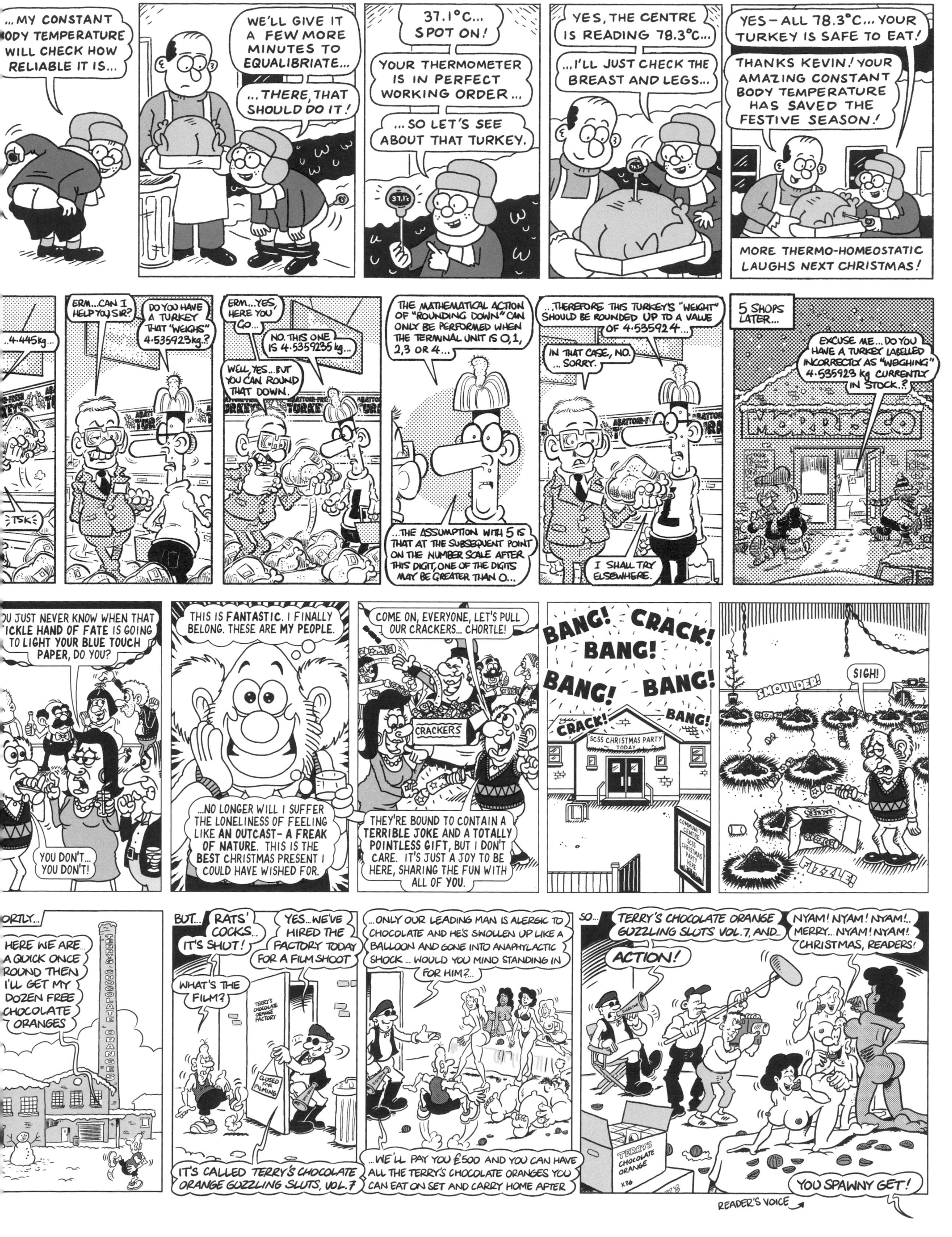
...MY CONSTANT
ODY TEMPERATURE WILL CHECK HOW RELIABLE IT IS...
WE'LL GIVE IT A FEW MORE MINUTES TO EQUALIBRIATE...
...THERE, THAT SHOULD DO IT!
37.1°C... SPOT ON!
YOUR THERMOMETER IS IN PERFECT WORKING ORDER...
...SO LET'S SEE ABOUT THAT TURKEY.
37.1°c
YES, THE CENTRE IS READING 78.3°C...
...I'LL JUST CHECK THE BREAST AND LEGS...
YES – ALL 78.3°C... YOUR TURKEY IS SAFE TO EAT!
THANKS KEVIN! YOUR AMAZING CONSTANT BODY TEMPERATURE HAS SAVED THE FESTIVE SEASON!
MORE THERMO-HOMEOSTATIC LAUGHS NEXT CHRISTMAS!
..4.445kg...
TSK
ERM...CAN I HELP YOU SIR?
DO YOU HAVE A TURKEY THAT "WEIGHS" 4.535923kg..?
ERM...YES, HERE YOU GO...
NO. THIS ONE IS 4.5359235 kg...
WELL, YES...BUT YOU CAN ROUND THAT DOWN.
THE MATHEMATICAL ACTION OF "ROUNDING DOWN" CAN ONLY BE PERFORMED WHEN THE TERMINAL UNIT IS 0, 1, 2, 3 OR 4...
...THE ASSUMPTION WITH 5 IS THAT AT THE SUBSEQUENT POINT ON THE NUMBER SCALE AFTER THIS DIGIT, ONE OF THE DIGITS MAY BE GREATER THAN 0...
...THEREFORE THIS TURKEY'S "WEIGHT" SHOULD BE ROUNDED UP TO A VALUE OF 4.535924...
IN THAT CASE, NO. ... SORRY.
I SHALL TRY ELSEWHERE.
5 SHOPS LATER...
EXCUSE ME... DO YOU HAVE A TURKEY LABELLED INCORRECTLY AS "WEIGHING" 4.535923 kg CURRENTLY IN STOCK..?
OU JUST NEVER KNOW WHEN THAT ICKLE HAND OF FATE IS GOING TO LIGHT YOUR BLUE TOUCH PAPER, DO YOU?
YOU DON'T... YOU DON'T!
THIS IS FANTASTIC. I FINALLY BELONG. THESE ARE MY PEOPLE.
...NO LONGER WILL I SUFFER THE LONELINESS OF FEELING LIKE AN OUTCAST- A FREAK OF NATURE. THIS IS THE BEST CHRISTMAS PRESENT I COULD HAVE WISHED FOR.
COME ON, EVERYONE, LET'S PULL OUR CRACKERS... CHORTLE!
CRACKERS
THEY'RE BOUND TO CONTAIN A TERRIBLE JOKE AND A TOTALLY POINTLESS GIFT, BUT I DON'T CARE. IT'S JUST A JOY TO BE HERE, SHARING THE FUN WITH ALL OF YOU.
BANG! CRACK! BANG! BANG! BANG! BANG! CRACK!
SCSS CHRISTMAS PARTY TODAY
COMMUNITY CENTRE SCSS CHRISTMAS PARTY HERE
SMOULDER!
SIGH!
FIZZLE!
ORTLY...
HERE WE ARE... A QUICK ONCE ROUND THEN I'LL GET MY DOZEN FREE CHOCOLATE ORANGES
TERRY'S CHOCOLATE ORANGES
BUT...
RATS' COCKS... IT'S SHUT!
YES...WE'VE HIRED THE FACTORY TODAY FOR A FILM SHOOT
WHAT'S THE FILM?
TERRY'S CHOCOLATE ORANGE FACTORY
CLOSED FOR FILMING
IT'S CALLED TERRY'S CHOCOLATE ORANGE GUZZLING SLUTS, VOL.7
...ONLY OUR LEADING MAN IS ALERGIC TO CHOCOLATE AND HE'S SWOLLEN UP LIKE A BALLOON AND GONE INTO ANAPHYLACTIC SHOCK ... WOULD YOU MIND STANDING IN FOR HIM?...
...WE'LL PAY YOU £500 AND YOU CAN HAVE ALL THE TERRY'S CHOCOLATE ORANGES YOU CAN EAT ON SET AND CARRY HOME AFTER
SO...
TERRY'S CHOCOLATE ORANGE GUZZLING SLUTS VOL.7, AND...
ACTION!
NYAM! NYAM! NYAM!.. MERRY...NYAM! NYAM! CHRISTMAS, READERS!
DIRECTOR
TERRY'S CHOCOLATE ORANGE X36
YOU SPAWNY GET!
READER'S VOICE

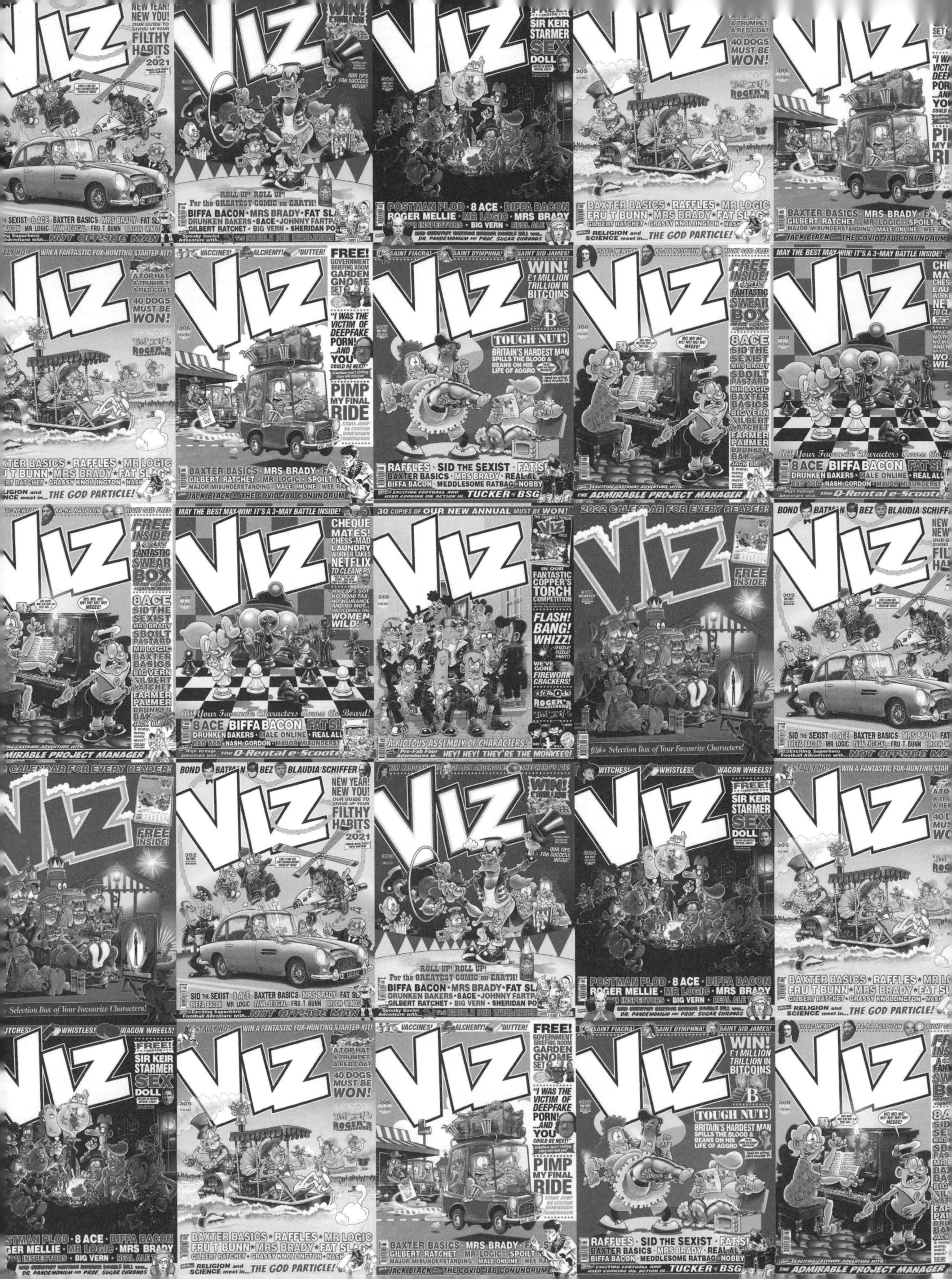

VIZ
NEW YEAR! NEW YOU! OUR GUIDE TO GIVING UP YOUR FILTHY HABITS 2021
ROLL UP! ROLL UP! For the GREATEST COMIC on EARTH!
BIFFA BACON · MRS BRADY · FAT SLAGS
DRUNKEN BAKERS · 8ACE · JOHNNY FARTPANTS
GILBERT RATCHET · SHERIDAN PO
SIR KEIR STARMER SEX DOLL
POSTMAN PLOD · 8 ACE · BIFFA BACON
ROGER MELLIE · MR LOGIC · MRS BRADY
BIG VERN · REAL ALE
DR. PANDEMONIUM AND PROF. SUGAR CHRONOS
A TOP HAT, A TRUMPET, A RED COAT AND 40 DOGS MUST BE WON!
BAXTER BASICS · RAFFLES · MR LOGIC
FRU T BUNN · MRS BRADY · FAT SLAGS
GILBERT RATCHET · GRASSY KNOLLINGTON · NASH
RELIGION and SCIENCE meet in... THE GOD PARTICLE!
TALLY HO! WIN A FANTASTIC FOX-HUNTING STARTER KIT!
VACCINES! ALCHEMY! BUTTER!
FREE! GOVERNMENT BRIEFING ROOM GARDEN GNOME SET
"I WAS THE VICTIM OF DEEPFAKE PORN! ...AND YOU COULD BE NEXT!"
PIMP MY FINAL RIDE
BAXTER BASICS · MRS BRADY · FAT SLAGS
GILBERT RATCHET · MR LOGIC · SPOILT
MAJOR MISUNDERSTANDING · MALE ONLINE · WEE RAB
JACK BLACK IN... THE COVID JAB CONUNDRUM
SAINT FIACRA! SAINT DYMPHNA! SAINT SID JAMES!
WIN! £1 MILLION TRILLION IN BITCOINS
TOUGH NUT!
BRITAIN'S HARDEST MAN SPILLS THE BLOOD & BEANS ON HIS LIFE OF AGGRO
RAFFLES · SID THE SEXIST · FAT SLAGS
BAXTER BASICS · MRS BRADY · REAL ALE
BIFFA BACON · MEDDLESOME RATBAG · NOBBY
EXCITING FOOTBALL AND USED COOKING OIL ACTION IN... TUCKER'S BSG
ISAAC NEWTON! RA-RA RASPUTIN! RIGHT SAID FRED!
FREE INSIDE! A FANTASTIC SWEAR BOX
MEE! MEE! MEE! MEEEE!
8ACE · SID THE SEXIST · MRS BRADY · SBOILT BASTARD · MR LOGIC · BAXTER BASICS · BIG VERN · GILBERT RATCHET · FARMER PALMER · DRUNKEN BAKERS
THE ADMIRABLE PROJECT MANAGER
MAY THE BEST MAY WIN! IT'S A 3-MAY BATTLE INSIDE!
CHEQUE MATES! CHESS-MAD LAUNDRY WORKER TAKES NETFLIX TO CLEANERS
MY CAR'S GOT NO ROAD TAX, NO INSURANCE AND NO MOT... WOMEN WILD!
All Your Favourite Characters Across the Board!
8ACE · BIFFA BACON · FAT SLAGS
DRUNKEN BAKERS · MALE ONLINE · REAL ALE
BAD BOB · NASH GORDON · MAJOR MISUNDERSTANDING
the Q-Rental e-Scooter
30 COPIES OF OUR NEW ANNUAL MUST BE WON!
IN OUR FANTASTIC COPPER'S TORCH COMPETITION
FLASH! BANG! WHIZZ!
WE'VE GONE FIREWORK CRACKERS!
A RIOTOUS ASSEMBLY OF CHARACTERS!
HEY! HEY! THEY'RE THE MONKEES!
2022 CALENDAR FOR EVERY READER!
FREE INSIDE!
With a Selection Box of Your Favourite Characters!
BOND · BATMAN · BEZ · BLAUDIA SCHIFFER
SID THE SEXIST · 8 ACE · BAXTER BASICS · MRS BRADY · FAT SLAGS
BIFFA BACON · MR LOGIC · IVAN JELICAL · FRU T BUNN · BROON WINDS
Exciting Superhero Football Adventure with... NOT OFFSIDE MAN
WITCHES! WHISTLES! WAGON WHEELS!